D1532683

DISCARDED

WIDENER UNIVERSITY

DISCARDED

United States Army in Vietnam

Advice and Support:
The Final Years, 1965–1973

by
Jeffrey J. Clarke

MILITARY INSTRVCTION

Center of Military History
United States Army
Washington, D.C., 1988

DS
558
.U55
1988

Library of Congress Cataloging-in-Publication Data

Clarke, Jeffery J.
   Advice and support

   (United States Army in Vietnam)
   Bibliography: p.
   Includes index.
   Supt of. Doc. no.: D 114.7/3:Ad 9/965–73
   1. Vietnamese Conflict, 1961–1975—United States.
2. United States. Military Assistance Command, Vietnam—
History. 3. Vietnam—Politics and government—1945–1975.
I. Title. II. Series.
DS558.C58   1988   959.7804'33'73   87–600379

CMH Pub 91–3

WIDENER UNIVERSITY
WOLFGRAM
LIBRARY
CHESTER, PA

First Printing

For sale by the Superintendent of Documents, U.S. Government Printing Office
Washington, D.C. 20402

United States Army in Vietnam

David F. Trask, General Editor

Advisory Committee

(As of 23 October 1987)

Charles P. Roland
University of Kentucky

Maj. Gen. Robert H. Buker
Deputy Surgeon General, USA

Frank G. Burke
National Archives and Records
Administration

Edward M. Coffman
University of Wisconsin

Brig. Gen. Roy K. Flint
U.S. Military Academy

Maj. Gen. Raymond E. Haddock
U.S. Army Training and
Doctrine Command

L. Eugene Hedberg
H. D. Reid Foundation

Ernest R. May
Harvard University

David B. Miller
City Government of
Scranton, Pennsylvania

Jamie W. Moore
The Citadel

Brig. Gen. Stephen Silvasy, Jr.
U.S. Army War College

Donald W. Smythe, S.J.
John Carroll University

Maj. Gen. Gordon R. Sullivan
U.S. Army Command and
General Staff College

Russell F. Weigley
Temple University

U.S. Army Center of Military History

Brig. Gen. William A. Stofft, Chief of Military History

Chief Historian
Chief, Histories Division
Editor in Chief

David F. Trask
Lt. Col. Richard O. Perry
John W. Elsberg

. . . to Those Who Served

Foreword

Well before the end of the American involvement in the Vietnam War, the U.S. Army Center of Military History committed itself to producing a comprehensive and objective multivolume series of one of our nation's most complicated and controversial foreign involvements. To this end Army historians began work on a number of studies treating our broad advice and assistance effort in Vietnam. Among these is *Advice and Support: The Final Years, 1965–1973,* the third of three historical works that tell the story of the U.S. Army's advisory program in Vietnam. The initial volume deals with the early advisory years between 1941 and 1960, and a second, treating the 1961–64 period, is in preparation.

In *Advice and Support: The Final Years* the author describes the U.S. Army advisory effort to the South Vietnamese armed forces during the period when the U.S. commitment in Southeast Asia was at its peak. The account encompasses a broad spectrum of activities at several levels, from the physically demanding work of the battalion advisers on the ground to the more sophisticated undertakings of our senior military officers at the highest echelons of the American military assistance command in Saigon. Among critical subjects treated are our command relationships with the South Vietnamese army, our politico-military efforts to help reform both the South Vietnamese military and government, and our implementation of the Vietnamization policy inaugurated in 1969. The result tells us much about the U.S. Army's role as an agent of national policy in a critical but often neglected arena, and constitutes a major contribution to our understanding of not only the events that occurred in Vietnam but also the decisions and actions that produced them.

Washington, D.C.   WILLIAM A. STOFFT
1 June 1987   Brigadier General, USA
                                                         Chief of Military History

The Author

Dr. Jeffrey J. Clarke has been a historian at the U.S. Army Center of Military History since 1971. He has also taught history at Rutgers University and the University of Maryland–College Park and is currently adjunct associate professor of history at the University of Maryland–Baltimore County. Dr. Clarke holds a Ph.D. in history from Duke University, is a lieutenant colonel in the Army Reserve, and commanded a military history detachment in Vietnam, 1969–70, spending part of his tour with Advisory Team 95 in the III Corps Tactical Zone. In addition, he has contributed many articles and essays on military history to a wide variety of professional publications, and is presently completing a combat volume in the World War II series and preparing another in the Vietnam War series.

Preface

In the spring of 1975 the military leaders of North Vietnam launched their final offensive against the forces of the South. What had begun so many years before as a nationalist revolt against foreign overlords, now appeared to be ending in a regional civil war, North against South. For the southerners, the Republic of Vietnam, the end was an unmitigated disaster—its defenders vanquished, its leaders scattered, and even the name of its capital city, Saigon, banished from the dictionary of current geography. In Southeast Asia the final verdict was thus swift and sure. But for the United States, Saigon's twenty-year ally, the results were more puzzling, and the abrupt defeat seemed to pose as many questions as it answered. What had caused the debacle and who was responsible? Were the South Vietnamese "stabbed in the back" by an American Congress reluctant to legislate further support for a war that seemed to have no end? Or, was the blame to be found closer to Saigon, in a domestic insurgency that South Vietnam had been unable to stamp out or in a host of internal problems that the American advisory effort had been unable to resolve? Given the almost limitless assistance that the United States had poured into South Vietnam, the lack of a successful American outcome appears almost inexplicable. Yet, what has been called "America's longest war" had both begun and ended with little American involvement. Perhaps it was never truly an American war, and a final assessment may conclude that the problems faced by the American advisory mission in Saigon were insurmountable and that, in the end, the South Vietnamese were simply "stabbed in the front" by a stronger, more determined enemy.

Seeking to answer some of these questions, this volume closely examines the relationship between the United States and the Republic of South Vietnam, and focuses not only on U.S. military strategy and policy but also on South Vietnamese politics and society, a filter through which all American advice and assistance had to pass. The historical questions to be asked are complex. What was the nature of this country of South Vietnam, its people, its government, and its army? What challenges did it face and what was the role of the United States in helping it meet those challenges? More specifically, what was American "advice and support," how was it formulated and implemented, and what was its impact? What role was played by the American tactical advisers, the school and training center advisers, and those at the higher American military headquarters, and how influential were the Washington-level decision-makers on the other side of the ocean? Although definitive answers to all of these questions may be elusive, their exploration will serve as the basis for a broader understanding of the American experience in the Vietnam War.

This third advice and support volume covers the period 1965 to early 1973, a time when American military leaders in Saigon made critical decisions affecting the course of the war. The American troop buildup, the disintegration of the South Vietnamese government, and the unconventional nature of the war thrust American military personnel deep into the local and national politics of a foreign country. Senior American officers, especially the chiefs of the American military mission in Saigon, found themselves serving both as military advisers and political counselors. Ironically, the same circumstances reduced the role of the lesser American advisers in the field to combat support coordinators, and many served as no more than a conduit for the increasing amounts of American combat and materiel assistance received by the South Vietnamese. Although American political leaders in Washington began to reassert their control over the war in 1968, senior U.S. military advisers continued to play a vital role in the political as well as the military survival of Saigon. In many ways their mission remained unique, and their accomplishments, their frustrations, and, ultimately, their failures formed the core of American advice and support during those troubled times.

In the course of research and writing, the author has received generous support from many individuals. Charles B. MacDonald, the former chief of the Current History Branch (now the Southeast Asia Branch), laid the foundation for the Vietnam War series and provided much assistance on my draft chapters, as did his successors, Drs. Stanley L. Falk and John Schlight. I also owe a special debt of gratitude to the center's successive Histories Division chiefs, Cols. John E. Jessup, James W. Ransone, James W. Dunn, and Lt. Col. Richard O. Perry, for their support, as well as to the former and the present Chief of Military History, Brig. Gens. James L. Collins, Jr., and William A. Stofft. I would also like to acknowledge my deep thanks to my colleagues in the Southeast Asia Branch who were always willing to share their research and knowledge with me: John Albright, Lt. Col. John D. Bergen, Dr. John M. Carland, Ann E. David, Vincent H. Demma, Dr. William M. Hammond, Dr. Richard A. Hunt, George L. MacGarrigle, Dr. Joel D. Meyerson, Jefferson L. Powell, Lt. Col. William K. Schrage, Dr. Ronald H. Spector, and Lt. Col. Adrian G. Traas.

The study also benefited greatly from the advice of the official review panel under the chairmanship of Dr. David F. Trask, Chief Historian, which included General William B. Rosson, Lt. Gen. William E. Potts, Dr. Guenther Lewy, and Dr. Gerald C. Hickey. Outside readers whose comments were also of value were General Frederick C. Weyand, Generals Cao Van Vien and Ngo Quang Truong, Maj. Gen. David R. Palmer, Drs. John H. Hatcher and Lewis Sorley, and many former advisers who read those portions of the manuscript that touched on their personal experiences. I am also indebted to Dr. Hatcher's records management staff (formerly part of TAG—The Adjutant General's office), especially Paul L. Taborn and Steven M. Eldridge, to Dr. Jack Shulimson of the U.S. Marine Corps History and Museums Division, to Larry A. Ballard of the center's Historical Services Division, to Theresa Farrell of the State Department's records service, and to the staff at the U.S. Army Military History Institute, including its director, Col. Rod Paschall; archivist Dr. Richard J. Sommers and his able assistant, David A. Keough; Michael J. Winey; and Randy W. Hackenburg.

A large amount of praise is also owed to Gustinia B. Scott of the Southeast Asia Branch, who typed much of the manuscript; to Arthur S. Hardyman,

Howell C. Brewer, Linda M. Cajka, and Michael Hertz Associates for their valuable graphics and cartographic support; to John A. Grier of the Government Printing Office for his expert typography and design assistance; and to the center's Editor in Chief, John W. Elsberg, who provided guidelines on style and format. Much credit is also owed to my diligent editor, Joanne M. Brignolo, who worked closely with the manuscript through all phases of production. Finally, I should like to thank my principal advisers at Duke University, Professors Theodore Ropp and Joel Colton, for their inspiration; the many American advisers who were willing to share a few stories with a wandering historian; and my students at the University of Maryland–Baltimore County who somehow always managed to spark new insights into the war they now seem to be so curious about.

The author alone is responsible for all interpretations and conclusions in the following work, as well as for any errors that may appear.

Washington, D.C.   JEFFREY J. CLARKE
1 June 1987

Contents

PART ONE

The Historical Perspective

Chapter   *Page*

1. The Road to War   5
   The Long Fuse   5
   The Land and Its People   8
   Challenge and Response 10

2. The Army of the Directory 19
   An Army Divided 20
   Organization for War 25
   The Field Army 32
   Personnel and Morale 39
   Combat Effectiveness 46

3. The Advisers 49
   The American High Command 49
   The Advisory System 53
   The Soldier-Adviser 61
   Special Forces as Advisers 69
   Paying the Bills 74

PART TWO

A New War (1965)

4. Searching for Stability 81
   Military Expansion 82
   Combined Command 85
   Roles and Missions 93

5. Toward a New Strategy 97
   At the Crossroads 99
   Roles and Missions 106

6. Enter the Americans 109
    Appeasing Saigon's Generals 109
    Quality Versus Quantity 111
    South Vietnamese Performance 113
    Prisoners of War 118
    Roles and Missions 120

PART THREE

Turmoil and Reform (1966–1967)

7. Revolt in the I Corps 127
    The Seeds of Crisis 127
    The Struggle Movement in Control 130
    Saigon Acts 136

8. The Reform Effort 145
    Organizing for Success 146
    Managing Saigon's Manpower 151
    Training 159
    Logistics 163
    Prisoners of War 167

9. The Pacification Campaign 171
    Organizing for Pacification 171
    The Security Mission 176
    Revolutionary Development Support 177

10. Advising in the Field 183
    Combined Operations 184
    The Advisory Ethos 187
    Trouble in the 25th 188
    Imbroglios Elsewhere 191

11. Heyday of the Special Forces 195
    Roles and Missions 195
    FULRO 199
    The Continued Expansion 200
    Border Operations 203

12. The Reform Effort Stalls 209
    Reorganizing for Pacification 209
    The Ground Army Expands 213
    The Failure of Reform 218
    Corruption: The Perennial Problem 229

13. The Security Mission Examined 233
    Supporting Revolutionary Development 233
    The Advisers 236
    Measuring Success 241
    Leadership 245
    Performance in the Field 247

14. Generals and Politics 255
    A Balance of Power 256
    Toward a New Regime 258
    Elections 263
    A Transition of Power 265

15. Image and Reality 271
    An Image of Progress 273
    A Change in Policy 278
    Support for Saigon 283

PART FOUR

Reevaluating the Effort (1968)

16. A Year of Planning 291
    The Tet Expansion 293
    The May Plan 294
    New Guidance 298
    Plan Six 299
    The Improvement and Modernization Plans 300
    T–Day Plans 302
    An Assessment 304

17. Saigon Takes Action 307
    Changes in Command 308
    Mobilization 313
    The Reform Effort 316

18. Progress or Stagnation? 321
    Advising on the Ground 321
    Evaluating the South Vietnamese 324
    Roles and Missions 331
    Conflicting Assessments 335

PART FIVE

A New Direction (1969–1970)

19. Vietnamization 341
    National Security Study Memorandum 1 341
    Decision for Withdrawal 346
    Withdrawal Planning 349
    A Self-Sufficient Saigon 351
    Washington Takes Control 357

20. Spotlight on Saigon 361
    One War, One Strategy 361
    New Generals, New Leadership 363
    The Advisers 368
    Internal Reform 372
    Organization and Training 377
    Manpower 384
    Evaluating Saigon 387

21. One War: The Highlands 391
    Combined Operations: I CTZ 392
    Combined Operations: II CTZ 393

22. One War: Cambodia 405
    Combined Operations: IV CTZ 405
    Combined Operations: III CTZ 408
    The 5th Division 412
    The Airborne 415
    Cambodia: A Test 418

23. Vietnamizing Military Support 427
    Early Planning 428
    The Ports 432
    Vietnamization by Function 435
    Rotary-wing Aviation 441
    An Assessment 443

PART SIX

Successes and Failures (1971–1973)

Chapter   *Page*

24. The Last Buildup 449
    The Advisory Drawdown 449
    A Final Military Expansion 455
    The Failure of Reform 464

25. A Matter of Leadership 471
    LAM SON 719 472
    Leadership Changes 476
    The Easter Offensive 481
    Ceasefire 490
    The Last Assessment 493

26. Trojan Horses 497
    Roles and Missions 497
    The Political Dimension 500
    The American Military Commanders 505
    The Advisers 508
    Advising From the Top 511

Appendixes

A. U.S. Army Advisory Buildup 523
B. South Vietnamese Armed Forces Officer and NCO Strength,
    December 1968 524
C. U.S. Troop Redeployments 524

Bibliographical Note 525

List of Abbreviations 545

Index 549

Tables

No.
  1. South Vietnamese Military Strength, 1965 20
  2. South Vietnamese Infantry Battalions by Corps Area, March 1965 . . 34
  3. Estimated Desertions in the South Vietnamese Armed Forces 43
  4. South Vietnamese Military-Civilian Pay Comparison, March 1965 . . 45

5. Average Strength of South Vietnamese Battalions, 31 May 1965 . . . 47
6. Headquarters, MACV, Personnel by Service Component,
   31 December 1965 51
7. Headquarters, MACV, Personnel by Staff Section, 1965 53
8. Field Advisory Strength, 1965 56
9. Status of South Vietnamese Ground Combat Battalions, June 1965 . . 100
10. South Vietnamese Armed Forces Expansion Plan 148
11. South Vietnamese Armed Forces Desertions, 1966 152
12. South Vietnamese Army Maneuver Battalion Strength, 1966 158
13. South Vietnamese–initiated Actions Per Week 253
14. Comparative Military Casualty Figures 275
15. Selected Annual Promotions for Calendar Year 1969 316
16. South Vietnamese Officer Strength, Regular Forces, December 1968 . 317
17. Advisory Team Personnel Reductions, September 1969 369
18. Approximate Field Advisory Strength, 1969–1970 373
19. Cost of South Vietnamese Army and Territorial Forces 380
20. CIDG Conversions, December 1970 381
21. South Vietnamese Defense Budget 463
22. Official Piaster Exchange 503
23. Comparative Estimates of Annual Military Base Pay 504

Charts

1. South Vietnamese Military Structure, 1965 . . . . *Facing* 26
2. Organization of Headquarters, MACV, January 1965 . . . . . *Facing* 50
3. Organization of MACV Field Advisory Network, 1965–1966 . . . *Facing* 56
4. Comparative Strengths and Losses of South Vietnamese Military Forces,
   1965 86

Maps

1. Geographic Regions of South Vietnam 9
2. Corps Areas of Responsibility, 1965 35
3. South Vietnamese Armed Forces Training System 160
4. I and II Corps Unit Locations, January 1969 394
5. III and IV Corps Unit Locations, January 1969 407
6. Cross-Border Operations, May–June 1970 419
7. LAM SON 719, February 1971 474
8. The Easter Offensive, April–May 1972 480

Illustrations

Page

Fortune-tellers in Gia Dinh Province 2
Vietnamese Fishing Village 11
U.S. Helicopter Support in the Delta 13
Saigon Besieged During Another Attempted Coup 16
General Nguyen Van Thieu 23
Air Vice-Marshal Nguyen Cao Ky 23
IV Corps Troops Boarding U.S. Helicopters 33
Montagnard Strike Force in the Central Highlands 38
Airborne Troops Carrying M1s 39
General William C. Westmoreland 50
MACV Headquarters 52
Field Adviser on Operations 58
Tactical Adviser in the Field 66
Maj. Donald A. Seibert 68
Special Forces Team 70
American Commanders Taking Charge of the Battlefield 80
Training an Expanding Army 83
Ambassador Maxwell D. Taylor and General Westmoreland 87
"Soldiers, meet your advisors!" 92
General Nguyen Huu Co Welcomes Secretary of Defense Robert S.
  McNamara 101
President Lyndon B. Johnson and Ambassador-designate Henry Cabot
  Lodge 104
Static Security Defenses in III Corps 115
Airborne Adviser Comforting Wounded Counterpart 117
Enemy Prisoners Captured in II Corps 119
President Johnson Conferring With Taylor 121
Johnson and Ky in Honolulu Discussing Reforms 126
Demonstrations in Hue, Spring 1966 128
Government Troops on the Move Against Dissidents 136
Rebel Stronghold at Thinh Hoi Pagoda in Da Nang 139
Buddhist Demonstrations Spread to Saigon 142
Regional Forces Company in Formation 147
Lunch in the Field 157
Brig. Gen. Richard M. Lee 162
Prisoner-of-War Camp at Bien Hoa 168
U.S. and South Vietnamese Leaders Agree on Pacification 173
Revolutionary Development Cadre Team Entering Its Assigned Hamlet . . 174
Weakly Armed Popular Forces Soldiers Providing Local Security 178
South Vietnamese Soldiers Flush a Viet Cong Suspect From the Jungle . . 180
Conducting a Village Search in Binh Duong Province 186

Lt. Col. Cecil F. Hunnicutt 189
General Phan Trong Chinh 189
Special Forces Adviser With *LLDB* and CIDG Leaders 197
Y Bham Enoul 200
Special Forces Camps, IV Corps and II Corps 202
Project Delta Members 204
Robert W. Komer and Ellsworth Bunker 211
New Territorial Recruits at a Basic Training Center 214
Main Commissary, South Vietnamese 2d Commissary Division, Qui Nhon . 223
Komer Discussing Revolutionary Development Plans 238
Field Adviser and His Counterparts 240
Lt. Gen. John A. Heintges and General Vinh Loc 249
Brig. Gen. John F. Freund and Lt. Col. Dao Ba Phuoc 250
General Nguyen Duc Thang 257
Thieu and Ky, February 1967 260
Manila Conference, October 1966 272
National Press Club Address, November 1967 281
American Leaders Charting a New Course 288
Secretary of Defense Clark Clifford Holding a Press Briefing 292
General Creighton W. Abrams, Jr. 294
M16 Training for South Vietnamese Soldiers 297
V–100 Armored Car 297
Presidents Johnson and Thieu Meeting Again in Honolulu 299
New Recruits Entering an Induction Center 315
Red Cross Representatives at Phu Quoc Island POW Facility 319
Advising Vietnamese Trainees on M60 Firing Techniques 323
Adviser in II Corps Checking Weapon of a Popular Forces Soldier . . . 324
Fighting To Hold Saigon 326
Vietnamization Becomes Policy 338
Maj. Gen. Richard G. Stilwell and General Ngo Quang Truong 343
Secretary of Defense Melvin R. Laird's Second Trip to Saigon 357
Abrams Discussing His Strategy in I Corps 362
General Nguyen Van Toan 366
Advisers' Living Conditions 370
Teaching Through Demonstration 371
Maj. Gen. William R. Peers 395
South Vietnamese 23d Infantry Division Troops 398
Lt. Gen. Arthur S. Collins, Jr. 402
General Do Cao Tri and Lt. Gen. Julian J. Ewell 410
Dong Tien Infantry Operations 414
South Vietnamese Troops En Route to Cambodia 421
Cambodian War Booty 422
Lt. Gen. Joseph M. Heiser, Jr. 429
Instruct and Advise Team Member at South Vietnamese Logistical Depot . 431
Training South Vietnamese in Harbor Operations 434

Transporting Supplies on Upgraded Roads in the Delta 437
U.S. Advisers: The First To Come and the Last To Leave 446
Transferring an American Base to Saigon 451
Project ENHANCE PLUS Equipment 454
Armor Engine Maintenance Class for the New M48 Tank 457
South Vietnamese Soldiers Pushing Through the Laotian Jungle 472
John Paul Vann 477
South Vietnamese 3d Infantry Division and 20th Tank Battalion Soldiers . 482
Col. Tran Van Nhut and Maj. Gen. James F. Hollingsworth 485
President Richard M. Nixon and Henry A. Kissinger 492
General Frederick C. Weyand 494

Illustrations courtesy of the following sources: pp. 121 and 288, Lyndon Baines Johnson Library; p. 260, National Geographic Magazine; p. 281, United Press International; pp. 33, 58, 68, 70, 115, 117, 147, 157, 174, 178, 204, 240, 249, 297 (bottom), 315, 324, 343, 395, and 422, U.S. Army Military History Institute; p. 257, Wide World Photos; and on the dust jacket, Terrence LaMarr Offer. All other illustrations from the files of the Department of Defense and U.S. Army Center of Military History.

I Did Not Die

Do not stand by my grave and weep:
I am not there. I do not sleep.
I am a thousand winds that blow.
I am the diamond's glint on snow.
I am the sunlight on ripened grain.
I am the gentle autumn's rain.
When you awake in the morning's hush,
I am the swift uplifting rush
Of quiet birds in circled flight.
Do not stand by my grave and cry:
I am not there. I did not die.

—Anonymous
Central Highlands
Circa 1969

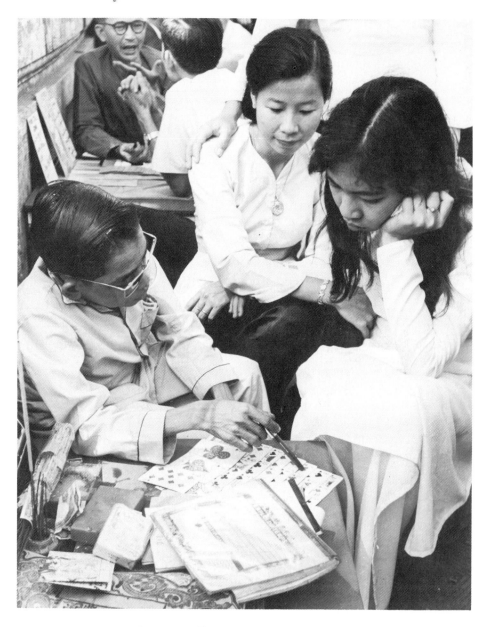

Fortune-tellers in Gia Dinh Province

PART ONE
The Historical Perspective

1

The Road to War

Until World War II, America's interests in the affairs of the Far East were marginal and her few involvements there almost accidental. Neither the acquisition of the Philippines nor the survival of China was vital to the United States. The war with Japan and the Korean conflict changed little, and throughout the Second World War and after, Europe remained America's primary overseas concern. The shores of the Asian mainland were still half a globe away, and Vietnam, for the few Americans who had ever heard of it, was hardly regarded as the gateway to the Far East, or anyplace else. Saigon was about 800 miles west of the Philippines and the nearest American bases and some 7,800 miles from California, or nineteen sea days from the West Coast of the United States and about thirty-four from the East. That such a small faraway land might someday figure in the destiny of the United States, no one could have foreseen or foretold.[1]

The Long Fuse

The American involvement in Southeast Asia had its origins in the Cold War, that international rivalry between the Western democracies and the East European totalitarian states following the end of World War II. The success of Communist revolutionaries in mainland China and the renewed commitment of international communism to "wars of national liberation" greatly complicated this conflict in the 1950s. By then, some of the ideological and tactical differences between the major Communist leaders had become more evident. In the West the older Leninist revolutionary model, stressing the key role of the urban work-

[1] For background, see Ronald H. Spector, *Advice and Support: The Early Years, 1941–1960*, United States Army in Vietnam (Washington, D.C.: U.S. Army Center of Military History, 1983), pp. 5–50. Unless otherwise stated, all manuscript sources cited in this volume may be found in the Center of Military History (CMH) Vietnam War Records collection. Those on file at the historical office in Washington, D.C., are identified by the three-letter abbreviation CMH, with the branch location (SEAB for Southeast Asia Branch, HRB for Historical Records Branch, SSB for Staff Support Branch) also given. Those stored at the Washington National Records Center (WNRC), National Archives and Records Administration, in Suitland, Maryland, are identified by the four-letter abbreviation WNRC, with the specific box, accession, and record group (RG) numbers also given.

ing class, predominated, while in underdeveloped countries the Chinese agrarian-based model became more popular. In each case the appeal was the same— the establishment of a highly centralized government that eventually, through intensive economic planning, could challenge the more advanced, freewheeling, and often aggressive industrial states of the West and, at the same time, could offer a certain degree of political stability and social justice. Western opposition was based primarily on a mix of eighteenth- and nineteenth-century liberalism and national self-interest. The pugnacity and stubborn individualism that had characterized the rise of the West seemed diametrically opposed to the egalitarian conformism of the socialist utopia. The inability of established Communist states to solve their own economic problems and their overt use of military force confused the issues at stake, as did the rapid growth of socialism in the Western democracies. Fear of nuclear war greatly reduced the chances of global conflict, but both sides continued to employ a wide range of less destructive politico-military alternatives to achieve their international objectives. American leaders attempted to "contain" Communist expansion by maintaining a large peacetime military force, by making regional defense agreements with non-Communist states, and by supplying direct military assistance to friendly governments. Such assistance usually consisted of excess military equipment and military advisory groups tailored to the needs of the supported country. The results were mixed. American officials often tried to encourage democracy, economic growth, social reform, and the expansion of individual liberties but sometimes found themselves supporting socially and economically inegalitarian societies in the interests of local and world stability.

The position of the United States toward the French involvement in Indochina between 1945 and 1954 reflected the inherent contradictions in American cold war diplomacy.[2] Although regarding the Viet Minh insurgency as part of a larger Communist conspiracy, Americans were not unsympathetic to Vietnamese aspirations for national independence. In the end, the United States supported French military efforts while encouraging Vietnamese independence under French tutelage. Neither policy was successful, and the ensuing defeat of the French brought an end to the first stage of what was to be a thirty-year struggle.

The Indochina ceasefire agreement (Geneva Accords) of 21 July 1954 led to the creation of separate states in Laos and Cambodia, and the artificial division of Vietnam into two republics. In the North the Communist Viet Minh established the Democratic Republic of Vietnam, and in the South a heterogeneous collection of non-Communist factions, led by Ngo Dinh Diem, formed the Republic of Vietnam.[3] The general elections provided for by the agreement never took place,

---

[2] For treatment of the early U.S. military involvement in Vietnam, see Spector, *Advice and Support: The Early Years*; James Lawton Collins, Jr., *The Development and Training of the South Vietnamese Army, 1950–1972*, Vietnam Studies (Washington, D.C.: Department of the Army, 1975); Robert F. Futrell, assisted by Martin Blumenson, *The Advisory Years to 1965*, The United States Air Force in Southeast Asia (Washington, D.C.: Office of Air Force History, 1981); and Robert H. Whitlow, *U.S. Marines in Vietnam: The Advisory and Combat Assistance Era, 1954–1964* (Washington, D.C.: U.S. Marine Corps History and Museums Division, 1977).

[3] In Vietnamese the family name normally precedes the given name (thus, Ngo Dinh Diem was a member of the Ngo family); but, because the number of different family names is small, an individual is referred to by his given name (thus, President Diem), a practice this study follows.

and the two states quickly grew apart. Almost immediately the United States threw its support behind the new southern regime and extended military aid through a Military Assistance Advisory Group (MAAG) under Lt. Gen. John W. O'Daniel. Despite a great deal of rhetoric, American objectives in South Vietnam were relatively simple and remained so—the establishment and preservation of a non-Communist government in South Vietnam. Initially, the most pressing problem was the weakness of the Saigon government and the danger of civil war between South Vietnam's armed political and religious factions. Diem, however, acting as a kind of benevolent dictator, managed to put a working government together, and O'Daniel's advisory group, about three to four hundred strong, went to work creating a national army.[4]

Much had to be done. Although thousands of Vietnamese had served in French military units, few had had any leadership or staff experience, and fewer still had received any kind of technical training (and those who had fought with the Viet Minh were not wanted). A military school and training system had to be built from the ground up; tactical units formed, trained, equipped, and quartered; and a command and supply system developed to direct and support them. The entire process took years of work, during which time many Vietnamese received command and staff or technical training in the United States, and many more received training from MAAG advisers and U.S. Army instructors on temporary duty to South Vietnam.

Slowly, under the direction of O'Daniel and his successor in October 1955, Lt. Gen. Samuel T. Williams, the new army took shape. At its core were seven infantry divisions, controlled by several regional headquarters and an army field command. The primary mission of this 150,000-man force was to repel a North Vietnamese Army invasion across the Demilitarized Zone that separated North and South Vietnam. Diem and his American advisers thus organized and trained the new army for a Korean-style conflict, rather than for the unconventional guerrilla style of warfare that had characterized the earlier Franco–Viet Minh struggle. President Diem also maintained a substantial paramilitary force almost as large as the regular army. This force had the primary task of maintaining internal security, but also acted as a counterweight to the army, whose officers often had political ambitions that were sometimes incompatible with those of Diem. From the very beginning, such tensions greatly weakened the Saigon government and severely hampered its ability to deal with South Vietnam's social and economic problems.

In 1960 an internal insurgency that had been simmering unnoticed for several years suddenly began to boil over throughout the length and breadth of the country. With but limited assistance from the North, the southern Communists had managed to rebuild their political organization and openly challenge the government of Saigon. Diem's new state, once regarded as a model bulwark against communism, began to totter, and the elaborate military machine constructed by the American advisers seemed incapable of dealing with the new situation. The second Indochina war had begun.

[4] For treatment of U.S. advisory efforts during the Diem era, see Spector, *Advice and Support: The Early Years*, pp. 219–379.

The Land and Its People

The world these men sought to master was both old and new, a mixture of rugged, unexplored jungle and cultivated ricelands that had sheltered man since almost the dawn of measured time.[5] Totaling approximately 66,000 square miles—about the size of Georgia or Alabama—the land of South Vietnam formed an upright crescent some 700 miles long, with a width of about 40 miles at its slender top slowly growing to approximately 120 at its broader base. In the northern and central portions of the country, steep, heavily forested mountains and hills marched east from the Laotian and northern Cambodian borders almost down to the sea, broken up in a few areas by small pockets of coastal lowlands; there, in scattered communities along the coast, lived most of the Vietnamese people of northern and central South Vietnam. Inland, steep mountains and deep valleys were interrupted only by the central plains, or "Highlands," of mid–South Vietnam, actually a broad, isolated plateau region inhabited chiefly by primitive mountain tribesmen. In the southern third of the country the mountains finally gave way to a hilly, rolling plain that rapidly flattened out into the wide low deltas of the Mekong River, heavily laced with streams, canals, dikes, and rice paddies, and home for most of the people of this agrarian land (*Map 1*). The climate was generally tropical and hot by European standards, temperatures averaging somewhere in the eighties (Fahrenheit), with seasonal variations caused by two monsoonal wet seasons.

Although demographic data on South Vietnam is almost nonexistent for this period, the total population was roughly 16 million.[6] About 85 percent were ethnic Vietnamese, and the remainder were divided about equally among the native Highlanders, or Montagnards (various mountain tribes of Malayo-Polynesian stock); the Khmer, or ethnic Cambodians; and the nonindigenous Chinese. Buddhism was the nominal religion of about 80 percent of the inhabitants, leavened by some 1.5 million Catholics and an assortment of local sects. Vietnamese culture was derived primarily from China, including the traditional social, economic, and political patterns based on the extended family system, intensive rice farming, and an authoritarian government. Buddhism, Taoism, Confucianism, and ancestor worship also came from China, but Western culture had made major inroads through French colonial administration and Roman Catholic proselytizing. Vietnamese society was, in fact, in a state of transition. Although the average Vietnamese lived in the rural countryside as farmers, fishermen, and small artisans, most had some property and education and were noted for their energy, resourcefulness, and ambition. While their primary loyalties were to their families and the lands they worked, their lives were inevitably linked to the

[5] For geographical, social, economic, and political background, see Central Intelligence Agency (CIA), National Intelligence Survey 43D, "South Vietnam: General Survey," April 1965, copy in SEAB, CMH; Nguyen Duy Hinh and Tran Dinh Tho, *The South Vietnamese Society*, Indochina Monographs (Washington, D.C.: U.S. Army Center of Military History, 1980).

[6] A formal census had never been taken, and as late as 1970 a U.S. Army report noted "almost a total lack of knowledge of the number, characteristics, and distribution of the [South Vietnamese] population and labor force." See Office of the Chief of Staff of the Army, *Army Activities Report: SE Asia*, 27 May 70, pp. 32–33.

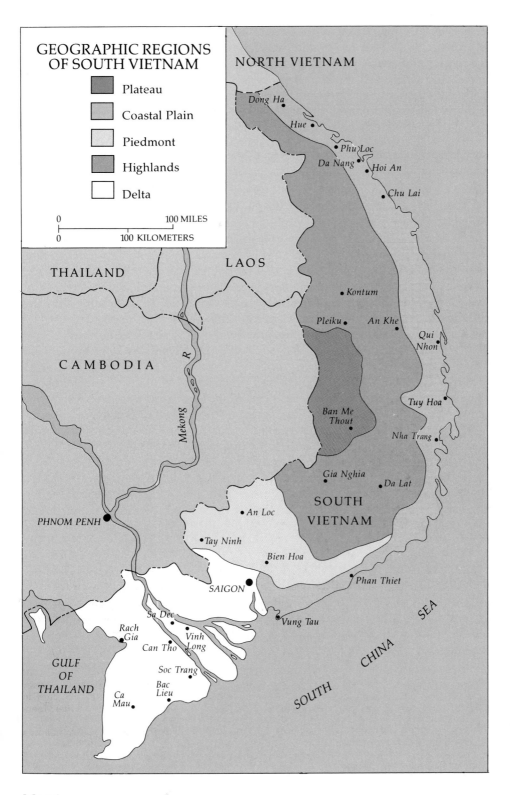

GEOGRAPHIC REGIONS
OF SOUTH VIETNAM

- Plateau
- Coastal Plain
- Piedmont
- Highlands
- Delta

0   100 MILES
0   100 KILOMETERS

NORTH VIETNAM

Dong Ha

Hue

Phu Loc

Da Nang

Hoi An

Chu Lai

THAILAND

LAOS

CAMBODIA

Kontum

Pleiku

An Khe

Qui Nhon

Mekong R

Ban Me Thout

Tuy Hoa

Nha Trang

Gia Nghia

Da Lat

SOUTH VIETNAM

An Loc

PHNOM PENH

Tay Ninh

Bien Hoa

Phan Thiet

SAIGON

Vung Tau

Sa Dec

SEA

Rach Gia

Vinh Long

Can Tho

Soc Trang

CHINA

GULF OF THAILAND

Bac Lieu

Ca Mau

SOUTH

MAP 1

larger villages, towns, and cities by a complex of trails, roads, and waterways; by a growing "transister radio" communications system; and by their own strong personal bonds with relatives and neighbors who had left the rural hamlets for other occupations. Of the 20 percent or so urban dwellers, over half lived in the capital, Saigon, a major port just north of the Mekong Delta, and the rest were scattered in smaller coastal communities to the north and south.

Most South Vietnamese considered themselves well-off and culturally and economically superior to their Southeast Asian neighbors. Vietnamese ethnocentrism had its roots in a history, two thousand years old, whose major themes were the successful resistance of the Vietnamese people to foreign domination and a continuous expansion to the South. Within South Vietnam, the "ricebowl of Asia," the great productivity of the land softened the local culture. However, significant social and economic problems existed. The urban-based upper class, about 3 percent of the population and distinguished primarily by its European education and wealth, provided most of the civilian and military leaders. The vast majority of the population had little political or economic influence and supplied most of the common soldiers, wage laborers, and domestic servants. In the countryside the growth of absentee landlordism and tenant farming since the 1930s had steadily eroded the economic position of the average peasant, causing widespread discontent and making land ownership a major issue. In the cities and towns, rising expectations, as well as growing disparities between rich and poor, also contributed to social unrest.[7] Social mobility could be achieved through education, but education was expensive. Commercial and industrial development in South Vietnam was slow, far too slow to act as a safety valve for a growing population. Although Diem's regime provided a certain degree of internal order, it was unable to address South Vietnam's social and economic problems. The absence of any sense of national identity magnified traditional tensions between the country's various ethnic and religious groups, and President Diem's open favoritism toward the Roman Catholic community only caused greater dissatisfaction. With minimal participation in national politics at the village and hamlet levels, where most of the people lived, the Saigon government had little grass roots support to help it through the coming struggle.

Challenge and Response

While Diem offered political stability and measured economic growth, the Communists promised immediate social and economic change, broadcasting the same message that Mao Tse-tung had spread successfully throughout the Chinese countryside several decades earlier.[8] The southern Communists, or Viet

---

[7] William Bredo et al., *Land Reform in Vietnam*, SRI Project no. IU-6797 (Menlo Park, Calif.: Stanford Research Institute, 1968), pp. 38–43, points out the partial success of the Diem government in reversing this trend.

[8] For background, see appropriate sections of Richard A. Hunt, *Pacification*, United States Army in Vietnam (Washington, D.C.: U.S. Army Center of Military History, forthcoming); *(Continued)*

Vietnamese Fishing Village

Cong,[9] promised land reform, education, social and sexual equality, responsive government, and social welfare, appealing mainly to the rural peasant. Many Viet Cong cadre were experienced and well-trained native southerners who had the added prestige of having fought and defeated the French. With little interference from Diem's government, they proselytized large segments of the Vietnamese rural population, especially at the hamlet and village levels, and, through a mixture of persuasion and force, organized them into an insurgent political structure. Participation was the key element; the better cadre relied on the people themselves to carry out the promised economic and social programs at the lower levels. Under Viet Cong direction, the peasants formed their own local governments, committees, judicial boards, and their own police, intelligence, and mili-

---

(Continued) Douglas Pike, *Viet Cong: The Organization and Techniques of the National Liberation Front of South Vietnam*, Studies in International Communism, no. 7 (Cambridge, Mass.: M.I.T. Press, 1966); and Douglas S. Blaufarb, *The Counterinsurgency Era: U.S. Doctrine and Performance, 1950 to the Present* (New York: Free Press, 1977). For ground accounts, see Jeffrey Race, *War Comes to Long An: Revolutionary Conflict in a Vietnamese Province* (Berkeley: University of California Press, 1972); James W. Trullinger, Jr., *Village at War: An Account of Revolution in Vietnam* (New York: Longman, 1980); and, for early theory and practice, Mao Tse-tung's *Basic Tactics*, trans. Stuart R. Schram (New York: Praeger, 1966), *Selected Military Writings of Mao Tse-tung* (Peking: Foreign Languages Press, 1963), and *Selected Works*, 4 vols. (Peking: Foreign Languages Press, 1961–65).

[9] "Viet Cong," a generic term used by the South Vietnamese government, means Vietnamese Communist(s).

11

tia forces. To outlying Saigon administrators, the first open signs of trouble might come months and even years later when taxes or rents went unpaid, minor officials were harassed, or confrontations took place between Viet Cong militia forces and province police. Normally, Viet Cong cadre used terror as a last resort, employing such measures only against recalcitrant or unpopular government officials. As the insurgency spread, the Viet Cong formed larger political and military organizations, combining, for example, several of their better militia units into company-size rifle formations that might some day form the core of a larger regional battalion. In 1961 the political structure created by the Viet Cong in the South officially became the National Liberation Front, but it remained under the control of the People's Revolutionary Party, essentially the southern branch of the North Vietnamese (*Lao Dong*) Communist Party. However, as in revolutionary China, there was little to differentiate the people from the military and political apparatus at the lower echelons, where direct control by Communist Party members was weakest.

In Saigon, American and South Vietnamese officials found it difficult to comprehend what was actually occurring in the countryside. Based on rough tallies of reported skirmishes, abductions, assassinations, and other such incidents in the hinterlands, they concluded—and not surprisingly—that the Viet Cong were waging a campaign of terror against the Vietnamese peasantry. Yet most remained puzzled by the inability of the South Vietnamese armed forces to stamp out the lightly armed Viet Cong, attributing the survival of the rebels to superior guerrilla warfare tactics. They failed to appreciate the significance of the Viet Cong political organization and believed that the defeat of the guerrillas would bring about an end to the insurgency. But the guerrillas were only one aspect of the problem. Although they generally avoided direct confrontations with Diem's regular troops and attacked only after extensive planning, especially when they believed they had local military superiority, their real strength lay in their parent political organizations. Until Saigon responded to the political activities of the Viet Cong, a military solution to the guerrilla problem would remain elusive.

Between 1960 and 1964 American and South Vietnamese prescriptions for the insurgency were basically identical.[10] First, increase the number and mobility of the South Vietnamese ground forces, improve their small unit training and leadership, and use them to destroy the enemy of the battlefield. Second, provide more armed security for the people, or, if this proved infeasible, separate the people from the Viet Cong by a variety of population control measures, to include massive resettlement programs. Accordingly, the strength of the South Vietnamese armed forces rose from 150,000 to 250,000 between 1960 and 1964, and the paramilitary militia grew to about the same level. The United States also supplied increasing amounts of military assistance to the paramilitary units, and the government gradually incorporated them into the armed forces. Equally important, entirely new organizations came into being to spearhead what U.S.

[10] For this period, see Vincent H. Demma, *Advice and Support: The Middle Years, 1961–1965*, United States Army in Vietnam (Washington, D.C.: U.S. Army Center of Military History, forthcoming); Collins, *Development and Training of the South Vietnamese Army*, pp. 17–46; Futrell, *Advisory Years to 1965*, pp. 63–76, 85–91, 151–56.

U.S. Helicopter Support in the Delta

military and civilian leaders called the "counterinsurgency" effort. With American impetus and materiel assistance, the South Vietnamese created military intelligence organizations to monitor the enemy's actions; activated special "ranger" units to hunt down the guerrillas; put "political warfare" units in the field to push local "psychological warfare" campaigns; and agreed to an American-sponsored paramilitary program to provide security for the isolated Montagnard tribes. To control this vast internal effort, Diem divided the country into three, and later four, military "corps tactical zones," each under the control of an army corps headquarters. The South Vietnamese Army corps commanders became, in effect, area as well as tactical commanders, responsible for both internal security and tactical combat operations.

Direct American support for the military effort also increased. The number of uniformed American soldiers in South Vietnam rose from a little over 500 in 1960 to more than 23,000 by the end of 1964. This increase included not only more advisers at all echelons but also hundreds of support units, including helicopter, light aviation, and air transport formations, and a wide variety of medical, engineer, signal, and intelligence detachments. The U.S. Air Force established an elaborate tactical air support network and supplied a growing fighter-bomber force, while an expanding U.S. Army Special Forces element served as both advisers and operators for a host of unconventional warfare programs. American air and naval support from areas adjacent to South Vietnam also increased.

13

Gradually, Americans became involved in the fighting. In 1960 American advisers, hitherto involved primarily with training and higher-level staff work, started assisting ground combat units in the field. U.S. Army advisers began to operate regularly at the regimental level in 1960, at the battalion level in 1961, and with the paramilitary forces in 1964. At the same time, other advisory teams began to assist provinces and their subordinate districts. By 1965 a five-man U.S. advisory team accompanied each South Vietnamese infantry battalion, allowing some advisers to work at the rifle company level and below. These tactical advisers coordinated the growing amount of direct American combat support available to the South Vietnamese on the battlefield, and, as this support steadily increased, their importance as combat coordinators grew accordingly.

The U.S. military command structure in South Vietnam also grew with the increased American participation. In February 1962 the United States established a unified (Army, Navy, Air Force) headquarters, the Military Assistance Command, Vietnam (MACV), to coordinate all American military activities in South Vietnam. Headed by General Paul D. Harkins, MACV initially controlled all U.S. Army support units in Vietnam as well as the MAAG advisory program, and also worked directly with the South Vietnamese government on overall military plans and operations. With the disestablishment of MAAG in May 1964, its functions were integrated into those of the MACV staff, and the advisory effort ceased to have a separate command and support organization. MACV thus became a hybrid headquarters that lay somewhere between a theater-level unified command and a country advisory group. Technically, the new headquarters was subordinate to the U.S. Pacific Command in Hawaii, but its commander worked closely with the American ambassador in Saigon and the U.S. Joint Chiefs of Staff in Washington. However, MACV's jurisdiction was limited to U.S. military operations within South Vietnam, and the Pacific Command controlled the subsequent air campaigns against North Vietnam.

In the field American advisers did their best to cope with the changing war. U.S. Army counterinsurgency doctrine was at a formative stage. Contemporary field manuals dealt only with tactical guerrilla operations and treated them as secondary activities conducted behind a main, or linear, battlefield. None took into account the experiences of the Chinese civil war, or those of the French in Indochina and Algeria. Later manuals were more detailed but continued to focus on antiguerrilla tactics and techniques. The instructions published by Lt. Gen. Lionel C. McGarr, who became the MAAG chief in June 1960, were more useful. Recognizing that extensive "*psycho-political* action" preceded almost all successful Viet Cong combat operations, they pointed out that it was the enemy's careful political preparations that enabled guerrillas to operate among the civilian population. McGarr's guidance, however, made little distinction between the Viet Cong cadre and the Viet Cong guerrillas and tended to regard the armed insurgents as the root, rather than the outgrowth, of the problem. Later manuals passed over these questions entirely and concentrated on remedies that included not only counterguerrilla operations but also environmental improvement and population and resource control. However, the role of regular military forces in the last two areas was generally limited to civic action—local community assistance projects—and general support for the civilian South Vietnamese and American agencies responsible for planning and carrying out programs in these areas. U.S. Army counterinsurgency doctrine remained devoted almost exclusively to counterguerrilla operations.[11]

The question of doctrine had a direct impact on operations. For example, the projected division of responsibility meant that Saigon's counterinsurgency, or "pacification," effort depended on a variety of military and nonmilitary organizations to plan and carry out a large number of overlapping programs. Without unified direction, successful counterinsurgency operations depended on cooperation and coordination between competing offices and agencies, making it extraordinarily difficult to put together and carry out a comprehensive response to the Viet Cong politico-military war strategy. One example was the Strategic Hamlet Program, a South Vietnamese effort to regroup the rural population into fortified camps. Whatever its potential for success, it proved impossible to implement effectively because of the difficulties in meshing population regroupment goals with increased demands for security and other government services. The assumption that the Viet Cong guerrilla could somehow be separated from the people was another misconception. In many cases, especially in those areas that the Viet Cong had controlled for many years, the two were identical. Another counterinsurgency problem was the lack of intelligence, and especially the lack of the proper kind of intelligence. By concentrating on "order of battle" intelligence of Viet Cong fighting units,[12] the collection and analysis of other types of information suffered neglect. Declining Viet Cong guerrilla activity did not necessarily signify success if the armed insurgents were merely resting while the political activity of the cadre continued apace. On the other hand, significant increases in terrorism might actually reflect serious resistance to the Viet Cong by local officials and the rural population. Neither MACV nor Saigon knew what such statistics really signified.

In the face of major setbacks on the battlefield and internal dissatisfaction with the Diem government, Saigon's counterinsurgency effort began to unravel in 1963. In November a group of South Vietnamese generals assassinated Diem and took control of the Saigon government. The coup had the tacit support of the United States, but both parties may have miscalculated the importance of the deposed president. His fall marked the end of civilian authority and political stability in South Vietnam, and the succession of military juntas, coups, and attempted coups in 1964 and early 1965 weakened the government still further. Changes at the top often led to corresponding changes in key government positions and major military commands, causing widespread confusion throughout

[11] Quoted words from Military Assistance Advisory Group, Vietnam, Tactics and Techniques of Counter-Insurgent Operations, rev. February 1962, p. 2, copy in SEAB, CMH. See Department of the Army Field Manual no. 31–15, Operations Against Irregular Forces, 31 May 61; Field Manual no. 31–16, Counterguerrilla Operations, 19 Feb 63; Field Manual no. 31–21, Guerrilla Warfare and Special Forces Operations, 29 Sep 61; and Field Manual no. 31–73, Advisor Handbook for Counterinsurgency, 23 Apr 65. See also Stephen Lee Bowman, "The United States Army and Counterinsurgency Warfare: The Making of Doctrine, 1946-1964" (M.A. thesis, Duke University, 1981), and especially the articles by Roger Hilsman, Peter Paret and John W. Shy, and Walter W. Rostow in T. M. Greene, ed., *The Guerrilla—And How To Fight Him: Selections From the Marine Corps Gazette* (New York: Praeger, 1962).

[12] Order of battle is a technical military intelligence term for the identification, strength, location, structure, and deployment of enemy combat forces.

15

Saigon Besieged During Another Attempted Coup

the armed forces and the civil administration. Military and civilian officials were increasingly preoccupied with merely surviving in office and devoted less and less attention to their primary responsibilities. The militarization of the civilian administration, begun under President Diem, continued unabated, but the net effect was to further politicize the armed forces and spread military factionalism throughout the government. As military and civilian activities lost drive and direction, the Viet Cong insurgency gained momentum and grew more daring. Sporadic U.S. air strikes against North Vietnam did little to deter the Viet Cong or stop support from the North, including the arrival of regular North Vietnamese Army combat units at the end of 1964 in the remote border areas of central South Vietnam. Perhaps the insurgent leaders, sensing imminent victory, were preparing an all-out conventional military effort to topple the ailing Saigon regime and bring the war to an early end.

In Washington the mood had become increasingly gloomy throughout 1964. Reports of South Vietnam's political disarray and battlefield defeats, growing American combat casualties, and mounting Viet Cong strength increased pressure for direct American action. President Lyndon Baines Johnson ordered retaliatory air attacks against North Vietnam in August and approved sustained bombing campaigns against Viet Cong supply lines in Laos (BARREL ROLL) the following December and against North Vietnam itself (ROLLING THUNDER) in February 1965. In March he finally agreed to commit two U.S. Marine Corps

16

battalions, ostensibly to provide security for the Da Nang Air Base, and in April and May increased the stakes with more Marines and a U.S. Army infantry brigade. Johnson hoped that these measures would demonstrate American resolve, boost South Vietnamese morale, and help reverse the tide of the war. But the exact role of the newly arrived U.S. ground combat units was ambiguous, and more reinforcements seemed likely. Many key decisions regarding America's military commitment and strategy for the coming conflict had yet to be made.[13]

One American who found himself trying to sort out these matters was General William C. Westmoreland. Westmoreland had succeeded Harkins as the MACV commander in June 1964 and was to hold the post for four long years. He had come to Saigon five months earlier as Harkins' deputy, with no special preparation for the turmoil of Vietnamese politics or the type of war that was being waged in South Vietnam.[14] His expertise lay in the areas of tactics, training, and management, and his abilities in the realms of strategy and politics were untested. Along with his fellow advisers of all ranks, Westmoreland would have to learn and grow with the job. As the senior American military commander in South Vietnam, he was soon to preside over one of the most powerful military forces ever assembled, and his influence over the formulation and execution of U.S. policy within South Vietnam was to grow accordingly. But in May of 1965 his command included few ground troop units of any size or consequence. In seniority and prestige he was still very much junior to the American ambassador to South Vietnam, Maxwell D. Taylor, a retired Army general and a former chairman of the Joint Chiefs of Staff. Westmoreland's most significant decisions and contributions lay in the future.

---

[13] For discussion of the decision to deploy U.S. ground combat troops, see Larry Berman, *Planning a Tragedy: The Americanization of the War in Vietnam* (New York: Norton, 1982); Lyndon B. Johnson, *The Vantage Point: Perspectives of the Presidency, 1963–1969* (New York: Holt, Rinehart and Winston, 1971), pp. 112–53; William C. Westmoreland, *A Soldier Reports* (Garden City, N.Y.: Doubleday, 1976), pp. 119–36; Alexander S. Cochran, Jr., "American Planning for Ground Combat in Vietnam, 1952–1965," *Parameters* 14 (Summer 1984): 63–69.

[14] See Westmoreland, *Soldier Reports*, for biographical data.

2

The Army of the Directory

At the beginning of 1965 the military strength of the Saigon government was, on paper, impressive.[1] The regular armed forces consisted of about 250,000 men, organized into a conventional army, navy, air force, and marine corps, well equipped with tanks, artillery, ships, and aircraft. Behind the regulars was a similar-size militia-like organization, the Territorial Forces (*see Table 1*).[2] Although consisting mainly of small rifle units, the territorials had begun to receive modern radios, vehicles, and small arms during the early 1960s, and their capabilities had increased considerably. The formal organization of the armed forces mirrored that of most Western nations; a civilian Ministry of Defense directed a military general staff that, in turn, headed a hierarchy of operational commands and various support and training facilities. The Territorial Forces, a formal component of the armed forces since 1964, was apportioned among the forty-four province chiefs, the principal administrators of South Vietnam. In comparison, the Viet Cong army looked weak. With some 40,000 lightly equipped regulars, backed by about 80,000–100,000 part-time guerrillas and supported by a few thousand North Vietnamese troops and a fragile supply line hundreds of miles long, it was hardly an imposing force.[3] Nevertheless, this force had inflicted a series of defeats on the South Vietnamese troops, all but throwing them out of the countryside and back into the cities and towns.

---

[1] For general surveys of the South Vietnamese armed forces, see Collins, *Development and Training of the South Vietnamese Army*; and the Vietnamese-authored Indochina Monographs published by the U.S. Army Center of Military History (CMH), especially Dong Van Khuyen, *The RVNAF* (Washington, D.C., 1980); Ngo Quang Truong, *Territorial Forces* (Washington, D.C., 1981); and Cao Van Vien, *Leadership* (Washington, D.C., 1981). See also Memo, Maj Gen Ben Sternberg, MACV J–1, to COMUSMACV, 7 Jul 65, sub: RVNAF Strength Summary, SEAB, CMH (also in History file 17–11, William C. Westmoreland Papers, HRB, CMH).

[2] The name Territorial Forces was not adopted officially until much later, but the term is used throughout this work in the interest of clarity. The Territorial Forces, or "territorials," consisted of the Regional Forces (formerly the Civil Guard) and the Popular Forces (formerly the Self-Defense Corps), but not the People's Self-Defense Force formed in 1968 or the variety of other paramilitary forces.

[3] There was no agreement on the size and composition of Viet Cong and North Vietnamese forces throughout this early period. For example, see National Intelligence Survey 43D, CIA, "South Vietnam: General Survey," April 1965, p. 78, copy in SEAB, CMH; Military History Branch, Headquarters, United States Military Assistance Command, Vietnam (hereafter cited at USMACV), "Command History, 1965" (Saigon, 1966), p. 268, HRB, CMH; Interv, author with Lt Gen *(Continued)*

TABLE 1—SOUTH VIETNAMESE MILITARY STRENGTH, 1965

Force	1 January	30 June	30 June
	Assigned Strength	Programmed Strength	Estimated Strength
Army	220,360	233,200	237,800
Air Force	10,521	12,200	12,000
Navy	8,194	9,000	9,000
Marine Corps	7,209	6,600	6,700
Total Regulars	246,284	261,000	265,500
Regional Forces	96,049	110,000	106,500
Popular Forces	168,317	161,500	151,000
National Police	31,395	40,800	40,800
Civilian Irregular Defense Group	21,454	21,000	21,000
Coastal Force [a]	3,747	3,900	3,900

[a] Later integrated into the navy.

Source: Memo, Sternberg to COMUSMACV, 7 Jul 65, sub: RVNAF Strength Summary, SEAB, CMH.

An Army Divided

In practice, the greater size and materiel strength of the South Vietnamese armed forces counted for little. Just beneath the surface of this army lay great weaknesses, the most evident being its heavy involvement in national and local politics. Following the overthrow of Diem, the army corps commanders had transformed themselves into regional governors, and a host of lesser military officers had taken over the province and district administrations, causing political and military responsibilities to become hopelessly intertwined. By 1964, for example, the entire country was divided into four corps tactical zones,[4] each under an army corps headquarters, and subordinate division commanders controlled division tactical areas, smaller zones consisting of two or more provinces. Below the division level, responsibilities for security and other military-related pacification efforts were shared by regimental and battalion commanders; by territorial and paramilitary troop leaders; by military installation commandants; by province, district, and village chiefs; and even by mayors and police officials.

The army officers might have provided the mortar needed to hold the country together. Instead they became a major divisive force. Senior generals vied among themselves for political power, spreading military factionalism still further, and

(Continued) William E. Potts (hereafter cited as Potts Interv), MACV J–2 (1969–72), 12 Apr 84, SEAB, CMH; William C. Westmoreland, *Report on Operations in South Vietnam, January 1964–June 1968,* Section II of U.S. Pacific Command, *Report on the War in Vietnam (as of 30 June 1968)* (Washington, D.C.: Government Printing Office, 1969), p. 100; and, for one major dissenter, Samuel Adams, "Vietnam Cover-Up: Playing War With Numbers," *Harper's,* May 1975, pp. 41–44; and the ensuing intelligence controversy treated in Don Kowet, *A Matter of Honor* (New York: Macmillan, 1984) and other publications under way dealing with the Westmoreland-CBS libel suit.

[4] These administrative areas were known variously as regions, military regions, and corps tactical zones. The latter term is the most accurate and the most common, and is used throughout the text.

proved unable to pursue any unified course of action. By 1965 they had institutionalized a system of military patronage throughout the armed services and government. The power of each senior general, whether he occupied a military or a civilian post, had come to depend, not on competency, position, or rank, but on the number of rifles—or, more accurately, on the number of combat commanders whose loyalty he could command. In practice, the link between a junta general and, for example, an infantry battalion commander or a province chief rested on a complex network of political, professional, and familial relationships that shifted from time to time. Because their authority depended on these informal relationships, the generals made almost all promotions and appointments on the basis of favoritism and loyalty rather than merit. Thus for their advancement and economic well-being, South Vietnamese line and staff officers as well as province and district chiefs looked to some higher-placed military patron rather than to the army as a whole or to the state. Officers had to be ever alert for political and military changes that might affect their tenures and careers. Survival depended on political shrewdness rather than military ability. The result was a system of military patronage based on an intricate pattern of mutual obligations, responsibilities, and conventions. Any military endeavors or programs that ignored this system were bound to encounter serious difficulty.[5]

Institutionalized corruption held much of the government and army together. Although by no means unique, corruption in the Far East had long ago acquired a certain degree of Confucian respectability that was alien to the West. Historically, Asian civil servants supplemented fixed incomes through extralegal methods that in the West would have been labeled graft and corruption. Traditional Asian societies considered prosperity a product of good administration and expected successful administrators to supplement their generally low governmental salaries in this fashion. It was also acceptable for administrators to provide jobs for members of their extended families as long as those relatives were reasonably competent. Asian officials were, however, expected to exhibit a certain undefinable degree of "moderation" in these activities. Excessive profit taking was a sign of poor administration, which, if unchecked, could lead to general dissatisfaction and political upheaval.[6] Revolutionary communism, with its strong puritanical bent, posed a direct challenge to such traditions, both in North and South Vietnam. How the South Vietnamese Army officers would fare in their role of administrators remained to be seen.

Within the armed forces, the most common forms of abuse were the misappropriation of military funds or equipment, the padding of unit rolls ("ghosting"), and the sale of military assignments and services. While harmful, such practices were limited in scope and degree. But once in a position of political authority, the officer corps found that the range of these types of activities

---

[5] For further comments see Gerald Cannon Hickey, *The American Military Advisor and His Foreign Counterpart: The Case of Vietnam* (Santa Monica, Calif.: Rand Corp., 1965); Msg, Westmoreland MAC 3099 to Harris, 190620 Jun 64, COMUSMACV Message file, Westmoreland Papers, HRB, CMH.

[6] In Msg, Bunker SGN 17199 to SecState, 291145 Jan 68, sub: Senator Kennedy's Speech, Ellsworth Bunker Papers, U.S. Department of State (DS), the U.S. ambassador to South Vietnam held that corruption moved beyond tolerable limits when Vietnamese family interests took precedence over public responsibilities.

widened considerably and included such things as organizing entertainment enterprises; transporting stolen or smuggled goods and drugs; black marketing in rice, cement, and other commodities; demanding protection fees from businessmen and farmers; selling deferments from regular military service; controlling Vietnamese facilities and land used by American forces; and so forth.[7] Small fortunes could be made from the sale of political offices alone. The most lucrative posts were in Saigon and in the heavily populated provinces and districts, especially those close to the capital. Office seekers sometimes purchased appointments to such posts for a flat fee or for a percentage of the total profit. (For the acquisition of some of the more dangerous posts, such as district seats and Special Forces camps in the Central Highlands, no financial blandishments were involved, because there were no buyers.) As these practices became more entrenched, reform proved exceedingly difficult, and the occasional housecleanings that did occur were often only the product of internal political maneuvering. In many cases, because the wives or female relations of the involved officers handled such illicit transactions, outsiders found it extremely difficult to discover their full nature and extent. Yet given the low pay of the South Vietnamese officers, and the immense wealth that the United States began to funnel into the country, many thought it reasonable to supplement their incomes in this manner as long as their profit taking was not excessive and did not interfere directly with their military duties. But the total effect of such venality was disastrous for the army. Increases in military security and greater American aid often led to increases in graft and corruption, without any commensurate rise in the quality of public service. Although these practices kept the government in business, they compromised the integrity of the officer corps, fostered military factionalism, dealt a severe blow to South Vietnamese military professionalism, and retarded the war effort.

The various factions and cliques of the South Vietnamese officer corps were rooted in family ties, personal loyalties, and financial emoluments.[8] Rank, age, religion (Buddhist or Roman Catholic), area of origin (northern, central, or southern Vietnam), source of commission (officer candidate school or military academy), and past assignments also played a part. At the top the alliances between senior officers tended to be transitory. During 1964 a rising coterie of younger officers, almost all in their late thirties and early forties, gradually displaced the older generals who had toppled Diem and slowly emerged as the real arbiters of power in Saigon. Most were corps and division commanders, each with their own followings in subordinate staffs and units, who, in the course of

---

[7] For details, see Vien, *Leadership*, pp. 117–23, and files on corruption, SEAB, CMH.

[8] For a detailed treatment, see Allan E. Goodman, *An Institutional Profile of the South Vietnamese Officer Corps* (Santa Monica, Calif.: Rand Corp., 1970), and, located in SEAB, CMH, the following: Airgram (72 pages), State A–131 to Saigon, 13 Aug 71, sub: Some Aspects of Personal Relations Among Senior RVNAF Officers; DIA South Vietnamese officer biographies (on microfilm); copy of Intelligence Memorandum CIA/CR M66–20, Directorate of Intelligence, CIA, 27 Jul 66, sub: Selected Personalities, Republic of Vietnam; and South Vietnamese officer dossiers. The officer corps was about 20,000 strong, with 16,000 aspirants and lieutenants, 3,000 captains, 1,000 majors, 250 lieutenant colonels, and 100 colonels and generals.

General Nguyen Van Thieu   **Air Vice-Marshal Nguyen Cao Ky**

their long military careers, had come to know one another intimately. The most prominent of these so-called young turks were General Nguyen Van Thieu, who became minister of defense in early 1965; Air Vice-Marshal Nguyen Cao Ky, head of the South Vietnamese Air Force; and General Nguyen Chanh Thi, commander of the I Corps Tactical Zone.[9] Dissatisfied with the series of military and civilian regimes that they had supported since the fall of Diem, this group of officers staged their own coup in June 1965 and took direct control of the South Vietnamese government.

The constitution of the new regime, the Convention of 19 June 1965, was actually a makeshift agreement between these younger generals.[10] Under its provisions ten of them constituted themselves as the Committee for the Direction of the State—or, more simply, the Directory.[11] Theoretically, the Directory acted as a standing committee of an armed forces congress, a group of some thirty to forty lesser generals and senior colonels who were supposed to represent the interests of the armed forces as a whole. In practice, the Directory ruled South Vietnam. It named its chairman, General Thieu, as chief of state and its

---

[9] Because the ranks of South Vietnamese generals constantly changed, all South Vietnamese general officers are referred to as "general," and, as noted in Chapter 1, given names are used in place of family names.

[10] On the organization of the South Vietnamese government and high command in 1965, see Joint Chiefs of Staff, "Southeast Asia Military Fact Book," January 1967, MACV Microfilm files, reel no. 1, frame 2745 (hereafter cited as MICRO reel/frame numbers, with the latter, if available, generally referring to the first page of the document), RG 334, WNRC; Bernard B. Fall, *The Two Vietnams: A Political and Military Analysis*, 2d rev. ed. (New York: Praeger, 1967), app. 7, pp. 451–54.

[11] Also called the National Leadership Committee, its initial members were Ky, Thieu, Thi, and Generals Linh Quang Vien, Cao Van Vien, Le Nguyen Khang, Pham Xuan Chieu, Nguyen Huu Co, Vinh Loc, and Dang Van Quang.

vice-chairman, Air Marshal Ky, as commissioner in charge of the executive. Ky, acting as a kind of appointed prime minister, or premier, was to run the day-to-day Saigon administration and to work closely with Thieu on broad matters of national policy. Both kept their military ranks and were to share power equally with the other Directory members. The Directory, as a body, was to rule on all senior military and civil promotions and appointments, but its individual members were free to conduct their affairs more or less independent of the Ky administration. In the beginning, few Americans leaders felt that this patchwork affair had any great promise of effectiveness or permanency.[12]

Once in power the individual factions within this new generation of generals became more apparent. Most visible was the so-called Ky clique. The 34-year-old air force general had many powerful friends but, with few ground troops under his direct command, had always lacked the soldiers that provided the grist for every serious coup. His appointment as administrative chief may have been a compromise among the bickering army generals, too wary to give one of their own members so much power. Like most of them, Ky had served his military apprenticeship under the French and later attended American military schools. Unlike many, he held a commission from the Nam Dinh Reserve Officers School and, although a native of North Vietnam, was a Buddhist, the religion of most South Vietnamese. His most distinguishing characteristic, however, was his exuberant style and flashy appearance, which made him considerably more popular among the younger officers and the general public than the saturnine Thieu. Closely allied to Ky were two older members of the Directory, Generals Linh Quang Vien, a military staff chief, and Le Nguyen Khang, who headed the South Vietnamese Marine Corps and also commanded the Capital Military District,[13] a command encompassing Saigon and its immediate environs. Also included in the Ky circle were three of his former classmates at Nam Dinh: General Nguyen Bao Tri, commander of an infantry division stationed close to Saigon; Col. Nguyen Ngoc Loan, chief of the army counterintelligence agency; and Col. Nguyen Duc Thang, the army operations chief. Coincidentally, all of these supporters were born in North Vietnam.

Representing somewhat of a counter to Ky was the 42-year-old Directory chairman and president, General Thieu. A native of the South but a Roman Catholic, Thieu had served with French military forces until 1954 and then joined the new South Vietnamese Army. After attending the U.S. Army Command and General Staff College at Fort Leavenworth, Kansas, he commanded a division near Saigon that supported the revolt against Diem and a subsequent coup d'etat early in 1964. He was later chief of staff of the army, then a corps commander, and, at the time of the June coup, minister of defense. Among his peers, Thieu was best known for his political shrewdness and patience. Known as the Old Fox, he possessed what the Vietnamese called *khon* or *khon vat*, the ability to listen without committing oneself, a special kind of intelligence or cunning that

---

[12] For example, see Westmoreland, *Soldier Reports*, p. 138; Maxwell D. Taylor, *Swords and Plowshares* (New York: Norton, 1972), pp. 345–46.

[13] Prior to 7 June 1966 the Capital Military District was called the Capital Military Region and technically was coequal with a corps tactical zone (CTZ). After that date it was a subordinate command of the III CTZ commander.

emphasized calculated self-interest. As president, Thieu quietly watched over the interests of the other army generals, as well as his own, and also served as a bridge between the officers in the field and the administrators in Saigon.

Other prominent generals included Nguyen Huu Co, a former corps commander who now headed both the military and defense staffs, and the four corps commanders: Nguyen Chanh Thi, the fiercely independent leader of the I Corps Tactical Zone, made up of the northern provinces of South Vietnam; Vinh Loc, a former cavalry officer in the French Army who had returned from exile to parlay a divisional command into control of the II Corps Tactical Zone, encompassing what was known as the Central Highlands; Cao Van Vien, a sometime Ky supporter, who headed the III Corps Tactical Zone, consisting of the provinces around Saigon; and Dang Van Quang, a close ally of Thieu, who had succeeded him as commander of the IV Corps Tactical Zone, comprising the rich lowlands of the southern Mekong Delta. All were members of the Directory, and each had his own followings and interests.

From its inception, the government of the generals was thoroughly fragmented. Although Ky supervised the central administration, he had little real authority over the military-related ministries or over the province and district chiefs, who actually implemented policy. Co's Ministry of Defense had jurisdiction over finance, veterans affairs, mobilization, and military justice but had no authority over the military staffs or the operational commands. The general staff, in turn, had little control over the semiautonomous corps commanders, and Co himself derived most of his real power and prestige from his close working relationship with General Westmoreland. A later Directory decree formalized this dispersion of power by officially scattering appointment and promotion authority among the generals. For example, the Directory chairman appointed corps commanders; the defense minister, corps chiefs of staff; the chief of the armed forces, division and sector (province-level) commanders; and corps commanders, all deputy division and subsector (district-level) commanders in their zone. Staff appointment and promotion authority were apportioned similarly. These arrangements established a system of checks and balances that prevented any general officer from acquiring too much power, thus ensuring that the senior generals undertook extensive negotiations on the most important administrative actions.[14] Personalities and personal relationships thus remained critical, and in matters of any importance Co and the corps commanders dealt directly with Ky and Thieu as fellow generals rather than as subordinates.

Organization for War

To be effective, every U.S. adviser had to understand how the South Vietnamese military system worked, or at least how it was supposed to work. The many organizational similarities between the American and South Vietnamese armed forces were, in many cases, deceptive. The South Vietnamese military

---

[14] Khuyen, *The RVNAF*, pp. 54–55 and 87. The decree also made the appointment and transfer of general officers and province chiefs the prerogative of the Directory chairman.

body that carried out administrative and planning functions for the entire armed forces was the Joint General Staff (*Chart 1*). Actually an army headquarters, it ran the army's training and logistical system and directly controlled a number of support units in the Saigon area. As the highest South Vietnamese military headquarters, it also dealt directly with the theater-level American military headquarters in South Vietnam, the Military Assistance Command, Vietnam (MACV). However, it possessed only limited authority over the corps commanders and other major military elements.[15]

The Joint General Staff itself consisted of five functional elements, supervised by a chief of staff. An Operations Directorate controlled five staff sections (J–2, J–3, J–5, J–6, and J–7);[16] a Personnel Directorate had three staff sections (the J–1, Military Police, and Adjutant General); a Logistics Directorate (J–4) managed the technical service branches (ordnance, signal, engineers, and others); and a Training Directorate and a General Political Warfare Department had smaller staffs. The last three also operated their own semiautonomous agencies.

Associated with the Joint General Staff were semi-independent commands for the air force, navy, marine corps, and airborne forces.[17] The Navy Command, after an abortive mutiny of its senior officers in April 1965, remained under the close scrutiny of the Joint General Staff chief, but the other three were more autonomous. Separate administrative commands also existed for rangers, armor, artillery, military police, Special Forces, and Territorial Forces, but they had no operational responsibilities. An inspector general's office also existed, but, lacking a network of subordinate offices, its authority was limited.[18]

The Operations and Personnel Directorates were the heart of the Joint Staff, providing guidance to the corps commands and monitoring their activities. Neither directorate had any command responsibilities, and both worked closely with American planners on organization, general campaign plans, and various administrative projects. The Operations Directorate also allocated the marine and airborne battalions to the corps commanders and served as the focal point for army intelligence efforts; however, it had little say over either the employment or the administration of the airborne and marine forces and little control over the

---

[15] For detailed treatments of RVNAF organization and evolution, see Briefing, MACJ–311 [to U.S. Senate Investigation Committee], 25 Oct 67, sub: RVNAF Organization and Force Structure, MICRO 1/1587, RG 334, WNRC; appropriate sections of the MACV command histories for the period 1964–73, HRB, CMH; appropriate volumes of CMH Indochina Monographs; and files on the South Vietnamese military, SEAB, CMH.

[16] In the American, French, and South Vietnamese armies the military headquarters of a commander was supervised by a chief of staff and divided into functional sections. Each number signified responsibility for a different functional area: "1" for personnel; "2" for intelligence; "3" for operations; "4" for logistics; "5" for plans (or psychological operations and civil affairs); and others for communications, counterintelligence, and so forth. The letter prefix signified the type of headquarters: "S" for battalion or brigade; "G" for division, corps, and larger army headquarters; "J" for interservice; and "C" for combined, or multinational, commands.

[17] The air force and navy chiefs were special assistants to the Joint General Staff (JGS) chief, and thus the two services were technically not subordinate JGS commands.

[18] Office of the Inspector General, MACV, "Inspector General History, 1964–1972," p. 99, MACV IG files, box 1, accession no. 77/0074, RG 334, WNRC. Normally, an inspector general's office handles general complaints and inspects units for mission performance, discipline, and adherence to orders and directives. The provost marshal's office, another organization, deals with criminal investigations.

26

many intelligence agencies operating outside of its immediate authority. In fact, the South Vietnamese government had no centralized intelligence system, and its information-gathering capabilities at the village and hamlet levels, where Viet Cong activity was most intense, were almost nonexistent.[19]

General Bui Huu Nhon, a political appointee who had commanded a division in the Diem regime, supervised the joint-level logistical staff (J–4) and a separate army supply organization, the Central Logistics Command. The command controlled agencies for ordnance, engineers, quartermaster, procurement, medical, signal, and transportation. Except for procurement and transportation, each operated its own base depot, which undertook complex repairs, stored equipment and supplies, and supported logistical units assigned to the four corps headquarters.[20]

In the field, area logistics commands, engineer groups, and signal battalions provided direct support to the South Vietnamese corps. From north to south, the area logistics commands were based at the port cities of Da Nang, Qui Nhon, Nha Trang, Saigon, and Can Tho; each consisted of ordnance, quartermaster, and medical units and their field storage and maintenance depots. These units, as well as corps, divisions and port commands, had their own depots and transportation (vehicle and boat) units that were supported through ordnance and quartermaster channels. The South Vietnamese Air Force and Navy provided logistical support peculiar to their services (for example, special fuels, complex maintenance) but relied on the army supply system for most items. The navy maintained a shipyard and supply center in Saigon, but the army supplied almost all logistical support for the marine corps. The air force had its headquarters at Tan Son Nhut Air Base on the northwest outskirts of Saigon and operated a supply complex at Bien Hoa, a few kilometers to the east.

The South Vietnamese logistical system was a well-developed but limited organization, designed to support an army that operated from fixed bases in carefully defined areas at a continuous but relatively low level of activity. The most immediate logistical needs of the ground combat units were food and ammunition. Consequently, Vietnamese commanders stocked ample supplies of these items in unit depots and storage areas, enabling them to dispense almost completely with detailed logistical planning for most tactical operations. The dispersion of the ground forces in pacification-related missions and the interdic-

---

[19] See Hoang Ngoc Lung, *Intelligence*, Indochina Monographs (Washington, D.C.: U.S. Army Center of Military History, 1982), pp. 37–83; Cao Van Vien and Dong Van Khuyen, *Reflections on the Vietnam War*, Indochina Monographs (Washington, D.C.: U.S. Army Center of Military History, 1980), p. 37; Potts Interv, 12 Apr 84, SEAB, CMH.

[20] Briefing, 1969, sub: RVNAF Log. Systems, MICRO 2/2652; Briefing, MACJ–46, 26 Oct 67, sub: Republic of Vietnam Armed Forces Logistics System, MICRO 1/1624. Both in RG 334, WNRC. For a detailed treatment, see Dong Van Khuyen, *RVNAF Logistics*, Indochina Monographs (Washington, D.C.: U.S. Army Center of Military History, 1980). The Logistics Command also included a logistics management school. The signal agency controlled a signal group in Saigon, a central base depot, and a signal battalion supporting the Joint General Staff; the signal staff section (J–6) of the Operations Directorate was responsible only for interservice communications and general signal planning and coordination. South Vietnamese engineer construction and combat groups (of several battalions each) operated in each corps area with their own supply and maintenance depots, and several area construction offices engaged in local contracting.

27

tion of roads and waterways by the Viet Cong furthered this practice.[21] Corps and agency logistical units, on the other hand, were inexperienced and found it difficult to adjust to the rising tempo of combat activity and the resulting demands on supply and maintenance facilities. Their own depots were overspecialized, understocked, and poorly maintained. Unit supply and maintenance requests tended to become bogged down in bureaucratic procedures, especially when the requests could not be satisfied quickly; depot personnel often shunted aside complex repair and maintenance tasks for easier ones that lower-echelon workers ought to have done.

Poor maintenance in the field and marginal repair facilities in the depots compounded the supply problems. With little confidence in their logistical support units, combat units frequently chose to retain damaged equipment and often failed to even submit requests for parts and supplies, which they felt would not be honored. The U.S. Military Assistance Program provided most of the equipment and supplies for the logistical agencies, but MACV found it difficult to constantly adjust the twelve-month program to the changing needs of the war effort. For items not supplied by the program, the agencies relied on frequent small purchases on the local market, a practice that also kept depot stock low. In the depots, storage and accounting procedures were time-consuming and prone to error and falsification, and the corruption and political rivalries of the officer corps militated against the hard work and cooperation needed to make any military logistical system successful. Almost incidently, Americans suspected General Nhon, the logistics director, of corruption, and he was one of the very few senior Vietnamese officers later dismissed from the army on such charges.[22]

No more successful was the Central Training Command under General Ton That Dinh. Described by Americans as "an aggressive, arrogant officer frequently erratic in personal behavior, . . . ambitious and flamboyant," Dinh had figured prominently in many of the previous coups, but his assignment to the Training Command reflected his waning influence. The command had little direct authority and supervised instruction in the armed forces by determining the location, type, and duration of courses, and the number of trainees. While it had direct control over the five large national training centers that provided recruit and unit training for the regular army, it had less authority over the Regional Forces training camps and almost none over those maintained by the air force, navy, marines, airborne, rangers, and Special Forces. The many small camps run by the province chiefs and most of the infantry divisions were also independent. Americans felt that the facilities and cadre at all camps were generally poor and the training rudimentary. But, as one adviser observed, "it's kind of hard to say exactly what the hell they're teaching when they're teaching all in Vietnamese." American influence was largely limited to providing training aids and manuals and to reviewing scheduled instruction. The camps could accommodate roughly

---

[21] Cao Van Vien et al., *The U.S. Adviser*, Indochina Monographs (Washington, D.C.: U.S. Army Center of Military History, 1980), pp. 65–66; Khuyen, *RVNAF Logistics*, pp. 98 and 450.

[22] See Memo, T. P. H. Dunlop, Chairman, Inter-Agency Committee on Corruption, to Frank Wisner, 5 Jul 67, sub: Request from Amb. Komer for Information on GVN Officials Dismissed for Corruption, SEAB, CMH; Khuyen, *The RVNAF*, p. 359.

forty thousand to fifty thousand trainees, but most did not operate at full capacity or on a twelve-month schedule.[23]

The Central Training Command also maintained specialized schools for artillery, infantry, armor, signal, engineer, military police, ordnance, transportation, psychological warfare, the adjutant general, quartermaster, administration and finance, social training, medicine, and language. The branch-affiliated schools gave basic and advanced courses for officers and noncommissioned officers; the medical school provided training for medical assistants, but not for physicians or dentists; and the language school taught English to those Vietnamese scheduled to receive military training in the United States. The instruction was roughly similar to that offered at comparable U.S. Army institutions, and the schools depended on their parent agencies in the Joint General Staff for cadre and course material. Most were located in the general Saigon area, with the largest, the infantry school, situated at Thu Duc, about 5 kilometers north of the capital.

The officer and officer candidate schools had more independence. Two schools, the Officer Candidate School at Thu Duc and the National Military Academy at Da Lat, supplied the army with most of its officers. The French had established both, but American advice and assistance had modified them to reflect American military methods and doctrine. Thu Duc offered nine months of military instruction to high school–level officer candidates, and graduates received a reserve commission, the rank of aspirant (one level below second lieutenant), and a four-year active duty obligation. The Da Lat academy, located in a former resort town in the Central Highlands, conducted a two-year program and awarded graduates a regular commission and the rank of second lieutenant, with a ten-year active duty obligation. But Da Lat produced less than two hundred new officers each year, while Thu Duc turned out several thousand annually, and remained the army's primary source of small-unit leaders. More important, admission into either program depended on advanced educational qualifications, a requirement that effectively eliminated most of the rural leaders from the Saigon officer corps and, over the years, ensured that the economic and social distinctions of South Vietnamese society were carried over into the armed forces.

Other key schools included a National Noncommissioned Officers Academy at the central coastal town of Nha Trang and, for mid-level officers, a Command and Staff College at Da Lat. The South Vietnamese Navy and Air Force also offered special training courses, as did U.S. mobile training teams assigned temporarily to various schools and camps. Through the U.S. Offshore Training Program, American advisers also sent thousands of South Vietnamese officers to U.S. service schools for both advanced technical and command instruction.[24] However, an evaluation in mid-1965 showed that about half of the Vietnamese

[23] First quotation from Briefing Book for SECDEF Honolulu Conference, 20–21 Nov 63, box 2, accession no. 69A702, RG 334, WNRC. See also Special Rpt, CIA, 8 Nov 63, sub: The Members of the New Regime in South Vietnam, SEAB, CMH. Second quotation from Interv no. 250, Lt Col Benjamin Russell, Senior Adviser, ARVN Armor School, June 1966–January 1967 (hereafter cited as Russell Interv), 29 Jan 74, Fort Knox Armor School Interviews, U.S. Army Military History Institute (MHI). See also Fact Sheet, MAC–RF/PF (for U.S. Senate briefing), 25 Oct 67, sub: Training Center Capacities, MICRO 1/1778, RG 334, WNRC.

[24] For a breakdown, see Talking Paper, Lt Col Herbert Y. Schandler, DA, 23 Jul 67, sub: MACV Advisory Structure, SEAB, CMH.

students lacked the "minimum" English-language comprehension needed to understand the courses attended. One American senior adviser termed the entire program a waste, viewing the incomplete knowledge that was acquired as "a dangerous thing." Another felt that Saigon sent only its "duds" or those "in a holding pattern" while temporarily out of favor.[25]

The South Vietnamese General Political Warfare Department had no true American equivalent. The junta generals had established it in 1964 under the guidance of a Nationalist Chinese advisory team invited to South Vietnam several years earlier by President Diem. Its commander, General Huynh Van Cao, a onetime favorite of Diem, had survived the political turmoil of 1964 and 1965 through his various political connections, but neither Americans nor Vietnamese thought highly of his abilities, and he may have served only as a figurehead in his new assignment. Cao's organization included staff sections for political indoctrination, psychological warfare, military security, social services, and the three chaplaincies (Roman Catholic, Buddhist, and Protestant), as well as special sections for public relations and recreation. It also provided support and direction to the political warfare battalions assigned to tactical commands, and was in the process of establishing its own branch school.[26]

The department focused its activities primarily on its own troops rather than those of the enemy. The Political Indoctrination Section, assisted by Nationalist Chinese advisers, concentrated on boosting morale and patriotism in the armed forces and on countering enemy propaganda. Although the section had begun training political warfare staff officers and school instructors, most of its existing activities centered around news and entertainment programs for the military. Much of its material was Confucian in content, emphasizing personal conduct and traditional morality. The army's *Small Unit Commander's Handbook*, for example, stressed not only sacrifice for country but also respect for the aged, correct behavior, and prohibitions against excessive "drinking, gambling, love affairs, and opium-smoking."[27] More ambitious projects, such as the development of a political warfare cadre system throughout the armed forces, had political ramifications that led to continued delays.

The Social Services Section was responsible for dependent housing, school, and medical programs, and the post exchange and commissary. Most of its

[25] First quotation from Memo, Col Jack M. Duncan, Director, Defense Language Institute, U.S. Naval Station, Anacostia, to Asst SecDef for ISA, 22 Apr 65, sub: English Language Training Provided for Foreign Military Personnel, Foreign Officer Training file, Henry C. Newton Papers, MHI. Second quotation from Msg, Westmoreland MAC 3099 to Harris, 190620 Jun 64, COMUSMACV Message file, Westmoreland Papers, HRB, CMH, quoting the words of Col Wilbur Wilson, the III Corps senior adviser. Third and fourth quotations from Interv, author with Lt Col Edward F. McGushin, Battalion and Staff Adviser, Airborne Division, August 1966–June 1967 (hereafter cited McGushin Interv), 27 Feb 76, SEAB, CMH.

[26] For the early development of political warfare in South Vietnam, see Fact Sheet, MACPD, 20 Jan 67, sub: RVNAF Political Indoctrination Program, MICRO 75/1710, RG 334, WNRC; Monte R. Bullard, "Political Cadre Systems in the Military" (Student paper written at U.S. Army Command and General Staff College, Fort Leavenworth, Kans., June 1970), pp. 20–23 and 128–41; USMACV, "Command History, 1965," annex L, and "1969," 3 vols. (Saigon, 1970), 3:XI–33 to XI–34. On Cao, see Westmoreland, *Soldier Reports*, p. 41; Robert Shaplen, *The Lost Revolution: The U.S. in Vietnam, 1946–1966*, rev. ed. (New York: Harper and Row, 1966), pp. 170–71. Cao later became a senator in the South Vietnamese legislature.

[27] Vien, *Leadership*, p. 177.

programs were overmanaged and underdeveloped. Those involving money and materiel were rife with corruption, and characterized by mismanagement and a general absence of command interest. Lack of attention to the problems of the ordinary soldier was the primary villain. Despite Vietnam's martial tradition, soldiering on the Asian mainland never ranked as a notable occupation, especially in the enlisted ranks, and the pervasiveness of class distinctions throughout the army militated against the closer rapport needed between officers and men.

The Psychological Warfare Section, which supervised military civic action and psychological operations, exhibited the same weaknesses. The army's civic action programs, mostly conducted by the territorials through psychological warfare–civic action teams operating in each province, were somewhat rudderless attempts to win the support of the civilian population. The section's own operations generally supported the Ministry of Information's *Chieu Hoi* ("Open Arms") Program, encouraging Viet Cong soldiers to surrender voluntarily. Although initially weak, the program had strong American backing from the U.S. Information Agency staff in Saigon and promised the most immediate results on the battlefield.

The most mysterious organ of the department was the Military Security Service (MSS). Although nominally under the deputy chief of staff for political warfare, the security service, like the Central Intelligence Office, the South Vietnamese equivalent of the American Central Intelligence Agency, operated directly under Premier Ky. MSS personnel supervised all counterintelligence and security activities, including the often lucrative task of awarding security clearances to military and civilian job seekers. Under the direction of Colonel Loan, the service focused less on the enemy than on domestic intelligence, acting as a watchdog for political discontent within the military community, and, with about seventeen hundred members stationed throughout the country, was able to keep a close watch on local officials and military commanders. However, its effectiveness in preventing enemy infiltration of South Vietnamese military ranks was doubtful, and by 1965 many Americans believed that Viet Cong agents had heavily penetrated Saigon's armed forces, especially at the lower levels.[28]

The Joint General Staff indirectly supervised a number of ground combat forces based in the Saigon area. The six parachute battalions of the Airborne Command and the five infantry battalions of the Marine Corps Command constituted the South Vietnamese "general reserve," the last vestiges of the French mobile task forces (mechanized mobile groups and amphibious commands) that had once operated throughout Vietnam. These units were the only true regulars in the South Vietnamese ground forces, because they alone were not recruited from any fixed geographical locale. They also received better training, pay, food, quarters, medical care, and dependent benefits than the rest of the armed forces. When not in Saigon, they operated in multibattalion task forces, gener-

---

[28] Vien et al., *U.S. Adviser*, p. 82; Fact Sheet, MACV, 5 Mar 65, sub: Increase in MSS Advisory Effort, SEAB, CMH. On the Viet Cong's penetration, see Msg, Walt to Westmoreland, 261345 Aug 65, COMUSMACV Message file, Westmoreland Papers, HRB, and Interv, author with Samuel Adams, May 1975, SEAB, both in CMH. Adams, the controversial Central Intelligence Agency analyst, wrote several official studies on the subject, which the author has reviewed.

ally reinforcing local South Vietnamese units in difficulty.[29] However, both airborne and marine units had a significant political role to play in Saigon. With General Khang, Ky's friend, heading the marines, and General Du Quoc Dong, Thieu's ally, commanding the airborne, the general reserve troops represented the real muscle of the Saigon-based Directory members and also constituted a balance of power between the rival officer cliques of Thieu and Ky.

The Joint General Staff "honor guard" battalion and a similar unit, the Capital Security Group, had the primary function of supporting the central military and political administration. The Security Group was a palace guard regiment composed of one bodyguard company, two infantry battalions, an armor detachment, and a signal company; it provided security for government offices in Saigon and for the residences and families of important officials. Both units stood outside the American-supported South Vietnamese military force structure, and MACV had no control over their deployment or activities.[30]

Command and control of the South Vietnamese Navy and Air Force was also centered in Saigon. The navy, with about eleven thousand men, consisted of six Riverine Assault Groups, each capable of transporting one infantry battalion; the Coastal Force, a paramilitary junk fleet that was officially incorporated into the navy that July; and a tiny seagoing force that worked closely with small American fleet units. Following the short-lived naval mutiny, the Joint General Staff made the marine corps, up to that time a component of the navy, an autonomous service.[31] The air force was about the same size as the navy, with 282 aircraft in four fighter-bomber, four helicopter, two transport, and four liaison squadrons, and was in the process of forming two more fighter-bomber and four more liaison squadrons. While specific air and naval units supported each corps tactical zone, they took orders only from their service headquarters in Saigon and not from the local corps commanders. The aviation arm had played such a significant role in previous coups, transporting friendly troops and threatening the movement of others, that Ky thought it wise to retain his command of the air service.

The Field Army

Below the Joint General Staff, the division between political and military responsibilities became even more blurred.[32] The four army corps commanders also acted as regional governors for each corps zone, which they ran almost as individual fiefs. Each zone was divided into division tactical areas, a few regimental-size special zones, and several autonomous cities. Saigon and its

---

[29] Vien, *Leadership,* pp. 92–94; McGushin Interv, 27 Feb 76, SEAB, CMH; and Interv (transcribed), Benis M. Frank and U.S. Marine Corps History and Museum Division historians with General Le Nguyen Khang, 30 Sep 75, pp. 7 and 31–32, U.S. Marine Corps Oral History Collection, U.S. Marine Corps Historical Center (MCHC), Washington, D.C.

[30] Khuyen, *The RVNAF,* p. 72.

[31] USMACV, "Command History, 1965," pp. 2–3, 87, 90, HRB, CMH.

[32] For a general survey of the RVNAF in 1965, see copy of Intelligence Memorandum OCI 1699/66, Directorate of Intelligence, CIA, 12 Dec 66, sub: The South Vietnamese Army Today; Memo, Sternberg to COMUSMACV, 7 Jul 65, sub: RVNAF Strength Summary; Memo, Col A. P. Wade, Chief, Military History Branch, MACV, to CofS, MACV, 8 Dec 66, sub: RVNAF Organizational Background and Employment. All in SEAB, CMH.

IV Corps Troops Boarding U.S. Helicopters *for area security operations*

environs were considered too sensitive to be under the control of a single commander, and authority was divided between the commander of the Capital Military District and various civilian officials. Under these military commands were the original civil administrative areas: 44 provinces and 219 districts, most headed by military officers who commanded local territorial and police units. For military matters, provinces were known as sectors and districts as subsectors, and their military chains of command wound through the division and corps headquarters and up to the Joint General Staff. For nonmilitary affairs, the province administrators dealt directly with the civil ministries in Saigon.

By 1965, in order to combat the Viet Cong insurgency, almost all South Vietnamese ground units had assumed area security missions. Saigon had apportioned its combat forces more or less equally among the four corps zones (*see Table* 2). General Thi held the I Corps Tactical Zone in the north with two infantry divisions, the 1st and 2d, the 51st Infantry Regiment, a few armor and ranger units, and the territorial troops of the five large but sparsely populated provinces (*see Map* 2). The proximity of North Vietnam made the zone a potentially dangerous battlefield. Although the recent arrival of U.S. Marine Corps units was reassuring, the political machinations of the charismatic and ambitious Thi posed an equally worrisome threat to security and stability. To the immediate south, General Loc secured the Central Highlands with a similar force, including the 22d and 23d Infantry Divisions and the 42d Infantry Regiment. In general,

TABLE 2—SOUTH VIETNAMESE INFANTRY BATTALIONS BY CORPS AREA,
MARCH 1965

Type of Battalions	I Corps Tactical Zone	II Corps Tactical Zone	III Corps Tactical Zone	IV Corps Tactical Zone	Total
Divisional	18	15	18	27	78
Separate Regiment	3	3	9	..	15
Airborne	1	3	2	..	6
Ranger	3	4	8	5	20
Marine	..	2	3	..	5
Total	25	27	40	32	124

Source: RVNAF organization files, SEAB, CMH.

the 22d Division and the territorials guarded the coast, while the 23d Division and the 42d Regiment operated in the interior, working mainly on the central plateau. Below the Highlands, General Vien's III Corps protected the approaches to the heavily populated Saigon area with two infantry divisions, the 5th and 25th; two independent infantry regiments, the 43d and 48th; and several independent battalions. Three more infantry divisions, the 7th, 9th, and 21st, garrisoned the rich rice-growing areas of the IV Corps Tactical Zone under General Quang. Both Vien and Quang had ranger and armor units in support, and substantially more Territorial Forces, because of the higher population density and greater number of province and district seats. The buildup of U.S. Army ground combat units around the capital gave an added measure of security to both southern zones. However, the deep involvement of many of the Vietnamese southern troop commanders in national politics was a constant cause for concern.

The organization of the nine South Vietnamese infantry divisions and the four independent regiments was fairly standard. With the exception of the 23d, each division controlled three infantry regiments of three battalions each, two artillery battalions (one of 105-mm. howitzers, one of 4.2-inch mortars), and support units (an engineer battalion, administrative, reconnaissance, signal, medical, quartermaster, ordnance, and transportation companies, and a military police detachment). The 23d Division was similar, but had only two rifle regiments. The four separate regiments, also with three infantry battalions each, normally operated under a "special zone" headquarters controlling an area somewhat smaller than a division zone. The corps commanders also controlled twenty ranger battalions, seven independent artillery battalions, six armored cavalry squadrons, and those airborne and marine units that the Joint General Staff had assigned to them.

Armor, artillery, rangers, and Special Forces constituted somewhat independent components of the field army. In 1965 the South Vietnamese armor force consisted of five tank troops with M24 light tanks dating from World War II, three scout troops with M8 armored cars of similar vintage, and twenty-one mechanized rifle troops with the new amphibious M113 armored personnel carrier. Each troop had about fifteen to twenty vehicles, and the twenty-nine existing troops were organized into six armored cavalry squadrons under the direct control of the corps commanders. Given the absence of enemy armor, these units

NORTH
VIETNAM

LAOS

THAILAND

CAMBODIA

Hue

1st Division

Da Nang
Hoi An   51st Regiment

I CORPS

Quang
Ngai   2d Division

42d Regiment
Kontum

Pleiku
Qui Nhon

II CORPS

22d Division

SOUTH
VIETNAM   *Tuy Hoa*

23d Division   *Ban Me Thuot*

Nha Trang
Da Lat *Cam Ranh*

An Loc

PHNOM PENH

III CORPS
Tay Ninh
5th Division   48th Regiment
Xuan Loc
25th Division ● SAIGON
43d Regiment
9th Division *My Tho*
Sa Dec   *Vung Tau*
IV CORPS
Rach Gia *Can Tho*   7th Division

SOUTH CHINA SEA

Soc Trang

GULF
OF
THAILAND

Bac Lieu
Ca Mau   21st Division

Mekong R

CORPS AREAS OF
RESPONSIBILITY
1965

0   100 MILES

0   100 KILOMETERS

MAP 2

constituted a formidable force. They were, however, often road-bound and were employed piecemeal supporting infantry sweeps, protecting fixed installations as palace guards, or spearheading army coups. Although training and maintenance were superior to the rest of the army, armor was not living up to its expectations.[33]

South Vietnamese artillery was fairly uniform and modern. Supplementing the eighteen divisional 4.2-inch and 105-mm. battalions were the equivalent of ten separate artillery battalions, including six of heavy 155-mm. howitzers under corps control and several 75-mm. and 105-mm. batteries of the general reserve. Both divisional and corps artillery normally fell under the control of the corps commander, and, like armor, these units were deployed in small packets in area support missions. The decentralized deployments, in turn, caused serious command and control problems, battalion and battery headquarters deteriorated from disuse, and the individual two-gun artillery platoons rarely went out on field operations.[34]

The ranger battalions also operated directly under the corps commanders. In theory, the rangers, light infantry dressed in special tiger-striped camouflaged fatigues, specialized in counterguerrilla operations (patrols, raids, ambushes); but, in practice, corps commanders used them as their personal reserve and generally employed them in the same manner as regular infantry battalions or as palace guards. Without the administrative, logistical, and combat support available to the divisional infantry battalions, the ranger units were plagued by serious morale and discipline problems and acquired an extremely poor reputation among American advisers. By 1965 they had lost their commando role to a variety of units led by American and South Vietnamese Special Forces.

The South Vietnamese Special Forces (*Lac Luong Dac Biet*) had begun in 1956 as the Presidential Survey Office, became the 77th Special Forces Group in 1960, and simply the Special Forces in 1962. Throughout this period the organization reported directly to President Diem and often carried out special military and political tasks. Organized into small hierarchical detachments similar to its American equivalent, it worked closely with U.S. Army Special Forces units and South Vietnam's ethnic minorities; participated in cross-border operations; kept surveillance over local military and civilian political activities; and trained and armed paramilitary groups, such as Diem's Catholic Youth Corps. Its early leadership was highly politicized, and the fall of Diem in 1963 brought purges and chaos, with the junta generals placing one of Co's proteges, General Doan Van Quang,[35] in charge of the force and moving its command elements under the

---

[33] Nicholas A. Andreacchio, "An Historical Analysis of ARVN Armor Operations From Conception to the Present, Focusing on the Two Northern Provinces," circa 1969, copy in SEAB, CMH; Raymond R. Battreal, "Ky Binh Viet Nam—Muon Nam!," *Armor*, July–August 1974, pp. 8–14; Donn A. Starry, *Mounted Combat in Vietnam*, Vietnam Studies (Washington, D.C.: Department of the Army, 1978), pp. 17–49; Russell Interv, 29 Jan 74, MHI.

[34] For further treatment, see the early sections of David Ewing Ott, *Field Artillery, 1954–1973*, Vietnam Studies (Washington, D.C.: Department of the Army, 1975), which notes on p. 216 that U.S. artillery units suffered similar problems when employed in area support missions.

[35] General Quang should not be confused with the IV Corps commander, General Dang Van Quang.

Joint General Staff and its field components under the corps commanders. But in 1965 the organization was still in disarray and its performance marginal.[36]

South Vietnam's Territorial Forces were light infantry units formed in the mid-1950s as the Civil Guard and Self-Defense Corps.[37] Their official mission was to provide local security for towns, villages, and hamlets, freeing regular military forces for mobile combat operations. The early territorials, poorly led, trained, and equipped, were completely independent of the regular armed forces. Civil Guard units served under presidentially appointed province chiefs and were little more than a personal army of President Diem. The Self-Defense Corps was a village-level militia, many of whose members even lacked arms. Following the fall of Diem, the ruling Saigon generals reorganized both services. The Civil Guard became the Regional Forces and the Self-Defense Corps was combined with several other paramilitary organizations to become the Popular Forces. Collectively, they became the Territorial Forces—better known in American circles by the combined initials RF/PF, or by the term *Ruff-Puff*. Subsequently the two were placed under the Joint General Staff and given a single chain of command, but remained separate from the regular army until 1970. In general, province chiefs controlled Regional Forces companies, and district and village chiefs directed Popular Forces platoons. Normally the province chief was also the sector, or military, commander of his province, and the district chief was the subsector commander. For military affairs, both reported to the local division commander.

In mid-June 1965 the number of authorized Regional Forces rifle companies stood at 959 and Popular Forces rifle platoons at 3,892. To accommodate this huge force, many province chiefs established their own training camps, with little if any direction from the Central Training Command. The Regional Forces also included separate mechanized (armored car) platoons, boat companies, railway guard detachments, and, in each province, at least one company to provide administrative and logistical support. The primary mission of all territorial combat units remained local security.

The South Vietnamese National Police and the Civilian Irregular Defense Group (CIDG) were paramilitary organizations entirely separate from the armed forces. The CIDG consisted of company-size rifle units, organized and led by American and South Vietnamese Special Forces teams but supported financially and logistically by the United States alone. Its members were recruited from South Vietnamese religious and ethnic minority groups living in remote areas inaccessible to the South Vietnamese government. Hired and paid by U.S. Army Special Forces "advisers," the CIDG troops swore allegiance "to no flag, no government."[38] Their loyalty to the Saigon regime was marginal and their legal

---

[36] Historical Study by 21st Military History Detachment, Encl to Transmittal Ltr, Col Harold R. Aaron, HQ, 5th Special Forces Group (Airborne), 1st Special Forces, 24 May 69, sub: Vietnamese Special Forces (VNSF); South Vietnamese officer dossiers. Both in SEAB, CMH.

[37] For general surveys of the Territorial Forces, see Briefing, MACV, 23 Oct 67, sub: Role of RF/PF in Pacification [for U.S. Senators], MICRO 1/1726, RG 334, WNRC; Irving Heymont et al., "Cost Analysis of Land Combat Counterinsurgency Operations: Vietnam, [1957–1964]" (Draft working paper of the Preliminary Report, Research Analysis Corp., McLean, Va., n.d.), copy in SEAB, CMH.

[38] Interv, Col C. E. Spragins, Deputy Commander, 5th Special Forces Group (hereafter cited as Spragins Interv), 29 Aug 65, file 206-02, Interviews with General Officers, box 6, accession no. 69A702, RG 334, WNRC. For a more detailed discussion, see Chapter 3, pp. 69–74.

Montagnard Strike Force in the Central Highlands

standing vague. The National Police, on the other hand, was an organ of the central government that included special combat and intelligence units as well as smaller uniformed detachments in province, district, and city precinct headquarters. In mid-1965 the CIDG program had between twenty thousand and twenty-five thousand members and the National Police between forty thousand and forty-five thousand men.

Regulars, territorials, and paramilitary troops had American weapons that dated from World War II and the Korean War, plus a sprinkling of leftover French and Japanese equipment. The predominant infantry weapons for the regulars were M1 rifles, light M1 carbines, Browning automatic rifles, and air-cooled .30-caliber and .50-caliber machine guns, augmented by 60-mm. and 81-mm. mortars, 2.36-inch and 3.5-inch rocket launchers, and 57-mm. and 75-mm. recoilless rifles. Boots, helmets, and other uniform accoutrements were also American, or American-inspired. The territorials were much less well equipped and had begun to receive extensive amounts of American military aid only in 1962. They used a variety of individual weapons, including the M1 carbine and American-made shotguns, depending on the regulars for artillery, air, and logistical support. The Popular Forces continued to wear a locally produced black uniform that was hard to distinguish from the black pajama-like garment commonly worn by both the Vietnamese peasant and the Viet Cong.

Airborne Troops Carrying Mls *at the start of a truck-borne operation*

Other standard equipment included the U.S. family of multiwheel drive trucks (1/4-, 3/4-, 2 1/2-, and 5-ton) and portable field radios, the artillery and armored vehicles noted earlier, and a host of ancillary materiel from land mines to generators and dial telephones. By 1965 much of the equipment was worn and, by Western standards, obsolete, and certain sophisticated materiel, such as high-frequency radios, antiaircraft weapons, radar, and sensors, was lacking. Nevertheless, the South Vietnamese Army was considerably better off than its Viet Cong opponent, which still used captured equipment and had virtually no supporting arms. Only the heavy semiautomatic M1 rifle was plainly unsatisfactory. The average South Vietnamese soldier, weighing about 100 pounds and standing a little over five feet, found the big M1 difficult to handle and unable to match the heavy volume of fire put out by the AK47, a Russian-designed automatic rifle that was becoming the standard weapon of the Viet Cong soldier.[39]

Personnel and Morale

In the less glamorous area of personnel administration, the South Vietnamese had many serious shortcomings. An adjutant general's branch, created in

[39] See Jac Weller, "Good and Bad Weapons for Vietnam," *Military Review* 48 (October 1968): 56–64.

1964, was not yet firmly established. The Vietnamese lacked, for example, an accurate personnel records system so that determining actual strength was difficult. In mid-1965 authorized strength was 261,000 for the regulars (army, navy, marine corps, and air force) and 271,500 for the territorials (*see Table 1*), but nobody could say with any certainty how many men were actually on hand.[40] Unit roles were poorly maintained, and personnel officers had little reliable information, except that obtained from periodic head counts by small unit leaders. The large number of Vietnamese with identical names contributed to the confusion, as well as the lack of individual efficiency reports and other personnel records that might indicate the length of service and amount of training completed, medical background, or even data on age and family. Although some enterprising commanders had begun their own system, most failed to give the matter any serious attention. Without a centralized records system, most personnel management actions—including pay, training and job assignments, and lower-ranking promotions and appointments—were done in the field and subject to the whims of local unit commanders.

The names of deserters, men absent without leave, and those hospitalized, physically disabled, discharged, and even deceased often remained on unit rolls as "ghosts," primarily because no standard procedures existed for deleting them quickly, allowing unit commanders to pocket the pay and allowances of the absent soldiers. Deserters from one unit often enlisted in another without discovery by changing their names and falsifying their personal identity records or by simply bribing the new commander. Combat units suffered from these maladies more often than headquarters or support units. As the pressure from combat operations rose, the personnel picture became more indistinct, and the ability of the Joint General Staff to monitor manpower steadily declined.

The draft and recruiting system for filling the ranks was complex and difficult to administer.[41] In theory, Saigon adhered to a Western model of military conscription. Youths registered with local draft boards at age seventeen and were subject to the draft between the ages of twenty and thirty-three. Obligatory service was three years for enlisted men in the regulars and territorials, and four to ten years for reserve officers and noncommissioned officers. Discharged veterans were in a reserve status until age forty-five. Men with less than seven years of schooling filled the enlisted ranks; those with the equivalent of a junior high school education received training as noncommissioned officers; and those with eleven to twelve years of education and who had received a baccalaureate degree were seen as potential officers. While officer candidates were called up individually, drafts for noncommissioned officers and enlisted men were collective by birth date (for example, in February 1965 all those who had less education than a baccalaureate I and were born in March 1945 might be called for induction).

---

[40] For strength estimates as of 31 May 1965, see Memo, Sternberg to COMUSMACV, 7 Jul 65, sub: RVNAF Strength Summary, SEAB, CMH.

[41] On conscription, recruitment, and deferments, see Briefing, MACV J–1 to Members of the Preparedness Investigating Subcommittee, Senate Committee on Armed Forces, 25 Oct 67, MICRO 1/1327; Joint Chiefs of Staff, "Southeast Asia Military Fact Book," January 1967, MICRO 1/2745; Briefing, MACV to Wheeler and MacNamara, circa 1967, sub: Manpower, MICRO 3/2711. All in RG 334, WNRC.

Provinces and districts had conscription quotas based on population and projected military needs. New army draftees reported to district capitals, where they were transported to province recruitment-induction centers and then sent to one of the five national training centers or the Thu Duc Infantry School.

In 1964 the Saigon government had extended the three-year term of enlisted service, but later began a "phased discharge" of those affected by the extension. At the time Westmoreland did not object, feeling that a limited service term was "essential to morale and recruitment."[42] Saigon had yet to institute a general mobilization, and military manpower policies and practices remained on a peacetime footing.

The Mobilization Directorate, a component of the Ministry of Defense, ran the conscription program, maintained a manpower inventory for the country, monitored reservist availability, and administered deferments. From the beginning the lack of reliable data crippled the work of its staff and field offices. Records for the civilian population were even less accurate than those for the armed forces. The last nationwide census had been conducted before World War II, and current population data was based on "a tenuous sampling" taken in 1959, with age and sex statistics extrapolated from a pilot census done in a single province that same year. In 1965 MACV roughly estimated that out of a total population of 15.7 million, evenly divided between both sexes, 66 percent of the males, or 5.19 million, lived in territory controlled by the government; of these, 1.97 million were of military age, from sixteen to forty-five years old. Subtracting those already in service—veterans, medical rejects, and others who might be deferred—1.04 million were available for conscription: 367,000 eighteen- to thirty-year-olds for the regular armed forces and 676,000 of other ages for the territorials. The usable manpower pool was smaller because the government applied conscription only to those between the ages of twenty and thirty.[43]

As in the United States, military service could be avoided or delayed by official deferments. Starting at age twenty, individuals could apply for renewable deferments for reasons of health, education, occupation, and family hardship, but recipients could generally not be deferred beyond their last year of eligibility at age thirty. A variety of administrators at the province and national levels handled the application and approval process, and bribery and the sale of deferments were common. Furthermore, the lack of accurate census data made it easier for those who never registered or who never reported when called to avoid detection. These problems, in turn, made it impossible to implement a fair deferment program. In the field, inequities centered around what one American

---

[42] Quoted words from Msg, Westmoreland MAC 1840 to Wheeler, 030855 Apr 65, COMUSMACV Message file, Westmoreland Papers, HRB, CMH. See also Ltr, Col Charles R. Fox and Wayne G. Althaus to Ambassador Taylor, 30 Sep 64, U.S. Mission Council (Working File), box 2, accession no. 67A4604, RG 338, WNRC. But according to Intelligence Memorandum OCI 1699/66, Directorate of Intelligence, CIA, 12 Dec 66, sub: The South Vietnamese Army Today, note on p. 15, copy in SEAB, CMH, many South Vietnamese officers, noncommissioned officers, and conscripts were never released from duty at the end of their official active service obligation.

[43] Quoted words from Briefing, MACV to Wheeler and MacNamara, circa 1967, sub: Manpower, MICRO 3/2711, RG 334, WNRC. See also Msg, CINCPAC to JCS and DIA, 29 Oct 69, sub: Availability of GVN Manpower, MICRO 74/1065, RG 334, WNRC; Msg, Westmoreland MAC 1840 to Wheeler, 030855 Apr 65, COMUSMACV Message file, Westmoreland Papers, HRB, CMH.

adviser called "inservice draft deferments." For a fee, unit commanders allowed locally recruited soldiers to return home for extended periods of time. Labeled "ornamental soldiers," they could easily be recalled for periodic head counts to satisfy visiting superiors, but few ever performed any military duties.[44]

Unlike conscription, recruiting took place at the tactical unit level, and divisions, regiments, and even battalions and companies conducted their own programs. Each formed small recruiting teams that canvased local towns, villages, and hamlets for potential soldiers. Coercion was generally unnecessary. Under the pressure of the draft, voluntary enlistments satisfied over half of the personnel requirements of the regulars and almost all of the territorials. Induction procedures were similar to those applied to draftees, with the exception that army volunteers often went directly to divisional training centers and territorial recruits to province training camps. Motives for enlisting varied. Military service offered a certain amount of independence, prestige, and adventure to teenagers and young men weary of the dawn-to-dusk routine on the average Vietnamese rice farm. Because each unit recruited in its own area of operations, many volunteers joined specific units in order to remain close to their native villages and hamlets. Territorial units almost never moved outside their home provinces, and most remained in a specific district or even within the environs of a single village. Except for the airborne troops and the marines, units of the regular army also remained in one general locale. This policy had the virtue of accommodating the South Vietnamese peasant's deep attachment to his family and home soil, an important factor in view of the inability of the Saigon government to provide adequate facilities for military families. Potential draftees often paid bribes to join units stationed close to their homes, and assignments in the small Popular Forces platoons were especially sought after.

In the long run, the practice of local recruitment and stationing was dangerous. For example, in 1964, when the Joint General Staff moved the 25th Infantry Division from Quang Ngai Province in the northern zone to Hau Nghia Province near Saigon, desertions in the division skyrocketed. Men whose families could not follow refused to go, and even those accompanied by their immediate dependents left with extreme reluctance. Long months were to pass, during which the Joint Staff transferred many men back to their home provinces and recruited others in the Saigon area, before the 25th Division was again capable of anything like normal operations.

Even in units that remained fixed, desertions were a perennial problem. By 1965 desertions were averaging about nine thousand a month, more than four times the U.S. Army's desertion rates in World War II and eight times that of the U.S. Army in the Korean War. American advisers had never seen losses of this magnitude and were deeply alarmed. Desertion rates were highest in infantry units, often amounting to 10 percent of a unit's strength each month, theoretically forcing a complete turnover of unit personnel in less than a year. More

---

[44] Memo, John Paul Vann, Deputy Senior Adviser for Civil Operations and Revolutionary Development Support (CORDS), IV Corps, to George D. Jacobson, Asst CofS, CORDS, MACV, 13 Aug 70, sub: Inquiry From Ambassador Bunker About "Ghosts on the Payroll," John Paul Vann Papers, MHI.

TABLE 3—ESTIMATED DESERTIONS IN THE SOUTH VIETNAMESE ARMED FORCES

Year	Regulars	Regional Forces (Civil Guard)	Popular Forces (Self-Defense Corps)	Total
1962	11,203	6,764	11,957	29,924
1963	9,666	8,235	18,540	36,441
1964	21,441	14,961	36,608	73,010
1965	47,297	16,647	49,224	113,168

Source: Statistical Table, "Vietnam: Desertions—RVNAF," 15 Aug 67, prepared by the Office of the Deputy Chief of Staff for Operations, DA. For monthly averages for the years 1963–66, see Rpt, MACJ–341, 27 Apr 67, sub: Analysis of Republic of Vietnam Armed Forces (RVNAF) for CY 1966, p. 111. Both in SEAB, CMH.

worrisome, desertion counts steadily increased during 1964–65 in direct proportion to the rise in combat activity (*Table 3*).[45]

Like all South Vietnamese statistics, these figures were only general approximations. Poor personnel accounting procedures made it difficult for Vietnamese commanders to apply Saigon's complex set of criteria for what constituted desertion. The army considered soldiers deserters if they had more than ninety days in service and were absent without leave (AWOL) at least six days; if they had less than ninety days in service and were AWOL as long as thirty days; or, if in transit to a unit, if they were AWOL as long as fifteen days. With so many opportunities for errors, mix-ups, and outright falsifications, it was questionable whether even the army's overall desertion statistics had any measure of accuracy. Where the deserters went—back to home and family, to the cities and towns for jobs, to other less demanding military units or to ones closer to home, or to the Viet Cong—was hard to determine. The Viet Cong undoubtedly recruited many into their ranks, and the "new recruits" provided the enemy with a ready reserve of trained manpower.[46] How many later returned to their units was also a question mark. Whatever the case, the resulting personnel turbulence was obviously damaging to the armed forces.

Military justice in the South Vietnamese armed forces was rudimentary. Only corps commanders had the authority to convene courts-martial, and only the minister of defense could bring charges against officers. Military tribunals tried criminal cases involving both servicemen and civilians, but with a Military Justice Corps of only forty-four officers and almost no investigating powers, their work was limited. Most unit commanders dealt with disciplinary problems through nonjudicial methods—work details, beatings, and confinements in makeshift unit prisons. Civilian police had little control over military personnel and lacked the authority even to check military identifications, making it difficult to apprehend AWOL soldiers or deserters. Much to the consternation of Americans, the South Vietnamese did not consider desertion a serious offense. Their corrective measures were normally limited to sporadic attempts to round up

[45] For an overview of the personnel problem, see Briefing, Brig Gen Donald H. McGovern, MACV J–1, circa October 1966, sub: Morale and Personnel Matters, MICRO 2/2565, RG 334, WNRC. See also Statistical Table, "Vietnam: Desertions—RVNAF," 15 Aug 67, prepared by the Office of the Deputy Chief of Staff for Operations, DA, copy in SEAB, CMH.
[46] Intelligence Memorandum OCI 1699/66, Directorate of Intelligence, CIA, 12 Dec 66, sub: The South Vietnamese Army Today, p. 16, copy in SEAB, CMH.

possible deserters in urban areas, with little attention paid to prevention or punishment.[47]

Relationships between soldiers and dependents caused special problems. Young servicemen often deserted to be with families, a practice that was spurred by overly restrictive leave and pass policies. In other cases, especially when a serviceman was the principal wage earner and head of household, dependents felt impelled to live with him, or at least nearby. However harsh the living conditions, proximity to a base provided a measure of protection from the Viet Cong, and dependents might share a soldier's rations and sometimes save a little extra money mending and washing clothes or doing other odd chores. Close family ties, local recruiting, and the need to be at hand on payday also encouraged this trend. As a result, clusters of makeshift civilian housing surrounded almost every South Vietnamese military base. Although these practices gave the South Vietnamese soldier added incentive to defend home bases, they also made him extremely reluctant to spend much time in the field or to move far from his home area.

A typical example was the base camp of Tan Hung, home in many ways to the South Vietnamese 2d Battalion, 9th Regiment, an infantry unit of the 5th Division. Like many others, the camp was basically a square enclosure, several hundred meters on each side, formed by interlocking earthenwork bunkers, barbed wire, and other barriers. The unit commander encouraged his married soldiers to bring their families into the camp, and each bunker also served as a communal home. When the camp was subject to enemy attacks, the Vietnamese soldiers, not surprisingly, defended the base fiercely and successfully. On the other hand, the troops were understandably reluctant to conduct field operations far from the base for any length of time. Although affording the Vietnamese soldiers and dependents a sense of security, the Tan Hung camp greatly reduced the mobility of the battalion and effectively tied it to one small geographical area. Similar situations existed throughout the armed forces, and General Westmoreland later observed that "when the fighting began, the soldiers were often torn between defeating the enemy and looking after their wives and children."[48]

Efforts by the South Vietnamese government to help military families were limited. Over the years the government had provided some primitive housing for enlisted dependents, but the numbers and quality were inadequate. In 1965, for example, the Joint General Staff allocated the equivalent of almost ten million U.S. dollars to the four corps headquarters and the Capital Military District to build two hundred thousand housing units, but the funds were never obligated. Major obstacles were graft, bureaucratic delays, lack of interest by local commanders, the absence of centralized planning, and the preoccupation of engineer units and private contractors with other construction projects.[49]

---

[47] Khuyen, *The RVNAF*, pp. 129–37; George F. Westerman, "Military Justice in the Republic of Vietnam," *Military Law Review* 31 (January 1966): 137–58.

[48] Quoted words from *Soldier Reports*, p. 253. See also USARV Combat Lessons Learned Bulletin no. 18, 15 Aug 67, Donald A. Seibert Papers, MHI.

[49] USMACV, "Command History, 1970," 4 vols. (Saigon, 1971), 2: IX–55, HRB, CMH. See also the general comments of advisers in 1965 noted in Office of the Inspector General, MACV, "Inspector General History, 1964–1972," pp. 11–12, MACV IG files, box 1, accession no. 77/0074, RG 334, WNRC.

TABLE 4—SOUTH VIETNAMESE MILITARY-CIVILIAN PAY COMPARISON, MARCH 1965

Job Categories	Average Number of Dependents	Yearly Salary (piasters)
Foot Soldier (Private)	2.4	38,988
Laborer	2.4	27,551
Maid	2.4	31,808
Janitor	2.4	33,500
Squad Leader (Corporal)	4.1	65,876
Chauffer	4.1	46,774
Cook	4.1	54,553
Clerk	4.1	58,443
Administrative Supervisor (Master Sergeant)	5.8	89,954
Accounting Clerk	5.8	72,362
Clerk Typist	5.8	66,174
Telephone Operator	5.8	70,074
Company Commander (1st Lieutenant)	3.7	100,386
Cashier	3.7	108,108
Engineering Draftsman	3.7	93,704
Secretary	3.7	126,880
Interpreter	3.7	113,616
Division/Regimental Commander (Colonel)	5.6	162,085

Source: Information Sheet, Office of the Deputy Chief of Staff for Operations, DA, sub: ARVN, RF and PF Pay Allowances, SEAB, CMH.

Another factor contributing to low morale and desertions was low pay, aggravated by a growing inflation rate. In the regular forces, pay was graduated by rank and time in service and supplemented by allowances for dependents, for the high cost of living in certain areas, and for special jobs, such as technicians. Assuming a generous exchange rate of 50 piasters to the U.S. dollar, the yearly pay of lower enlisted ranks was $600 to $1,200; for noncommissioned officers, $1,200 to $1,800; and for company-grade officers (aspirant to captain), $1,200 to $2,400. A division commander, from a full colonel to a major general, received an annual salary of $3,200 to $4,000. Pay for the Regional Forces was somewhat lower than the regulars, but Popular Forces personnel, because they supposedly defended the villages in which they lived, received a uniform $600 per year regardless of rank. Pay for enlisted men in the armed forces was nevertheless comparable to civilian salaries in 1965, but that for officers lagged (*Table 4*).[50]

Pay and rations were closely related. As units often had no centralized mess, soldiers purchased food individually at local markets and ate informally in small groups or with families. In addition, they received a "garrison ration," financed by payroll deductions, to supplement their diet; however, by the end of 1965

[50] Information Sheet, Office of the Deputy Chief of Staff for Operations, DA, sub: ARVN, RF and PF Pay and Allowances, SEAB; "Comparison of RVNAF to Civil Guard Pay and Allowances, 10 May 1964," History file 5–14, Westmoreland Papers, HRB. Both in CMH.

inflation had so reduced its purchasing power that the supplement normally consisted only of rice provided by U.S. aid programs. The cost of emergency field rations, similar to American C-rations, was deducted from a soldier's pay and was thus unpopular; few units other than those of the general reserve used them. A commissary system was supposed to make basic commodities available at reasonable prices, but most of its twenty-two outlets were poorly stocked and offered little but rice. Food shortages contributed to the tendency of soldiers in the field to confiscate or steal from the peasants, a practice that did little to increase the government's popularity in the countryside.[51]

Difficulties also existed with other amenities. Medical facilities, for example, were too small to treat the large number of casualties that the fighting had begun to generate by 1965. The number of physicians was inadequate, and most supplemented their military pay with extensive civilian practices. Medical assistance for dependents was minimal, and rehabilitative programs for wounded soldiers were nonexistent. Veterans benefits were so negligible that many paternalistic commanders retained disabled but loyal soldiers on their payrolls. For those who did well, rewards were few. Enlisted promotions, passes, leaves, awards, and decorations demanded so much paper work that commanders often declined to grant them. Again it was the infantry units that suffered most, especially those engaged in heavy combat.

Combat Effectiveness

The military capabilities of Saigon are difficult to judge. By 1965 the insurgency had stretched the South Vietnamese armed forces thin, and most of the regular and territorial combat units were busy guarding their own bases or strung out in countless wire-enclosed mud forts protecting roads, bridges, hamlets, villages, city gates, airstrips, and those commercial and military installations deemed critical. In these units, mobility was marginal, morale low, and leadership poor. Although troop deployments were extremely decentralized, overall military direction was vested in the hands of a few senior officers, further stifling initiative and movement. Knowledge of enemy dispositions and intentions was hazy and a comprehensive military plan of action lacking. Only the airborne and marine troops conducted regular offensive operations, and these generally consisted of two-battalion task forces searching an area for two to three weeks before returning to Saigon. The offensive operations of other regular infantry units were

---

[51] For background on military rations and other amenities, see Ltr, Westmoreland to Nguyen Van Vy, Minister of Defense, 30 Dec 67, COMUSMACV Signature file, 1967, Westmoreland Papers, HRB, CMH. See also Briefings, Brig Gen Albert R. Brownfield to Congressman Chet Holifield (hereafter cited as Brownfield Briefing), 11 Jan 68, sub: Improvement of RVNAF, MICRO 3/3048, and McGovern, circa October 1966, sub: Morale and Personnel Matters, especially Annex, Fact Sheet, MACPD, sub: Status of U.S. Support for GVN Exchange System, MICRO 2/2565. Both in RG 334, WNRC.

TABLE 5—AVERAGE STRENGTH OF SOUTH VIETNAMESE BATTALIONS,
31 MAY 1965

Type of Unit	Authorized	Assigned	Present for Duty	Present for Operations
Infantry	714	557	434	376
Ranger	646	532	409	384
Airborne	889	795	641	496
Marine	931	969	797	634

Source: Memo, Sternberg to COMUSMACV, 7 Jul 65, sub: RVNAF Strength Summary, SEAB, CMH.

normally limited to one-day sweeps through a series of terrain objectives, so long in the planning that the enemy, often aware that the troops were coming, either made his getaway or prepared elaborate ambushes.

In the field, the situation sometimes appeared hopeless to some American officers. According to Col. Wilbur Wilson, the III Corps senior adviser in 1964, the basic Vietnamese military weakness was leadership, a product of the officer corps' obsession with "politics, corruption and nepotism." "The generals got to be generals," he went on, "by virtue of their ability in political intrigue, not as a result of their ability as military men." In terms of actual military experience, Wilson felt that the senior officers, despite their long service records, had about as much combat background as their juniors. Leadership in the Vietnamese army was "a question of the blind leading the blind."[52]

The South Vietnamese 25th Division operating west and northwest of Saigon was a good example of Wilson's generalizations. Under Col. Phan Trong Chinh, a friend of both Ky and Thi, the division guarded Highway 4, the major rice supply route to the Delta, and protected the roads and towns of Tay Ninh, Hau Nghia, and Long An Provinces (with a total of fourteen districts). Strong enemy forces operated in both Hau Nghia and Long An, close to the capital, but the 25th, although reinforced by four ranger battalions, appeared unable to come to grips with the local Viet Cong, or otherwise interfere with their activities. American advisers at MACV and in the field were puzzled and angry, blaming Chinh's lack of aggressiveness. Unbeknownst to the Americans, however, Ky had instructed Chinh to orient the bulk of his unit south as an anticoup force, perhaps as a counter to the neighboring South Vietnamese 5th Division commanded by General Pham Quoc Thuan,[53] a close friend of General Thieu. Ky had given him strict orders not to commit any more than one battalion of each regiment to combat at any one time. Chinh thus had his hands full providing static security for those provinces under his authority and keeping an eye on the political situation in Saigon. Some of his most critical military operations consisted of merely opening the main roads from time to time so that produce could be brought into the capital and supplies and other goods taken out to the towns and

[52] As quoted in Msg, Westmoreland MAC 3099 to Harris, 190620 Jun 64, COMUSMACV Message file, Westmoreland Papers, HRB, CMH.
[53] Thuan served as Thieu's chief of staff in the early 1960's, when the latter commanded the 5th Division.

military bases within his jurisdiction. Defeating the enemy was not his first priority.[54]

Seeking better ways to measure the war effort, senior American advisers had begun to rely heavily on statistical indicators: kill and casualty ratios; comparisons of authorized, assigned, present-for-duty, and actual operational strengths; the number of small and large unit operations that a unit had conducted; the number of day and night operations; the percentage of operations resulting in engagements; and the ratio of weapons captured to weapons lost. But the data was difficult to verify, and accurate information on enemy strength and intentions was even scarcer. Totaling enemy casualties was problematic and often resulted in inflated enemy loss figures, especially when South Vietnamese casualties were high.[55] Because the performance of American advisers was inevitably judged, at least to some degree, on the performance of the units they advised, it seldom behooved them to lower the so-called body count.

Even when weighted in favor of the tabulators, the statistics available in 1965 were depressing. South Vietnamese losses in men and equipment had moved steadily up, and by the end of June Saigon was losing about 2,000 men each month on the battlefield and 10,000 more a month from desertions. Overall manpower losses were outstripping enlistments and conscription, with infantry units suffering the heaviest losses. In just one month, between May and June, the average strength of the South Vietnamese infantry battalion dwindled from 376 to 338 men, compared to an authorized strength of 714 and a estimated average strength of 425 for Viet Cong battalions (*see Table 5*).[56] Moreover, most of the combat losses had come at the hands of the Viet Cong and not the North Vietnamese, who had yet to make their weight felt. Changes obviously were necessary if South Vietnam was to survive.

---

[54] Donald A. Seibert, "The Regulars," pp. 1035–91, Seibert Papers, MHI (Seibert was the deputy senior adviser of the 25th Division at the time); Race, *War Comes to Long An*, pp. 135–40; Eric M. Bergerud, "The War in Hau Nghia Province, Republic of Vietnam, 1963–1973" (Ph.D. diss., University of California, Berkeley, 1981), pp. 67–86 and 108–109.

[55] Msg, Westmoreland MACV 4114 to Wheeler, 131245 Aug 65, COMUSMACV Message file, Westmoreland Papers, HRB, CMH.

[56] Msg, Taylor to SecDef, 18 Jun 65, History file 16–29, Westmoreland Papers, HRB; Memo, Sternberg to COMUSMACV, 7 Jul 65, sub: RVNAF Strength Summary, SEAB. Both in CMH.

3

The Advisers

With over ten years of experience by 1965, the American advisory effort in South Vietnam was well established. The focus of the effort, however, had changed during the past five years from advising a peacetime army to advising one at war. Obviously, the exigencies of assisting a wartime army differed markedly from those involving one at peace. But the basic role of the adviser was unchanged. Advice remained advice, and, although accountable for both the advice they gave and the receptivity it received, advisers remained advisers, with no legal command responsibilities. Any changes in their relationships with their South Vietnamese counterparts involved far-reaching political, rather than military, decisions.[1]

The American High Command

The U.S. Military Assistance Command, Vietnam (MACV), was the supreme American military headquarters in South Vietnam. Although technically a subtheater command,[2] it combined elements of both a country Military Assistance Advisory Group (MAAG) and an independent joint operational command. MACV not only supervised an extensive field and staff advisory effort but also controlled several combat commands, such as the U.S. Army 5th Special Forces Group (Airborne) and the U.S. Air Force 2d Air Division. In addition, MACV had a growing number of political responsibilities—an unusual state of affairs brought about by the deep involvement of the South Vietnamese officer corps in local and national politics and by the politico-military nature of the war itself. These combined political, advisory, and operational responsibilities presented unique challenges to the MACV headquarters and the officers who led it.

[1] The term *counterpart* technically applied to both adviser and advisee, but almost always referred to the Vietnamese being advised.
[2] A theater command encompasses all military forces in a fixed geographical area. Subordinate commands generally control a fixed number of military units from one service. Because MACV was a geographical command within the Pacific Theater area, it was considered a subtheater command.

General Paul D. Harkins, the commander of MACV from its establishment
in February 1962 until his replacement
by General Westmoreland in June 1964,
worked under the general supervision of
the American ambassador, Henry Cabot
Lodge, and had immediate responsibility for all U.S. military policy, operations, and assistance in South Vietnam.
However, when Maxwell D. Taylor, a retired senior Army officer, replaced
Lodge in July 1964, President Johnson
gave the new ambassador broad coordinating authority over the entire American military and political effort in South
Vietnam, and the MACV commander
became, in effect, Taylor's deputy for
military affairs until the ambassador's
departure one year later. But Taylor's
span of control was limited; he operated
mainly through a Mission Council

General William C. Westmoreland

composed of the heads of the major U.S. agencies in South Vietnam, such as MACV,
the Central Intelligence Agency (CIA), the U.S. Information Agency (USIA), and the
U.S. Agency for International Development (USAID). Chaired by Ambassador Taylor, the Mission Council met weekly, but each of the member agencies retained
strong ties with their parent organizations in Washington and, for all practical purposes, continued to enjoy a great deal of local independence.[3]

MACV itself was a joint, or interservice, headquarters directly under Admiral
U.S. Grant Sharp's U.S. Pacific Command in Hawaii. Technically, Sharp was the
theater commander and Westmoreland's immediate superior, but in practice the
MACV chief often dealt directly with General Earle G. Wheeler, chairman of the
Joint Chiefs of Staff in Washington, and later even with the secretary of defense and
the president himself. In the same manner, Westmoreland also bypassed the Army
component command in Hawaii, preferring to deal directly with the Army chief of
staff in Washington, General Harold K. Johnson. Outside of South Vietnam, Admiral Sharp continued to control the air war over North Vietnam, while Ambassadors
Graham Martin and William H. Sullivan, respectively, supervised U.S. military
efforts in Thailand and Laos.[4]

MACV was an extraordinarily complex headquarters (*Chart 2*), made up of a
number of major and minor staff sections spread throughout the city of Saigon. Its
work was coordinated by Westmoreland himself and his chief of staff, Maj. Gen.

---

[3] Westmoreland, *Soldier Reports*, pp. 67–68. For a revealing treatment of command relationships and
personalities, see Bruce Palmer, Jr., *The 25-Year War: America's Military Role in Vietnam* (Lexington, Ky.:
University Press of Kentucky, 1984), pp. 17–22 and 25–33. Lodge, the ambassador to South Vietnam
from 1963 to 1964, returned to replace Taylor in August 1965 and served until April 1967, when
Ellsworth Bunker assumed the post.

[4] Westmoreland, *Soldier Reports*, pp. 74–76.

TABLE 6—HEADQUARTERS, MACV, PERSONNEL BY SERVICE COMPONENT,
31 DECEMBER 1965

Service	Authorized	Assigned
U.S. Army	1,665	1,673
U.S. Navy	218	136
U.S. Marine Corps	131	56
U.S. Air Force	413	277
Total	2,427	2,142

Source: USMACV, "Command History, 1965," table II-6, p. 274, HRB, CMH.

Richard G. Stilwell, and Stilwell's replacement as of July 1965, Maj. Gen. William B. Rosson. Although manned by officers of all services *(Table 6)*, the conglomerate headquarters was in essence an Army organization, staffed largely by U.S. Army personnel who used U.S. Army staff procedures. Westmoreland felt that this balance was only natural because the war in South Vietnam was primarily a ground effort, and both the South Vietnamese high command and its armed forces were primarily "army" organizations. However, because of the size of the American air effort, a separate U.S. Air Force headquarters was established under MACV, the 2d Air Division, which later became the Seventh Air Force.[5]

During 1965 the size of the MACV headquarters increased rapidly. Although in July Westmoreland organized a separate Army component command, the United States Army, Vietnam (USARV), to provide administrative and logistical support to U.S. Army field units, the authorized strength of MACV more than doubled, from 1,016 to 2,464, during the year *(see Table 7)*.[6] Most of the increases were in the critical areas of operations, intelligence, and logistics, enabling MACV to become a full-fledged combat command while retaining its advisory functions. Only in the politico-military pacification area did the U.S. military command and control organization exhibit serious weaknesses, and MACV continued to share authority over this critical area with several other major U.S. agencies in South Vietnam.

As the MACV chief, General Westmoreland had diverse responsibilities. He was concurrently commander of all U.S. military forces in South Vietnam; senior adviser to the South Vietnamese armed forces; and, almost as a footnote, commander of the Army component command. Because of the nature of the new South Vietnamese government in mid-1965, he was also a major adviser to the principal Directory leaders: General Thieu, who was both chief of state and a senior army officer; Air Marshal Ky, who continued to head the South Vietnamese Air Force; and General Co, the chief of both the Joint General Staff and the Ministry of Defense. Hardworking and well organized, the MACV commander worked closely with a few key subordinates, attended Taylor's weekly Mission Council meetings, met with the South Vietnamese military chiefs also on a weekly basis, and conferred personally with the American ambassador and the South Vietnamese generals as necessary. He also met with his senior field com-

[5] Intervs, Stilwell, 11 Jul 65, and Lt Col Richard A. Naldrett, USAF, Secretary Joint Staff (SJS), MACV, 22 Jun 65, file 206–02, Interviews with General Officers, box 6, accession no. 69A702, RG 334, WNRC.

[6] USMACV, "Command History, 1965," table II-6, p. 274, HRB, CMH.

MACV Headquarters, *with Tan Son Nhut Air Base in the background*

manders regularly, although, unlike General Harkins, he spent much of his time with his staff in Saigon and used his deputy, Lt. Gen. John L. Throckmorton, as a troubleshooter in the field. Within MACV he relied primarily on Stilwell, his chief of staff, and Maj. Gen. William E. DePuy, Stilwell's successor as J–3 (Operations). Both were highly experienced and trusted officers who worked well with Westmoreland. A close associate, General Bruce Palmer, Jr., later characterized both Westmoreland and Stilwell as "workaholics,"[7] and he also might have included DePuy in the category. For personal and practical reasons, Westmoreland made less use of his J–1 (Personnel), J–4 (Logistics), and J–5 (Plans) early in the year, and the MACV J–2 (Intelligence) staff was still too weak to be of much use on its own. In addition, Westmoreland often took a project manager approach in areas he considered important, appointing committees to direct, investigate, or monitor certain efforts that cut across functional staff lines. He also supplemented his personal advice to the Joint General Staff through a constant flow of formal letters, prepared by the various MACV staff sections for his approval and signature. Indeed, in many ways General Westmoreland was the principal American military adviser in South Vietnam during his long tenure as the MACV commander. But throughout 1965 both he and the MACV staff became increas-

---

[7] Palmer, *The 25-Year War,* p. 40.

TABLE 7—HEADQUARTERS, MACV, PERSONNEL BY STAFF SECTION, 1965

Staff Section	1 January		31 December	
	Authorized	Assigned	Authorized	Assigned
Command Group	. . .	. . .	78	70
J-1 (Personnel)	35	46	91	97
J-2 (Intelligence)	135	133	476	339
J-3 (Operations)	130	153	318	243
J-4 (Logistics)	43	47	433	342
J-5 (Plans)	30	35	49	42
J-6 (Communications-Electronics)	132	147	182	152
Adjutant General	136	147	248	260
Staff Judge Advocate	7	9	34	23
Provost Marshal	. . .	. . .	26	26
Chaplain	. . .	. . .	7	7
Headquarters Commandant	49	48	65	60
Inspector General	. . .	. . .	6	4
Surgeon	21	23	33	28
Office of Information	59	57	123	76
Comptroller	18	21	26	22
Political Warfare Directorate[a]	. . .	. . .	49	42
Training Directorate	194	226	68	49
Allied Military Assistance Office	. . .	. . .	22	18
Joint Research and Test Activity	12	13	16	20
MAP Directorate	15	14	13	13
Army MAP Logistics Directorate[b]	. . .	. . .	. . .	. . .
Flight Detachment	. . .	. . .	81	63
Pacification Committee	. . .	. . .	20	16
Total[c]	1,016	1,119	2,464	2,012

[a] Established in May.
[b] Combined with J-4 in May.
[c] Approximate figures. Note: The figures in Tables 6 and 7 do not correspond precisely due to differences in service personnel accounting procedures.

Source: USMACV, "Command History, 1965," table II-6, p. 274, HRB, CMH.

ingly involved in the deployment and operations of U.S. ground combat units, and their advisory responsibilities received correspondingly less attention.[8]

The Advisory System

The core of the U.S. advisory system was the individual adviser, both military and civilian. Normally operating in small teams at various levels of the South Vietnamese politico-military structure, he focused his efforts on the specific programs and goals of an expanding mission. Up to 1965 the general American public perceived all U.S. military personnel in South Vietnam as "advisers"—to include clerks, mechanics, radio operators, administrative officers, and other

---

[8] Intervs, Stilwell, 11 Jul 65; Naldrett, 22 Jun 65; Brig Gen Ben Sternberg, MACV J-1, circa July 1965; Maj Gen Milton B. Adams, USAF, MACV J-5, circa July 1965; Col M. J. L. Greene (hereafter cited as Greene Interv), SJS, MACV, 6 Jun 65; Maj Gen C. A. Youngsdale, USMC, MACV J-2, circa July 1965. All in file 206-02, Interviews with General Officers, box 6, accession no. 69A702, RG 334, WNRC. See also Vien et al., *U.S. Adviser*, pp. 38–42 and 189.

support personnel who did little or no actual advising—simply because their general mission was to support the South Vietnamese armed forces. In practice, however, a very small number of individuals provided direct advice to the Vietnamese. In the smaller military teams the team chief, informally called the senior adviser, normally performed this function; in the larger teams the senior adviser's deputy and four or five of his key staff officers also contributed. The USAID, CIA, and USIA civilian advisers were even less visible because their organizations were more informal, their roles and missions more nebulous, and their mobility limited by their inability to provide for their own security. As in the military network, many of the civilian advisers also had only supply, administrative, or internal planning functions.

The command and staff advisers at MACV headquarters and the U.S. Embassy in Saigon were among the most important and the most prominent. They included the MACV commander, the U.S. ambassador, and at least a portion of the senior officers and executives in their subordinate staff sections and offices. In general, the counterparts of these command and staff advisers were the corresponding national-level Vietnamese leaders. More numerous but less prominent were the military field advisers that permeated almost every echelon of the South Vietnamese Army, Navy, Marine Corps, and Air Force. They constituted the heart of the military advisory system and included the U.S. Army advisory teams assigned to the South Vietnamese corps, divisions, regiments, and battalions; those teams assigned to provinces and districts; those to combat support organizations, schools, and training centers; the separate U.S. Naval and Air Force Advisory Groups;[9] and the bulk of the U.S. Army Special Forces teams. Supplementing the work of these advisory elements were special U.S. military training teams that visited South Vietnam on a temporary basis and a smaller civilian field advisory network that had quasi-military responsibilities.[10]

The MACV staff had a variety of advisory-related duties. Advisory cells within each of the major staff sections closely monitored the activities of their Joint General Staff counterparts, and several MACV offices were devoted entirely to the advisory mission.[11] Most prominent was the Training Directorate. This office advised the South Vietnamese Central Training Command; commanded the U.S. Army advisory teams assigned to schools and training centers and to the Ranger, Artillery, and Armor Commands; and supervised the Offshore Training Program. Most of its work involved supplying training program data and equipment to subordinate detachments, assisting the Central Training Command in drawing up master training schedules, and reviewing all training in

---

[9] The Naval Advisory Group had operational control of the Marine Advisory Unit, which advised the South Vietnamese Marine Corps forces. On the unit's role, see Jack Shulimson and Charles M. Johnson, *U.S. Marines in Vietnam: The Landing and the Buildup, 1965* (Washington, D.C.: U.S. Marine Corps History and Museums Division, 1978), pp. 204–10.

[10] For detailed treatments, see Fact Sheet, MACMA, "Description of the Organization, Mission, and Scope of the Advisory Effort," in COMUSMACV Fact Book, 1968, vol. 2, Westmoreland Papers, HRB; Talking Paper, Schandler, 23 Jul 67, sub: MACV Advisory Structure, SEAB; MACV Directive 10–11, 10 Nov 65, sub: Organization and Function: Command Relationships and Terms of Reference for USMACV, SEAB; appropriate section of USMACV, "Command History, 1964" (Saigon, 1965) and "1965," HRB. All in CMH. See also Vien et al., *U.S. Adviser.*

[11] For a detailed organizational breakdown, see USMACV, "Command History, 1965," pp. 91–97, HRB, CMH, and organization charts in MICRO 40/1429–31, RG 334, WNRC.

progress. The Training Directorate was under the staff supervision of the MACV J-3, which also controlled the American staff elements assigned to a combined U.S.–South Vietnamese operations center that monitored all combat activities in South Vietnam.

Several organizations shared responsibility for logistical support to the South Vietnamese armed forces: the MAP (Military Assistance Program) Directorate; the Army MAP Logistics Directorate; and, for items peculiar to their service, the U.S. Air Force and Naval Advisory Groups. The MAP Directorate, originally a planning group of the MACV J-5, became an independent body working directly for the MACV chief of staff in December 1965. The Army MAP Logistics Directorate managed the technical service advisory programs (signal, quartermaster, engineer, ordnance, transportation, and medical) under the staff supervision of the MACV J-4. In May 1965, when the logistics office was dissolved, its functions were integrated into the J-4 staff. Henceforth, one of the three deputy J-4s was responsible for all assistance to South Vietnamese and allied forces, including supervision of the technical service advisory personnel. In December the five area logistics command advisory teams also came under the MACV J-4's supervision. These changes reduced the importance of the logistical advisory effort, and reflected the reorientation of the MACV headquarters toward the overwhelming construction and supply requirements of arriving U.S. troop units.[12]

In May 1965 a Political Warfare Directorate replaced the smaller psychological warfare–civil affairs branch of the MACV J-3 staff. The new directorate had staff responsibility for monitoring psychological warfare and civic action conducted by American tactical units and for coordinating political warfare advisory activities. It also advised the Joint General Staff's General Political Warfare Department and supplied guidance to U.S. Army psychological warfare advisers at the corps, division, and province levels. But the American psychological warfare advisory effort remained weak. For example, as of March 1965, MACV had only one U.S. adviser assisting the important but semipolitical Military Security Service that had hundreds of agents assigned throughout the South Vietnamese armed forces.[13]

The field advisory network expanded at a moderate pace during 1965. The network included the U.S. Army and Marine Corps tactical teams, those assigned to Vietnamese province and district commands, and those assigned to logistical support units and training camps. Together they totaled about 4,700 personnel in over one hundred autonomous teams.[14] Increases during the year, which resulted from augmenting existing teams and establishing new ones,

---

[12] See Interv, Col K. W. Kennedy, MACV engineer, 10 Nov 65, file 206–02, Interviews with General Officers, box 6, accession no. 69A702, RG 334, WNRC.

[13] USMACV, "Command History, 1966" (Saigon, 1967), pp. 554–86, HRB; Fact Sheet, MACV, 5 Mar 65, sub: Increase in MSS Advisory Effort, SEAB. Both in CMH. The Joint U.S. Public Affairs Office (JUSPAO), created in 1965 as an organ of the U.S. Embassy in Saigon, had overall responsibility for American psychological warfare programs and supplied guidance to MACV.

[14] MACV assigned each team a number, but the size, function, and composition varied greatly. For example, Advisory Team 99 consisted of the South Vietnamese 25th Division advisory team and all subordinate regimental and battalion teams; Advisory Team 90 included the Tay Ninh Province team and all subordinate district teams; Advisory Team 101 assisted the South Vietnamese 40th Engineer Base Depot in Saigon; and an unnumbered team of a few officers advised the South Vietnamese National Military Academy at Da Lat. Few kept or retired any permanent records.

TABLE 8—FIELD ADVISORY STRENGTH,[a] 1965

Component	January	December
Army and Marine Corps	4,741	5,377
Special Forces	1,264	1,828
Air Force	309	391
Navy [b]	192	636
Total	6,506	8,232

[a] Approximate figures.
[b] Less Marine Corps personnel.
Source: USMACV, "Command History, 1965," pp. 74–90 and 274–75, HRB, CMH.

raised the end-of-year total to over 5,300. During the same period, the U.S. Special Forces command grew from 1,264 to 1,828 assigned personnel and began providing advisers to remote border provinces. The U.S. Air Force Advisory Group rose from 309 to 391, and the U.S. Naval Advisory Group jumped from 192 to 636 assigned (and 1,538 authorized). U.S. Marine Corps advisers, already included in the advisory counts above, numbered 64 officers and enlisted men assigned to MACV field elements, 131 to the MACV staff, and 30 more to the Naval Advisory Group. Thus in 1965, the number of U.S. military personnel concerned with advisory duties in the field totaled about 6,500 at the beginning of the year and almost 8,250 at the end *(Table 8).*[15]

Prior to the deployment of American combat units, a U.S. Army advisory group assisted each of the four South Vietnamese corps headquarters. These groups supervised not only the local division advisory teams, which in turn controlled the regimental, battalion, province, and district advisory detachments, but also the five area logistics command advisory teams until their subsequent transfer to the MACV J–4 in December 1965. The major mission of each field detachment was to advise the Vietnamese commander and staff of the unit to which it was assigned on all aspects of military operations and to coordinate all direct American assistance for that unit. The advisers were also the eyes and ears of MACV headquarters, enabling it to keep tabs on almost every South Vietnamese unit and command. MACV itself provided most of the administrative support for these scattered detachments but funneled most supplies and equipment to them through the South Vietnamese chain of command. For food, building materials, and other items, individual detachments had to rely on the local marketplace and their own ingenuity.

A corps senior adviser, normally a senior colonel, headed each corps advisory group and reported directly to General Westmoreland. However, with the arrival of large U.S. combat units in South Vietnam and the creation of U.S. corps-level headquarters—I and II Field Forces, Vietnam, and III Marine Amphibious Force—in the I, II, III Corps Tactical Zones in 1965 and 1966 *(Chart 3),*[16] the authority of the corps advisory group commander greatly diminished. As each U.S. corps-

[15] USMACV, "Command History, 1965," pp. 74–90 and 274–75.
[16] On 7 August 1965 the I Corps Advisory Group was placed under the Commanding General, III Marine Amphibious Force; on 25 September the II Corps Advisory Group came under what later became I Field Force; and on 1 December the III Corps Advisory Group was subordinated to the senior U.S. military commander in the III Corps Tactical Zone (initially, the Commanding General, 1st Infantry Division, and on 15 March 1966 the Commanding General, II Field Force).

level headquarters was established, Westmoreland placed the local advisory group under its direction. The group commanders became deputy senior advisers and the new corps-level commander, usually a lieutenant general, became the corps senior adviser. In this way the advisory groups and their subordinate teams became part of the local U.S. tactical chain of command. This included not only the division, regimental, and battalion advisory detachments but also the province and district teams. As a result, the bulk of the field advisers lost their direct operational link with MACV headquarters. Only in the IV Corps, where no U.S. ground combat units were quartered, did the local corps advisory group remain directly under MACV.

Other advisers continued to enjoy a certain amount of independence. In addition to the four corps advisory groups, MACV retained separate advisory detachments for the Capital Military District; the Territorial Forces; the Airborne, Ranger, Armor, and Artillery Commands; the school and training centers; and the Railway Security Force. The U.S. Navy, Marine, and Air Force advisers remained attached to their service component commands. Westmoreland vetoed a proposal by the Army Staff to place the bulk of the field advisers under the Army component command because he believed that it would have decentralized the advisory effort still further.[17]

By 1965 MACV had stabilized the size of the basic field advisory teams (*see Appendix A*). Battalion and district detachments consisted of 5 men each, and province teams were now 20 strong (not counting representatives from nonmilitary U.S. agencies); regimental teams remained small, a mere 3; and division and corps teams averaged 52 and 143, respectively, with most members providing administrative support to a smaller number of key staff advisers. Although personnel shortages sometimes reduced the actual strength of the advisory teams by as much as 50 percent, their authorized strength remained fixed at these levels for the next four years.[18]

Far more important than the structure of the advisory system in 1965 was its basic philosophy, which emphasized technical proficiency and personal relationships. Originally, the United States had stationed military advisers in Vietnam to ensure that MAP equipment provided to France was maintained properly and used for the purpose intended. With the departure of the French, the advisers extended their work throughout the South Vietnamese armed forces—first to the staffs, training centers, and schools, and then to the tactical units and military area commands. During this transition the advisory system began to take on its unique characteristics. Its most distinguishing trait was its extreme decentralization. Assistance and guidance from MACV itself was minimal. The advisory chain of command became primarily administrative, an apparatus for placing and maintaining the individual adviser within the South Vietnamese military structure. Once installed, the field adviser—relying on his American military experience and know-how—faced the challenge of not only recommending solutions to his counterpart's tactical, operational, and administrative problems but also persuading him to implement those solutions. To accomplish this feat,

[17] Msg, Westmoreland MAC 1724 to Johnson, 301340 Mar 65, COMUSMACV Message file, Westmoreland Papers, HRB, CMH.
[18] See Talking Paper, Schandler, 23 Jul 67, sub: MACV Advisory Structure, tab A, SEAB, CMH.

Field Adviser on Operations

MACV expected the adviser to befriend and influence his counterpart within the context of the existing South Vietnamese politico-military system. It was not his task to solve, or even to address the deeper political and social problems that beset South Vietnam and its armed forces.[19]

General Westmoreland himself had accepted the decentralized "one-on-one" advisory system as he had found it in 1964 and had even modeled his own relationships with the senior Vietnamese generals after it. As he understood it, the task of the adviser was "to appraise the situation and . . . give sound advice . . . based on an objective analysis grounded on fundamental military knowledge." Whether the advice was taken depended, according to Westmoreland, on the adviser himself—his "knowledge, past experience, and common sense."[20] In his view the foundation of the advisory effort was the personal relationship between the adviser and his counterpart, and both the quality of the advice and the receptivity of the individual being advised were measures of the adviser's worth. In this context Westmoreland urged his field advisers to "accentuate the positive, and . . . work out solutions to [their] problems in [a] dy-

---

[19] For example, see HQ, USMAAG, Vietnam, U.S. Army Section, Lessons Learned no. 28, 18 Apr 63, sub: Guidelines for Advisors, in History file 1–30, Westmoreland Papers, HRB, CMH.

[20] This and the preceding quotation from Westmoreland's preface to MACV, Combat Fundamentals for Advisors, 1 Oct 64 (a wallet-size fold-out card issued to advisers), SEAB, CMH.

namic way."[21] Above all, he believed that they had to encourage the Vietnamese to establish "realistic goals" and to "place [a] premium on leadership, imagination and drive." Fostering leadership was critical. Advisers had to steer themselves and their counterparts clear of the "frustration and stagnation" that were the "occupational hazards" of larger commands and staffs. Their personal relationships with their Vietnamese charges were the key. Reminding them that "victory and positive achievements are contagious," he exhorted his advisers to "emphasize constantly all aspects of leadership and professionalism" and to "help develop and maintain in your counterparts the positive attitudes necessary to inspire their troops on to victory."

The politico-military turmoil in the South Vietnamese high command made Westmoreland lean hard on his low- and mid-level advisers to hold the field army together. To accomplish this, advisers had to exercise as much leverage and influence as possible. But the lower the adviser in the chain of command, the more diluted his power. While tactical and pacification advisers might control the availability of various types of American support, they found it difficult to deny such support to their counterparts in a crisis, nor could they force them to use such support if they chose otherwise. Neither the "carrot and stick" nor the "buddy" approach was foolproof, and, from the start, Westmoreland recognized their limitations. He noted with approval a recent agreement between the United States and South Korea requiring that the senior U.S. military commander there endorse all senior Korean military appointments and voiced a "hope to give the proposal a try with the US policy makers."[22] But not until the arrival of U.S. combat units in the spring and summer of 1965 was the entire American–South Vietnamese military relationship critically assessed.

Even prior to 1965 the role of the American tactical advisers had expanded far beyond that of military advice to their counterparts. As early as 1962 they had begun to serve as combat air support coordinators, directing American fixed- and rotary-wing support in the field. This responsibility had given them greater control over battlefield firepower and transport, and, as a by-product, more influence over Vietnamese plans and operations. The growth of this influence, however, was concomitant with the advisers receiving tactical radios (AN/PRC–10s) that enabled them to communicate directly with supporting aircraft (equipped with complementary AN/ARC–44 sets).[23] The continued expansion of combat operations and the growing number of American support units available severely overextended the MAP-equipped advisory communications system, and by 1965 it was barely able to support the tempo of combat activity. Nevertheless, the provision of air support was one of the chief responsibilities of the tactical advisers.

---

[21] This and following quotations from Msg, Westmoreland MAC 6468 to Brig Gen Dunn, 15 Dec 64, COMUSMACV Message file, Westmoreland Papers, HRB, CMH, which paraphrased his New Year's message to all senior advisers.

[22] Msg, Westmoreland MAC 5645 to Gen Howze (Korea), 26 Oct 64, COMUSMACV Message file, Westmoreland Papers, HRB, CMH.

[23] On air–ground communications, see John D. Bergen, *Military Communications: The Test of Technology*, United States Army in Vietnam (Washington, D.C.: U.S. Army Center of Military History, 1986), pp. 55–58.

The field advisers also had a third major task, gauging the performance of the South Vietnamese armed forces and thereby providing MACV with a rough idea of how the war was progressing. Because of the small size of the field detachments, their internal staff and administrative capabilities were weak. But throughout 1964 face-to-face talks with superiors became less frequent and written reporting requirements of the advisory teams more demanding. As the war grew in size and complexity, so did the paper work demands on individual advisers, and some were preparing as many as forty reports every month. Two became major bellwethers of the war effort: the senior adviser monthly evaluation (SAME) report, which forced advisers to rate each South Vietnamese unit being advised; and the province monthly evaluation report, prepared jointly by the MACV sector senior adviser and the USAID province representatives. Higher military commands all the way up to Washington scrutinized both, and an adviser's career often seemed to depend on the content and acceptability of these reports.

The American troop buildup in 1965 forced other changes in the lives of the field advisers. Almost overnight, the corps, division, and province advisory teams began furnishing liaison officers to U.S. units operating in the territorial jurisdiction of the Vietnamese commands that they advised. In addition, they found it necessary to establish 24-hour operations centers similar to those in U.S. troop units so that tactical information could be exchanged on a moment's notice. Advisers at all levels also found themselves forced to spend more time addressing such matters as law enforcement, morale and recreation, post exchanges, living facilities, and press and community relations in response to policies and procedures established by American commanders. As the size of the U.S. ground commitment increased, these requirements increased proportionately, and, without additional personnel, the field detachments had to perform these tasks at the expense of their normal advisory duties.[24]

During a meeting at MACV headquarters in March 1965, General Westmoreland offered a sober reappraisal of the tactical advisory program. Noting that the advisory mission had evolved from training to tactical advice, and then to combat support, he directed his staff to study the best way for advisers to carry out this "new support role." The duties of the "adviser," he explained, had grown considerably and now included coordinating both artillery and helicopter and fixed-wing air support; acting as a conduit for intelligence; developing supply and service programs; improving communications between combat units and area commands (provinces and districts); and providing special assistance in such areas as psychological warfare, civic action, and medical aid.[25]

At about the same time, General DePuy also underlined the "increased US [adviser] involvement in operational activities." He told a conference of senior advisers that the "optimum objectives of the US advisory effort in SVN should be increased influence in planning and control of military operations," although it "should not overlap into command." He went on to point out that the Ameri-

[24] For a general discussion, see Vien et al., *U.S. Adviser*, pp. 46–76.
[25] Quoted words in this and the following paragraph from Memo, MACV, sub: Meeting—100830 Mar 65: Advisors in the Support Role, History file 14–28, Westmoreland Papers, HRB, CMH.

can battalion advisers were younger and less experienced than their counterparts and that American influence at this level was, in any case, greatly circumscribed by their counterparts' lack of operational flexibility. Advisory detachments at this level functioned primarily as "support teams," and the role of most advisers, he noted, did not go beyond this. As American ground combat units entered the fray, DePuy foresaw an increasing number of combined American–South Vietnamese operations and the eventual need for "the integration of US staff officers into the GVN military staffs from division through the national level." In summation, he recommended that battalion and regimental advisory detachments be redesignated as "combat support teams" and that the remaining field advisers be formed into a combined American–South Vietnamese staff.

The Soldier-Adviser

The task of the ground-level adviser was extraordinarily difficult. He had to be a jack-of-all-trades, not only advising but also solving his own supply and administrative problems, often living on the local economy and training his own subordinates as best he could. Most were unfamiliar with their strange Asian allies and the type of war they were supposed to be fighting. Their morale was high but their work frustrating. With only sporadic contact with the echelons above them, they often had only their own individual resources to guide them in their unusual mission.

The selection, training, and placement of the advisers themselves received relatively little attention. Prerequisites for advisory duty were generally identical to those demanded for advancement in regular military service: attendance at key military schools, and successful command tours with U.S. tactical units. Colonels (corps senior advisers) were to be graduates of senior service schools, such as the U.S. Army War College, and lieutenant colonels (division senior advisers) and majors (regimental and province senior advisers) graduates of the U.S. Army Command and General Staff College, with neither having been passed over for advancement to the next higher rank.[26] Prior to 1965, candidates were normally volunteers anxious to serve in one of the few assignments that offered operational experience in a combat environment. In Vietnam, MACV tried to assign newly arrived officers to units appropriate to their U.S. military backgrounds—combat arms officers to combat units, engineer officers to engineer units, and so forth. But by 1964, with the flood of junior officers and noncommissioned officers needed to fill battalion and district advisory teams, the importance of military experience in advisory posting at the lower levels had become irrelevant.

Preparation for advisory duty was minimal. The U.S. Army Special Warfare School at Fort Bragg, North Carolina, offered a short six-week military assistance

---

[26] Talking Paper, MACV, circa June 1964, sub: Quality of Military Personnel in Vietnam, History file G–1, Westmoreland Papers, HRB, CMH.

training and advisory (MATA) course for advisers. The instruction stressed counterinsurgency tactics, small arms training, psychological operations, and civic action, and included some general background on Vietnam. About one-half of the course (120 hours) consisted of training in the Vietnamese language, and this was sometimes followed by eight to twelve weeks of more intensive instruction at the Defense Language Institute in Monterey, California. Priority for language training went to battalion, province, and district advisers who worked with their counterparts on a daily basis. But the limited capacity of Monterey, and the length of time needed to acquire a working knowledge of the complex Vietnamese tonal language, greatly restricted advanced linguistic training. Within South Vietnam, only district advisers received additional instruction and others reported immediately to their assignments. All continued to rely heavily on the Vietnamese military interpreters assigned to almost every detachment.[27]

Another important aspect of the advisory system was the length of the assignment, or tour, in South Vietnam.[28] The Joint Chiefs of Staff originally had authorized a two-year tour for advisers with dependents and, because of the "primitive living conditions, dietary effect . . . , isolation involved, adverse climatic conditions, and health problems," an unaccompanied one-year tour for those assigned outside of Saigon. Early in 1965, with the increased tempo of combat activity, the president of the United States ordered all American military dependents home, leaving U.S. military personnel with a uniform one-year tour. In the field, corps senior advisers further shortened specific assignments by having subordinate advisers serve in hardship posts, especially in battalions and remote districts, for no more than six months, after which the individual rotated to a new position, normally on a higher-level staff.[29]

During 1965 American military leaders critically examined the length of the service tour in Vietnam. In February Westmoreland recommended that 130 individuals in key positions be authorized an extended tour of nineteen months, and in May the secretary of defense approved a tour of nineteen to twenty-four months for general and flag officers and for selected colonels and naval captains, including the chiefs of the four corps advisory groups. In August the Army Staff considered a general extension of the twelve-month tour and the deputy chief of staff for personnel prepared a fifteen-month tour proposal. However, General Johnson, the Army chief of staff, and the heads of the other services were strongly opposed to longer tours. Dissenting views cited the "adverse impact on morale due to family separation, possible decline in enlistments, . . . greater reliance on the draft . . . , increased exposure to health hazards, especially for personnel in rural areas, . . . [and the] debilitating effects of climate and envi-

---

[27] Vien et al., *U.S. Adviser,* p. 195; Report of the Department of the Army Board To Review Army Officer Schools (Haines Board Report), February 1966, Newton Papers, MHI. From 1958 to 1968 Newton was the director of the Military Assistance Institute. Established by a government contract in Arlington, Virginia, this school offered four weeks of orientation to senior officers scheduled to fill top advisory posts in South Vietnam and other countries.

[28] Following quotations and discussion from Staff Study, Dep CofS for Personnel, DA, 29 Jan 70, sub: Study of the 12-Month Vietnam Tour, SEAB, CMH.

[29] USMACV, "Command History, 1966," pp. 472–73, HRB, CMH.

ronment. . . ." Finally, in December 1965 Westmoreland endorsed the twelve-month tour, declaring its maintenance critical for morale.[30]

To the Vietnamese, the American advisers were simply *dai dien* ("representatives") of the U.S. government. In the field, most understood the advisory function of their American counterparts and treated them almost as assistant commanders. Inevitably conflicts arose, especially when Americans failed to understand or accept the political and social roles of the Vietnamese officers, or when they were too belligerent or too demanding towards their counterparts. Most Vietnamese tended to be wary of the younger advisers who normally had little military and no combat experience, while, in some cases, the Vietnamese battalion commanders might have ten to twenty years of fighting under their belts and had seen many advisers come and go on their one-year tours. To them, the war was alway there, unending. Lacking the short-range goals that might have given them a sense of accomplishment, they found it difficult to share the need for action imparted by almost all of the aggressive young American officers. Nevertheless, Vietnamese commanders highly valued the American combat support that the advisers made available and, at the division and corps levels, the detailed staff work that made their more ambitious operations possible.[31]

The generalized selection process, limited training, and the relatively short tours understandably caused many problems. An American Southeast Asian scholar, Gerald Cannon Hickey, summed up most of them early in 1965.[32] Based on field work done in Vietnam in 1964 and interviews with some 320 advisers, Hickey concluded that the success of an adviser lay in not only his professional competence but also his ability to establish "rapport" with his counterpart. He found the closest adviser-counterpart relationships at the lowest levels, and noted that advisers at higher echelons rarely saw their opposites informally and had an ever-increasing amount of nonadvisory duties. Advisers at all levels appeared to be compartmentalized and had little knowledge of what others were doing. The one-year tour in general and the six-month tour in operational units greatly limited the effectiveness of the average adviser, for by the time he had become accustomed to his surroundings and had established a working relationship with his counterpart, his tour with the unit was nearly over. In addition, the lack of any overlap between departing advisers and their replacements, and the absence of any historical records at these levels, made it difficult for the advisory effort to achieve continuity. Hickey, realizing that other factors also came into play, contrasted the good relations between South Vietnamese ranger and airborne units and their advisers with the often miserable ones shared between the

---

[30] Quoted words from Staff Study, Dep CofS for Personnel, DA, 29 Jan 70, sub: Study of the 12-Month Vietnam Tour, SEAB, CMH. See also Interv, Col Richard Jensen and Lt Col Rupert F. Glover with Johnson (hereafter cited as Johnson Interv), 21 May 73, sess. 13, p. 44, Senior Officers Debriefing Program, MHI. Because of the high fatigue factor of continuous combat operations, Johnson favored the six-month rotation of field commanders (sess. 12, p. 39).

[31] For Vietnamese attitudes, see USMACV, "Command History, 1970," 2: VII-79, HRB, CMH, and Vien et al., *U.S. Adviser*, pp. 46-76.

[32] Unless otherwise stated, the following discussion on adviser-counterpart relations is from Hickey, *The American Military Advisor and His Foreign Counterpart.*

U.S. and South Vietnamese Special Forces. Difficulties between the two latter organizations, he felt, could be traced to internal South Vietnamese political problems, Saigon's prejudicial policies toward the Montagnards, and the underlying racial animosity between the ethnic Vietnamese and Highland people.

Hickey's research also showed that the field advisers felt they were being held accountable for their counterparts' mistakes. In their eyes, their superiors viewed South Vietnamese shortcomings as failures of the adviser to do his job properly, even with all extenuating circumstances considered. A later outside study agreed, noting the emphasis that MACV placed on "harmonious relations" between adviser and counterpart and the prevalent attitude that "the advisor only exposes his own incapacity when he complains to his own superiors about the stupidity, want of integrity, laziness, ingratitude, or lack of competence of his counterpart."[33] The burden of establishing a mutually agreeable working relationship was on the adviser who often went out of his way to please his counterpart, scavenging for supplies and equipment, minimizing everyday problems, and emphasizing even insignificant improvements and successes. But such habits inevitably hampered the effectiveness of the adviser, undermined the veracity of the advisory reporting system, and masked serious faults in South Vietnamese units.

Hickey suggested many remedies: screening adviser candidates for aptitude in foreign languages, ability to work with foreign nationals, and availability for extended overseas assignments; doubling the MATA course length to twelve weeks; and adding eight hundred to one thousand hours of Vietnamese-language instruction to the pre-tour preparation. Hickey also felt that the practice of using the advisory network as the prime source of statistical information on the South Vietnamese armed forces made little sense and only overworked advisers. Such data ought to come directly from the South Vietnamese Joint General Staff. Finally, he recommended a nine-month field tour for advisers; longer, overlapping tours; a training program in South Vietnam to supplement the MATA course; centralized historical files on advised units and their commanders; and greater communication between advisers at all levels.

In 1965 the Army Staff put together a special report based, in part, on interviews with over three hundred senior advisers. The study showed that advisers were concerned with their own performance and especially their lack of influence, or leverage. They considered their missions too general and objected strongly to the practice of measuring the progress of the South Vietnamese armed forces in terms of statistical yardsticks. Without more clearly defined goals and greater leverage, their jobs had little sense of immediacy, producing a bureaucratic nine-to-five job mentality. The report concluded that the entire advisory system needed to be strengthened by a unified chain of command, greater control over direct and indirect American military support, longer tours, and a comprehensive debriefing and evaluation program for departing advisers.[34]

---

[33] Paul S. Ello et al., *U.S. Army Special Forces and Similar Internal Defense Advisory Operations in Mainland Southeast Asia, 1961–1967* (McLean, Va.: Research Analysis Corp., 1969).

[34] Office of the Deputy Chief of Staff for Military Operations, DA, "A Program for the Pacification and Long-Term Development of South Vietnam" (hereafter cited as PROVN Study), March 1966. See also Rpt, Military History Branch, MACV, circa April 1966, sub: Report on Interview *(Continued)*

While the field advisers had legitimate grievances, most felt that their presence was necessary and beneficial. Differences in personalities, backgrounds, and missions also meant that each individual adviser had his own unique style and experience. One young adviser firmly believed that he and his colleagues at the battalion level performed the bulk of the real advisory work. "The battalion adviser," he felt, "is in a key position. . . . He doesn't look to any body for help and, because of this, he doesn't have to write reports and tie himself down with administrative business. He is forced into the Vietnamese Army; if he is effective, he eats with them and sleeps with them. This is where you get the advising done." In the young adviser's eyes, the corps, division, and province advisory teams were only burdens to the Vietnamese, who spent too much time "just trying to placate the Americans—trying to either keep them informed or come up with some pet project that some American . . . [was] trying to jam down their throats—rather than fighting the day-to-day war." Such sentiments were common. In the field, at the nuts-and-bolts tactical level, the American military adviser somehow seemed more in his element; here he left his bureaucratic constraints behind and could personally see, touch, hear, smell, and taste what was going on, things that were only words and statistics at the echelons above him. As he planned operations with his counterpart, helped him train his troops, and called American air support when needed, he became an integral part of the unit he was technically only advising, and in turn, the Vietnamese battalion commanders regarded the adviser as their personal support element, providing radio communications, armed helicopters, aerial resupply and medical evacuation, and intelligence. Many even considered any lengthy combat operation without their American advisers as almost suicidal.[35]

Another adviser, at the same level, likened the effort to a burr under a saddle: "Often we are the burr. We're not sure which way the horse is going to go; but its bound to go some way or another if we just keep the burr there." The problem then, as he saw it, was to direct the horse, or to persuade the Vietnamese to accept the proffered advice. He admitted, however, that it was not so much their lack of military competence that bothered him as their lack of "spiritual aggressiveness." Perhaps the burr was not having the desired effect.

He also questioned how much his superiors knew or wanted to know about what was really happening in the field. In terms of an officer's career, he thought it "obvious to anybody what you must do in order to succeed as an advisor," for, in this respect, it was "possibly the easiest job in the Army." If things weren't going well, he explained,

you can always say that you told your counterpart to do something else and who can prove that you're wrong. You can always keep up statistics, turn in your reports, say you

(Continued) Program of U.S. Army Advisers in Vietnam. Both in SEAB, CMH. The history branch report was a synopsis of interviews with 128 advisers, supplementing the Hickey Rand study. The MACV J–3 recommended against publishing or distributing the report, alleging that its conclusions were too vague and unsupported by empirical evidence.

[35] Quoted words from MFRs, MACV J–3, 29 May 65, sub: Debriefing of Departing Advisor, pp. 1–2, 5, 9–10, and, 19 Apr 65, same sub, p. 5, SEAB, CMH. The MACV command historian, Lt. Col. W. R. Stroud, prepared a memorandum for the record for each of the interviews he or his staff conducted with departing advisers. The identity of the adviser was not recorded, only the date of the interview.

Tactical Adviser in the Field

enjoy good relations with your counterpart, go on the operations. If somebody says that there aren't enough operations, you can say that you tried to get them to conduct more.

The temptation to minimize real problems and turn in glowing reports of progress was great, a situation that was to test the integrity of the entire American officer corps in Vietnam.[36]

For the province and district advisers, the tasks were more complex. The counterinsurgency, or pacification, campaign demanded much more than just military skills. In 1971 John Paul Vann, one of the foremost American field advisers throughout the war, defined the tasks of these officers succinctly if not briefly:

I expect each advisor within 30 days after his assignment, to be the world's leading expert on the functional and geographical area of his assignment. As an example, for a District Senior Advisor, this involves a knowledge of the size, ethnic makeup, religious adherence and political breakout of the population of the district; the authorized, assigned and present-for-duty strengths of RF/PF, National Police, RD Cadre, and People's Self-Defense Force; the family name, age, education, place of birth, religion, political connections, past assignments, strengths and weaknesses of the District Chief, and only to a slightly lesser degree, the other major personalities within the district, both GVN and VC; the price of

---

[36] Quoted words in this and the preceding paragraph from ibid., 18 Jun 65, pp. 1, 6, 10, SEAB, CMH.

rice, fish sauce, beef, fish, pork, beer, soft drinks, labor, sampan motors, transport, etc., and their trend over the past 12 months; a history of the district, its physical characteristics and its potential for development; the number of identified and estimated VCI and their *de facto* organizational structure; the number of primary and secondary classrooms, the shortage (if any) of school teachers and the percentage of children eligible who are enrolled at both primary and secondary school levels; the number, types and productivity and potential of major private industries within the district; the enemy order of battle and how it has changed in the past two years; an intimate knowledge of the name and location of all contested hamlets and the actions necessary to improve them to an acceptable level; the number and type of medical facilities either in the district or accessible from the district and an evaluation of their adequacy; the most decorated or otherwise outstanding RF soldier and PF soldier within the district; the average daily number of rounds fired by each tube of sector artillery and a knowledge of whether or not the fire was observed and to the extent that it was H&I [harassment and interdictory fires]; the status of major items of equipment authorized within the district, to include radios (PRC–25s, PRC–10s, and HT–1s), mortars, machine guns, starlight scopes, M–79s, Claymore mines and vehicles; effectiveness and organization of the DIOCC [District Intelligence Operations Coordination Center] and the performance of principal personalities within the DIOCC; knowledge of the ten 'most wanted' VCI on the black list; status of RF and PF housing and plans for improvement; knowledge of the existence or non-existence of an RF/PF recruiting plan, steps underway to improve it, monthly attrition rate of RF/PF and number of individual fillers currently at the training center.[37]

Yet even for the early pacification advisers, these job requirements were only a beginning. The heart of the pacification program in 1965 was security, and province and district advisers had to work closely with not only their counterparts but also a myriad of higher, lower, and adjacent elements, all of which had to come together before anything substantial could be done.

At the division and corps levels the advisory experience was different, although equally challenging and frustrating. The problems faced by Col. Jesse G. Ugalde, senior adviser to the South Vietnamese 25th Infantry Division, were typical. As the chief of Advisory Team 99, Ugalde was responsible for the division, regimental, and battalion detachments; for three province teams and fourteen district detachments; for a U.S. Air Force tactical air control party; and for several small direct-support Army aviation units. His command also included a Special Forces B team, which served as the district advisory detachment for Tay Ninh Province, and several ranger battalion advisory teams whose units were temporarily under the control of the South Vietnamese division. From the beginning Ugalde had his hands full supervising these diverse elements while serving as the senior adviser to the Vietnamese division commander.[38]

To Ugalde's newly arrived deputy, Maj. Donald A. Seibert, the confusion inherent in Team 99's activities was readily apparent. In mid-1965 three hundred men were scattered throughout the division tactical area in many small detach-

---

[37] Memo, Second Regional Assistance Group, 5 Jun 71, sub: Policy Guidance and Information Memorandum no. 1, Vann Papers, MHI. DIOCCs were not established until 1966. Vann served as a division senior adviser in 1962–63 and then resigned from the Army, but returned to Vietnam in 1965 as a USAID official, later becoming a province adviser, then the senior pacification adviser for first the III CTZ and then the IV CTZ, and finally, still as a civilian, the senior U.S. commander in the II CTZ. See Palmer, *The 25-Year War*, pp. 21–23 and 55–56. Journalist Neil Sheehan is currently completing a biography of Vann.

[38] This and the following two paragraphs from Seibert, "The Regulars," especially pp. 1035–91, Seibert Papers, MHI.

Maj. Donald A. Seibert *(second from right) visiting the 10th Infantry Division*

ments, where, according to Seibert, living conditions were generally primitive. Most of the advisory compounds centered around a patchwork of French-style Vietnamese buildings, prefabricated American structures, and various types of troop-constructed shelters. Security was poor, and none of the compounds could have withstood a determined enemy attack. The operations center of the division detachment, supposedly the heart of the advisory team, was located in an old temple that had to be vacated at times for local religious services. Discipline was lax. When not in the field, team members performed military duties in a leisurely fashion, paid more attention to social functions than the war, and wore civilian clothing during "off-duty" hours. In manner and taste they reflected the slow, unhurried tempo of the unit they advised.

Seibert's main task was to work with the assistant division commander, Col. Hoang Van Luyen, who directed most of the division's military operations while the division commander took care of political affairs. But, according to Seibert, Luyen was more concerned with his Saigon business interests (he reportedly had a monopoly on ice in the downtown area), and the few division-level military endeavors were fruitless, compromised by poor security. MACV blamed the advisers for the lackluster performance of the division, and Seibert recalled that General DePuy personally reprimanded the team. Ugalde, however, pointed out that the division commander's political preoccupations had kept the unit almost stationary. Asked to use his own influence with the Joint General Staff to get the 25th moving, DePuy in turn admitted that he also had no control over his counterparts and let the matter drop. Ugalde, Seibert, and their subordinates had to make the best of a bad situation. This perhaps typified the advisory predicament, for Seibert also noted that those advisers who became too frustrated with the performance of their counterparts, or those whose reports were too critical, were quietly but promptly relieved and transferred to presumably less demanding jobs.

Special Forces as Advisers

As the protege of President John F. Kennedy, the U.S. Army Special Forces enjoyed a great deal of public attention in the early 1960s. Their jaunty green berets quickly captured everyone's attention and became the trademark of the new branch. Billed as counterinsurgency experts, the highly visible Special Forces soldiers embodied something of the youth culture in America that the Kennedy administration sought to harness. Trained in both guerrilla and counterguerrilla tactics, as well as in civic action, the new organization represented one of America's first military responses to Communist wars of national liberation. The individual Special Forces soldier also was viewed as a ground-level exporter of the American way of life and as a sort of folk hero in the tradition of the American frontiersman. However, despite a certain amount of naivete that surrounded their early missions and operations, the Special Forces seemed to have successfully carried out their WHITE STAR counterinsurgency program in Laos by 1962, and Washington had high hopes for the employment of similar endeavors in South Vietnam. But Special Forces personnel were soon to discover that it was much more difficult to export American social and political beliefs than American economic and military expertise.[39]

The size and organization of the U.S. Army Special Forces varied considerably during this period. Prior to 1963 U.S. Army Special Forces personnel in South Vietnam operated under the Combined Studies Division, an organ of the Central

---

[39] Good studies on the Army Special Forces in Vietnam are Ello, *U.S. Army Special Forces . . . , 1961–1967*; and Frederick H. Stires, *The U.S. Special Forces C.I.D.G. Mission in Vietnam: A Preliminary Case Study in Counterpart and Civil-Military Relationships* (Washington, D.C.: Special Operations Research Office, American University, 1964). See also general material in Special Forces and CIDG files, SEAB, CMH; and USMACV, "Command History, 1964," pp. 56–58, and "1965," pp. 77–79 and 347–52, HRB, CMH. For a narrative with flavor, see Robin Moore's fictional *The Green Berets* (New York: Crown, 1965), which is based on the author's experiences with U.S. Special Forces detachments in 1964. On Montagnard ethnic minorities, see Gerald Cannon Hickey's *Sons of the Mountains: Ethnohistory of the Vietnamese Central Highlands to 1954* (New Haven, Conn.: Yale University Press, 1982), *Free in the Forest: Ethnohistory of the Vietnamese Central Highlands, 1954–1976* (New Haven, Conn.: Yale University Press, 1982), and *The Highland People of South Vietnam: Social and Economic Development* (Santa Monica, Calif.: Rand Corp., 1967). On organization and operations, see Charles M. Simpson III, *Inside the Green Berets: The First Thirty Years* (Novato, Calif: Presidio Press, 1983); Francis J. Kelly, *U.S. Army Special Forces, 1961–1971*, Vietnam Studies (Washington, D.C.: Department of the Army, 1973); Blaufarb, *Counterinsurgency Era*; and Shelby L. Stanton, *The Green Berets at War: U.S. Army Special Forces in Asia, 1956–1975* (Novato, Calif.: Presidio Press, 1986).

Special Forces Team

Intelligence Agency. Small Special Forces teams served temporary duty tours in South Vietnam of approximately six months. Between November 1962 and July 1963 control of the Special Forces effort was transferred to MACV, and in September 1962 a provisional U.S. Army Special Forces command arrived in South Vietnam to act as a central headquarters. At the same time, Special Forces personnel began serving on a permanent status with a normal one-year tour. In October 1964 the provisional Special Forces headquarters, by then located at Nha Trang, became the 5th Special Forces Group (Airborne) and, at the end of the year, was managing four C (corps-level) detachments, five B (province- and division-level) detachments, and forty-four A (district- or unit-level) detachments, with 1,227 assigned personnel. During 1965 MACV placed all Special Forces field detachments under the corps senior advisers, but the Special Forces program remained apart from the regular field advisory effort. Due to inherent weaknesses in their Vietnamese counterparts, American Special Forces servicemen were not true advisers and normally provided most of the leadership for all of the Special Forces programs in South Vietnam.

The original mission of the U.S. Army Special Forces in South Vietnam was to develop paramilitary forces loyal to Saigon in remote areas—especially those inhabited by non-Vietnamese ethnic minorities—where there was little, if any, government presence. Initially, American and South Vietnamese Special Forces soldiers concentrated on organizing, training, and advising primitive village defense teams among the various Montagnard tribes of central South Vietnam. Once a degree of security was achieved, the Americans planned to withdraw the advisers and to convert the militia teams into territorial units. The early program was entirely defensive in nature and an adjunct to the larger pacification effort. However, as the insurgents began to form larger military units in 1963 and 1964, Special Forces advisers responded in kind by establishing a standing Montagnard army, by building heavily fortified operational bases, and by expanding their programs to include the ethnic and religious minorities of the northern and southern areas of South Vietnam.[40]

Despite the later incorporation of Cambodians, Laotians, Chinese, and the Hoa Hao and Cao Dai religious sects into the Special Forces programs, the Montagnard tribes in the Highland (or plateau) region of the II Corps Tactical Zone constituted the bulk of the minority advisory effort. Although the small Highland cities of Ban Me Thuot, Kontum, and Pleiku had important Montagnard populations, most Montagnards were poor upland farmers and hunters living in small forest communities. Unfortunately, their strategically located settlements along the Vietnamese-Laotian border slowly embroiled the peaceful tribes in the growing war, an involvement greatly complicated by the traditional, intense racial animosity between the ethnic Vietnamese and Montagnards. Most Vietnamese, North and South alike, tended to regarded the tribesmen as *moi* ("savages"). While the insurgents often used extreme force to extract Montagnard support for their cause, the South Vietnamese government had done little better and, under Diem, had continued its century-old movement to "Vietnamize" the western plateau. The Montagnard people often had no legal titles to the lands they occupied, and disputes with new ethnic Vietnamese landowners and speculators were common. Local officials and South Vietnamese Special Forces personnel were generally unsympathetic toward the Montagnards and often thwarted American efforts to aid them. Most of the organizing work on the ground thus devolved to the American Special Forces teams, with little constructive assistance from Saigon.

Montagnard units trained by the Special Forces were referred to collectively and separately as Civilian Irregular Defense Groups, CIDGs, or "Cidges." U.S. Special Forces A detachments, consisting of 12 men each, established area development centers and attempted to organize and train several thousand tribesmen into local militia units with one standing mobile strike force (known variously as CIDG companies, a Camp Strike Force, or just Strikers) of 300–450 full-time soldiers for each center. The mobile units operated from fixed bases, or camps, and served as reaction forces. The strength of the CIDG militia units peaked at about 38,000 in late 1963, but the force was gradually phased out over the next two years; some units were converted to Territorial Forces, others upgraded into Strikers, and still others simply dissolved. In contrast, membership in the CIDG companies mushroomed from 13,000 in 1963 to about 22,000 in mid-1965,[41] organized into about two hundred rifle companies performing all manner of small

---

[40] See Simpson, *Inside the Green Berets*, pp. 113–19.

[41] Kelly, *U.S. Army Special Forces*, p. 82, notes that all strength figures are only approximate because of "numerous irreconcilable differences" in official Special Forces reports.

unit combat operations. Although the worth of many of the early militia units and CIDG companies was questionable, the ambitious Special Forces program completely undercut a similar organizational and recruiting effort of the Viet Cong, preventing their domination of the isolated Highlands.

As the pace of the war quickened, the Special Forces teams took on the additional task of border surveillance. Originally, the mission had belonged to the Central Intelligence Agency, which in June 1962 had begun a clandestine intelligence program along the border, using small teams (called Trailwatchers and later Mountain Scouts) trained by American and South Vietnamese Special Forces. In October 1963 the U.S. Army Special Forces headquarters assumed responsibility for the program and in November integrated it into the CIDG effort. As part of its new intelligence-gathering mission, the U.S. Army Special Forces command also organized Project Delta in 1964, consisting of several mixed American–South Vietnamese Special Forces scout teams backed by a special South Vietnamese reaction force, the 81st Airborne Ranger "Battalion." During 1965, American Project Delta advisers also began training special CIDG scout units for each CIDG camp.

The year 1965 also saw the groundwork laid for several other Special Forces–led units. In June General Westmoreland approved the organization of battalion-size reserve units composed of ethnic minorities for each of the four U.S. Army Special Forces C detachments. These units, called mobile strike (or MIKE) forces, conducted long-range patrols and served as reinforcement and reaction forces for the CIDG camps. By the end of the year the Special Forces command had organized a MIKE force in each of the corps zones and formed a fifth at Nha Trang under its direct control. The MIKE units, each led by a Special Forces A detachment, were better armed and trained than normal CIDG elements and were designed strictly for offensive operations. Initially, no South Vietnamese cadre participated, and many were composed of Nungs, Vietnamese of Chinese origin who traditionally performed military service.[42]

American Special Forces personnel also served in MACV's Studies and Observation Group (SOG). Staffed by U.S. military and CIA personnel, this small organization was tasked with conducting clandestine operations outside the borders of South Vietnam under the supervision of the U.S. Joint Chiefs of Staff in Washington. It also advised its South Vietnamese counterpart, the Strategic Technical Directorate, and organ of the Joint General Staff, and, in practice, directed all its operations. The group maintained a training camp with sixteen American Special Forces instructors and two operating offices. One, the Combined Military Operations Studies Office, organized several commando companies, but the Vietnamese had diverted them into a special palace guard security battalion and had never deployed them in the field. The other, the Combined External Operations Studies Office, placed a series of ethnic agent teams into North Vietnam, but Washington was reluctant to support a larger subversive

---

[42] Nungs previously made up the core of the 5th Infantry Division and the 81st (formerly 91st) Airborne Ranger "Battalion." But when these units were "Vietnamized" prior to 1965, many of the Nungs gravitated to various U.S. Special Forces elements or served as bodyguards to Vietnamese commanders.

campaign in the North, and the office's activities had only a nuisance value at best.[43]

The Special Forces programs showed a steady evolution from local security to intelligence-gathering and offensive combat operations.[44] The use of Special Forces detachments as province and district advisory teams in areas containing large CIDG elements slowed this trend. However, as enemy infiltration became a more serious problem, MACV began to position CIDG camps away from the tribal farming areas and closer to the borders, often in extremely remote locations accessible only by helicopter. These isolated CIDG camps were more vulnerable to attack, creating a pressing need for the larger reaction forces described above. The CIDG program exhibited serious internal weaknesses; the disintegration of the South Vietnamese Special Forces during 1964 and the continued hostility between the minorities and ethnic Vietnamese were the most evident. Too often American Special Forces "advisers" personally led CIDG units and openly favored the primitive tribesman over the ethnic Vietnamese, especially in the face of official corruption and sometimes blatant racial prejudice. Much to the chagrin of the Vietnamese, many Montagnard soldiers became intensely loyal to their American advisers, and some Vietnamese attributed the rise of the *Front unifie de la lutte des races opprimees (FULRO)*, the autonomous and armed Montagnard separatist movement, to American machinations. A major Montagnard uprising in 1964 had only underlined the fragile nature of the entire effort.[45]

Throughout 1965 internal problems continued to bedevil the CIDG program, and the underlying hostility between Montagnard and ethnic Vietnamese refused to subside.[46] Despite many promises, Saigon failed to grant the Montagnards their basic rights as citizens, and *FULRO* remained unreconciled to Vietnamese rule and continued to press for political autonomy. *FULRO* leader, Y Bham Enoul, distanced himself from the movement's Communist supporters in April 1965, maintaining his headquarters and an army of several thousand troops just inside the Cambodian border.[47] From there, with the tacit support of the Cambodian government, he bargained for concessions from both sides. Like Saigon, the Viet Cong apparently had promised much, but their sometimes brutal treatment of the Montagnard people had alienated most of the tribes.

[43] For details, see the Studies and Observation Group (SOG) annexes to the MACV command histories, HRB; Strategic Technical Directorate (STD) Assistance Team 158, MACV, "Command History, 1 May 1972–March 1973," HRB; and comments of Col Rod Paschall on draft manuscript, "Advice and Support: The Final Years," 25 Apr 85, SEAB. All in CMH. See also Westmoreland, *Soldier Reports*, pp. 106–09; Simpson, *Inside the Green Berets*, pp. 143–52. SOG, replaced in 1972 by the STD Advisory Team 158, also directed an intelligence-gathering effort separate from its South Vietnamese counterpart.

[44] This trend is discussed at length in HQ, 5th Special Forces Group (Airborne), 1st Special Forces, "Commander's Debriefing Letter, Col John H. Spears, 31 July 1964–1 July 1965," circa 1965 (about 200 pages), SEAB, CMH, and Spragins Interv, 29 Aug 65, file 206–02, Interviews with General Officers, box 6, accession no. 69A702, RG 334, WNRC.

[45] See Hickey, *Free in the Forest*, pp. 90–131. *FULRO* also cited as *Front unifie pour la liberation des races opprimees*.

[46] For summaries, see USMACV, "Command History, 1965," annex A, pp. 347–52, and "1966," annex B, pp. 697–706, HRB; Rpt, 13th Military History Detachment, 6 Sep 69, sub: FULRO—Overview as of 15 Aug 69, SEAB. Both in CMH. See also Hinh and Tho, *South Vietnamese Society*, pp. 96–103.

[47] At the time, MACV estimated that Y Bham had somewhere between two thousand and ten thousand armed men. See USMACV, "Command History, 1965," p. 347, HRB, CMH.

Saigon, in the meantime, had agreed in principle to certain reforms sought by the Montagnards, but had stopped short of approving the almost complete political and military autonomy demanded by Y Bham.

On 29 July, as a show of force, *FULRO* troops seized a Highland CIDG border camp at Buon Brieng in Darlac Province, withdrawing several days later with 176 CIDG personnel. When elements of the South Vietnamese 23d Division reoccupied the camp, and forced several hundred *FULRO* supporters to join local Regional Forces units, tensions increased further. In mid-December *FULRO* launched a series of coordinated attacks in the Highland Provinces of Quang Duc and Phu Bon, seizing a province headquarters and killing 32 South Vietnamese troops before government forces, including an airborne battalion flown in, restored order. The incidents were more a demonstration than a genuine revolt, and after the initial attacks, *FULRO* military activity subsided. In an ensuing crackdown on *FULRO*, Saigon arrested 92 suspected members in Pleiku city, accusing them of planning an uprising to coincide with a forthcoming visit of Premier Ky. Of the *FULRO* suspects arrested throughout the Highlands, most received minor disciplinary action, several were jailed, and four were sentenced to death and executed. Vietnamese-Montagnard relations seemed as poor as ever.

The American position was ambiguous. Advisers who worked closely with the Montagnards tried to stay aloof from these controversial matters, and MACV officially regarded them as an internal affair of the South Vietnamese government. However, individually, many American Special Forces personnel adopted a protective attitude toward their Montagnard charges, shielding them from Vietnamese discrimination. Saigon, in turn, remained suspicious of American motives, fearing that U.S. officials were sympathetic to the Montagnard nationalists, and purposely excluded U.S. representatives from their negotiations with *FULRO*. In August 1965 MACV had advocated supporting South Vietnamese military contingency plans against *FULRO* and informing Montagnard leaders that the United States would not tolerate further disturbances. But the American embassy overruled this approach, fearing that the South Vietnamese might interpret it as a blank check for overt military action against the Montagnards, and instead favored continued negotiations. The December incidents showed *FULRO* possessing greater strength and organization than either Saigon or MACV had suspected, making a policy of conciliation even more desirable. At the time, Westmoreland himself labeled the situation "ticklish" and was concerned "that the [South Vietnamese] government is not proceeding along enlightened lines in its attitude towards the Montagnards."[48]

Paying the Bills

While the glamour of the early American advisory effort went to the Special Forces and, to a lesser extent, to the field advisers, American military advice and support in the areas of materiel, equipment, and finance were also

---

[48] Notes of 30 Jan 66, History file 4–A, Westmoreland Papers, HRB, CMH.

critical. In these fields American control was more complete, though less visible. The U.S. Military Assistance Program provided almost all South Vietnamese military supplies and equipment. Other costs, such as military salaries, were also heavily dependent on American support of the annual Saigon defense budget. Without this assistance it is doubtful whether Saigon could have put up more than token resistance to the growing insurgency.

The United States supplied direct financial aid to the Saigon government primarily through the U.S. Agency for International Development, an arm of the Department of State.[49] In the early 1960's four major types of USAID assistance to South Vietnam were under way: development loans, the Commercial Import Program, surplus agriculture commodity programs, and various projects to aid the public sector. While these endeavors sought to improve the South Vietnamese economy in general, they also were used to create large financial accounts, called joint support funds (JSF), to support the Saigon government. For example, under the Commercial Import Program, local Vietnamese importers ordered certain goods from the United States and other foreign countries. After the American government paid for the goods in dollars or other foreign currencies, the importers reimbursed the United States in piasters, the local currency of South Vietnam. The American government then deposited the piasters into a special account and used them to support the South Vietnamese defense budget. The agricultural commodity program worked in much the same manner. Although importers benefited from the favorable piaster-dollar exchange rate maintained by the United States, the South Vietnamese government soaked up a portion of their profits through import duties.

MACV and the U.S. Embassy controlled joint support funds and apportioned them to specific areas within the South Vietnamese budget. They designated some as assistance-in-kind funds and used them to defray local costs incurred by the advisory effort, but American officials used most of the joint support funds to support the payroll of the South Vietnamese armed forces, giving MACV a great amount of influence over their size and composition.

Joint support funds accounted for approximately 55 percent of the South Vietnamese defense budget in 1963 and 38 percent in 1964.[50] These statistics, however, were only approximate. Because U.S. and South Vietnamese fiscal years were different, funds appropriated in a U.S. fiscal year were not necessarily disbursed, or even obligated, in a parallel Vietnamese budgetary time unit, making it extremely difficult to trace the source of specific expenditures.

Other American assistance was even less direct. For example, U.S. construction activities boosted local businesses, increased governmental tax revenues

---

[49] For basic information, see Heymont et al., "Cost Analysis of Land Combat Counterinsurgency Operations: Vietnam," copy in SEAB, CMH; Irving Heymont, *Resource Allocations for the RVN Army, Regional Forces, Popular Forces, and U.S. Army Advisory Program: FY65–FY67*, RAC–TP–333 (McLean, Va.: Research Analysis Corp., 1968), pp. 11–15.

[50] For background, see Staff Study, Advisory Division, Office of the Comptroller, MACV, 17 Jan 66, sub: 1966 Vietnamese Defense Budget Summary for Presentation to U.S. Mission Council by COMUSMACV; Staff Study, Office of the Assistant Chief of Staff for Intelligence, DA, 11 Sep 64, sub: Republic of Vietnam Manpower. Both in SEAB, CMH. See also Fact Sheet, MACCO, 23 May 68, sub: Growth of the Republic of Vietnam Defense Budget During the Period 1964–1968, in COMUSMACV Fact Book, vol. 2, Westmoreland Papers, HRB, CMH.

accordingly, and provided the basis for the more permanent U.S. installations that later would dominate much of the economy. The United States also funded the Military Assistance Program and the CIDG effort entirely from its own re- sources, and their costs were not included in the South Vietnamese defense budget. In addition, regular U.S. Army units provided assistance in such areas as maintenance, repair and rebuilding of equipment, emergency logistical support, and construction, which never surfaced as either JSF or MAP expenses. Ameri- can support of favorable dollar exchange rates for the declining Vietnamese pias- ter was another major financial prop, as were several other U.S. programs supporting nonmilitary activities, such as the resettlement of refugees, that were related to the war effort.

Another aspect of the financial picture was the soaring inflation rate. Nonde- fense expenditures constituted roughly 50 percent of the Saigon budget. Al- though the proportional U.S. monetary share of the defense budget had fallen between 1961 and 1965, U.S. support of nondefense expenditures had risen dramatically, but not enough to cover all of Saigon's mushrooming expenses. The result was a growing deficit and, by 1965, a severe inflation that had an immedi- ate effect on the fixed salaries of civil service and military personnel. The eco- nomic disruptions of the growing war further reduced government revenues, making the inflation problem worse.

MACV was responsible for supervising the South Vietnamese defense budget. Within MACV, a budget advisory committee, a budget screening board, budget project officers, and an Office of the Comptroller were directly concerned with its planning, programming, formulation, execution, and administration.[51] The MACV comptroller was responsible for preparing the original guidelines in coordination with the rest of the MACV staff. One MACV project officer super- vised each budget chapter and worked closely with his Vietnamese counterparts in the Ministry of Defense. The MACV screening board, which constituted the working body of the budget advisory committee, worked closely with budget project officers to ensure that budget guidelines were followed and that requests for funds were justified adequately. The board referred unresolved differences with the Vietnamese to the budget advisory committee, composed of senior MACV officers, and, if necessary, to the MACV commander himself. This proc- ess gave MACV almost complete control over the entire South Vietnamese defense budget.

Occasionally, the Vietnamese requested reconsideration of certain portions of the budget deleted by the American managers. The budget advisory committee studied such reclamas and, if necessary, modified the budget to reflect the change. Only after U.S. representatives had approved a draft budget, did the two partners draw up a formal budget support agreement.

American control did not end with the approved budget. The South Vietnam- ese minister of defense also needed MACV concurrence to disburse funds each quarter. The United States also released joint support funds to the Ministry of Defense on a monthly basis, giving MACV managers yet another check over their counterparts. The South Vietnamese also had to submit monthly reports to

---

[51] Fact Sheet, MACMAP, 3 Jul 67, sub: Budget Screening Board, MICRO 3/0451, RG 334, WNRC.

MACV detailing credits released, total obligations, and total expenditures by budget chapter and article. These reports were then used by the MACV comptroller and the budget project officers to monitor expenditures.

The Military Assistance Program provided MACV with a second powerful means of influence. Annual U.S. congressional appropriations financed the program, and MACV administered it under the supervision of the Department of Defense. The program paid for military equipment and supplies and services to Saigon, including expenses associated with training and advisory activities; provided for the repair and rehabilitation of excess U.S. stock furnished without cost and all expenses incurred in shipping such materiel; and directly supported some aspects of unconventional and psychological warfare activities, civic action programs, and paramilitary forces. The Defense Department determined the funding levels for South Vietnam, and the availability and costs of military items and services. With this information MACV drew up requests for equipment, supplies, and services on a fiscal year basis. Among the basic planning factors were detailed tables of personnel and equipment for each planned South Vietnamese unit, personnel information (if available) by rank and specialty, rates of consumption or usage, and equipment and supply inventories needed.

Within the MACV headquarters, the MAP Directorate had primary responsibility for the implementation of the program in South Vietnam.[52] Its actions were closely coordinated with special MAP officers in the Naval and Air Force Advisory Groups, the J–3 (Operations) and J–5 (Plans), and the MACV comptroller. Based on guidance from the MACV commander, the J–3, and the comptroller, the J–5 staff prepared the MACV Joint Strategic Objectives Plan that, in Annex J, delineated the proposed South Vietnamese military organization for the next five years. The MAP Directorate also had representatives on both the budget advisory committee and the budget screening board, and supervised the Offshore Training Program prepared by the MACV Training Directorate and by the Naval and Air Force Advisory Groups.

By 1965 the Military Assistance Program had begun to exhibit serious weaknesses. During the year the MAP Directorate was forced to revise its plans several times because of General Westmoreland's decisions to expand the South Vietnamese armed forces and the expectation of an increased tempo of operations. Inflation, requests for more supplies and materiel, and military construction costs also pushed up the projected MAP budget, making additional funding necessary. Normally the Defense Department could increase the South Vietnamese share of the program only by reducing the share of other nations, by making more use of "excess" materiel, by buying cheaper products, or by asking Congress for supplementary monies. The arrival in Vietnam of large Korean and Thai military forces supported by separate American MAP appropriations further complicated funding priorities. Although the program gave the top echelons of the U.S. advisory effort a great deal of potential leverage, it was too rigid to finance a military situation in constant flux.

---

[52] Briefing, MACMAP, 29 Jan 69, sub: MAP Directorate Mission, Organization and Function, MICRO 3/0396, RG 334, WNRC.

American financial support of the CIDG program was awkward but effective. Special funding procedures were required because of the restrictive language of Defense Department appropriation acts and the sensitive nature of the program. Under the code name PARASOL-SWITCHBACK, the comptroller of the Army informed the Central Intelligence Agency in Washington of the approved budget and then allocated funds directly to a special office of Army Finance, from where they were transferred to a special CIA account. This caused the funds to lose their identity and freed them of restrictions applicable to Army funds.[53] CIA representatives in Saigon then drew cash from this secret account and passed it on to the 5th Special Forces Group finance officer, who, in turn, disbursed the laundered money to the field teams for daily expenditures. With this cash U.S. Army Special Forces team leaders, or their South Vietnamese counterparts under extremely close American supervision, paid the CIDG soldiers. Control of both funds and materiel remained in American hands, and local purchases of goods and services were made in cash. American Special Forces officers also controlled air transport and depot stockage, and both requisitioning and accounting procedures were informal. Auditing was done by the 5th Special Forces Group headquarters and the Central Intelligence Agency.[54] Although cumbersome, the process gave the American Special Forces advisers in the field a great amount of control over the units they were technically only advising and also offered a working alternative to the regular MACV advisory system.

The advisory system that had evolved by 1965 was thus a low-key, oblique, almost surreptitious effort. Although it encompassed the totality of Saigon's armed forces, its effectiveness in molding that force was in no way commensurate with the size and scope of its actual power. Neither the U.S. ambassador nor the MACV commander, for example, had been able to use his control over the South Vietnamese military budget to limit the involvement of armed forces in national politics. The Vietnamese generals appeared almost immune to American advice in certain critical areas: Westmoreland and his subordinate corps senior advisers experienced more success in influencing South Vietnamese military deployments, plans, and operations than leadership and morale. As the war began to pass into another stage, American officials now had the opportunity to evaluate their advisory relationships and to make those changes and adjustments that they deemed necessary.

---

[53] MAP funds could not be used to pay indigenous troops.
[54] Memo, Maj Gen Joseph A. McChristian, Asst CofS for Intelligence, DA, 8 Apr 70, sub: Audit of Army Use of Other Agency Funds, SEAB, CMH; Simpson, *Inside the Green Berets*, pp. 165–69.

PART TWO

A New War
(1965)

American Commanders Taking Charge of the Battlefield

4

Searching for Stability

As early as September 1964 Westmoreland made political stability one of his primary advisory objectives. He realized that before any significant military improvements could be made, the South Vietnamese government had to settle down to business and the army had to be taken out of politics. Its officer corps had to be "protected against purge solely by reasons of religious or political affiliation," its commanders assured "that their careers and reputations will not be sacrificed for political expediency," and its rank and file convinced that they would not be "punished or expelled from the Armed Forces" if they carried out their responsibilities as efficiently as possible. Restoring military professionalism was paramount; however, this task proved easier said than done. During his first year in command Westmoreland found it impossible to keep the Humpty-Dumpty Saigon regimes in one piece and the military out of the political process. By March of 1965, with political stability as remote as ever, he predicted "a VC takeover of the country sooner or later if we continue down the present road at the present level of effort."[1]

A contemporary MACV staff study arrived at some of the same conclusions. According to the study,[2] the "lack of stability in [the] GVN and RVNAF" was responsible for dissipating American advisory efforts. With six coups to their credit in the last eighteen months, Vietnamese generals had devoted too much time to power politics and had let their other responsibilities slide. The basic problem was the "power appetite and irresponsibility of several of the VN senior officers," which made it necessary for all commanders to be politically informed for their own survival. The military juntas, and not the Joint General Staff, remained the "focal point of power within the RVNAF." As a remedy, the study recommended establishing a combined American-Vietnamese military staff to bolster the South Vietnamese high command and to increase American influence over the war effort; creating a centralized American logistical support organization to replace the MAP system over which the field adviser had no control or

[1] First, second, and third quotations from Msg, Westmoreland MAC 4830 to Wheeler 061000 Sep 64, sub: Assessment of the Military Situation. Fourth quotation from Msg, Westmoreland MAC 1190 to Wheeler, 060500 Mar 65. Both in COMUSMACV Message file, Westmoreland Papers, HRB, CMH.
[2] In Memo, MACV, sub: Meeting—100830 Mar 65: Advisors in the Support Role, History file 14–28, Westmoreland Papers, HRB, CMH.

leverage; or, as another alternative, eliminating both the Military Assistance Program and the Joint General Staff and placing all Saigon forces under an American command. But because "the issue of sovereignty and national pride appear to render this alternative unacceptable, and for US purposes at this time, infeasible," the study favored a combined military command reporting to a political council consisting of the South Vietnamese chief of state and the American ambassador. MACV would become a small Southeast Asia headquarters, with its major operational responsibilities assumed by the combined command. Its chief of staff, J–1, J–2, J–3, and navy component would have Vietnamese heads with American deputies; its J–4, J–5, J–6, and air force element would have American chiefs with Vietnamese deputies. The U.S. corps-level senior advisers would become deputies to the Vietnamese corps commanders, and their staffs would be integrated. Presumably, Westmoreland would assume the position of combined commander, with the current Joint General Staff head serving as his deputy.

Among the more exotic suggestions in the study was a "coup inhibitor" proposal to establish trust accounts of $5,000–$20,000 for each South Vietnamese general officer. For every month that the officer avoided involvement "in a coup, attempted coup or other actions not in GVN/US interest," he would receive between $250 and $1,000 in his account. Failure would result in forfeiture of the entire sum. Other proposals along the same line included trust funds for the dependents of generals and generous pensions for cashiered officers. To further inhibit military meddling in political affairs, the study proposed removing all Vietnamese armored units from the sensitive Saigon area, stationing an American "anti coup" brigade there, and establishing U.S. espionage units to detect any antigovernment plots at an early stage. Apparently neither Westmoreland nor Ambassador Taylor pondered such measures seriously, but both realized that immediate action was needed to halt the deterioration of the military situation. Expanding the South Vietnamese armed forces, reinforcing them with American ground combat units, and establishing a combined command all merited careful consideration.

Military Expansion

Despite South Vietnamese shortcomings in leadership and the shaky political foundation in Saigon, Westmoreland was hopeful that the situation would soon improve. In November 1964 he noted that the South Vietnamese military had "weathered" many months of political turbulence without any defections or insubordination, that division and corps commanders were "stronger and more able than heretofore," and that strength increases brought about by more volunteers and conscripts were a "most encouraging development." Desertion rates, however, were still too high, and Westmoreland believed that they were "directly related to frequent changes of senior commanders, unit relocations on short notice and the resultant family separation." The MACV commander's critical objectives for 1965 thus included reducing desertions, rebuilding combat ineffective battalions, increasing enemy losses, and pacifying

Training an Expanding Army

more hamlets. He reasoned that stronger leadership, greater discipline, a better troop information program, additional family housing, and more attention to morale and welfare by the Vietnamese, would lower desertions. To overcome tactical deficiencies, which ran "the entire gamut" in the armed forces, Westmoreland stressed better leadership and, "in the long run," the development of "a tradition which disassociates the military from politics. . . ."[3]

Westmoreland's favorable assessment of the South Vietnamese armed forces in late 1964 fostered thoughts of future military expansion. During 1965 he planned to enlarge the Vietnamese force structure, adding almost 94,000 new troops—about 47,500 regulars and another 46,200 territorials. For the regular army he proposed 31 new infantry battalions, 1 for each regular army regiment (giving each regiment 4 battalions instead of the traditional 3), thereby increasing the number of maneuver units without adding more headquarters and administration overhead. This increase, he believed, would be both inexpensive and rapid, requiring only a few officers or highly skilled personnel. The proposed expansion of the territorials, 35,387 for the Regional Forces and 10,815 for the Popular Forces, had the same advantage. All of the increases would greatly enlarge the number of security forces available, and the territorial expansion would release more regulars for offensive operations. The buildup also included

[3] Msg, Westmoreland MAC 6191 to Wheeler, 280530 Nov 64, sub: Assessment of the Military Situation, COMUSMACV Message file, Westmoreland Papers, HRB, CMH.

grouping several independent regiments and battalions into a new infantry division and raising four new armored cavalry squadrons. The new division was to be "austere," with spaces for its "essential" command and support components coming from regimental and special zone commands around Saigon so as not to interfere with activation of the new rifle units. If the buildup went as planned, the regular armed forces would increase to 155 ground combat battalions (124 infantry, 20 ranger, 6 airborne and 5 marine); 10 armored cavalry squadrons (1 per division), 27 artillery battalions; and 10 division, 31 regimental, 1 airborne, and 1 marine corps tactical headquarters.[4] No expansion was intended for the general reserve units (marines and airborne); although American advisers considered them the best and most versatile South Vietnamese combat forces available, their involvement in Saigon politics had always been a major drawback.[5]

Political instability and an intensification of the war continually threatened the successful execution of Westmoreland's proposals. South Vietnam was still plagued by civil disturbances, and there were ominous signs of a major Viet Cong offensive in the offing. The MACV commander became concerned about the expansion in the spring of 1965. His optimism of November 1964 momentarily shaken, he viewed the increased manpower acquisitions as too ambitious. Desertions were still too high and recruitment had dropped off. Although South Vietnamese leaders had pledged that the needed conscription measures would be "vigorously implemented," Westmoreland had misgivings and confided to the Joint Chiefs chairman, General Wheeler, that "it will be necessary to push the GVN in order to get maximum performance."[6]

Despite his underlying reservations, Westmoreland remained "convinced [that] we must press on" and accelerate the buildup. MACV studies showed that South Vietnam had ample young men to provide the requisite manpower, and he was confident that Saigon would adopt and pursue the manpower measures needed to carry out the expansion. Even though the government's past performance in this area left something to be desired, the MACV commander noted that Saigon had already taken important steps to revitalize its "conscription-recruitment-psywar effort," such as creating a mobilization directorate and drafting twenty-six and thirty year olds.[7]

To solve the manpower problem, Westmoreland proposed establishing a combined American-Vietnamese manpower committee to coordinate U.S. advice and South Vietnamese programs. He believed that enlistment and reenlistment bonuses, an expansion of the Women's Armed Forces Corps (to release men for combat duty), better pay, more liberal promotions, increased dependent benefits, more awards and decorations, and more generous pensions and death bene-

---

[4] Nine of the ten divisions had 3 regiments each, the tenth division (the 23d) had 2 regiments, and two regiments remained independent, giving a total of 31 regiments, each with 3 (to be raised to 4) infantry battalions of 400–500 men.

[5] Quoted words from Msg, Westmoreland 1463 to Wheeler, 171825 Mar 65, COMUSMACV Message file, Westmoreland Papers. See also USMACV, "Command History, 1965," pp. 57–64. Both in HRB, CMH.

[6] Msg, Westmoreland MAC 1463 to Wheeler, 171825 Mar 65, COMUSMACV Message file, Westmoreland Papers, HRB, CMH.

[7] First quotation from ibid. Second quotation from Msg, Westmoreland MAC 1840 to Wheeler, 030855 Apr 65. Both in COMUSMACV Message file, Westmoreland Papers, HRB, CMH.

fits could attract recruits and reduce desertions. But to rebuild damaged units and make good the new expansion program more was needed. Desertions had to be reduced, accessions stabilized at about 8,000 recruits per month, deferments curtailed, and conscription extended to a wider age bracket. Specifically, the MACV commander hoped to see Saigon issue a "national public service decree" that would subject all males in the 20- to 45-year-old age group to some type of service for three years, and another law reducing the draft age to eighteen and ultimately to seventeen. Experience had shown that the threat of the draft was enough to induce recruits to enlist in territorial or regular units close to their homes, where they were also less likely to desert.[8]

The only bottleneck to the rapid completion of the South Vietnamese buildup was the army's limited training facilities. Westmoreland remained confident, however, stating that Saigon's manpower program "is meeting realistic and obtainable goals." In May the new 10th Infantry Division and about half of the planned thirty-one infantry battalions were activated, desertions seemed to be leveling off, and army strength had risen from a little over 218,000 in January to about 229,000. But the optimism of the spring soon gave way to despair. In June and July combat losses took a turn for the worse and rose dramatically, especially in the rifle units, which also had the highest desertion rates (*see Chart 4*). By mid-year many infantry battalions were at half-strength, with between six to nine of them completely "combat ineffective," and another seventeen newly activated infantry battalions needing several months of training before becoming operational. As an emergency measure, the Joint General Staff, with Westmoreland's approval, briefly suspended the activation of new battalions and assigned all newly trained recruits to existing ones. But the benefit derived from the desertion-prone recruits was fleeting, and the politico-military turmoil of May and June made the military situation appear only worse.[9]

Combined Command

The arrival of American ground combat troops gave a new dimension to U.S. efforts in South Vietnam. The first Marine battalions came ashore in March, followed by the U.S. Army 173d Airborne Brigade in May. Ambassador Taylor wanted U.S. troops restricted to enclaves along the coast. Westmoreland temporarily agreed, but had more ambitious plans, feeling that American firepower and mobility would be wasted defending ports and airfields. Warned about enemy intentions in the Central Highlands, he continued to press for an entire airmobile division to secure the interior plateau. At the same time, both he and

---

[8] Quoted words from Msg, Westmoreland MAC 1840 to Wheeler, 030855 Apr 65, COMUSMACV Message file. See also MACV, Index: Status Report on Non-Military Actions, April 1965, History file 15–26. Both in Westmoreland Papers, HRB, CMH. On the Women's Armed Forces Corps, see USMACV, "Command History, 1972–1973," 2 vols. (Saigon, 1973), 1:C–23, HRB, CMH.

[9] Quotation from MACV, Recommendations, April 1965, History file 15–27, Westmoreland Papers, HRB. See also Memo, Sternberg to COMUSMACV, 7 July 65, sub: RVNAF Strength Summary, SEAB. Both in CMH.

CHART 4—COMPARATIVE STRENGTHS AND LOSSES OF SOUTH VIETNAMESE MILITARY FORCES, 1965

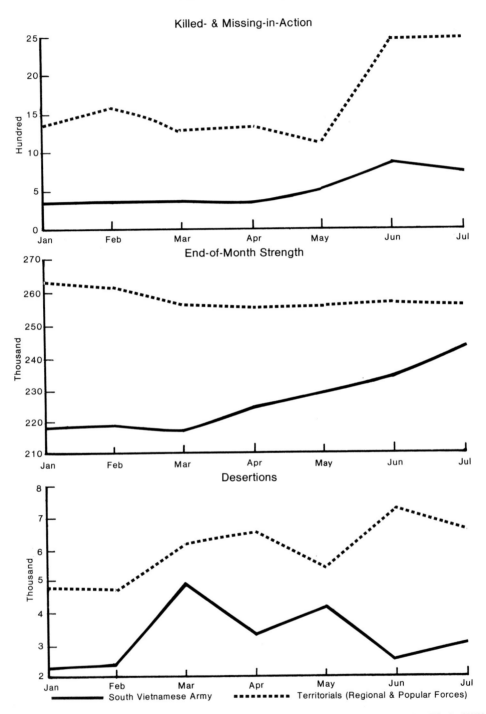

Sources: Adapted by author from USMACV, "Command History, 1965," pp. 270–72; Msg, Westmoreland MAC 6191 to Wheeler, 280530 Nov 64, sub: Assessment of the Military Situation, COMUSMACV Message file, Westmoreland Papers. Both in HRB, CMH.

Ambassador Maxwell D. Taylor (left) and General Westmoreland *discussing the future role of U.S. combat forces in South Vietnam*

Taylor approved the dispatch of South Korean and Australian contingents, as well as several more Marine battalions.[10]

As all these forces deployed to South Vietnam, the prospect of some sort of unified command similar to that employed by the United Nations in the Korean War seemed imminent. On 18 March 1965 Westmoreland told General Wheeler "that a transition phase, based on cooperative rather than formal authority, to [a] combined command and staff arrangement is in order and would be accepted by the Vietnamese." Building on a combined corps commander–senior adviser conference hosted by him every month, and agreements with the Vietnamese high command to consult with MACV before making any further senior appointments or major troop displacements, Westmoreland believed that the next step was "a small combined, coordinating, operational staff, at the outset superimposed on

[10] For details on the decisions leading to the deployment of U.S. ground combat forces, see John M. Carland, *Combat Operations, June 1965–October 1966*, United States Army in Vietnam (Washington, D.C.: U.S. Army Center of Military History, forthcoming); Stanley Robert Larsen and James Lawton Collins, Jr., *Allied Participation in Vietnam*, Vietnam Studies (Washington, D.C.: Department of the Army, 1975), pp. 5–14; Westmoreland, *Soldier Reports*, pp. 131–43; U.S. Department of Defense, *United States–Vietnam Relations, 1945–1967* (commonly known as the *Pentagon Papers* but hereafter cited as *U.S.-Vietnam Relations*), 12 vols. (Washington, D.C.: Government Printing Office, 1971), 4:secs. IV. C. 4. and IV. C. 5.; and appropriate sections of Historical Division, Joint Secretariat, U.S. Joint Chiefs of Staff, "The Joint Chiefs of Staff and the War in Vietnam, 1960–1968" (hereafter cited as "Joint Chiefs of Staff in Vietnam, 1960–1968"), Part 2, History of the Joint Chiefs of Staff (Washington, D.C., 1970), HRB, CMH.

the present structure, to be headed jointly by COMUSMACV and CINCRVNAF. . . ." Initially, "this organization would deal only with problems that are of a combined nature," while the existing headquarters would handle "normal, unilateral, national functions." However, once "sizeable contingents of U.S. troops" had arrived, Westmoreland felt that he "would assume control of those operations where American troops were involved" and, at the same time, devise "a politically palatable and operationally effective transition command arrangement" whose "organization and functions" he himself could shape.[11]

In a message to Admiral Sharp one week later Westmoreland elaborated on his proposed combined command. Such a command "would have only limited directive powers" but would assure "U.S. direction at [the] highest common working level. . . ." An American general officer with a South Vietnamese deputy would head what he now called a combined coordinating staff. Below this level, "whenever U.S. and RVN forces are geographically colocated or adjacent or have agreed combined missions assigned to them," the MACV commander intended that they might issue combined directives but would execute them "unilaterally through [their own] national chain of command." To facilitate these arrangements, he proposed the creation of ad hoc combined staffs by tactical commands or an exchange of liaison officers between these headquarters. He noted that such arrangements would provide a transition "if and when it becomes politically palatable or militarily essential for the U.S. to take full command." His deputy, General Throckmorton, was to "oversee [the] coordination process," which "would be a logical precedent to his assumption of a field command role should the U.S. take full command of the deployed RVNAF." But until that time Westmoreland was convinced that, "in view of current relationships and leverage at hand," the United States would have "de facto operational control of RVNAF forces in bilateral operations."[12]

In a revised estimate on 26 March Westmoreland was even more insistent on the need for a combined command. Citing the continued instability in Saigon, he related that the "RVNAF . . . has begun to show evidence of fragmentation and there is no longer an effective chain of command." A committee ran the armed forces and was itself an "area for intrigue and personal ambition." He called for immediate action and warned that "unless the U.S. can effectively enter the command and control structure of RVNAF through integration or creation of combined staffs and thus exert leadership and moderation, it seems likely that additional coups will take place and the completely irresponsible game of musical chairs will continue among and between the highest command and staff positions." Once a few more U.S. combat battalions had arrived, he felt sure that

---

[11] Quoted words from Msg, Westmoreland MAC 1463 to Wheeler, 171825 Mar 65, COMUSMACV Message file, Westmoreland Papers, HRB, CMH. See also *U.S.-Vietnam Relations*, 3:sec. IV. B. 3., pp. 61–63. But according to General Harold K. Johnson, then the Army chief of staff, in early March both Taylor and Westmoreland felt that the Vietnamese would not accept a combined command. See Informal Discussion 7 March, 1150 Hours, in file General Johnson's Trip to South Vietnam in March 1965, box 35, Harold K. Johnson Papers, MHI.

[12] Msg, Westmoreland MAC 1566 to Sharp, 221655 Mar 65, COMUSMACV Message file, Westmoreland Papers, HRB, CMH.

the South Vietnamese generals would accept "a small combined staff" that could be expanded as the American ground commitment increased.[13]

A subsequent message on 1 April to the Army chief of staff, General Johnson, continued this theme. Predicting that the creation of a small combined headquarters was "highly probable . . . in the near future," Westmoreland asked if he could retain Brig. Gen. James L. Collins, Jr., to organize and manage it. The matter was still touchy, he explained, calling for great tact and diplomacy. In his opinion the "time is not yet ripe to propose [the] staff organization to [the] GVN so we cannot openly move ahead."[14]

Concurrently, Westmoreland also proposed creating unified tactical commands at the corps level and establishing a "field command" under General Throckmorton to "coordinate" American, South Vietnamese, and South Korean operations in the I and II Corps Tactical Zones. Several days later Throckmorton suggested creating a U.S. "Northern Area Command" to control all American, South Vietnamese, and Korean forces in the two northern zones. The commander and principal staff officers of the command would be American, each having a Vietnamese deputy. The new command would supervise the existing Vietnamese I and II Corps headquarters, with the Vietnamese I Corps commander responsible for the U.S. 3d Marine Division. As an alternative, a central area command could be established on a similar basis in the II Corps area alone. In relating this concept to Admiral Sharp, Westmoreland described it as "a corps size field force in the northern part of South Vietnam which would be international in complexion albeit built around the solid frame of a U.S. corps force."[15]

On 11 April Westmoreland proposed the alternative possibility of an International Military Security Task Force, or IMSTAF, for the Da Nang area in the northern I Corps Tactical Zone. The force would be built around a U.S. Marine Corps regiment consisting of "attached or assigned" Vietnamese and South Korean elements. "Combined staff representation" on the IMSTAF headquarters would give it an "international flavor while retaining the strength and authority of U.S. forces." He suggested that a second IMSTAF might be created around Saigon and envisioned that "upon deployment of major [U.S.] forces, the IMSTAFs would phase into a larger international force." At the national level Westmoreland affirmed his desire for "the formation of a small single combined staff headed by a U.S. general officer, a Vietnamese Deputy Chief of Combined Staff, and a multi-national staff," and now held that "informal discussions" with Vietnamese leaders on "such a concept would be palatable . . . [if] introduced on a low-key basis."[16]

---

[13] Commander's Estimate of the Military Situation in South Vietnam, March 1965, 26 Mar 65, History file 14–38, Westmoreland Papers, HRB, CMH.

[14] Msg, Westmoreland MAC 1776 to Johnson, 010240 Apr 65, COMUSMACV Message file, Westmoreland Papers, HRB, CMH.

[15] First and second quotations from Msg, Westmoreland MAC 1724 to Johnson, 301340 Mar 65, COMUSMACV Message file. Third quotation from Memo, Throckmorton to Westmoreland, 4 Apr 65, sub: Organization of Northern Area, History file 15–7. Fourth quotation from Msg, Westmoreland to Sharp, 9 Apr 65, sub: Planning for Deployment of Logistic Support and Combat Forces to Southeast Asia, History file 15–14. All in Westmoreland Papers, HRB, CMH.

[16] Msg, Westmoreland to CINCPAC, 11 Apr 65, sub: Additional Deployments and Command Concepts, History file 15–15, Westmoreland Papers, HRB, CMH.

On 14 April General Collins, tabbed by Westmoreland to be his point of contact with the South Vietnamese on combined planning, tied most of the MACV proposals together. He outlined a working plan for a combined command under the dual control of General Westmoreland and his Vietnamese counterpart. The command would have an American chief of staff and a Vietnamese deputy, assisted directly by an American secretariat and a Vietnamese executive office for national military regions. The American chief of staff would supervise six staff sections, with those for personnel (C–1) and intelligence (C–2) headed by a Vietnamese, each with an American deputy, and those for logistics (C–4), plans (C–5), and communications (C–6) by an American, each with a Vietnamese deputy. The nationality of the operations staff section chief (C–3) was left open, but all sections would have a mix of American and Vietnamese personnel. Representatives of other nations could be added later, "in proportion to the strength of their forces committed in Vietnam." At first this new headquarters would have no operational responsibilities, but Collins foresaw it slowly evolving into a multinational combined command controlling Westmoreland's IMSTAFs as well as specific national field commands. As this combined command assumed greater responsibility for directing military operations, MACV and the Joint General Staff would become components of it and deal primarily with unilateral administrative and logistical support. In retrospect, the Collins proposal marked the high point of the combined command concept in South Vietnam.[17]

On 15 April President Johnson himself tossed a new idea into the planning hopper. Searching for some way to turn the war around, he endorsed the "experimental encadrement by U.S. forces of South Vietnamese ground troops both to stiffen and increase their effectiveness and also to add to their own firepower." As a trial, American combat soldiers could be placed in several South Vietnamese infantry battalions. The following day McGeorge Bundy, the president's national security adviser, wired Ambassador Taylor of Johnson's "personal desire for a strong experiment in the encadrement of U.S. troops with Vietnamese." But, perhaps feeling that the proposal was ill-advised, Bundy suggested that a few combined operations between American and South Vietnamese infantry battalions might satisfy the president. He also noted that such endeavors, if successful, might ease the approval of additional troop deployments and indicated that the entire matter of American–South Vietnamese command relationships would be discussed further at the meeting in Honolulu scheduled for 20 April, four days later.[18]

But even before the Honolulu conference the enthusiasm for a unified command had begun to waver. Admiral Sharp cautioned Westmoreland on 14 April that any organizational changes in the Vietnam military command structure

---

[17] Memo, Collins to CofS, MACV, 14 Apr 65, sub: Development of Combined Staff Organization, History file 15–20, Westmoreland Papers, HRB, CMH.

[18] First quotation from Msg, DOD 9164 to AmEmbassy, Saigon (info CINCPAC and COMUSMACV), 15 Apr 65, sub: Joint State-Defense Message, History file 15–23, Westmoreland Papers, HRB. Interv, Thomas W. Scoville and Charles B. MacDonald with Robert W. Komer, 7 May 70, sub: Organization and Management of the New Model Pacification Program, 1966–1969 (hereafter cited as Komer Interv), Rand Limited Document D(L)–20104–ARPA, copy in SEAB, also mentions Johnson's initial interest in encadrement. Second quotation from Msg, McGeorge Bundy and Rusk to Taylor, 15 Apr 65, History file 15–24, Westmoreland Papers, HRB. All in CMH.

should be "evolutionary" and insisted that "we simply can't afford another one-year shakedown period for a new and difficult set-up." Westmoreland noted his "complete agreement," seconded the necessity of "evolutionary change in our organization structure," and suggested only that one or two proposed U.S. corps-level headquarters might also command Vietnamese forces at some future date. He also rejected Washington's proposals for encadrement. He and Throckmorton concluded that the language barrier and the extra support needed to maintain large numbers of American personnel in Vietnamese units made the practice unworkable. If Washington insisted, Westmoreland was willing to experiment with encadrement but was more hopeful regarding the creation of IMSTAF-type task forces.[19]

On 20 April Westmoreland, Ambassador Taylor, and Admiral Sharp met in Honolulu with Secretary of Defense Robert S. McNamara, General Wheeler, John T. McNaughton, the assistant secretary of defense for international security affairs, and William P. Bundy, the assistant secretary of state for Far Eastern affairs. The participants recommended sending nine more American battalions to Vietnam, in addition to the four Marine battalions already deployed, and formally agreed to request ground combat forces from Australia and South Korea. According to McNaughton, Westmoreland dismissed the concept of encadrement as "neither required nor feasible" and instead planned "to assign Vietnamese liaison personnel to each independent U.S. platoon and to 'brigade' U.S. forces with ARVN troops in counter-insurgency actions." He also reiterated his intention of creating international brigade-size military forces.[20]

Plans for a combined command soon encountered a major setback. On 28 April Westmoreland met with the current chief of the Joint General Staff, General Tran Van Minh, and his then chief of staff, General Thieu. The MACV commander found Minh "politically sensitive" to the formation of a combined staff, even though he had previously favored it. Westmoreland backed down and suggested that MACV's small International Military Assistance Office might serve as a coordinating mechanism. He later confided to Taylor that, although Minh intitially had approved the formation of a combined staff that would "prepare studies, analyses and guidance to be promulgated to the Vietnamese and U.S. field commands through our respective communications channels," he now "swung perceptively [sic] away from anything suggestive of [a] 'combined' headquarters." When Thieu and Ky followed suit, each issuing press statements on the "undesirability" of a unified or combined command, the matter became a political football. Taylor felt that someone had leaked the American proposals for a combined command to the Saigon press, which "interpreted [them] as the

---

[19] First and second quotations from Msg, Sharp to Westmoreland, 142345 Apr 65, sub: MACV Organization. Third and fourth quotations from Msg, Westmoreland MAC 2135 to Sharp, 171110 Apr 65, sub: MACV Organization. Both in COMUSMACV Message file, Westmoreland Papers, HRB, CMH. See also *U.S.-Vietnam Relations*, 3:sec. IV. B. 3., pp. 59–60; COMUSMACV's Notebook, Honolulu, Hawaii Trip, 18 April 1965, tab 2–A, SEAB, CMH; and MACV, Recommendations, April 1965, History file 15–27, Westmoreland Papers, HRB, CMH.

[20] Quoted words from Memo, McNaughton, 23 Apr 65, sub: Minutes of the Honolulu Meeting, History file 15–36, Westmoreland Papers, HRB, CMH. See also COMUSMACV Notebook, Green I, "8 Experiments With Summary Recommendations," circa 1965, box 2, accession no. 67A4604, RG 338, WNRC.

"Soldiers, meet your advisors!" *This cartoon, which appeared in the Hungarian journal* Ludas Matyi, *reflected the sensitivity of the South Vietnamese to American domination.*

U.S. taking charge," resulting in a variety of commentaries "critical of any yielding of Vietnamese authority over its forces." "The incident is a reminder," he warned, "that we will have to proceed cautiously in proposing arrangements in this area."[21]

Westmoreland's proposals for an international military force also began to fall by the wayside. In discussions with the Australian ambassador on 29 April he proposed an international force of American, Australian, Korean, and Filipino troops but averred "that initially Vietnamese forces would not be a part of the task force although their attachment was possible at a future date." This time South Korean sensitivities to U.S. command over their troops convinced Westmoreland that this idea was also infeasible. With the deteriorating military situation, he found it more expedient to assign the different national forces separate tasks without the complication of experimental combined commands.[22]

[21] First quotation from MFR, Westmoreland, 28 Apr 65, sub: Conference With Generals Thieu and Minh, 28 April, History file 15–45. Second and third quotations from Memo, Westmoreland to Taylor, 21 May 65, sub: Combined Command, History file 16–8. Remaining quotations from Msg, Taylor EMBTEL 3552 to Rusk, 29 Apr 65, History file 15–50. All in Westmoreland Papers, HRB, CMH.

[22] Quoted words from MFR, Westmoreland, 29 Apr 65, sub: Conference With Australian Ambassador, History file 15–47, Westmoreland Papers, HRB, CMH. See also Larsen and Collins, *Allied Participation in Vietnam*, pp. 131–34; Westmoreland, *Soldier Reports*, p. 133.

In the second half of May Westmoreland began to distance himself from the entire concept of a combined command. On the twenty-first, while reviewing the matter for Taylor, he asserted that plans for a national-level combined headquarters had originally emanated from the Office of the Secretary of Defense and were "not related to any specific recommendations . . . from this headquarters." Considering current Vietnamese attitudes, he maintained that it was still "clearly premature to propose the creation of a combined coordinating staff with our counterparts." Moreover, the sensitivity of the issue had prevented the drafting of any such plans, primarily because they involved "something approaching de facto U.S. control of the RVNAF" and could not "be aired with our Vietnamese counterparts prior to submission." Westmoreland also held that his lack of authority to discuss additional U.S. troop deployments, "which are the conditions precedent for such a command arrangement," hindered frank consultations with the Vietnamese. Nevertheless, he still hoped to establish a U.S. Army corps headquarters in Vietnam to control "all U.S. and Allied ground forces deployed in the northern half of the country . . . [and] prepared to assume operational control of ARVN ground forces in the area." Such a command would not be "a fully integrated corps headquarters but rather [would include] certain ARVN augmentation to . . . [its] staff." He was also hopeful that the situation might warrant the "creation of a combined organization" in the future and confirmed that General Collins would remain his "special representative" to the Vietnamese on these matters. Collins would represent MACV on joint field inspections and help coordinate combined operations between U.S. and South Vietnamese tactical units. If and when a formal discussion of a combined "organization with the GVN and the JGS" was politically feasible, the Collins proposal would serve as a basis for such an arrangement. Meanwhile, Westmoreland held, the "accreditation" of Collins to the South Vietnamese high command "is as far as we can go." Ambassador Taylor supported Westmoreland's analysis, and shortly thereafter Washington agreed to drop the matter.[23]

Roles and Missions

The absence of a combined command made the definition of roles and missions—who was to do what to whom—much more complex. Even before the arrival of foreign combat units in South Vietnam, the articulation of missions and assignments was a major problem. In 1964 MACV had reduced military tasks to three general categories: *search and destroy* operations against large enemy units, *clearing* operations to force enemy units out of an area, and *securing* operations to destroy the remaining Viet Cong militia and cadre. These missions, in turn, supported the larger pacification campaign that consisted of clearing (including

---

[23] Quoted words from Memo, Westmoreland to Taylor, 21 May 65, sub: Combined Command, History file 16–8, Westmoreland Papers, HRB, CMH. See also Msgs, Taylor SGN 3855 to Rusk, 240905 May 65, and Rusk STATE 2730 to Taylor, 272027 May 65, SEAB, CMH; *U.S.-Vietnam Relations*, 3:sec. IV. B. 3., pp. 61–62; comments of Vien in Vien et al., *U.S. Adviser*, p. 23, and of Taylor in Taylor, *Swords and Plowshares*, pp. 349–50.

military search and destroy and clearing operations), securing (including but not limited to military securing operations) and developing (no military participation outside of civic action) phases. So far that was about as close as MACV, the American embassy, or the South Vietnamese had come to creating an overall war strategy.[24]

Theoretically, regular units under corps and division control conducted search and destroy operations, territorials and detached regular forces under province control performed clearing missions, and territorial and police units under province and district control undertook securing missions. In practice, however, the assignment of missions depended on the availability of forces, the enemy threat, the personalities and relationships of local commanders and officials, and such factors as terrain, population density, and the political or military importance attached to a region. For example, in areas where territorial and police forces were weak, regular army units had to perform all three missions. In other cases the absence of regulars meant that province and district forces might have to perform all three tasks. In fact, many area commanders found that all missions had to be performed simultaneously because of enemy aggressiveness at all levels and the limited number of forces available to them.

General Westmoreland gave the first U.S. combat units to arrive in South Vietnam a defensive mission of providing local security for vital air and naval bases. But soon after their arrival he began reviewing the entire American military role in South Vietnam, which he divided into two general categories. First was the general effort to implement the Military Assistance Program in South Vietnam. Most advisory activities fell somewhere within this category. Second was the provision of direct combat support to the South Vietnamese armed forces, which included staff support for tactical operations, long-range communications, air transportation, and tactical air support. The mission of the American ground combat units now arriving also fell into this second category. Given their greatly restricted missions at the outset, Westmoreland believed that no new command arrangements were necessary and, until combined command arrangements were finalized, that direct assistance was possible "thru coordination and cooperation in the mutual self-interest of both commands."[25]

In his official assessment of 18 March 1965 Westmoreland pointed out that existing logistical and support bases, especially ports and airfields, would have to be both expanded and effectively protected before American ground combat units could fulfill more ambitious roles. At a conference with his Vietnamese counterparts the following month he repeated this theme: U.S. ground combat forces would first secure key installations and "eventually [conduct] offensive or reaction operations against the VC." As American troops passed into this second stage, "the principles of combat support of RVN tactical commands which had

---

[24] USMACV, "Command History, 1964," pp. 65–67, HRB, CMH; Commander in Chief, Vietnamese Armed Forces, *Chien Thang* ["National Pacification"] Plan, 22 Feb 64, SEAB, CMH; MACV, Organization and Mission of Forces, 11 Dec 64, MACV files, Working file no. 2, box 2, accession no. 67A4604, RG 338, WNRC.

[25] MACV, Concept for U.S./Allied Combat Operations in Support of RVNAF, March 1965, History file 14–1, Westmoreland Papers, HRB, CMH.

worked so successfully with respect to U.S. helicopter units would be applicable to the use of [U.S.] ground tactical units."[26]

From March to June 1965 MACV and the Joint Chiefs of Staff championed an American troop buildup in South Vietnam and an expanded combat role for U.S. ground units. President Johnson and Ambassador Taylor were more hesitant. Taylor warned that introducing divisional-size U.S. combat units "will raise sensitive command questions with our GVN allies and may encourage them to [sic] an attitude of 'let the United States do it.'" The ambassador still favored an "enclave strategy" in which U.S. units remained in easily defended and supplied coastal enclaves, reinforcing South Vietnamese units in difficulty. Westmoreland, however, wanted a more offensive role for the arriving U.S. troops, viewed them as the cutting edge of an allied counteroffensive, and specifically requested large airmobile (helicopter) formations to operate in the Vietnamese interior.[27]

While plans for enlarging the U.S. ground combat role were under discussion, American commanders of the first ground combat units to deploy to Vietnam coordinated with local South Vietnamese leaders on specific operational zones for securing their bases. Called tactical areas of responsibility (TAORs), the zones were arbitrary geographical areas created by joint agreements between local American and South Vietnamese ground commanders and generally superimposed on existing Vietnamese operating zones. Within these TAORs American units conducted specific combat operations, or other limited tasks. At first these zones included only defensive perimeters and adjacent areas along the coast, but they quickly grew as the need for more far-reaching operations became evident.[28]

In May Westmoreland continued to portray these arrangements as a "logical extension and expansion of [the] advice and support role already performed by a wide range of U.S. units and forces throughout RVN."[29] Although the "general mission" of all American tactical forces remained "combat support of RVNAF," the MACV commander now divided it into four specific missions: security of base areas, deep patrolling and offensive operations around base areas, direct support of South Vietnamese forces, and "U.S. contingency operations as required." While South Vietnamese corps commanders retained overall responsibility for military affairs in each corps tactical zone, he agreed that American commanders could "accept responsibility for segments of defense perimeters and for larger security zones or Tactical Areas of Responsibility. . . ." After American forces had secured their base areas, he wanted them to "initiate

[26] Quoted words from MFR, Westmoreland, 28 Apr 65, sub: Conference With Generals Thieu and Minh, 28 April, History file 15–45. See also Msgs, Westmoreland MAC 5875 to Wheeler, 210905 Nov 65, and Westmoreland MAC 1463 to Wheeler, 171825 Mar 65, COMUSMACV Message file. All in Westmoreland Papers, HRB, CMH.

[27] Quoted words from Msg, Taylor EMBTEL 3003 to Washington, 18 Mar 65, cited in *U.S.-Vietnam Relations*, 4:sec. IV. C. 5., p. 57. For detailed accounts, see Edward C. Janicik, "Evolution of Missions for US Land Forces, March 1965–July 1966" (Study of the Institute for Defense Analyses, Arlington, Va., 1968), copy in SEAB, CMH, and Westmoreland, *Soldier Reports*, pp. 119–53.

[28] For the initial arrangements made by U.S. Marine Corps commanders, see Shulimson and Johnson, *U.S. Marines in Vietnam*, especially pp. 18–35, 48–49, 58–65.

[29] Following discussion from Msg, COMUSMACV MAC 15125 to CINCPAC, 071516 May 65, sub: Concept for US/Allied Combat Operations in Support of RVNAF, SEAB, CMH. All quotations from this source.

reconnaissance and offensive operations against VC bases and forces . . . unilaterally in easily identifiable Tactical Areas of Responsibility from which, for [the] duration of [the] operation, all ARVN and Regional Forces have been excluded."

Westmoreland now envisioned a future battlefield with all U.S. and South Vietnamese units "in adjacent but separated and clearly defined TAOR's." If combined operations between American and South Vietnamese units materialized, he held, they would have to be undertaken with care "because of the coordination problems and the absence of a positive [?] command chain controlling all units." In the meantime, he planned to "avoid close and intricate maneuvers between U.S./Allied and RVNAF forces" by assigning each national element to "clearly defined zones and objectives . . . which are readily identifiable on the ground and on the map." Field advisers were to serve as "combat liaison officers" and to "report positions, actions and intelligence directly" to the appropriate U.S. commander and to MACV.

Without a combined command, Westmoreland enjoined his subordinates to accommodate themselves "to a new environment in which responsibility is shared and cooperatively discharged without benefit or traditional command arrangements." The American mission, he emphasized, was "one of combat support through coordination and cooperation in the mutual self-interest of both commands." Policy dictated that the forces of one national army would never be placed under the operational control of another, except in "particular circumstances and as mutually agreed by the appropriate commanders" of the national armies involved. But even then, the MACV commander stressed, "national command integrity will be maintained at all levels."

At the end of May American strategy in Vietnam was only in its incipient stage. Westmoreland had not yet determined how U.S. ground combat forces would fit into the larger war effort; what role, if any, they would have in clearing operations; whether they would undertake both securing and search and destroy missions; or how their presence would fit into the overall pacification campaign. Straining the military situation was the continued turmoil in Saigon and in the upper echelons of the South Vietnamese armed forces, which made his proposal for establishing a combined command impossible. Unable to predict what larger strategies President Johnson, Secretary McNamara, or General Wheeler might come up with in Washington, the MACV commander had no choice but to make the best of an unfortunate situation and faced the future hopeful that an expanded bombing campaign and further U.S. troop deployments would keep it under control.

5

Toward a New Strategy

During the first half of 1965 American efforts to improve South Vietnamese combat effectiveness had been no more successful than their efforts to establish a stable government. Neither the Saigon government nor its army appeared to have much staying power, and a collapse of one or the other seemed increasingly possible. How long the new Directory coalition of generals would survive was unknown. In meetings with his new counterpart, General Co, that summer Westmoreland urged him not to make any major policy decisions or senior appointments without consulting American officials. Privately, he worried that the Directory generals would "tear down the good things developed by the previous regime and . . . pursue some new pet idea." Changes at the top usually meant changes all the way down the line, with little continuity in military policies or activities. Glumly, he later concluded that "the ability to organize a project, execute it step by step, and supervise it to insure that things are done properly, is not typical of the Vietnamese mentality."[1]

With all hope of a combined command abandoned, Westmoreland now saw his plans to expand the South Vietnamese military forces in grave difficulty. Desertions and high combat losses were making it impossible to keep existing units up to strength, let alone to create new ones. To salvage as much as possible, he advised Co to tighten up his manpower controls through a new personnel committee headed by Co himself and Maj. Gen. Ben Sternberg, the MACV J–1. Co's leadership, he hoped, would ensure that desertion control received "forceful action" at the "highest levels." Westmoreland also proposed reducing recruit training from twelve to nine weeks; using men in eleven of the newly activated infantry battalions as general replacements; and having the combined training inspection team, created earlier under Generals Collins and Dinh, closely monitor ineffective combat units. He also encouraged Co to liberalize battlefield promotions by expanding quotas and automatically promoting all combat commanders to their authorized rank. To "strengthen morale and sustain the loyalty within the RVNAF," he approved a new political warfare program and the

---

[1] Quoted words from Notes of 30 Aug 65, History file 1–4. See also MFR, Westmoreland, 29 Jun 65, sub: Meeting With General Co, Minister of Defense, GVN, History file 16–42. Both in Westmoreland Papers, HRB.

assignment of political warfare officers to every regular unit. Finally, he reminded Co of the Directory's promise to convene special military courts to try
deserters.[2]

Despite Co's acceptance of this advice, American confidence in Vietnamese
ability to get the job done was diminishing daily. Admiral Sharp informed him of
Defense Secretary McNamara's reluctance "to depend on further ARVN buildup
since thus far it had not been sufficient to offset losses plus VC gains and further
it was too unreliable a factor." Westmoreland also realized that many of his
manpower proposals would not come to fruition. He admitted to Ambassador
Taylor that a full mobilization of South Vietnamese manpower was "doubtful."
Saigon's ability to process and adequately train massive numbers of troops was
highly questionable, and South Vietnamese society was unprepared to accept
the drastic measures needed to carry out such a policy. Mobilization would have
to remain selective and American advice aimed at "developing a favorable mobilization environment," for example, through information programs publicizing
government intentions to enforce conscription and punish deserters and through
increased psychological warfare efforts to explain the nature of the war and the
American presence to the Vietnamese people. The MACV commander also
wanted to see Saigon shut down South Vietnam's universities, or at least tie
student deferments to some kind of reserve officer training program, but realized
that any such actions would be extremely unpopular. Nevertheless, he considered it mandatory that Saigon mobilize for war and dismiss its "business as
usual attitude." Competition between private and military efforts in the fields of
construction, land acquisition, and transportation, continued inequities in the
conscription program, and the government's lax attitude toward desertions was
sapping the war effort and undercutting the morale of the fighting soldier.[3]

Assessing South Vietnam's manpower difficulties in early July, General Sternberg confirmed the depth of the problem.[4] He noted that the average strength of
the eighty-two "combat effective" South Vietnamese battalions was 376, or about
half of their authorized complement. None of the battalions could probably put
even that many men in the field at any one time. In accordance with Westmoreland's recommendations to rebuild unit strength, the Joint General Staff had
increased monthly recruiting from 8,000 to 9,500, reduced individual training to
nine weeks and unit training from twenty-one to eighteen weeks, and put off
activating all but four of the projected thirty-one new battalions. All of the technical services and four infantry divisions had begun their own basic training centers to supplement those of the Central Training Command, and other major
units planned to follow that example. Sternberg predicted that these measures
would enable the Vietnamese to not only bring their units rapidly up to strength
but also activate all of the projected new units by the end of the year.

[2] Quoted words from *Aide Memoire*, Westmoreland to Co, 29 Jun 65, sub: Current Programs of
Material Interest, History file 16–42. See also Memo, Westmoreland to CofS, MACV, 22 Jun 65,
History file 16–32. Both in Westmoreland Papers, HRB, CMH.
[3] First quotation from Msg, Sharp to Westmoreland, 30 Jun 65, History file 16–44. Remaining
quotations from Memo, Westmoreland to Taylor, 6 Jul 65, sub: Mobilization, History file 17–6. Both in
Westmoreland Papers, HRB, CMH.
[4] Following discussion from Memo, Sternberg to COMUSMACV, 7 Jul 65, sub: RVNAF Strength
Summary, SEAB, CMH.

Westmoreland was less optimistic and realized that improving the ability of the South Vietnamese to fight was a much tougher task. More men, battalions, pay, promotions, awards, and so forth, did not automatically produce better leaders. The American field advisers could only do so much with marginal commanders, or those preoccupied with politics. Any American efforts to reform the upper echelons of the South Vietnamese officers corps threatened to undermine the Directory government. Political stability still came first. He could only hope that more American troops would eventually tip the scales of the war in Saigon's favor.

At the Crossroads

A merican strategy within South Vietnam now became centered around the employment of U.S. ground troops. By May Westmoreland began to plan for three stages of employment. During the first, or enclave, stage American combat units would secure their coastal base areas; during stages two and three they would conduct increasingly more extensive ground operations from bases in the interior. Arriving at the precise number of American combat battalions needed to reinforce the South Vietnamese in this manner was difficult because it depended on matters outside the MACV commander's control, such as enemy recruitment and infiltration, the status of the South Vietnamese armed forces, and events on the battlefield. As the military situation worsened, his requirements rose accordingly. At the beginning of June, based on Westmoreland's estimates, Washington contemplated increasing the American-sponsored commitment to forty-four combat battalions.[5]

Although concerned that the United States might be "cast in the role of the French," fighting an antinationalist colonial war, Westmoreland saw no alternative to greater American participation. Worried about the fragile military situation in the countryside and the political instability in Saigon, he was convinced that American forces would have to take up much of the combat slack, especially in remote, sparsely populated areas where their presence would not be so obtrusive. But American troops or not, he told the Joint Chiefs chairman, General Wheeler, that no "quick fix" for South Vietnam's troubles was likely and warned that "we are in for the long pull."[6]

Sympathetic to Westmoreland's plight, Wheeler indicated that the administration probably would agree to increase U.S. combat strength if the American units were used to free South Vietnamese battalions from static security missions. American forces, he suggested, could function as a strategic, mobile reserve; assume the defense of the northern Demilitarized Zone (DMZ); secure

[5] Westmoreland, *Soldier Reports*, p. 135. The combat units included one Australian and nine American battalions already in South Vietnam, and twenty-five more American and nine South Korean battalions. For an analysis of the decision-making, see Berman, *Planning a Tragedy*.

[6] Quoted words from Msg, Westmoreland MAC 3240 to Wheeler, 241220 Jun 65. See also Msg, Wheeler JCS 2331–65 to Westmoreland, 230144 Jun 65. Both in COMUSMACV Message file, Westmoreland Papers, HRB, CMH.

TABLE 9—STATUS OF SOUTH VIETNAMESE GROUND COMBAT BATTALIONS,[a]
JUNE 1965

Corps Tactical Zones	Static Security	Security Clearing	In Reserve	In Training	Ineffective	Total
I	12	6	5	5	2	30
II	6	14	5	6	1	32
III	2	30	3	4	3	42
CMD [b]	1	1	2	1	. . .	5
IV	11	15	5	1	. . .	32
Total	32	66	20	17	6	141

[a] Types of battalions specified are infantry, airborne, ranger, and marine. To complete the 31-battalion program, 14 additional battalions had yet to be activated.
[b] Capital Military District.
Source: Msg, Westmoreland MAC 3275 to Wheeler, 261000 Jun 65, COMUSMACV Message file, Westmoreland Papers, HRB, CMH.

selected major military installations; or "replace ARVN mobile security battalions in the Saigon area."[7]

Westmoreland reacted hotly to some of these proposals, perhaps fearing the imposition of some sort of enclave strategy by Washington. He urged Wheeler to "stick with the principle that it is a Vietnamese war; that the Vietnamese must fight it; and that they are the only ones that can win it." He warned against any "attempt to usurp their basic prerogatives as a nation or the basic responsibilities which maintenance of sovereignty entail," noting Saigon's unwillingness to turn the decisive missions of the war over to American military forces. Using American combat units to "free" South Vietnamese forces for offensive operations was unnecessary, because a reasonable number—approximately 40 percent—of the South Vietnamese ground combat battalions were always available for or committed to offensive combat operations (*Table 9*). Furthermore, bringing U.S. troops into Saigon was neither necessary nor desirable, because the Vietnamese had no "mobile security battalions" there and kept only a few airborne and marine units temporarily in reserve in the capital area.

Westmoreland viewed any commitment of U.S. ground combat troops to Saigon as dangerous. The risk of becoming involved in Vietnamese politics, especially as an "anti-demonstration force," simply was too great. Once again pleading for more helicopter, artillery, and engineer units to support the South Vietnamese, the MACV commander stressed to Wheeler that the American combat forces already requested were needed to reinforce the DMZ and to back up South Vietnamese units in difficulty and that "he be allowed to use these troops in accordance with his best judgment." Such determinations, he chided Wheeler, certainly were not within the purview of "one remote to the scene" of this "complex and rapidly changing situation." Only the commander on the ground was in the best position to evaluate the situation and to make decisions on how to best use American forces.[8] Perhaps it was Wheeler's interference rather than his suggestions that Westmoreland objected to.

[7] Msg, Wheeler JCS 2360–65 to Westmoreland, 242123 Jun 65, COMUSMACV Message file, Westmoreland Papers, HRB, CMH.
[8] Quotations in this and the preceding paragraph from Msg, Westmoreland MAC 3275 to Wheeler, 261000 Jun 65, COMUSMACV Message file, Westmoreland Papers, HRB, CMH.

General Nguyen Huu Co (right) Welcomes Secretary of Defense Robert S. McNamara *(left) to Saigon. At center is U. Alexis Johnson, the deputy ambassador to South Vietnam.*

In preparation for Secretary McNamara's visit to Saigon in mid-July to discuss U.S. troop increases and their employment, Assistant Secretary of Defense John McNaughton called for more specific guidelines pertaining to "the number and effectiveness and uses of the South Vietnamese forces, exactly where we would deploy ours and exactly what we would expect their mission to be, . . . the time frames in which things would be done, command relationship, etc." McNaughton suggested a strategy in which the bulk of the South Vietnamese armed forces would "retain control over areas now held" (that is, securing) and "extend pacification operations and area control where possible" (that is, clearing), while "U.S. and Allied forces, in conjunction with GVN national reserve . . . , possibly augmented by [a] limited number of ranger and infantry battalions, [would] by offensive land and air action locate and destroy VC/PAVN forces, bases and major war-supporting organizations in South Vietnam" (that is, search and destroy). This concept, which made Wheeler's earlier proposals more compatible with Westmoreland's own plans, gave the bulk of the South Vietnamese regular army area security missions and left only the eleven reserve battalions to participate in mobile offensive operations with U.S. ground units.[9]

---

[9] *U.S.-Vietnam Relations*, 5: sec. IV. C. 6. (a), pp. 1–7. First quotation on p. 4; remaining quotations on p. 5.

101

As a presidential decision on MACV's larger troop requests became imminent, Westmoreland continued to clarify his military objectives and to refine the troop levels he thought necessary to achieve those objectives. Both were contingent on the changing military situation. In July he and Taylor met in Saigon with Secretary McNamara, General Wheeler, and Henry Cabot Lodge, Taylor's designated replacement, to thrash out these issues face to face. McNamara was unhappy with Saigon's military performance, questioning the accuracy of South Vietnamese intelligence information and their battlefield reports. General DePuy, representing Westmoreland's staff, noted the low morale of the South Vietnamese commanders, their inability to locate the enemy, and the low strengths of their combat battalions. Westmoreland himself labeled one-third of the South Vietnamese officers "unsatisfactory" and the remainder as just "adequate." The airborne units were still "the best," but the rangers were "substandard" and the marines "disappointing," a problem he traced to General Khang, "a poor leader [with] . . . influential political connections." Ambassador Taylor wanted more American say in the selection of major South Vietnamese military commanders, but no one had any ideas on how to accomplish this.[10]

Putting Vietnamese capabilities to the side, Westmoreland then laid out a newly conceived ground strategy. He visualized three phases. In Phase I South Vietnamese forces, reinforced by allied combat units, would defend all areas under friendly control and halt the "losing trend" by the end of 1965. During Phase II, whose length depended on American force commitments and enemy reactions, allied forces would take the offensive to destroy enemy forces and provide security for an expanded pacification effort. If the enemy persisted, Phase III called for the complete destruction of enemy units and the expansion of the pacification campaign throughout South Vietnam. Within each phase Westmoreland listed the tasks to be performed, but the phases did not differ markedly from one another. He estimated enemy strength at ten "main force," or regular, regiments (composed of thirty-three battalions, including three North Vietnamese Army battalions) and another twenty-three local force (territorial) battalions. Total enemy strength was about 53,000 combat troops, 17,000 headquarters and support troops, and about 80,000 to 100,000 militia, although the North Vietnamese could reinforce these forces at any time from units stationed just across the border. Westmoreland felt that the forty-four battalion force level currently under consideration was adequate for Phase I but could not predict the number of troops needed for Phases II and III. He did, however, suggest that an additional twenty-four allied battalions, plus more combat support and logistical forces, would put MACV in the Phase II offensive stage in 1966. All told that meant about 175,000 American troops for Phase I and another 100,000 to begin Phase II.[11]

---

[10] Memo, MACV, sub: Meeting With Secretary of Defense and Party, 16–17 July 1965, MICRO 2/2100. See also Memo, MACV, sub: Secretary of Defense Visit to Vietnam, 10–14 October 1966, MICRO 2/2136 (which refers to the earlier meeting). Both in RG 334, WNRC. For the MACV J–2's version of meeting, see Joseph A. McChristian, *The Role of Military Intelligence, 1965–1967*, Vietnam Studies (Washington, D.C.: Department of the Army, 1974), pp. 4–5. For the U.S. ambassador's account, see Taylor, *Swords and Plowshares*, pp. 348–51.

[11] *U.S.-Vietnam Relations*, 5: sec. IV. C. 6. (a), pp. 8–10. See also Westmoreland, *Soldier Reports*, pp. 140–43; MACV, Concept Study on Operations in Vietnam, 23 Jul 65, SEAB, CMH.

Returning to Washington, McNamara learned that President Johnson had already approved the strength increases desired by Westmoreland, even though there had been little discussion of the role that the American ground forces were to play in Vietnam. During his visit the secretary had learned that the South Vietnamese leaders wanted American units "to operate in the big, sparsely populated provinces such as Kontum, Pleiku and Darlac" and to "hold strategic points so that the GVN could carry out pacification,"[12] but MACV apparently had not approved such a division of roles and missions. Thus, in follow-up recommendations to the president, McNamara only noted that the additional troops would be used "however they can be brought to bear most effectively." In general, he explained, American forces would continue to "operate in coordination with South Vietnamese forces," at first only defending their own bases, contributing to security in neighboring areas, and augmenting Vietnamese units guarding "key logistical areas and population centers." The additional American troops would provide MACV with "a small reserve-reaction force, conducting nuisance raids and spoiling attacks, and opening and securing selected lines of communication"; they would carry out more offensive missions only "when the Vietnamese government and General Westmoreland agree that such active missions are needed."[13] McNamara championed a "strategy for winning" based on offensive combat operations, but he did not further elaborate except to note that, after the destruction of the enemy's conventional forces, Saigon would have to "reinstitute" the pacification campaign. Several days later, McNamara further advised President Johnson that the war had, in his opinion, now become a conventional struggle and that the American combat forces could best serve in a "quick-reaction reserve role," backing up South Vietnamese forces whenever necessary.[14]

Upon returning from Saigon, Lodge concurred with McNamara's analysis and recommendations, adding that, "with ARVN and police providing security," pacification still had a good chance of success. He cautioned Johnson that Saigon had to run this side of the war by itself and, in the interest of facilitating "a true revolution," that American desires for rapid progress based on "flashy and misleading statistics" had to be held in check. Success in this area was possible if "an affirmative, highly political oil spot procedure . . . seeking solid and *durable* gains" was pursued. Like McNamara, Lodge wanted the American combat units to play a reserve reaction role, advising that they "should not be committed to prolonged 'search sweeps' in the jungle or to being permanently stationed in the jungle." However, the ambassador-designate also added that, "if the opportunity offers, U.S. troops can fight the pitched battles with large units of the Viet Cong—as they attack our strong points, and possibly, in other places where they

---

[12] Draft Msg, Lodge to Rusk (forwarded to Westmoreland, 16 Sep 65, for comment), History file 1-C4, Westmoreland Papers, HRB, CMH.

[13] Above quotations from Memo, McNamara to Johnson, 20 Jul 65, sub: Recommendations of Additional Deployments to Vietnam, SEAB, CMH (also reproduced in Gareth Porter, ed., *Vietnam: The Definitive Documentation of Human Decisions*, 2 vols. [Stanfordville, N.Y.: Coleman, 1979], 2: 385-91).

[14] Above quotations from Memo, McNamara to President, 26 Jul 65 (rev. 1 Aug 65), sub: Program of Expanded Military and Political Moves With Respect to Vietnam, SEAB, CMH.

President Lyndon B. Johnson (left) and Ambassador-designate Henry Cabot Lodge *(right) discussing Vietnam at the White House*

[the enemy] can be identified and where the circumstances are such that the outlook for destroying them is propitious."[15]

President Johnson's principal military and civilian advisers thus agreed on the need for more troops but offered no specifics regarding timetables, objectives, or responsibilities. Both McNamara and his military subordinates had assigned only the most general priorities to future military tasks and had presented only a vague concept of sequence and timing. They contemplated no division of responsibilities between the growing number of national forces and their services and subservices, although they had not discussed the subject in any detail. Greatly concerned, President Johnson on 22 July met with McNamara, Wheeler, Lodge, National Security Adviser McGeorge Bundy, Secretary of State Dean Rusk, and others, to review the matter. He noted that the troop recommendation "gives no sense of victory, but rather [one] of continuing stalemate." While believing "that our mission should be as limited as we can make it," he saw no alternative to even greater American involvement. All agreed that much depended on the enemy's response to the American military buildup. General Wheeler, reflecting the views of Westmoreland, predicted that the Viet Cong "will have to 'come out and fight,'" probably in the Highlands, but also added that American forces "should engage in offensive combat operations to seek out

[15] Memo, Lodge (Saigon) to President, 20 Jul 65, SEAB, CMH.

104

and fight the VC main forces" regardless. McNamara was less certain, stressing the lack of information on Viet Cong intentions, and recommended that the American combat units be prepared to fight either guerrillas or main force units as the situation dictated. Little more, it appeared, could be resolved in Washington.[16]

Gordon L. Jorgensen, the Central Intelligence Agency's station chief in Saigon, made a more cohesive analysis of American alternatives in July. The intelligence expert viewed the South Vietnamese proposals to have the American forces assume responsibility for the Highlands and the more critical border regions above Saigon as absolutely necessary. The U.S. Marine units around Da Nang in the northern zone could play the same role along the Laotian border. Referring to the recent series of meetings in Saigon, Jorgensen noted that many members of McNamara's staff and some MACV senior officers were skeptical of Saigon's recommendations, "feeling that the Vietnamese were trying to put one over on the U.S. by persuading the Americans to carry the brunt of the war, while the Vietnamese took life easy in pacification tasks in the lowlands." But, in balance, he felt that a division of missions was logical. The possibility of Americans getting caught in some sort of Dien Bien Phu debacle was remote because of the overwhelming air support available to U.S. ground combat units, and the South Vietnamese—"for political and psychological reasons"—were much better suited for providing security in the heavily populated delta and coastal regions. The enemy's military concentrations in the remote border areas and Saigon's weakened military strength further argued for such an operational strategy. The assignment of separate missions to the different national forces would also ease the combined command problem by giving American units distinct areas of responsibility. Jorgensen judged Saigon incapable of rallying Montagnard support in the border regions, and greater American participation here the only way to avoid a major disaster. The concern over the increase in American casualties that would result from the assumption of the border war was "not fully justified," considering that Saigon suffered most of its combat losses in relatively small-scale security actions. In summary, Jorgensen thought a division of missions inevitable and any delay in implementing the concept would have to be paid for later at a much greater cost.[17]

General Rosson, Westmoreland's new chief of staff, later agreed and regarded the July troop deployment decision as pivotal. According to Rosson, "it meant American assumption of responsibility for the war . . . [and] made it an American war." Several key factors, he felt, decisively influenced the decision. Paramount was the conviction in Washington that a political or military collapse in Saigon was imminent. A second factor was President Johnson's personal determination to avoid a defeat in Southeast Asia that might forever mar the record of his administration. Related considerations were the desire to uphold America's

[16] MFR, Office of the President, 22 Jul 65, sub: Meetings on Vietnam, July 21, 1965, SEAB, CMH. The meetings consisted of a morning session without the president, 10:30 to 11:00 A.M., and two meetings with Johnson, from 11:30 A.M. until 1:00 P.M. and 2:30 to 5:30 P.M. Other attendees included Under Secretary of State George Ball, Deputy Secretary of Defense Cyrus R. Vance, Assistant Secretary of State William Bundy, and Assistant Secretary of Defense John McNaughton.
[17] Memo, Jorgensen to Chester Cooper, 20 Jul 65, sub: Comments on Vietnam Highlands Concept, SEAB, CMH.

credibility as an ally and the belief that the Communist powers were testing the will of the United States. None of these factors, however, explain the absence of any coherent American war strategy in either Saigon or Washington and the continued confusion in roles and missions. Apparently the American leaders in Washington accepted neither the views of Westmoreland nor those of Jorgensen and the Saigon generals as the basis for a new strategy for fighting the war. The continued reluctance of the president, the secretary of defense, or the Joint Chiefs of Staff to deal with this problem is puzzling. The future role of South Vietnamese forces in offensive combat operations and the future role of American forces in the security campaign—still supposedly the foundation of the war effort—remained ill-defined, with the matter of expanding the ground war into Laos or the southern portion of North Vietnam never broached. Boiled down to its essence, American "strategy" was simply to put more U.S. troops into South Vietnam and see what happened.[18]

Roles and Missions

In August the Joint Chiefs of Staff published its own concept of operations study, which essentially approved Westmoreland's plans. The study defined four U.S. objectives in Southeast Asia: keeping Communist China out of the war, forcing North Vietnam to end its support for the insurgency, defeating the Viet Cong, and extending Saigon's authority throughout South Vietnam. The "strategy for accomplishing the above tasks" was limited almost entirely to military actions, such as interdicting enemy supply routes and destroying enemy forces. Added was the need for a strategic reserve to deter the Chinese and the promise "to improve the combat effectiveness of the RVNAF." Within Vietnam, the study specified only that American combat forces were "to participate with the RVNAF in search and destroy operations while assisting the RVNAF in clearing and securing operations in support of the rural reconstruction [that is, pacification] effort."[19]

In mid-September Westmoreland formally detailed his own concept of operations to his subordinates. Basically, he rearticulated the proposals that he had made in July. The American objective, or "ultimate aim," in South Vietnam was "to pacify the Republic of Vietnam by destroying the VC . . . while at the same time reestablishing the government apparatus, strengthening GVN military forces, rebuilding the administrative machinery, and re-instituting the services of the Government." He repeated his three-phase strategy: halting the enemy offensive ("to stem the tide"), resuming the offensive ("to destroy VC and pacify selected high priority areas"), and winning the war (by restoring "progressively the entire country to the control of the GVN"). The missions to be conducted encompassed search and destroy, clearing, and securing operations. Regional

---

[18] William B. Rosson, "Nine Steps Into the Maelstrom," *Army* 34 (August 1984): 54–55. Quotation on p. 54.

[19] See *U.S.-Vietnam Relations*, 5: sec. IV. C. 6. (a), pp. 13–16; "Joint Chiefs of Staff in Vietnam, 1960–1968," Part 2, pp. 23–2 to 23–11, HRB, CMH.

Forces would have "primary responsibility" for securing operations and for re-lieving "ARVN or US forces that have cleared the area to enable them to move onward and outward to clear additional areas thus expanding the pacification zones"; however, where territorial forces were weak, South Vietnamese regulars would remain in a "securing role." As a supplemental operation, Westmoreland noted that U.S. ground combat elements often would provide "reserve/reaction forces to support the defense of bases, province and district towns, hard pressed units and other US and ARVN forces involved in clearing or securing opera-tions." Apparently the MACV commander envisioned American forces working side by side with Vietnamese regulars in search and destroy and clearing opera-tions—and, as necessary, serving in a reserve or mobile reaction role—and the territorials and police performing securing operations, assisted, as necessary, by South Vietnamese regulars.[20]

Westmoreland played down any sharp delineation of roles and missions be-tween American and South Vietnamese forces. A MACV directive in September urged "the participation of Vietnamese forces in operations . . . so that the war does not appear to be a U.S. action against the Vietnamese people." The secre-tary of defense shared this view, as did the JCS chief. Reacting to speculation that South Vietnamese leaders "apparently contemplate a plan of operations which would give separate missions to GVN forces and to U.S. forces," Wheeler ad-vised MACV "that maximum benefit can accrue to our efforts in South Vietnam only by joint and cooperative endeavors."[21] Westmoreland reassured Wheeler that his fears were groundless. He and General Co, the chief of the Vietnamese Joint General Staff, were hard at work developing combined war plans, entailing operations by American and regular South Vietnamese forces against enemy main force units, while the territorials dealt with the Viet Cong guerrillas. No division of responsibilities along national lines was contemplated.[22]

As American combat forces arrived in South Vietnam, similar guidance was given to new units. Addressing a MACV commanders conference in October, General Rosson stressed that the "primary mission" of MACV was to "assist and support the RVNAF" through "cooperation and coordination between com-manders at all echelons." He indicated that planning for combined activities was the sole responsibility of the "senior responsible RVNAF and U.S. commanders" at corps-level headquarters; they alone would determine objectives, operational zones, and combat support for subordinate units. For security reasons, Rosson recommended that the number of personnel involved with planning be limited to as few as possible and, when appropriate, that temporary multinational com-mand posts could be established for operational purposes.[23]

---

[20] MACV Directive 525-4, 17 Sep 65, sub: Tactics and Techniques for Employment of US Forces in the Republic of Vietnam, SEAB, CMH.

[21] First quotation from MACV Directive 525-3, 7 Sep 65, sub: Combat Operations Minimizing Non-Combatant Battle Casualties, para. 3a (9), History file 1–B1. Second quotation from Msg, Wheeler JCS 3428 to Sharp and Westmoreland, 16 Sep 65, History file 1–C5. Both in Westmoreland Papers, HRB, CMH.

[22] Msg, Westmoreland MAC 4643 to Wheeler and Sharp, 17 Sep 65, History file 1–C6, Westmore-land Papers, HRB, CMH.

[23] Rosson, "Planning and Controlling Combined Operations by Republic of Vietnam and United States Forces," 17 Oct 75 (Presentation delivered by Westmoreland at Qui Nhon, 18 October 1965), History file 1–H1, Westmoreland Papers, HRB, CMH.

Thus by the end of October, despite that lack of a combined command, neither MACV nor Washington appeared to view the arrival of more U.S. ground combat units as changing the nature of the war or the basic pacification strategy. American forces would reinforce and supplement those of South Vietnam. The missions to be performed remained the same, regardless of increases in enemy strength or activity. And with the South Vietnamese command structure intact and independent, no one could accuse the United States of taking over the war effort.

Yet the JCS concept of operations study and some of the earlier ideas expressed by Westmoreland and McNaughton had already hinted at an important change in American strategic thinking toward the war. The ROLLING THUNDER bombing campaign against the North, which steadily increased in intensity throughout the year, sought not only to interdict the enemy's supply lines but also to force North Vietnam to cease its support of the insurgency in the South. Almost unspoken was the growing assumption in Washington—if not in Saigon—that sufficiently high North Vietnamese losses in men and materiel would force Hanoi out of the war. A second, related assumption, also largely unvoiced, was that the insurgency itself had no indigenous roots and would collapse without continued outside assistance. If so, then a strategy of attrition against North Vietnam and North Vietnamese troops appeared a more direct way of winning the war. It made better use of America's great superiority in firepower and mobility, obviated the need to work through Saigon's quarrelsome generals, and relegated the more complex and frustratingly slow strategy of pacification to the background. As one MACV staff officer explained at the time, pacification was "too slow for the Americans" and "not an action word." Americans wanted immediate improvement—"action" and "results"—and, as everyone at MACV knew, "the way you get action, in the military sense, is to have U.S. units."[24] Whether anyone admitted it or not, the strategy of pacification was being replaced by the strategy of attrition.

---

[24] Greene Interv, 6 Jun 65, file 206-02, Interviews with General Officers, box 6, accession no. 69A702, RG 334, WNRC.

6

Enter the Americans

The U.S. buildup in South Vietnam was rapid. Two full American combat divisions were in place by August 1965 and the equivalent of over four by the end of the year. Almost all were crack units—like the 3d Marine Division; the "airmobile" 1st Cavalry Division; and the "Big Red One," the 1st Infantry Division, the best that the country had to offer. These divisions plus myriad support elements increased the American military commitment in South Vietnam from about 23,000 at the end of 1964 to around 184,000 one year later. Supplementing the Americans were several thousand "third-country" forces, including an entire South Korean infantry division and a small Australian contingent, each with its own separate logistics, administration, and combat support. The presence of these units soon made Westmoreland's concern over South Vietnamese political instability and military effectiveness less pressing. But despite these reinforcements, the MACV commander soon found his politico-military responsibilities to the new Saigon regime steadily rising.

Appeasing Saigon's Generals

While Westmoreland, Wheeler, McNamara, and their staffs pursued the matter of future military strategy and American troop levels, the Directory generals continued to squabble among themselves. With the replacement of the autocratic Taylor as ambassador by the less forceful Lodge in August 1965, the MACV commander became deeply involved in these internal disputes. Westmoreland's relationship with his counterpart, General Co, proved brief. In September, when the Joint General Staff chief was in the United States for a short visit, Thieu and Ky announced his replacement with General Cao Van Vien, the III Corps commander. They probably considered Vien, a friend of Thieu, more tractable than Co and gave General Nguyen Bao Tri, an ally of Ky, Vien's corps command. Without his knowledge or acquiescence, Co remained minister of defense,[1] technically a higher-level post, but in reality a position of considerably less authority.

This political shuffling infuriated Co. Without direct access to Westmoreland he had little power or influence. Immediately after returning in early October, Co sought Westmoreland's assistance to rectify his diminished status. He demanded that he remain Westmoreland's counterpart and insisted that General Rosson, the MACV chief of staff, be Vien's adviser. Probably as a delaying tactic, he asked Westmoreland to help him retain his post as chief of the Joint General Staff to oversee the preparation of new pacification plans. According to Co, Thieu and Ky had agreed to this and only Westmoreland's ratification was necessary.[2]

In pleading his case to Westmoreland, Co warned about "rumbling within the [South Vietnamese] officer corps [because] . . . too many northern born Vietnamese officers were being placed in command positions. South Vietnamese looked upon northern born Vietnamese as refugees from the north and did not feel they had the same interest in the south as those officers who were born in the area." According to Co, Vien was "a good soldier" who "will do what he is told," but Buddhist leaders distrusted both Vien, because of his family ties with Diem and his refusal to support the uprising against the former president in 1963, and Tri, because he was northern-born and a Roman Catholic. Co, a Buddhist himself, cautioned Westmoreland that Thieu and Ky "should not allow any cracks to develop within the leadership group."[3]

All this verbiage was, of course, designed to make Co look indispensable to Westmoreland. But the MACV commander declined to take the bait. He made no commitments to Co, regretted that he "could not be of more help to him," and remained concerned about the possible disintegration of the Directory. Thieu had warned him earlier of the animosity that many southerners harbored toward northern-born Roman Catholics who had once formed the mainstay of the Diem regime, a resentment easily directed against either Thieu or Ky. Two weeks later Co continued his personal campaign, accusing Ky of "losing touch with the real problems of the country," but once again Westmoreland failed to respond. The MACV commander was not about to fuel an internal revolt against the two officers who had put the current government together, and especially now that Vien had begun to take over the Joint General Staff. Co formally gave up the fight at the end of November, when he informed Westmoreland that the Directory generals no longer disagreed among themselves. Without an open show of American support, Co had little room to maneuver. American officials were relieved at the peaceful transition between Co and Vien, and the brief stability shown by the Directory government. However, the leadership changes in the Joint General Staff made it more difficult for Westmoreland to bring the Vietnam-

---

[1] Co's actual title was deputy premier for war and reconstruction, giving him nominal authority over several ministries.

[2] MFRs, Westmoreland, 6 Oct 65, sub: Conference With General Co on Monday, 4 October 1965, History file 1–F1, and 8 Oct 65, sub: Meeting With General Co, History file 1–F4, Westmoreland Papers, HRB, CMH.

[3] MFR, Westmoreland, 7 Oct 65, sub: Meeting With General Co on 7 October, History file 1–F3, Westmoreland Papers, HRB, CMH.

ese into the American planning and strategy discussions that were currently under way.[4]

Quality Versus Quantity

For the time being, Westmoreland was not inclined to press for further expansion of the South Vietnamese armed forces beyond that planned for 1965. With Saigon already strapped to meet current manpower authorizations, he intended to work on qualitative improvements, especially in the areas of leadership and personnel management. Further strength increases in the territorials depended on the extension of Saigon's control over the countryside and the speed at which CIDG units could be converted to Regional Forces. Perhaps more important, the continuing U.S. troop buildup now made the expansion of South Vietnamese regulars and territorials less critical.[5]

South Vietnamese leaders, however, continued to push for more new units, often less for military than political reasons. Col. Pham Van Lieu, the National Police chief, began secretly organizing three battalions of "riot control police" in the Saigon area, Co talked about forming a huge "Home Guard" to supplement the Territorial Forces, and Vien and the Joint General Staff pushed for more airborne and marine battalions, units over which they had greater control.[6]

The police units caused Westmoreland the most chagrin. Lieu, an alleged supporter of the politically ambitious I Corps commander, General Thi, appeared to be organizing a private army "to be used for possible Thi-supported coups." Westmoreland feared that the Joint General Staff might station three general reserve battalions permanently in the capital "to nullify the presence of the police battalions." Over American opposition, but with the approval of Ky and Co, Lieu formed the new units, arming them from non-American sources. The Directory placed the troops under the supervision of the Capital Military District commander, General Khang, with the mission of acting as a reserve, supporting Saigon's eight police precincts, protecting government offices and important officials, and coping with "national disasters." As police units they received no support from the Military Assistance Program, and Westmoreland had little say over their employment. Of limited combat value, they nevertheless

[4] First quotation from ibid. Second quotation from MFR, Westmoreland, 25 Oct 65, sub: Meeting With General Co on 23 October 1965, History file 1–H3. See also Notes of 8 Oct 65, History file 1–F; MFR, Westmoreland, 31 May 65, sub: Call on General Thieu, History file 16–17; Notes of 1 Dec 65, History file 2–F. All in Westmoreland Papers, HRB, CMH.
[5] MFR, Westmoreland, 5 Nov 65, sub: Meeting of US/GVN Council, this date; Discussions With Generals Co and Vien, this date; and Discussion With Ambassador Lodge on 4 November, History file 2–B3, Westmoreland Papers, HRB, CMH. Many other documents repeat Westmoreland's desire to deemphasize expansion and concentrate on qualitative improvement.
[6] On the Home Guard and general reserve units, see GVN Briefing to McNamara, circa 29 Nov 65, History file 2–F2. On Lieu's battalions, see Notes of 26 Nov 65, History file 2–F. Both in Westmoreland Papers, HRB, CMH.

111

bore scrutiny and concern because of their presence near Saigon and were testaments to Westmoreland's limited influence over his rambunctious allies.[7]

Despite his misgivings, Westmoreland continued to expand the South Vietnamese military forces in November 1965. Having agreed in June to form two more airborne battalions (bringing the total to eight) by deferring the activation of three infantry battalions until 1966, he now approved eight infantry battalions (including the three deferred in 1965, a new four-battalion regiment, and the sixth marine battalion), one artillery battery, two military police companies, one civil affairs company, and four pyschological warfare companies. These increases raised the authorized strength of the regular armed forces from 292,305 to 311,454 in 1966 and 325,256 in 1967, for a total increase of nearly 33,000. The expansion also included increases in headquarters units; more political warfare cadre; and an enlarged "pipeline," or manpower, reserve. Westmoreland found the additional marine battalion difficult to justify, believing it to have some function in restoring the "political balance of forces within the RVNAF," perhaps as a counter to the growth of the pro-Thieu airborne force of General Dong. Nevertheless, McNamara approved all of the force increases verbally during a visit to Saigon in November, though by then the continuing U.S. troop buildup, the participation of American units in combat against North Vietnamese regulars, and the bombing campaign against North Vietnam had almost completely overshadowed the issue of expanding the South Vietnamese armed forces.[8]

The Territorial Forces, depending entirely on voluntary recruitment and shorter training periods than the regular army, had fared better in meeting force-level goals. The Regional Forces, the principal arm of the province and district chiefs, grew to about 130,000 soldiers by the end of 1965, coming so close to their planned strength that Westmoreland thought it safe to approve another increase of 20,000 for 1966–67. The hamlet-based Popular Forces, however, declined during the year, with a net loss of 25,000 from casualties and desertions, leaving them with about 135,000 troops out of an authorized 185,000 at the end of the year. Their losses were the highest in the armed forces, and recruiting had become a major problem. Earlier in the year the Joint General Staff had prohibited the Popular Forces from taking twenty to twenty-five year olds and, in July, had widened the ban to the seventeen- to thirty-year age bracket. As intended, the prohibitions improved regular force recruiting at the expense of the territorials and were halted at the end of the year. Other difficulties included competition for recruits with the National Police, whose authorized strength of 51,500 was scheduled to rise to 72,000 by June 1966, and the failure to fully incorporate some 39,000 members of the Armed Combat Youth, a hamlet militia force, into the Popular Forces organization. Nevertheless, Westmoreland felt that these prob-

[7] Quoted words from Notes of 26 Nov 65, History file 2–F. See also Memo, Charles A. Mann, Director, U.S. Operations Mission, USAID, to Westmoreland, 20 Dec 65, sub: Order Police, History file 3–A4. Both in Westmoreland Papers, HRB, CMH.

[8] Quoted words from USMACV, "Command History, 1965," p. 70, HRB, CMH. See also MFR, Westmoreland, 5 Nov 65, sub: Meeting of US/GVN Council, this date; Discussions With Generals Co and Vien, this date; and Discussion With Ambassador Lodge on 4 November, History file 2–B3, Westmoreland Papers, HRB, CMH; MFR, MACJ03, 1 Dec 65, sub: Summary of Major Points Covered During 28–29 November 1965 Meeting With Secretary of Defense, MICRO 3/2127, RG 334, WNRC.

lems were manageable and ordered an increase of some 200,000 in the Popular Forces strength during 1966.[9]

As the South Vietnamese organized the new units, field advisers and Vietnamese officials pressed MACV for new equipment. Ky wanted B–57 jet bombers ("since jets are now in the hands of the Thais, the Cambodians and the North Vietnamese") and the Air Force advisers wanted to reequip South Vietnam's eight fighter squadrons with F–5 jet fighters. Westmoreland initially resisted, hesitant to supply Saigon with more advanced aircraft that might be used independently to take the war to the North, and argued that the slower, propeller-driven A–1 fighter bombers were better suited to the battlefields of South Vietnam. However, he finally agreed to transfer a few B–57 bombers to Saigon to convert two A–1 squadrons to F–5s, and to provide new landing and patrol craft for the navy and more heavy equipment for the army. In addition, the South Vietnamese mortar battalions exchanged their short-range pieces for field howitzers (giving each division two towed 105-mm. battalions); armored units replaced their aging M24 light tanks with newer M41 models; and, a successful local innovation, the Vietnamese added extra machine guns, recoilless rifles, and armored shields to their M113 armored personnel carriers, making them suitable for mounted combat. In December, Westmoreland also requested that all American, South Korean, and South Vietnamese infantry battalions be equipped with the lightweight Colt-designed M16 automatic rifle. Some 250,000 were needed for these battalions, but he estimated that about 100,000 "will solve immediate problems."[10]

South Vietnamese Performance

Based on reports from the field, MACV had little hope for greater South Vietnamese contributions to the war effort. From July to December 1965 American advisers saw negligible, if any, improvement in the military performance of the South Vietnamese units. The only positive news came from the northern zone, where, according to Maj. Gen. Lewis W. Walt, the commander of the U.S. III Marine Amphibious Force and the I Corps senior adviser, the South Vietnamese 1st Infantry Division under General Nguyen Van Chuan was "waging a skillful campaign" and "consistently destroying the VC in all significant encounters." South of Hue, his evaluation was less optimistic. The South Vietnamese 2d Infantry Division had done little, and the independent 51st Infantry Regiment had not budged from its static defensive positions. Westmoreland and DePuy blamed the 2d Division's temerity on its "less aggressive" commander,

---

[9] USMACV, "Command History, 1965," pp. 61–62, HRB, CMH.

[10] USMACV, "Command History, 1965," pp. 64–69, HRB, CMH. For Ky on jets, see Notes of 10 Dec 65, History file 2–G, and for M16 rifles and source of quotation, see Msg, COMUSMACV MAC 42787 to CINCPAC, 6 Dec 65, History file 2–G2. Both in Westmoreland Papers, HRB, CMH. U.S. armored cavalry units later adopted the M113 modifications.

General Hoang Xuan Lam, who had been either unwilling or unable to get the unit moving during the year.[11]

In the II Corps Tactical Zone Westmoreland regarded the South Vietnamese leadership as shaky. He had passed on his dissatisfaction with the corps commander, General Loc, to Ky and Co several times, characterizing Loc's abilities as "marginal" and his retention "a calculated risk." Westmoreland felt that the isolated Highlands was an allied weak point and expected heavy fighting there. The local senior adviser, Col. Theodore C. Metaxis, held similar opinions and, as an alternative, suggested that Loc be made political governor of the Highlands and his military responsibilities delegated to someone else. Advisory assessments of Loc's two infantry division commanders, Generals Nguyen Thanh Sang of the 22d Division and Nguyen Van Manh of the 23d, were more favorable, but advisers judged the regimental commanders as poor and gave high marks only to the head of the remote 24th Special Tactical Zone.[12]

In the III Corps Tactical Zone the situation was worse. By June 1965 the pacification effort was falling apart and the new corps commander, General Vien, showed little interest in the campaign. Westmoreland reported that many of Vien's units had "pulled into defensive positions with the resultant lack of aggressiveness in saturation patrolling and the limiting of night activities to manning fixed positions." All three South Vietnamese divisions had higher than average desertion rates and, according to Co, were filled with locals "who had little difficulty in getting back to Saigon and becoming lost." Vien's replacement in October, Nguyen Bao Tri, had been unable to rectify the situation. The American corps senior adviser considered Tri's staff marginal at best, with "no G–1, a weak G–3 and a lazy G–4" and a chief of staff who was "a fine fellow" but a "buffoon."[13]

American advisers considered the three division commanders little better. Westmoreland viewed Col. Phan Trong Chinh's leadership of the 25th Infantry Division as uninspired. The corps senior adviser had requested Chinh's immediate relief, but the MACV commander chose not to press the matter, hoping that combined operations with American forces "will be able to develop the unit." Several months later he noted that the recent arrival of U.S. combat troops in the area was "already causing some increase in the morale of the 25th ARVN Div[ision]," but the unit was still "the weakest division in the ARVN," barely "hanging on by its teeth in Hau Nghia Province," just north of Saigon. Westmoreland

---

[11] First and second quotations from Msg, Walt to Westmoreland, IN 9425, 140019 Nov 65, COMUS-MACV Message file. Third quotation from Notes of 30 Dec 65, History file 3–B. Both in Westmoreland Papers, HRB, CMH.

[12] Quoted words from Notes of 10 Dec 65, History file 2–G. See also Notes of 29 Oct 65, History file 2–A; Msg, Westmoreland MAC 2812 to Wheeler, 091345 Apr 66, COMUSMACV Message file; MFR, Maj Carl M. Putnam, 30 Dec 65, sub: COMUSMACV Conference With FFORCEV Commander and II Corps Advisers (held 29 Dec 65), History file 3–B1. All in Westmoreland Papers, HRB, CMH.

[13] First quotation from Memo, Westmoreland to Lodge, 14 Sep 65, sub: Hop Tac, History file 1–C1. Second quotation from Notes of 22 Nov 65, History file 2–E. Remaining quotations from MFR, Kenneth W. Accousti, 25 Dec 65, sub: COMUSMACV Visit to 1st Inf Div and 173rd Abn Bde, 24 Dec 65, History file 3–A2. All in Westmoreland Papers, HRB, CMH.

Static Security Defenses in III Corps

was well aware that Chinh's close ties with members of the Directory made his replacement difficult.[14]

Leadership in the South Vietnamese 5th Infantry Division was equally poor. The division commander, General Thuan, had recently gone to pieces when his 7th Regiment had been badly mauled in the Michelin Rubber Plantation, about 50 kilometers north of Saigon, and the unit was notorious for its high desertion rate and low morale. Just about the only positive items that the division senior adviser discerned were an expanded dependent care program and Thuan's efforts to fly his paymaster to each subordinate unit on a regular basis. Both were probably major accomplishments from the viewpoint of the advisory team.

In the new South Vietnamese 10th (later 18th) Infantry Division American advisers regarded the "moody and vacillatory" General Lu Mong Lan as "a marginal commander who would have to be worked with." They gave Lu Lan high marks for his "perceptiveness and dexterity in civil affairs and troop morale" but saw his interest in local politics as too distracting. Although they found his three regimental commanders "capable and willing people," they felt that it

---

[14] First quotation from Notes of 24 Dec 65, History file 3–A. See also MFR, Accousti, 25 Dec 65, sub: COMUSMACV Visit . . . , History file 3–A2. Remaining quotations from Msg, Westmoreland MAC 1450 to Wheeler, 172520 Feb 66, COMUSMACV Message file. All in Westmoreland Papers, HRB, CMH.

was too early to judge if the 10th was going to jell into a fighting unit. Again optimistic, Westmoreland predicted that combined operations with the U.S. 1st Infantry Division and the 173d Airborne Brigade would inspire both the 5th and 10th to higher standards.[15]

The Americans regarded the delta-based South Vietnamese IV Corps as a mixed bag. Westmoreland considered the senior Vietnamese officer, General Dang Van Quang, to be "an excellent corps commander and leader." Yet continued charges of corruption and his close political ties with Thieu clouded his professional reputation. According to common rumors, Quang had "a virtual monopoly on the economic life of the Delta," ran a "brisk trade in rice and opium," and had amassed a small fortune through official corruption. His senior adviser, Col. George Barton, denied the allegations but admitted that Quang's wife and brother ran a club that catered to both Vietnamese and Americans. Whatever the case, the charges were not unusual, and putting an end to them was difficult because no mechanism—legal or otherwise—existed to investigate them or stop further speculation.[16]

Assessments of Quang's three major subordinates were, in the main, positive. The highest rated was Col. Nguyen Viet Thanh, commander of the 7th Infantry Division. The division senior adviser considered Thanh an aggressive commander who demanded "clear, correct and frank" reports from his subordinates and who had a "sound tactical sense of the war." In contrast, advisers labeled Col. Lam Quang Thi, commander of the 9th Infantry Division, as "fair" but lacking in "confidence and aggressiveness." His unit had suffered over eighteen hundred desertions in the last six months of the year and morale was low. Desertions were also a problem in the 21st, the last of the ten regular infantry divisions, but the American advisers thought well of its commander, General Nguyen Van Minh, and reported that the division was "getting more aggressive" and had "a good potential not yet fully realized."[17]

Advisory evaluations of the supposedly elite South Vietnamese ranger, airborne, and marine units were disappointing. Tasked with much of the heavy fighting, they were in poor condition by the second half of the year. In October Westmoreland complained about the unsatisfactory conduct of these units toward the civilian population, implying a lack of discipline, and in November he feared that even the airborne units "might get involved in more than they could handle" and that "a bloody nose for the ARVN general reserve would be adverse

[15] Quoted words from MFR, Accousti, 25 Dec 65, sub: COMUSMACV Visit . . . , History file 3–A2. See also Msg, Westmoreland MAC 5875 to Wheeler, 210905 Nov 65, COMUSMACV Message file. Both in Westmoreland Papers, HRB, CMH.

[16] First quotation from Notes of 1 Jan 66, History file 3–B, Westmoreland Papers, HRB, CMH. Second quotation from William T. Seeber, "A Study in Leadership," copy of draft article (circa 1967) in SEAB, CMH. Third quotation from Francis Fitzgerald, *Fire in the Lake* (Boston: Little, Brown, 1972), p. 311. See also Braddock Political file no. 5, SEAB; Notes of 2 May 66, History file 6–B, Westmoreland Papers, HRB. Both in CMH.

[17] For American evaluations of IV CTZ commanders, see MFR, Lt Col David F. Bird, 24 Dec 65, sub: Conference at Can Tho on 23 Dec 65, History file 3–A1, Westmoreland Papers, HRB. See also Rpt, HQ, 7th Infantry Div Advisory Detachment, MACV, 22 Jul 65, sub: Debriefing of Officers Returning From Field Assignments (end-of-tour report of Col Robert A. Guenthner, Senior Adviser, 7th Div, 16 Sep 64–8 Aug 65), SEAB. Both in CMH.

116

to government morale." To keep the paratroopers out of trouble, the MACV commander considered having the U.S. 1st Cavalry Division work closely with them or, as suggested by DePuy, sending them to quieter areas to "reduce the risk of unsuccessful operations."[18]

The senior airborne adviser, Col. Francis E. Naughton, was unhappy with the performance of the airborne force, blaming leadership problems on an "inbred organization where change comes hard and new ideas are regarded with suspicion." Naughton considered only two of the eight battalion commanders adequate and was concerned that, despite the high cadre combat losses in 1965, "no provision for replacing key leaders" existed. He was unimpressed with the airborne commander, General Dong, but praised his deputy, Col. Ngo Quang

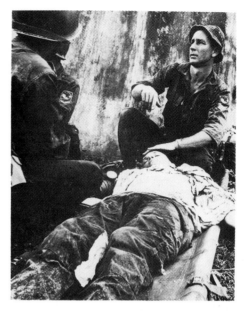

Airborne Adviser Comforting Wounded Counterpart

Truong, who provided most of the operational leadership. But notwithstanding Truong's efforts, the combat performance of the airborne units in 1965 steadily declined. Saigon's employment of the airborne units as fire brigades, back and forth across the country, and the marginal support available from local corps and divisions had worn them thin. After losing an entire battalion in midyear, Dong had become extremely conservative, trying to reduce casualties at all costs, and his subordinates equally cautious.[19]

Although the South Vietnamese armed forces looked better on paper at the end of 1965, they still had to overcome their major weaknesses in leadership and combat effectiveness. The general reserve units were tired, and most of the other ground combat units were in static defensive positions. Exhausted by encounters with large Viet Cong and North Vietnamese Army units, neither the regulars nor the territorials had the energy to seriously challenge the local Viet Cong cadre and militia. Westmoreland expected little improvement in the forseeable future. Wholesale replacements of South Vietnamese corps, division, regimental, province, and district officers would only undermine the shaky Saigon regime. And where would their successors come from? Under these circumstances, American "leverage"—the ability to influence the South Vietnamese government and mili-

---

[18] Quoted words from Notes of 19 Nov 65, History file 2–D. See also MFR, Westmoreland, 6 Oct 65, sub: Conference With General Co on Monday, 4 October 1965, History file 1–F1. Both in Westmoreland Papers, HRB, CMH.

[19] Quoted words from MFR, Naughton, 8 Jan 66, sub: Airborne Brigade Personnel Status (Officers), History file 3–C2, Westmoreland Papers, HRB. See also Interv, author with Lt Col Donald G. Wells (hereafter cited as Wells Interv), Bn and Staff Adviser, Airborne Div (August 1965–August 1966), 25 Mar 75, SEAB. Both in CMH.

tary—was negligible. Salvation appeared to lie in greater American participation in the war effort by continuing the U.S. troop buildup and escalating the air war over Laos and North Vietnam. If the South Vietnamese could not win the war, the Americans would have to do it for them.

Prisoners of War

While American troops entered the fray, a new issue fell into the American advisory lap—the treatment of enemy prisoners of war.[20] Two major aspects of the issue were the classification and interrogation of prisoners for intelligence information and compliance with the provisions of the Geneva Conventions of 12 August 1949. Two of the four separate conventions dealt with the treatment of wounded or ill captives; a third covered the treatment of prisoners of war; and the fourth concerned the protection of civilians. Both the United States and South Vietnam were signatories, while the North Vietnamese and Viet Cong were not.

Under the Conventions of 1949, the classification and care of captives was the responsibility of the "detaining power." In the case where the opposing troops belonged to a nonsignatory power, only members of its "regular armed forces" received prisoner-of-war (POW) status; members of militias and similar paramilitary bodies were not included in this category. When the detaining power could not readily determine the status of a captive, it was obliged to establish special tribunals to make an investigation and a final decision. Captured individuals who were not accorded POW status were still due humane treatment and, if legal proceedings were initiated, a fair and just trial.

Officially the Saigon government regarded captured enemy soldiers as political prisoners, calling them "Communist rebel combat captives," and refused to accord them POW status. In the field, treatment of prisoners was capricious. While some were undoubtedly badly tortured and murdered, others were freed without question. Despite the establishment of a National Interrogation Center in the early 1960s, South Vietnamese commanders gave the interrogation of prisoners only summary attention. Saigon maintained no camps for prisoners of war, confining them in provincial and national jails along with political prisoners and common criminals. The South Vietnamese kept no records on the classification and disposition of military prisoners, and the magnitude of the problem was a matter of guesswork. According to one American inspection team, "when the

---

[20] For background, see Fact Sheet, Lt Col Marcello Guiang, Office of the Center of Military History, DA, 2 Nov 66, sub: Vietnamese Communist Prisoners, SEAB, CMH; Department of the Army Field Manual no. 27–10, The Law of Land Warfare; Department of the Army Pamphlet no. 27–1, Treaties Governing Land Warfare; USMACV, "Command History, 1965," annex I, pp. 429–34, and "1966," annex A, pp. 675–96, HRB, CMH; Molton Moss et al., "U.S. Preparedness for Future Enemy Prisoner of War/Detainee Operations" (Study prepared under the auspices of the Engineer Studies Group, 1977), especially Bibliography, copy in the U.S. Army Corps of Engineers Library; Office of the Provost Marshal, MACV, "Provost Marshal History, 1964–1973," SEAB, CMH; and POW files, SEAB, CMH.

Enemy Prisoners Captured in II Corps

jails became overcrowded it has been the practice to release a proportionate number of inmates to make room for new arrivals." Prison officials maintained that some Viet Cong prisoners were captured and released repeatedly. But most had their freedom within two months to two years after capture.[21]

The arrival of U.S. ground combat forces in Vietnam brought a new dimension to the issue. Influenced perhaps by the difficulties in maintaining POW camps during the Korean conflict, Westmoreland directed that all individuals captured by American units be transferred to South Vietnamese custody. Although the Geneva Conventions provided for such transfers, they also specified that the original detaining power had continued responsibility for the treatment and disposition of those transferred. But the American position that the enemy forces were part of a legal if not a "recognized" foreign government, the Democratic Republic of Vietnam, and the South Vietnamese assertion that the foe be regarded as internal insurgents, made compliance with the conventions impossible. The result was complete chaos in POW accounting. For example, MACV claimed that American and South Vietnamese military forces had taken about six

[21] Quoted words from Memo to Asst SecDef for Manpower, 22 Apr 65, sub: Selected Facts and Problems Resulting [sic] From Our Recent Trip to CINCPAC and MACV, SEAB. On the treatment of prisoners, see Memo, Westmoreland to Taylor, 15 May 65, sub: Comments on Draft, History file 16–3, and Commander's Estimate of the Military Situation in South Vietnam, March 1965, 26 Mar 65, History file 14–38, Westmoreland Papers, HRB. See also Memo, Brig Gen John C. F. Tillson III, OPS–OD, DA, to Gen Palmer, 19 Jan 65, SEAB. All in CMH.

thousand Viet Cong prisoners during 1965, but a later search of South Vietnamese jails could identify less than four hundred of them.[22]

South Vietnamese and American compliance with the Geneva Conventions was thus initially marginal. The Saigon government refused to grant POW status to combat captives, to construct prison camps for them, or to ensure humane treatment during their incarceration. The fratricidal nature of the war and the poor treatment accorded to civil and military captives by the Viet Cong all militated against reform. In August 1965 Westmoreland confided to the U.S. Marine commander, General Walt, that the whole matter was "a difficult problem since we have no command authority over Vietnamese troops" and urged him to "try to moderate the conduct of the [South] Vietnamese in their treatment of prisoners so that it conforms to the spirit" of the conventions. But if this proved impossible, the MACV commander directed Walt to "do everything humanly possible to disassociate our presence with any indiscriminate use of force, brutality, or violations. . . ."[23]

The following month Co reassured Westmoreland that Saigon would rectify the situation. The MACV commander hoped that better treatment of enemy prisoners would spur the Viet Cong and North Vietnamese to reciprocate and would also ameliorate domestic and international criticism of the war. On 2 September Co agreed to establish a combined American–South Vietnamese military interrogation system from the provincial to the national level. A few days later, on the seventh, he approved a troop training program on the handling of prisoners of war and Vietnamese participation on a combined commission that would study the entire problem. But Saigon's enthusiasm for what it considered a minor issue was limited, with Co soon claiming that he lacked a Vietnamese translation of the Geneva Conventions. Perhaps like many South Vietnamese, he hoped for some reciprocal agreement with the enemy first and only gradually bowed to American pressure for unilateral action. However, Co's transfer abruptly interrupted the discussions, and by the end of the year the two parties had accomplished little.[24]

Roles and Missions

With additional U.S. troop deployments under consideration, the issue of roles and missions and command relations remained a constant concern to officials in Washington. In early November the Joint Chiefs of Staff (JCS) noted that "complex, detailed U.S. conceived programs . . . [were not being] picked

---

[22] See Walter G. Hermes, *Truce Tent and Fighting Front*, United States Army in the Korean War (Washington, D.C.: Office of the Chief of Military History, 1966), pp. 233–62, on the problems encountered in running POW camps during the Korean War. See also USMACV, "Command History, 1965," pp. 262–63, HRB; Msg, COMUSMACV MAC 13366 to CINCPAC, 110550 May 68, sub: Vietnamese Prisoners of War, SEAB. Both in CMH.

[23] Ltr, Westmoreland to Walt, 14 Aug 65, History file 17–21, Westmoreland Papers, HRB, CMH.

[24] Notes of 1 Sep 65, History file 1–A; MFR, Westmoreland, 10 Sep 65, sub: Meeting With General Co, 7 September 1965, History file 1–B4. Both in Westmoreland Papers, HRB, CMH. For South Vietnamese attitudes, see Khuyen, *The RVNAF*, pp. 303–10.

President Johnson Conferring With Taylor *upon return from his ambassadorial duties in Saigon*

up and executed by the Vietnamese," forcing the MACV commander to deal "with them in terms of simple tasks and short step by step objectives." For these reasons, the Joint Chiefs agreed to endorse a revised concept of operations, specifying that "the bulk of operations against the VC forces and bases outside the secure areas will be undertaken by US/Third Country and RVNAF general reserve forces, while the bulk of RVN forces will be committed to the defense of GVN installations and securing operations." Both MACV and the South Vietnamese generally agreed to this logical simplification of roles and missions and the matter at first seemed to pass without comment.[25]

At the end of November, however, the controversy over roles and missions suddenly sharpened. Former Ambassador Maxwell Taylor, who had returned from Saigon in the summer to become a special military adviser to the president, took exception to the drift of U.S. operational strategy. Basing his comments on the new JCS study and a recent briefing by General DePuy, Taylor observed that "the concept of assistance as the primary role of U.S. ground forces seems to have dropped out and that of primary doer to have taken its place." Westmoreland, he felt, intended to have U.S. ground forces "move into the forefront of offensive operations against the VC, supported to some degree by VN general

[25] *U.S.-Vietnam Relations*, 5: sec. IV. C. 6. (a), pp. 16–17. Quoted words on p. 17.

reserve units." The role of the bulk of the South Vietnamese units was "unspecified." He asked whether "we are prepared to undertake this preponderant ground role and allow ARVN to fall behind our units . . . [in] pacification duty" without evaluating "the effect of adopting such a concept on U.S. and VN public opinion, on VN military performance and on command and control procedures governing the employment of our troops." In considering future troop requests and assigning combat responsibilities, he insisted that American planners take into consideration expected improvements in the military capabilities of the South Vietnamese and increase their role accordingly.[26]

Under the proposed concept, Taylor pointed out, the mission assigned to U.S. forces "will result in the heaviest fighting," with U.S. casualties rising sharply in relation to those of the Vietnamese, possibly swaying American public opinion against the war. He predicted that 50 to 75 percent of the South Vietnamese infantry battalions would end up playing static defensive roles, and not the 15 to 39 percent suggested by the Joint Chiefs of Staff and Westmoreland. Taylor concluded that "giving the primary combat role to U.S. forces and reserving ARVN for secondary combat missions and a large share of the static defense" was "a mistake from the point of view of GVN psychology and U.S. domestic opinion." He suggested that securing missions be given to the Territorial Forces and clearing missions to South Vietnamese regular army units, with American and Vietnamese forces sharing major combat missions. Every effort, he urged, should "be made to avoid the impression and the fact that U.S. forces are taking over the bulk of the heavy fighting and thereby providing a shield for GVN forces to engage in less hazardous operations." Taylor believed that the more numerous Vietnamese infantry should locate and engage enemy main force units, with mobile American units waiting in reserve to move up and destroy them. Unlike Westmoreland, who wanted American forces to take advantage of their mobility and firepower and actively seek out the enemy, Taylor continued to champion a concept in which Americans occupied secure enclaves and served primarily as a reaction force.[27]

Advised of Taylor's reservations, Westmoreland and Sharp both insisted that there would be no significant division of roles and missions. Although the MACV commander recognized the validity of Taylor's major points, he diffused the former ambassador's criticisms by indicating that "each ARVN corps commander and each ARVN Division commander retains . . . mobile reserve forces . . . for offensive operations" and that many South Vietnamese Army units were employed in this manner. Because of their superiority, American forces would "inevitably find themselves involved in many of the tougher fights," but Westmoreland promised "a major effort to fill in behind U.S. and ARVN forces in areas to be pacified with Regional and Popular Forces." Where Territorial Forces were insufficient, South Vietnamese regulars would have to perform securing operations.[28]

[26] As related in Msg, Wheeler JCS 4500–65 to Westmoreland, 201906 Nov 65, COMUSMACV Message file, Westmoreland Papers, HRB, CMH.

[27] Quoted words from ibid. See also Taylor, *Swords and Plowshares*, p. 364.

[28] Msg, Westmoreland MAC 5875 to Wheeler, 210905 Nov 65, COMUSMACV Message file, Westmoreland Papers, HRB, CMH.

Responding separately, Admiral Sharp pointed out that the "roles and mission of Vietnamese regular and paramilitary forces must be considered in terms of both their present capabilities and their future potential," with any expansion of their roles and missions based on improvements in their military performance. Meanwhile, unilateral American operations would be necessary at times. However, he agreed that "U.S. strategy and operations in both the short and longer time frames" should not become a "shield of foreign power behind which the RVNAF hopefully operates." According to Sharp, "the heart of the offensive program is a combined U.S./RVNAF effort, coupled with a significant number of unilateral GVN actions," and "any other arrangement would result in our fighting their war for them." He assured Washington that "we are not prepared to undertake the preponderant ground role and allow the ARVN to fall back behind our units in pacification duty." Such a division of responsibilities "would contravene the basic U.S. policy for prosecution of the war, dampen Saigon's motivation to fight, and force the United States into the mold of the French." Thus both Sharp and Westmoreland maintained that no division of military roles and missions in South Vietnam would occur and that the bulk of the South Vietnamese regulars would operate side-by-side with American ground combat units.[29]

Secretary of Defense McNamara was unconvinced. During his forthcoming trip to Vietnam to review Westmoreland's new troop requests, he planned to examine closely the roles and missions of the South Vietnamese armed forces. The secretary was reasonably comfortable with MACV's plans for U.S. military forces in 1966, but troubled by the roles intended for Saigon's army. As a result, he requested that MACV prepare a complete breakdown of the projected availability, placement, and mission of the South Vietnamese forces.[30]

Visiting Saigon between 28–30 November 1965, McNamara received extensive briefings from both American and Vietnamese staffs on the current situation. General Nguyen Duc Thang discussed the status of the eleven general reserve battalions (six airborne and five marine); one was currently "inoperative" and six "permanently reinforced" units in the I and II Corps Tactical Zones, leaving only four to form a mobile reserve. To augment these reserve forces, he requested American approval for more airborne, marine, and ranger units. The Vietnamese high command approved American proposals for deploying more U.S. Marines in the northern zone and additional U.S. divisions in the II and III Corps areas. According to Thang, the Vietnamese leaders also agreed that American and allied (that is, South Korean and Australian) combat units had the "primary mission" of "search and destroy" and a secondary one of defending strategic bases and that South Vietnamese forces, both regulars and territorials, had the primary mission of "pacification" and would operate in populated areas. From a *"purely military* point of view," Thang envisioned a South Vietnam divided into two areas: a "populous area . . . the direct responsibility of the Republic of VN armed forces; the other . . . the responsibility of U.S. and Allied forces." Elaborating on Thang's remarks, General Westmoreland broke down the employ-

---

[29] Msg, Sharp to Wheeler and Westmoreland, IN 9529, 230148 Nov 65, COMUSMACV Message file, Westmoreland Papers, HRB, CMH.

[30] Msg, McNamara SECDEF 4539–65 to Lodge and Westmoreland, 231925 Nov 65, COMUSMACV Message file, Westmoreland Papers, HRB, CMH.

ment of South Vietnamese infantry battalions during 1966. Of 162 projected battalions, 69 would defend "government centers and critical installations" (only 1 protecting a U.S. base), 22 would provide "security for [the] expansion of government control," and 71 would conduct "offensive operations and major reactions."[31]

The precise role of the South Vietnamese forces, however, was still unclear. They lacked the airlift support to perform a reserve or reaction role, and Westmoreland had earmarked over half of the South Vietnamese infantry battalions— 56 percent—for static security missions, a role that the South Vietnamese high command willingly accepted. Thus, as Taylor predicted, Americans were to take over most of the offensive combat missions entailing the heaviest fighting. Westmoreland was increasingly doubtful of the ability of the South Vietnamese Army to operate alone and, after McNamara's departure, told his staff and principal commanders that, in the future, "we would have to take the ARVN even more under our wing and earn for them greater [battlefield] victories."[32]

The combined campaign plan published by American and South Vietnamese staff officers at the end of the year added little. Although the document broke the war effort down geographically and functionally, it was not a true operational plan and, as in similar MACV and JCS documents, made no assignment of tasks or goals. Westmoreland hailed its formal signature on 31 December 1965 as "the first time we have been able to work out plans so far in advance with our Vietnamese associates," but he cautioned that it was no panacea for Saigon's ills and that "the ability of . . . [the Thieu-Ky] government to maintain itself in power . . . [was] essential to success in the future." Political stability still came first.[33]

A major part of the war in Southeast Asia had thus become Americanized by the end of 1965, as vividly demonstrated by the Ia Drang campaign of the U.S. 1st Cavalry Division in November. The implications were clear. Despite protestations to the contrary, two different wars were now under way in South Vietnam: the "big battalion," or conventional, war, carried out by American military forces through a strategy of attrition; and the "other war," pursued by the South Vietnamese through the strategy of pacification. American attention, both inside and outside the government, quickly became riveted to the first while the second slowly faded into the background.

---

[31] Quoted words of Thang from GVN Briefing to McNamara, circa 29 Nov 65, History file 2–F2, Westmoreland Papers, HRB, CMH. Previously the Joint General Staff J–3, Thang now headed the Ministry of Rural Construction (later Revolutionary Development). Quoted words of Westmoreland from *U.S.-Vietnam Relations*, 5:sec. IV. C. 6. (a), p. 24.

[32] Notes of 10 Dec 65, History file 2–G, Westmoreland Papers, HRB, CMH. The word *battlefield* was penciled into the reproduced, typed copy on file.

[33] Quoted words from Notes of 31 Dec 65, History file 3–B, Westmoreland Papers, HRB. See also JGS-MACV, Combined Campaign Plan 1966, AB 141, 31 Dec 65, SEAB. Both in CMH.

PART THREE

Turmoil and Reform
(1966–1967)

Johnson and Ky in Honolulu Discussing Reforms

7

Revolt in the I Corps

At the beginning of 1966 the stability of the Saigon government still remained the chief concern of the American advisory effort. The South Vietnamese civil and military apparatus continued to rest on a precarious balance of power between rival military factions. The most prominent leaders remained Thieu, chairman of the Directory; Ky, titular head of the Saigon government and also chief of the air force; Vien, chief of the Joint General Staff; and the commanders of the four corps tactical zones. Any changes involving these men, or their supporters, pointed the way to civil war and chaos.

Both General Westmoreland and Ambassador Lodge were well aware of the Directory's narrow basis of political support and the deep divisions within its own membership. The danger of political turmoil colored almost every bit of advice they tendered to their Vietnamese counterparts. Yet, despite the growing American involvement in Southeast Asia, the South Vietnamese could often be remarkably resistant to American advice, as a new politico-military crisis was soon to show.[1]

The Seeds of Crisis

Since 1964 the failure of the military to establish a stable political structure had led many American and Vietnamese leaders to favor the return of civilian government in South Vietnam. Although the first attempts in early 1965 had failed, the belief that such a transition would take place continued to enjoy widespread support. On 15 January 1966, at the Second Armed Forces Congress in Saigon, Ky announced the intent to restore civilian rule. Rather than holding elections for a national constituent assembly, the Directory planned to appoint its own committee to draft an acceptable constitution that would provide for a

[1] Unless otherwise indicated, material in this chapter is based on the following: Military History Branch, MACV, "The March-June 1966 Political Crisis in South Vietnam and Its Effect on Military Operations," December 1966, SEAB, CMH; files on Vietnam-South (GVN): Buddhism, 1966, in Richard A. Gard Papers, HRB, CMH; U.S.-Vietnam Relations, 7:sec. IV. C. 9. (b), pt. 2, pp. 11-22; and History files 5-6, Westmoreland Papers, HRB, CMH.

Demonstrations in Hue, Spring 1966

popularly elected government in Saigon. The draft constitution was to be subject to a referendum sometime in 1966 and, if approved, followed by general elections in 1967. Thieu and Ky repeated that proposal at a conference with President Johnson in Honolulu the following month and received the blessings of their American supporters.

In South Vietnam the response was less enthusiastic. Distaste for a dictated constitution united domestic critics of the military regime under two prominent religious leaders, the militant Thich Tri Quang, heading the High Council of the Buddhist Hierarchy in Central Vietnam, and the more moderate Thich Tam Chau, presiding over the Buddhist Institute for Secular Affairs in Saigon. Both religious leaders railed against government corruption and inefficiency, declining economic conditions, and the regime's subservience to American influence. They demanded the immediate resignation of the Thieu-Ky government, its replacement by an elected national assembly to draw up a constitution, and a rapid settlement of the war. The bonzes drew immediate support from Buddhists and students in the major South Vietnamese cities. Hue, the former imperial capital of Vietnam and a focal point for regional interests in the northern I Corps Tactical Zone, quickly became the center of the protest for dissidents, who, by March, had formed a loose confederation known as the Struggle Movement.[2]

[2] Intelligence Memorandum 0806/66, CIA, 20 Apr 66, sub: Thich Tri Quang and Buddhist Political Objections in South Vietnam, and other documents in box 11, Gard Papers, HRB, CMH.

128

During the antigovernment demonstrations that followed, General Thi, the commander of the I Corps zone, failed to take action against the protestors. Apparently he was unwilling to see his popular support in the northern zone eroded by heavy-handed treatment of the Buddhist-led rallies, aware that many general officers' careers had already come to grief by such action. From his headquarters at Da Nang, Thi regarded himself as the equal of both Thieu and Ky, which, given the collegial nature of the Directory, was accurate. The general felt free to run the northern zone as he wished. He was also cognizant that he had powerful supporters within the central government, including the National Police director and the commander of the 25th Infantry Division located just outside of Saigon. His relationships with his American advisers were excellent, and perhaps his ambitions extended south, to the capital.

None of these factors carried much weight in Saigon. Ky accused the I Corps commander of seeking to topple the regime and strengthen his own political base by supporting the Struggle Movement.[3] U.S. officials at the time speculated that the Saigon government was using the Struggle Movement in the I Corps as an excuse to attack Thi's independence and enhance its own power—or, alternatively, to attack the popular Thi in order to bait the leaders of the movement into rash actions that would serve as a pretext for crushing them.

Whatever the case, the Saigon generals decided to fire Thi. On 11 March Ky made the dismissal public, and a rump Armed Forces Congress approved the decision the following day. They named the commander of the South Vietnamese 1st Infantry Division based at Hue, General Chuan, the new corps commander, and put the head of the Ranger Command in Saigon, General Pham Xuan Nhuan, in charge of the division. Thi, visiting Saigon at the time of his relief, returned to the northern zone, ostensibly to wind up his personal affairs.

The abrupt dismissal of Thi displeased U.S. officials. In American eyes Thi, a former airborne brigade commander, was one of the better South Vietnamese military leaders. The units under his command, the 1st and 2d Infantry Divisions and the independent 51st Infantry Regiment in the Quang Nam Special Zone, included some of the best in the army. U.S. Marine Corps generals in the I Corps had praised Thi's cooperation with U.S. combat forces and cited his devotion to pacification. When informed of the impending dismissal, Secretary of State Dean Rusk noted his complete surprise, warned that "there is something more in [the] picture than meets the eye," and expressed concern that the move would further exacerbate Saigon's relations with the Buddhists.[4]

Citing no specific misdeeds, Ky, Thieu, and Co found it difficult to justify Thi's dismissal to Lodge and Westmoreland. If it were a matter of corruption and military incompetence, then other general officers were more likely candidates. The Saigon leaders denounced Thi solely on the basis of not cooperating with the central government, of nurturing personal political ambitions, of consorting with both the Communists and the Struggle Movement, and of having little

---

[3] See also Nguyen Cao Ky, *Twenty Years and Twenty Days* (New York: Stein and Day, 1976), pp. 89–90.
[4] Msg, Lodge 3260 to SecState, 9 Mar 66, History file 4–E1; Msg, Rusk 2653 to Saigon, 9 Mar 66, History file 4–E3. Both in Westmoreland Papers, HRB, CMH. See also Interv, author with Maj Gen John F. Freund (hereafter cited as Freund Interv), 25–26 May 72; Airgram, State A–42 to Saigon, 16 Mar 72, sub: General Nguyen Chanh Thi's Non-Return. Both in SEAB, CMH.

popular support in the northern provinces. When queried by Lodge on the availability of evidence, Ky admitted that he had none but cleverly added that it was not as important as the question of U.S. confidence in his government, for any action to thwart the dismissal would force him to resign.

The American ambassador was perturbed. Lodge felt that he "was being brought in long after a decision had been made to try to do something" and noted that Ky was "definitely committed." Although at first he intended to advise the South Vietnamese leaders against the move, he recalled his own "long disapproval of the corps system," compared it to Chinese warlordism of the 1920s, and concluded that the "subordination of corps commanders to central authority may be part of Viet-Nam's march toward nationhood." In the end the United States would neither support nor oppose the maneuver, which, given Ky's proclivity for action, was tantamount to endorsing it.[5]

The Struggle Movement in Control

Following the dismissal of Thi, the northern zone erupted into a seething inferno of political dissent. The number and intensity of strikes, marches, and rallies steadily increased, fueled by soldiers, police, and local officials loyal to the general. Major disturbances took place in Hue and in the port city of Da Nang, the logistical center of the I Corps zone, where labor strikes brought harbor and transportation activities to a standstill and threatened to cripple military operations in the area. The return of Thi to Da Nang, from which he then refused to leave, added further to the confusion. On 29 March several Roman Catholic leaders joined the dissidents in a demand for a return to civilian rule. By the beginning of April Struggle Movement forces appeared to control most of Hue, Da Nang, and Hoi An and had the support of the South Vietnamese I Corps headquarters and the 1st Division. At the same time, South Vietnamese combat operations in the northern zone began to peter out, and the danger that the crisis presented to the war effort became evident.

What the Struggle Movement lacked was a charismatic leader and a unified program. Its supporters were united only in their dissatisfaction with the central government. While some factions demanded new political institutions, others called for the resignation of Thieu and Ky, the reinstatement of Thi, and the return of those generals who were more acceptable to the Buddhists. No strong personage emerged, and the movement essentially continued unfocused and unguided.

The protest activities of the dissidents alarmed American leaders more than their South Vietnamese counterparts. State Department and Saigon embassy officials, as well as President Johnson, saw the hand of Communist organizers behind the disturbances and viewed the movement as strongly anti-American, even though most Struggle activists stressed their solidarity with American aims

---

[5] First and second quotations from Msg, Lodge 3260 to SecState, 9 Mar 66, History file 4–E1. Third and fourth quotations from Msg, Lodge 3265 to SecState, 9 Mar 66, History file 4–E2. Both in Westmoreland Papers, HRB, CMH. See also Memo, Robert W. Komer to President, 9 Mar 66, 7:50 P.M., SEAB, CMH.

and goals. Lodge himself insisted throughout March that Ky disregard Buddhist demands and push through his original plans for an appointed constitution-writing body. He blamed the disturbances on the Communists and "French trouble-making," as well as on the ambitions of those currently out of power. Westmoreland saw student leaders as the principal agitators, constituting a "5th column" in Da Nang and Hue, and urged that they "be brought in line by terminating their deferment from the draft and putting them in uniform." Westmoreland's deputy, Lt. Gen. John A. Heintges, seconded that view, called it "a crying shame to let the students up there get away with their anti-government and anti-US activities," and recommended a "terrific psychological campaign" to counter the Struggle Movement. If that failed, Heintges advised that "martial . . . law be declared and these young upstarts severely dealt with." From Washington, Rusk urged that U.S. officials take a more active role in ending the crisis. All agreed that the Saigon regime should take forceful action and that Americans should avoid becoming directly involved.[6]

Ky, Thieu, Co, and their supporters were more cautious than their American advisers. On 2 April Westmoreland related that Ky apparently accepted the American advice but seemed "to be biding his time, either hoping that the problem will go away or waiting for favorable conditions for him to use military force."[7] That in fact proved to be the case. On the following day the Armed Forces Congress announced that the government would convene a committee with representatives from all social, economic, and religious groups to discuss creating some kind of constitutional convention or assembly. While the regime made that concession to the Buddhists, Ky also declared that Da Nang was in the hands of the Communists and that the government intended to restore order by force of arms. One day later the Saigon government began military operations against the city.

On the night of 4 April Ky, Co, Vien, and Col. Nguyen Ngoc Loan, the Military Security Service (MSS) chief, flew to the Da Nang Air Base, accompanied by National Field Force Police, MSS personnel, psychological warfare teams, and two South Vietnamese Marine Corps battalions. A third marine battalion and two ranger battalions soon followed. The Directory hoped that a strong show of force, combined with a pro-government propaganda campaign and a willingness to negotiate, would persuade any military units supporting the movement to come to terms. The South Vietnamese generals had briefed Lodge and Westmoreland prior to the operation and secured their approval. Westmoreland provided U.S. air transport for the government troops and, expecting blood-shed, withdrew American advisers from both sides.

The reaction to the troop deployment was immediate. Generals Thi and Nhuan joined the Struggle Movement, and many local officials and officers

---

[6] Quoted words of Lodge from Msg, Lodge SGN 3589 to President, 300822 Mar 66, Bunker Papers, DS. Quoted words of Westmoreland from Notes of 24 Mar 66, History file 5–B (see also MFR, Westmoreland, 24 Mar 66, sub: Meeting at Chu Lai on 24 March 1966, History file 5–B1), and quoted words of Heintges from Ltr, Heintges to Westmoreland, 23 Mar 66, sub: Demonstrations in I Corps, History file 5–B2, Westmoreland Papers, HRB, CMH. See also Johnson, *The Vantage Point*, pp. 246–47; *U.S.-Vietnam Relations*, 4:sec. IV. C. 9. (b), pp. 12–14; Telg, Rusk to Lodge, 1 Apr 66, in Porter, *Vietnam*, 2:420–21.

[7] Notes of 2 Apr 66, History file 5–C, Westmoreland Papers, HRB, CMH.

quickly followed their lead. As the new 1st Division commander, Nhuan placed infantry and armored forces in blocking positions along Route 1, between Hue and Da Nang, and stood ready to reinforce Struggle units in Da Nang. The situation inside the port city was tense. The commander of the Quang Nam Special Zone, Col. Dam Quang Yeu, headed the rebel military units that, according to American estimates, included an infantry battalion from the 51st Regiment, three Regional Forces companies, eleven Popular Forces platoons, and six armored vehicles, plus about six thousand South Vietnamese administrative troops and two hundred military police. When Yeu quickly positioned some of his units on the approaches to the downtown area, the start of civil war seemed imminent.

The Saigon generals, seeing the strong forces that confronted them, decided against direct action. The government task force remained at the air base and made no move to enter Da Nang. Instead, the generals stalled for time and hoped that the rebel military units would disintegrate through prolonged inactivity. Ky returned to Saigon almost immediately and took a conciliatory position. On 6 April he announced that Da Nang was not occupied by Communists and that the confrontation in the northern zone was basically a political problem that did not necessitate the use of force. In a letter to the Buddhist Institute he later suggested that the government would convene an elected constitutional convention within six months.

Westmoreland wanted no interference by the local American troops. He ordered the temporary evacuation of Americans from Hue and Da Nang, instructing Lt. Gen. Lewis Walt, the American corps-level commander, to "confine all American troops to their billets, keep them off the streets, and trucks off the roads, . . . [and] close down all port operations until the dust settles." He also directed remaining U.S. military personnel to adopt a "detached, . . . calm and polite attitude toward all the Vietnamese."[8]

Privately, Westmoreland was disappointed. He had hoped for more decisive action at Da Nang and now began using his own influence to end the affair. On 7 April he told Walt to withdraw American advisers from all rebellious South Vietnamese units in the northern zone as a sign of American displeasure, and later sent Brig. Gen. John F. Freund, who since mid-1964 had worked closely with various South Vietnamese leaders on other sensitive matters, to assist. Westmoreland instructed Freund to "do all possible to put the struggle forces in a bad light by blaming the entire situation in I Corps on the group of hot headed students" and to use the advisers to bring rebel military units back into the fold.[9]

More alarmed than Westmoreland by the government's failure to pacify Da Nang, Ambassador Lodge saw the situation in an increasingly pessimistic light. On 8 April he reported that "a rebellious combination of Buddhist control, student agitation, police and civil servant complicity, mob participation, undisciplined armed forces personnel in units and individually, and a numerically

---

[8] Msg, Westmoreland MAC 2650 to Walt, 3 Apr 66, History file 5–D1, Westmoreland Papers, HRB, CMH.

[9] Quoted words from MFR, Westmoreland, 7 Apr 66, sub: Record of Telephone Conversation With General Platt, Chief of Staff, III MAF, 0925 hours, this date, History file 5–D4. See also Notes of 9 Apr 66, History file 5–D. Both in Westmoreland Papers, HRB, CMH.

unknown but undeniable and increasing Viet Cong influence" had supplanted government authority in Da Nang and north of the city. Seeing no legitimacy in the demands of the Struggle Movement organizers, Lodge asserted that "when stripped of hypocrisy and cant, they boil down to a naked grab for power." He went on to castigate Ky for failing to use force at Da Nang and, despite U.S. Army advisory reports to the contrary, continued to portray the Struggle Movement as anti-American and Communist-inspired. He also publicly disagreed with Ky's decision to hold elections for a constituent assembly, fearing that such a body, with its popular mandate, might challenge the authority of the military government.[10]

General Walt had more immediate concerns. Any military confrontation at Da Nang would threaten a number of American and South Vietnamese supply depots, the large air base there, and Walt's own headquarters. Walt had the thankless task of limiting the conflict without interfering too obtrusively. A test of his skill came on 9 April, when the rebel military leader, Colonel Yeu, led a large armed force against the air base, where the government troops were stationed. The approaching column included both armor and artillery, and again a major battle appeared inevitable. With the hasty approval of General Westmoreland, Walt intervened by blocking Yeu's force with a small U.S. Marine Corps convoy and sent his operations officer, Col. John R. Chaisson, out to negotiate. Tension was high as U.S. Marine Corps fighter bombers circled overhead, Yeu's artillerymen unlimbered their pieces, and both parties threatened to open fire. The South Vietnamese officer finally backed down and called off the attack, and the immediate danger to the air base was over.[11]

On the following day, 10 April, Ky, feeling nothing more could be accomplished, began withdrawing the government task force, again using American aircraft. At the same time, the Directory replaced General Chuan as the official I Corps commander with General Ton That Dinh. Dinh was an older general who had commanded a French mobile group in North Vietnam prior to 1954 and thereafter had become one of President Diem's leading commanders. Early American evaluations characterized Dinh as "ambitious" and "frequently erratic in personal behavior."[12] However, as a native of Hue and a favorite of the Buddhist leaders, he appeared to be an excellent political choice for the job. Four days later, with Dinh installed and the government troops withdrawn from Da Nang, Thieu declared that elections for a constitutional assembly would take place in three to five months, and the Buddhist Institute quickly agreed that the Ky government should remain in office until then. Who would rule in Saigon after the assembly had convened was still open to conjecture, but the Buddhists seemed to have won the first round.

Once the government troops had departed Da Nang, the tense political situation appeared to quiet down. General Walt, despite Lodge's foreboding, began to

---

[10] Quoted words from Telg, AMEMB 3817, 8 Apr 66, as given in MACV, "The March–June 1966 Political Crisis," p. 21, SEAB, CMH. See Telg, Lodge to Rusk, 7 Apr 66, in Porter, *Vietnam*, 2:421–22, where Lodge's position is much milder. See also *U.S.-Vietnam Relations*, 7:sec. IV. C. 9. (b), pt. 2, p. 17.

[11] MACV, "The March–June 1966 Political Crisis, pp. 23–24, SEAB, CMH; Lewis W. Walt, *Strange War, Strange Strategy: A General's Report on Vietnam* (New York: Funk and Wagnalls, 1970), pp. 118–22.

[12] Briefing Book for SECDEF Honolulu Conference, 20–21 Nov 63, box 2, accession no. 69A702, RG 334, WNRC.

relax. He sponsored meetings between Dinh and Yeu, later reporting that Dinh was slowly bringing order to the I Corps zone, and approved the use of U.S. helicopters to fly Buddhist leader Tri Quang around the corps area in an effort to appeal for moderation among his adherents. Thi remained hidden, probably in Da Nang. Although Thi and his former appointees still constituted a potential danger, U.S. advisory reports indicated that, outside of the I Corps headquarters and the 1st Division, the Struggle Movement had little support in the armed forces. Westmoreland noted that the Viet Cong had failed to exploit the situation and seemed as surprised as American officials at the turn of events. Only the U.S. Embassy remained suspicious and held that enemy inactivity might signify some sort of secret agreement between the Struggle Movement and the Communists.

The apparent calm was misleading. On 26 April Ky informed Lodge that the Directory had no intention of surrendering its executive authority to the projected constitutional assembly, and three days later he removed a powerful Thi supporter, Colonel Lieu, from his post as director general of the National Police, replacing him with his close friend, MSS Chief Loan. In the I Corps Tactical Zone Dinh proved either unwilling or unable to restore the normal tempo of combat operations. During a visit to the zone on 1 May Westmoreland found crowds of local combat troops in the streets of Hue and Da Nang and rejected Dinh's assertion that the political situation there was settling down. Finding the corps commander "talkative and emotional," Westmoreland concluded that his "control of the situation was tenuous to the point where we should not fully accept his judgment."[13] Dinh later retorted that he himself had ordered troops to remain in the two cities to control unruly civilian elements.

As Westmoreland visited Da Nang, General Freund, now officially designated as the MACV commander's special assistant for the South Vietnamese armed forces, toured the II Corps headquarters at Pleiku, where he learned that the deputy Buddhist chaplain, Thich Ho Giac,[14] had visited the city on 27 April and had spoken to troops of the South Vietnamese 3d Armored Cavalry Squadron. Ho, according to Freund's sources, had stressed three themes: that South Vietnamese soldiers should lay down their arms; that the objectives of the war were solely American; and that China, not North Vietnam, was the real enemy. When Freund relayed that story to the chief of the South Vietnamese Joint General Staff, he added that Ho Giac was directing his campaign against the army's best units and that "the other Buddhist chaplains are also busy in similar operations all over the army."[15]

Although providing no specific evidence for either contention, Freund reported that Vien was deeply concerned over the situation, believing that "the army is being destroyed from within." According to Freund, Vien recommended deactivating the chaplain's corps and replacing the Directory with a one-man dictatorship to deal with the emergency. Fearing that the Buddhists were estab-

[13] Notes of 1 May 66, History file 6–B, Westmoreland Papers, HRB, CMH.
[14] Ho Giac was also a leader of the Buddhist Institute's political branch and a protege of Tri Quang.
[15] Quoted words from MFR, Freund, 2 May 66, sub: Records of Conversation With Lieutenant General Cao Van Vien on 2 May 1966, History file 6–B1. See also Notes of 2 May 66, History file 6–B. Both in Westmoreland Papers, HRB, CMH.

lishing some sort of religious commissar system, he reported that Vien had also suggested that Ky manufacture an incident requiring governmental intervention. The regime could then use force to clamp down on the Buddhists and restore order. (Vien later denied making any of these statements.)[16]

Dismayed by the threat of Buddhist subversion, other American officials expanded on the original tale. Barry Zorthian, chief of the Joint U.S. Public Affairs Office in Saigon, related Freund's story almost word-for-word to Ambassador Lodge and added that "an insidious organizational technique" existed whereby each unit had senior Buddhist leaders acting as "religious (political) commissars." Because the matter of who commanded the South Vietnamese 3d Armored Cavalry Squadron was already "somewhat questionable," he speculated that the unit would defect to the Struggle Movement within a few months. The II Corps commander, General Vinh Loc, also had "stated publicly that he was neither for Thi nor Ky," which raised the possibility of his defecting too. Taking into consideration the "very apparent deterioration in [South Vietnamese] troop morale" and the fact that "local police forces are completely demoralized," Zorthian concluded that a major disaster was imminent. The American embassy immediately passed the information on to Washington, insisting that Vien's personal and Tri Quang's public comments had corroborated the charges and stressing the danger of an impending collapse.[17]

On 6 May Ky gave Westmoreland an even blacker picture of the situation. He contended that the Struggle Movement had passed to the control of a mysterious Dr. Tam,[18] who, according to rumor, had recently come from the Soviet Union by way of Switzerland. The three northern provinces of South Vietnam, Ky said, were virtually independent of Saigon; liaison between the politically oriented bonzes and the Viet Cong was suspected; and irresponsible Buddhist leaders had privately urged him to stage a coup to oust the other members of the Directory.[19]

The next day, in an apparent move to demonstrate the authority of the Directory, Ky announced at a press conference his intention to continue in office at least until sometime in 1967 and said that the military would oppose, by force, any elected government that had neutralist or Communist sympathies. Reports also surfaced that Colonel Loan was secretly shipping arms to groups hostile to the Struggle Movement, but American officials had no indication that the Saigon government was preparing to move militarily against the dissidents.

---

[16] Quoted words from MFR, Freund, 2 May 66, History file 6–B1, Westmoreland Papers, HRB, CMH. In discussing the matter in 1978, Vien pointed out that even replacing the dissident Buddhist chaplains would have caused more trouble and that there was no need for the government to create new incidents when so many existed already. See Ltr, Potts to MacDonald, 23 Jan 78, sub: Comments by General Cao Van Vien, SEAB, CMH.

[17] Quoted words from Memo, Zorthian to Lodge, 2 May 66, sub: Record of Conversation Between Brigadier General John F. Freund and Senior ARVN Officers, History file 6–B2. See also Msg, AmEmbassy SGN 4401 to SecState, 6 May 66, History file 6–B4. Both in Westmoreland Papers, HRB, CMH.

[18] Perhaps referring to Nguyen Van Man, the mayor of Da Nang.

[19] MFR, Westmoreland, 6 May 66, sub: Meeting With Prime Minister Ky, 11–1130 hours, 6 May 1966, History file 6–B3, Westmoreland Papers, HRB, CMH.

Government Troops on the Move Against Dissidents

Saigon Acts

Both Lodge and Westmoreland were out of the country attending a planning conference in Honolulu when government forces, commanded by Vien, seized Da Nang in the early morning hours of Sunday, 15 May. Two South Vietnamese Marine Corps battalions, supported by tanks of the South Vietnamese Army and covered by planes of the South Vietnamese Air Force, moved quickly into the city and secured the mayor's office, the radio station, the I Corps headquarters and other military installations, and the police stations. Two airborne battalions under the command of General Dong provided reinforcements. Little fighting transpired, as most of the dissidents fell back inside several Buddhist pagodas, which the troops refrained from attacking. Ky and Co later joined Vien, and during the next four days an uneasy truce prevailed inside the city.

When the current commander of the I Corps, General Dinh, objected to the action, the Directory replaced him with the political warfare director, General Huynh Van Cao. Dinh fled first to General Walt's headquarters and then north to Hue, where he joined Thi, Nhuan, several dissident province chiefs, and leading Buddhists in publicly denouncing the return of government troops. Nhuan placed units of the 1st Division on the approaches to Hue and at the nearby Phu Bai airfield but made no move to reinforce Da Nang. The commander of the 2d Division, General Lam, remained loyal to the government, but some elements of

136

his unit made their way to Da Nang to take part in the revolt. Lam warned that any attack on the pagodas would cause more troop defections and even recommended reinstating Thi as corps commander.

American participation in the second Da Nang operation was minimal. According to General Westmoreland, the Directory had not informed him of the impending operation and U.S. officials had been taken by surprise. Still in Hawaii, both Westmoreland and Lodge disassociated themselves from the politically explosive action. Secretary of State Rusk, disturbed that his representatives were not consulted prior to the attack, ordered Deputy Ambassador William J. Porter to halt the fighting immediately. He instructed Porter and, upon Lodge's return, the ambassador himself to insist that U.S. officials be apprised of all government actions, that the pagodas be left alone, and that a compromise solution be reached as soon as possible. Also on Rusk's advice, MACV vetoed all Directory requests for U.S. air support and again withdrew advisers from all involved units. The secretary was worried lest the United States throw its weight behind an unsuccessful endeavor that might backfire and weaken the Saigon government further.[20]

On 16 May Walt met the new (and fourth) Vietnamese commander of the I Corps, General Cao. He was unimpressed. In talks with both Freund and Walt, Cao revealed that he had no interest in commanding the corps and that other Directory members had coerced him into taking the assignment. Westmoreland belatedly recommended that Dinh be retained, but by then he had joined the Struggle Movement in Hue.

On 17 May Cao flew in a U.S. Marine Corps helicopter to Hue to confer with Thi and Nhuan. Accompanying him were Walt's chief of staff, Brig. Gen. Jonas M. Platt (USMC), and the I Corps deputy senior adviser, Col. Archelaus L. Hamblen, Jr. After Thi and Nhuan declined to see him, Cao returned to the helicopter and prepared to depart when about a hundred students and soldiers rushed the helicopter pad. Cao scrambled aboard, but as the aircraft began to rise, a South Vietnamese lieutenant began firing at it with a .45-caliber pistol. Returning the fire, the American helicopter's door gunner killed the lieutenant and wounded several other South Vietnamese soldiers.[21] Although the local province chief later claimed that the incident was an attempt to assassinate Cao led by a nephew of Tri Quang, the 1st Division's headquarters company commander, Quang denied the allegation and blamed the American gunner for starting the incident. Badly frightened, Cao went on to General Lam's 2d Division headquarters at Quang Ngai, where the reception was more cordial.

Hardly had Cao returned to Da Nang when he encountered more trouble in the person of Colonel Loan, now chief of the National Police. Loan insisted that Cao order an immediate attack on the pagodas in Da Nang and apparently threatened the corps commander with bodily harm if he refused. Sometime during an ensuing argument, Colonel Hamblen arrived unannounced to find Cao surrounded by Loan and several of his armed police. Terrified, Cao departed with Hamblen and subsequently begged General Walt for asylum. Writing to

[20] *U.S.-Vietnam Relations*, 7:sec. IV. C. 9. (b), pt. 2, pp. 17–20.
[21] Interv, author with Col Archelaus L. Hamblen, Jr., Deputy Senior Adviser, I CTZ (March–June 1966), January 1979, SEAB, CMH.

137

Westmoreland shortly thereafter, Cao asked to be flown to the United States and volunteered to join the U.S. Marine Corps and fight communism "anywhere in the world."[22] He later explained that had he ordered attacks on the pagodas, the Buddhists might have taken reprisals against his Roman Catholic parents, who resided in Hue, and other Catholics. Although first Vien, then Co, flew to Da Nang to try to calm the reluctant corps commander, neither was able to coax him out of the U.S. Marine Corps compound.

General Walt also became personally involved in securing a vital bridge over the Tourane River in Da Nang on 18 May. The bridge linked the city with a depot complex known as Da Nang East. U.S. Marines secured the Da Nang end, while rebels held the other. When Walt found out that South Vietnamese engineers supporting the Struggle Movement had wired both the bridge and the depot with explosives, he arranged a personal meeting with the South Vietnamese officer commanding the engineers. While the two had a lively discussion on the bridge, a U.S. Army engineer secretly cut the wires leading to the explosives. As Walt waved his marines across the span, the South Vietnamese officer ordered the charges blown. Much to the officer's surprise, the explosives failed to go off, and Walt's forces secured the entire bridge without further opposition.[23]

On the afternoon of 19 May Ky and Thieu at last decided to act decisively. Because Cao continued to refuse to order an attack on the pagodas, they finally told General Vien to do the job. Under the deputy airborne commander, Colonel Truong, five battalions, numbering some thirty-three hundred troops, forcibly occupied most of the pagodas and the remaining military installations within the city. In an effort to hold down casualties Truong surrounded the two main centers of resistance, located in the Tan Linh and Thinh Hoi pagodas, and offered amnesty to any who would surrender.

American officials were again upset by the renewed fighting, but there was little they could do. General Walt brought in a U.S. Marine Corps rifle company to protect his own headquarters, and, in the days that followed, U.S. Marine Corps and Air Force installations received stray small arms fire, mortar rounds, and aircraft rocket and cannon fire, causing several casualties. When South Vietnamese propeller-driven attack aircraft mistakenly shot up portions of the U.S. Marine Corps headquarters, Walt threatened to have the offending aircraft shot down, and the skies were soon filled with American and South Vietnamese jet fighters wheeling back and forth over the city. Finally, after a heated exchange of messages between Da Nang, Saigon, and Washington, the Vietnamese agreed to suspend all air attacks within the city limits.[24]

While Truong directed the government troops in Da Nang, the operations officer of the South Vietnamese Joint General Staff, General Tran Thanh Phong, assumed temporary command of the I Corps. At the same time, the selection of yet another corps commander began. This time the Directory considered moving General Vinh Loc up from the II Corps area or, on Westmoreland's recommendation, importing the exiled professional, General Do Cao Tri, from Hong Kong. Finally, perhaps because of his steadfast loyalty, the government settled on the

[22] Ltr, Cao to Westmoreland, 24 May 66, History file 7–A1, Westmoreland Papers, HRB, CMH.
[23] Walt, *Strange War, Strange Strategy,* pp. 125–30.
[24] Ky, *Twenty Years and Twenty Days,* pp. 94–97; Walt, *Strange War, Strange Strategy,* pp. 122–23.

Rebel Stronghold at Thinh Hoi Pagoda in Da Nang

commander of the 2d Division, General Lam, and at the end of the month he officially took office. Lam was the sixth corps commander in the northern zone in less than three months.

Distressed by the deterioration of the political situation in South Vietnam and the adverse reaction of the American public to it, Washington began to pressure American officials in Vietnam to take a more active role in what was on the way to becoming a civil war. Upon his return to Saigon on 20 May, Westmoreland found a strongly worded message from General Wheeler directing him to use all his influence to end the political crisis quickly. A feeling now prevailed in the United States that American units were doing all the fighting while the South Vietnamese dabbled in political intrigue. The JCS chairman wanted to know whether the South Vietnamese now felt that we were "firmly hooked in Vietnam" and, consequently, that they could ignore our wishes.[25]

The following day General Wheeler asked that Westmoreland and Lodge make American dissatisfaction with the situation unequivocal and sponsor a meeting between the two factions at a safe location. Wheeler himself and Ambassador-at-Large W. Averell Harriman were prepared to head a special team to assist in the negotiations. In the interim, the JCS chairman suggested cutting off all U.S. military and economic aid to the I Corps zone, withdrawing all military

---

[25] Msg, Wheeler JCS 2837 to Westmoreland, 20 May 66, History file 6–D1, Westmoreland Papers, HRB, CMH.

and civilian advisers from the zone, and perhaps halting all American offensive combat operations there.[26]

Westmoreland responded that, contrary to Wheeler's impression, the situation in the northern zone was "serious" but "not desperate" and had been "blown out of perspective by the headlines. . . ." His own appraisal was now optimistic. The government controlled most of Da Nang, the 2d Division had remained loyal, the defecting Quang Nam Special Zone headquarters had returned to government control, and the rebellious 11th Ranger Battalion had disintegrated. He also noted that General Phong was now assisting the timid Cao and that even General Nhuan, still heading the 1st Division at Hue, "seems to be taking more interest in commanding his division against the Viet Cong. . . ." Thi and Dinh, the two ex-corps commanders hiding in Hue, were only an annoyance to Nhuan, while the Buddhist leader, Tri Quang, "may be running scared." Westmoreland felt that Thi was "the only man with sufficient influence to return the I Corps area to normal in short order" and was urging General Walt to sponsor a meeting between Thi, Ky, and Dinh at Chu Lai, a local American base. Thi might cooperate, he added, if his avowed enemy, Defense Minister Co, "was removed from the scene."[27]

Later in the day the MACV commander repeated his contention "that the whole matter is [being] blown out of proportion . . . because of . . . reporters on the scene attempting to make a name for themselves and to play a role." He considered the measures proposed by Wheeler too drastic. Withdrawing advisers or U.S. assistance was untenable, serving only to decrease American influence; halting U.S. combat operations was "unacceptable" and "inconceivable"; and redeploying U.S. forces from the I Corps zone was unconscionable. His staff, Westmoreland noted, had already "come up with practical means of restoring order with minimum wounds" and was currently trying to bring representatives from both sides together.[28]

On 21 May Westmoreland flew to Chu Lai, where he advised General Walt to "start using our influence behind the scene in order to try and break off any ARVN . . . from the Struggle Group" and to take over the dissident-held Da Nang East ammunition depot "by negotiations rather than military action if possible."[29] The next day he met with his personnel and logistical staff officers and the head of the U.S. Naval Advisory Group to discuss taking control of all South Vietnamese logistical operations in the northern zone in order to deny supplies to the dissidents, a step which General Vien subsequently approved enthusiastically.

General Walt in the meantime opened negotiations with the rebel forces at the Da Nang East ammunition depot and, on 23 May, gained approval for a combined American–South Vietnamese operation of it. Two days later he started

---

[26] Msg, Wheeler JCS 2480 to Westmoreland, 21 May 66, History file 6–D3, Westmoreland Papers, HRB, CMH.

[27] Msg, Westmoreland MAC 4070 to Wheeler, 22 May 66, History file 6–D5, Westmoreland Papers, HRB, CMH.

[28] Quoted words from Msg, Westmoreland MAC 4081 to Wheeler, 22 May 66, History file 6–D7. See also MFR, Westmoreland, 22 May 66, sub: Telephone Conversation With Mr. Habib, History file 6–D8. Both in Westmoreland Papers, HRB, CMH.

[29] Notes of 21 May 1966, History file 6–D, Westmoreland Papers, HRB, CMH.

rationing fuel to the South Vietnamese 1st Division, and a day after that his marines began a series of combined operations with units of the division in an effort to pull its attention away from the center of the rebellion at Hue.

Back at Da Nang, Westmoreland's optimism was soon justified. On 21 May the dissidents in the Tan Linh pagoda, including Colonel Yeu, surrendered and two days later the remaining hold-outs capitulated. While Colonel Loan's police arrested the mayor of Da Nang, planes of the South Vietnamese Air Force dispersed a dissident battalion marching on the city from Hue. By the twenty-fourth Da Nang was under complete government control. According to rough U.S. estimates, casualties for both sides included 150 South Vietnamese dead and 700 wounded, and another 23 American soldiers wounded.

During the same period Westmoreland, Walt, and their representatives conducted a series of formal and informal talks with the major South Vietnamese military leaders: Ky, Thieu, Co, Vien, Cao, Thi, and Dinh. The Americans tried to win over Thi and Dinh by blaming the Struggle Movement on Buddhist extremists, especially Tri Quang, and intimating that both generals would receive important posts upon their return to the fold. To General Thieu, Westmoreland underlined the importance of American public opinion in future decisions to deploy more U.S. troops to South Vietnam and the danger of Americans "receiving the impression of serious disunity." Thieu welcomed the American initiative and complained that Westmoreland's previous policy of noninvolvement had only encouraged the Struggle Movement.[30]

On 27 May and 1 June General Walt sponsored formal meetings at Chu Lai between members of the opposing military factions. The American mediators emphasized their support for the existing Saigon government and guaranteed the safety of the dissident generals should they accept offers of amnesty. Continued government control of Da Nang and the announcement of an agreement between the Directory and the Buddhist Institute reinforced the government's position. Cao finally agreed to return to Saigon, and although Thi and Dinh elected to remain in the northern zone, they indicated their willingness to cooperate. When the chief of Thua Thien Province (who was also mayor of Hue) also threw his lot in with the government, only Nhuan and his 1st Division remained to be persuaded.

The Directory already had a plan to bring Nhuan and his division into line. General Vien estimated that two of the division's three regiments would remain neutral, but he expected trouble from a few division headquarters elements and the third regiment commanded by a nephew of Thi. Vien intended to send the potentially difficult regiment north to Quang Tri Province for combined operations with U.S. Marine Corps units. Should Nhuan refuse to cooperate, the Directory would dismiss him. Government troops would blockade the remaining rebel forces at Hue and offer them amnesty. Force was to be used only as a last resort.

---

[30] Quoted words from MFR, Westmoreland, 23 May 66, sub: Call on General Thieu, Chairman, Military Directorate, at 1700 hours, 22 May 1966, History file 6–D9. See also MFR, Westmoreland, 26 May 66, sub: Guidance for General Walt, 26 May 1966, History file 6–D22. Both in Westmoreland Papers, HRB, CMH.

Buddhist Demonstrations Spread to Saigon

The Directory's plan had yet to be put into effect when the activities of the Struggle Movement took a decidedly anti-American turn. During riots in which a number of South Vietnamese soldiers participated, demonstrators burned the U.S. Information Agency's library in Hue on 26 May and, six days later, sacked the U.S. consulate there. American observers blamed the acts on the Buddhist leader, Tri Quang. A few days later the Saigon government's understanding with the more moderate Buddhist Institute broke down, and Buddhist clergy once again were aligned against the regime. Lodge predicted that the episode was now entering its "fanatic if not actually macabre stage" and cited the "plentiful supply of Buddhists—mystics and mental defectives—ready to burn themselves and men ruthless enough to use them."[31] Communist professionals were using the Buddhists, he maintained, and the evidence was everywhere.

Alarmed by the increasing violence in Hue, the new commander of the I Corps decided on direct military action. On 1 June General Lam proposed sending contingents of the 1st Division's most loyal regiment, supported by armor attached to the division, into Hue from the north to occupy the city while airborne and armored forces from Da Nang moved up from the south as a reserve. Should General Nhuan decline to command the operation, Lam intended to place the deputy commander of the 2d Division, Col. Nguyen Van Toan, in

---

[31] Msg, Lodge SGN 5178 to President, 1 Jun 66, Bunker Papers, DS.

142

charge. The plan, however, proved premature. Nhuan not only refused to cooperate but also secretly drove to Hue and warned Tri Quang of the impending assault. With surprise and the possibility of conducting the operation without major fighting lost, Lam canceled it.

On 7 June, as turmoil in Hue continued, Buddhist priests placed altars as roadblocks on the main thoroughfares of Hue, Da Nang, Quang Tri, and Qui Nhon, and military and civilian traffic ground to a halt. When local troops refused to remove the altars, the Directory decided to use government forces. Starting on 10 June, Ky began a steady buildup of special riot police under Colonel Loan on the outskirts of Hue and, on the fifteenth, sent a task force of two airborne and two marine battalions under Colonel Truong into the city for a final showdown.

Intermittent fighting lasted in Hue for four days. Opposition was disorganized and consisted of about a thousand 1st Division troops, mostly soldiers from support units. Protected by Truong's forces, Loan's police removed the Buddhist altars and arrested most of the remaining leaders of the Struggle Movement, including Tri Quang. The Directory gave Truong command of the 1st Division, and by the end of June both the division and Hue were under firm government control. On 23 June government troops and police swept through the Buddhist Institute in Saigon, eliminating the last stronghold of the Buddhist leaders, and on 9 July a special tribunal retired Thi, Dinh, Cao, Nhuan, and Chuan.[32]

The revolt in the I Corps was finally over. Aside from a comparatively slight reduction in military operations, the crisis had little effect on the battlefield. Although surprised by the turmoil, the Viet Cong failed to take advantage of it. The Thieu-Ky regime successfully tested its power against the Buddhists and a popular corps commander and, as a consequence, seemed to increase its political standing. While the government agreed to hold elections for a constituent assembly, it successfully resisted demands to have the projected assembly replace the Ky government. On the other hand, several good commanders—notably Thi and Chuan—were gone, and the chief virtue of Lam, the new I Corps commander, was his loyalty to the current Saigon regime. The crisis also marked the last stand of the Buddhists as an intermediate political force, leaving the Vietnamese people little choice between the Saigon generals on one end of the political spectrum and the Viet Cong on the other.

The influence of the American advisers during the revolt is difficult to assess. Although the Vietnamese participants often sought U.S. support for their actions, they did not necessarily adhere to American advice or plans. The Americans wanted the crisis ended as soon as possible, but were in no position to dictate solutions. In many cases the pessimistic American analyses failed to stand up. The disintegration of the army through Buddhist subversion predicted by Freund and Zorthian never occurred, and the great influence that Ambassador Lodge attributed to the Communists in the drama remained unproven. West-

---

[32] A four-day trial of twenty-six leaders of the rebellion ended on 22 December 1967. Nguyen Van Man, the ex-mayor of Da Nang, and Colonel Yeu were sentenced to ten years of hard labor, two others received ten-year prison terms, and the remaining twenty-two were acquitted. See Msg, Bunker SGN 14556 to President, 281200 Dec 67, Bunker Papers, DS.

moreland's concern with left-wing student activists and his recommendation to close down the University of Hue and draft the student body also failed to address the larger issues raised by the episode.[33] Nevertheless, the U.S. commander's policy of limiting American involvement and his insistence that the Vietnamese generals work out their own solutions helped produce an end to the crisis without any major political or military upheaval.

[33] MFR, Jones, 20 Jun 66, sub: MACV Commanders Conference, 5 June 1966, History file 7–B1, Westmoreland Papers, HRB, CMH.

8

The Reform Effort

During 1966 the U.S. troop buildup changed the basic nature of the war. From 184,000 troops at the end of 1965, the American military presence in South Vietnam swelled to over 385,000, with more arriving every day. New combat units included a second Marine Corps division for the northern zone, the 4th Infantry Division in the II Corps Highlands, and the 25th Infantry Division north of Saigon, as well as a second South Korean division. To support this force, the Americans constructed fifty-nine new airfields and shipped over 600,000 tons of supplies to South Vietnam each month. North Vietnam responded by moving an estimated 58,000 men into the South, which, according to rough MACV estimates, increased the combined Viet Cong and North Vietnamese Army troop strength to over 282,000.[1]

As American military commanders sought to wear down this growing enemy force through a conventional "big unit" war of attrition, MACV became a true operational command, directing American air, sea, and ground forces in South Vietnam, and its staff advisory effort quickly became a secondary endeavor. The U.S. Pacific Command in Hawaii continued to control the bombing campaigns in North Vietnam and Laos but had little influence over U.S. ground operations in South Vietnam, the new heart of the American war effort. In the field the less visible and widely dispersed advisory effort also diminished in importance, and its activities became minor adjuncts to the operations of the larger American ground combat units in almost every locale.

The U.S. troop deployments ought to have given the South Vietnamese armed forces the respite that it needed to reform and repair the damages of 1964–65. Saigon's many military problems were now well known to American leaders in Saigon and Washington. From MACV headquarters General Westmoreland continued to initiate, encourage, and monitor improvements through his weekly meetings with General Vien, chief of the Vietnamese staff, and, less directly, through his senior field advisers in each corps zone. The Department of Defense, the Joint Chiefs of Staff, the Department of the Army, and the Pacific Command monitored Westmoreland's efforts through regular reports, summaries, and briefings. In the field General Heintges remained the MACV com-

[1] Pacific Command, *Report on the War in Vietnam*, p. 114.

mander's liaison to the senior American advisers, assisted by General Collins and his successor in May 1966, General Freund. Prior to becoming involved in the I Corps revolt, Freund had mediated a series of disputes between Vietnamese and Montagnard leaders, earning the reputation of being able to work closely with the Vietnamese generals. Although he also became the MACV training director later in the year, Freund generally operated alone, engaging in frequent informal contacts with South Vietnamese generals and keeping Westmoreland well informed of their views and personal activities.[2] The MACV staff advisory effort thus remained fragmented between the various staff sections, and coordination between the MACV staff advisers and those in the field remained minimal.

Organizing for Success

Throughout 1966 MACV reviewed the size and organization of the South Vietnamese armed forces almost continuously.[3] Believing that a larger and more balanced army would produce better combat results, Westmoreland wanted to continue the expansion program that he had begun in 1965. During the first half of the year he expected the Joint General Staff to deploy the 10 newly organized maneuver battalions (all infantry) currently in training and to form 10 additional units (8 infantry and 2 armored); during the last half he wanted 4 more infantry battalions activated, thus completing the 1964 expansion program (giving each infantry regiment 4 battalions). Added to the original buildup was the new regiment for the II Corps zone (giving the 23d Infantry Division 3 regiments), the sixth battalion for the marines, the seventh and eighth battalions for the airborne force, and the ninth and tenth armored cavalry squadrons, all to be activated sometime in 1966. He also approved the organization of 5 ranger group headquarters to improve the command and administrative support of the often neglected ranger battalions. The entire expansion would stabilize the South Vietnamese force structure at 10 twelve-battalion infantry divisions; 2 four-battalion separate regiments; 8 airborne, 6 marine, and 20 ranger battalions; 26 artillery battalions; and 10 armored cavalry squadrons. Future force increases, primarily limited to combat support and combat service support units, included engineer, military police, medical, and transportation units, and 9 prisoner-of-war detachments. The only new combat units authorized by MACV after 1966 were 10 mortar platoons.[4]

[2] See Westmoreland's comments in *Soldier Reports*, pp. 75–81. Freund headed the MACV Training Directorate in early 1965 and thereafter served as assistant director to the Joint U.S. Public Affairs Office in Saigon. See also Freund Interv, 25–26 May 72, SEAB, CMH.
[3] Unless otherwise stated, treatment of organization and administration, manpower, training, and logistics (to include relevant statistics) in this chapter is based on Rpt, MACJ341, 27 Apr 67, sub: Analysis of Republic of Vietnam Armed Forces (RVNAF) for CY 1966, SEAB, CMH; USMACV, "Command History, 1966," pp. 100–22 and 451–93, HRB, CMH; Special Studies Group, Office of the Chief of Staff of the Army, "Programs To Improve ARVN (PIARV)" (hereafter cited as PIARV Study), December 1966, Document no. ASDIRS 2589, Pentagon Library.
[4] In January the regular ground forces consisted of 139 combat maneuver battalions (infantry and armored units) and 26 similar-size artillery units. In addition, each corps had at least one unauthorized "palace guard" infantry battalion and Saigon several more.

Regional Forces Company in Formation

Westmoreland was even more eager to see the strength increases approved for the Territorial Forces realized early in 1966. These units were needed to provide security of those areas that he expected American troops to clear during the next two years. Regional Forces strength was to rise from 134,999 to 155,322 and the number of rifle companies from 767 to 888 during 1966 and 1967, with personnel for 40 of the new companies coming from deactivated CIDG units. Similarly, if losses could be held down, Popular Forces strength was to reach 200,000 as soon as possible. As in 1965, Westmoreland felt that the Joint General Staff could easily and cheaply expand the territorials because they required little training and drew from a much broader pool of manpower. With all these additions, the total South Vietnamese armed forces strength would thus rise to 631,457 by mid-1966 and 680,578 by mid-1967 (*see Table 10*).

Almost immediately, however, Westmoreland was again forced to reconsider the continued expansion. The problem was still the vital line infantry battalions. A recent MACV study showed that, while the assigned strength of these units averaged 85 percent of authorized strength, only 62 percent were being mustered for operations. South Vietnamese unit strength reports were hazy and included deserters, casualties, and soldiers in all types of ad hoc units, from bodyguard squads to unit recruiting teams. Unable to persuade the Joint General Staff to remedy the problem, Westmoreland took direct action. On 24 March 1966 he

TABLE 10—SOUTH VIETNAMESE ARMED FORCES EXPANSION PLAN

Component	Planned		Freeze	Revised
	FY 1966	FY 1967	Mid-1966	FY 1967
Regulars [a]	311,458	325,256	315,660	322,072
Regional Forces	134,999	155,322	141,731	152,560
Popular Forces	185,000	200,000	176,254	147,440
Total	631,457	680,578	633,645	622,072

[a] Army, navy, air force, and marines.

Sources: Fact Sheet, MACV J-3, 8 Oct 66, sub: RVNAF Force Structure Plan for FY 67, MICRO 2/2419, RG 334, WNRC; USMACV, "Command History, 1966," pp. 100–101, HRB, CMH.

ordered his field advisers to monitor South Vietnamese authorized, assigned, present-for-duty, and present-for-operations strength and to report the number, type, and composition of all unauthorized units. In May he postponed activating 7 of the new infantry battalions until September and in June extended the delay until the end of the year. He also refused to approve the activation of any of the new infantry battalions until the existing ones had reached a strength of at least 450 men. These measures, he hoped, would force the Joint General Staff to funnel recruits into understrength units. However, he did not apply these strictures to the general reserve battalions or the armored units, which were activated on schedule, or to the ranger group headquarters, three of which were operating by the end of the year.[5]

By June 1966 the situation was worse. High desertion rates and recruiting shortfalls in the territorial components finally led Westmoreland to freeze the authorized force structure at 633,645 and to make drastic reductions in his projected increases. During the course of the year he trimmed the proposed strength of the Popular Forces from 200,000 to 147,440; that of the Regional Forces from 155,322 to 152,560; and that of the regulars from 325,256 to 322,072.[6] However, he regarded these measures as temporary, believed the continued expansion vital, and planned to resume it as soon as Saigon's manpower problems could be solved.

Despite these measures Westmoreland found it difficult to hold the line on the growth of Saigon's military force structure, that is, the *number* of units in the armed forces. It always seemed easier to solve South Vietnam's military organizational problems by adding to, rather than reducing, its various components. Field advisers, for example, indicated that almost all regimental commanders kept company-size elements directly under their personal control for security,

[5] For discussion, see Notes of 8 May 66, History file 6–C; Notes of 11 May 66, History file 6–C; Notes of 27 Jun 66, History file 7–D; and MFR, Jones, 17 Aug 66, sub: MACV Commanders Conference, 24 July 1966, History file 8–B1. All in Westmoreland Papers, HRB, CMH.

[6] Fact Sheet, MACJ-3, 8 Oct 66, sub: RVNAF Force Structure Plan for FY 67, MICRO 2/2419, RG 334, WNRC; USMACV, "Command History, 1966," pp. 100–101. The size of the South Vietnamese Women's Armed Forces Corps rose from 1,436 to 2,203 in 1966 and to about 4,000 in fiscal year 1967. Thereafter a South Vietnamese law limited its growth to 1 percent of the regular forces, reflecting a traditional bias against the use of women in the military. See USMACV, "Command History, 1972–1973," 1:C–23, HRB, CMH.

reconnaissance, and garrison duties, and to act as a combat reserve. Because these units generally were effective in the field, Westmoreland felt that it was best to sanction their existence by authorizing a reconnaissance company for each regiment. The MACV commander hoped his approving additional person- nel for these units would prevent them from draining soldiers from the infantry battalions. Temporarily, spaces for the new units were to come from forces pro- grammed for activation in 1967.

Increased American demands for tactical intelligence led Westmoreland to approve increases in the South Vietnamese military intelligence service, allowing the Joint General Staff to deploy ten military intelligence detachments to support U.S. and allied combat units. Additional personnel raised the strength of the Vietnamese intelligence staff section from 124 to 220 and provided personnel for four new U.S.–South Vietnamese intelligence centers (Combined Intelligence Center, Vietnam; Combined Military Interrogation Center; Combined Document Exploitation Center, and Combined Materiel Exploitation Center). However, ac- tual Vietnamese strength at the centers remained low because of the lack of trained personnel.

Westmoreland gave less emphasis to Saigon's political warfare corps. Headed by General Cao, the sometime commander of the I Corps, and later by General Nguyen Bao Tri, the close friend of Premier Ky, the General Political Warfare Department was a potentially powerful organization, and the Directory generals still regarded it with suspicion. In October Ky approved a political cadre system down to the company level throughout the armed forces, modeled after the Nationalist Chinese system; however, without personnel and funds, the pro- jected organization remained dormant. The new Political Warfare College still occupied temporary quarters at Thu Duc, training its academic staff, while politi- cal warfare instructors offered short courses to several hundred officers and noncommissioned officers in each zone. A shortage of qualified U.S. psychologi- cal operations advisers and differences in doctrine continued to limit American participation in the effort.[7]

Westmoreland's expansion plans did little to alter the structure and doctrine of the South Vietnamese armed forces. Despite years of advice and training for counterinsurgency, their basic organization remained conventional. In Washing- ton Robert W. Komer, one of President Johnson's new special assistants, voiced his concern, pointing out that the expansion was inflationary and increased the competition for Saigon's slim manpower resources. He concluded "that our mili- tary, having gotten moving first and being better forward planners to boot, have outdistanced the civil side of the bidding up [for] available manpower." As a remedy, Komer recommended "a more rational dividing of the pie" between Saigon's military and civilian organizations and "a freeze on further Vietnam military manpower support authorizations until an overall manpower review can

---

[7] See Fact Sheet, MACPD, 20 Jan 67, sub: RVNAF Political Indoctrination Program, MICRO 75/1710; Ltr, Westmoreland to Vien, 30 Jan 67, MICRO 75/1728. Both in RG 334, WNRC. See also Bullard, "Political Cadre Systems in the Military," pp. 20–23. U.S. Army doctrine did not consider propa- ganda directed at friendly troops a psychological operations function.

be completed." But officials in Washington hesitated to take action, and John McNaughton, Komer's superior, curtly informed him that "security require-ments" based on current campaign plans determined the South Vietnamese force structure and that Lodge's Mission Council, and not Washington, was responsible for manpower priorities.[8]

Lodge, however, was also concerned about the continued expansion. Citing the poor showing of South Vietnamese troops on the battlefield and their impor-tant role in pacification, he suggested that perhaps MACV was making a mistake in trying to increase their conventional combat forces as quickly as possible. But Westmoreland immediately took exception to what he felt was now an old accu-sation, explaining that "it takes a conventionally organized military force to fight VC main forces as well as guerrillas." The basic problem of fighting an uncon-ventional war, he maintained, was "not a matter of organization, but a matter of tactics which differ depending upon the mission or task." A battalion, for exam-ple, might fight as a unit against conventional enemy forces or break down into smaller patrols to track down guerrillas. Westmoreland believed that Lodge lacked "a deep feel of military tactics and strategy," and felt that top U.S. civilian officials like the ambassador were "inclined to over-simplify the military situa-tion and to deal with it on a simple formula basis." Obviously troubled, the MACV commander commissioned his historical section to refute Lodge's criti-cisms in detail.[9]

The misgivings of Komer and Lodge went to the heart of the basic question of allied strategy and roles and missions. Adding more and more infantry-type battalions and territorial companies and platoons only increased the tendency of the South Vietnamese armed forces to resemble a large decentralized police force, able to maintain law and order but unable to fight conventional battles or institute the economic and social reforms needed to win the support of the people. On the other hand, what was the point of having a large conventional military organization if the Vietnamese were to conduct only battalion- and smaller-level operations? The mobile airborne and marine task forces seemed one alternative, although Westmoreland still viewed them as too expensive in terms of mobility, training, and support to serve as models for the rest of the ground forces.[10] But if current trends continued, the static corps, division, and regimental headquarters seemed superfluous. Westmoreland's own desire to expand the territorials underlined the point. Again, organizational questions stemmed primarily from the confusion over roles and missions. Perhaps West-moreland was on the right track in seeking to stabilize the South Vietnamese regulars and increase the territorials as quickly as possible. But other factors always seemed to thwart his intentions.

---

[8] First quotation from Memo, Komer to McNaughton, 30 Apr 66, sub: Increases in ARVN Force Structure. Second quotation from Memo, McNaughton to Komer (undated). Both in SEAB, CMH.

[9] Quoted words from Notes of 2 Dec 66, History file 11–D. See also MACV Historical Study, circa 1966, History file 11–D6. Both in Westmoreland Papers, HRB, CMH.

[10] See Wells Interv, 25 Mar 75, SEAB, CMH, in which Wells recalled the cost arguments that MACV used to oppose further expansion of the general reserve units.

Managing Saigon's Manpower

In the eyes of MACV one of the most serious problems of Saigon's armed forces was a chronic shortage of manpower, caused partially by a continuously high rate of desertion. Perceiving the primary culprit as poor leadership, MACV also viewed the matter as an administrative problem easily corrected by better management. Westmoreland's subordinates thus tended to treat the various aspects of the manpower problem in isolation, monitoring them closely through detailed statistical reports from the field and expressing Vietnamese shortcomings in easily understood mathematical terms. The simplicity and objectivity of the data was compelling—so difficult to ignore and yet, in appearance, so susceptible to correction.

Westmoreland made solving Saigon's manpower problems one of MACV's primary advisory tasks throughout 1966. The MACV commander knew that he would also have to redouble his personal efforts in this area if his expansion plans were to succeed. As a first step, he recommended that Saigon not only lower the age of conscription to eighteen in 1966 but also, in order to sustain the armed forces the following year, greatly expand the draft and lengthen the service obligation. Although curtailing desertions was critical, he felt that these administrative measures were also necessary and hoped that Saigon would incorporate them all into a general mobilization package. However, both Westmoreland and Ambassador Lodge pursued the matter only halfheartedly throughout the year and accomplished little. Efforts of the MACV staff to encourage greater use of veterans in paramilitary units, to reduce medical standards for recruits, and to trim deferments also had little success.[11] Concerned with political stability, both the MACV commander and the ambassador remained reluctant to force unpopular measures on the Saigon government. In their view a more pleasant solution appeared to be success in the pacification campaign, which would expand government control and increase Saigon's recruiting base. As for the high desertion rates, MACV often rationalized that deserters returned to the pool of available manpower and could be picked up again at some future time. The most significant advance in 1966 was in the mechanics of recruitment, when, responding to American advice, the Joint General Staff began to replace unit recruiting with a corps- and province-run system.

The real problem was not in finding soldiers but in keeping them. During the first six months of 1966 the monthly desertion rate (desertions per 1,000 troops assigned) of the regulars leapt from the already high 1965 average of 14.2 to over 21.5, signifying a loss of 7,000–8,000 men each month. The Popular Forces had an even higher desertion rate of 27.0, an average that was more than double that of the Regional Forces rate of 12.3 (*see Table 11*). The armed forces of South Vietnam had become a giant sieve, and expanding the size of the military only seemed to increase the size of the holes.[12]

[11] For details, see Rpt, MACV, circa 1967 (?), sub: Manpower Mobilization, MICRO 3/2762, RG 334, WNRC.
[12] Rpt, MACJ–341, 27 Apr 67, sub: Analysis of Republic of Vietnam Armed Forces (RVNAF) for CY 1966, p. 111, SEAB, CMH. See Table 3 of this volume for statistics for the years 1962–65.

TABLE 11—SOUTH VIETNAMESE ARMED FORCES DESERTIONS,[a] 1966

Month	Regulars		Regional Forces		Popular Forces	
	Number	Rate	Number	Rate	Number	Rate
January	5,790	18.8	1,086	8.2	2,375	17.4
February	7,951	25.7	1,859	13.8	4,300	31.9
March	7,529	23.9	1,119	8.2	4,628	34.3
April	6,439	20.5	2,086	15.3	4,376	32.2
May	7,169	23.1	2,554	18.5	2,965	21.6
June	5,723	17.0	1,466	10.4	3,553	25.9
July	4,882	15.4	1,006	7.1	3,333	24.0
August	4,133	12.9	887	6.2	3,220	23.1
September	3,541	11.0	635	4.4	1,915	13.6
October	3,440	10.8	674	4.5	1,848	12.7
November	3,638	11.3	997	6.7	2,341	15.7
December	3,529	10.9	1,105	7.4	2,364	15.4

[a] Number and rate per 1,000 assigned strength by component.

Source: Rpt, MACJ–341, 27 Apr 67, sub: Analysis of Republic of Vietnam Armed Forces (RVNAF) for CY 1966, p. 111, SEAB, CMH.

To staunch the loss of men through desertions, Westmoreland examined several options. He considered halting the South Vietnamese military expansion to stabilize the force structure, having Saigon increase the number of military recruits, and working with the Joint General Staff to plug up the holes. Because of his control over the South Vietnamese defense budget and military force structure, Westmoreland had the power to retard or accelerate the growth of Saigon's military establishment. On the other hand, he continued to feel that administrative reforms and improvements in leadership and morale were the best ways to lower desertions. Consequently, the MACV commander used a combination of all three remedies during the year.

The South Vietnamese usually treated deserters leniently and returned them to their units without formal punishment. After constant urgings by Westmoreland, the Joint General Staff finally changed this policy in April 1966 and approved stiff penalties for desertion. The minimum punishment was five years of hard labor, with greater penalties for repeated offenders and those deserting during combat. Convicted deserters were to serve their sentences as "battlefield laborers" attached to regular units, receiving no pay and performing unskilled construction work and other odd jobs. By making these measures effective as of 1 October, Saigon provided a grace period to allow deserters to voluntarily turn themselves in. A decree in August also granted amnesty to individuals who had deserted from one component of the armed services in order to join another. Using area dragnets and checkpoints, Saigon also initiated a series of drives by military and civilian police in urban areas to apprehend deserters prior to the October deadline, while MACV required all American military agencies to screen their Vietnamese civilian workers for deserters, and Westmoreland urged the embassy to compel other U.S. agencies to take similar action. He also persuaded Defense Minister Co to delegate court-martial authority down to the division commanders to speed up the administration of military justice.[13]

[13] Notes of 28 Sep 66, History file 9–B, Westmoreland Papers; USMACV, "Command History, 1966," pp. 103–05. Both in HRB, CMH.

Saigon's new punitive policy led to a steady rise in the number of deserters apprehended. In one ten-day period in October, for example, a large-scale police operation netted 7,495 deserters, many of whom had surrendered voluntarily. Yet MACV could hardly have been pleased with the final results. Between 1 October and 31 December 1966 the government tried only some 1,383 individuals for desertion and related crimes, convicting and sentencing 1,243 to battlefield labor groups.[14] What had happened to the over 6,000 others caught back in October, or the 7,000 or so that MACV statistical reports claimed were deserting every month, was not explained.

In addition to its new punitive policy, Saigon began taking more steps to prevent desertions, including a wide range of personnel reforms to improve morale and leadership. After preliminary discussions between Westmoreland and Vien in April and May 1966, the MACV staff formulated a series of reforms for consideration by the South Vietnamese high command. Most of the measures were personnel management policies and procedures previously recommended but ignored. They included the posting and promotion of officers and noncommissioned officers on merit; command emphasis on the training, discipline, and health, welfare and morale of the individual soldier; regular officer evaluation reports; and centralized control of assignments, promotions, dismissals, retirements, schooling, and transfers. MACV also recommended that Saigon stress small-unit leaders training and general leadership courses and establish a court-martial and nonjudicial punishment system down to the battalion level.[15] Finally, the staff suggested handling individual complaints by expanding the Vietnamese inspector general's office to the field units.

In response, the Joint General Staff established a special leadership committee to consider these suggestions. However, despite Westmoreland's continued encouragement, progress was negligible.[16] The Vietnamese agreed in principle to several measures, including the development of a career management program that promised assignments based on merit and rotation of assignments between command, staff, and school posts similar to that practiced by the U.S. Army, but did little. They also endorsed the idea of annual officer efficiency reports, centralizing the management of officer and noncommissioned officer promotions, and having the training command select staff school students rather than giving student quotas to individual commands. But given the system of patronage in the officer corps, MACV's recommendations not surprisingly went nowhere. Just about the only achievement of the committee in 1966 was the publication of a pocket-size small-unit leaders guide, the impact of which is difficult to measure. Both Westmoreland and Vien were wary of usurping the existing prerogatives of the corps and division commanders, and considered the Thieu-Ky regime still too weak to make sweeping changes in practices and policies traditionally left to the Vietnamese senior commander in the field.

[14] Rpt, MACJ–341, 27 Apr 67, sub: Analysis of Republic of Vietnam Armed Forces (RVNAF) for CY 1966, pp. 111–12, SEAB, CMH.
[15] At the time only corps commanders could convene courts-martial for enlisted men and only the Joint General Staff for officers.
[16] For example, Notes of 25 Jul 66, History file 8–B; Notes of 22 Dec 66, History file 12–A. Both in Westmoreland Papers, HRB, CMH.

Surprisingly, however, Saigon made some progress in lower-level promotions and appointments. Temporarily waving the officer educational requirements, the Joint General Staff pushed some 1,700 noncommissioned officers through a special officer candidate course at Thu Duc and commissioned them as aspirants, and also approved direct commissions to about 500 senior noncommissioned officers, mostly regular army personnel. A similar program to expand the non-commissioned officer ranks reduced the educational requirements and made enlisted men with the equivalent of a sixth-grade education eligible. Another program awarding direct commissions based on battlefield performance fared poorer and produced only 16 new officers. The Joint General Staff also limited special promotions to officers performing well in command positions to 12.5 percent of the annual promotions, and applied the provision to only 365 officers during 1966. Although Vien's staff was more generous in awarding battlefield promotions, approving 3,553 out of 7,867 allocated in the first half of 1966, only 159 went to officers. Most officer promotions still depended on unit quotas; fixed time-in-grade criteria; and, equally or more important, the support of influential superiors. The higher the rank, the more important political considerations became. American analysts described the promotion system in the upper military echelons as "erratic, inequitable, [and] often made without regard to ability or merit." However, American analysts had no real way of judging the merits of the system and the officer appointment effort was encouraging.[17]

Efforts to improve leadership in the upper military echelons met with little success. American advisers had a clearer idea of what was needed here; however, paradoxically, their influence was, if anything, less. Reports of high-level corruption in the South Vietnamese military reached Westmoreland regularly, but he was often unable to evaluate them and suspected that many were politically motivated "character assassinations." He was reluctant to use his advisers as "spies," believing such a practice would irreparably damage their existing influence, but was willing to pass any evidence of corruption to "the top and then let Thieu and Ky deal with it as they see fit." Yet when General Vien's leadership committee suggested bringing charges against Defense Minister Co, General Quang of the IV Corps, and Admiral Chung Tan Cang, commander of the South Vietnamese Navy, Westmoreland, after consulting with the U.S. Embassy, urged the committee to "do nothing to rock the boat." Until the planned constituent assembly had convened to sort out the political problems, unity and stability in the armed forces was paramount. The dismissal of either Co or Quang, coming on the heels of the Thi affair, looked too risky. In the case of Cang, Westmoreland believed that the allegations of corruption were true, but U.S. naval advisers could recommend no suitable replacement. Like Westmoreland, Thieu was reluctant to move against high-level corruption until the assembly had produced a new constitution, elections were held, and a new government was installed. That Quang was an able general, and a personal friend and principal supporter of Thieu, was another consideration. In the mean-

---

[17] Quoted words from PIARV Study, December 1966, unpaginated, Document no. ASDIRS 2589, Pentagon Library. See also Draft Rpt, SACSA, JCS, circa 1967, sub: Assessment of the Republic of Vietnam Armed Forces (RVNAF). Both in SEAB, CMH.

time, younger South Vietnamese officers would have to look elsewhere for professional inspiration.[18]

American advisers also sponsored several administrative reforms designed to produce a more accurate picture of South Vietnam's true military strength. At MACV urging, the army adopted a computerized "by name" strength accounting system on 1 January 1966. This proved a major administrative undertaking, and American advisers at all levels spent much time during the year seeing that the information was accurately recorded, posted, and updated. In one division, for example, the American personnel adviser spent several months putting the unit's personnel records into order, eliminating in the process some two thousand soldiers from the unit roles of whom he could find no trace.[19] With such data, MACV felt that it could piece together a more comprehensive picture of South Vietnamese military strength, making it possible to correlate data on rank, age, service longevity, training, pay, and marital status.

Other administrative reforms recommended by American advisers included creating a personnel records folder for each soldier, requisitioning replacements by grade and skill, completing a military identification card system, using aptitude tests for training and assignment selection, adopting U.S. military procedures for casualty reporting, and switching from a decimal to a functional-file system similar to that used by the U.S. Army. Westmoreland felt that these seemingly routine measures were necessary to ensure the Joint General Staff's ability to properly administer its combat forces. The adoption of most of these recommendations, however, was put off until the following year. Again, a sense of immediacy was lacking. The only signs of progress in the field of personnel management during 1966 were increased enrollments in the adjutant general school, the great proliferation of forms and regulations, and the rising number of awards and decorations granted. But even this last measurement raised questions in Washington. The U.S. Army Staff contended that a disproportionate number of awards for valor went to officers, including many "staff favorites who played little part in [combat] engagements or were absent altogether," and that the recipients often had to purchase their own medals and ribbons.[20]

Saigon made little headway improving the living conditions of the average soldier. Low pay scales, an inadequate commissary, and poor dependent housing made it difficult for the average family-oriented Vietnamese serviceman to get by and fostered moonlighting, corruption, theft, and desertion in all branches and ranks. Although Saigon brought Popular Forces salaries up to the level of the other military components, Westmoreland felt that money was not the answer. Pay raises only increased the South Vietnamese budget deficit and, through inflation, decreased the value of the piaster, further depressing the soldier's earning power. Vietnamese soldiers were competing among each other and with the general population for a limited number of goods and services. Larger pay-

---

[18] First quotation from MFR, Westmoreland, 6 Oct 66, sub: Visit With Prime Minister Ky, 5 October 1966, History file 9–C2. Second quotation from Notes of 3 Dec 66, History file 11–D. Third quotation from Notes of 22 Aug 66, History file 8–D. See also Msg, Lodge SGN 6836 to SecState, 120024 Sep 66, History file 9–4A. All in Westmoreland Papers, HRB, CMH.

[19] Interv, author with Lt Col Lawrence W. Hoffman (hereafter cited as Hoffman Interv), Battalion, S1/S4, and S2/S3 Adviser, Airborne Division (January–December 1966), 25 Mar 75, SEAB, CMH.

[20] PIARV Study, December 1966, unpaginated, Document no. ASDIRS 2589, Pentagon Library.

checks only upped the bidding. Instead, Westmoreland considered direct American support to improve the lot of the South Vietnamese soldier and investigated the possibilities of giving USAID foodstuffs to Vietnamese military dependents or providing direct monetary support for their shaky post exchange–commissary system. The South Vietnamese Ministry of Economy was lukewarm, fearing a loss of tax revenues, and when the Pacific Command pointed out the need for special congressional approval, MACV tabled the project until this last issue could be resolved in Washington.

Saigon's failure to accomplish any significant improvements in this area by the end of the year upset Westmoreland. He put the blame on "inadequate management, insufficient allocation of commodities by the [South Vietnamese] Minister of Economy, the general economics of the country, and the lack of concerted effort by the [South Vietnamese] service commanders and staff to develop a system adequate to the requirement." Noting that direct subsidies were alleged to be illegal, he hoped at least to have the U.S. Army and Air Force Exchange Service support the South Vietnamese military post exchange–commissary system on a simple cost basis by 1967.[21]

Westmoreland also tried to breathe new life into Saigon's moribund dependent housing program. Of the standing 1965 requirement for about 200,000 family units for the regular forces, the Joint General Staff planned to have roughly 50,000–60,000 by the end of 1966, but, due to rising costs in other areas, had budgeted for only 3,000 more for 1967. To accelerate the construction rate, Westmoreland asked permission to use MAP funds to support an experimental self-help shelter construction program in the III Corps Tactical Zone. Using building materials supplied by the United States, local Vietnamese troops would perform the construction. Monitored by American field advisers, the program promised to bypass Saigon's bureaucracy and harness the enthusiasm of the benefactors. But Westmoreland's superiors attached no urgency to the proposal. After a review by the Pacific Command, the Joint Chiefs of Staff, the Army Staff, and the Department of Defense, Defense Secretary McNamara approved a portion of the proposal on 19 December 1966, specifying some 9,130 "trial" shelters for the South Vietnamese 5th, 18th, and 25th Infantry Divisions around Saigon. If successful, he agreed to provide funds for an additional 26,000 units in 1967 for the other seven regular divisions, the navy, and the air force.

American advisers also pushed several other programs to improve the quality of life for the South Vietnamese soldier. These included the construction of unit cantonments, improving health care, and expanding the military postal system as a means of transferring funds from soldiers to dependents. To accommodate the many new units activated in 1965 and 1966, more bases and quarters were needed. As in the dependent housing program, rising costs and competition with other construction projects, especially U.S. programs, contributed to a shortage. Lack of adequate quarters, in turn, tended to limit troop mobility by forcing them to depend more heavily on overcrowded existing bases. Lack of unit messes and a shortage of field rations had the same effect. Some improvements were made in medical and health care when General Westmoreland extended

---

[21] Notes of 29 Dec 66, History file 12–B, Westmoreland Papers, HRB, CMH.

Lunch in the Field

medical civic action programs conducted by U.S. tactical units to nearby South Vietnamese military units and dependents. But the American advisers' efforts to improve the infrequently used military postal system were unsuccessful because of the problem of illiteracy and a lack of command interest.[22] In all these areas infantry troops fared worse; however, senior Vietnamese commanders did not consider the absence of such amenities a great hardship for those soldiers serving in their native areas.

The South Vietnamese Army's reluctance to use combat and garrison rations was another unresolved problem. In 1965, after several years of research, MACV approved an adequate South Vietnamese field ration—the equivalent of the American C-ration. But Saigon refused to purchase it in sufficient quantity, and South Vietnamese troops in the field continued to take time out from operations to cook their rice or, in some cases, to live off the land by pillage and theft.[23] With a modest operational requirement of approximately 1.5 million field rations— enough to feed roughly 30 infantry battalions one hundred days annually—in 1966, the Joint General Staff either procured or contracted for only 219,000 rice and 591,000 meat components by the end of the year. Increased purchases were planned in 1967, with any deficiencies to be made up through direct U.S. military assistance. Yet even if these measures were carried out, the amount of combat

[22] See Khuyen, *The RVNAF*, p. 126.
[23] Notes of 25 Jun 66, History file 7–D, Westmoreland Papers, HRB, CMH.

TABLE 12—SOUTH VIETNAMESE ARMY MANEUVER BATTALION [a] STRENGTH, 1966

Month	Assigned		Present for Duty		Present for Operations	
	Average	Percentage of Authorized	Average	Percentage of Authorized	Average	Percentage of Authorized
January	638	100	511	80	481	75
February	596	93	492	77	462	72
March	581	91	462	72	410	64
April	572	90	460	72	423	66
May	554	87	453	71	422	66
June	547	86	456	71	422	66
Average for 6 months	581	91	472	74	437	68
July	541	85	453	71	411	64
August	532	83	449	70	416	65
September	548	86	471	74	444	69
October	598	94	508	79	477	75
November	596	93	529	83	499	78
December	604	95	548	86	517	81
Average for 6 months	570	89	493	77	461	72
Average for CY 1966	576	90	483	76	449	70

[a] Infantry, airborne, ranger, marine, and armored units.

Source: Rpt, MACJ-341, 27 Apr 67, sub: Analysis of Republic of Vietnam Armed Forces (RVNAF) for CY 1966, p. 118, SEAB, CMH. Figures in above table are approximate only.

rations available to each of the over 150 combat battalions would be minimal. The status of garrison rations—unit messes—was even more dismal. Financed through obligatory payroll deductions, the rations proved inadequate because inflation, despite compensating increases, steadily eroded buying power. In addition, pay deductions were unpopular, and most soldiers preferred to prepare their own meals. A model mess established at the quartermaster school showed what could be done, but the possibility that any tactical units would follow the example was doubtful.

Despite all this miniscule progress, some of the measures taken by the Joint General Staff to improve leadership and reduce desertions seemed to have taken root by the end of the year. At MACV the evidence was in the statistics for all to see. The operational strength of the combat battalions had risen dramatically, and the activation of new units was again feasible (*Table 12*). From a low of 31 out of 121 battalions meeting Westmoreland's 450-man operational strength goal in July 1966, 100 of 120 rated battalions met this criterion in November, and by the end of the year all components of the armed forces were within reach or had surpassed their interim strength goals. These gains reflected significantly reduced desertion rates for all components during the last six months of the year (*see Table 11*) and an upsurge of voluntary and draft enlistments. Westmoreland's staff saw these favorable trends as "indicators that the positive actions taken by RVNAF to control desertions, reduce the number of ineffectives on unit rolls and improved [*sic*] personnel management and assignment procedures have proven effective." Still no one could be certain how many of the supposed "effectives" on unit rolls were actually serving in the units and how many either were "ghost" or "ornamental" soldiers performing odd jobs, or were excused from military service altogether through bribes or other understandings with unit commanders. Westmoreland himself suspected that as many as 10 percent of the armed forces fell into these categories, and other MACV officials put the number of ghost and ornamental soldiers in the territorials alone at 60,000. Neither could the statistics tell how well the soldiers were trained, led, and supported. More information was necessary.[24]

Training

From Westmoreland's vantage point, command attention by senior South Vietnamese officers could have easily rectified many of their administrative problems. More responsible and better trained leaders were needed. But American advisers encountered considerable frustration in the realm of training. The quality of South Vietnamese junior officers and noncommissioned officers was especially poor. While potentially competent, their motivation was weak. Most cared little for their men and failed to accept responsibility or to delegate authority. Nomination for officer and noncommissioned officer training schools was based on education rather than leadership, and few candidates came from the enlisted ranks. But MACV's answer was better leadership training through improved course material and instruction. In the MACV Training Directorate American staff advisers translated instructional programs from U.S. Army branch schools and the U.S. Army Command and General Staff College for final consideration by the South Vietnamese Central Training Command. Better instructors, however, were hard to find, and the small two- and three-men advisory teams at the various schools and training centers had limited influence over student and cadre selection, or the greater problem of merit promotions.

In September 1966 Westmoreland directed General Freund to examine the officer training program of the National Military Academy at Da Lat, believing it should reflect a leadership philosophy stressing "the obligation and responsibility of the graduates to the country as opposed to self-interest." Freund's investigation was devastating. He found the existing two-year program "simply an enriched OCS [Officer Candidate School] course" and a planned four-year curriculum heavily weighted toward science and engineering but weak in leadership, social sciences, humanities, political warfare, and military science. The quality of the South Vietnamese instructors was poor, the instruction worse, and learning minimal. Students were graded on a curve so that most passed, which explained the low attrition rate of 3–4 percent. According to the American advisers at the academy, the commandant, General Lam Quang Tho, was one of the

---

[24] Quoted words from Rpt, MACJ–341, 27 Apr 67, sub: Analysis of Republic of Vietnam Armed Forces (RVNAF) for CY 1966, p. 8. See also Memo, Montague to Komer, 22 Dec 66, sub: Other Ideas on Improving ARVN Effectiveness. Both in SEAB, CMH.

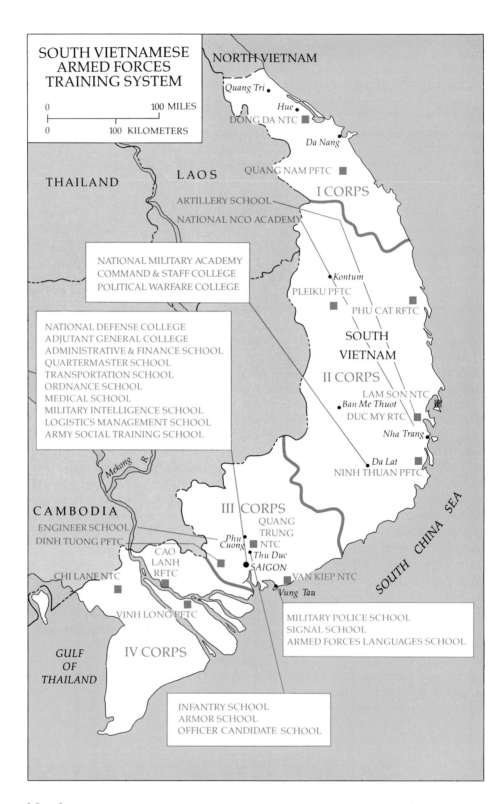

SOUTH VIETNAMESE
ARMED FORCES
TRAINING SYSTEM

0   100 MILES
0   100 KILOMETERS

NORTH VIETNAM

Quang Tri

Hue

DONG DA NTC

Da Nang

THAILAND

LAOS

QUANG NAM PFTC

I CORPS

ARTILLERY SCHOOL

NATIONAL NCO ACADEMY

NATIONAL MILITARY ACADEMY
COMMAND & STAFF COLLEGE
POLITICAL WARFARE COLLEGE

Kontum

PLEIKU PFTC

PHU CAT RFTC

SOUTH
VIETNAM

NATIONAL DEFENSE COLLEGE
ADJUTANT GENERAL COLLEGE
ADMINISTRATIVE & FINANCE SCHOOL
QUARTERMASTER SCHOOL
TRANSPORTATION SCHOOL
ORDNANCE SCHOOL
MEDICAL SCHOOL
MILITARY INTELLIGENCE SCHOOL
LOGISTICS MANAGEMENT SCHOOL
ARMY SOCIAL TRAINING SCHOOL

II CORPS

LAM SON NTC

Ban Me Thuot
DUC MY RTC

Nha Trang

Da Lat
NINH THUAN PFTC

Mekong R.

CAMBODIA

ENGINEER SCHOOL

DINH TUONG PFTC

CAO
LANH
RFTC

CHI LANE NTC

VINH LONG PFTC

III CORPS

QUANG
TRUNG

Phu   NTC
Cuong
Thu Duc
SAIGON

VAN KIEP NTC

Vung Tau

MILITARY POLICE SCHOOL
SIGNAL SCHOOL
ARMED FORCES LANGUAGES SCHOOL

GULF
OF
THAILAND

IV CORPS

SOUTH CHINA SEA

INFANTRY SCHOOL
ARMOR SCHOOL
OFFICER CANDIDATE SCHOOL

MAP 3

least effective South Vietnamese general officers. Freund recommended hiring competent civilian instructors, establishing academic departments, and planning a 30-percent failure rate for the projected four-year curriculum.[25]

The MACV commander passed the findings to Vien in November, with the hope that the Joint General Staff might adopt them in 1967 and initiate a similar review at the South Vietnamese Command and Staff College. Reversing his favorable attitude toward the college at the beginning of the year, Westmoreland believed that South Vietnamese commanders used the institution as a dumping ground for inept officers from their units. He sought more selectivity in students and recommended that the college concentrate on practical instruction for battalion commanders and junior staff officers. For more senior officers, he suggested establishing a "National Security College." As usual, the MACV commander dutifully submitted the suggestions to the Joint General Staff for its consideration.[26]

Other advisers reported that basic and unit training remained a morass. No coordination existed between the helter-skelter South Vietnamese manpower efforts and the elaborate training schedules of the Central Training Command. National training centers were often underused, while the more poorly equipped divisional training centers were overcrowded (*Map 3*). Poor scheduling often jammed the centers for several months, especially July and August, and left them nearly vacant during other periods. Both training camp and school staffs continued to include many "homesteaders" who either had no field experience or were not wanted in the field. Westmoreland wished to close down the divisional training camps but recognized their value to local commanders. He recommended closing five of the seven Regional Forces training centers in 1967 and using the slack period of the national training centers to train Regional Forces recruits.

Because the influx of new recruits and the constant losses from casualties and desertions damaged unit cohesion, MACV proposed a six-week refresher training program for all South Vietnamese infantry battalions. The Joint General Staff scheduled forty-two battalions for such training in 1966, but the results were disappointing. Only a few battalions actually received the training, and the instruction for those that did was marginal. Unit commanders at all levels showed little interest in the program, and participating units were far below even their field strengths. Most regarded the training as a rest period for officers and troops, and at times the training was broken up or postponed by unexpected operational commitments. A similar program for the territorials had even less success. Province chiefs flatly refused to relinquish control of their forces to regular army training camps outside their jurisdiction. Almost all efforts by the Joint General Staff and American advisers to have South Vietnamese combat units conduct in-place training in the field also met with failure. Commanders simply were not interested in training and found excuses to avoid it. The Joint

---

[25] First quotation from Notes of 23 Sep 66, History file 9–A (see also Notes of 13 and 18 Sep 66, History files 8–E and 9–A, respectively). Second quotation from MACV, "Comprehensive Study of the Vietnamese Military Academy (VNMA)," November 1966, History file 11–D5. All in Westmoreland Papers, HRB, CMH. On General Tho, see South Vietnamese officer dossiers, SEAB, CMH.
[26] Notes of 15 Nov 66, History file 11–E, Westmoreland Papers, HRB, CMH.

General Staff had to content itself with forming mobile training teams to work with particularly poor units in the field.

The American Offshore Training Program to send selected South Vietnamese military personnel to U.S. Army service and staff schools also had unresolved problems. Despite the program's favorable publicity, academic reports in 1966 continued to show that poor English comprehension by Vietnamese students greatly reduced the amount of meaningful learning. In many cases students were chosen for their superfluousness rather than for their ability, and in others student quotas simply went unfilled. South Vietnamese commanders generally saw no profit in sending their best men away for one or more

Brig. Gen. Richard M. Lee

years of training, especially when they had no guarantee that the student would ever return to his original unit. Efforts of the Central Training Command increased the number of trainees in 1966 and 1967, but not the quality. To improve Vietnamese facility in English, MACV recommended expanding the courses at the South Vietnamese language school and, as an interim measure, directed some Vietnamese officer students to the Defense Language Institute at Lackland Air Force Base, Texas, for further English-language instruction.

Reviewing the year's accomplishment, MACV lamented that training remained another weak spot because of the "lethargy and lack of initiative of [Vietnamese] commanders at all echelons . . . to implement effectively programs or actions recommended by advisors."[27] Vietnamese officers put a low value on training and regarded battlefield experience as a more desirable substitute. But the two were not comparable. Improvements in training were dependent on improvements in other areas: a more equitable merit promotion system, a systematic officer rotation policy, the elimination of marginal or ineffective officers, and better officer instruction. All were necessary to cultivate leadership without which better training could never be attained.

Maj. Gen. Richard M. Lee, who served as deputy senior adviser of II Corps from June 1966 to July 1967, saw a close relationship between South Vietnamese attitudes toward training and administrative reform and South Vietnamese combat effectiveness.[28] Lee reasoned that on the surface the lack of attention to

---

[27] Rpt, MACJ–341, 27 Apr 67, sub: Analysis of Republic of Vietnam Armed Forces (RVNAF) for CY 1966, p. 91, SEAB, CMH.

[28] Discussion of Lee's position in this and the following paragraph is based on Ltr, Lee to Freund, 8 Jul 71, in Brig Gen John F. Freund, "ARVN Training," SEAB, CMH. All quotations are *(Continued)*

training reflected the war weariness of the line officers and the preoccupation of senior commanders with political, social, and economic concerns but, in reality, was symptomatic of deeper weaknesses in the South Vietnamese officer corps. Noting that this relatively small group came almost entirely from the southern society's upper class—those who had associated with the French, the rising urban commercial and business elites, especially from Saigon, and a few of the old royal aristocracy that had managed to survive—he believed that, as a group, they "seemed to lack aggressiveness, leadership ability and a full professional commitment to their profession," all of which "had a pervasive, adverse impact on training." Too many of the Vietnamese officers wanted rear area assignments and political jobs, rather than combat commands, preferring to avoid "the rigors, boredom and dangers of training and combat" and "to use their positions for personal or even financial gain." The Vietnamese noncommissioned officers simply reflected the attitudes of the officers. Although both ranks had many exceptional leaders, they still were too few to offset the nonprofessional mindset of the army leaders in general.

Lee maintained that the answer lay not in more leadership training or more American advice, but in the basic selection of officer and noncommissioned officer candidates and their ensuing advancement. His remedy for the officer corps "was an infusion of fresh, competitive leadership" from the "large, untapped pool in the peasant classes." In the South Vietnamese Army, however, such men were barred from even the lower ranks of the officer corps by a "military caste system" based on social and economic class distinctions. Because the average Vietnamese peasant sought to benefit from the "vast social revolution" under way as a result of the conflict, Lee felt that opening the officer corps to the peasantry would help satisfy this need and, in the process, commit the new recruits "irrevocably" to Saigon. He envisioned the molding of "tough, dedicated young combat leaders who learn quickly and who can train their men effectively and lead their platoons and companies into enemy positions because the young officers' personal future stake in the society and the state tends to flow from their performance in training and on the battlefield." Despite the magnitude of the training involved in transforming a peasant into an officer, Lee concluded that "the general leavening effect of integrating and broadening the officer base, making it more egalitarian and opening a means of sought-after upward mobility," was well worth the effort.

Logistics

Logistics in South Vietnam presented unique problems to the advisory effort. Geared to support a peacetime army, the supply system lacked the organiza-

---

(Continued) from this source. See also the briefer comments of Lee's deputy and successor, Col. Charles A. Cannon, Jr., in Senior Officer Debriefing Rpt, Cannon (hereafter cited as Cannon Debriefing Rpt), 17 Nov 67, pp. 8–9 and 117–18, SEAB, CMH.

tion, skill, and size to support a sustained war effort. Coordination between the Central Logistics Command, the five area logistics commands, and the individual branch agencies was poor. The lines of authority between them were exceedingly hazy, and further obscured by the independence of the corps headquarters and their subordinate units. For example, the Movement Branch of the Central Logistics Command vied with the Office of the Chief of Transportation, the service branch, for authority. But neither of the two offices controlled the zone transportation officers of the area logistics commands, which were responsive to the corps they supported. The lack of command interest in field maintenance and depot accounting increased the strain on the logistical system, as did the burgeoning size of the South Vietnamese, American, and allied combat forces, all of which demanded an ever-growing volume of materiel funneled through a common logistical pipeline from the United States to South Vietnam. A considerable part of the burden fell to the American logistics advisers in the field. They found themselves unraveling the innumerable tangles caused by the ineffective supply system and spent most of their time identifying minor short-range problems and trying to "sell" solutions to their Vietnamese counterparts.

During 1966 American and South Vietnamese logisticians made a start at reform in several areas. They centralized inventory lists, conducted monthly reviews of current stocks of supplies and equipment, identified and redistributed excess stocks, and established minimum levels of stockage at each supply level. As the American ground combat commitment allowed the South Vietnamese more breathing room, logistical improvements were easier to make. However, the shortage of skilled Vietnamese managers and technicians at all levels remained a long-term problem. Depots and smaller supply facilities were overloaded with work, short of personnel, and subject to pilferage and poor accounting. Procedural defects were rampant, such as the lack of suspense control for repair orders so that older requests often languished or were lost while newer ones were filled. Rear depots and port facilities depended heavily on civilian labor and had the greatest personnel problems. Since mid-1965 higher-paying jobs with civilian contractors and U.S. military commands had continually drained skilled labor from the South Vietnamese supply organizations without any relief in sight. Even with direct American assistance, it would take much planning and cooperation between all logistics and training commands to develop and retain the mixed civil-military work force needed to operate the existing system. The creation of new support units in 1967 or 1968 promised only to complicate the personnel problem. For now, as long as the combat units were relatively stationary, the South Vietnamese seemed content with the functioning of its jerry-built system.

Of all the elements of the overtaxed logistical system, the South Vietnamese transportation service functioned reasonably well. Better roads and local security enabled the amount of cargo moved inland to increase from 1,258,707 metric tons in 1965 to 1,574,083 for 1966. But more was needed. With minimal improvements in air or rail transport expected and only one medium boat company (with landing craft) and three light truck companies scheduled to be activated in 1968, continued progress by the transportation service would require greater operational efficiency.

164

Off-loading and storage problems in the Saigon port area remained the major physical bottleneck. Lack of dock space, workers, cargo-handling equipment, trucks, barges, and depot storage all impeded the unloading of ships and the movement of cargo. Delays at almost every stage of movement increased opportunities for pilferage, misappropriation, and misdirection of goods and materiel. Some progress was made during the year by centralizing all South Vietnamese military shipping under the Saigon Terminal Transportation Command and using personnel from the U.S. 4th Terminal Command to advise and assist. Eventually American advisers hoped to end the congestion in the Saigon area by diverting overseas cargos to ports in the I and II Corps Tactical Zones. The use of up-country ports would reduce transport time to local depots but, at the same time, necessitate more accurate, up-to-date depot inventories and usage rates by the Central Logistics Command.

The Vietnamese handled certain high-priority shipments more efficiently. Civilian contractors delivered petroleum products directly to the ports of Saigon, Can Tho, Da Nang, Qui Nhon, and Nha Trang. Because these items required special transport and storage facilities, American advisers had an easier time keeping a close watch over them. The same was true of munitions, but foodstuffs were another matter. Only in December, after several area logistics commands had run out of rice while ships filled with the commodity waited to be off-loaded in Saigon, were American advisers able to persuade the minister of economy to ship imported rice destined for the armed forces directly to the appropriate command without unloading and temporarily storing it in the Saigon area.[29] As these problems were resolved, new ones—overcrowded depots, confused inventories, bottlenecks in local transportation, bureaucratic confusion at the local field supply points, long delays in procuring certain hard-to-manufacture munitions—always cropped up. Overall, however, no serious supply shortages existed in South Vietnam.

Advisers made less headway in the realm of maintenance. In the field South Vietnamese units rarely performed preventive maintenance due to a lack of training and command attention. For the same reasons, direct support maintenance by the maintenance platoons of the divisional service companies and the Regional Forces administrative and logistical companies at the province level was minimal. Technical service units and depots in each area logistics command and those directly under the Central Logistics Command in Saigon were competent but unable to handle the backlog of work orders caused by improper maintenance at lower levels. Age and constant use also took its toll, compounding routine maintenance problems. A lack of spare parts made a direct exchange program impossible,[30] and a scarcity of skilled civilians limited depot rebuilding projects. Development of a national reporting system for equipment status and improvements in inventory control made it possible to make some forecasts of future demands for spare parts and replacements. American logistics advisers at all levels tried to oil the Vietnamese system as much as they could, but South

---

[29] Briefing, MACV J-46, 1967, MICRO 1/1624, RG 334, WNRC.
[30] Direct exchange programs allowed users to receive operating parts immediately upon turning in an identical damaged item if the depot had the component in stock.

Vietnamese unit commanders increasingly sought to remedy serious maintenance problems by having their advisers talk neighboring U.S. support units into
performing critical repair work or obtaining needed components.

Although Saigon was eager to obtain more modern military equipment, General Westmoreland kept South Vietnamese requirements at the bottom of his
shopping list. More sophisticated materiel would only strain the already weak
logistical system and stretch the pool of skilled manpower even thinner. A major
exception to this policy was the introduction of the Colt-designed M16 automatic
rifle. Westmoreland had requested these small but powerful weapons for Saigon
late in 1965 to counter the introduction of the Russian-designed AK47 by the Viet
Cong. Adoption of the new rifle would have greatly increased the firepower of
the average South Vietnamese infantryman without presenting any complex
training or supply problems. However, the Colt's limited production capacity, a
priority distribution to American combat battalions, and Washington's desire to
hold down the costs of the war pushed South Vietnamese military needs into the
background. MACV revised its plans by allocating M16 rifles only to the South
Vietnamese airborne and marine battalions, but Defense Secretary McNamara
disapproved even this moderate proposal in December 1966. At this time only
387 M16s were in use at a few South Vietnamese training centers, and neither
MACV, the Joint Chiefs of Staff, nor the Defense Department gave the distribution of the weapon to Saigon's regular forces much priority.[31]

The other military components did a little better. In 1966 the Military Assistance Program added over 5,500 vintage American small arms and almost 1,000
trucks to the Territorial Forces, helping standardize their hitherto diverse arsenal.
For the air service the United States agreed to outfit the six fighter squadrons
with jet aircraft over a period of several years, almost a necessity because of the
lack of propeller-driven A–1 aircraft to replace current losses. A similar problem
affected the old H–34 helicopters used by the South Vietnamese since 1961. Their
air force had only 65 of 98 authorized H–34s, and Washington was considering
proposals to modernize the rotary-wing squadrons with the new UH–1 models.
But, as in the case of the M16 rifle, the needs of American units in South Vietnam
came first. Helicopters were in short supply and an early replacement was
unlikely.

The South Vietnamese Navy's sea and coastal units remained stable, but the
strength of the riverine force rose from 165 to 192 craft. By the end of the year the
riverine area commands in the III and IV Corps Tactical Zones could support
ground operations with thirteen river assault groups. But both the air and naval
services were desperately short of qualified personnel, a problem compounded
by the length of time needed to give Vietnamese students adequate English-
language training before attending technical schools in the United States. Maintenance at most levels was also marginal and more critical than in the army. Both
services also shared the army's problem of a supply system geared to area sup-

---

[31] On M16 rifles, see Notes of 13 Jul 66, History file 7–F, Westmoreland Papers, HRB; Memo,
Director, FPAO, to General Johnson, 7 Nov 66, sub: Findings on Small Arms Weapons Systems
(SAWS), SEAB; and various papers in M16 Vietnamization file, SEAB. All in CMH.

port and, despite their inherently greater mobility, found it difficult to shift their forces about at will without encountering severe logistical problems. In general, U.S. Navy and Air Force advisers could do little to accelerate the long training needed to bring the technical services up to a satisfactory level.

The American logistics advisers with the most clout were those in the Budget Branch and the Financial Management Branch of the MACV Office of the Comptroller. MACV budget officers carefully monitored all South Vietnamese defense expenditures and worked closely with other MACV advisory branches. On several occasions in 1966 Westmoreland used financial leverage to make the South Vietnamese adopt certain American-sponsored measures. One example was the diversion of funds for the construction of prisoner-of-war camps. In other instances MACV pressured Saigon to purchase barrier material for territorial outposts, to raise Popular Forces salaries, to increase allowances for military rations, to procure additional rations and clothing, and to increase funds for dependent housing and locally manufactured items. But Westmoreland used the tactic sparingly, and only in minor matters.

American comptroller advisers also monitored the use of funds through a regular auditing program carried out by the Vietnamese but assisted closely by the MACV Financial Management Branch. About 50 percent of the regular armed forces and 80 percent of the territorial units were audited in 1966, disclosing sixty-two cases of fraud and misappropriation involving 20 million piasters. Auditors, audit advisers, and field advisers scrutinized unit payrolls and also tried to determine the actual number, rank, and time in grade of assigned individuals. As in logistics, the success of one endeavor depended on success in others. In this case the prerequisite for accurate payroll audits was the implementation of other personnel administration reforms. With more auditors and more finance advisers planned for 1967, MACV hoped to put more emphasis on unit audits and put a brake on corruption.

Prisoners of War

Progress on the prisoner-of-war (POW) issue—sorting out the interrogation system and establishing POW camps—was agonizingly slow.[32] The combined American–South Vietnamese commission established in 1965 agreed to apply the Geneva Conventions to all North Vietnamese Army and Viet Cong prisoners and, in October, disseminated guidelines on the proper handling of prisoners. Under the guidance of the advisory section of the MACV provost marshal, the Joint General Staff also developed a plan for the construction of five permanent POW camps in 1966, one for each corps zone and a fifth for the capital region.

---

[32] For an overview, see Briefing, McGovern, circa October 1966, sub: Morale and Personnel Matters, and annexes, Fact Sheets, MACJ, "Status of Prisoners of War in Vietnam" and "Status of Prisoners of War Camps in Vietnam," MICRO 2/2565, RG 334, WNRC; Rpt, Lt Col Angus B. MacLean, Chief, Vietnamese Military Police Advisory Branch, 11 Nov 66, sub: MP Advisor End of Tour Report, SEAB, CMH.

Prisoner-of-War Camp at Bien Hoa

However, each was to have a capacity of only 500 prisoners, making them little more than a token solution. As an interim measure the South Vietnamese established a small, temporary stockade at Bien Hoa, on the northern outskirts of Saigon. The South Vietnamese Military Police Corps also planned to recruit and train eight hundred soldiers to staff the camps, while MACV was to contribute five camp advisory teams. These teams were to act as both advisers and observers, ensuring that the South Vietnamese abided by the conventions. Finally, Saigon planned to form combined interrogation stations at all division- and corps-level headquarters to supplement the Combined Military Interrogation Center in Saigon.

The response of the South Vietnamese to the prison construction program was halfhearted. Only two camps opened in 1966: the first in May at Bien Hoa to serve the III Corps Tactical Zone, and the second in October at Pleiku to support the II Corps area. Despite Westmoreland's personal urging, the South Vietnamese failed to establish similar camps in the I and IV Corps Tactical Zones and the Capital Military District, due essentially to a lack of command interest. In October the prisoner population of the two existing camps was only 605, which included the 162 military prisoners transferred from local prisons and jails as a result of an earlier search. MACV's statistics were considerably higher and indicated that at least 1,980 identified prisoners of war existed as of that date. To ensure proper facilities for the growing number of prisoners, MACV would have to force Saigon not only to complete the planned camps but also to expand both the existing and future ones.

Another area of concern for MACV was the proper classification of captives. MACV published elaborate guidelines in May 1966, specifying that all apprehended enemy personnel were to be placed in one of three categories: "prisoner-of-war," "returnee," or "suspect." Members of the North Vietnamese Army and Viet Cong main force units captured in combat were considered official prisoners of war. Returnees, or "ralliers," were personnel who had actively supported the Viet Cong—including North Vietnamese Army members—and had voluntarily surrendered to the South Vietnamese government. All other captives were classified as suspects, or "detainees," a temporary category until South Vietnamese officials could determine their status. As of 1966 MACV refused to accord POW status to members of the Viet Cong Local Force, village militia, or guerrilla units. Captured members of these units, together with those from Viet Cong governmental organizations, normally became civil defendants and "political prisoners," subject to incarceration in provincial and national jails. MACV took no responsibility for their subsequent treatment and fate.[33]

MACV regulations pertaining to the disposition of captives, however, conflicted with guidance concerning their interrogation. According to the regulations on captives, all personnel apprehended by U.S. forces and classified as prisoners of war were to be first interrogated by the capturing unit and then sent directly to South Vietnamese POW camps. Returnees and civil defendants were to be turned over to civil agencies (provinces or districts), and all others returned to their homes by U.S. military civil affairs personnel. "Very important" prisoners could be sent to the national-level interrogation center at Saigon, but the United States was to retain custody until their transferral to a Vietnamese POW camp. Where South Vietnamese corps commanders had not yet established such camps, temporary detention centers at the Vietnamese corps headquarters would have to make do.

Regulations on POW interrogation, on the other hand, sought to broaden, rather than restrict, prisoner evacuation channels by having captives interrogated and screened at every possible level. They specified that American commands were to forward prisoners to South Vietnamese agencies only after all American intelligence needs had been satisfied. They made no mention of POW camps or tribunals ruling on the status of suspects. Suspected Viet Cong or individuals with an undetermined status were to be handed over to South Vietnamese province intelligence personnel for further interrogation and disposition.[34]

MACV also stationed American interrogation teams at all major South Vietnamese headquarters (corps, division, special zone, and province) and created a country-level combined military interrogation center to ensure that their information gathering was as comprehensive as possible. As a by-product, this enabled MACV to better monitor the treatment of prisoners in South Vietnamese cus-

---

[33] MACV Directives 20–5, 17 May and 21 Sep 66, sub: Inspections and Investigations: Prisoners of War—Determination Status, SEAB, CMH.

[34] See ibid., 190–3, 24 May and 29 Oct 66, sub: Military Police: Evacuation of Prisoners of War (POWs), and 381–11, 5 Mar 66, sub: Military Intelligence: Intelligence Procedures for Handling, Processsing, and Exploitation of Captives, Returnees, Suspects and Documents. All in SEAB, CMH.

tody.[35] But for those political and military captives processed by the South Vietnamese National Police, MACV had no authority, and American advice was handled by other U.S. agencies. The overriding emphasis was thus on the acquisition of intelligence, and until the South Vietnamese constructed more and larger prisoner camps and gave more command emphasis to the entire POW question, the United States was unable to comply with even the minimum provisions of the Geneva Conventions. Saigon's decision in 1966 to halt all inspections of its prisoner facilities by the International Red Cross made the situation worse. On the other hand, neither the Viet Cong nor North Vietnamese indicated that they would comply with the treaty provisions, and their handling of American and South Vietnamese military prisoners continued to be equally capricious and often brutal.

The POW issue typified MACV's new approach to the war. Engrossed in the strategy of attrition, it did not give such matters a high priority. Throughout the year Westmoreland and the MACV staff had ever so gently prodded Saigon to comply with the Geneva Conventions and to make numerous reforms. That few of their suggestions were adopted failed to daunt either Westmoreland or his senior generals, for they clearly regarded the South Vietnamese as having a secondary, less important, and less immediate role in the war effort. Because most of the advisory effort had no direct impact on the conduct of the war by American military ground tactical units, American advice could be soft-peddled to the South Vietnamese, put off until the following year, or, in the military jargon of the time, "put on the back burner." Exceptions to the rule were few, and generally made only when the matter in question had a direct impact on American military operations. The production of tactical intelligence, for example, from enemy prisoners or CIDG patrols in the interior was critical for American commanders, and stemming the revolt in the I Corps Tactical Zone, which threatened to disrupt the entire conventional war effort in the region, also fell into this category. MACV gave these areas immediate priority and resolved the problems as quickly as possible. Still, Westmoreland could not be expected to reform the South Vietnamese military apparatus and government by himself in the space of a year. Nor could MACV ignore what had been the heart of the war effort for so many years, the pacification campaign. If the American advisers could rapidly redirect the South Vietnamese armed forces towards their new task of population security, many of their shortcomings in other areas could be easily forgiven.

---

[35] Described briefly in McChristian, *Role of Military Intelligence,* pp. 14–16 and 26–32.

9

The Pacification Campaign

As the danger of an immediate collapse became less threatening to the Saigon regime, American leaders returned some of their attention to the general pacification campaign. In the minds of many U.S. officials the term *pacification* had undergone a radical revision: Originally used to describe a comprehensive strategy for achieving American political and military objectives in South Vietnam, it now often served as no more than a catchall expression for either the nonconventional or, alternatively, the nonmilitary aspects of the war. As the U.S. ground combat forces assumed more responsibility for the conventional war effort based on a strategy of attrition, the South Vietnamese armed forces, both regulars and territorials alike, became increasingly associated with what was incorrectly called "pacification support"—providing area security for the nonmilitary portions of the overall pacification strategy. The result was a growing gap between the two allied national armies that would continue to widen during 1966.

The groundwork for this division of roles and missions had already been laid in 1965, in part by circumstance—the nature of the war—and in part by conscious decision. A U.S.–South Vietnamese conference in Honolulu in early February 1966 further solidified these changes. There, Thieu and Ky agreed to increase direct South Vietnamese military participation in area security missions and to shift authority for local security and development programs to the province chiefs. They also approved a host of related American-sponsored measures, ranging from fiscal reforms and refugee assistance to progressive health, education, and agricultural programs. President Johnson, for his part, pledged greater American economic aid to Saigon and reaffirmed America's military commitment to the country.[1]

Organizing for Pacification

The heart of the pacification strategy, from the military point of view, was providing adequate security. All aspects of the nonmilitary nation-building

---

[1] *U.S.-Vietnam Relations*, 7: sec.IV.C. 9. (b), pp. 9–10.

process—called rural construction, rural reconstruction, and, in early 1966, revolutionary development—had to be closely tied with area security if the overall effort was to have any chance of success. As before, coordinating the multiple activities in the endeavor was a major problem. On the South Vietnamese side, the Ministry of Revolutionary Development under General Nguyen Duc Thang supplied broad administrative guidance for population security and nation-building programs.[2] Thang also headed a hierarchy of revolutionary development councils, extending from the National Central Revolutionary Development Council in Saigon down through corps- and division-level councils to those in each province. On the American side, the U.S. Embassy's Mission Liaison Group, led by Deputy Ambassador Porter, provided general guidance and supervision at the national level while Komer, who became a special assistant for pacification matters to President Johnson in March 1966, tried to unify support for these programs in Washington. Within MACV headquarters, the chief of the Revolutionary Development Division in the operations staff (J–3), Col. Joel M. Hollis, was Porter's military adviser until November 1966, when the division became part of a larger Revolutionary Development Support Directorate headed by Brig. Gen. William A. Knowlton.[3]

Providing security for government officials and the population in general remained the task of the Territorial Forces (Regional Forces companies and Popular Forces platoons), buttressed, as necessary, by regular South Vietnamese troops and the growing number of U.S. ground combat units. In practice, the regular ground forces of both armies had many recurring area security missions. Varying from unit to unit, these included protecting such critical installations as roads, bridges, power plants, and airfields; providing security for province and district capitals, where the rear bases often were located; and serving as reaction forces for beleaguered territorial units. However, the precise responsibility of the regular forces in territorial security was still unclear, with their degree of involvement left to the discretion of the corps- and division-level commanders. In areas where the recruitment of territorial troops was the most difficult, the dependence on regulars for security was still the greatest. But in all zones the peculiar South Vietnamese politico-military chain of command that subordinated the province and district administrations to division and corps commanders ensured that the South Vietnamese Army retained overall control of territorial security at the local level. Whether Thieu and Ky could make good their promise in Honolulu to take the regular army commanders out of the security chain of command and give province and district chiefs direct authority for local security remained to be seen.

The employment of special revolutionary development cadre teams at the village and hamlet levels was one critical new element of Saigon's pacification strategy for 1966.[4] Organized for training in late 1965, each team had about sixty

---

[2] Thang, an ally of Ky and former J-3 of the Joint General Staff, was appointed to head the new ministry in late 1965 following the death of the former minister in an air crash.

[3] For detailed treatments, see Hunt, *Pacification*, forthcoming, and Thomas W. Scoville, *Reorganizing for Pacification Support* (Washington, D.C.: U.S. Army Center of Military History, 1982).

[4] Villages usually consisted of two or more adjacent hamlets.

U.S. and South Vietnamese Leaders Agree on Pacification. *Clockwise from foreground: President Johnson, General Thieu, Ambassador Vu Van Thai, Admiral U.S. Grant Sharp, and Premier Ky.*

members. About half, equipped with light arms, performed security functions, while the other half set up a political structure within the villages and hamlets and also oversaw short-range development projects. Specifically, the teams collected simple census data and built rudimentary assembly halls, where local inhabitants could meet with district officials to initiate small improvement projects involving schools, roads, irrigation, dispensaries, and so forth. They also had a propaganda mission, explaining the war effort to the local peasants and the position of the South Vietnamese government.

The pacification campaign came under close scrutiny in March 1966, when the Army Staff in Washington proposed several changes in the current organization of the war effort.[5] It recommended replacing the U.S. ambassador's Mission Council and MACV with a higher military command that would have jurisdiction over all security and national development support efforts. The military advisory effort was again to have its own headquarters separate from the combat commands, and American influence, or leverage, over the South Vietnamese was to be clarified and formalized through negotiated, written agreements. It

[5] PROVN Study, March 1966, SEAB, CMH.

173

Revolutionary Development Cadre Team Entering Its Assigned Hamlet

also proposed that the South Vietnamese divisions be removed from the security chain of command; the authority of division commanders over province and district chiefs ended; and, when necessary, regular army battalions assigned to province headquarters to beef up territorial defenses.

During a visit to Honolulu in May General Westmoreland reviewed the proposals. Although agreeing with many of the recommendations, he regarded them as too ambitious. He believed that greater American control over the South Vietnamese would lend credence to enemy propaganda that the Saigon government was a puppet regime, and that any major changes in American and South Vietnamese command arrangements would cause turmoil and confusion. Removing South Vietnamese divisions from the security chain of command was desirable, but senior South Vietnamese commanders would strongly oppose the measure and, in all likelihood, would resist the detachment of regular infantry battalions to province chiefs. The MACV staff was already addressing all of the problems noted in the Army study, but progress had to be gradual and evolutionary. For now, the MACV commander saw no need for major changes in these areas and suggested that the proposals serve only as a contingency plan.[6]

Westmoreland was soon to change his mind. As the first class of revolutionary development cadre graduated in the spring of 1966, the prospects for increasing security for the pacification campaign were dim. The Territorial Forces were

[6] USMACV, "Command History, 1966," p. 512, HRB, CMH.

174

experiencing severe recruiting problems and steadily rising losses through casualties and desertion. Through necessity, American combat units—especially U.S. Marine Corps forces in the I Corps Tactical Zone—had to perform an increasing number of area security tasks, but without any specific mandate or design. Westmoreland still regarded population security as primarily a nonmilitary undertaking and coordination of the program the purview of the U.S. ambassador's staff, rather than MACV. His views in this respect had solidified by the end of 1965 and were now shared by most American military leaders.[7] Nevertheless, he desperately needed more forces to provide security for the population and his rear bases.

Toward the end of May, with the political situation in Da Nang settling down, Deputy Ambassador Porter asked Col. George Jacobson to chair a study group of American military and civilian experts to examine pacification strategy, organization, and division of labor. The result, three months later, was eighty-one separate recommendations. Included were the removal of the South Vietnamese division headquarters from the security chain of command and the assignment of the bulk of the regular South Vietnamese infantry battalions to province commands to perform area security duties. The group also proposed merging the Territorial Forces and the Field Force Police into some type of constabulary to exempt the territorials from any future peace negotiations that might limit the size of the armed forces. The CIDG organization was to be relieved of territorial security functions and operate only in remote areas, while the rangers, because of their limited combat effectiveness, were to be dissolved and their personnel reassigned to regular infantry units.

Westmoreland again declined to endorse any major changes. Removing the territorials and the regular infantry battalions from the South Vietnamese Army chain of command would only cause confusion and invite defeat in detail. The MACV commander believed that, on a case-by-case basis, some South Vietnamese corps commanders might attach or assign some infantry or ranger battalions to specific provinces. However, he felt that using his advisers to encourage regular army commanders to take a greater interest in territorial security was a better solution. He considered transforming the territorials into some type of police force premature and disbanding the rangers unwise. Although agreeing that the rangers were not being used effectively, he felt that they should be assigned offensive combat missions more in keeping with their training and organization. Population security, Westmoreland argued, remained the responsibility of all commands and was not a separate effort. American combat commanders could assist advisers by conducting combined operations with South Vietnamese units that had proved particularly reluctant to accept their area security roles.[8]

To further these ends, Westmoreland persuaded Vien to issue a formal directive in July, declaring area security operations equal in importance to conven-

---

[7] Comments of Gen William B. Rosson on draft manuscript "Advice and Support: The Final Years," 16 Mar 84, SEAB, CMH.

[8] Ltr, Westmoreland to Lodge, 7 Sep 66, sub: Report of the Inter-Agency "Roles and Missions" Study Group, file 206–02 ARVN/RF/PF/CIDG, box 6, accession no. 69A702, RG 334, WNRC; Notes of 25 Aug 66, History file 8–D, Westmoreland Papers, HRB, CMH; *U.S.-Vietnam Relations*, 6:sec.IV. C.8., pp. 83–86.

tional combat operations and urging all South Vietnamese commanders to pay more attention to this vital mission. Vien also asked them to correct or improve specific weak points relating to this task, such as local intelligence capabilities, the conduct of their troops toward the local population, the cooperation of army commanders with civil authorities and territorial troops, and the degree of continuity in security-related activities. Westmoreland issued similar guidance to his advisers, adding that at least 50 percent of the South Vietnamese Army units in the I, II and III Corps Tactical Zones should be supporting the pacification campaign in area security missions. In addition to helping the South Vietnamese remedy the deficiencies cited by Vien, advisers were to encourage night operations, saturation patrolling by small units, and cordon-and-search operations with territorial troops and police.[9]

The Security Mission

Between August and October the idea that the greater part of the South Vietnamese armed forces should devote itself to population security solidified in the minds of the top American officials. Meeting with Lt. Gen. Jonathan O. Seaman, the II Field Force commander, and Deputy Ambassador Porter on 20 August, Westmoreland declared it "extremely important that we do all possible to get the ARVN more involved during future months in providing general security for the people." The participants also agreed that South Vietnamese division headquarters could not be taken completely out of the security chain of command. At his Commanders Conference on the twenty-eighth Westmoreland expanded on these points, declaring that U.S. forces were now strong enough "to go after the [North Vietnamese and Viet Cong] main force, and release the ARVN for securing the population." The annual campaign plan for 1967 would "incorporate the concept that ARVN will get more into the pacification business [and] do more security with less punching." Although the South Vietnamese were still to perform some conventional combat operations—the "punching"— "both for their own prestige and for their share of the casualties," their major task would be "securing their people." The American military chief conceded that there would be "a tremendous educational task in getting them [the South Vietnamese] to accept it," and both he and several of his key subordinates expressed reservations regarding the speed at which this could be accomplished. To start the transition, Westmoreland urged his corps senior advisers to sponsor special "pacification" training for South Vietnamese Army battalions to prepare them for their new role.[10]

In Washington Special Assistant Komer presented a similar concept to Defense Secretary McNamara. According to Komer, the "underlying rationale" of

[9] USMACV, "Command History, 1966," p. 523, HRB, CMH.

[10] First quotation from Notes of 20 Aug 66, History file 8–D. Remaining quotations from MFR, Jones, 3 Oct 66, sub: MACV Commanders Conference, 28 August 1966, History file 8–D4. See also Notes of 16 Sep and 8 Oct 66, History files 8–E and 9–C, respectively; MFR, Col James H. Dyson, DepCofS, II FFV, 9 Oct 66, sub: Visit of COMUSMACV, 7 October 1966, History file 9–C4. All in Westmoreland Papers, HRB, CMH.

the change in missions "seems to be that, as the growing U.S. forces take over the 'big war,' we might as well use ARVN for something else. Amen." Paradoxically, the Americans had the job of "teaching ARVN how to pacify." Yet to be decided, however, was the "key question" of who would control the military forces supporting the revolutionary development programs: General Thang's Ministry of Revolutionary Development and the province chiefs, or Vien's Joint General Staff through the corps and division commanders.[11]

Another unresolved area was the security role of the ranger units. Westmoreland termed their notoriously bad behavior toward civilians an "age-old subject" and hoped that the new head of the Ranger Command, Col. Tran Van Hai, could somehow instill a new spirit into these lightweight ground combat battalions. Their proper employment was "in jungles and on reaction missions," and he even suggested ending U.S. military assistance to the rangers if they failed to improve. Westmoreland conveyed his strong concern over the rangers to Vien, who in turn recommended conducting a combined American–South Vietnamese study of the problem and possibly forming the twenty ranger battalions into separate divisions. The new divisions could be part of the general reserve forces controlled by the high command, ensuring that the now widely scattered ranger units had proper logistical and administrative support. Although regarding Vien's proposal too ambitious, the MACV commander endorsed the creation of ranger group headquarters to act as the administrative and logistical link between the corps headquarters and the individual battalions. Vien and Hai's Ranger Command, however, gained no greater control over the individual battalions. Ranger units continued to work directly for the corps, division, and regimental commanders and had little to show for their efforts during the year.[12]

Revolutionary Development Support

In actuality, MACV's position on population security was readily accepted by the South Vietnamese, who had repeatedly urged such a policy throughout 1965. In early October, while discussing what he now called his "favorite subject, . . . how to persuade South Vietnamese regular troops and commanders to support the RD program," Westmoreland found that Vien and Co were in complete agreement. Co proposed that American units devote themselves entirely to conventional combat operations, aided by South Vietnamese rangers, airborne, and marines, while the rest of the armed forces provided territorial security. To strengthen his mobile reserve forces, Co recommended creating five ranger group headquarters and regrouping the marine units into a division. Agreeing in principle, the MACV commander informed Co that he planned to use American troops as a "shield behind which the ARVN, RF and PF would

[11] Memo, Komer to McNamara, 9 Sep 66, sub: Key Matters on Which October Decisions Needed, SEAB, CMH.
[12] Quoted words from MFR, Jones, 3 Oct 66, sub: MACV Commanders Conference, 28 August 1966, History file 8–D4. See also Notes of 29 Aug 66, History file 8–D; MFR, Dyson, 9 Oct 66, sub: Visit of COMUSMACV, 7 October 1966, History file 9–C4. All in Westmoreland Papers, HRB, CMH.

Weakly Armed Popular Forces Soldiers Providing Local Security

provide local security" and that, "for the time being," they could even assist the Vietnamese in this effort. While favoring the creation of ranger group headquarters, further expansion was out of the question until current South Vietnamese recruitment and desertion problems were corrected. More important was the regular army's need for special training to prepare for its population security mission. Many senior South Vietnamese officers, he pointed out, "neither understand nor would support the use of ARVN for this purpose." Before leaving, Westmoreland also cautioned Co to discuss such matters with him before bringing them up with senior American officials like McNamara, who was scheduled to arrive in Vietnam the following day.[13]

During Secretary McNamara's October visit Premier Ky forcefully presented the case for a shift in roles and missions. Ky, who had suggested such a division of responsibilities over a year ago, claimed that the retraining of the South Vietnamese Army for its area security tasks could easily be accomplished in two months by using one mobile training team for each division. He also proposed regrouping the airborne and marines into a single reserve division and assigning at least half of the ranger battalions to a centralized Special Forces command that would operate along the border. Thieu seconded these recommendations, add-

[13] MFR, Westmoreland, 10 Oct 66, sub: Discussions With Generals Vien and Co Preliminary to Secretary McNamara's Visit, History file 9–D5, Westmoreland Papers, HRB, CMH.

ing that "the entire military chain of command [must] be held responsible for supporting Revolutionary Development. . . . Otherwise, there will be a tendency for the ARVN to rely on the U.S. troops to fight the war and Minister Thang to run Revolutionary Development."[14]

American officials found the Vietnamese proposal sensible but balked at making any major command reorganizations to strengthen the general reserve. Westmoreland, in addition, felt that at least eight months were necessary to retrain the South Vietnamese Army and remained reluctant to approve any further expansion of the regulars. Nevertheless, the decision to employ most of Saigon's military forces in an area security role was now official.

In Manila in late October President Johnson and General Thieu publicly announced the change in mission for the South Vietnamese Army, specifying that Saigon would commit a "substantial share" of its military forces to provide security for the revolutionary development campaign. According to one participant, as an "interim measure" the South Vietnamese were to assign half of its infantry forces—some fifty to sixty battalions—to population security tasks.[15] Everyone agreed on the need for special training for the new mission, and Westmoreland called on General Freund, the new chief of the MACV Training Directorate, to see that proper instruction was provided.

For the remainder of the year, Westmoreland and his staff worked closely with the Joint General Staff to push the new revolutionary development program off the ground. The U.S.–South Vietnamese Combined Campaign Plan for 1967 assigned the South Vietnamese Army the "primary mission" of population security and listed five specific tasks: clearing populated areas of enemy forces; providing physical security; assisting police in locating Viet Cong political cadre; opening and securing roads, bridges, and canals; and civic action. To Thieu, Ky, and Vien, Westmoreland continued to personally emphasize the need to overcome the "resistance" of the corps and division commanders to the new role.[16]

The MACV commander also briefed his senior subordinates on the details of the regulars' new population security mission. At his Commanders Conference in November Westmoreland pointed out that, with American units engaging the Viet Cong main forces, the South Vietnamese Army "can now provide protection to the area, people and resources and participate in Revolutionary Development programs."[17] At his Commanders-in-Chief Conference that same month he repeated the same theme and asked that the "reorientation of ARVN in connection with support of Revolutionary Development" be "intensified" and the South Vietnamese Army weaned from "its habitual favoritism" for "conventional battalion and regimental operations and from [its] reluctance to conduct operations

[14] Quoted words from MFR, Westmoreland, 11 Oct 66, sub: Secretary McNamara's Meeting With General Thieu, Chairman, National Leadership Council, History file 9–D3. See also ibid., sub: Secretary McNamara's Meeting With Prime Minister Ky, History file 9–D2. Both in Westmoreland Papers, HRB, CMH.

[15] Komer Interv, 7 May 70, Rand Limited Document D (L)–20104–ARPA, copy in SEAB, CMH.

[16] First quotation from JGS-MACV, Combined Campaign Plan 1967, AB 142, 7 Nov 66, p. 4 (see also annex B), SEAB, CMH. Second quotation from Msg, COMUSMACV to CINCPAC, 23 Nov 66, COMUSMACV Message file, Westmoreland Papers, HRB, CMH.

[17] MFR, Jones, 19 Dec 66, sub: MACV Commanders Conference, 20 November 1966, History file 11–C3, Westmoreland Papers, HRB, CMH.

South Vietnamese Soldiers Flush a Viet Cong Suspect From the Jungle

without artillery support. . . ."[18] In December, to the same audience, he asked that "no stone . . . be left unturned" in the effort to "reorient and re-educate" the South Vietnamese Army in its new security mission. His new deputy chief of staff for RF/PF operations, Brig. Gen. Albert R. Brownfield, he announced, was currently developing doctrine for the tactical employment of military forces in area security roles. When completed, this guidance would be disseminated to American commanders and advisers, and possibly "directly to the JGS."[19] Although at first discouraged by Vietnamese footdragging in organizing pacification mobile training teams for the regulars, Westmoreland was confident at the end of the year that all of the Vietnamese infantry battalions could be trained in "saturation patrolling, ambush security and checkpoint operations, and hamlet search" by mid-1967, significantly "reorienting the ARVN soldier's attitude toward working with the people."[20]

Some key commanders disagreed with this particular allocation of roles and missions. General Walt, the U.S. Marine Corps commander in the northern

[18] MFR, Rosson, 26 Nov 66, sub: CIIC Meeting, 25 November 1966, History file 11–C6, Westmoreland Papers, HRB, CMH.

[19] MFR, Rosson, 17 Dec 66, sub: CIIC Meeting, 17 December 1966, History file 12–A4, Westmoreland Papers, HRB, CMH.

[20] Quoted words from Msg, Westmoreland MAC 10608 to Sharp, 041204 Dec 66, COMUSMACV Message file. See also Notes of 7 Nov and 1 Dec 66, History files 11–B and 11–D, respectively. All in Westmoreland Papers, HRB, CMH.

180

zone, took exception, feeling that U.S. forces should become directly involved in local security. Influencing Walt were Marine Corps experiences in Haiti and Nicaragua and British practices in Malaya during the 1950s. In August 1965 he had begun a Combined Action Program (CAP), integrating small Marine Corps rifle units with local Popular Forces platoons. By 1966 Walt viewed the practice a success—stiffening the morale of the poorly trained and equipped territorials, pushing them out of their fixed fortifications, and putting them to work in the field. Over the next several years he gradually extended the program to each of the five provinces in the I Corps Tactical Zone, guarding about 350 hamlets with 114 CAP units comprised of two thousand American marine and naval corpsmen and three thousand Popular Forces soldiers. Through a formal written agreement with the South Vietnamese corps commanders, Walt had his Marine noncommissioned officers leading—not advising—the mixed contingents under supervisory CAP elements at the district and province headquarters.

Westmoreland, however, continued to feel that U.S. combat forces were best employed away from the populated areas. Although approving some assistance to the territorials by Army ground combat units, he opposed expanding the CAP concept to the other corps zones, believing that it would drain the strength of his maneuver battalions, duplicate the advisory effort, and make the territorials dependent on American support. The division in roles and missions was now official, and henceforth area security was to be Saigon's primary responsibility. In the end, the South Vietnamese armed forces had to protect their own people.[21]

---

[21] Shulimson and Johnson, *U.S. Marines in Vietnam*, pp. 133–38; William R. Corson, *The Betrayal* (New York: Norton, 1968), pp. 177–98; Ngo Quang Truong, *RVNAF and US Operational Cooperation and Coordination*, Indochina Monographs (Washington, D.C.: U.S. Army Center of Military History, 1980), pp. 115–16 and 119–27. The Marines, however, did not advocate an "enclave" strategy. See Memo, Gen Leonard F. Chapman, Jr. (USMC) to President, 2 Feb 68, sub: Strategy for the Conduct of the War in SEASIA, box 127, Johnson Papers, MHI. On Westmoreland's decision, see Pacific Command, *Report on the War in Vietnam*, pp. 214–15.

10

Advising in the Field

The official change in the South Vietnamese combat mission is somewhat of a paradox. Was it a calculated move based on changing battlefield conditions or the result of poor South Vietnamese performance in the field? Or was the mission change only a recognition of an existing state of affairs? With the exception of the airborne and marine battalions of the general reserve, most of the regular South Vietnamese combat units were already performing security missions, and most of their offensive sweeps were close to populated areas. Rarely did they venture deep into Viet Cong jungle base areas or confront North Vietnamese regulars. In October a survey of American field advisers showed that only 23 percent of the South Vietnamese ground combat battalions (regular infantry, ranger, airborne, marine, and armor units) were conducting what could be termed offensive operations. Some 28 percent were in reserve and 49 percent were performing area security missions (defined as "clearing and securing operations to support Revolutionary Development"). If accurate, the need to make an official mission change appears superfluous or, at the least, cosmetic.[1]

Advisory ratings told little regarding the true status and activities of South Vietnamese units. For example, in July 1966 advisers considered 2 of the 158 South Vietnamese infantry-type battalions "ineffective" and 20 "marginal." In August the number of battalions rated ineffective rose to 7 and the following month increased to 14, with 36 more rated marginal. The remaining 108 fell into the nebulous category of "satisfactory," a subjective label that conveyed no idea of a unit's actual effectiveness. The monthly evaluations were simply too brief, eclectic, and bland to be useful. Later studies revealed that field advisers were still inflating the ratings of South Vietnamese units, had serious reservations about many of those that had received a "satisfactory," and continued to fear that negative reports reflected badly on their own performance. Aware of the problems, Westmoreland knew that South Vietnamese military performance had to be improved, irrespective of any changes in the roles and missions performed by the South Vietnamese units. The shuffling of roles and missions would not, by itself, produce more effective units. To turn the situation around, either Ameri-

[1] Percentages in Talking Paper, MACJ-341, 8 Oct 66, sub: Analysis of Performance of ARVN, MICRO 02/2624, RG 334, WNRC.

can advisers would have to exercise more authority or U.S. combat commanders would have to lend a hand.[2]

Combined Operations

In February 1966 Westmoreland advised his senior subordinates that South Vietnamese combat units could not be expected to fight "at our tempo" and that American commanders would somehow have to "make them part of our victories." In April he urged his senior commanders to use "diplomacy, tact, and finesse to get them more and more into the act . . . [through] joint [combined] operations [and to] share in any battlefield victory." Traditionally, armies learned to fight best by fighting, and experience was what Saigon's fighting forces needed. The poorest South Vietnamese units, he felt, should receive the most assistance.[3]

In 1966 the two worst units in the South Vietnamese Army were still the 5th and 25th Infantry Divisions, both guarding the approaches to Saigon. Here the brunt of the fighting had been assumed by American combat units—the U.S. 1st and 25th Infantry Divisions and three separate brigades. Under their protection, the local Vietnamese regular forces performed static security missions. But rather than using this respite to regroup and retrain their forces, or to hunt down the local Viet Cong, the Vietnamese commanders had let their units degenerate through inactivity, and American advisers now rated them lower than even the neighboring territorials.

To remedy this unsatisfactory situation, Westmoreland's staff suggested four courses of action: deactivating the two division headquarters and assigning their subordinate units to local province chiefs; exchanging the two divisions with two from another zone; limiting the two divisions to population security tasks; or somehow using direct American pressure to relieve marginal officers and force the units to correct problems like desertions, poor combat tactics, and lax discipline. The staff also recommended using leverage by withdrawing advisers, financial support, or both. General Westmoreland rejected all of the suggestions and instead proposed that U.S. combat units lend a hand to the ailing Vietnamese forces and to the area security campaign in general.[4]

In early May Westmoreland ordered the U.S. 1st and 25th Divisions to "start working more closely with elements of these two [South Vietnamese] divisions on operations in order to improve their morale, efficiency and effectiveness." He suggested a "buddy" effort, matching the U.S. 1st and the South Vietnamese 5th

---

[2] In Encls to Ltr, Westmoreland to Vien, 26 Sep 66, ARVN Effectiveness file, box 6, accession no. 67A702, RG 334, WNRC, the July and August rating descriptions are "combat ineffective" and "marginally effective." In Talking Paper, MACJ-341, 8 Oct 66, sub: Analysis of Performance of ARVN, MICRO 02/2624, RG 334, WNRC, the September rating descriptions are "unsatisfactory" and "marginal." See also Frederick C. Rockett et al., *SEER Revision* (Greenwich International, 1969), Document no. ASDIRS 2650, Pentagon Library.
[3] First and second quotations from MFR, Jones, 10 Mar 66, sub: MACV Commanders Conference, 20 February 1966, History file 4–C1. Third quotation from ibid., 10 May 66, sub: MACV Commanders Conference, 24 April 1966, History file 6–A1. Both in Westmoreland Papers, HRB, CMH.
[4] USMACV, "Command History, 1966," p. 465, HRB, CMH.

Divisions; the U.S. 25th and the South Vietnamese 25th Divisions; and the U.S. 173d Airborne Brigade and the Australian Task Force with the South Vietnamese 10th (later redesignated 18th) Infantry Division. The MACV commander directed that the association begin immediately on a "tactical basis" in order "to bolster the effectiveness of the elements in the III Corps"; later he wanted it extended "to administrative support and advice with primary emphasis on improving the dependent housing situation in the ARVN units" and to "give a boost to the ARVN Post Exchange and Commissary arrangements by perhaps assisting them in effecting better management." Vien agreed and Westmoreland asked General Seaman, the II Field Force commander, to get together with his counterpart, III Corps commander General Nguyen Bao Tri, to implement the buddy program.[5]

The buddy concept of operations also raised the issue of an integrated command once again. In late May Westmoreland asked General Freund "to deal with matters of combined operations and revolutionary development." Westmoreland's J–5, Maj. Gen. John N. Ewbanks, Jr. (USAF), went further, recommending that a post be created for a lieutenant general to serve as a "resident" adviser to the South Vietnamese high command and that the American and South Vietnamese logistical systems be "integrated." Westmoreland, who was already the senior adviser to the South Vietnamese high command, rejected the idea of a resident adviser and asked only that Ewbanks' staff study the logistical proposal in more detail. Westmoreland also discouraged hopes aired by the South Vietnamese III Corps commander that the buddy program might lead to a national-level combined command, maintaining that "the present [command] arrangement was working adequately."[6]

In the meantime, the commanders of both the U.S. 1st and 25th Divisions began to assist the South Vietnamese regular units in performing area security missions. In mid-May the commander of the U.S. 25th Division, Maj. Gen. Frederick C. Weyand, started a series of combined operations with South Vietnamese regular and territorial forces in Hau Nghia Province, just northwest of Saigon; tasked his subordinate brigade commanders to assist the three infantry regiments of the South Vietnamese 25th Division in constructing housing for military dependents; and sponsored a propaganda program entitled "The Brotherhood of the 25th Division," which he dedicated to the "fight for freedom against the communists." In neighboring Binh Duong Province the new commander of the U.S. 1st Division, General DePuy, began a similar effort, with one of his three brigades supporting the South Vietnamese 5th Division. Initially each unit contributed one infantry battalion to the project. Combined activities consisted of small unit patrolling, village seals and searches, propaganda campaigns, intelligence collection efforts, and various civic improvement projects. In July, however, with the bulk of his units engaged in heavy fighting north of Saigon, DePuy had to abandon the combined operations task force concept.

---

[5] First quotation from Notes of 2–7 May 66, History file 6–B. Remaining quotations from Notes of 9–11 May 66, History file 6–C. Both in Westmoreland Papers, HRB, CMH. The II Field Force was the U.S. corps-level headquarters in the III Corps Tactical Zone.

[6] First quotation from Msg 4074, Westmoreland to Johnson, 22 May 66, History file 6–D6. Second quotation from Notes of 25 Jun 66, History file 7–D. See also Notes of 4 Jun 66, History file 7–A. All in Westmoreland Papers, HRB, CMH.

Conducting a Village Search in Binh Duong Province. *On the right a soldier carries his food for lunch.*

Thereafter, he monitored and supported the 5th Division's activities in Binh Duong through the division's 2d Brigade headquarters, only occasionally assigning ground units to the effort. Westmoreland enthusiastically applauded these endeavors, especially Weyand's propaganda program, and both he and Seaman claimed major improvements for the participating South Vietnamese units. Whether real progress existed, however, remained to be seen.[7]

Elsewhere in South Vietnam similar combined efforts took place. Westmoreland encouraged all his combat commanders to coordinate their endeavors more closely with local South Vietnamese forces, to exchange liaison teams whenever possible, and to include Vietnamese forces in their major endeavors. He hoped that closer relations between the two armies would push South Vietnamese military commanders out of their old two- or three-day battalion sweep routines

[7] Quoted words from Notes of 20 Aug 66, History file 8–D. See also Notes of 28 May and 9 Jun 66, History files 6–D and 7–B, respectively; MFR, Jones, 20 Jun 66, sub: MACV Commanders Conference, 5 June 1966, History file 7–B1. All in Westmoreland Papers, HRB, CMH. On DePuy's efforts, see 17th Military History Detachment, "Project LAM SON," n.d., inputs and rough drafts of an unfinished 1st Infantry Division after-action report; Combat Operations After-Action Report (hereafter cited as COAAR), 2d Bn, 16th Infantry, 29 Nov 66, sub: Operation LAM SON II (SOUTH ALLENTOWN), 21 Oct–5 Nov 66; COAAR, 1st Bn, 18th Infantry, 3 Nov 66, sub: Operation LAM SON II (BETHLEHEM, BELTON ALLENTOWN WEST), 20–28 Oct 66. All in HRB, CMH. For a favorable treatment of one operation, see John H. Hay, Jr., *Tactical and Materiel Innovations*, Vietnam Studies (Washington, D.C.: Department of the Army, 1974), pp. 137–42.

and into the more intensive small-scale patrolling that was needed to provide security in the Vietnamese countryside. Should serious trouble develop, the more mobile American combat units could always step in quickly. The major obstacle in implementing the concept was the preoccupation of most American combat units with large-scale offensive combat operations in the interior. Few American commanders had spare troops to assist the South Vietnamese regulars for any length of time. In addition, American corps and division commanders usually assigned secondary missions, guarding roads or serving as static blocking forces, to those South Vietnamese forces that were supporting some of their larger offensive operations. In light of these difficulties Westmoreland decided on a more ambitious approach, deploying three U.S. infantry battalions to the Saigon area in late 1966 to work directly with South Vietnamese security forces in the extremely heavily populated region. It was several months, however, before the new operation could begin.[8]

The Advisory Ethos

Throughout 1966 General Westmoreland continued to shy away from using force to attain his advisory goals and, on the battlefield, expected increasingly less from his Vietnamese allies and his field advisers.[9] Early in the year the MACV commander declared that "the number one priority in importance in this theater of war is the quality of [the] commanding officers of U.S. units." American troops deserve the best leadership that the Army can provide, and, if necessary, he was ready to transfer personnel from the advisory organization to satisfy this need. His guidance to the field advisers was, if anything, even more circumspect. He warned them against overwhelming their counterparts with advice, taking over their units, or even publicly praising them. Public praise by an American, he explained, was the "kiss of death" for a Vietnamese commander who would then be labeled "an American boy" and "eased out." The converse was also true. Overt American criticism of a Vietnamese commander sometimes raised his status among compatriots as one who could stand up to Americans.[10]

Westmoreland also instructed his field advisers not to refer Vietnamese leadership problems to MACV. "Deficiencies involving policy," he stated, should be brought to his attention, but those "involving non-compliance with directives, apathy on the part of the command, etc., are to be resolved in RVNAF channels." While again recognizing that the role of the adviser was "difficult and often frustrating," he felt that success in this area was a measure of each adviser's "military acumen, dedication, selflessness, and perserverance," and instructed the corps senior advisers "to complement tactical advice with improvement in

---

[8] For origins of what was later termed Operation FAIRFAX, see Msg, Westmoreland MAC 9974 to Wheeler, 150418 Nov 66, COMUSMACV Message file, Westmoreland Papers, HRB, CMH.

[9] For example, see Talking Paper, MACJ-341, 8 Oct 66, sub: Analysis of Performance of ARVN, MICRO 02/2624, RG 334, WNRC.

[10] First quotation from MFR, Jones, 10 Mar 66, sub: MACV Commanders Conference, 20 February 1966, History file 4–C1. Remaining quotations from ibid., 10 May 66, sub: MACV Commanders Conference, 24 April 1966, History file 6–A1. Both in Westmoreland Papers, HRB, CMH.

the quality, efficiency, and reliability of the RVNAF structure as a whole."[11] But the ground-level American advisers had expressed their deep dissatisfaction with this outlook many times before, and it is doubtful whether even Westmoreland expected the U.S. advisory ethos to be any more successful in 1966 than it had been in the past.

Trouble in the 25th

The continuation of the soft-sell approach made it increasingly difficult for American advisers to deal with ineffective commanders who had proved impervious to advice, however tactfully offered. The Chinh-Hunnicutt affair in late 1966 was an example of the tensions that existed at the field advisory level.[12] MACV advisers, from Westmoreland on down, had consistently criticized the performance of General Phan Trong Chinh since he had taken command of the 25th Division in 1964. In American circles he was considered one of the worst Vietnamese division commanders. However, his continued friendship with Premier Ky allowed him to ignore American advice with impunity, and the presence of strong U.S. ground forces within his division tactical area made the performance of his own unit less critical to Saigon. Yet given the temperament of the average American officer, it was inevitable that Chinh would butt heads with his more able advisers.

On 9 May 1966 Col. Cecil F. Hunnicutt became senior adviser to the 25th Division. His immediate superior, Col. Arndt Mueller, the III Corps deputy senior adviser, ordered him to put some life in the unit and somehow get it moving. At the time, Chinh had delegated control of many of his battalions to the province and district chiefs and had made little effort to supervise their activities. Hunnicutt, later described as a "competent, dynamic officer," pushed Chinh, Chinh's subordinates, and his own advisers to greater efforts, and the performance of the 25th slowly began to improve.[13]

From April to September, relations between Hunnicutt and Chinh were apparently cordial. The American adviser was frank with his counterpart, proposed many operational and personnel changes, and passed on his judgments to Mueller when Chinh failed to act. For example, when Hunnicutt recommended the removal of the Cu Chi district chief for blatant graft and corruption, Chinh unofficially acknowledged the situation but explained that his personal friendship with the accused prevented him from acting. Hunnicutt, however, reported both the case and Chinh's views to Mueller, who promptly informed General Khang,[14] the new III Corps commander. Khang took immediate action and relieved the offending officer, severely embarrassing General Chinh in the process.

---

[11] *U.S.-Vietnam Relations*, 7:sec. IV. V. 9. (b), pp. 41–42.

[12] Material on the affair may be found in the Chinh-Hunnicutt file, SEAB, CMH.

[13] Memo, Heintges to Porter, circa December 1966, sub: The Chinh/Hunnicutt Situation in the 25th ARVN Division, SEAB, CMH.

[14] Khang, also a Ky supporter, had replaced Nguyen Bao Tri as III Corps commander in June 1966.

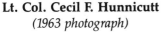

Lt. Col. Cecil F. Hunnicutt
(1963 photograph)

General Phan Trong Chinh

In August, the relationship between Hunnicutt and Chinh grew steadily worse. Frustrated over the performance of the division, the American adviser began to exert more pressure, recommending several of Chinh's major commanders for relief and threatening to withdraw the field advisers from units whose performance failed to improve. Shortly thereafter, Hunnicutt pulled his advisory team from the division's reconnaissance company following several incidents of Vietnamese drunkenness and misbehavior, and he also accused several battalion commanders of avoiding engagements with enemy units and falsifying their operational reports. Hunnicutt informed Chinh that the United States could not afford to support operations that were not pursued aggressively and achieved so little. He also believed that Chinh was cognizant of his critical monthly evaluation (SAME) reports but unaware that MACV routinely passed on much of the information directly to the South Vietnamese Joint General Staff.

Tired of Hunnicutt's constant badgering and humiliated by his complaints, Chinh decided to sever his relationship with the troublesome American officer. On 28 September he sent a memorandum to Khang, accusing Hunnicutt of submitting "sneaky reports on his division, threatening to pull advisors from units and of being insulting to the 46th and 50th Regiments."[15] He demanded that the III Corps commander remove Hunnicutt as senior adviser within twenty-four hours. The same day Chinh left his headquarters at Duc Hoa, a few kilometers west of Saigon; spent two days in the capital; and, upon his return,

---

[15] As quoted in Study, MACV J–3, circa October 1966, sub: The Chinh-Hunnicutt Situation, SEAB, CMH.

remained in his quarters for several days on the pretext of being ill. Thereafter he avoided Hunnicutt whenever possible.

Upon Hunnicutt's scheduled departure two months later, Chinh made the dispute public through a special "order of the day" to his troops and a slightly more detailed letter to his commanders. Both communications criticized Hunnicutt and those Vietnamese officers in his command who, Chinh felt, had cooperated too closely with their American advisers. Charging that Americans like Hunnicutt had little respect for the Vietnamese and were trying to take over the army by demanding control over all important appointments, Chinh stated that he was currently punishing one subordinate (later identified as the province chief of Long An) because "he only forwards reports to advisors"; "fails to keep his immediate commanders informed"; and, "having first let the means subjugate his mind, . . . has put himself in the hands of the provider of those means"—namely, the Americans. He went on to lecture his subordinates on the need to avoid being subverted by American wealth and power, as well as on the importance of keeping their self-respect and their loyalty to their own superiors. Chinh's accusations were quickly picked up, first by the Vietnamese and then by the American press, causing a sensation in Washington and forcing MACV to take a closer look at the matter.[16]

Several days later General Heintges flew to Duc Hoa to talk with Chinh. The Vietnamese general, Heintges reported, appeared contrite and apologetic, worrying about the ruckus he had stirred and blaming irresponsible translators and careless news reporters for misconstruing his words and taking them out of their proper context. Neither Heintges nor Westmoreland believed Chinh's explanation, but felt that his regret was sincere and that Hunnicutt "may have been a little too aggressive in his approach to this supersensitive, complex ridden, apprehensive, unsure, and relatively weak division commander." Heintges considered Chinh's excuse plausible enough for public relations purposes, allowing him to rescind the statements on the pretext that outsiders had misunderstood them. In closing the case, Heintges termed it an isolated incident. Hunnicutt rotated at the end of his normal tour, the recipient of the Legion of Merit for his outstanding performance as senior adviser. And Chinh, after publicly recanting his words, now appeared more amicable toward his new adviser, Col. John P. Arntz.[17]

---

[16] Quoted words from Ltr, Samuel V. Wilson, Long An Province representative, to John Hart, U.S. Embassy, Saigon, 3 Dec 66, History file 11–D2/D3, Westmoreland Papers, HRB, CMH. See also, in SEAB, CMH, the following: Chinh, "Order of the Day From Brigadier-General Commanding the 25th Infantry Div., C.O. Strategic Zone [i.e., DTA] 31, to Officers and Commanding Cadre of All Grades," 28 Nov 66; Memo, Chinh to Unit Cdrs of the 25th Div and the 31st Div Tactical Zone, 26 Nov 66 (rough English translation); Msg, Westmoreland (in Hawaii) to Rosson (in Saigon), 140740 Dec 66; Msg, SecState STATE 101802 to AmEmbassy, Saigon, and COMUSMACV, 132240 Dec 66 (Joint State-DOD Msg); Msg, COMUSMACV MAC 53642 to CINCPAC, 171245 Dec 66, sub: The Chinh/Hunnicutt Affair: Situation in the 25th ARVN Division.
[17] Quoted words from Msg, COMUSMACV MACJOO 53829 to CINCPAC, 191251 Dec 66, sub: Chinh/Hunnicutt Cause Celebre. See also Memo, Heintges to Porter, circa December 1966, sub: The Chinh/Hunnicutt Situation in the 25th ARVN Division. Both in SEAB, CMH. Colonel Hunnicutt had extended his twelve-month tour by six months to take the senior adviser assignment and had served his full eighteen months prior to his departure. In *U.S.-Vietnam Relations*, 7:sec. IV. C. 9. (b), p. 42, the authors imply, incorrectly, that Hunnicutt was relieved from his assignment in disgrace.

While Heintges visited Chinh, General Rosson had the MACV staff take a deeper look at current MACV advisory "techniques, procedures and regulations." Subsequent interviews with Hunnicutt and the four corps senior advisers revealed the absence of any written directives in this area and their general agreement that the advisory relationship was "a highly personal one" and that "success . . . at any level depends to a large degree on the rapport established between the two individuals concerned." General Brownfield, the acting J–3 at the time, noted that Hunnicutt was using MACV guidance issued back in June 1965—which allowed senior advisers to withdraw subordinate teams from South Vietnamese units if their security was endangered unnecessarily—as a rationale for pulling his teams out of Chinh's units. Feeling that Hunnicutt had abused the guidance as a means to pressure Chinh into action, he proposed that it be employed only during a true battlefield emergency. The corps senior advisers agreed, according to Brownfield, and his only recommendation was to publish clarifying instructions.[18]

The restrictive guidance was soon forthcoming. A new MACV directive cautioned field advisers to "avoid becoming involved with their counterparts' minor, everyday problems"; "to be discreet in applying . . . pressure"; and "under no circumstance," to use a "threat of removal . . . as a means of exerting pressure on a counterpart." Perhaps a more useful result of the affair was a small essay prepared by the Joint U.S. Public Affairs Office and distributed by MACV in March. The handout discussed the nature and origin of Vietnamese ethnocentrism and suggested ways of dealing with the people in the context of their own culture. However, the real problem was not the American tactical adviser's limited knowledge of Vietnamese culture and society but the inability of MACV to integrate the South Vietnamese commands and units into the war effort.[19]

Imbroglios Elsewhere

Unfortunately for MACV advisers, the Chinh-Hunnicutt affair was hardly the isolated case described by Heintges. The situation in South Vietnam's elite airborne force, for example, was similiar. The airborne commander, General Dong, also seemed highly resistant to American advice. Because of his close relationship with Thieu, General Vien, his nominal superior, was reluctant to discipline Dong and instead passed on American misgivings to Thieu. Thieu valued the support of Dong's Saigon-based paratroopers highly, but, to appease his American critics, apparently reprimanded Dong in private over his lackadaisical approach to the job. The result was a supposed "changed attitude" in Dong

---

[18] Quoted words from DF, MACV J–3 to CofS, MACV, 25 Jan 67, sub: Chinh/Hunnicutt Situation. See also Msg, COMUSMACV MACJ3 23815 to Corps Senior Advisers, 100025 Jun 65, sub: The Continuing Ambush Problem. Both in SEAB, CMH.

[19] Quoted words from MACV Directive 525–20, 26 Jan 67, sub: Combat Operations, Guidance for US Advisors, SEAB, CMH. The directive did recommend Hickey's Rand study, *The American Military Advisor and His Foreign Counterpart* (1965), as a reference. See also Ltr, MACV (to each adviser), 4 Mar 67, sub: Relationships Between U.S. Advisors and GVN Officials and Armed Forces, SEAB, CMH.

that, unhappily for his advisers, proved too brief. By the end of the year the airborne senior adviser, Col. James B. Bartholomees, again reported that Dong "was still not applying himself to his job."[20]

Examples of this nature existed in every corps area and at every echelon of command. Given Westmoreland's policy of noninterference, the Vietnamese had to do their own housecleaning. Both the Thi and Chinh affairs showed how explosive the matter was.[21] The next shake-up in the South Vietnamese politico-military government caught the Americans again by surprise. In November 1966, in the midst of the Chinh imbroglio, the Directory replaced General Quang, the IV Corps commander, with General Nguyen Van Manh and in January 1967 told Defense Minister Co, who was visiting Formosa, not to return. The two were key Directory members. In both cases Ky instigated the dismissals after securing the support of other senior generals, including Thieu. In doing so Ky probably felt that he had the full support of Ambassador Lodge, because the latter had previously labeled Quang and Co as the two most prominent "corruptionists" in the South Vietnamese government.[22]

In contrast to Co's removal, Quang's purge was potentially more divisive. Relieved to see the eclipse of Co, a rival, Thieu in all likelihood went along with the demise of his old friend Quang only because of constant pressure from the American embassy for his removal. Ky obviously was not as troubled. Apparently he had hoped to oust both Thi, the I Corps commander, and Quang in one sweep at the beginning of the year, but the Buddhist turmoil had temporarily stayed his hand. The American position on Quang was ambivalent. Like Thi, he had proved an excellent corps commander and Westmoreland was reluctant to see him go. Yet Ky's charge of corruption appeared to be accurate; Quang had amassed considerable wealth through the sale of offices, furthering the financial interests of his wife and relatives. To complicate matters, rumors reaching Westmoreland claimed that Co was pushing for Quang's relief and, at the same time, urging Quang to resist dismissal. If true, Co may have hoped to profit from any resulting turmoil between Quang's supporters and Premier Ky. In the end, however, both Co and Quang accepted the dismissals graciously. But to head off any possible trouble, Westmoreland himself attended the IV Corps change of command ceremony on 25 November. The MACV commander later urged Thieu to bring Quang to trial for his alleged corruption, but Thieu demurred, noting the absence of evidence and the chance that the former corps commander might be acquitted and the government embarrassed.[23]

---

[20] First quotation from Notes of 19 Sep 66, History file 9–A. Second quotation from Notes of 1 Dec 66, History file 11–D. Both in Westmoreland Papers, HRB, CMH. See also Seibert, "The Regulars," pp. 1117–19, Seibert Papers, MHI; Hoffman Interv, 25 Mar 75, SEAB, CMH.

[21] See Chapter 7 of this volume for details on the Thi affair.

[22] On Lodge's assessments of Quang and Co, see Statement of H. C. Lodge, Monday, October 10, 1966, MACV Conference Room, to Secretary of Defense Robert S. McNamara and Party, MICRO 2/ 1074, RG 334, WNRC. While retaining his post as chief of the Joint General Staff, General Vien carried out Co's duties until General Nguyen Van Vy, an apolitical senior general, took over permanently in November 1967.

[23] On the Quang affair, see Seeber, "A Study in Leadership," circa 1967, SEAB, CMH. See also Notes of 1 Jan, 2 May, and 11 and 21 Nov 66, History files 3–B, 6–B, and 11–C, respectively; MFR, Westmoreland, 11 Nov 66, sub: Visit With Prime Minister Ky, 6 November 1966, History *(Continued)*

The rapid shifts greatly perplexed Westmoreland. Despite Lodge's assessments of Quang and Co, the MACV commander regarded both officers as extremely competent. Describing the defense minister as "the victim of a character assassination campaign," he attributed his purge to personal jealousies between the wives of Co and Vien and to the humble origins of Co and his family. Nevertheless, the moves were handled deftly, with little interference or influence from either MACV or the U.S. Embassy and with none of the disruption that had accompanied the earlier dismissal of General Thi. The net result was again to strengthen the Directory government, now essentially the government of Thieu and Ky. However, from a military standpoint, it also meant the loss of two more able commanders, while generals like Dong and Chinh continued in office. Saigon was still too weak either to discipline its field commanders at will or to effect the sweeping changes in Vietnamese military leadership that Westmoreland and his field advisers thought necessary.[24]

Unwilling to do anything that might upset Saigon's new-found stability, Westmoreland thus chose to accept existing Vietnamese weaknesses in leadership for the time being, hoping that Saigon's forces could accomplish the supposedly less demanding chore of pacification security. The ensuing division of labor between American and South Vietnamese combat units also allowed Westmoreland to deploy more of his forces against conventional enemy units along the western borders and to minimize the presence of U.S. troops in the populated areas. But his lenient stand toward the senior South Vietnamese military leaders tended to undercut the entire field advisory effort. Without more support from MACV, the field advisers were relatively impotent. In Washington, one observer pointed out that a few more Chinh-Hunnicutt affairs "resolved in favor of poor Vietnamese commanders could destroy advisor confidence and initiative."[25] Certainly no one could have agreed more with such judgments than the U.S. Army Special Forces soldiers trying to bring some degree of order to the remote border areas.

(Continued) file 11–B2; ibid., 16 Nov 66, sub: Conference With General Thieu From 1630 to 1750 Hours, 15 November 1966, History file 11–C4. All in Westmoreland Papers, HRB, CMH. Ky gives his version in *Twenty Years and Twenty Days*, p. 110. Ky also tried to move Vinh Loc out of the II Corps command, but he did not push the matter when Loc proved "reluctant" to leave. See Msg, Larsen NHT 882 to Westmoreland, 15 Nov 66, COMUSMACV Message file, Westmoreland Papers, HRB, CMH.

[24] Quoted words from MFR, Westmoreland, 3 Jan 67, sub: Conferences With Generals Vien and Co, 3 January 1967, History file 12–B6. For comments on Quang, see Notes of 1 Jan and 2 May 66, History files 3–B and 6–B, respectively. All in Westmoreland Papers, HRB, CMH. On other personalities, such as Nguyen Van Vy, see copy of Intelligence Memorandum, CIA, July 1968, sub: Members of the Cabinet of the Republic of VN, SEAB, CMH.

[25] Memo, Montague to Komer, 22 Dec 66, sub: Other Ideas on Improving ARVN Effectiveness, SEAB, CMH.

11

Heyday of the Special Forces

In the remote interior of South Vietnam the U.S. Army Special Forces faced many of the same problems that beset the rest of the advisory effort. The CIDG program reflected all the inherent contradictions of American military policies in South Vietnam. Was the program part of the strategy of attrition or the strategy of pacification? Were the American Special Forces teams supposed to lead or merely advise the various types of CIDG units? By 1965 MACV had already expanded the original Special Forces mission of providing military security in remote areas with the tasks of conducting border surveillance and collecting order of battle intelligence. With the expansion of the ground war in 1966 Westmoreland also began to view the organization as an anti-infiltration force, while American tactical commanders wanted their assistance in locating the elusive enemy. The subordination of the Special Forces field detachments to the U.S. corps-level commanders and the steady growth of the Special Forces mobile reaction units only helped to increase their involvement in the conventional military effort.[1]

Roles and Missions

By 1966 the U.S. Army Special Forces were stretched thin trying to satisfy too many different requirements. One B (mid-level) detachment noted that its multiple missions included aiding, advising, supporting, and assisting the local Vietnamese Special Forces; organizing, equipping, and training its CIDG contingent; conducting border surveillance operations; and interdicting enemy infiltration routes. Satisfying everyone called for bewildering amounts of coordination and tightrope walking, with many adjacent and higher commands looking over a unit's shoulder. For example, when a sizeable enemy force attacked and almost overran one of the isolated A (unit-level) detachments at Ton Le Chon, the nearby U.S. 1st Infantry Division rushed in two full combat battalions, the local South Vietnamese division provided air and artillery support, and the Special Forces Group headquarters in faraway Nha Trang reinforced with two Mobile Strike

[1] See comments of one of the 5th Special Forces Group commanders, in Kelly, *U.S. Army Special Forces*, pp. 77–85. For a general background on the Special Forces, see sources cited in Chapter 3, p. 69.

(MIKE) Force companies. In the process the tiny Special Forces detachment—almost totally occupied with trying to lead, advise, and fight the immediate battle—was almost overwhelmed, not by the enemy, but by the massive support requirements generated by the reinforcements. Not surprisingly, American combat commanders found their relationships with the Special Forces units confusing, and only gradually came to understand the complex political and social problems the Special Forces faced and the ambiguities of their advisory role. But many others continued to regard the CIDG forces as tactical combat units, rather than part-time militia, and expected them to perform accordingly. Perhaps the self-nurtured image of the Special Forces Green Berets as elite jungle commandos had begun to catch up with them and their exotic allies.[2]

Trying to put the CIDG fighting ability into perspective, a veteran Australian adviser noted that the Montagnard soldiers had been hired for pay, "aren't subjected to military discipline in any way, shape or form, and aren't really required to obey orders they don't like." The CIDG was not part of the American or South Vietnamese armed forces, or of any organized army. The American and South Vietnamese Special Forces "commanders" of the units had no legal authority over the indigenous troops who could come and go as they pleased. CIDG troopers were willing to defend the traditional lands of their people, he added, but were "not really fighting for a cause that they either understand or believe in." As a result, Montagnard soldiers generally would not maneuver aggressively against strong enemy forces, or otherwise put their lives in jeopardy needlessly, but, if attacked, would instinctively "dig in and . . . stay there and fight to the end." Another adviser, Lt. Col. Medley M. Davis, observed that the Montagnards exhibited more hostility toward the North Vietnamese than toward the Viet Cong soldiers, who often had family ties with the local tribes. Both Davis and another career Special Forces officer, Col. Charles M. Simpson III, also pointed out that the CIDG forces were light infantry, lacking the equipment and trained cadre of similar-size American units, as well as the physical stamina of the Americans. In conventional ground operations these irregulars best served as static blocking forces, around which American troops could maneuver and American and air and artillery firepower could be employed. However, almost all Special Forces advisers agreed that their most suitable use was reconnaissance, small unit patrolling, and defending their home bases and villages from prepared positions.[3]

Special Forces advisers also continued to have serious problems with the *Lac Luong Dac Biet (LLDB)*, the separate Vietnamese Special Forces organization of the regular army whose members theoretically commanded the CIDG units.

---

[2] Rpt, HQ, Detachment B–33, to CO, Co A, 5th Special Forces Group (Airborne), 1st Special Forces, 14 Aug 67, sub: After-Action Report of the 165th NVA Regiment Attack on Ton Le Chon, 7 August 1967, VNIT 225, HRB, CMH; Kelly, *U.S. Army Special Forces*, pp. 172–73.

[3] Quoted words from Interv, Maj Roy S. Barnard with Capt Shulsten (Australian Army Training Group), CO, 1st Mobile Strike Force Bn, circa 1970, pp. 231–32, VNIT 677, HRB. Shulsten, a twenty-year veteran, was a member of the Australian Army advisory group that supported the MACV field advisory effort. For similar comments on CIDG units composed of ethnic Cambodians in the Delta, see interviews and documents in VNIT 126, HRB. On Davis, see Interv, author with Davis (hereafter cited as Davis Interv), Special Forces A Detachment, Khe Sanh, and S–3, Special Forces C Detachment, Da Nang, I CTZ (November 1966–September 1967), 27 Feb 76, SEAB. All in CMH. See also Simpson, *Inside the Green Berets*, p. 205.

Special Forces Adviser With *LLDB* and CIDG Leaders *planning ambush operations*

LLDB assignments to units in remote areas whose inhabitants were traditionally hostile to Vietnamese culture were decidedly unpopular. *LLDB* members rarely spoke the Montagnard tribal languages and, according to Colonel Davis, most continued to look down on the Highlanders as *ngoui thuong* ("mountain people" or "hicks"). Not surprisingly, few *LLDB* officers, most of whom were ethnic Vietnamese, developed any close ties with their troops or, in fact, any enthusiasm for their job. Lt. Col. Kenneth B. Facy, a C (corps-level) detachment commander, viewed Saigon's *LLDB* soldiers as almost hopeless, exhibiting a "lack of ethical standards, dedication to duty, patriotism, courage, and professional competence. . . ." Most *LLDB* members were apathetic, and the worst misfits were normally reassigned within the component rather than dismissed. As a result, Facy felt that the CIDG program was only marginally effective in some areas and that American lives were being unnecessarily jeopardized by the unfitness of their counterparts. His only solution was a complete purge of the entire organization, and a concentrated politico-military training program for those few that remained. At the lowest levels, reports of the Special Forces A detachments varied. Some noted that *LLDB* cadre refused to go into combat or even to accompany CIDG units on operations; others related that officers sold enlistments to prospective recruits and even their own equipment on the black market; and still other reports told of more dedicated *LLDB* members—those who worked hard, fought hard, and sometimes died at the sides of their American advisers. The situation appeared to vary greatly from camp to camp and from individual to individual. In general, however, it was evident that, until leadership in the *LLDB* improved, American personnel had to assume the task of both advising and leading the CIDG program.[4]

Another Special Forces problem was internal. As early as 1965 Col. Charles E. Spragins, the deputy group commander, noted that many of the more conventional American officers viewed the semiautonomous organization with suspicion and even "distrust." With its own chain of command, funding, and supply system, it may have appeared too independent and too steeped in "unconventional warfare" to be part of the Army "team." The varied and often conflicting roles and missions of the Special Forces made the problem worse. Spragins felt that Army field advisers envied the greater power and leverage that Special Forces officers enjoyed over their counterparts, their almost direct control of the CIDG effort, and their ability to call on their own combat reserve forces when necessary. Col. Francis J. Kelly, who commanded the 5th Special Forces Group in 1966 and 1967, was "continually conscious of mistrust and suspicion on the part of many relatively senior field grade U.S. military men" toward his command. As a remedy, he recommended more familiarization by senior American Army personnel with Special Forces organization and missions, and perhaps the appointment of a general officer to command the group. Another Special Forces veteran, Col. Rod Paschall, later added that the C (corps-level) detachment commanders were normally lieutenant colonels and thus lacked the rank to advise a lieutenant general commanding a U.S. Army corps or field force whose deputies and primary staff officers were also general officers and senior colonels.[5]

The feelings of Army Chief of Staff Harold K. Johnson typified some of the attitudes that worried Kelly. Although the tough, experienced General Johnson had survived the Bataan Death March and many harsh years as a Japanese prisoner of war, he was confused and unhappy with the activities of the Special Forces. They were "supposed to be training guerrillas," he observed, "and what they did was build fortifications out of the Middle Ages and bury themselves . . . with concrete." After visiting some of their more exposed Highland camps, he expressed "horror" that an organization that prided itself on being a "highly mobile, disdainful of fixed installations, innovative, [and] not requiring organized logistical support" should find itself "in fortified installations with mortars in concrete emplacements with fixed range cards printed on the concrete, and literally . . . locked in by their own actions." In his estimation the CIDG program drained manpower from Saigon and was too expensive; the indigenous soldiers spent too much time protecting their own dependents who lived nearby.

---

[4] Davis quote from Davis Interv, 27 Feb 76. Facy report of 21 Mar 66 from Historical Study by 21st Military History Detachment, Encl to Transmittal Ltr, Aaron, HQ, 5th Special Forces Group (Airborne), 1st Special Forces, 24 May 69, sub: Vietnamese Special Forces (VNSF), pp. 1.3–1.12. Quotation on p. 1.10. Both in SEAB, CMH. The latter study of the *LLDB* includes hundreds of comments by Special Forces advisers about their counterparts during the period 1964–69. See especially interview excerpts on pp. 9.5–9.6, 10.11–10.12, 10.25.

[5] Quoted words by Spragins in Spragins Interv, 29 Aug 65, file 206–02, Interviews with General Officers, box 6, accession no. 69A702, RG 334, WNRC. Quoted words by Kelly in Kelly, *U.S. Army Special Forces*, p. 172 (see also pp. 80, 85, 173). On Paschall, see Interv, author with Paschall (hereafter cited as Paschall Interv), Special Forces adviser (1962–63), 15 Oct 84, SEAB, CMH.

198

Furthermore, he felt that U.S. Special Forces members "viewed themselves as something separate and distinct from the rest of the military effort," describing them as "fugitives from responsibility" who "tended to be nonconformist, couldn't quite get along in a straight military system, and found a haven where their actions were not scrutinized too carefully, and where they came under only sporadic or intermittent observation from the regular chain of command." For those who shared Johnson's judgments, it was easy to write off the CIDG program and, indeed, the entire American advisory effort as almost a waste of time and money. Trained in conventional methods of warfare, many American commanders looked down on such unconventional endeavors and regarded the results of U.S. ground operations as the principal gauge for measuring progress in the war. Others, such as General Heintges, had extensive experience with Special Forces units in South Vietnam and elsewhere, and were thus more knowledgeable of both their capabilities and their limitations.[6]

FULRO

Stabilizing the political status of the CIDG was the first order of business in 1966. In Saigon Westmoreland remained irritated by the poor relationships between the Special Forces advisers and their Vietnamese counterparts, fearing that *FULRO (Front unifie de la lutte des races opprimees)*, the Montagnard separatist movement led by Y Bham Enoul, might have misinterpreted the situation and expected Americans to support Montagnard autonomy, as the French had done. Consequently, he forbade his advisers to deal with *FULRO* representatives in any manner, and throughout 1966 the U.S. 5th Special Forces Group commanders, Col. William A. McKean and his successor, Colonel Kelly, tried to put the CIDG advisory effort on a more harmonious footing.[7]

Meanwhile, urged by Westmoreland, Saigon began to take several steps towards reaching an accord with the Montagnards and *FULRO*. On 22 February 1966 the government established a Special Commissariat for Montagnard Affairs headed by Paul Nur, a respected French-educated administrator of Montagnard descent. Shortly thereafter, Nur and General Vinh Loc, commander of the II Corps Tactical Zone (the Highlands), agreed upon a package of economic, social, and administrative reforms for the Montagnard tribes. Loc promised to increase the number of Montagnard civil servants, to reestablish tribal courts, and to widen educational and medical services for the Montagnards. He also promised to resolve the long-standing issue of land ownership by granting land titles to the Highland tribes. Nur produced an even more comprehensive program, allegedly approved by both General Loc and Premier Ky, and Ky reserved several seats for

[6] Quoted words from Johnson Interv, 8 Jan 73, sess. 9, p. 27; 23 Apr 73, sess. 12, p. 7; and 23 Apr 73, sess. 12, pp. 9–10, Senior Officers Debriefing Program, MHI. See also Paschall Interv, 25 Apr 85, SEAB, CMH.

[7] On *FULRO*, see Notes of 27 and 30 Jan 66, History files 3-F and 4-A, respectively; Remarks Made by CO, 5th Special Forces Group, to All Incoming Personnel, circa February 1966, History file 4–A2. All in Westmoreland Papers, HRB, CMH. See also Cannon Debriefing Rpt, 17 Nov 67, pp. 18–21; and sources cited in Chapter 3, p. 69.

Montagnard representatives in the forthcoming constituent assembly. Despite the fanfare accompanying these promises, American officials remained skeptical, recalling the government's poor performance in the past. For the time being MACV remained aloof from the matter, looked for hard results, and felt it best that Saigon resolve the problem on its own.

To avoid further disturbances that could embarrass both governments, the American embassy encouraged Ky to continue his negotiations with *FULRO*. After prolonged talks, the two parties reached a tentative understanding in September 1966. *FULRO* leaders agreed to return their forces to areas under Saigon control in exchange for a release of *FULRO* prisoners, a Montagnard "bill of rights," and the incorporation of

Y Bham Enoul

FULRO military units into the South Vietnamese armed forces without losing their special identity. *FULRO* apparently abandoned its demands for political autonomy and a separate army. But only about 250 *FULRO* troops initially returned from Cambodia, and Y Bham remained across the border with the bulk of his forces waiting to see if Saigon would fulfill its promises. His caution proved wise. Saigon again did nothing, and in December American embassy officials and the II Corps senior adviser urged Vinh Loc to take unilateral actions that would demonstrate Saigon's good intentions. Thus at year's end, despite almost continuous negotiations, Vietnamese-Montagnard relationships were still "ticklish."

The Continued Expansion

Amid this turmoil MACV continued to expand the CIDG program and other Special Forces advisory activities. CIDG forces grew from about 22,000 in mid-1965 to about 30,000 by the end of 1966 and leveled off at about 40,000 troops in 1967, spread throughout eighty different camps. Each camp had two to three rifle companies and a specially trained reconnaissance platoon, known collectively as a camp strike force. These units, however, had neither the strength nor organization of an infantry battalion. Westmoreland had decided against adding new rifle companies but authorized the reconnaissance platoons to boost intelligence-gathering capabilities. American Special Forces members also continued to serve as province and district advisers along the border, while others advised or led the various commando-type units established earlier. In 1966 the size of the Territorial Forces under Special Forces supervision increased from about

18,000 to 70,000 and the strength of the commando units from 1,500 to 3,200. Like the CIDG, both were composed primarily of South Vietnamese ethnic or religious minorities and included not only Montagnards but also large numbers of Cambodians and Cao Dai adherents.[8]

The expanding CIDG program, the establishment of Special Forces province and district advisory teams, and the creation of the Special Forces–led commando units fueled the growth of the 5th Special Forces Group. During 1966 the group grew from 1,828 men (in 4 C, 11 B, and 61 A detachments) to 2,745 (in 5 C, 16 B, and 80 A detachments). Approximately 40 detachments served as province and district advisory teams, and Westmoreland even toyed with the idea of transferring the entire pacification advisory effort to the Special Forces. But qualified experienced personnel were now at a premium. Many of the small A detachments were understrength, a product of the rapid expansion and the scarcity of officers and noncommissioned officers from combat arms branches, and the group would have been hard pressed to assume a responsibility of such magnitude without completely bowing out of the CIDG program.[9]

In 1966 the 5th Special Forces Group also beefed up its own headquarters. Comptroller, judge advocate, aviation, engineer, and inspector general sections were added and the operations and intelligence staffs enlarged. To satisfy the growing demand for more and better intelligence for American combat units, the group overhauled its information-gathering, analysis, and dissemination procedures and tried to assign Special Forces liaison officers to all major U.S. Army units close to CIDG camps. As an economy measure, it replaced officers in staff positions whenever possible with noncommissioned officers.[10]

Poor relationships between ethnic Vietnamese and the minority groups hamstrung all CIDG operations. Only in the Highland camp of Plei Mrong, Pleiku Province, were Special Forces advisers able to transfer operations completely to their South Vietnamese counterparts. In the III and IV Corps Tactical Zones, where large numbers of ethnic Cambodians and Vietnamese religious minority groups had entered the program, similar problems existed but were less intense. Nevertheless, American Special Forces advisers continued to provide the necessary leadership and also to direct the financial and logistical support that, together with the draft exempt status of the CIDG, made service in the irregular organization attractive. But in the eyes of the Saigon government, the CIDG still had no legal status.

MACV efforts to convert the CIDG into territorials had little success. To put these irregulars on a legal footing, Westmoreland had intended to convert the majority of the companies into Regional Forces during 1965 and 1966. However, the lack of security in the border regions and the continuing friction between the Vietnamese and Montagnards militated against the transition. No conversions

---

[8] The Cao Dai was a religious sect concentrated in Tay Ninh Province, northwest of Saigon. On the expansion, see USMACV, "Command History, 1965," pp. 78–79, HRB, CMH; Ello et al., *U.S. Army Special Forces . . . , 1961–1967*; and especially MICROs 2/2205, 2/2208, 2/2194, 2/2195, RG 334, WNRC, for various 5th Special Forces Group (Airborne) fact sheets for this period.

[9] Ello et al., *U.S. Army Special Forces . . . , 1961–1967*; Fact Sheet, 5th Special Forces Group (Airborne), 8 Oct 66, MICRO 2/2195, RG 334, WNRC; and Briefing of 15 Mar 66, History file 4–E, Westmoreland Papers, HRB, CMH, which discusses the transfer proposal.

[10] Kelly, *U.S. Army Special Forces*, pp. 97–101.

Special Forces Camps, IV Corps (top) and II Corps (bottom). *Geography played a major role in preparing defenses in each camp.*

took place in 1965 and only nine camps successfully made the transition in 1966, while twelve had to be returned to the CIDG program. Most of the successful conversions occurred in the more secure coastal lowlands or where U.S. Special Forces members were serving as province and district advisers. In general, the Montagnards were dissatisfied with the lower rank structure and pay rates of the territorials, the reduced logistical support, the separation from home villages that conversions sometimes entailed, and the loss of their special relationship with their American advisers. Many tribesmen refused to serve under South Vietnamese officers and, at the first opportunity, either returned home or enlisted in other CIDG units in more remote areas, where recruitment was difficult. The loyalty of the Montagnards and other participants to the U.S. Special Forces personnel, the control of the Special Forces "advisers" over CIDG finances and logistical support, and the new emphasis on conventional combat missions continued to give the entire effort a mercenary character that was inimical to the original program. Although Westmoreland hoped that better territorial logistical support would make conversion more attractive, his continuing need for these unconventional forces kept him from pressing the matter strongly.[11]

Border Operations

CIDG operations continued to consist primarily of small-scale patrolling to provide local security and to gather information. A lack of regular combat support elements, an insufficient number of radios, and the absence of organic crew-served weapons made it difficult for CIDG units to engage Viet Cong and North Vietnamese regular units on an equal basis. In addition, CIDG members often had close family ties within the areas they defended and refused to serve far from home camps. The camps themselves, especially those along the border, were vulnerable to attack and often depended entirely on air resupply. In the face of strong enemy concentrations, MACV even ordered several abandoned in 1965.

During 1966 and 1967 American field commanders used the Special Forces–led MIKE units increasingly for long-range reconnaissance missions, employing them as scouting or security elements for American ground tactical units. For example, in the fall of 1966 Lt. Col. Eleazar ("Lee") Parmley IV, commanding a B detachment at Pleiku, led a battalion-size task force of two local CIDG companies and one MIKE Force company into the Plei Trap woods to the west, covering the northern flank of a multibattalion sweep of the U.S. 4th Infantry Division. During the ensuing operation, Parmley's patrolling rifle units engaged scattered enemy forces in a running fight, but finally bumped into the *88th North Vietnamese Regiment*, which had been preparing to attack the relatively inexperienced American division from the rear. In a series of firefights that followed, the rapidly withdrawing CIDG force took several casualties before the more powerful 4th Division units could relieve it and take over the battle. However, the CIDG action prevented the division from being surprised and enabled it to bring the normally

[11] See Ello et al., *U.S. Army Special Forces . . . , 1961–1967*; USMACV, "Command History, 1966," pp. 110–11, HRB, CMH; Notes of 1 Feb 66, History file 4–A, Westmoreland Papers, HRB, CMH.

Project Delta Members

elusive enemy unit to battle, illustrating how the U.S. tactical unit commanders would have liked to have used the Montagnard irregulars in the field.[12]

Strike forces were better at such mobile operations than the average CIDG company. Consequently, during 1966 Westmoreland increased the number of these units from five to eighteen and began introducing South Vietnamese Special Forces personnel into the program. Under the direction of Kelly, the Strikers were seconded by smaller but similar units called mobile guerrilla forces.[13] Operating under the direction of the C detachments, these units entered suspected enemy base areas in South Vietnam and conducted hit-and-run guerrilla operations against regular enemy units. Initially, no South Vietnamese Special Forces personnel participated. Such tactics represented, in fact, a return to the pre-Vietnam era Special Forces missions and, ironically, a reaffirmation of the role of the Special Forces in conventional warfare.

The Special Forces–led Delta, Sigma, and Omega units serving as reconnaissance and reaction forces also grew in size and employment. The Delta Force continued to perform missions assigned jointly by MACV and the Joint General Staff and to operate under the combined supervision of the U.S. and South Vietnamese Special Forces commands. By 1967 the reconnaissance elements of

[12] See Simpson, *Inside the Green Berets*, pp. 205–14.
[13] Each was led by a U.S. Special Forces A Detachment and consisted of a guerrilla company of 150 soldiers and a 46-man reconnaissance platoon.

the unit had grown from six to twenty-four teams and the reaction force, the South Vietnamese 81st Airborne Ranger "Battalion," from three to six rifle companies. The Delta Force operated primarily in the I and IV Corps Tactical Zones. The 5th Special Forces Group raised similar units in 1966, the Sigma and Omega "projects," to serve in the II and III Corps areas directly under the American field force commanders. Each organization consisted of sixteen reconnaissance teams and several MIKE Force units as reaction forces. No South Vietnamese Special Forces initially participated, and Sigma and Omega were under complete American command and control. For both the MIKE and Greek-letter forces, the Special Forces recruited heavily among the Nungs, Vietnamese of Chinese extraction who had traditionally served as mercenaries in Vietnam.[14]

As members of the Studies and Observation Group (SOG) assigned to MACV, Special Forces personnel also continued to advise the South Vietnamese Strategic Technical Directorate and to support its reconnaissance operation in North Vietnam. However, in 1965 American cross-border operations into Laos, under the code name SHINING BRASS, steadily grew in size and scope. Directed first by the 5th Special Forces Group and then by SOG, the SHINING BRASS reconnaissance and harassment operations were much more extensive and successful than those conducted against North Vietnam. Here again, South Vietnamese military personnel were not involved and the Special Forces recruited extensively from minority groups to fill out the teams. However, in coordination with SOG and under U.S. Army Special Forces advisers, the Vietnamese directorate gradually developed their own cross-border reconnaissance programs into Laos and Cambodia.[15]

In addition to their operational advisory roles, American Special Forces personnel continued to advise the South Vietnamese Special Forces training center at Dong Ba Thin and the Strategic Technical Directorate camp at Long Thanh. In September 1966 the 5th Special Forces Group also opened a "Recondo School" at Nha Trang to train regular American troops in long-range reconnaissance techniques and to conduct special courses for future Delta, Sigma, and Omega personnel. But the regular CIDG units located in the widely dispersed camps received little training aside from the individual instruction offered by the Special Forces A team members.

During 1967 the involvement of the Special Forces in the conventional war effort became even greater. Throughout South Vietnam, Special Forces soldiers led, cajoled, and advised their heterogeneous collection of troopers—'Yards, 'Bods, "Cidges," Strikers, and what not—against regular enemy forces, carrying the war into his most remote base areas and supply routes. Repeatedly the 5th Special Forces Group closed out camps in quiet areas and opened new ones in traditional enemy strongholds, always expanding the conventional operations of

[14] The Omega Force was also known as B–50 and Sigma Force as B–56, referring to the Special Forces B detachments that led them.

[15] Cross-border activities are covered in USMACV, "Command History, 1965," annex N, and "1966," annex M (both published separately), HRB, CMH; Fact Sheet, MACSOG, 8 Oct 66, sub: Shining Brass Assets, MICRO 2/2191, RG 334, WNRC; and Strategic Technical Directorate Assistance Team 158, MACV, "Command History, 1 May 1972–March 1973," pp. 2–5, which discusses two major subordinate elements: the Liaison Service, responsible for operations in Cambodia; and the Special Missions Service, with jurisdiction over similar operations in Laos.

their growing forces. In May 1967, for example, the group employed a total of eleven MIKE and CIDG companies in a single operation against enemy units in the seven mountains border region of the IV Corps Tactical Zone (Operation BLACKJACK 41C), while during the same month the commander of the U.S. 1st Division put a combination of Special Forces guerrilla units, Project Sigma reconnaissance teams, and MIKE units into War Zone D, a vast, ill-defined enemy base region in the III Corps Tactical Zone. The first was essentially a search-and-destroy operation that led to encounters against conventional enemy units, while the second, led by Lt. Col. Clarence T. Hewgley and Capt. James ("Bo") Gritz, harassed larger North Vietnamese Army units in their own sanctuaries. Meanwhile, in a remote northwestern corner of Vietnam, between the Laotian border and the Demilitarized Zone, Special Forces elements had the distinction of repelling a North Vietnamese armored attack on 4 May 1967, marking the first use of enemy tanks in South Vietnam. The action was a harbinger of things to come.[16]

Elsewhere, Special Forces soldiers often had a tougher and more lonely row to hoe. For 1st Lt. Charles R. Lloyd, on his first combat operation with Detachment A–416 out of camp My Dien II in swampy Dinh Tuong Province (IV Corps Tactical Zone), the working conditions were challenging. When an estimated reinforced Viet Cong platoon ambushed his lead element on 22 May 1968, the young officer's *LLDB* counterpart and many of the troops fled. Undaunted, Lloyd and his noncommissioned officer put together a makeshift defense by physically threatening the remaining soldiers and, with the assistance of air support, managed a painful withdrawal. However, a dozen men were left behind, dead or missing, including Lloyd's senior sergeant, who had been caught in the initial ambush, and the detachment's interpreter, whose body was found four days later floating in a canal by the base camp, "spread-eagled on a log with 30, 40, or 50 bullet holes in him."[17] Although CIDG units often came out ahead in such encounters, the story of A–416 that day was not especially unusual.

The experiences of Sfc. William T. Craig were even more trying. Stationed at the lonely Lang Vei camp just west of besieged Khe Sanh on the eve of the Tet offensive, Craig watched his base overrun by enemy armor on the night of 6–7 February 1968. With a Soviet-made PT76 tank perched atop the team's command bunker and many of his fellow advisers dead or wounded, the sergeant attempted to organize a relief force outside the perimeter of the camp, only to be first wounded and then buried alive by supporting U.S. air strikes. In the morning, only the disorganization of the enemy and the confusion of battle allowed Craig and the remnants of his force to escape. Until the end, it was such small-scale operations, endless patrols and ambushes, and the defense of their isolated camps that continued to form the core of the Special Forces' experience in the war.[18]

---

[16] See the operations chronicled in Kelly, *U.S. Army Special Forces*, pp. 102–48, 204–13, app. F; Stanton, *Green Berets at War*, pp. 109–67, and the ORLLs of the 5th Special Forces Group for this period, HRB, CMH.

[17] Interv, Capt Nicholas Sellers, Unit Historian, Co D, 5th Special Forces Group (Airborne), with Lloyd and M Sgt Donald H. Chase, 19 Jun 68, to include synopsis by Capt Thomas B. Edwards, CO, 21st Military History Detachment, 25 Jun 68, VNIT 126, HRB, CMH.

[18] Interv, Edwards with Craig, 25 Apr 68, VNIT 173, HRB, CMH. For Lang Vei action, see also interviews and documents in VNIT 138.

Considering the small size of the Special Forces organization and the small amount of materiel invested in the CIDG effort, the contributions of the 5th Special Forces Group to the overall war effort were substantial. With no more than about twenty-five hundred men at any one time, the group raised an army of about fifty thousand in some of the worst and certainly the most dangerous terrain in South Vietnam. In doing so, it not only provided security and organization in areas whose populations might have been conceded entirely to the enemy but also supplied American commanders with reliable tactical intelligence by systematically patrolling the border infiltration areas. In many cases, enemy attacks on remote CIDG camps and enemy encounters with patrolling CIDG, MIKE Force, and Greek-letter detachments led to larger engagements with reinforcing U.S. units. The Ia Drang campaign of the U.S. 1st Cavalry Division in August 1965 following the siege of the Special Forces camp at Plei Me was only the first example. Wary of American firepower, Viet Cong and North Vietnamese Army units often chose to bypass CIDG camps and patrols whenever possible. Still, serious problems remained. Because of the poor quality of the South Vietnamese Special Forces, the American advisers continued to perform as the *de facto* leaders of the CIDG camps and units. The failure of the 5th Special Forces Group to build an effective *LLDB* counterpart organization was perhaps its greatest shortcoming.[19] The continued hostility between ethnic Vietnamese and the minority groups also sapped the military efforts of the CIDG units, especially in the Montagnard camps. The increasing employment of CIDG forces in conventional combat operations confused their leaders, and the continued status of the CIDG as almost a private mercenary army irritated both MACV and Saigon. In many ways the Special Forces programs stood outside the mainstream of the American war effort and, in the aggregate, remained one of the many "separate" wars of the Vietnam conflict.

[19] Stanton, *Green Berets at War*, p. 293; Paschall Interv, 19 Aug 86, SEAB, CMH.

12

The Reform Effort Stalls

As the United States passed through its second year of attrition strategy in 1967, the advisory effort appeared to have taken a permanent back seat in the American war effort. The attention of both MACV and Washington remained fixed on the question of further U.S. troop deployments, enemy losses on the battlefield, and the continued infiltration of men and materiel from North Vietnam. Seeking to measure progress in the war, military and civilian analysts debated endlessly over the accuracy and significance of a bewildering number of battlefield statistics. Meanwhile, in both Saigon and Washington, senior American leaders were more concerned with the continued stability of the South Vietnamese government and its public image in America than with the effectiveness of its fighting forces in the field. If anything, the first six months of 1967 marked the lowest ebb of the overall advisory effort.

Reorganizing for Pacification

At the beginning of 1967 the U.S. advisory effort still remained thoroughly fragmented from top to bottom. Coordination of this vast effort depended greatly on General Westmoreland himself and his deputy, General Heintges. While Westmoreland and Heintges, and the latter's successor in May, General Creighton W. Abrams, Jr., focused on specific military and political problems, the advisory effort suffered from a lack of daily supervision and guidance. In June Maj. Gen. Walter T. Kerwin, Jr., the new MACV chief of staff, directed the MACV J–5 (Plans), General Ewbanks, to study the problem and consider either reestablishing a separate advisory headquarters or improving the existing organization. The result was an advisory organization study code-named Project 640.[1]

Project 640 identified five possible courses of action: maintaining the current organization; establishing a separate advisory headquarters; assigning all Army staff advisers to USARV, the U.S. Army component command; withdrawing all

[1] For background, see USMACV, "Command History, 1967," 3 vols. (Saigon, 1968), 1:221–35, HRB, CMH; Briefing, MACMA, 5 Jul 67, sub: Army Programs for Military [?] Vietnam, MICRO 3/0404, RG 334, WNRC. Maj. Gen. Don O. Darrow (USAF) succeeded Ewbanks on 5 July 1967.

advisory functions from the Army component command and returning them to MACV; or creating a separate focal point for advisory matters within the MACV headquarters. Ewbanks' staff dismissed the first two alternatives, as the existing system was unsatisfactory and creating yet another headquarters would be too cumbersome. Alternative three, assigning all staff advisers to USARV, even if possible, involved too much disruption of existing command arrangements. By the process of elimination, the study group settled on the last two courses of action. General Abrams agreed and, in September, began transferring the logistics advisers back to MACV and establishing a major staff section for military assistance. The ensuing reorganization transformed the existing MAP Directorate into the larger Office of the Assistant Chief of Staff for Military Assistance under Brig. Gen. Donnelly P. Bolton. Bolton's new office assumed responsibility for the technical service advisers (ordnance, quartermaster, transportation, medical, engineer, and signal) and the advisory teams assigned to South Vietnam's five area logistics commands. The logistics school advisers joined the Training Directorate, and the MACV J–4 (Logistics) staff took on the country-level logistical advisory function. MACV completed the realignment early in 1968. At the time, the authorized MACV headquarters advisory strength numbered about 1,000, of which 370 were logistics advisers, 270 were assigned to schools and training centers, and the remainder was spread throughout the headquarters staff and the national-level South Vietnamese component commands.[2]

These changes did little to reduce the fragmentation of the headquarters advisory effort. Each major and most special staff sections still carried out minor advisory functions. When General Freund left the MACV staff in February 1967 to take a field command, Brig. Gen. Albert R. Brownfield became Westmoreland's representative to the Joint General Staff and Brig. Gen. Edward M. Flanagan, Jr., took over the Training Directorate. Under Flanagan, the directorate continued to advise the South Vietnamese Central Training Command and to supervise the school and training camp advisory detachments. The U.S. Naval and Air Force Advisory Groups also remained separate entities, as did the advisers to the Airborne, Ranger, Armor, Artillery, and Special Forces Commands. In the field, the tactical and territorial advisers remained completely apart from the MACV staff advisers and continued to work directly for the senior U.S. military commander in each corps zone.

The most far-reaching reorganization of the advisory effort, perhaps the most important realignment made during the entire war, was MACV's assumption of all responsibilities for both military and nonmilitary support of the pacification campaign in 1967. The issue had been a point of heated controversy in 1966, with military leaders wary of taking on political, economic, and social advisory functions and the civil agencies in Saigon unwilling to surrender their areas of responsibility to a competing agency. Westmoreland had rejected earlier proposals to replace the divided military and civilian advisory network at province and district levels with U.S. Army Special Forces detachments or U.S. Army civil

---

[2] Briefing, MACMA, 5 Jul 67, sub: Army Programs for Military [?] Vietnam, MICRO 3/0404, RG 334, WNRC; Memo, Westmoreland to Palmer, 17 Feb 68, sub: U.S. Logistical Advisory Effort on Behalf of ARVN, COMUSMACV Signature file, 1968, Westmoreland Papers, HRB, CMH.

Robert W. Komer (left) and Ellsworth Bunker *(right) conferring with General Westmoreland*

affairs teams; the Special Forces corps was too small, and the majority of the Army's civil affairs servicemen were reservists.[3] Nevertheless, in April 1967 President Johnson finally settled the dispute in favor of military control. Shortly thereafter, the American embassy's Office of Civil Operations, a loose confederation of U.S. civilian agencies that maintained a network of representatives at corps and province levels, became part of MACV and its new director, Robert Komer, the deputy commander for civil operations and revolutionary development support (CORDS) under Westmoreland. The replacement of Ambassador Lodge with the astute Ellsworth Bunker around the same time eased the transfer of the civilian advisory apparatus to the military command.

The able Komer, nicknamed the "Blowtorch" for his aggressive management style, quickly hammered out a completely new organization. At the corps level he established CORDS advisory groups composed of both civilian and military personnel under the senior U.S. military adviser (normally the U.S. corps-level commander); at the province level he merged civilian and military advisory staffs, making the senior U.S. military adviser, a lieutenant colonel, the team commander, and the senior civilian, his deputy. The new CORDS province teams also supervised the subordinate district detachments, which remained entirely military. Komer also established the Hamlet Evaluation System, or HES,

[3] Briefing of 15 Mar 66, History file 4–E, Westmoreland Papers, HRB, CMH.

a new computer-compatible reporting system to monitor the progress of pacification in the countryside. The organizational and reporting changes not only unified the American revolutionary development and population security support effort but also put the pacification field advisory network on a much firmer footing.[4]

The U.S. Army tactical advisory teams had no part in the CORDS chain of command. Most teams continued to encourage and monitor conventional combat operations; to push improvements in staff work, training, maintenance, logistics, and administration; to coordinate American combat support; and, most important, to supply adjacent American commands with detailed information on all current South Vietnamese operations and activities. Nevertheless, the assignment of security tasks to the South Vietnamese regular units constantly involved the tactical advisers in nonmilitary affairs. Several tactical senior advisers even insisted that the province teams be returned to their control to unify the military advisory chain of command.[5] Although Komer was able to resist such proposals successfully, the continued presence of the South Vietnamese division headquarters in the Vietnamese area security chain of command remained a source of confusion, necessitating almost continuous coordination between the tactical and CORDS advisers to sort out the roles and missions of the various ground combat elements tasked with providing security.[6]

The question of a combined command also raised its head briefly in 1967. Komer, prior to his arrival in Vietnam to head the CORDS staff, believed such an arrangement desirable and raised the issue with McNamara. In Komer's colorful language, McNamara "read me the riot act." According to Komer, the defense secretary had "considered it earlier and was talked out of it by Westy . . . , [who] was very much against it." In April, when Komer brought up the matter with Westmoreland and suggested some sort of unified command arrangement that would place South Vietnamese army units under American commanders, he again received his "comeuppance on joint command." Westmoreland felt that he already had immense influence through his personal relationships with Cao Van Vien and other senior generals; that formalizing these relationships would lessen that influence; and that, with a combined command, "we would be committed much more than we wanted to." Several months later the related issue of encadrement was raised again, this time by the Office of the Secretary of Defense, and again Westmoreland rejected it as impractical. American and South Vietnamese military forces thus continued to operate under two entirely separate chains of command.[7]

---

[4] For details on the origins and establishment of CORDS, see Hunt, *Pacification*, forthcoming, and Scoville, *Reorganizing for Pacification Support*.

[5] See comments in Cannon Debriefing Rpt, 17 Nov 67, pp. 9–12, SEAB, CMH, and p. 25 of appended Status Report on the 24th Special Tactical Zone, March–November 1967, by Col. E. H. Kaufman, Senior Adviser, 24th STZ.

[6] See Msg, COMUSMACV to Senior U.S. Commanders, 030333 Aug 67, sub: Role of the ARVN Division in CORDS, History file 19–A24, Westmoreland Papers, HRB, CMH.

[7] Quoted words from Komer Interv, 7 May 70, Rand Limited Document D(L)–20104–ARPA. See also Memo, SACSA, JCS, sub: Comments Pertaining to Memorandum for Sec of Defense, 4 Jul 67, sub: Improvement in RVNAF Force Effectiveness prepared by Mr. Enthoven, OASD SA, p. 10. Both in SEAB, CMH.

The Ground Army Expands

The MACV staff continued to review the size and organization of the South Vietnamese armed forces during 1967.[8] In January Westmoreland noted that the continuous expansion of the armed forces had prevented any qualitative improvements. The demands of new units for officer and noncommissioned officers had stretched South Vietnam's "marginally effective" leadership pool, and, according to Westmoreland, poor leadership was the root cause of all South Vietnamese military problems. He reiterated his determination to hold down the expansion of the South Vietnamese armed forces and to concentrate on qualitative improvements. Further increases or adjustments would be minor and based strictly upon three prerequisites: the creation of a more balanced military structure, the availability of men, and a reduction in the inflation rate.[9]

The MACV commander was also still concerned about the low operational strengths of Saigon's combat battalions, now believing the cause to be the "malassignment" of personnel rather than a shortage of soldiers. Consequently, he ordered his field advisers to pressure their counterparts into eliminating unauthorized units, paring down overstrength garrisons and headquarters, reducing unauthorized absences, and insisting on a more accurate administration of unit roles. The high turnover of men in the infantry-type battalions, Westmoreland observed, also continued to make periodic unit retraining necessary, and field advisers had to make South Vietnamese commanders recognize this requirement. As a minimum, he wanted each battalion retrained at one of the national training centers every thirty-one months.

Despite reservations about expanding Saigon's armed forces, Westmoreland again found it necessary to support substantial strength increases in both its size and structure. At the beginning of 1967 the authorized South Vietnamese military strength was still frozen at 633,645. In March, at Westmoreland's suggestion, General Vien activated 88 new Regional Forces companies and 333 more Popular Forces platoons, but MACV had to reduce the authorized strength of the existing territorial units by almost 20,000 spaces to keep the force within the approved manpower limits. On 26 April Westmoreland decided to end his imposed freeze and agreed to a general increase of 45,000 spaces, mostly to support the larger number of territorial units needed to provide security for the revolutionary development effort. In July he raised this figure by 7,000 and suggested a further increase of 78,000 by mid-1969, for a total expansion of 130,000. He wanted most of the additional men allocated to the territorials, roughly 85,000 to the Regional Forces and 35,000 to the Popular Forces, to provide men for new rifle companies and platoons and for province and district military staffs, territorial support companies, and territorial pipeline strength (personnel in training, hospitalized, on leave, and so forth). Even this, Westmoreland felt, was insufficient, but he

---

[8] Unless otherwise noted, this section is based on USMACV, "Command History, 1967," 1:167–217, HRB, CMH; Briefing, MACJ–311, 25 Oct 67, sub: RVNAF Organization and Force Structure [for U.S. Senate Investigating Committee], MICRO 1/1587, RG 334, WNRC.

[9] Command Ltr, Westmoreland, 16 Jan 67, sub: Improvement Within the RVNAF, COMUSMACV Signature file, 1967, Westmoreland Papers, HRB, CMH.

New Territorial Recruits at a Basic Training Center

believed that it was the most that South Vietnam's recruiting and training systems could handle.

By October 1967 the Territorial Forces consisted of 896 Regional Forces companies (equipped with carbines, machine guns, M79 grenade launchers, radios, and trucks); 24 riverine companies (with eight landing boats each), all in the delta area; and, in each province, 1 logistics company, 1 mechanized platoon (with six armored cars), 1 intelligence or scout platoon, and 1 training camp. The Popular Forces consisted of 242 intelligence squads (1 per district) and 4,121 rifle platoons (still armed primarily with carbines and old Browning automatic rifles). Of this force, MACV estimated that only 213 Regional Forces companies and 754 Popular Forces platoons were providing direct support for the revolutionary development effort. The remaining territorial units were presumably either in the process of formation, in training, defending bases and installations, outposting roads, or conducting conventional combat operations.

Command and control of the territorials had also become a serious problem. Their chain of command extended from the Territorial Directorate of the Joint General Staff (now advised by Komer's MACV CORDS staff section), down through a deputy chief of staff for territorial affairs at each corps headquarters (advised by an American CORDS team), and through another deputy on each South Vietnamese division staff, until it finally reached the province and district commands, where deputy province and deputy district chiefs for security (each

214

assisted by an American advisory team) directed territorial military operations.[10]
With an average of 20 Regional Forces companies and 100 Popular Forces platoons in each province, the province and district military staffs were swamped
with staff work, and MACV considered establishing some sort of intermediate
tactical command (for example, a territorial group or battalion headquarters) to
ease their growing control problems.

The province Territorial Forces adviser, normally an Army captain, and the
small district advisory teams (still about four men each) assisted the territorial
units as best they could. Smaller advisory cells also operated with Popular Forces
training centers, the territorial logistics companies, and the smaller specialized
units. But the Territorial Forces advisory effort was too small to have much
of an impact, and advisers spent most of their time working behind the scenes to
make the weak territorial command, administration, and supply system work.
The South Vietnamese regular army continued to support the territorials with
some training and supplies, but showed little interest in their deployment and
operations.[11]

Strength increases planned for the regulars in 1967 were moderate. Westmoreland hoped to complete all of his older expansion programs and to activate 3
new infantry-type regiments, including a special ranger regiment to protect Saigon, a new fourth regiment for the 1st Infantry Division to man a fortified line
along the Demilitarized Zone; and a third regiment for the 23d Infantry Division.
Other additions included a ninth battalion for the airborne force, regimental-
level headquarters for the ranger battalions, and 10 new artillery battalions
spread among the four corps to bolster Vietnamese organic fire support.

Westmoreland's expansion plans raised many questions. How, for example,
could they be reconciled with his promise to emphasize quality over quantity?
Why did he continue to favor the activation of more infantry units instead of
combat support forces? And what of the impact of the expansion on Saigon's
inflation and manpower problems? Concerned over the inflationary impact of
larger military payrolls, the U.S. Joint Chiefs of Staff suggested assigning all
ranger battalions to the regular South Vietnamese divisions and moving the
proposed ranger administrative and control spaces elsewhere. Westmoreland
rejected the idea. The corps commanders, he stated, would lose their independent reserve force and the rangers their special esprit de corps and aggressiveness. In October 1967 the Joint Chiefs questioned Westmoreland on the feasibility
of redirecting funds slated to support new South Vietnamese units to other
areas—higher salaries or improved dependent housing, for example. Westmoreland answered that, despite their inflationary impact, all proposed force increases were necessary and that any funds saved by a few reductions could not
be usefully expended elsewhere in South Vietnam.[12]

Realizing that some economy was essential, Westmoreland himself suggested
deactivating a number of units to provide spaces for the new ranger regiment and

[10] For military affairs, provinces were still referred to as sectors and districts as subsectors.
[11] Briefing, MACV, 23 Oct 67, sub: Role of RF/PF in Pacification [for U.S. Senators], MICRO 1/1726,
RG 334, WNRC.
[12] Msg, COMUSMACV MAC 37104 to CINCPAC, 120655 Nov 67, sub: FY 69 RVNAF Force Level,
COMUSMACV Signature file, 1967, Westmoreland Papers, HRB, CMH.

taking one existing infantry battalion from every corps to form the new DMZ formation. Vien, however, disagreed and went ahead to form the ranger regiment simply by assigning three existing ranger battalions in the Saigon area to a strengthened ranger group headquarters. In the case of the new regiment for the DMZ area, Vien argued that the strong socioeconomic ties of battalions to their home stations made Westmoreland's idea impractical, and instead persuaded him to approve stationing an existing regiment of the 1st Division on the border zone and having the latter form a new regiment through a local recruiting campaign.[13] Inexorably, the expansion of the armed forces thus continued.

During 1967 Westmoreland also pursued his goal of having each South Vietnamese infantry battalion to put at least 450 men (70 percent of its authorized strength) in the field, hoping that the additional personnel approved for the regimental reconnaissance companies would make it easier to attain this goal. Again, he was disappointed. Although the Vietnamese dutifully filled their units with the appropriate numbers, many still ended up in a welter of unauthorized detachments, such as recruiting teams, bodyguard squads, and various special purpose units. Some South Vietnamese commanders may even have included battlefield laborers in their strength reports in order to meet the 450-man goal. To clarify the problem, General Abrams suggested changing South Vietnam's strength reports to reflect soldiers performing "supporting tasks" or detached for other assignments. He also felt that raising the present-for-operations target from 470 to 550 and activating more regimental reconnaissance companies might also help. At worst, the spaces for the companies could provide a manpower reservoir that units could draw on for special needs. His objective, however, was to persuade the regimental commanders to use the reconnaissance companies as special combat forces, augmenting the operations of their infantry battalions.[14]

To realize all of these proposed increases, the MACV staff believed that Saigon would have to institute some mobilization measures in the next two years, such as lowering the draft age, extending terms of service, and recalling reservists.[15] Decreasing desertion rates were one hopeful sign, as were Saigon's efforts to apprehend and punish deserters in larger numbers. The new "by name" strength reports made it easier for military and civil officials to identify and apprehend deserters, and during the first half of 1967 over 15,000 were taken into custody, 6,531 tried, and 4,186 assigned to battlefield labor units.[16] But, although the U.S. Joint Chiefs made their support of MACV's new expansion plans conditional on Saigon's enactment of mobilization, Westmoreland decided to go ahead and authorize the activation of the new units as soon as possibile. Mobilization measures could be put off until the following year. Accordingly, between July and December 1967, the Joint General Staff activated 446 Popular Forces platoons, 99 Regional Forces companies, an infantry regiment, an airborne battalion, 2 prisoner-of-war (POW) camp companies, and 22 regimental reconnaissance com-

---

[13] Notes of 4 Sep 67, History file 21–A, Westmoreland Papers, HRB, CMH.

[14] Msg, Abrams to Desobry, 27 Nov 67; Ltr, Abrams to Vien, 18 Nov 67. Both in DEPCOMUSMACV Signature file, 1967, Westmoreland Papers, HRB, CMH.

[15] See MACV, Preliminary Report on Manpower Mobilization, 1967, MICRO 2/322, RG 334, WNRC, for a detailed breakdown of projected losses and accessions.

[16] Sec Def Visit Vietnam, 7–11 Jul 67, Brig Gen McGovern Briefing: Morale-Leadership US/RVNAF (hereafter cited as McGovern Briefing), MICRO 2/1251, RG 334, WNRC.

panies. Westmoreland planned to authorize the activation of the remaining units by April 1968, and, because it took nearly a year or longer before newly activated units became fully operational, he and Abrams reasoned that the desired mobilization steps would be taken before the new units were actually in the field, thus satisfying Washington's conditions.[17]

In 1967 MACV also approved strength increases for the South Vietnamese Marines, Navy, and Air Force without altering their organization or missions. The marines still consisted of 6 infantry-type battalions, supported by 3 artillery batteries and an amphibious support battalion. The heart of the navy remained the three river assault groups of 237 craft, while the small ocean-going fleet and the coastal (or "Junk") force continued to complement U.S. Navy coastal surveillance operations. The Vietnamese air force, now with about 350 aircraft and 550 pilots, flew one-fifth of the combat air sorties in South Vietnam in 1967 and was preparing to receive more advanced fighters, helicopters, and transports. Both the air and naval services had about 15,000 personnel each and their greatest difficulties centered around repair and maintenance, a problem underlined by the air service's excessively high accident rate.

While the U.S. Air Force and Naval Advisory Groups concentrated on solving these problems, the U.S. Army Special Forces teams worked at the other end of the spectrum on the discipline and small unit operations of the CIDG, over which the South Vietnamese Special Forces still had only nominal control. The CIDG program and associated Special Forces efforts remained unchanged. The 5th Special Forces Group continually closed bases in relatively quiet areas and opened new "fighting camps" along the border, but stabilized the number of native troops at about 31,000 men out of an authorized strength of 41,000. Westmoreland and Abrams were undecided about the future of the CIDG program, wavering between two alternatives: "legalizing" the CIDG units as part of the South Vietnamese armed forces by converting them into territorials, or retaining the present CIDG organization and employing the troopers to support the larger, more conventional American operations. The CIDG troopers themselves finally decided the issue when they showed little enthusiasm for enlisting in the Territorial Forces, forcing MACV to retain the separate CIDG program.[18]

Westmoreland also entertained several ideas about changing the roles and missions of the ranger battalions, the South Vietnamese Special Forces, and the CIDG units. One proposal envisioned withdrawing the lightweight ranger units from their now traditional reserve and security roles and to use them as mobile strike forces against regular enemy units in remote areas. Another involved creating some kind of independent anti-infiltration force along the Laotian and Cambodian borders or on the Demilitarized Zone. With this in mind, the MACV staff continued to study the merger of the rangers and the South Vietnamese Special Forces, and moving the CIDG effort closer to the border by converting existing camps into Regional Forces bases. MACV staff officers also proposed

---

[17] Ltr, Abrams to Vien, 26 Nov 67, DEPCOMUSMACV Signature file, 1967, Westmoreland Papers, HRB, CMH.
[18] See Kelly, *U.S. Army Special Forces*, pp. 82 and 96; JGS/RVNAF Staff Agency Reports: Problem Areas and MACV Staff Positions, Encl to Ltr, Abrams to Vien, 9 Sep 67, DEPCOMUSMACV Signature file, 1967, Westmoreland Papers, HRB, CMH.

forming some kind of international task force to man a "strong-point obstacle system" along the Demilitarized Zone, backed up by five to eight National Police companies. But Westmoreland opposed the idea of a special border command, believing that border control forces should remain under the corps commands. Cross-border operations were another matter. These remained under MACV's Studies and Observation Group (SOG) and the South Vietnamese Strategic Technical Directorate. In April 1967 MACV staff officers studied the possibility of launching extensive ground operations into Laos, using an elite "Rainbow" division composed of South Vietnamese marine, airborne, and ranger battalions supported by Vietnamese helicopter and logistical units, but they never developed the proposal very far.[19]

From this potpourri of ideas and proposals, the Joint General Staff, with MACV support and encouragement, took three actions. First, it activated an airborne division headquarters and a ninth airborne battalion, and enlarged the airborne support base. The Vietnamese hoped to have the unit operating as a full division by March 1968. Second, it withdrew and reequipped one of the 1st Division's regiments with M16 rifles and ground radar sets, and assigned it responsibility for guarding a portion of the Demilitarized Zone. The new regiment approved by Westmoreland would make up for the loss. Finally, upon the recommendation of the U.S. 5th Special Forces Group commander, the Joint General Staff established the 44th Special Tactical Zone along the Cambodian frontier in the IV Corps area to control all border surveillance and interdiction efforts there. The American Special Forces advisers had sought a Vietnamese Special Forces commander for the new zone, but instead Vien gave the command to Col. Nguyen Huu Hanh, a senior army officer from the nearby 21st Infantry Division. Like the other South Vietnamese special zones, the command was subordinate to the local corps commander.[20]

The Failure of Reform

Although South Vietnamese administrative reform remained a critical area, Americans continued to give it little serious attention.[21] In 1967 the MACV staff bundled all of its reform programs into a single package called the Program Review and Analysis Improvement System (with the suggestive acronym of PRAISE). PRAISE matched specific reforms with responsible MACV staff agen-

[19] Msg, CG, II FFV, to COMUSMACV, 181030 Jan 67, sub: Visit by COMUSMACV to HQ, II FFORCEV, 171400 Jan 67, History file 12–D4; MFR, Westmoreland, 23 Feb 67, sub: Separate Meetings With General Thieu, General Ky, and General Vien on 17 and 20 February 1967, History file 13–B15; Notes of 16 and 17 Mar 67, History file 13–C, p. 16; Notes of 17 Apr 67, History file 15–B, p. 7; Notes of 8 Apr 67, History file 15–A, p. 9. All in Westmoreland Papers, HRB, CMH.

[20] USMACV, "Command History, 1967," 1:201–02; Ltr, Kerwin to CO, 5th Special Forces Group (Airborne), 18 Dec 67, sub: 44th Special Zone, IV CTZ, Chief of Staff Correspondence file, 1967, Westmoreland Papers. Both in HRB, CMH.

[21] For general background, see McGovern Briefing, MICRO 2/1251; Brownfield Briefing, 11 Jan 68, MICRO 3/0348; Briefing, MACJ-3, 25 Oct 67, sub: Effectiveness of RVNAF [for U.S. Senate Investigating Committee], MICRO 1/1531. All in RG 334, WNRC. See also Draft Rpt, SACSA, JCS, circa 1967, sub: Assessment of the Republic of Vietnam Armed Forces (RVNAF), SEAB, CMH.

cies, and the latter in turn advised, monitored, and reported on South Vietnamese progress in these areas. But PRAISE couched objectives for many of the programs only in the most general terms. Although the initial forty-four "subprograms" covered everything from CIDG conversions to training, logistics, administrative reform, desertions, and leadership, MACV assigned no priorities to any one area. In July Westmoreland agreed to transfer management of this so-called system to the Joint General Staff and to retain a private contractor to train the Vietnamese to operate it. In the realm of administration, PRAISE became the official means by which MACV gauged South Vietnamese progress.[22]

By itself, PRAISE did little to solve immediate South Vietnamese problems. The lack of able field- and general-grade officers (that is, majors and above) continued to bedevil the army. In June 1967 the South Vietnamese armed forces had only about 30 percent of the authorized generals, colonels, and lieutenant colonels, 60–70 percent of the authorized majors and captains, but 126 percent (17,277) of the authorized lieutenants and an excess of about 8,000 aspirants. Most of the senior officers were political appointees with little actual practical experience and, with the army in area support missions, little opportunity to learn. According to Brig. Gen. Donald H. McGovern, the MACV assistant chief of staff for personnel (J–1), massive promotions could have solved the officer grade shortage, but MACV and the Joint General Staff felt that such a solution was harmful and favored retaining the lengthy time-in-grade requirements for promotion eligibility. Good officers were experienced officers, McGovern maintained, and South Vietnam's weak leadership was due primarily to inexperience. Westmoreland agreed, and, despite the common practice of having lieutenants and captains fill major and lieutenant colonel positions, MACV recommended against promoting such officers until they had acquired the requisite experience after perhaps two to five years in command. Only time could correct the situation.[23]

Some headway was made during 1967 in tying promotions to ability as well as experience. A central promotion board, a reform pushed by MACV and adopted by the Joint General Staff in 1966, met to consider all officers above the rank of first lieutenant who had satisfied specific time-in-grade requirements. Recommendations for promotion were based on officer efficiency reports and a new point system that gave credit for time in grade, current assignment, civilian and military education, and military decorations.[24] Promotions remained automatic in the two lowest grades: aspirant to second lieutenant after eighteen months, and second to first lieutenant after another two years. Promotions to colonel and above and appointments to high-level staff, command, and administrative posts

[22] Rpt, USMACV, 24 May 67, sub: Program Review and Analysis of RVNAF Progress, SEAB, CMH; USMACV, "Command History, 1967," 1:194–95, HRB, CMH; Briefing, MACJ-3, 25 Oct 67, sub: Effectiveness of RVNAF [for U.S. Senate Investigating Committee], MICRO 1/1531, RG 334, WNRC.
[23] McGovern Briefing, MICRO 2/1251, RG 334, WNRC.
[24] For details, see MACJ-1, circa 1969, Briefing on ARVN Promotion System, MICRO 74/1191, RG 334, WNRC; Draft Rpt, SACSA, JCS, circa 1967, sub: Assessment of the Republic of Vietnam Armed Forces (RVNAF), SEAB, CMH. Using the U.S. Army's officer efficiency report system as a model, Vietnamese commanders awarded subordinates a varying number of points based on their annual performance, but ratings were too inflated and subject to political influence to be of much use. See Khuyen, *The RVNAF*, p. 105.

remained highly political. The board thus dealt almost exclusively with the captain, major, and lieutenant colonel ranks.

Intense lobbying by MACV forced the Joint General Staff to continue supplementing annual officer promotions with battlefield and special merit advancements. But Saigon tied merit promotions closely to appointments and normally awarded them to those in positions calling for a higher grade (for example, captains commanding battalions or filling high-level staff posts). The criteria for battlefield promotions were more exacting; prerequisites included the award of no less than three decorations in "successful" combat actions, as well as stringent time-in-grade and time-in-command requirements. During 1967 the Joint General Staff granted 1,535 merit promotions to officers, but only 157 battlefield promotions, leading Westmoreland to urge greater selectivity in the first category and more liberality in the other.[25] Either the South Vietnamese officers were not doing much fighting or they were not rewarding those who did.

Linked to promotions was the procurement of officers. As in 1966, Westmoreland sought to strengthen the officer corps by opening it to the enlisted ranks, but was less successful. During the year the Joint General Staff almost abandoned its noncommissioned officer commissioning program and scheduled only about six hundred for 1968. The Vietnamese generals felt that the freeze in the expansion ended the need for the program and continued it only at Westmoreland's insistence. Moreover, Saigon also stipulated that promotion to captain required a high school diploma, thus prohibiting the advancement of many officers commissioned from the ranks. Merit and battlefield appointments of noncommissioned officers, also a reform encouraged by Westmoreland, was another disappointment. In both 1966 and 1967 merit appointments numbered about five hundred and battlefield appointments averaged about fifteen. McGovern noted that the Joint General Staff nominated only the most senior noncommissioned officers whose service longevity and assignments rarely exposed them to front-line combat duty. The MACV J–1, however, declared himself "reasonably satisfied" with the overall effort. The Vietnamese, he argued, had at least abandoned the practice of allocating promotions to subordinate commands on the basis of raw unit strength and was exercising some central direction.[26]

To improve officer retention rates, the Joint General Staff began awarding regular commissions to reserve officers, mostly first lieutenants. As regular army commission holders, they could be promoted faster and be eligible for retirement pensions, but their service obligation was longer than those with normal reserve commissions awarded at Thu Duc. The results were also disappointing. Only 335 reserve officers accepted commissions out of a 1,141 target in 1966 and only 272 of a 3,145 goal in 1967. Taking a different approach, Westmoreland suggested that

[25] Ltr, Westmoreland to Vien, 17 Feb 68, COMUSMACV Signature file, 1968, Westmoreland Papers, HRB, CMH; MACJ–1, circa 1969, Briefing on ARVN Promotion System, MICRO 74/1191, RG 334, WNRC; USMACV, "Command History, 1968," 2 vols. (Saigon, 1969), 1:284–90, HRB, CMH.
[26] Quoted words from McGovern Briefing, MICRO 2/1251, RG 334, WNRC. See also Notes of 10 Jan 67, History file 12–C, pp. 8–9, Westmoreland Papers, HRB, CMH; Fact Sheet, MACJ–14, 15 Jan 68, sub: RVNAF Command Leadership and Personnel Effectiveness Program, MICRO 3/0331, RG 334, WNRC.

the Vietnamese award bonuses to those who agreed to extend their service tours and promised Vien that MACV would somehow obtain the necessary funding.[27]

While the war-weary officer corps appeared to suffer from a shortage of high-ranking officers and experienced leaders, an underlying problem was the almost total absence of a central career management system. Earlier efforts to institute an officer career program, although strongly supported by Westmoreland and his staff, had foundered. During 1967 the Joint General Staff discussed developing standard selection criteria for school and training assignments; rotating officers between command, staff, and school posts; and making combat assignments mandatory for new officers. Initially the staff hoped to apply these measures to the infantry officers and later to extend them to those in other branches. But the limited control exercised by the Vietnamese high command over officer assignments prevented it from putting any of these measures into practice. With so few able officers in the field, commanders were highly reluctant to lose experienced cadre and often blocked their transfer elsewhere. McGovern maintained that the shortage of experienced officers made it impossible to establish an equitable rotation policy. Yet many officers had commanded the same battalions for years, while others had remained in less demanding staff and training posts. But the refusal of the Joint General Staff to make officer records available to MACV made it extremely difficult for staff advisers to ascertain the scope of the problem and to make suitable recommendations.[28]

One concrete administrative achievement was the completion of the computerized personnel roster, listing each member of the regular armed forces by name, rank, serial number, and military specialty or skill. Although a personnel accounting rather than a managerial advance, it represented a major improvement from the ragtag strength reports of 1965, and the Joint General Staff planned to extend the practice to the Territorial Forces by 1968. An October 1967 audit revealed a 15-percent error in the reporting of enlisted strength (10.8 percent missing data and 4.4 percent incorrect data), sloppy reporting procedures by submitting units, and daily strength reports at least one month in arrears. The new accounting procedures enable the armed forces to purge some 20,000 ghost soldiers from unit rolls during 1967; however, if Westmoreland's earlier estimates of the size of the problem were accurate, this figure was only a small proportion of the total.[29]

Throughout 1967 Westmoreland continued his efforts to improve the lot of the individual South Vietnamese soldier. He approved small wage supplements for the armed forces and had his staff take a closer look at the Saigon army's postal money system, which still constituted almost the only way soldiers could send

[27] Notes of 9 Oct 67, History file 23–A, Westmoreland Papers, HRB, CMH.
[28] Fact Sheet, MACJ–14, 15 Jan 68, sub: RVNAF Command Leadership and Personnel Effectiveness Program, MICRO 3/0331; McGovern Briefing, MICRO 2/1251. Both in RG 334, WNRC. See also Ltr, Locke to Westmoreland, 16 Oct 67, sub: Manpower Data, COMUSMACV Signature file, 1967, Westmoreland Papers, HRB, CMH.
[29] Ltr, Locke to Westmoreland, 16 Oct 67, sub: Manpower Data, COMUSMACV Signature file, 1967; JGS/RVNAF Staff Agency Reports: Problem Areas and MACV Staff Positions, Encl to Ltr, Abrams to Vien, 9 Sep 67, DEPCOMUSMACV Signature file, 1967. Both in Westmoreland Papers, HRB, CMH. See also Brownfield Briefing, 11 Jan 68, MICRO 3/0348, RG 334, WNRC.

funds to dependents.[30] Westmoreland also agreed to a proposal of the new minister of defense, General Nguyen Van Vy, to establish special banking facilities for the military, but advised that any such ventures should have the concurrence and cooperation of South Vietnam's National Bank and be tied closely with the commercial banking system. He promised assistance from the MACV Office of the Comptroller in formulating suitable arrangements, but neither he nor his advisers had any easy answer for the inflation and low military pay scale, which, they felt, encouraged corruption and indifference.[31]

Inflation and low pay scales also made it increasingly difficult for the armed forces to hire and retain skilled civilian labor. A closer look at Vietnam's civil service revealed a wage system based on education rather than on responsibilities, and an overtime pay rate that was less than half the regular hourly rate. Moonlighting was common; skilled, experienced workers, rare in Vietnam, continued to find better-paying jobs elsewhere. As manpower shortages delayed repairs, the backlog of work continued to mount. Westmoreland's decision in late 1967 to replace 12,545 U.S. soldiers in combat service support units with Vietnamese civilians only increased the scarcity of skilled labor. To relieve the overloaded depots Westmoreland recommended that U.S. Army ordnance units in the Far East help rebuild South Vietnamese military vehicles and that increased overtime pay rates be established for depot civilian workers on a trial basis. But both proposals cost money that was unavailable. If necessary, U.S. support units in South Vietnam could have easily pitched in and rectified the backlog of work, but most were fully occupied with their primary duties. In any case, few South Vietnamese units conducted mobile combat operations in 1967, and Saigon's chronic problems with supply and maintenance were easy to ignore.[32]

American efforts to improve South Vietnamese military subsistence, especially in combat units, continued to run into trouble. In September 1967 MACV noted that many units had managed to scrape together enough gear and soldiers to run informal unit messes, with some even having their own gardens and livestock, but that most units that stayed in the field for any length of time still tended to live off the land. Payroll deductions to support unit messes remained inadequate and unpopular. Soldiers still had to acquire most food locally, primarily because the quantities of certain staples, rice, tea, and sugar supplied by the Ministry of Economy through the Central Logistics Command were insufficient.

[30] The raise consisted of about $5 per month for each Popular Forces soldier; another $2 per month, in the form of a "rice allowance," for both the territorials and regulars, including regular and Regional Forces dependents; and another scheduled $5 per month raise for all servicemen in 1968. Although the military postal system was rudimentary, operating with only twenty-nine offices supplemented by twenty-seven two-man route teams, it handled about between $1 and $2 million worth of transactions annually, which MACV felt was sufficient. See USMACV, "Command History, 1967," 1:174–76, HRB, CMH.
[31] Ltr, Westmoreland to Vy, 3 Jan 68, COMUSMACV Signature file, 1968, Westmoreland Papers, HRB, CMH. Vy replaced Vien as defense minister on 9 November 1967.
[32] Memo, Abrams to Eugene Locke, 17 Nov 67, sub: GVN Civil Service Reforms; Ltrs, Westmoreland to Vien, 16 Jan and 3 Aug 67. All in COMUSMACV Signature file, 1967, Westmoreland Papers, HRB, CMH. Westmoreland wanted to free more slots for combat personnel in view of the reluctance of Washington to raise overall U.S. troop strength in South Vietnam. See USMACV, "Command History, 1967," 2:714–15, HRB, CMH.

Main Commissary, South Vietnamese 2d Commissary Division, Qui Nhon.
The commissary system was an attempt by Saigon to supply some basic necessities for soldiers and their dependents.

When MACV offered to supply such items without cost, the U.S. Agency for International Development opposed the proposal; when MACV later provided some seventy thousand individual field rations free of cost from U.S. Army stocks, most of the rations never reached troops in the field due to a combination of South Vietnamese bureaucratic inefficiency and corruption. Westmoreland's stipulation that priority for the rations be given to units performing security duties may have only confused matters, for units performing conventional combat missions had the greatest need.[33]

One bright spot was the improvement of the South Vietnamese commissary–post exchange system through direct American support. In April 1967 Westmoreland finally received approval from Washington to transfer $1.3 million worth of canned meats to the South Vietnamese commissary from local U.S. Army stocks and in July, under a cost-free grant, began funneling $42 million worth of basic foodstuffs (rice, sugar, milk, salt, oil, canned meat, and fish) into the commissary. Under the supervision of American advisers, the commissaries sold these goods to soldiers at reduced prices (about two-thirds of the basic cost) and retained the proceeds to finance further purchases and the construction of more outlets. To supervise the program, Westmoreland assigned seven full-time commissary advisers to the MACV J–4 (Logistics) staff section. He also urged Vien to transfer the South Vietnamese commissary agency from the General Political Warfare Department to the Central Logistics Command. By September over 12,000 tons of foodstuffs were arriving each month, almost overwhelming existing commissary facilities, but the steady expansion of depots and outlets promised to alleviate this situation early in 1968. To supplement the American aid, Vien had his quartermaster staff begin planning a military farm network to raise livestock, poultry, fish, and vegetables for the army.[34]

Efforts to provide adequate care for military dependents languished during the year. Rough estimates still indicated a shortage of about 250,000 family quarters for regular and Regional Forces dependents, with the shortfall continually rising. The self-help program planned at the end of 1966 appeared promising, but the test program of 9,000 units in the III Corps Tactical Zone quickly ran into trouble. The purchase of land was subject to political influence, and South Vietnamese units had little time to do the actual construction work. By the end of the year MACV had handed over some 4,000 prefabricated houses to III Corps units, but less than half of these had been erected and many had simply disappeared. Until better results could be achieved, Westmoreland postponed any expansion of the program.[35]

[33] Ltr, Westmoreland to Vy, 30 Dec 67, COMUSMACV Signature file, 1967, Westmoreland Papers, HRB, CMH; Supplemental Data Sheet, MACV, AVHGD–AP/AQ, 3 Apr 67, sub: Actions To Improve the Effectiveness of the ARVN Soldier, MICRO 3/0879, RG 334, WNRC.

[34] Ltrs, Westmoreland to Vien, 9 Jan 67 and 21 Jan 68, COMUSMACV Signature files, 1967 and 1968, respectively, Westmoreland Papers, HRB, CMH; Supplemental Data Sheet, MACV, AVHGD–AW, 10 Apr 67, sub: Actions To Improve the Effectiveness of the ARVN Soldier, MICRO 3/0881, RG 334, WNRC.

[35] Ltr, Vien to Westmoreland, 5 Dec 67, sub: Procurement of Dependent Quarters in 1968, COMUSMACV Signature file, 1967, Westmoreland Papers, HRB, CMH, which also notes that *(Continued)*

Again disheartened by the lack progress, Westmoreland in October 1967 asked Vien to transfer responsibility for dependent housing construction from the corps headquarters to the engineer office of the Central Logistics Command. He felt that better results could be achieved by having the command run the entire housing construction program, assisted by U.S. Army engineers at MACV and the Army component command and by engineer advisers in the field. Assuring Vien that MACV could make the necessary funds available in 1968, he wanted priority given to combat units. Each unit was to purchase the necessary real estate by December 1967 and submit its construction requirements to the engineers through its area logistics command. After preparing building plans, the Central Logistics Command would invite construction bids by civilian contractors. The total cost of completely satisfying the dependent housing requirement was about $7.6 million, including land purchases and the construction of one-story partitioned barracks-type buildings of the most simple design.[36] But even with this support the chances that the program could be completed rapidly were dim. Most military and civilian constructors were almost completely preoccupied building billets and bases for new South Vietnamese units and newly arrived American troops. Dependent housing was still a secondary chore.

The South Vietnamese veterans program, termed "grossly inadequate" by General Westmoreland, also continued to limp along throughout the year.[37] The Ministry of Veterans Affairs, established by the Directory in March 1966, had accomplished little. The ministry oversaw two homes for invalid servicemen, with a combined capacity of 188; a small overburdened prosthetic center in Saigon; and a small vocational school for disabled soldiers at Cat Lai, about 16 kilometers east of the capital. Early in 1967 MACV estimated that the names of about 10,000 disabled soldiers still appeared on unit roles as a result of the commanders unwillingness to abandon the men to an uncertain fate. Concerned, Westmoreland asked the U.S. Agency for International Development, which was responsible for supporting South Vietnam's veterans programs, to expand its support of hospitals, rehabilitation programs, and job training and placement programs. But with little hope of immediate action, he finally recommended to Ambassador Bunker that veterans affairs be placed under the South Vietnamese Ministry of Defense, where its programs could be supported through Saigon's American-subsidized defense budget. Instead, the embassy worked out an agreement with the South Vietnamese, allowing MACV to advise the Ministry of Veterans Affairs and to assist officials in developing adequate

---

(Continued) Popular Forces soldiers were supposedly living at home and thus had no need for dependent accommodations; Supplemental Data Sheet, MACV, AVHGD–AE, 3 Apr 67, sub: Actions To Improve the Effectiveness of the ARVN Soldier, MICRO 3/0883, RG 334, WNRC. See also Westmoreland-Vien correspondence in COMUSMACV Signature file, 1967, Westmoreland Papers, HRB, CMH, especially letters of 29 Oct and 19 Dec 67.

[36] Ltr, Vien to Westmoreland, 25 Oct and 5 Dec 67, sub: Procurement of Dependent Quarters in 1968, COMUSMACV Signature file, 1967, Westmoreland Papers, HRB, CMH.

[37] Memo, Westmoreland to Lodge, 14 Feb 67, sub: Veterans Affairs, COMUSMACV Signature file, 1967, Westmoreland Papers, HRB, CMH.

vocational programs. Much had to be done. But without more authority and time, MACV made little headway. By the end of 1967 only eleven veterans had graduated from the vocational training school, and MACV estimated that the names of about 16,000 physically impaired soldiers remained on unit roles—a 60-percent increase from the beginning of the year.[38]

Although MACV was unable to make substantial gains in dependent housing construction or in improving the lot of the veteran, Westmoreland was able to realize two of his major aspirations. In 1967 the Vietnamese Military Academy at Da Lat emerged as a four-year institution, with a curriculum and teaching methods modeled after West Point, and the Joint General Staff established a National Defense College in Saigon for senior military and civilian officials. The military academy limited each class to 250 students, while the defense college handled about 20 each year. American funds to support the academy's expansion totaled about $8 million, more than had been suggested for the entire dependent housing program.[39] Whether the long-term gains in improved leadership justified the money lavished on Da Lat, or whether such funds ought to have supported the more immediate gains in improved morale that might have been realized had the same money been spent on such programs as dependent housing, was problematic. The schools were isolated projects where American advice and support were much easier to direct and control.

In other schools and training centers MACV made little headway improving the cadre and facilities. Although Westmoreland persuaded the Joint General Staff to open the Noncommissioned Officers Academy at Nha Trang to the lower enlisted ranks, his staff was unable to improve the selection of students and cadre.[40] Field commanders still feared that those nominated would never return to their units and continued to use training and school assignments as dumping grounds for their less able officers and noncommissioned officers. Although Westmoreland urged Vien to close down some of the training centers, he also recommended that center enrollments exceed planned capacities by about 10 percent to compensate for expected losses through desertions.[41] Revolutionary development training by mobile training teams continued to be weak, and refresher training for both regular and territorial units lagged.

Revolutionary development and political warfare both had the primary mission of generating support for the South Vietnamese government. Political warfare instructors and cadre attended the Political Warfare College at Da Lat, while training teams from the college and unit political warfare officers carried out training and indoctrination in the field. The indoctrination, which stressed discipline, proper troop behavior, and patriotism, was similar in content to the propa-

---

[38] Ibid.; Ltr, Westmoreland to Bunker, 26 Aug 67, sub: Veterans Affairs; Ltr, Westmoreland to Vy, 27 Jan 68. All in COMUSMACV Signature files, 1967 and 1968, respectively, Westmoreland Papers, HRB, CMH. See also Brownfield Briefing, 11 Jan 68, MICRO 3/0348, RG 334, WNRC.

[39] USMACV, "Command History, 1967," 1:180–82, HRB, CMH.

[40] Previously the academy had been open only to those with at least ten years of education.

[41] Notes of 17 Jan 67, History file 12–2, pp. 2–3; Ltr, Westmoreland to Vien, 12 Jul 67, COMUSMACV Signature file, 1967. Both in Westmoreland Papers, HRB, CMH.

ganda employed by the revolutionary development teams. During 1966 and 1967 visiting indoctrination training teams conducted short in-place sessions for troop units and slightly more intensive sessions for individuals designated as political warfare cadre at company, district, and province levels.[42] The political warfare officers had little real power and were in no way the equivalent of military commissars.

Although limited in scope, American and South Vietnamese intelligence efforts continued to be more closely integrated. The U.S. 519th Military Intelligence Battalion provided American staff for the four national-level combined intelligence centers, as well as for the military intelligence detachments serving in each South Vietnamese corps, division, and province headquarters. The Americans at the combined centers trained their Vietnamese counterparts as they became available, and the detachments supported the field intelligence advisers and funneled information into American intelligence channels. Similar Vietnamese intelligence detachments continued to work with almost all U.S. tactical headquarters. The degree of cooperation in intelligence matters, however, was still marred by Saigon's poor counterintelligence capabilities, especially at lower military echelons, and the widespread suspicion that the Viet Cong had penetrated South Vietnamese military and civilian agencies. Although Americans could not ascertain the degree of penetration, U.S. commanders and intelligence officers continued to be reluctant to share information and methodology with their South Vietnamese opposites.[43]

Despite the construction of new POW camps in 1966 and closer cooperation between Americans and South Vietnamese in the handling of prisoners, the situation remained muddled throughout 1967. The camps constructed in each corps tactical zone in 1966 and early 1967 were too small. In the II Corps Tactical Zone alone over 7,000 prisoners of all types were crowded into jails and camps whose combined capacity was less then 3,000. Although South Vietnamese officials had classified about 5,800 of these prisoners as civil defendants, they had tried and convicted only 139, sent 851 to *Chieu Hoi* "reeducation centers," and held the remaining 4,836 without trial. The process of classifying and trying prisoners was slow, disorganized, arbitrary, and often punctuated by demonstrations within the prisons and holding areas. The entire matter made few friends for Saigon, while its contribution to the war effort was questionable.[44]

The situation was the same in every corps area. Separating military prisoners from civil defendants was time-consuming and difficult in the absence of good

[42] Fact Sheet, MACPD, 20 Jan 67, sub: RVNAF Political Indoctination Program, MICRO 75/1710; Ltr, Westmoreland to Vien, 30 Jun 67, MICRO 75/1728. Both in RG 334, WNRC. See also Bullard, "Political Cadre Systems in the Military."
[43] McChristian, *Role of Military Intelligence*, pp. 21–93; Truong, *RVNAF and US Operational Cooperation and Coordination*, pp. 28–36; Memo, Westmoreland to Bunker, 2 Nov 67, sub: Charges Against the South Vietnamese, COMUSMACV Signature file, 1967, Westmoreland Papers, HRB, CMH; Intervs, author with Samuel Adams, April and May 1975, SEAB, CMH.
[44] Memo, Westmoreland to Porter, 17 Jan 67, sub: Detention Facilities in the Republic of Vietnam, COMUSMACV Signature file, 1967, Westmoreland Papers, HRB, CMH; Msg, Larson to Westmoreland, 15 Jan 67, sub: Incident at PW Camp, Pleiku, MICRO 75/1182, RG 334, WNRC.

records and able personnel. Many prisoners either escaped or bribed officials to buy their way out. Others were simply declared to be refugees and released. MACV estimated that since 1963 another 10,000 had switched sides and enlisted in the South Vietnamese armed forces.[45] American advisers from MACV and the U.S. Embassy advocated better screening, greater use of the judicial process, and the expansion of detention and prisoner facilities, but did little to influence the situation directly.

American involvement centered around the issue of sovereignty. Although recognizing its international responsibilities, the United States hesitated to become entangled in an issue that might have significant political repercussions at some later date. Like the combined command, American assumption of direct responsibility for the care of enemy prisoners entailed a permanent commitment to what American officials still viewed as a political problem. The International Red Cross was puzzled by the situation. After it failed to gain visitation rights to prisoners of war held by the Viet Cong and the North Vietnamese, the Directory barred it from inspecting camps in the South during 1967. Vien even objected to inspections by MACV teams. Westmoreland, growing increasingly sensitive to the issue, convinced Vien of the advantages of cooperating with the Red Cross and offered American engineer assistance to construct and expand the POW camps in each zone. He also proposed establishing a central POW camp on Phu Quoc Island to end the need for large camps on the mainland. But he made no move to change basic U.S. policy regarding the custody of enemy prisoners.[46]

American support of the South Vietnamese military budget remained firm. While overall American financial assistance for the Saigon government varied from year to year (about $268.5 million in 1965, $707.9 million in 1966, and $541.9 million in 1967), the size of the South Vietnamese defense budget and the proportion of that budget supported by the United States was relatively constant: about $335 million (38 percent) in 1964, $506.6 (35 percent) in 1965, $583.3 (39 percent) in 1966, and $569.6 (40 percent) in 1967. The defense budget covered only military salaries. Funding for war materiel, including both equipment and expendable items like ammunition, came from the U.S. military service budgets, except for a few items still supported by the Military Assistance Program. Materiel assistance from the U.S. Army budget alone totaled $474 million in fiscal year (FY) 1967, with steady increases projected for the 1968 and 1969 budget years. As before, the bulk of this direct materiel assistance was devoted to munitions

---

[45] MACV, Preliminary Report on Manpower Mobilization, 1967, MICRO 2/322, RG 334, WNRC. Most had been classified or perhaps reclassified as *hoi chanhs*, enemy soldiers or supporters who had surrendered voluntarily.

[46] Ltrs, Westmoreland to Vien, 8 Jul, 28 Aug, 25 Oct 67 and 22 Feb 68; Ltr, Vien to Westmoreland, 17 Oct 67, sub: Observations on Activities of Communist PW Camps Made During Visits by Guest and Armed Forces Personnel. All in COMUSMACV Signature files, 1967 and 1968, respectively, Westmoreland Papers, HRB, CMH. See also MFR, Westmoreland, 3 Jan 67, sub: Conferences With Generals Vien and Co, 3 January 1967, History file 12–B6, Westmoreland Papers, HRB, CMH; MFR, MACJ03 (prepared by Deputy Ambassador Eugene M. Locke), 2 Nov 67, sub: Blueprint for Vietnam, and app. 13, "The Screening Detention Problem," MICRO 2/1641, RG 334, WNRC. For camp operations, see Interv, Maj Charles C. Pritchett with Capt Marion R. Morehouse, Adviser POW Compound, III Corps, 19 Dec 68, VNIT 310, HRB, CMH.

($246.9 million in FY 66, and $269 and $307.85 million projected for FY 67 and FY 68).[47]

Corruption: The Perennial Problem

Corruption and poor management continued to bedevil internal Vietnamese military finances. To help stem both, Westmoreland convinced the Directory to issue a decree in June 1967 making officers "who commit a serious offense pertaining to military discipline, mission or obligation" subject to demotion. But the provision was rarely used, and grappling with corruption in the officer corps proved difficult. Guided by the MACV Office of the Comptroller, the South Vietnamese Office of the Director General for Finance and Audit slowly expanded, and the number of audits and investigations increased. In September MACV assigned advisers to each of Saigon's six field finance detachments to improve American monitoring of financial controls and expenditures. These advisers accompanied Vietnamese auditors in the field and reported irregularities to the MACV comptroller, who referred them to the finance and audit director for action. They found the practice of carrying deserters on unit rosters and pocketing payroll funds the most common abuse. But investigations were time-consuming and, with only eleven of its authorized twenty-five auditors, the powers of the Vietnamese office were still extremely limited.[48]

General Westmoreland tried to assist by assigning his own inspector general the additional task of advising his South Vietnamese counterpart, and subsequently placing staff advisers directly in the South Vietnamese office. A U.S. Army inspector general training team from the United States also helped Saigon establish a network of inspector general field offices throughout the army, greatly expanding its investigatory powers. At the same time, both MACV and the U.S. Embassy urged the Directory generals to take more forceful action against corruption in the armed forces.[49]

For once, American advice appeared to produce results. In late 1966 and early 1967 a series of investigations by Joint General Staff representatives caused a

[47] Fact Sheet, MACCO, 23 May 68, sub: Growth of the Republic of Vietnam Defense Budget During the Period 1964–1968, in COMUSMACV Fact Book, vol. 2; Memo, Col J. L. Clancy, MACV comptroller, to COMUSMACV, 17 Sep 67, sub: Briefing on the Overall Status of the CY 1967 and CY 1968 GVN Defense Budget, History file 22–A7. Both in Westmoreland Papers, HRB, CMH. See also Briefing, MACMA, 5 Jul 67, sub: Army Programs for Military [?] Vietnam, MICRO 3/0404, RG 334, WNRC. The figures for the South Vietnamese defense budget show greater variation in piasters due to the steady devaluation of South Vietnamese currency.

[48] Quoted words from Fact Sheet, MACJ–14, circa June 1969, sub: RVNAF Leadership, MICRO 3/0213, RG 334, WNRC. See also McGovern Briefing, MICRO 2/1251, RG 334, WNRC; Ltr, Westmoreland to Bunker, 2 Oct 67, sub: Corruption Within the RVNAF, COMUSMACV Signature file, 1967, Westmoreland Papers, HRB, CMH.

[49] Rpt, MACSJS–01, 14 Jul 67, sub: Historical Summary 2d Quarter 1967, Inspector General, MICRO 40/1517; Rpt, MACSJS–01, sub: Historical Summary CY 67, Inspector General, MICRO 40–1566. Both in RG 334, WNRC. See also MFR, Westmoreland, 3 Jan 67, sub: Conferences With General Vien and Co, 3 January 1967, History file 12–B6, Westmoreland Papers, HRB, CMH; Office of the Inspector General, MACV, "Inspector General History, 1964–1972," especially pp. 33–43, MACV IG files, box 1, accession no. 77/0074, RG 334, WNRC, which notes that MACV did not provide a full-time IG adviser until 6 March 1967.

sensation in Saigon. One case involved Col. Vu Ngoc Tuan, commandant of the large Quang Trung Training Center near Saigon, who apparently had used military real estate, materiel, and trainee labor to build an ice-making plant nearby. Acting on information supposedly contained in an unsigned letter, Vien launched an official inspector general investigation that resulted in the relief and demotion of Tuan and several other officers, including the director of the Central Logistics Command, General Nhon. A few months later, Maj. Tran Tien Khang, the Kien Tuong Province deputy chief, was accused of operating an opium smuggling ring that extended from Cholon (Saigon) to Cambodia and, in addition, of shipping explosives to his brother in Saigon for the manufacture of fireworks. The publicity associated with the case precipitated Khang's dismissal. However, as MACV and U.S. Embassy officials were well aware of by now, such charges, investigations, and the resulting courts-martial, reliefs, demotions, and transfers normally meant little. In the case of Major Khang, the accused moved over to command the local South Vietnamese 11th Regiment, 7th Infantry Division, for three years, where American advisers, not surprisingly, found him ineffective and recommended his relief. Tuan, temporarily demoted to lieutenant colonel and in disgrace, remained out of a job longer, but emerged in 1973 with his old rank as the III Corps chief of staff. Thus, while MACV often made much of such actions in its reports to Washington, the various investigations that were undertaken by Saigon never reflected any widespread reform effort.[50]

To Americans, the Vietnamese official most concerned over the entire matter of corruption was General Nguyen Duc Thang, Ky's handpicked minister of revolutionary development. Thoroughly discouraged by 1967, he confided to Edward G. Lansdale, the old Indochina hand who was currently serving as Bunker's assistant, that the army was "far more corrupt than anyone can imagine" and that "the 'Americanization' of the military effort was accepted by many ARVN leaders as an excuse to spend more of their time on personal, selfish affairs." Many of the better Vietnamese commanders had finally succumbed, becoming "playboys," constantly nightclubbing while sitting out the war in Saigon, Da Lat, or some other safe haven. Thang explained that, beginning rather early in one's military career, the pattern of corruption progressed in an almost standardized fashion. Frustrated with his job, a young officer spent increasing amounts of time at cafes and bars, gradually developing a series of relationships with local mistresses until one became what the Vietnamese called "the second wife." At the same time, to impress and satisfy the needs of both wife and mistress, and his families and friends, the officer gradually began using his position to acquire property, houses, and material goods, all of which demanded a constant supply of cash. The pressing need for money forced the officer to supplement his legitimate earnings with more lucrative, corrupt activities of all sorts. In the process he soon found himself protecting those above and below

---

[50] Memo, Frank Wisner to T. P. H. Dunlop, 5 Jul 67, sub: Request From Amb. Komer for Information on GVN Officials Dismissed for Corruption, SEAB, CMH; Khuyen, *The RVNAF*, p. 359; Supplemental Data Sheet, MACJ3–051, 10 Feb 70, sub: Assessment of ARVN/VNMC Organizations–B, MICRO 3/ 1438, RG 334, WNRC; South Vietnamese officer dossiers, SEAB, CMH. Tuan had been deputy commander of the 5th Division in 1965 and may thus have had close ties with General Thieu, the unit's former commander.

him engaged in similar practices, both to safeguard and to justify his own actions. He also discovered that managing his financial affairs was a full-time task and spent increasingly less time at his official duties. The need to incorporate family members and friends into the process complicated his affairs further. But the real tragedy, Thang concluded, was that many officers openly flaunted their wealth and money-making activities, encouraging others to take part and demoralizing those that abstained. To remedy the situation, the minister recommended a thorough house-cleaning of the upper echelons of the army. The tactical commanders in the field, especially those at regimental and battalion levels, he felt, would support such action and the possibility of a coup was remote. Generals Vien and Vy, Thang believed, were capable of supplying the drive and leadership for a massive reform effort, but would need considerably more American support in this area than they had been receiving in the past. American attitudes were critical.[51]

Westmoreland was also completely frustrated over the corruption issue. Acknowledging that "corruption is everywhere" in the South Vietnamese army, he felt that it was impossible to refute the charge when it periodically appeared in the American press or on the floor of Congress. In November he even sent Vien a copy of the U.S. Army Code of Ethics in hopes that it might somehow spark a higher standard of conduct among the Vietnamese. However, hesitant to intervene directly in South Vietnamese internal affairs, he believed the source of the problem to be much deeper, pointing out that the "Vietnamese traditionally have placed duty to family and friends over duty to the nation." Until the Saigon government could command more loyalty from its own officials, the MACV commander judged that little could be done to improve civic responsibility. Because the essentially political nature of the problem obviated any solution that MACV could recommend or impose, Americans would just have to live with the situation and hope for more success on the battlefield.[52]

As in 1966, MACV had thus accomplished little in the way of administrative reform. Other events continued to overshadow the staff advisory effort, and the whole endeavor continued to lack a sense of urgency. Few officers could see any direct relationship between such measures and the "real war" that was going on out in the field. Even if successful, the administrative reforms pushed by MACV could not have produced the immediate results desired by senior U.S. officials. With most American attention still focused on the battlefield or on Komer's new CORDS organization, the reform effort slipped through yet another year almost unnoticed and unchanged. Whether it really mattered that much for the future course of the struggle no one could yet tell.

[51] Memo, Lansdale to Bunker, 23 Jun 67, sub: Two Days With Thang, SEAB, CMH.

[52] First quotation from Msg, Westmoreland MAC 8875 to McConnell, acting JCS chairman, 20 Sep 67, History file 22–A16. Second quotation from Memo, Westmoreland to Bunker, 2 Nov 67, sub: Charges Against the South Vietnamese, COMUSMACV Signature file, 1967. See also Ltr, Westmoreland to Vien, 30 Nov 67, COMUSMACV Signature file, 1967. All in Westmoreland Papers, HRB; CMH.

13

The Security Mission Examined

America's fighting strategy remained unchanged in South Vietnam during 1967. The troop buildup continued with the arrival of three new brigades in the northern zone and the deployment of the 9th Infantry Division in the Delta, raising U.S. troop strength to almost half a million men. With an increasing number of Vietnamese forces providing area security, American units pursued the war of attrition, best characterized by the large multidivisional clearing operations MANHATTAN and JUNCTION CITY, northwest of Saigon. Hanoi had stepped up the infiltration of both regular units and individual replacements to match the American buildup, but casualties had been heavy. In February the Joint Chiefs chairman, General Wheeler, told President Johnson that Westmoreland now had the initiative, predicting that "we can win the war if we apply pressure upon the enemy relentlessly in the north and in the south." Even if North Vietnam could not be forced to the conference table, he felt that enemy losses could be made so high "that the North Vietnamese would be unable effectively to support the war in the south" and "at that point the war would be essentially won." Almost as an afterthought, he added that "much would remain to be accomplished in the revolutionary development field."[1]

Supporting Revolutionary Development

In Vietnam, progress in revolutionary development had indeed been slow, and Westmoreland had yet to create any enthusiasm in the South Vietnamese Army for the mission of area, or population, security. In adjusting South Vietnamese forces for a more significant role in revolutionary development, the U.S.–South Vietnamese Combined Campaign Plan for 1967 stressed the participation of Saigon's regular forces in securing operations. The plan envisioned attaching regular infantry battalions directly to province chiefs "to achieve unity of effort." With primary responsibility for pacification, each province chief was to prepare comprehensive plans encompassing both military and nonmilitary efforts. Corps

---

[1] Msg, Wheeler JCS 1284–67 to Sharp and Westmoreland, 170000 Feb 67, COMUSMACV Message file, Westmoreland Papers, HRB, CMH.

commanders would decide on a case-by-case basis when regular units would be attached to provincial authorities. South Vietnamese division commanders would continue to provide administrative, combat, logistical, and training support to these detached units and to have the authority to recall them in the event of a combat emergency. Units remaining under division control would serve as mobile reserve forces. Because regular units had performed similar missions in the past, the suggested command arrangements and deployments did not appear to represent any great departure from past practices. Westmoreland judged it logical to make the province chief (sector commander), rather than the division commander (division tactical area commander), the focal point of the area security campaign. Neither the U.S. Embassy nor any of the American civilian agencies in Vietnam had ever stationed advisers at the district level, and province and district advisers had been habitually frustrated by the bureaucratic delays in obtaining the approval of their security plans by the division tactical commands and their staffs. But no one, certainly not Westmoreland, suggested dissolving the division headquarters, even if such a solution was practicable. Although Westmoreland continued to emphasize the importance of the security mission to Vien, even suggesting that Saigon give regular forces providing territorial security priority in logistical support and other matters, he still regarded the detachment of infantry battalions to province chiefs as a temporary measure until more Territorial Forces could be raised.[2]

Throughout 1967 control of regular army battalions by province chiefs remained controversial. American and South Vietnamese commanders viewed the practice as exceptional, while the U.S. Embassy and other American agencies and the Saigon administration, especially the Ministry of Revolutionary Development, saw it as the only way the regular forces could be integrated into the area security effort. The crux of the problem was political. Loss of control over battalions, even temporarily, reduced not only the military but also the local economic and political powers of the division commanders. Understandably, they adamantly opposed the practice and discouraged it whenever possible. Despite his own endorsement, Westmoreland himself was concerned that the wholesale detachment of battalions would further fragment the regular army and complicate the field advisory chain of command. Thieu, as chairman of the Directory, was of the same opinion. Many of his supporters were division commanders, and perhaps he was wary of any organizational shifts that might increase the influence of Ky's revolutionary development network. Many officers serving as province chiefs were Ky-appointees. Lt. Col. Volney F. Warner, an Army CORDS official, saw the matter in a different light. Given the "gradual installation of military rule throughout rural Vietnam" since the fall of Diem, he thought the process now had to be reversed. Like many others in the U.S. mission, Warner thought removing the division commanders from the area sec-

---

[2] Quoted words from JGS-MACV, Combined Campaign Plan 1967, AB 142, 7 Nov 66, p. B–7, SEAB, CMH. See also Msg, COMUSMACV to CINCPAC, 9 Jun 67, sub: ARVN Support for RD, COMUSMACV Message file; Msg, COMUSMACV to CINCPAC, 220305 Nov 67, sub: 1968 Goals for Measurement of Progress in Southeast Asia, Chief of Staff Message file; Ltr, Westmoreland to Vien, 6 Sep 67, COMUSMACV Signature file, 1967. All in Westmoreland Papers, HRB, CMH. On the advisers' frustration, see Interv, Pritchett with Maj Francis C. Vossen (hereafter cited as Vossen Interv), Senior Adviser, Team 98, Nhon Trach Sensitive Area, 19 Jul 68, VNIT 198, HRB, CMH.

urity chain of command as "the best place to start." But most province and district officials were also active military officers and, without an experienced cadre of civil service personnel or an organized political party system, the prospects of truly civilianizing the administration were bleak.[3]

Throughout the year Westmoreland continued to have difficulties mustering support for the new security mission from the South Vietnamese tactical commanders. In January he expressed his concern to Vien over the special revolutionary development training given to the regulars, and in February General Freund confirmed his misgivings. Although twenty-four of twenty-eight battalions had received the training, Freund judged the quality of instruction as marginal. Division commanders had taken little interest in the training program, and the mobile training teams had tried to teach entire battalions in massive lecture sessions that were poorly attended. Westmoreland passed on these observations to Vien, urging him to place more emphasis on the program, but made no specific recommendations.[4]

Revolutionary development training nevertheless continued throughout 1967. The corps formed more training teams and extended the instruction to noninfantry units in the army and to the Territorial Forces. Eight combined American–South Vietnamese inspection teams reviewed the training and in March, following Westmoreland's comments to Vien, reported favorable changes in military attitudes and conduct toward civilians. Vien predicted that all infantry battalions would complete the instruction by December and declared the program a success. Later that month Westmoreland agreed, but asked that supplemental training in small unit tactics be provided as soon as possible.[5]

The judgment of Vien and Westmoreland may have been premature, for the long-term effectiveness of revolutionary development training had yet to be tested. Similar instruction was already part of the American and South Vietnamese basic training curriculum, and an almost identical "refresher" pacification training program began in early 1968 for all Vietnamese units. Later that year the MACV staff discussed the merits of sending South Vietnamese battalion commanders to the Vung Tau Revolutionary Development School for even more training in revolutionary development, but rejected the proposals as too disruptive. According to CORDS Director Robert Komer, it took pressure and time to develop a "pacification consciousness" in both American and South Vietnamese

---

[3] Quoted words from Memo, Warner to Clayton E. McManaway, 20 Mar 67, sub: Military Operation in Support of the RD Program, SEAB, CMH. Warner, a member of the Army Staff, became a White House military adviser in June 1967. See also MFR, Westmoreland, 17 Jan 67, sub: Meeting With General Thieu on 13 January 1967 at His Office in the Palace, History file 12–C5, Westmoreland Papers, HRB, CMH.

[4] MFR, Westmoreland, 3 Jan 67, sub: Conferences With General Vien and Co, 3 January 1967, History file 12–B6; Notes of 1 Feb 67, p. 15, History file 13–A. Both in Westmoreland Papers, HRB, CMH. See also Ltr, Westmoreland to Vien, 2 Feb 67, MICRO 75/1729, RG 334, WNRC; MFR, Maj Loren M. Eberhart, IV Corps Liaison Officer, 2 Feb 67, sub: Trip Report—Military Support for RD, 9th ARVN Division, SEAB, CMH.

[5] Memo, Westmoreland to Porter, 28 Mar 67, sub: RVNAF Training in Support of Revolutionary Development, COMUSMACV Signature file, 1967; General Vien's Remarks (at Unit Commander's Meeting, Nha Trang, 2 Apr 67), History file 15–A4; Ltr, Westmoreland to Vien, 13 Apr 67, COMUSMACV Signature file, 1967. All in Westmoreland Papers, HRB, CMH.

commanders, and he was still dissatisfied with this aspect of the war effort when he left South Vietnam in 1968.[6]

The Advisers

Following the creation of CORDS in April 1967, Westmoreland set about to strengthen the area security advisory organization. During the subsequent months he established mobile advisory teams (MATs), to work directly with the small territorial units in the field, and mobile advisory logistics teams (MALTs), to assist the territorial logistics companies in each province, deploying several hundred MATs and MALTs by the end of the year. Under the overall direction of the province senior advisers, each team consisted of two junior officers and three to four enlisted men. At the same time the MACV commander integrated similar teams, formed by American tactical units, into the field advisory organization and also enlarged the size of the province advisory teams by adding training, engineer, and personnel advisers. In 1967 the number of CORDS advisers for the provinces, districts, and Territorial Forces thus increased from about two thousand to over five thousand, while the strength of the tactical, or combat, advisers remained stable at about three thousand.[7]

During the process of strengthening the CORDS advisory organization, Westmoreland asked the chief of the MACV Training Directorate, General Flanagan, to conduct yet another review of the entire advisory effort. Westmoreland contemplated no changes in the role of the adviser, stipulating that they would continue to serve as tactical and technical advisers, support coordinators, and liaison officers for American tactical units and commands. Instead, he asked Flanagan to examine ways to reduce the number of advisers by eliminating duplication, by standardizing teams with similar missions, and by withdrawing advisers from units that had outgrown their need for them. He believed that security detachments for advisory teams were no longer needed now that American combat units were in country and that some savings could be realized by eliminating or consolidating advisory support activities and by using Vietnamese civilians or servicemen as drivers, translators, radio operators, guards, and clerks. The spaces thus saved could be better used, he felt, by his ground combat units and the forces that supported them.

In August Flanagan submitted his report, recommending drastic manpower reductions across the board. The report proposed deleting 165 advisory spaces from the MACV staff, 562 from the combat advisory groups, and 949 from the CORDS advisory net. The cuts, totaling 1,676 spaces, would have halved the size of the planned mobile advisory teams working with the Territorial Forces and reduced the battalion advisory teams to three. To make the advisory effort more

---

[6] Quoted words from Komer Interv, 7 May 70, Rand Limited Document D(L)–20104–ARPA, SEAB, CMH. See also Fact Sheet, MACJ–341, 11 Jul 68, sub: To Provide the Answer To . . . , MICRO 3/2147, RG 334, WNRC.

[7] Supplemental Data Sheet, MACCORDS, 10 Jul 68, sub: Deployment of MATs, MALTs, Engineer and S–1 Advisors, MICRO 3/2051, RG 334, WNRC; USMACV, "Command History, 1967," 1:221–26, and "1968," 1:233–37, HRB, CMH.

flexible, Flanagan suggested that senior advisers have the authority to shift subordinate advisers and adjust team strengths accordingly. Westmoreland approved the staff reductions, agreed to delete 296 spaces from the combat teams,
but left the size of the new territorial advisory teams intact.[8]

While Flanagan conducted his study, several other high officials also addressed the future of the advisory organization. General Wheeler, during his
visit to Vietnam in April 1967, suggested that MACV increase the strength of the
advisory teams assigned to Vietnamese battalions performing territorial security
to provide an adviser for each company. He also asked Westmoreland to assign
"our very best men" to these teams to ensure a smooth transition from normal
combat operations ("search-and-destroy" or "clear-and-hold") to "local security
activities." As an alternative, the MACV staff proposed assigning two extra men,
a captain and an experienced NCO (E–7) to each four-man battalion advisory
team serving with a security-tasked battalion. However, considering the shortage
of experienced personnel, Westmoreland decided against either proposal and the
matter was dropped.[9]

By the spring of 1967 the quality, experience, and morale of the advisers had
also become a serious issue. In May Westmoreland again asked General Johnson,
the Army chief of staff, to assign the Army's best officers to American tactical
units in South Vietnam (that is, the Army component command), and not to
MACV and the advisory network. The new MACV deputy commander, General
Abrams, felt that Westmoreland's priorities were inevitable, yet he was worried
and communicated his concerns to the Army Staff. Responding to Abrams,
Johnson confided that he was doing everything possible in Washington to enhance the status of the advisers but had to give priority to the requirements for
troop commanders, noting that the U.S. Army was "a fighting force and [the]
ability to command troops effectively is [its] primary measure of success."
Abrams responded that the advisers not only saw themselves as "second class
citizens" but also were treated as such, and felt that it was necessary to "make a
concerted effort to increase their status in their own eyes."[10]

Noting the increased attention given to area security, General Johnson felt
that he could best help by improving the quality and incentives for prospective
province senior advisers. Under Johnson's prompting, the Army Staff upgraded
standards for these posts and sought to identify qualified candidates several
months prior to their assignment to Vietnam. Nominees were to be superior
combat arms officers with the rank of colonel or promotable lieutenant colonel
who had commanded units in Vietnam; they were also to be graduates of the
U.S. Army War College, with the ability to speak or aptitude for learning Vietnamese. With Westmoreland's approval, the entire package included advanced
courses at the U.S. Foreign Service Institute, extensive Vietnamese-language

---

[8] USMACV, "Command History, 1967," 1:227–31, HRB, CMH.

[9] Ltr, Westmoreland to CINCPAC, 16 Apr 67, sub: Use of Additional Advisors To Support Revolutionary Development, COMUSMACV Signature file, 1967, Westmoreland Papers, HRB, CMH.

[10] First quotation from Msg, Johnson WDC 9205 to Abrams, 150210 Jul 67. Second and third quota-
tions from Msg, Abrams MAC 6712 to Johnson, 172324 Jul 67. Both in Creighton W. Abrams Papers.
See also Ltr, Westmoreland to Johnson, 28 May 67, COMUSMACV Signature file, 1967, Westmoreland
Papers. All in HRB, CMH.

Komer (right) Discussing Revolutionary Development Plans *with the regional CORDS adviser*

training, eighteen-month tours, and generous leave privileges, extra pay, and special consideration for their next assignment.[11]

Westmoreland and Johnson also agreed to award "command credit," an important factor in promotion consideration, to all province and district senior advisers. Abrams, for his part, supported the establishment of a special advisory school in Vietnam for future mobile advisory team members. Approved in October 1967 and staffed by handpicked advisers from each zone, the school began concentrated two-week training sessions in early 1968.[12] Abrams also insisted that only highly experienced personnel be assigned to the territorial advisory program, and when the Army Staff was unable to fulfill his requirements, he had the MACV and USARV staffs transfer personnel who had the requisite qualifications directly from American combat units in Vietnam.[13]

Komer, anxious to see more immediate progress in local security and revolutionary development, took a different approach. Prior to his arrival in Vietnam

---

[11] Fact Sheet, MACJ–12, July 1970, sub: Personnel Status of Selected MACV Advisory Program (by the MACV, J–1, Brig Gen L. V. Greene), MICRO 97/1360, RG 334, WNRC.

[12] For a detailed study of the school, see Rpt, Maj Charles G. Vemity, CO, 45th Military History Detachment, 13 May 69, sub: Historical Coverage of the United States Army Vietnam Advisor School, VNIT 382; USMACV, "Command History, 1968," 1:233–38. Both in HRB, CMH.

[13] Rpt, Maj Charles C. Pritchett, 20th Military History Detachment, 28 Aug 68, sub: The Mobile Advisory Team, VNIT 246, HRB, CMH.

he had considered having corps and province advisers directly control American-supported programs. Although he later realized that Vietnamese sensibilities made this impractical, he believed that CORDS advisers had to be able to deal effectively with inept or blatantly corrupt South Vietnamese administrators if pacification was to have a chance. Consequently, as CORDS director he actively solicited candid evaluations of the South Vietnamese commanders and staffs at corps, province, and district commands and worked vigorously through MACV and the American embassy to have those officials with the worst ratings replaced. He was also able to provide province senior advisers with their own funds so that they could influence the progress of various security and development projects that CORDS considered critical. These measures gave pacification advisers in the field greater leverage over their counterparts and represented a departure from the advisory policies generally followed by Westmoreland.[14]

The attention given to the CORDS advisory effort pushed the activities of the combat, school, and logistics advisers even further into the background. Early in 1967 General Westmoreland had called them the "heart and soul" of the American commitment to South Vietnam, but described their primary duty as preparing the Vietnamese armed forces "to assume the responsibility for the post-war security of the Vietnamese people with a minimum of external assistance." His recipe for the job remained unchanged. He called on each adviser "to provide the ingredients necessary for your counterpart to make valid judgments and then encourage his decision-making prerogatives."[15] But the old personal relationship formula had not improved with time. According to CORDS evaluators, the tactical advisers were still fighting the same problems. The adviser at division level and below, relying on his "own personality and persuasive powers and on the receptiveness of his counterpart," was generally unable to persuade Vietnamese commanders and officials to accept his advice, especially in the many areas that had political ramifications.[16] Hardly any advisers spoke Vietnamese and their communications with counterparts depended heavily on native interpreters. Departures of advisers without immediate replacements continued to be commonplace, damaging the continuity of the effort at the lower echelons. Under pressure to project a positive image of the South Vietnamese army, many advisers continued to avoid passing on adverse comments to their superiors. The problems were not new, having existed throughout the advisory network for years. But now they had become severe in the small battalion and regimental advisory teams, where the advisers were normally inexperienced younger officers who viewed advisory duty as detrimental to their careers.[17]

On the battlefield, field advisers continued to play their combat support role.[18] Whether the South Vietnamese were performing search and destroy, clear-

[14] For treatment, see Hunt, *Pacification*, forthcoming.

[15] Ltr, Westmoreland to All Advisers, 8 Jan 67, sub: US Advisor/VN Counterpart Relationship, COMUSMACV Signature file, 1967, Westmoreland Papers, HRB, CMH.

[16] For example, see CORDS Field Evaluation Rpt, Maj Stanley J. Michael, 29 Aug 67, sub: 18th ARVN Division in Support of RD, SEAB, CMH.

[17] For example, see CORDS Field Evaluation Rpt, Maj Philip Hurd and T. McAdams Deford, 2 Sep 67, sub: The ARVN 7th Division in Support of RD, SEAB, CMH.

[18] The general description that follows was distilled from advisory interviews at CMH, from the author's interviews with former advisers, and from the author's experiences with Advisory Team 85, III CTZ, 1970.

Field Adviser and His Counterparts *calling for an air strike*

ing, or securing missions, the requirements and tasks at the dirt level never really changed throughout the war. "In the boondocks" (on operations) the battalion adviser needed a good pair of legs and a strong back; water and perhaps a bit of food (rice); a variety of skin lotions (suntan, mosquito repellant, foot powder, and medicinal cremes); a pack of cigarettes; hard candy or chewing gum; and a good map, an accurate compass, and a reliable radio with extra batteries. His rifle, a few clips of ammunition, smoke grenades, and assorted odds and ends (pen and paper, some kind of small knife, rope, extra socks, a towel, and perhaps a good paperback book) completed his basic needs. The less he carried the better, for most operations involved long, difficult treks through overgrown marshes and jungles in stifling heat and humidity. Boobytraps and mines were his worst enemy, with fatigue, insects, and disease everpresent but minor irritations.

Most combat actions in the field were small-scale but fast-paced firefights, ambushes, or accidental "meeting engagements," reaching a climax in perhaps a few seconds and often lasting no more than a few minutes as the weaker side sought to disengage as quickly as possible. When his unit made "contact" with the enemy, the adviser quickly "got on the horn" (the radio) and sent a brief "sitrep" (situation report) "in the clear" (without code words) to his "six" (superior). Generally he reported his location (an eight-digit map coordinate, or, in a rush, something like "five clicks"—kilometers—north, south, east, or west of Chanh Thanh, Minh Tan, or wherever); described the enemy force ("estimated

240

Victor Charlie—VC—squad, platoon, or company"); and requested assistance ("What have we got up?"). The language was as terse and brief as possible. In most cases, FACs (U.S. Air Force forward air controllers) in "Birddogs" (light Cessna O–1 fixed-wing aircraft) were within a few minutes flying time of the adviser's location. Upon arrival overhead, the adviser would "pop smoke" (ignite a colored smoke grenade), identify himself (FAC: "I see green smoke"; Adviser: "Affirmative"), and explain his problem ("Victor Charlie so many hundreds of meters from my location at an azimuth—compass direction—of such and such degrees"). The "aloft" (the pilot/observer) then confirmed the transmission ("Roger that") and proceeded to direct all "assets" (artillery, air strikes, helicopter gunships) under his control onto the target area. In the meantime, the adviser continued to keep both his superiors and the FAC apprised of any changes in the tactical situation, as did the adviser's Vietnamese counterpart using his own communications gear. While calling for either "dust offs" (aeromedical evacuation of casualties) or resupply, if necessary, the adviser simultaneously assisted his counterpart in retaining or regaining control over his troops—a normal problem of any small unit in combat. The tempo of such battles usually gave the adviser little chance to do anything more coherent. But while much of his work and sacrifices went unnoticed and unrewarded, it was here on the hundreds of small battlefields in Vietnam that he continued to earn his room and board. Although larger actions, such as the extended defense of bases and installations, were more complex and tactical advice potentially more significant, without the immediacy of combat the influence of the adviser was greatly reduced.[19]

Measuring Success

To evaluate South Vietnamese military effectiveness in the new mission, MACV still relied heavily on the senior adviser monthly evaluation (SAME) reports.[20] During 1966 and 1967 advisers were still rating units as "satisfactory," "marginal," or "unsatisfactory" by weighing four categories: present-for-duty strength (measured against authorized and assigned strengths), overall morale, the state of training, and leadership (officers and noncommissioned officers). The ratings were deceptively simple. "Unsatisfactory" units were those "ineffective or incapable of accomplishing [their] basic mission," "marginal" units were "capable of accomplishing [their] basic mission with minimal effectiveness," and "satisfactory" units were "capable of performing [their] basic mission and functions with a reasonable degree of effectiveness." Advisers might rate a South

---

[19] For a treatment of some of the more vexing medical problems in the tropical Southeast Asian environment, see Alfred M. Allen, *Skin Diseases in Vietnam, 1965–72*, Medical Department, United States Army (Washington, D.C.: Office of the Surgeon General and the U.S. Army Center of Military History, 1977).

[20] See the 1966–67 SAME ratings found in MICRO 135, RG 334, WNRC, for following statistics and specific evaluations.

Vietnamese unit "marginal" in all areas, without rating the unit "unsatisfactory." For a "satisfactory" rating, advisers found it difficult to agree on what constituted "a reasonable degree of effectiveness." In August, to reduce the subjectivity inherent in the rating system, MACV raised the number of rated categories for each unit to twenty-seven and included such items as care of dependents, resupply, the status of equipment, tactics, and intelligence. The three basic ratings, however, remained unchanged.[21]

In general, senior officers regarded the narrative evaluations by individual advisers as too subjective and used them primarily to explain discrepancies in broader statistical trends. Statistical ratings, expressed in percentages and gross totals, remained the normal method of comparing units and assessing progress. Using 1964 or 1965 as a base, MACV evaluators concentrated on three sets of ratios: enemy killed compared with friendly killed (the "kill ratio"); weapons captured to weapons lost; and engagements with the enemy per unit days of operation. By 1967 MACV also considered such factors as the time of engagement, the initiator, the size of the units engaged, total casualties, and the circumstances of disengagement. The percentage of time battalions spent on particular missions (search and destroy, security, reserve) and the ensuing results constituted another set of measurements. A variety of statistics on strength and desertions (actual operational strength compared with authorized, assigned, or official present-for-duty strength; gross desertions, desertions per 1,000 men assigned, and status of deserters) were also part of the overall statistical picture. No one believed that the quantitative data could substitute for traditional evaluations based on territory conquered or enemy units destroyed. But by comparing current figures with past ones, General Westmoreland and his staff felt that the statistics yielded a general picture of both the status and progress of the South Vietnamese armed forces.[22]

How well all this information reflected the actual state of Saigon's army was questionable. MACV evaluators noted that both "unsatisfactory" and "satisfactory" battalions had poor kill ratios, but maintained that, when all the statistics were examined over a long period of time, correlations between subjective ratings and statistical results were evident.[23] Nevertheless, the interpretation of statistical and subjective evaluations often led to perplexing conclusions. For example, during 1967 the number of infantry-type battalions awarded an overall rating of "satisfactory" rose markedly. However, the number of such battalions considered unsatisfactory or marginal in the area of "combat effectiveness and security" also increased, and the status of the South Vietnamese divisions and regiments remained about the same.[24] What was one to make of such information?

---

[21] SAME Evaluation, October 1966, MICRO 135, RG 334, WNRC.
[22] Msg, Westmoreland MAC 8073 to Wheeler, 25 Aug 67, sub: Assessment of Progress by CTZ, COMUSMACV Message file, Westmoreland Papers, HRB; MACV Directive 335-13, 6 Jun 67, sub: Reports: Senior Advisors' Monthly Evaluation (SAME), SEAB. Both in CMH.
[23] SAME Evaluation, October 1966, MICRO 135, RG 334, WNRC.
[24] USMACV, "Command History, 1967," 1:197 and 204, HRB, CMH. In 1967 evaluators gave units overall ratings in both "combat effectiveness" and "readiness," but the text only considers the first category.

The individual SAME reports revealed similar confusion. A comparison of the last three months of 1966 and 1967 showed little change in the average ratings of the South Vietnamese combat forces, although the ratings of individual units might vary from month to month. Advisers downgraded some of the better South Vietnamese units, like the 42d Infantry Regiment, only because of heavy losses sustained in combat, and habitually rated as "satisfactory" other units that showed little aggressiveness but were at full strength. In some cases, fluctuations in specific ratings may have reflected only the arrival of a new adviser with different standards. At worst, ratings improved because of command pressures on advisers to show progress or because of the advisers' own desires to better their relationships with their counterparts.

Correlating the ratings of individual categories with overall evaluations was also confusing. In March, for example, advisers judged leadership in fifty battalions as "less than satisfactory," but gave only eight battalions "marginal" or "unsatisfactory" overall ratings. The reports also showed widespread improvement in the training status of units, but this reflected only the establishment of unit training programs rather than the frequency or quality of instruction. Strength figures improved in all categories in 1967, yet they appeared to have little correlation with combat results. For example, despite a low "paddy" (or operational) strength that hovered around 50–60 percent, the South Vietnamese airborne units consistently performed better in the field than the infantry and ranger battalions. In other cases regular units heavily involved with area security tasks often produced poor combat statistics but nevertheless had satisfactory ratings.

Subjective judgments were also mixed. In reports to higher headquarters MACV often highlighted successful South Vietnamese combat operations. Battlefield victories of the airborne and crack units of the South Vietnamese 1st Infantry Division stood side by side with successful actions by the 5th, 7th, and 18th Infantry Divisions, the worst units in the army. Such presentations were part of Westmoreland's effort to present a better image of the South Vietnamese armed forces not only to the American public but also to higher military commands. The MACV commander might have achieved a more balanced picture, however, had he mentioned the many less glorious episodes, such as the refusal of one battalion commander in the 1st Division to attack a minor Viet Cong unit or the disintegration of the 1st Armored Cavalry Squadron when fighting a small Viet Cong force. But accurate portrayals of South Vietnamese military performance as a whole depended so much on an understanding of individual leadership—personalities—and on specific circumstances, that Westmoreland avoided making any generalizations independent of the statistical evidence.[25]

How to remedy perceived shortcomings was a closely related factor. In early 1967, in an effort to apply more direct pressure on the South Vietnamese military to improve its performance, Westmoreland threatened to take an action he had

[25] Ibid., 1:197–99; Memo, Abrams to Bunker, 5 Jul 67, sub: Increased Effectiveness of ARVN, DEPCOMUSMACV Signature file, 1967, Westmoreland Papers. Both in HRB, CMH. See also SAME Evaluation, April 1967, MICRO 135, RG 334, WNRC.

hitherto avoided—withdrawing military assistance from "unproductive" South Vietnamese units. In January he ordered the MACV MAP Directorate to review all South Vietnamese forces to identify units "not contributing effectively to GVN and United States objectives." If Saigon failed to take measures to improve such units, MACV would cease supporting them. Through this ultimatum, Westmoreland hoped to force the South Vietnamese to redeploy some of their units in order to "get more military mileage out of them" and, as an example, suggested sending the ranger units out along the western borders. He considered the review a harsh but necessary measure, indicating that it might result even in the deactivation of certain regimental headquarters and combat battalions. He wanted the initial review by 15 March, with ensuing reviews every three months.[26]

In practice, Westmoreland applied these measures with great restraint. After reviewing the initial survey, he withdrew MAP support for only two ex-fishing boats employed by the South Vietnamese Navy, and placed other units under "close scrutiny" until they improved. Included were several underwater demolition teams, a cargo ship, two ranger battalions, and one armored cavalry squadron. Following a second evaluation in June, the MAP Directorate removed the probationary units from its black list but added several more: eighteen Regional Forces companies, sixteen Popular Forces platoons, fourteen Popular Forces squads, an engineer battalion, two more armored cavalry squadrons, a convalescent center, a dispensary, and an administrative company. In both reviews MACV's concern was with the *misemployment* of units rather than their inability to perform assigned missions. As a result, there was no correlation between units rated "unsatisfactory" and those under "scrutiny."[27] Inspecting the units on probation, General Abrams found the lack of correlation puzzling, although he judged that the corrective process was effective. Only in the case of the two fishing boats was financial support permanently withdrawn. But a withdrawal of financial support would not necessarily have forced the Joint General Staff to disband a unit, for, as noted by John Paul Vann, now the senior CORDS adviser in the III Corps Tactical Zone, Saigon could have spread any monetary reduction throughout the defense budget one way or the other. In any case, the dissolution of units was never Westmoreland's objective. While he threatened to withdraw "adviser, artillery, air or MAP support to units who are not carrying their load," his major goal was "better disciplined, better motivated, more effective units; [and] not unit . . . inactivations."[28]

---

[26] First quotation from Memo, Westmoreland to MAP Directorate, 26 Jan 67, sub: Optimum Programming of Military Assistance, COMUSMACV Signature file, 1967. Second quotation from MFR, Westmoreland, 29 Jan 67, sub: Meeting With General Vien at 1510 Hours on 23 January 1967, History file 12–D10. Both in Westmoreland Papers, HRB, CMH. See also USMACV, "Command History, 1967," 1:172–73, HRB, CMH.

[27] Ltrs, Westmoreland to Vien, 14 Apr (source of quoted words) and 27 Jul 67, COMUSMACV Signature file, 1967; Ltr, Kerwin to Senior Adviser, II Corps, 22 Aug 67, sub: Optimum Programming of Military Assistance, Chief of Staff Correspondence file. All in Westmoreland Papers, HRB, CMH.

[28] Comments of Westmoreland in MFR, Chaisson, 12 Oct 67, sub: MACV Commanders Conference, 24 September 1967, History file 22–A22, Westmoreland Papers, HRB, CMH. See ibid. for comments of John Paul Vann. See also Msg, Abrams MAC 8956 to Rosson, 220951 Sep 67; Msg, Abrams MAC 8956 to Palmer, 221111 Sep 67. Both in Abrams Papers, HRB, CMH.

Leadership

Despite better methods of evaluation and greater leverage to measure and improve South Vietnamese military effectiveness, Westmoreland remained stymied by the problem of leadership. Without improvement in this critical area, the shift in roles and missions would have little significance. But, although viewing the South Vietnamese officer corps as "completely inadequate to do the task at hand," the MACV commander still hesitated to dictate solutions and even avoided proposing specific changes. He continued to regard himself as merely an adviser to Ky, Thieu, and Vien, especially in the area of appointments, making his own wishes known only when consulted. Personnel matters were the responsibility of the Directory leaders, and Westmoreland hoped they would have enough confidence and perspicuity to do what was necessary themselves. In this area his own personal advisory effort can hardly be termed a success.[29]

In September Westmoreland went over the whole question of leverage with Admiral Sharp. He continued to believe that a "low key, behind the scenes approach" was the best way to exert American influence over the South Vietnamese, especially in view of the delicate political situation in Saigon. American pressure had to be applied quietly through the field advisory network, the MAP Directorate, and the MACV Office of the Comptroller. Although both MACV offices controlled the purse strings, the MACV commander preferred to rely on his senior field advisers to effect deeper changes in leadership and esprit. American control of air, artillery, and other direct support, he believed, "serves both as a restraint on RVNAF in the matter of conducting operations contrary to US policy or advice and as a strong inducement to make deployments and conduct operations that conform to US operational plans." Again he cautioned that, to be effective, all American leverage "must be applied with [the] utmost diplomacy and discretion . . . in a personal [manner] and hidden from the public view. . . ." Westmoreland still could not bring himself to endorse Komer's more direct methods, which he felt were unsuitable for the regular army advisory effort.[30]

In 1967 the three South Vietnamese divisions surrounding Saigon—the 5th, 18th, and 25th—had shown no improvement, and U.S. advisers considered their commanders, Generals Phan Trong Chinh (25th Division), Pham Quoc Thuan (5th Division), and Do Ke Giai (18th Division), flatly incompetent. The senior Directory generals had repeatedly agreed on the need to replace them, but, for political reasons, had taken no action. When Komer tried to enlist the aid of Secretary of Defense McNamara to relieve Chinh, Westmoreland upbraided him for bypassing the U.S. military chain of command. Referring to the affair with Colonel Hunnicutt in 1966, Westmoreland blamed the American press for Chinh's long tenure, asserting that critical news stories about Chinh had made it impossible for Ky to act without appearing to be an American puppet.[31]

---

[29] Quoted words from Notes of 2 Feb 67, p. 16, History file 13–A. See also Msg, Westmoreland MAC 7988 to Wheeler and Sharp, 23 Aug 67, History file 21–A5. Both in Westmoreland Papers, HRB, CMH.

[30] Msg, Westmoreland MAC 8807 to Sharp, 171340 Sep 67, sub: Post Election Priorities in Vietnam, History file 22–A32, Westmoreland Papers, HRB, CMH.

[31] MFR, Westmoreland, 23 Feb 67, sub: Separate Meetings With General Thieu, General Ky, and General Vien on 17 and 20 February 1967, History file 13–B15; Notes of 21 Jun 67, p. 14, *(Continued)*

As always, Westmoreland had a difficult time dampening the frustrations and public complaints of his leading senior advisers and field commanders over such matters. In 1967 he faced yet another imbroglio, this time over General Thuan, the commander of the South Vietnamese 5th Division since 1965. Although continually judged by American leaders as corrupt and incapable, Thuan had strong political ties with the Directory generals—in this case, Thieu. John Paul Vann noted the "widespread public belief that Thuan not only controlled most of the local bars and prostitution houses but also extorted protection fees for convoys moving through his division tactical area. General DePuy, commanding the nearby U.S. 1st Infantry Division, agreed. He made the convoy protection charge public, as did a local Vietnamese province chief, perhaps with Vann's encouragement. Westmoreland could do little. He already had taken up the matter previously with Vien, but to no avail. Thuan had been Thieu's chief of staff when the latter had commanded the 5th Division back in 1962, and the division, together with General Dong's airborne units, remained the Directory chairman's major basis of power. In the interests of political stability, nothing could be done.[32]

In August Vien finally came to Westmoreland's rescue with a list of about forty "corrupt, incompetent or old and tired" senior officers that he intended to discharge after the South Vietnamese presidential election scheduled for September. He promised that replacements would be found for Chinh and Thuan, and possibly Giai. Westmoreland sympathized with Vien's desire to avoid any "disruptive actions" prior to the elections and informed Washington that changes in key South Vietnamese military positions would be made "within the next several weeks." But his prediction proved to be optimistic, and again the Joint General Staff failed to act.[33]

After the elections, Westmoreland broached the leadership issue from a different tack. Meeting with Vien, he offered his personal evaluations of key South Vietnamese officers down to the battalion level. Vien initially declined but apparently agreed in October, when Westmoreland asked his new J-1 (Personnel), Brig. Gen. Franklin M. Davis, Jr., to supervise a general evaluation of all South Vietnamese commanders. He passed the information dutifully to Vien, but again nothing was done. Discouraged and perhaps embarrassed, Westmoreland felt that he had given his field advisers merely another administrative chore and had little to show for it.[34]

(Continued) and 29 Jun 67, pp. 14 and 22–23, History file 18–A. All in Westmoreland Papers, HRB, CMH. See also Memo, Heintges to Westmoreland, 7 Feb 67, sub: PPC by Maj. Gen. DePuy on LTG Thieu and General Vien, MICRO 75/1731, RG 334, WNRC. On the Chinh-Hunnicutt affair, see Chapter 10 of this volume.

[32] MFR, Vann, 21 Feb 68, sub: Binh My Nam Operation Base, Vann Papers, MHI. Vann relates that Khang, the III Corps commander and ally of Ky, supposedly had a thick Military Security Service folder on Thuan's activities, compiled by Loan, and used it to keep Thuan in line. See also MFR, Westmoreland, 10 Oct 66, sub: Discussions With General Vien and Co Preliminary to Secretary McNamara's Visit, History file 9–D5, Westmoreland Papers, HRB, CMH.

[33] Msg, Westmoreland MAC 7988 to Wheeler and Sharp, 23 Aug 67, History file 21–A5, Westmoreland Papers, HRB, CMH.

[34] MFR, Westmoreland, 2 Oct 67, sub: Conference With General Vien, 25 September 1967, History file 22–A23; Notes of 9 and 16 Oct 67, History file 23–A; Notes of 14 Dec 67, History file 26–A. All in Westmoreland Papers, HRB, CMH.

Finally, in December, perhaps to appease Westmoreland, Vien decided to "remove" Chinh by promoting him to the post of III Corps deputy commander. His American advisers had given Chinh some credit for his interest in the civil matters of his division tactical area and seemed pleased by his new appointment.[35] According to Komer, Chinh was always "a better pacificer than a Division Commander," and the new post would hopefully keep him out of mischief. Thieu was equally pleased to be able to replace Chinh, an old rival, with a supporter, General Nguyen Xuan Thinh. Westmoreland, noting that Thinh had been relieved as commander of the 22d Infantry Division in 1965 because of his poor performance, was not enthusiastic about the choice, but he could only hope that he would do better than his predecessor.[36]

The leadership issue—how to improve the quality of individual South Vietnamese commanders—thus remained unresolved. General Heintges continued to hold that Chinh and Thuan were special cases,[37] the result of the proximity of their units to the capital. He believed the overall performance of the South Vietnamese armed forces was exemplary and cited increased enemy attacks on pacification security forces as "an apparent reaction to the importance which the enemy attaches to the expanded RD program." While admitting that the South Vietnamese military had many problems, especially in the realm of leadership, he argued that "statistics do not tell the full story" and blamed adverse press reporting for Saigon's poor image in the United States. Rather than "leaning back in the foxholes," the South Vietnamese forces providing pacification security were taking on the brunt of the war effort. Fighting small-scale engagements throughout the countryside, they were suffering most of the casualties and were in fact the "unsung heroes of the war." General Abrams, Heintges' successor, later gave an equally optimistic assessment of the South Vietnamese armed forces, although his judgments were to the press and not to his military superiors.[38]

Performance in the Field

Assessments from the senior American advisers in each corps during 1967 were more encouraging. In the sparsely populated northern zone, after the

---

[35] For example, see Memo, Senior Adviser, 31st Division Tactical Area, to Director, Region III, OCO, circa October 1967, sub: Commanding General, 31st DTA, SEAB, CMH.

[36] Quoted words of Komer in MFR, Forsythe, 6 Sep 67, sub: Meeting With General Thang, 1430 Hours, 5 September 1967, History file 21–A25; MFR, Westmoreland, 13 Nov 67, sub: Conference With General Vien on 6 November 1967, History file 24–A21; ibid., 18 Feb 65, sub: Meeting With General Khanh, 18 February 1965, History file 13–47. All in Westmoreland Papers, HRB, CMH.

[37] At the time Westmoreland was in the United States and Heintges was in temporary command of MACV.

[38] Quoted words from Msg, Heintges MAC 03785 to Westmoreland, 211107 Apr 67, sub: ARVN Performance, DEPCOMUSMACV Message file, Westmoreland Papers, HRB, CMH. See also Abrams press interview in "Vietnamese Army Starts To Fight," *U.S. News and World Report*, 4 Dec 67, pp. 62–65.

Buddhist agitation had subsided, advisers reported that General Truong, the new 1st Division commander, had whipped the rebellious 1st Division into one of South Vietnam's best army units and that Lam, the I Corps commander, and Toan, commanding the 2d Division, had proven to be competent leaders. The allied troop commitment in the northern zone was also considerable and included two U.S. Marine Corps divisions, one South Korean Marine brigade, and three U.S. Army brigades that would later form the 23d Infantry Division ("Americal"). The Joint General Staff also reinforced the zone with marine and airborne units when necessary.

In the southernmost region, the IV Corps Tactical Zone, the news was also good. The American presence was small. Here, where the bulk of the population of South Vietnam lived, three South Vietnamese divisions and a growing number of territorial companies and platoons supplied local security. Although a traditional Viet Cong stronghold in the early 1960s, the delta region had never been subject to North Vietnamese influence, primarily because of its distance from Hanoi. Brig. Gen. William R. Desobry, the American senior adviser since August 1965, felt that the South Vietnamese now had the upper hand. He considered the 21st Infantry Division under General Nguyen Van Minh the best in the army, and the 9th Infantry Division not far behind. Only the 7th Division, whose area of operation included many traditional Viet Cong strongholds, was having difficulties, but Desobry expected that the recent arrival of the U.S. 9th Infantry Division would help the 7th pick up the pace.[39]

American advisers also rated the South Vietnamese general reserves and the Special Forces–sponsored units highly. The Joint General Staff continued to employ the airborne and marine units in regimental-size task forces, but had started to give them separate operational areas instead of merely attaching them to one of the corps commanders. On Westmoreland's advice, General Vien also tried to employ his reserve units with American ground forces whenever possible, to take advantage of the greater air and fire support available. However, division-level marine or airborne operations were still out of the question because of the marginal quality of the component commanders and staffs. The CIDG companies, the MIKE Force units, and the special Greek-lettered commando forces were also successful, normally operating closely with American combat units in the interior of the country. All of these forces were almost always understrength due to high casualty and desertion rates, but statistically they were the most active and, subjectively, according to their advisers, the most successful.

The state of the South Vietnamese military forces in the two middle regions, the II and III Corps Tactical Zones, was less noteworthy. Nevertheless, in August 1967 Lt. Gen. William B. Rosson, now the U.S. senior adviser and the senior American commander in the II Corps area, was hopeful. Combined operations between American and the South Vietnamese forces in the Highlands and the

---

[39] Senior Officer Debriefing Rpt, Desobry, 1 Jan 68. See also Msg, Westmoreland to CINCPAC, 11 Aug 67, sub: COMUSMACV Monthly Assessment, History file 20–A6, Westmoreland Papers. Both in HRB, CMH.

Lt. Gen. John A. Heintges (center) and General Vinh Loc *(left) conferring with the 24th Special Tactical Zone commander on field operations*

South Vietnamese revolutionary development training programs for both regular and territorial units along the coast were proving beneficial. Although nepotism and corruption were still serious problems, the Vietnamese corps commander, General Vinh Loc, had firm control over the province chiefs and was loyal to the Saigon regime. Vinh Loc's frequent consultations with Montagnard leaders also enhanced his stature and promised stability in this area.[40]

In the III Corps Tactical Zone around Saigon, General Weyand, now commanding the II Field Force, cultivated his relationship with General Khang, the III Corps commander, through weekly meetings. He bypassed the three incompetent division commanders by having American combat units work directly with South Vietnamese regiments, battalions, and territorials—thus repeating on a larger scale what he had done the year before as commander of the U.S. 25th Infantry Division. Weyand also began a six-week training program for local South Vietnamese infantry and ranger battalions, which he hoped to extend to

---

[40] Msg, Rosson NHT 0989 to Westmoreland, 041400 Aug 67, sub: Evaluation and Assessment of Situation in II CTZ, History file 20–A2. See also Maj Gen Tolson's presentation in MFR, Chaisson, 18 Sep 67, sub: MACV Commanders Conference, 27 August 1967, History file 21–A14. Both in Westmoreland Papers, HRB, CMH.

South Vietnamese engineer, signal, armor, and artillery units by the end of the year.[41]

In Gia Dinh Province surrounding Saigon City, Westmoreland sponsored a much larger undertaking, Operation FAIRFAX. Alarmed by deteriorating security in the capital area, he decided to use American infantry battalions to spark lethargic South Vietnamese regular and territorial units into action. American commanders were to "lead by example" and, through "good judgment, diplomacy and finesse," induce the Vietnamese to work together and improve security around Saigon through small unit actions against the local Viet Cong forces and political cadre.[42] FAIRFAX was, in effect, a large-scale advisory effort.

Brig. Gen. John F. Freund and Lt. Col. Dao Ba Phuoc

Confusion reigned at the outset of FAIRFAX. American and South Vietnamese units rotated in and out of the operation with little direction. To solve this problem, Westmoreland committed the U.S. 199th Light Infantry Brigade, now commanded by General Freund, and persuaded Vien to match the 199th with the Vietnamese 5th Ranger Group, commanded by Lt. Col. Dao Ba Phuoc. By July 1967 both units had achieved a close working relationship with the Gia Dinh Province headquarters and the Capital Military District command. Because each participating headquarters controlled considerable military or paramilitary forces, the operation proved difficult to conduct in a controlled manner. Despite extensive experimentation with combined command arrangements at various levels, the results were thus mixed. But, with American support and encouragement, ranger and territorial operations became bolder and more decentralized. According to American CORDS evaluators, security had improved in Gia Dinh by the end of 1967 as a result of successful actions against the local Viet Cong forces. However, due to the general disorder of the intelligence effort, FAIRFAX had made little progress in identifying and eliminating the Viet Cong political infrastructure and in improving the generally untrained and undisciplined territorials, whom the rangers regarded more as rivals than allies.[43] Nevertheless, by November Westmoreland considered Gia

---

[41] See Weyand presentation in MFR, Chaisson, 18 Sep 67, sub: MACV Commanders Conference, 27 August 1967, History file 21–A14; Msg, Weyand HOA 1162 to Westmoreland, 4 Aug 67, sub: II FFORCEV Situation for July 1967, History file 20–A1; Ltr, Weyand to Westmoreland, 21 Jul 67, COMUSMACV Signature file, 1967. All in Westmoreland Papers, HRB, CMH.

[42] MFR, Hyatt, HQ, 4th Bn, 9th Infantry, 30 Nov 66, sub: COMUSMACV Comments at HQ FF II, 291330 Nov 66 (Operation Fairfax), SEAB, CMH.

[43] MFR, MACCORDS–RE, Maj Stanley J. Michael and L. Craig Johnstone (Field Evaluators), 3 Aug 67, sub: Evaluation of Operation FAIRFAX/RANG DONG, SEAB, CMH. In Memo, L. S. *(Continued)*

Dinh secure enough to move the 199th Brigade elsewhere, leaving the security of the province in the hands of the rangers and the local territorial and police forces.[44]

FAIRFAX revealed the myriad problems of assigning regular South Vietnamese units direct responsibility for territorial security. Some of the usual ones were poor civil-military relations; dissatisfaction with billeting and rations; complex command relations between province, district, and army headquarters; and the boredom of static security assignments. Others were more unique. In April, for example, the Joint General Staff charged that regular army units performing security duties were helping local authorities and absentee landlords collect retroactive land rents and taxes from peasant tenants in formerly insecure areas. Vien and his chief of staff, Nguyen Van Vy, termed the practice illegal, if only because the owners themselves had paid no taxes for the period concerned.[45] But the ramifications were obviously much deeper. If the practice was indeed widespread during FAIRFAX, the Vietnamese farmers must have seen the returning government troops as oppressors, rather than liberators, and the Saigon regime that they represented as only concerned with the interests of a privileged minority. The entire concept of employing regular troops in this manner was thus open to question, and may explain why it was so easy for the Viet Cong to move men and supplies into the Saigon area for a major offensive scheduled for early 1968.

Elsewhere similar problems occurred. Without an adequate ration or mess system, the South Vietnamese soldiers continued to live off the land, stealing or expropriating food from local inhabitants, and the concentration of large numbers of troops in heavily populated areas during operations like FAIRFAX may have only made the practice more prevalent. Other problems included a tendency of South Vietnamese troops to operate only during daylight hours, the absence of civic action programs to bring the army closer to the rural community, and the continued reluctance of corps and division commanders to give province chiefs direct control of combat battalions.[46] Taken together, they were strong indictments of the regular army's performance of its new task.

Despite these trends, by the end of 1967 the Joint General Staff had committed some fifty-five infantry battalions, or almost half of its regular combat forces, to static security missions. Yet American CORDS advisers in every zone noted a lack of enthusiasm on the part of South Vietnamese commanders for the new

---

(*Continued*) Wehrle and J. Arthur to J. P. Grant, 29 Nov 67, sub: Discussion With John Vann, Wednesday, November 22, 1967, Vann Papers, MHI, Vann felt that the strength of the active Viet Cong was reduced from thirty-four hundred to six hundred but that "overall security in Gia Dinh had improved very little."

[44] For a more comprehensive treatment of FAIRFAX, see Jeffrey J. Clarke, "The Role of USARV Units in Vietnamization," CMH Monograph 192M (Washington, D.C.: U.S. Army Center of Military History, 1974), pp. 20–29; Truong, *RVNAF and US Operational Cooperation and Coordination*, pp. 128–34.

[45] MFR, W. R. Warne, EA/VN, 28 Nov 66, sub: Assignment of ARVN to Clear-and-Hold Operations (see also subsequent trip reports by MACV CORDS field evaluators, 1967–68), SEAB; JGS Memo 973, 12 Apr 67, sub: Prohibiting of Military Personnel From Helping Local Authorities To Retroactively Collect Taxes, and Landowners To Retroactively Collect Land Rents in Newly Secured Areas, COMUSMACV Signature file, 1967, HRB. Both in CMH.

[46] Notes of 13 Dec 66, History file 12–A; Ltr, Westmoreland to Vien, 29 Mar 67, COMUSMACV Signature file, 1967. Both in Westmoreland Papers, HRB, CMH.

mission, and their evaluations contrasted greatly from those of the senior military advisers noted above. In the Delta (IV Corps Tactical Zone) they reported that the commanders of the 9th and 21st Division rotated combat battalions with population security roles every three months, fearing that units performing static security for long periods of time would eventually disintegrate through inactivity. But the result, according to the local American advisers, was the lack of any continuity in the security effort. Nevertheless, in the area of the South Vietnamese 7th Division, where there was no unit rotation, CORDS advisers found the battalions charged with area security missions more concerned with their own static defenses than with protecting nearby villages and hamlets or with chasing the local Viet Cong. Perhaps the special revolutionary development training had not differentiated between static and offensive security operations, or perhaps the commanders assigned area security tasks viewed the mission only as an opportunity for their units to rest.[47]

Advisory evaluations of units performing population security missions in the III Corps Tactical Zone were more critical. They attributed most problems to poor leadership at all levels and the lack of coordination between the various commands. At times CORDS advisers reported that regular and territorial units were entrenched side by side, protecting the same hamlet. In other instances security-tasked battalions failed to even make a gesture at providing hamlet security, and Komer himself accused several battalion commanders in the 18th Division of using the new mission as an excuse to withdraw from all meaningful operations, except to provide for their own self-protection.[48]

A worse situation arose in the II Corps Tactical Zone, when soldiers of the 22d Division attacked and robbed inhabitants of a protected hamlet and members of the local revolutionary development team. After the high command investigated the case, the guilty parties were beaten and placed in regimental disciplinary cages. But the chief of the MACV Revolutionary Support Directorate, General Knowlton, termed the incident commonplace and demanded that the South Vietnamese generals do more to halt such occurrences. Americans, however, had no way of directly controlling the conduct of the indigenous troops toward their own people.[49]

American CORDS advisers in the I Corps Tactical Zone were more satisfied, but complained that combat battalions with population security roles spent too much time supporting community development projects and not enough time providing military security. Moreover, they also noted that the two local Vietnamese division commanders flatly refused to place any of their infantry battalions

[47] Notes of 13 Aug 67, History file 20–A, Westmoreland Papers, HRB, CMH. See also CORDS Field Evaluation Rpts, Hurd and John G. Lybrand, 27 Dec 67, sub: The ARVN 7th Division in Support of Pacification; 12 Sep 67, sub: The ARVN 21st Division in Support of Pacification; and Hurd and Deford, 2 Sep 67, sub: The ARVN 7th Division in Support of RD. All in SEAB, CMH.

[48] CORDS Field Evaluation Rpt, Michael, 29 Aug 67, sub: 18th ARVN Division in Support of RD (with attached Komer note); MFRs, Dale Pfetpfer, 31 Jul 67, sub: 5th ARVN Division Concept of Revolutionary Development Platoons, and 11 Jul 67, sub: 25th ARVN Division Support to Pacification in Long An. All in SEAB, CMH.

[49] Memo, Knowlton to Westmoreland, 15 May 67, sub: Conduct of 47th Regiment, 22d ARVN Division—Phu Yen Province, SEAB, CMH.

TABLE 13—SOUTH VIETNAMESE-INITIATED ACTIONS [a] PER WEEK

Time Period	Average Number of		Percentage
	Operations	Engagements	
1965			
January–June	16,227	83	.51
July–December	19,603	93	.47
Total	35,820	176	.49
1966			
January–June	20,490	55	.27
July–December	24,962	95	.38
Total	45,452	150	.33
1967			
January–June	25,842	100	.39
Grand Total	107,114	426	.40

[a] Company size or smaller

Source: Study, Vann, 13 Nov 67, sub: Improvement of Security Within South Vietnam, Vann Papers, MHI.

under the operational control of the province chiefs and preferred to direct their own security campaign.[50]

More damning was the independent evaluation made by John Paul Vann at the end of 1967. Vann's research indicated that between 1965 and 1967 South Vietnamese small unit offensive operations had shown a marked decline in effectiveness (*Table 13*). Saigon's military forces were not carrying the fight to the local enemy, and their performance in providing security for the revolutionary development program was a sham. As an example, he cited a twelve-day period, 17–28 March 1967, during which South Vietnamese regulars and territorials in the III Corps zone conducted a total of 13,228 military operations, large and small, that resulted in only sixteen engagements with enemy forces, or, for those at MACV who were statistically inclined, a rate of about .12 percent. The cause, he held, was simply a failure of leadership, and he went over some of the old ailments he considered most significant: corruption, especially the hiring out of troop labor, the educational requirements for entry into the officers corps, and the failure of Saigon to use its rural leadership.[51]

Despite Vann's pessimistic appraisal, MACV's new Hamlet Evaluation System (HES) showed steady improvement in Saigon's control over the countryside during 1967. But evaluators in Saigon and Washington were unsure if the new statistical reporting system reflected real gains in security. From its inception HES was subject to the same inconsistencies and data-gathering problems that beset MACV's other statistical reports. Moreover, if the observations of Vann and other

[50] Rpts, Lt Col Clarence W. Hannon, 4 Dec 67, sub: ARVN 1st Division Support of Pacification, and 19 Dec 67, sub: ARVN 2d Division Support of Pacification, SEAB, CMH.

[51] Study, Vann, 13 Nov 67, sub: Improvement of Security Within South Vietnam, Vann Papers, MHI. Vann sent copies to Komer, Abrams, and the III and IV CTZ senior advisers. For an earlier Vann analysis of the same problem, see MFR, Komer, sub: Contact Rate in ARVN Small Unit Actions, SEAB, CMH.

CORDS advisers were at all accurate, any success in this area did not appear to be the result of South Vietnamese military operations. In addition, MACV's efforts to increase military security for the revolutionary development campaign may have contributed substantially to the further deterioration of the regular army units, binding them tighter to static area security missions that had no clearly defined goals or objectives. Col. Robert M. Montague, a senior CORDS official who worked closely with Komer and his successors in the CORDS establishment, later concluded that the entire effort to assign the regulars population security tasks had been a mistake, "since the mission is almost always misinterpreted," and felt that some kind of less direct security role would have been more appropriate.[52]

By the end of the year Americans up and down the MACV chain of command had thus begun to question the wisdom of pushing the South Vietnamese regulars into the securing mission. The results had seemed counterproductive in almost every area, and the progress that had been achieved during the year in administration and organization did not appear to have been translated into improved performance in the field. Perhaps, however, too much had again been expected too soon, and the American penchant for "results" and "action" was leading to hasty judgments. Yet the leadership problem had existed since the start of the struggle, and little had been accomplished in this critical area. Obviously, if more was to be expected of Saigon's military forces, the South Vietnamese generals would have to decide among themselves who was going to run the army and who was going to operate the civil administration. The same officers could not do both.

---

[52] Quoted words from Memo, Montague to Colby, 18 Jan 69, sub: 1969 Pacification, SEAB, CMH. On HES, see Hunt, *Pacification*, forthcoming.

14

Generals and Politics

One of the major weaknesses of the South Vietnamese armed forces was the continued military involvement in local and national politics. With the elimination of the Buddhists as a political force in 1966, the army was left with a virtual monopoly of the political process. But Saigon purchased its political stability with military professionalism. As long as promotions in the armed forces depended more on political affiliations than on professional ability, any military reforms would be superficial. MACV wished to encourage military professionalism and leadership, but realized that any sweeping changes in the senior military leaders threatened to destroy the existing government because the two were the same. In order to bring about reform at this level, military leadership had to be separated from politics and civilian government restored. Although the task appeared incredibly difficult, the South Vietnamese generals themselves had already taken the first step with the establishment of the Directory government. The next task was to curb the powers of the semi-independent regional military leaders and to establish a sharper division of political and military authority in Saigon and the countryside. The dismissal of General Thi, the I Corps commander in early 1966, was a part of this process. On these objectives Ky, Thieu, and their American advisers were in complete accord. Where they differed was in the pace of the transition. Americans at the tactical level and in Washington wanted to make such changes as quickly as possible, while those at the Saigon level—as well as their South Vietnamese counterparts—feared that too rapid a shift might cause the entire edifice to come tumbling down once again.[1]

---

[1] For general information on military cliques and politics for the 1966–68 period, see Senior Liaison Office, U.S. Embassy, Saigon, "Nationalist Politics in Viet-Nam," May 1968, History file 32–57, Westmoreland Papers, HRB, CMH; Msg, Bunker to Landsdale, 7 Jan 68, and Airgram, State A–131 to Saigon, 13 Aug 71, sub: Some Aspects of Personal Relations Among Senior RVNAF Officers, SEAB, CMH; the appropriate sections of Hinh and Tho, *South Vietnamese Society*; the more vivid, Alfred W. McCoy, *The Politics of Heroin in Southeast Asia* (New York: Harper and Row, 1972), pp. 149–222; Ky's *Twenty Years and Twenty Days*; Tran Van Don's *Our Endless War: Inside Vietnam* (San Rafael, Calif.: Presidio Press, 1978); and Henry Cabot Lodge, *The Storm Has Many Eyes* (New York: Norton, 1973), pp. 214–16, which, unfortunately, says little about his second tour as ambassador. On the dismissal of Thi, see Chapter 7 of this volume.

A Balance of Power

As the most visible representative of the Saigon government, Premier Ky enjoyed strong American support. He had used it to quell the political turmoil in the I Corps and thereafter to consolidate his own power in Saigon. Throughout 1966 he steadily increased his authority by furthering the careers of his supporters—for example, making Colonel Loan, the Military Security Service chief, also director general of the National Police and General Nguyen Bao Tri, the III Corps commander, head of both the Political Warfare Department and the Ministry of Information. Ky replaced Tri with another close associate, General Khang. Khang, now at the height of his power, headed the III Corps Tactical Zone, the Capital Military District, and the South Vietnamese Marine Corps, all at the same time. Ky, who continued to head the South Vietnamese Air Force, also abolished the Ministry of the Interior in early July and transferred control of the police to a new Ministry of Security headed by his friend and former classmate, General Linh Quang Vien.[2]

Ky's relationship with his close friend, General Nguyen Duc Thang, the minister of revolutionary development, was complex. Thang had a reputation for honesty and hard work, which won him not only the respect of his American civilian and military advisers but also substantial American support for his revolutionary development campaign. But from Ky's point of view, Thang's political influence was potentially immense. His revolutionary development teams were busy throughout South Vietnam, working in thousands of villages and hamlets, where local army province and district chiefs had little control over their activities. Between Thang's revolutionary development teams and Tri's political warfare cadre, Ky had the potential of bypassing the senior military leaders and creating a constituency among the lower-ranking soldiers and the rural peasants in any future bid for political power in Saigon.[3]

To further strengthen his political position in 1966, Ky also tried to transfer the Territorial Forces command from the Joint General Staff to Thang's Ministry of Revolutionary Development. This ambitious move would have given Thang control over territorial appointments and promotions, as well as over the training and stationing of these troops. Claiming that the transfer would aid Saigon's national development efforts by forging a closer link between the weakly armed revolutionary development cadre and the territorials, Ky secured American support for the reorganization. The senior army leaders, however, were adamantly opposed to the shift. The transfer would have given Ky and his adherents too much political power. Although claiming that the proposed realignment would fragment military security efforts in the field, military commanders and province chiefs were primarily concerned with the threat that the proposed change posed to their own authority. Siding with the field commanders, the Joint General Staff

---

[2] Linh Quang Vien had been chief of staff under Cao Van Vien, who remained chief of the Joint General Staff.

[3] CORDS advisers noted that Vinh Loc, the II Corps commander, had even established his own "civil-military teams" in direct competition with Thang's revolutionary development cadre. See Memo, Frank G. Wisner to L. Wade Lathram, 14 Jun 67, sub: Revolutionary Development in Khanh Hoa and Formation of Civil/Military Teams, SEAB, CMH.

General Nguyen Duc Thang *on a revolutionary development inspection tour of the Vietnamese countryside*

took the opposite course by transforming the semiautonomous Territorial Forces command into a directorate of the Joint General Staff and by establishing separate staff sections for Territorial Forces in each corps headquarters to supervise province and district security forces. The net result was to strengthen, rather than diminish, army control over the territorials.[4]

American officials tried to stay out of these squabbles, but always found themselves somehow involved. Both General Westmoreland and Ambassador Lodge wanted the Directory replaced by some sort of constitutional democracy, regarding such a step as part of the national development of South Vietnam. But both were also wary of replacing the existing authoritarian government with a civilian one that might be more popular but weaker. The Americans believed they had to guide the South Vietnamese leaders on a course between these extremes. Since early 1966, many American analysts had been recommending that Saigon separate the military and political functions of the corps and division commanders, whom even the MACV staff regarded as "feudal warlords in twentieth-century uniforms," too preoccupied with local and national politics to de-

[4] Notes of 27 and 28 Jun 66, History file 7–D; Ltr, Westmoreland to CG, III MAF, 24 Jun 67, sub: Organization of I Corps RF/PF Advisory Effort, COMUSMACV Signature file, 1967. Both in Westmoreland Papers, HRB, CMH. For a speculative discussion of Ky's actions, see Corson, *The Betrayal,* pp. 112–22.

vote the requisite attention to their military responsibilities.[5] But despite similar recommendations from the U.S. Embassy,[6] Westmoreland continued to have serious reservations. Removing the South Vietnamese division headquarters from the revolutionary development chain of command or establishing some sort of territorial constabulary under the Revolutionary Development Ministry would undermine his efforts to draw the regular army closer to the entire security effort. He and several members of the country team also felt that the Ministry of Revolutionary Development was too weak to assume overall responsibility for territorial security. Westmoreland also rejected a proposal to create a separate pacification staff at the South Vietnamese division headquarters on the grounds that the addition would only further entangle these units in purely civilian matters.[7]

Thus, senior U.S. advisers continued to treat any proposal that would alter current South Vietnamese command relationships, especially those diminishing the political authority of the senior military commanders, with great circumspection. When Vien suggested that the current unity among the surviving Directory members might dissolve upon the end of the crisis in the I Corps, American officials took the warning to heart. Westmoreland and Lodge advised Ky to handle the corps and division commanders with caution—"whittle away at them, eliminate some of their functions, shrink them, isolate them," but make no abrupt changes that would threaten political stability. They wanted no repeat of the Thi affair.[8]

Toward a New Regime

Despite their own political ambitions, the ruling generals took major steps toward creating a responsive constitutional government in South Vietnam during 1966. Here lay the greatest hope for separating the military from politics, and Westmoreland and Lodge accordingly devoted much of their energy to see that the transition to some form of democratic government made steady progress. In early June, after several false starts, a civilian committee, appointed by Thieu and Ky, recommended that a constituent assembly be elected to draft a new constitution within six months. The Directory agreed, reserving the right to propose amendments, after which the draft would be automatically adopted

---

[5] Quoted words from MFR, Bengtson, 24 May 66, sub: Political and Military Functions in Corps Zones, History file 6–D13, Westmoreland Papers, HRB, CMH. See also "Briefing Paper for the [U.S.] President's Talks With Lodge on the Constitutional Assembly," 12 May 66, and "Briefing Paper for the President's Talks With Lodge (on the Duration of the Ky Government)," 12 May 66, both in Porter, *Vietnam*, 2:422–24; Msg, II FFV to COMUSMACV, 17 Nov 66, sub: Deputy CG for Revolutionary Development, SEAB, CMH.

[6] See *U.S.-Vietnam Relations*, 6:sec. IV. C. 8., pp. 83–86.

[7] Ibid.; Ltr, Brig Gen A. M. Hendry, Jr. (USAF), DepCofS, MACV, to CG, II FFV, 4 Dec 66, sub: Deputy CG for Revolutionary Development, SEAB, CMH.

[8] Quoted words from Statement of H. C. Lodge, Monday, October 10, 1966, MACV Conference Room, to Secretary of Defense Robert S. McNamara and Party, MICRO 2/1074, RG 334, WNRC. See also MFR, Freund, 24 Jun 66, sub: Meeting With General Vien, 23 June 1966, History file 7–D2, Westmoreland Papers, HRB, CMH.

unless rejected by two-thirds of the assembly. Thieu and Ky scheduled the assembly elections for 11 September 1966, but stipulated that the body was to have no interim legislative powers. They also declared that the Directory itself would establish the new national institutions specified by the constitution within three to six months after its promulgation. The entire process would take about one year. To leaven the authoritarian nature of the present regime, the generals agreed to add ten civilian members to the Directory and create an eighty-member People's and Armed Forces Council to advise Premier Ky.

Despite boycotts by Buddhist leaders and the Communist National Liberation Front, the assembly elections in September proved a success, if only because of a large voter turnout and the absence of any glaring irregularities. But the future of democracy in South Vietnam remained clouded. With no organized political parties and the Buddhist leadership in disarray, the army remained the only cohesive national-level interest group. While the new assembly went to work, speculation over the nature of the future government was endless. If the army withdrew from politics, who would fill the void? Would the province chiefs, now almost all military men, be appointed by the civilian government? Would the corps commanders continue to be the regional governors? How would the corps and division commanders react to all this? The attitudes of the senior military commanders was obviously crucial. Rumors of anti-Ky political groups coalescing around Thieu, Co, Quang, the current IV Corps commander, and Tran Van Don, a retired general heading several veterans groups, repeatedly upset both Westmoreland and Lodge. To the Americans, Ky's dismissal of Co and Quang toward the end of 1966 appeared particularly dangerous, but, for the moment, American fears proved groundless.[9]

By mid-January 1967 the constituent assembly had hammered out a new constitution for South Vietnam. Of its significant provisions, the constitution called for the direct election of a president and vice-president, for an elected bicameral legislature, for the presidential appointment of a prime minister to manage the central administration, and for a military council to advise the president. The Directory approved the constitution on 19 March, and eight days later—after some prodding from Thieu and Ky—the Armed Forces Congress endorsed it. The Directory set the presidential and upper house elections for 3 September and the lower house elections for 22 October.

Once the new constitution was proclaimed, American attitudes toward the transition to civilian rule became more evident. A contemporary MACV study pointed out that the military was the only body in South Vietnam with the experience and administrative skills to run the country and predicted that a rapid transition to a civilian government might lead to disaster. Whatever the value of a democratic representative government, the "political realities" were that South Vietnam was "at war, divided, underdeveloped, with a long authoritarian tradi-

---

[9] MFRs, Freund, 24 Jun 66, sub: Special Report Related to Conversation With General Vien, 23 June 1966, History file 7–D1, and 25 Jun 66, sub: Discussion With General Tran Van Don, 24 June 1966, History file 7–D2, Westmoreland Papers, HRB, CMH. On the dismissals of Co and Quang, see Chapter 10 of this volume.

Thieu and Ky, February 1967, *preparing for the coming presidential elections*

tion, . . . [and] beset by major social dislocation and widespread corruption." In the beginning a strong regent was needed for the new democracy.[10]

Both Lodge and Westmoreland agreed, feeling that the future government of South Vietnam, no matter what form it took, would have to be dominated by the military. Lodge saw the need for "adequate civilian participation" in any new regime, but he feared another coup if the military were denied "a proper role." He saw no civilian candidate strong enough to win a decisive electoral victory— or, once in office, able to control the senior officers. Convinced that the new president would have to be a military man, either Ky or Thieu, the ambassador insisted that American support must go to one or the other to prevent any open conflict among the two generals. Although he voiced no preference between the two, Lodge strongly recommended that the vice-presidential running mate be a popular civilian who, in his opinion, would attract more public support for the new government.[11]

The following month the Joint General Staff chief, General Vien, confirmed Lodge's belief that the military leaders would not tolerate a civilian regime. Victory by a civilian candidate, he told Westmoreland, would produce chaos. But Vien was more concerned that Thieu and Ky might run against one another and,

[10] Study, MACV SJSH, circa 1967, sub: Blueprint for Vietnam, MICRO 2/1, RG 334, WNRC.
[11] Msg, Lodge SGN 16463 to SecState, 25 Jan 67, History file 12–D9, Westmoreland Papers, HRB, CMH.

to avoid such a situation, recommended that the two place themselves on the same ticket as presidential and vice-presidential candidates. Speculating on possible electoral slates, he noted that many hopeful candidates were already claiming American support and contended that the neutral attitude of U.S. officials only encouraged political intrigue. The Americans, he told Westmoreland, must make their preference known. Although the Directory would convene in the near future to determine the army's position on the matter of candidates, it would probably do whatever Westmoreland and Lodge felt was best.[12]

Vien's fears were justified, for by the end of April an open feud between Ky and Thieu appeared likely. As the most visible South Vietnamese leader, Ky appeared the logical candidate. But in early May Thieu sounded out Westmoreland for support, claiming that Ky's northern origins made him a weak candidate and that, if elected, Ky would probably try to oust other generals, including himself, contributing to further unrest. While implying that he might challenge Ky in the presidential elections, Thieu suggested that, to avoid a confrontation between Ky and himself and splitting the military vote, an honest, respected civilian president might be best. Westmoreland, alarmed at the possibility of a military schism, assured Thieu that he considered him indispensable and the only person able to hold the armed forces together, and urged him not to take any rash actions. But by taking this stand, Westmoreland later admitted that he had "unwittingly" encouraged Thieu to challenge Ky for the presidency, thus bringing about the very situation that he had tried to avoid.[13]

The new American ambassador, Ellsworth Bunker, shared his predecessor's concern that a rivalry between Thieu and Ky would split the armed forces. Each of the two Vietnamese leaders insisted that he had the support of the other generals, and both probably told their peers that the Americans supported their candidacy. Ky, in an effort to head off Thieu, promised to make him head of the armed forces if elected. Thieu countered by recommending that the Directory back a compromise civilian slate. Bunker speculated that a victorious Ky might well dispense with Thieu altogether and place his old friend, General Khang, in charge of the military, despite Westmoreland's low opinion of him.[14]

In June Westmoreland tried to poll the leading South Vietnamese generals regarding their preference, but most were more worried about the inability of Thieu and Ky to produce a single military slate. Vien argued that the chief U.S. advisers should "umpire" the matter and ignore Vietnamese sensibilities for the sake of unity.[15]

Westmoreland and Bunker, however, remained neutral. They refused to endorse either Thieu or Ky, or any other candidate for that matter, and told the two

[12] Memo, Freund to Westmoreland, 21 Feb 67, sub: Discussion With General Vien, 18–20 Feb 67, History file 13–B16, Westmoreland Papers, HRB, CMH.
[13] Quoted words from Westmoreland, *Soldier Reports*, p. 218. See also Notes of 7 May 67, pp. 5–8, History file 17–A; MFR, Chaisson, 21 May 1967, sub: MACV Commanders Conference, 13 May 67, History file 17–A13; MFR, MACV, 9 May 67, sub: Synopsis of Private Meeting . . . , History file 17–A7. All in Westmoreland Papers, HRB, CMH.
[14] Msgs, Bunker SGN 26674 and 26779 to SecState, 25 and 26 May 67, History files 17–B3 and 17–B4, respectively; Notes of 24 May 67, p. 2, History file 17–B. All in Westmoreland Papers, HRB, CMH.
[15] Notes of 5 Jun 67 (source of quotation), p. 5, and 15 Jun 67, p. 13, both in History file 18–A, Westmoreland Papers, HRB, CMH.

contenders to reconcile their differences among themselves. Bunker urged Thieu, Ky, and Vien to commit themselves at least publicly to the principle of unity, thereby avoiding any split in the military vote that might set one faction of generals against the other. But Ky and Thieu continued to bicker, and Vien contended, more realistically, that any such statement ought to originate from the legal governing body of South Vietnam—the Directory.[16]

Toward the end of June General Wheeler relayed the general concern in Washington over the growing split between Thieu and Ky, but confessed that he was "at a loss as to what, if anything, we can and should do." Another coup, further politicizing the senior South Vietnamese officers, would be disastrous. According to Wheeler's sources, Generals Khang, Vien, and Lam, the I Corps commander, supported Ky and General Vinh Loc, heading the II Corps, and General Manh, the IV Corps chief, backed Thieu. Was this correct, he asked? What would happen to Thieu if Ky were elected? Should the United States "covertly" support a civilian candidate? Could some sort of deal be made between Thieu and Ky prior to the election?[17]

Westmoreland responded that Ky had the upper hand and, as president, might appoint Thieu head of the armed forces. Vien, currently the titular head of the armed forces, favored such an alignment. Although Thieu was still calling for a civilian president, Westmoreland felt that he would reach some sort of accommodation with Ky prior to the election. The powerful corps commanders, he added, were "[sitting] on the fence," hoping that either Ky or Thieu would give way.[18]

The South Vietnamese generals finally settled the matter themselves. Under Vien's leadership, the Armed Forces Congress met with the military members of the Directory and, in three long days and nights of meetings, on 28, 29, and 30 June, thrashed the question about. Apparently Thieu's refusal to give way to Ky was decisive, although the other generals may also have feared that Ky had already acquired too much power to be trusted. In the end Ky backed down and Thieu became the military candidate, with Ky as his vice-presidential running mate. Military unity was preserved.

Despite their endorsement of Thieu, the military members of the Directory also decided to form a secret organization, the Military Council, composed of senior officers who would guide Thieu on national policy, appointments, and promotions. Although the new constitution provided for a military committee, its function was only to "advise" the future president on military matters and not to act as a shadow government. Given the recent history of the Saigon regime, the mere existence of such a secret body indicated that the generals were reluctant to surrender any of their political powers. The elections would not create a democratic government overnight.[19]

[16] Msg, Bunker SGN 28409 to SecState, 20 Jun 67, History file 18–A16, Westmoreland Papers, HRB, CMH.

[17] Msg, Wheeler JCS 4736 to Westmoreland, 24 Jun 67, COMUSMACV Message file, Westmoreland Papers, HRB, CMH.

[18] Msg, Westmoreland MAC 5994 to Wheeler, 25 Jun 67, History file 18–A22, Westmoreland Papers, HRB, CMH.

[19] Airgram, Saigon A–37 to State, 28 Jan 70, sub: The Armed Forces Council Law, and Encl 1, "Law no. 017/69 Fixing the Organization and Operation of the Armed Forces Council," SEAB, CMH.

Confident of an electoral victory, the ruling generals also decided to compensate Ky somewhat by allowing him to name the future cabinet. They also ruled against the candidacy and even the return to South Vietnam of the popular General Duong Van Minh ("Big Minh"). Minh, the leader of the coup against Diem in 1963, still had many supporters in South Vietnam, and the Directory considered him a major political threat.[20]

The outcome of the Directory's three-day session pleased both Westmoreland and Bunker. Although evidence of American interference in the candidate selection is lacking, their preference for the cautious Thieu over the flamboyant Ky was well known. The ambassador cabled Washington that the generals "apparently very well understood . . . the importance of military unity in maintaining political stability and defending the nation—and also in retaining a strong military voice in government."[21]

Elections

The prospect of a democratically elected government again raised the possibility of establishing a multinational unified military command. With Saigon's high command one step removed from the chief executive, some Americans believed that the issue of South Vietnamese national sovereignty would be of less significance. Westmoreland again rejected the concept. He remained convinced that his personal influence over the senior South Vietnamese generals was adequate to ensure unity in the conduct of military operations, contending that a combined command would deepen American commitment to the war, restrict American freedom of action, and stifle South Vietnamese initiative. Ambassador Bunker, Admiral Sharp, and Defense Secretary McNamara all agreed with Westmoreland on the matter. Whatever the electoral results, American leaders were disinclined to become even more involved with the fate of South Vietnam than they already were.[22]

Neither the public appearance of unity between Thieu and Ky nor their promise to keep the army out of the electoral process calmed American anxieties

[20] For details of the meeting see Msg, Westmoreland MAC 6150 to Wheeler, 1 Jul 67, COMUSMACV Message file (also in History file 18–A27); Msg, Bunker SGN 344 to SecState, 5 Jul 67, Embtel/Deptel Message file; Notes of 14 Aug 67, History file 20–A; Msg, Bunker SGN 347 to SecState, 5 Jul 67, sub: Thang's Version of Armed Forces Council on Unified Thieu-Ky Ticket, Embtel/Deptel Message file. All in Westmoreland Papers, HRB, CMH. At the time Thieu and Ky denied the existence of any secret military council. See ibid., SGN 2972, 12 Aug 67. See also Ky's *Twenty Years and Twenty Days*, pp. 155–57; and Hinh and Tho, *South Vietnamese Society*, pp. 144–45.
[21] Quoted words from Msg, SGN 544, 5 Jul 67, COMUSMACV Message file, Westmoreland Papers, HRB, CMH. See also Interv, author with Bui Diem, former Vietnamese ambassador to the United States, 9 Nov 84, SEAB, CMH. After the war Bui repeatedly queried Ambassador Bunker about American influence on the outcome, and although Bunker assured him that the embassy in Saigon took no part in the selection of Thieu, he continued to feel that lower-ranking embassy officials may have influenced the decision without Bunker's knowledge.
[22] Komer Interv, 7 May 70, Rand Limited Document D(L)–20104–ARPA, SEAB, CMH. See also Notes of 27 Jun 67 (talk with General Do Cao Tri), pp. 21–22, History file 18–A; Study, Policy Planning Council, DS, 15 Jun 67, sub: Possible Alternatives to the Present Conduct of the War in Vietnam, History file 18–A13. Both in Westmoreland Papers, HRB, CMH.

toward the forthcoming elections. Embassy officials warned Westmoreland that the entire electoral control process depended heavily on "military officers who strongly desire to keep power, prestige and (in some cases) access to rapid wealth. . . ." Most South Vietnamese generals considered a civilian president "incapable of running the government and prosecuting the war effectively," questioned whether "any form of democracy is either possible or desirable" in South Vietnam, and feared a "civilian 'sell out' to the communists." With the exception of some converts to democracy like Vien or Thang, most of the generals regarded the elections as "necessary 'public relations' or 'optical' ploys" to fool both their own and the international public.[23]

Westmoreland took a rosier view. While acknowledging the deep involvement of the South Vietnamese officers in politics, and probably in the forthcoming elections, he believed that they would abide by the results. He saw no need for alarm and recommended that American involvement should be, if anything, minimal.[24]

Thieu and Ky were also concerned about the conduct of the elections, confident of victory but fearing that open violations might make a mockery of the elections. During a Directory meeting held on 18 July, Thieu reportedly urged his fellow generals to avoid taking any action to influence the elections and later requested that American advisers in the field convey the same message to their counterparts. A coup scare the following day and the possibility that the electoral committee provided for by the constitution might reject the Thieu-Ky slate were further worries, but nothing significant broke the apparent calm. In August Vien announced that there would be no official armed forces candidate, that members of the armed forces would not electioneer in any manner, and that soldiers were free to support the candidate of their choice. Thang, the revolutionary development minister, made an identical announcement, and both Thieu and Ky gave similar instructions to the province and district chiefs. Ky also emphatically denied a rumor that he might lead a military coup should a civilian candidate win.[25]

As the Americans held their breaths, the South Vietnamese presidential and senate elections took place on Sunday, 3 September 1967. The results were gratifying to Westmoreland and Bunker. According to official tabulations, 4,735,404 Vietnamese—representing 83 percent of those registered to vote—participated. Irregularities were minimal, and the final tally was evidence in itself that no manipulation of the balloting had occurred. The Thieu-Ky ticket received only 35 percent of the popular vote, a low plurality, while Truong Dinh Dzu, the leading civilian contender and a "peace" candidate, won 17 percent. Although some illegal machinations had taken place on behalf of the Thieu-Ky slate, its success probably demonstrated only the familiarity of the electorate with the two gen-

---

[23] Memo, Hudson to Lansdale, 6 Jul 67, sub: A Course of Action, History file 19–A5, Westmoreland Papers, HRB, CMH.
[24] Msg, Westmoreland MAC 7430 to Sharp, 8 Aug 67, COMUSMACV Message file, Westmoreland Papers, HRB, CMH.
[25] Msgs, Bunker SGN 1475 and 2972 to SecState, 20 Jul and 12 Aug 67, respectively, Embtel/Deptel Message file, Westmoreland Papers; Msg, Abrams MAC 6773 to Westmoreland (in Hawaii), 160634 Jul 67, Abrams Papers. All in HRB. CMH. Technically, active duty officers could not run for office.

erals and the larger number of voters closely associated with the armed forces. On the other hand, the slim margin of victory hardly constituted a popular mandate for the military candidates.[26]

A Transition of Power

The elections of 1967 only hinted at the turmoil taking place behind the political scenes in Saigon. In the interval between the nomination of Thieu in late June and the elections in early September, Ky desperately tried to shore up his waning power. As vice-president, his powers would be negligible and his supporters could not be expected to last long in office. Loan, his closest associate, was the most vulnerable, and Ky tried to broaden his own base by replacing him as head of the Military Security Service with another supporter, Col. Tran Van Thang. For the meantime, Loan remained director general of the National Police, a more influential post. Ky then proposed that the revolutionary development minister, Nguyen Duc Thang, be put in charge of an enlarged Political Warfare Department. In this capacity Thang was to control the Territorial Forces command and have administrative authority over all territorial troops. The attempt was actually a repeat of the ploy Ky had tried in 1966, but this time in the opposite direction. Ky also suggested dismissing several key generals—such as Vinh Loc of the II Corps and Thuan and Chinh of the 5th and 25th Infantry Divisions stationed around Saigon—prior to the elections as a sign that he and Thieu were intent on reform at the highest levels. Many of those suggested for dismissal were coincidentally friends of General Thieu.[27]

Although the idea of separating the territorials from the regulars had merit of its own, Ky supported these and several other measures to strengthen his own political base of power. At a meeting with Bunker and McNamara in July, Ky also urged that division and corps commanders be taken out of the territorial security chain of command to allow province and district chiefs direct control of both regular and territorial units and direct access to the central government. Thieu, familiar with Ky's proposals, disagreed, arguing that the South Vietnamese division commanders needed more not less responsibility for area security. Bunker at first sided with Ky, but the fight had only just begun.[28]

---

[26] For a breakdown of results, see Msg, Bunker SGN 5060 to President, 061142 Sep 67, Bunker Papers, DS. See also Msg, Bunker SGN 2972 to SecState, 12 Aug 67, History file 20–A10; Memo, Landsdale to Bunker and Westmoreland, 18 Sep 67, sub: The Situation, History file 21–A12. Both in Westmoreland Papers, HRB, CMH. Extensive material may also be found in DEPCORDS file no. 43 (GVN Elections (General) 1967), SEAB, CMH.

[27] Memo, Lansdale to Bunker, 7 Jul 67, sub: Talk With Thang, July 6, History file 19–A4; MFR, sub: Ky, Vien, Thang Meet of 15 August 1967, History file 20–A15. Both in Westmoreland Papers, HRB, CMH.

[28] Msg, Bunker SGN 1165 to SecState, 15 Jul 67, Embtel/Deptel Message file, Westmoreland Papers, HRB, CMH. In Memo, Komer to Bunker, 4 Jun 67, SEAB, CMH, the American CORDS chief noted that Thieu recommended placing "all pacification . . . under the ARVN" and that the issue over the control of revolutionary development was longstanding.

From July to September a committee headed by Generals Vien, Vy, Thang, and Vien's J-3, Tran Thanh Phong,[29] studied the South Vietnamese command system in close coordination with MACV and the American embassy. The group examined four major proposals: dissolving the division tactical area command, thus forcing South Vietnamese division commanders to relinquish control of Territorial Forces at province and district levels; expanding the province and district military staffs and creating Regional Forces "group" headquarters for better tactical control of the territorials;[30] appointing general officer assistants for each corps commander, one for combat operations and the other for area security and development; and establishing a "vice-chief" of territorial security in the Joint General Staff to control all Territorial Forces.[31] Ky, who inevitably became involved in the discussions, continued to push for a completely separate chain of command for the Territorial Forces and also for the dissolution of some division, regimental, and ranger headquarters.[32]

On 15 August Ky, Vien, and Thang met with Westmoreland, Komer, and Bunker to discuss specific aspects of the reorganization. Ky wanted to make Thang vice-chief of staff of the army, with responsibility for the Territorial Forces command, the Military Security Service, and the Political Warfare Department while retaining control of the revolutionary development cadre. He also proposed assigning province and district chiefs directly to the political warfare agency under Thang and having the Military Security Service spearhead a major effort to end corruption in the armed forces. Ky again recommended dissolving the division tactical area commands, as well as disbanding several divisions and converting their forces into territorial units. These measures would have removed the division commanders from the area security chain of command and provided more combat units for the provinces and districts. They also would have given an incredible amount of power to General Thang.[33]

Bunker and Komer were enthusiastic, but Westmoreland was more circumspect. Having learned about some of the proposals earlier during a private meeting with Vien, the MACV commander probably realized the political motivations behind the suggestions and declined to support them. He viewed the dissolution of the division tactical area commands too "disruptive" and the formation of a separate Territorial Forces chain of command too "impractical to effectively control or supervise." If transferred to the Defense Ministry, Thang, he felt, should be a special assistant to Vien rather than a semi-independent vice-chief of staff.[34]

[29] Phong, a well-known rival of Vien, had close ties with Generals Do Cao Tri and Tran Thien Khiem, both friends of Thieu, and may have been watching out for the interests of the Directory chairman. See Intelligence Memorandum CRM 69–43, Directorate of Intelligence, CIA, October 1969, sub: Key Appointees to the South Vietnamese Cabinet, pp. 25–26, copy in SEAB, CMH.
[30] A group headquarters was approximately the size of a brigade or regimental staff but more specialized.
[31] A vice-chief normally had much more authority than a deputy chief in the absence of the commander.
[32] See MACCORDS–PP, "Fact Book of Reorganization of RVNAF, 1967," SEAB, CMH.
[33] MFR, Komer, 16 Aug 67, Meeting With Prime Minister Ky, General Cao Van Vien and General Thang on 15 August 1967, History file 20–A15, Westmoreland Papers, HRB, CMH. It was at this time that Vien presented the list of forty officers marked for dismissal, which is discussed in Chapter 13 of this volume.
[34] Notes of 14 Aug 67, History file 20–A, Westmoreland Papers, HRB, CMH.

But three days later, on 18 August, Westmoreland went on record against any organizational changes in the South Vietnamese armed forces, especially the deactivation of regular units. He had worked too hard putting these forces into the field to see them summarily disbanded. If more territorials were needed, Westmoreland believed that the necessary men and funds could be found elsewhere. If the South Vietnamese were intent on reorganizing their command and force structure, he believed it prudent to wait until 1968, or at least until after the elections. Westmoreland became equally alarmed at the plans of Ky and Vien to replace many province and district chiefs during their anticorruption drive and again cautioned them against the "wholesale replacement" of government officials prior to the elections.[35]

After the Thieu-Ky electoral victory, the military reform and reorganization effort became, if anything, more rather than less political. Several competing lists of senior officers slated for dismissal went into circulation, each appearing to be politically motivated, and rumors of impending dismissals and appointments multiplied daily. But despite the charges and countercharges, little was done. Just about the only Vietnamese officer to lose his job was the commandant of the Noncommissioned Officers Academy at Nha Trang, Col. Pham Van Lieu, the former Thi-supporter whose outspoken opposition to the Thieu-Ky ticket had earned him the emnity of both leaders. Nevertheless, even the hint that a major command shake-up was forthcoming provided sufficient grist for several rumors, such as the one repeated by the South Vietnamese press suggesting the possibility of an imminent rebellion led by the I and II Corps commanders and General Chinh of the 25th Division. But more indicative of the new regime's intentions was the return of Quang as Thieu's new minister of planning and the promotion of Chinh to deputy III Corps commander. If anything, such changes must have reassured the other senior officers that no major housecleaning was forthcoming. Thus, when Vinh Loc, the II Corps commander, whom Westmoreland wanted to see replaced by the able Do Cao Tri, refused to step down, nothing seemed to have changed.[36]

Meanwhile, Ky's elaborate schemes to reorganize the Territorial Forces command foundered when Thang proved reluctant to leave the Revolutionary Development Ministry. Angered by the complete failure of the organizational reform effort, Thang charged that American advice repeatedly failed to take into consideration either the importance of personalities or the need for a greatly simplified chain of command and that American textbook command and staff procedures— the so-called Leavenworth solution—relied greatly on mutual cooperation and coordination, qualities normally absent in Saigon's politically oriented officer corps. If the Americans really wanted the revolutionary development effort to succeed, they had to put it under a single chief who would not be dependent on the whims of the corps and division commanders to get things done. Making Chinh a deputy corps commander just because he was supposedly "a better

---

[35] MFR, Komer, 18 Aug 67, sub: Chief JGS Briefing on RVNAF Reorganization Plan, History file 20–A19, Westmoreland Papers, HRB, CMH.

[36] Msg, COMUSMACV MAC 29383 to DIA, 5 Sep 67, sub: Corruption Charges Against Five Generals, Chief of Staff Message File; Msg, Bunker SGN 5550 to SecState, 9 Sep 67, History file 21–A29. Both in Westmoreland Papers, HRB, CMH. Thieu offered Vinh Loc the Ministry of Information.

pacifier than a fighter" was, Thang felt, a farce. If Chinh was incompetent, then he ought to be fired. Although Thang verbally agreed to accept the post of vice-chief for territorial security on the Joint General Staff, he remained minister of revolutionary development and never assumed his new staff duties. In November he submitted his resignation and was replaced by General Nguyen Bao Tri. Impatient and action-oriented, Thang would have made a poor partner for the cautious and methodical Thieu.[37]

Thang's problem marked the beginning of the end for Ky. Once elected, Thieu began consolidating his power. On 9 September, unbeknownst to Westmoreland, he met with the other Directory generals to discuss the future of the new regime. Westmoreland later learned that Thieu himself had proposed taking over all military and revolutionary development activities, leaving Ky responsible only for social, economic, and education programs. The generals also decided that the new prime minister was to be a southerner and a civilian chosen by Ky. Vien would continue as Joint General Staff chief; Phong would become chief of staff; and Vy, Vien's current chief of staff, would take over the Defense Ministry. No other command changes or reorganizations were recommended. Ky and Thang were unhappy, but Vien urged everyone to end their bickering and support Thieu for the sake of the war effort. Westmoreland, concerned over a renewed split between Thieu and Ky, endorsed Vien's stand and spent the next several months urging Ky, Thang, and the other generals to fall into line.[38]

What American leaders in Washington made of all the proposals and counterproposals is unclear. On 30 October, at the "suggestion" of MACV and the U.S. Embassy, Thieu formed a Committee for the Study and Conduct of the Anticorruption Program to plan a new anticorruption drive in the armed forces and on 3 November appointed a working group to supervise the investigations. Although most of the committee members were senior officers of minor importance, Westmoreland's chief of staff, General Kerwin, felt that the committee's establishment represented genuine progress in reform and cited the removal of several generals earlier in 1967 to be indicative of what to expect. Kerwin told officials in Washington that the South Vietnamese Joint General Staff was preparing to attack corruption "throughout the entire government" with a national-level committee of

---

[37] MFR, Forsythe, 6 Sep 67, sub: Meeting With General Thang, 1430 Hours, 5 September 1967, History file 21–A25, Westmoreland Papers, HRB, CMH. According to Msg, Bunker SGN 12347 to SecState, 011310 Dec 67, Bunker Papers, DS, Thieu and Ky had agreed that they would appoint all province chiefs from a list of 120 politically acceptable candidates, whom Thang would then train. Upon taking office, the province chiefs would report to the minister of the Interior rather than the corps commanders. See also Komer Interv, 7 May 70, Rand Limited Document D(L)–20104–ARPA, SEAB, CMH.

[38] Msg, Bunker SGN 5550 to SecState, 9 Sep 67, History file 21–A29; Notes of 10–18 Sep 67, History file 22–A; MFR, Westmoreland, 14 Sep 67, sub: Meeting With General Thieu, 1600–1730 Hours, 13 September, at JGS, History file 22–A2; MFR, Westmoreland, 15 Sep 67, sub: Meeting With Prime Minister Ky, 1130–1230 Hours, 15 September, at VNAF Headquarters, History file 22–A3; MFR, Westmoreland, 16 Sep 67, sub: Meeting With General Vien, 0820, 16 September, at JGS, History file 22–A5; Memo, Montgomery to Westmoreland, 17 Sep 67, sub: Secure Telephone Conversation With Mr. Calhoun, History file 22–A9 (on talk with General Lam, I Corps Commander); MFR, Westmoreland, 2 Oct 67, sub: Discussion With Generals Manh and Lam, 17 September 1967, History file 22–A10, Westmoreland Papers, HRB, CMH.

civilian and military officials and that the anticorruption program "appears to be functioning effectively and should serve as a deterrent to wrongdoers."[39]

Despite Kerwin's enthusiasm, little was done, and the absence of any significant changes illustrated Thang's point. Any true reform of the armed forces depended more on leadership changes than on changes in organization. Thang was probably not surprised when President Thieu began to push some of the same organizational reforms that he and Ky had championed earlier and that Thieu had previously opposed. These included removing the division commanders from the area security chain of command; enhancing the powers of the province and district chiefs; and curbing those of the corps commanders who, Thieu allowed, could "retain temporarily an intermediate role in supporting province chiefs, but should no longer be [the] civil government delegate."[40] Centralization of authority now worked to the president's advantage. With Westmoreland and Bunker supporting him, Thieu was now able to bypass his rivals and place his own followers in an increasing number of important posts. But he could not push the senior officers about too freely, lest they turn against him. The new president clearly realized that his own political fortunes depended on both American support and continued political stability. Rash actions on his part could jeopardize either. Although strengthening his political power base remained his major concern, he could not pursue his objectives in this area too ruthlessly. To Thieu and his Vietnamese compatriots, the conduct of the war effort was almost a secondary matter, one that was primarily an American responsibility, at least for as long as the Americans wished to claim it.

[39] Msg, Kerwin (acting COMUSMACV) to SecState and SecDef, 10 Dec 67, sub: Corruption and Inefficiency, Chief of Staff Signature file, 1967, Westmoreland Papers, HRB, CMH. Kerwin may have been referring to the dismissal of Bui Huu Nhon, director of the Central Logistics Command; Ton That Xung, commandant of the Command and Staff College; Nguyen Thanh Sang, deputy inspector general; and a General Lan (possibly General Pham Dong Lan, the Saigon port director).

[40] Msg, Locke and Komer SGN 1861 to SecState, 7 Oct 67, History file 23–A10, Westmoreland Papers, HRB, CMH.

15

Image and Reality

During 1967 domestic American political pressures began to have an influence on MACV policies toward the South Vietnamese armed forces. Ostensibly the Saigon army had taken a back seat in the war effort, concentrating on security missions and internal reform, while the more powerful American military forces destroyed the regular North Vietnamese Army and Viet Cong units. But the assumption that the insurgency would somehow collapse when Hanoi saw that it could not win a quick military victory proved fallacious, and the war in South Vietnam dragged on. In the Manila Communique of 1966 American and South Vietnamese leaders had suggested the possibility of a mutual withdrawal of U.S. and North Vietnamese forces from the South, leaving the South Vietnamese armed forces to handle the Viet Cong alone. President Johnson and Secretary McNamara were also increasingly reluctant to send more American troops to South Vietnam. Both were deeply concerned about the public image of the South Vietnamese combat units and the fact that American troops appeared to be doing all of the serious fighting. The lack of any discernible improvement in Saigon's forces threatened to become a political issue and contribute to the erosion of domestic American support for the war.[1]

In late 1966 General Wheeler complained to Westmoreland about "the apparent lack of military activity on the part of ARVN." His elaborate Pentagon briefings on the combat operations of the South Vietnamese had become tedious and disappointing. Too many of their operations lacked direction, and enemy-initiated actions seemed to cause most of their combat casualties. Was the enemy returning to guerrilla warfare, Wheeler chided? Perhaps the Vietnamese were placing too much emphasis on revolutionary development to the detriment of all else.[2]

---

[1] For background, see appropriate sections of William M. Hammond, *Public Affairs: The Military and the Media, 1962–1968*, United States Army in Vietnam, vol. 1 (Washington, D.C.: U.S. Army Center of Military History, forthcoming).

[2] Msg, Wheeler JCS 7859–66 to Westmoreland, 21 Dec 66, COMUSMACV Message file, Westmoreland Papers, HRB, CMH.

Manila Conference, October 1966, *where President Johnson again stressed the importance of political stability to Thieu and Ky*

Westmoreland responded in kind. The war was complex, but "everything falls into place if the difficulties are viewed through the eyes of those on the ground or those possessing a comprehensive grasp of the situation." Routine security missions were as important as the more spectacular conventional operations. Although most South Vietnamese units had not produced high enemy body counts, the MACV commander felt that local security was improving. He saw no evidence that the enemy had abandoned large-scale conventional operations, or any other reason to change MACV's operational plans. Improving "the effective employment of ARVN assets" was a "constant objective," but Westmoreland pointed out that increased South Vietnamese military support of revolutionary development freed more American combat forces for operations against enemy base areas and main force units. "Whenever possible," he maintained, South Vietnamese forces are "associated" with these actions. Although such arguments may have quieted Wheeler, Westmoreland was to find "selling" the South Vietnamese armed forces to his civilian superiors, to the American public, and to his own advisers a much tougher task.[3]

[3] Quoted words from Msg, Westmoreland MAC 0030 to Wheeler, 021137 Jan 67, COMUSMACV Message file, Westmoreland Papers, HRB, CMH. See also Westmoreland's critical comments on the press in *Soldier Reports*, pp. 250–52.

An Image of Progress

While encouraging greater South Vietnamese military support of revolutionary development, MACV faced the problem of how to present the new security role to the American press and public. Ambassador Lodge's staff worried that the United States might "appear to be pulling GVN chestnuts out of [the] fire at [the] cost of suffering [the] larger percentage of casualties." Embassy press briefers, he noted, were "carefully walking [a] tight rope between RVN sensitivity [and the truth] lest [the new] role be interpreted as degrading [to] ARVN . . . while free world forces monopolize [the] more glamorous job of fighting [the] main force enemy."[4] Some of the concerns that Taylor had raised in Washington back in 1965 were now becoming more apparent.

To end such impressions Westmoreland demanded that all American agencies project a positive image of Saigon's military forces. He found the disparaging remarks of his own field advisers about South Vietnamese military abilities particularly galling, insisted that his senior generals put an end to such complaints, and reminded them that it was the South Vietnamese army alone that had held the government together since 1963. The thousand of small patrols ambushes and skirmishes conducted by the South Vietnamese, he pointed out, were just as important as the larger American actions. "The story to get across" was that the South Vietnamese and not the Americans were doing most of the fighting. Such a "favorable image" would, he believed, improve the morale of the Vietnamese soldiers and dispel doubts over the course of the war in America. He also urged his American advisers to encourage their counterparts to improve the image of the South Vietnamese army among their own people. A subsequent directive repeated his advice and ordered U.S. military personnel to avoid any public statements questioning the capability or willingness of the South Vietnamese to fight.[5]

Several months passed before Westmoreland realized the serious domestic political implications of Wheeler's earlier remarks. In April 1967, while en route to Washington to discuss troop reinforcements, the MACV commander learned of President Johnson and Secretary McNamara's personal concern over the South Vietnamese role in the war effort and over the "wide[spread] impression that the South Vietnamese have now leaned back in their foxholes and are content for us to carry the major share of the combat activity." American congressmen apparently regarded the security mission as unimportant, reflecting what the president felt was probably the public's consensus and, for that matter, also the prevailing view of most American military commanders. With this in mind, Westmoreland underlined the need for "increased combat activity by ARVN forces" to his senior commanders and recommended increasing the frequency of combined operations "to get more mileage out the indigenous forces."

---

[4] Msg, AmEmbassy and MACV SGN 14983 to SecState, 6 Jan 67, SEAB, CMH.
[5] Quoted words from MFR, Chaisson, 9 Feb 67, sub: MACV Commanders Conference, 22 January 1967, History file 12–D11, Westmoreland Papers, HRB, CMH. See also MACV Directive 550–3, January 1967, sub: Public Awareness of RVNAF Operations and Activities, SEAB, CMH.

As a start, each major American combat operation was to include at least one South Vietnamese infantry battalion.[6]

Several days later, Wheeler informed Westmoreland that the secretary of defense was more interested in seeing better use made of South Vietnamese manpower than in sending more American troops. Extending duty tours for South Vietnamese regulars and territorials, recalling ex-servicemen, and lowering draft ages were all under discussion in Washington. More information was urgently needed on these matters.[7]

Westmoreland responded with what facts and figures he could marshal. The existing military service system in South Vietnam—drawing regulars from the 20- to 30-year-old age group, taking territorials from the 16- to 19- and 31- to 45-year-old age group, and discharging soldiers after about four years—could probably support the current armed forces through 1968. But even this estimate depended on many variables, and with the strength increases scheduled for 1968, some sort of general mobilization might well be necessary by 1969. To date, the MACV commander's efforts to elicit support from the U.S. Embassy on this point were unsuccessful. He promised to continue to press the embassy on the matter, but implied that it was out of his own jurisdiction. Although realizing that an early general mobilization "would make it more palatable at home for the U.S. to send additional troops to Vietnam, and could also have salutary psychological effects on the RVN itself . . . ," he cautioned Wheeler that the matter was highly sensitive and that nothing could be expected until after the South Vietnamese presidential elections in September. He might also have added that South Vietnamese casualties, especially battle deaths, were continuing to run higher than American losses, as they would throughout the war (*Table 14*).[8]

That same day Westmoreland dutifully sent another memo to Bunker, advising him that, due to public opinion in the United States, South Vietnam would have to mobilize before more American troops would be sent.[9] The MACV commander felt that the matter was now imperative, as it was interfering with his own military plans. He recommended that Saigon immediately lower the draft age from twenty-one to eighteen and extend terms of service indefinitely, or until the end of hostilities.

When Secretary McNamara, General Wheeler, and Admiral Sharp visited Saigon in July 1967, the subject of South Vietnamese contributions to the war effort again arose. Westmoreland, Komer, and other MACV representatives explained that, for political reasons, mobilization in South Vietnam had to be

[6] First quotation from Msg, Wheeler JCS 2861–67 to Westmoreland, 19 Apr 67, cited in Msg, Westmoreland HWA 1272 to Heintges, same date, COMUSMACV Message file. Remaining quotations from Msg, MAC 14391, 2 May 67, sub: Tempo of Combat Operations, COMUSMACV Signature file, 1967. Both in Westmoreland Papers, HRB, CMH. See also comments of Rosson on draft manuscript "Advice and Support: The Final Years," 16 Mar 84, SEAB, CMH.

[7] Msg, Wheeler JCS 3332 to Westmoreland, 5 May 67, History file 17–A2, Westmoreland Papers, HRB, CMH.

[8] Quoted words from Msg, Westmoreland MAC 4600 to Wheeler, 16 May 67, COMUSMACV Message file, Westmoreland Papers, HRB, CMH. On the South Vietnamese casualties, see data supplied by Directorate of Information Operations and Control, Office of the Comptroller (OASD/Comptroller), DOD, copies in SSB, CMH.

[9] Memo, Westmoreland to Bunker, 16 May 67, sub: Mobilization of the Republic of Vietnam, COMUSMACV Signature file, 1967, Westmoreland Papers, HRB, CMH.

TABLE 14—COMPARATIVE MILITARY CASUALTY FIGURES

Year	Killed in Action		Wounded in Action [a]	
	U.S.	RVNAF	U.S.	RVNAF
1960	....	2,223	....	2,788
1961	11	4,004	2	5,449
1962	31	4,457	41	7,195
1963	78	5,665	218	11,488
1964	147	7,457	522	17,017
1965	1,369	11,242	3,308	23,118
1966	5,008	11,953	16,526	20,975
1967	9,377	12,716	32,370	29,448
1968	14,589	27,915	46,797	70,696
1969	9,414	21,833	32,940	65,276
1970	4,221	23,346	15,211	71,582
1971	1,381	22,738	4,767	60,939
1972	300	39,587	587	109,960
1973	237	27,901	24	131,936
1974	207	31,219	....	155,735
Total	46,370	254,256	153,313	783,602

[a] Required hospitalization.

Source: Compiled by author from data supplied by Directorate of Information Operations and Control, Office of the Comptroller (OASD/Comptroller), DOD, copies in SSB, CMH.

approached carefully and in stages. The Directory, they claimed, had already "tacitly" agreed to lower the draft age to eighteen and extend terms of service by one year as soon as such measures were politically palatable.[10]

McNamara, thoroughly irritated by any hint of delay, was unsatisfied and demanded that more be done immediately. With the future of the entire country at stake it was nonsense, he countered, to induct so many people, push them through the elaborate training centers and schools, and then release them after their terms of service had expired. Lower draft ages, extension of service terms, and perhaps the importation of Korean civilian laborers were needed now if he were even to consider sending more American troops to South Vietnam. When General McGovern, Westmoreland's J-1, suggested that such measures might not be "psychologically" acceptable to the South Vietnamese leaders, an angry McNamara retorted, "Psychologically, I can't accept it" and "am sick and tired of having problems in what the GVN will accept when the American society is under the strain it is under today. . . . There is no damn reason why we should worry about whether the GVN will accept it psychologically." Again he repeated that no U.S. troop reinforcements would be forthcoming until Saigon mobilized.[11]

The need to squeeze more out of the South Vietnamese military effort was now unquestionable, if only to placate the American public. But, despite McNamara's admonitions, Westmoreland was loathe to force the South Vietnamese to do anything against their wishes, especially during the presidential campaign.

[10] For agenda, see Msg, SecDef 4563 to Bunker, 172115 Jan 67, COMUSMACV Message file, Westmoreland Papers, HRB, CMH. For meeting, see Memo, sub: SECDEF Briefing, 7–11 July 1967, MICRO 3/2838, RG 334, WNRC. Quoted word from memo.

[11] Memo, sub: SECDEF Briefing, 7–11 July 1967, MICRO 3/2838, RG 334, WNRC.

Extending service terms indefinitely or broadening the draft was sure to lose votes for Thieu and Ky, and might even swing the elections against them. In the meantime, the best he could do was persuade the Directory to suspend officer discharges for a four-month period starting July.

In mid-September, with the dust from the elections starting to settle, Westmoreland turned his attention back to the problem of the South Vietnamese military image. To counter what he felt was a problem in press relations, he assigned U.S. Army information advisers to each corps and division to monitor advisory comments and improve Saigon's public standing. At MACV headquarters he sponsored combined American and South Vietnamese daily military press briefings and directed his information office to provide a "more balanced" coverage of South Vietnamese military accomplishments in MACV-controlled media (Armed Forces Radio and Television, Vietnam, and the *Stars and Stripes* newspaper). He and Abrams also met personally with newsmen as often as possible to discuss South Vietnamese military contributions, and he ordered his subordinate commanders to do likewise, warning them to be fair and not to "overdo it," as the press was skeptical of excessive optimism. Westmoreland himself realized that optimistic statements alone would not suffice and that a "dramatic surge of improvement" from Saigon's armed forces was needed in 1968 "if [American] public backing to the war effort is to be maintained."[12]

In October Wheeler renewed his pressure on Westmoreland to improve the public image of the South Vietnamese soldier. Citing recent American press reports on South Vietnamese military failings, he noted the continued domestic opinion that "ARVN is not carrying its fair share of the combat support." Upset over what he considered hostile reporting, Westmoreland asserted that the American press had recently dealt "telling blows" to the South Vietnamese, portraying them as "less than aggressive in combat." Henceforth, if only for "political and psychological reasons," the South Vietnamese would participate in more combat operations. The MACV commander even directed that hereafter major operations would carry Vietnamese, rather than English, code names.[13]

The following month Westmoreland remained dissatisfied, despite the fact that MACV radio, news, and television medias were making a concerted effort to highlight South Vietnamese military successes. Complaining to his subordinate commanders that "press reports and comments of visitors to Vietnam which derogate the willingness and capability of the ARVN to fight" had caused the American public to believe that the South Vietnamese army was "not carrying its fair share of the combat effort," he again warned them against making any derogatory comments about South Vietnamese military performance.[14] He also

---

[12] MFR, Chaisson, 12 Oct 67, sub: MACV Commanders Conference, 24 September 1967, History file 22–A22, Westmoreland Papers, HRB.

[13] First quotation from Msg, Wheeler JCS 9298 to Westmoreland, 31 Oct 67. Remaining quotations from Msg, Westmoreland MAC 10451 to Sharp, 030422 Nov 67, sub: Amphibious Operations North of the DMZ. See also Msg, Westmoreland MAC 10453 to Sharp, 030609 Nov 67, sub: Nicknames for Combat Operations. All in COMUSMACV Message file, Westmoreland Papers, HRB, CMH.

[14] Msg, COMUSMACV MAC 36743 to Subordinate Commands, 090257 Nov 67, sub: Improving the Image of ARVN Among the U.S. Public, COMUSMACV Signature file, 1967, Westmoreland Papers, HRB, CMH.

assured Wheeler that MACV's ongoing program "to improve the image of ARVN" was in full swing, "getting the US public to understand the Vietnamese War, and especially the truly significant contributions that are being made by the ARVN in the prosecution of this war." Taking the offensive, Westmoreland urged that Washington do its part and suggested that the Department of Defense "recruit and organize a team of special consultants from the news media, public relations, and academic life to take a fresh look at the problem, and to study and propose ways of improving the ARVN image and telling its story to the world more effectively."[15] The subject was further discussed during Westmoreland's November trip to the United States, and at least one meeting, attended by Westmoreland, Bunker, Komer, General Wheeler, Secretary of Defense McNamara, Secretary of State Dean Rusk, presidential assistant Walter W. Rostow, and CIA Director Richard M. Helms, was devoted entirely to the poor press being given the South Vietnamese military by the American news media.[16]

On mobilization, Westmoreland had little success. On 24 October the lame duck Directory promulgated a partial mobilization decree, and on the following day Ky signed an implementing order authorizing conscription of 18- to 35-year-olds, the recall of selected veterans, and the "mobilization-in-place" of certain civilian technicians.[17] But the new government that took office on the thirty-first failed to act on the measures. To Westmoreland's chagrin, Thieu, making good one of his campaign promises, released those officers whose discharges were suspended back in July and, because of the opposition within the new National Assembly to widening the draft, postponed plans to call up 18- to 19-year-olds for military service.[18]

Westmoreland tried other ways to show that the South Vietnamese were picking up their share of the war effort. He publicized Operation FAIRFAX, the showpiece combined operation around Saigon, and announced his plans to enlarge the South Vietnamese airborne force into a division "to fight in-country along side US divisions and for future out-of-country operations."[19] He later presented the formation of the new South Vietnamese infantry regiment to guard the Demilitarized Zone and the creation of regimental reconnaissance companies as part of the same package. Although all these measures had diverse origins and purposes, when grouped together they gave the impression that

---

[15] Msg, Westmoreland MAC 10685 to Wheeler, 9 Nov 67, sub: Program To Improve the Image of ARVN Among the U.S. Public, History file 24–A15, Westmoreland Papers. See also USMACV, "Command History, 1967," 1:199. Both in HRB, CMH.

[16] MFR, Westmoreland, 22 Nov 67, sub: Breakfast Meeting at White House on 22 November, History file 25–A31, Westmoreland Papers, HRB, CMH.

[17] Mobilization-in-place refers to the involuntary enlistment of civilian workers, and is a normal mobilization action used to reduce personnel turbulence in industries vital to the war effort.

[18] Ltr, Westmoreland to Bunker, 24 Jan 68, sub: Discharge of RVNAF Officers; Memo, Westmoreland to Bunker, 4 Feb 68, sub: MACV Recommendations for Exemptions From the Draft. Both in COMUS-MACV Signature file, 1968, Westmoreland Papers, HRB, CMH.

[19] Action Memo 67–129, CofS, MACV, 28 Oct 67, sub: CIIB Meeting, 28 October 1967, History file 24–A6. On the origins of the Airborne ("Rainbow") Division, see Notes of 2 Jan 67, p. 3, History file 18–A, and Notes of 23 Sep 67, History file 22A. All in Westmoreland Papers, HRB, CMH. By "out-of-country operations," Westmoreland was probably referring to contingency plans to operate in Laos.

MACV was doing something coherent to increase the participation of the South Vietnamese armed forces in what Americans saw as the center of the war.[20]

A Change in Policy

Despite all the public relations hoopla, Westmoreland had not yet planned any new role for the South Vietnamese military. The combined campaign plan prepared in late 1967 differed little from its predecessor regarding the employment of South Vietnamese troops. The division of missions between American and South Vietnamese forces remained unchanged. One of the plan's goals was, in fact, to increase the number of South Vietnamese regular infantry battalions performing local security during 1968. However, the plan was general enough to allow for a flexible interpretation, stipulating, for example, that those regular combat battalions not assigned to the security campaign serve as "division mobile strike forces" and pointing out the need to develop a balanced South Vietnamese logistical system to support extended combat operations.[21] Perhaps feeling that changes in American war policies might be forthcoming, Westmoreland also advised his staff officers to be ready "to adjust our strategy in case there was any change in the nature of the war" and, as a first step, asked them "to develop better ARVN logistics so that . . . [the South Vietnamese] would be better prepared to take care of themselves. . . ."[22]

According to American advisers, marked improvements in the area of logistics already were under way. Assisted by U.S. Army port and transportation units, the South Vietnamese finally broke the logjam that had choked the Saigon port since 1965 and put an end to the lines of ships waiting offshore to be unloaded. Newly constructed port facilities also enabled advisers to simplify Vietnamese cargo handling and the transshipment of goods, thus expediting port clearance and freeing warehouse space.[23]

Logistical support of the South Vietnamese armed forces also improved significantly. In October 1967 Westmoreland reported that Saigon could supply 80–90 percent of its ground transportation, 55–60 percent of its sealift, and 20–30 percent of its airlift needs. Because most of the supplies moved by land, the air and sealift deficits did not pose a particularly serious problem, for American support could easily compensate for them. If American materiel, advisory, and training support continued at current levels, Westmoreland believed that the

[20] For example, Msg, Westmoreland MAC 10726 to Wheeler, 9 Nov 67, COMUSMACV Message file, Westmoreland Papers, HRB, CMH.
[21] JGS-MACV, Combined Campaign Plan 1968, AB 143, 11 Nov 67, pp. 4–7, SEAB, CMH. Quoted words on p. 7.
[22] Notes of 12 Aug 67 (at "weekly strategy session"), History file 20–A, Westmoreland Papers, HRB, CMH.
[23] For details, see USMACV, "Command History, 1967," 2:808–16; Ltr, Westmoreland to Donald G. MacDonald, Director, USAID, Vietnam, 18 Aug 67, sub: USAID Resumption of Advisory Responsibilities to Saigon Port Authority, COMUSMACV Signature file, 1967, Westmoreland Papers. Both in HRB, CMH.

existing logistical system would suffice to support the South Vietnamese military in its present posture.[24]

The effectiveness of Saigon's logistical system in a more mobile situation was another matter. Most South Vietnamese combat units continued to operate at a low tempo from fixed locations near major transportation routes, greatly easing the tasks of their support units and depots. Should the level of combat suddenly increase or the need to conduct large, extended operations in remote areas arise, or should the level of American support decrease, the strain on the logistical system might become intolerable. As a start at improving Saigon's tactical support system, Westmoreland recommended consolidating all division support elements (supply, maintenance, transportation, signal) into a single support battalion.[25] But there was no quick solution. At the other end of the logistical pipeline—in the field and base depots where materiel was stored, maintained, and repaired—many older problems remained unaddressed.

Despite their limitations, Westmoreland slowly began to increase the role of the South Vietnamese in the conventional war effort. During informal talks with Vietnamese leaders in early October, he reflected on the increasing number of American casualties, the sometimes marginal performance of the South Vietnamese forces, and the net effect of all this on American public opinion. All this had to be turned around, and he personally appealed to them to "instill a fighting and aggressive spirit, . . . reduce the desertion rate, . . . achieve significant victories on the battlefield, . . . and, . . . seize the initiative at every opportunity . . . ," reminding them "that God helps those who help themselves." Although the remarks were not particularly new or striking, the fact that Westmoreland later disseminated them to every major American command in South Vietnam gave them more weight. Several weeks later, on the twentieth, following a briefing on South Vietnamese modernization, the MACV commander even declared that "our mission, in essence, is to weaken the enemy, improve the Vietnamese Armed Forces and therefore, make the American troops superfluous." Perhaps Westmoreland was already beginning to consider a withdrawal of American troops—a withdrawal that would not necessarily be preceded by any truce or ceasefire.[26]

On 12 November Westmoreland went even further down this trail and presented General Wheeler with a rough plan for turning over the war to the South Vietnamese. He outlined measures that would or should be taken to improve the South Vietnamese armed forces within the next six, twelve, or twenty-four months, assuming that some sort of ceasefire and the beginning of negotiations, and possibly a mutual U.S.–North Vietnamese troop withdrawal, would follow each of these periods. These recommended measures reflected only current MACV programs. Six months would give MACV time to activate the new ranger group, the regiment for the Demilitarized Zone, and the airborne division head-

---

[24] Briefing, MACJ–46, 26 Oct 67, sub: Republic of Vietnam Armed Forces Logistic System, MICRO 1/1624, RG 334, WNRC.

[25] Ltr, Westmoreland to Vien, 9 Dec 67, COMUSMACV Signature file, 1967, Westmoreland Papers, HRB, CMH.

[26] First and second quotations from Msg, COMUSMACV to Subordinate Commands, 8 Oct 67, History file 23–A12. Third quotation from Notes of 20 Oct 67, History file 24–A. Both in Westmoreland Papers, HRB, CMH.

quarters; to transfer some equipment directly to the South Vietnamese from American stocks in Vietnam; and to make some logistical improvements. A one-year period would also allow MACV to supply Saigon with better small arms and trucks and to activate another infantry regiment, but a two-year scenario would provide little more than additional training in leadership and logistical skills. Westmoreland contemplated no organizational changes or new force increases, and ignored the American embassy's suggestion to combine elements of the regular army, the territorials, and the police into a national constabulary, which might be exempt from any negotiated indigenous troop reductions.[27]

In mid-November Westmoreland returned to Washington at the request of President Johnson. Though regarding the visit as a public relations exercise, he used the opportunity to announce a major change in American military policy. On Tuesday, the twenty-first, at an address given before the National Press Club, Westmoreland gave his "most optimistic appraisal of the way the war was going." The Saigon government, he declared, was "becoming stronger to the point where conceivably in two years or less the Vietnamese can shoulder a larger share of the war and thereby permit the U.S. to begin phasing down the level of its commitment." In a question period that followed, he repeated his prediction, adding that any U.S. troop withdrawals "at the onset . . . may be token, but hopefully progressive, and [that] certainly we are preparing our plans to make it progressive." A unilateral withdrawal of American troops now seemed official.[28]

Westmoreland's actual intentions are difficult to fathom. He later explained to General Abrams that he had made the announcement on his "own initiative" to give "the American people 'some light at the end of the tunnel.'" Rather than hasten U.S. troop withdrawals, he felt that his optimistic assessment would be an "incentive" to those supporting the war effort, smooth the way for further U.S. troop increases, influence the American presidential elections, and support the expansion and modernization of Saigon's armed forces. He believed he had encouraged a "protracted commitment" to the war effort by showing that a precipitious withdrawal was unnecessary. But at the same time he also asked Abrams to have the MACV staff explore "areas and time frames in which responsibility might be transferred from the U.S. to the Vietnamese," and devise a plan "to put the Vietnamese in a posture to make some transfer of responsibility at the earliest practical time."[29]

Westmoreland's motives at this point are open to question. While preparing his new policy, one that greatly increased the role of the South Vietnamese armed forces, the need to improve the image of that organization must have

[27] Msg, Westmoreland MAC 10817 to Wheeler, 12 Nov 67, History file 25–7, Westmoreland Papers, HRB, CMH. For the constabulary proposals, see MFR, MACJ03 (prepared by Ambassador Locke), 2 Nov 67, sub: Blueprint for Vietnam, MICRO 2/1641, RG 334, WNRC.
[28] Msg, Westmoreland HWA 3445 to Abrams, 26 Nov 67, sub: Concept of Situation Portrayed During Recent Visit to Washington, History file 25–A45, Westmoreland Papers, HRB, CMH. According to Notes for Talk With the President, November 1967, SEAB, CMH, Westmoreland had arrived in Washington with these ideas and intended to discuss them with President Johnson. See also Westmoreland, *Soldier Reports,* pp. 230–35.
[29] Msg, Westmoreland HWA 3445 to Abrams, 26 Nov 67, sub: Concept of Situation Portrayed During Recent Visit to Washington, History file 25–A45, Westmoreland Papers, HRB, CMH.

National Press Club Address, November 1967, *where Westmoreland presented his optimistic outlook for the future of the war*

weighed heavily on his mind, and may have influenced the timing of his announcement and even its contents. Nevertheless, no valid reason exists to doubt the MACV commander's sincerity or his belief that the enemy, who had not won a major battle since 1965, was all but defeated in the South. However, his optimism regarding the general military situation in South Vietnam was apparently the product of enemy losses on the battlefield rather than of any marked improvement in South Vietnamese capabilities.

Upon returning to Saigon, Westmoreland clarified his guidance. On 3 December he told his commanders to concentrate on two "co-equal objectives": first, "grind down the enemy," and second, "build up the Vietnamese armed forces . . . fighting qualities, logistic capabilities, and confidence." With steady progress in both of these areas, he predicted, "the future will take care of itself." South Vietnam "will be able to carry more and more of its share of the load and at some future date allow us to reduce our effort here." He saw the current campaign plan as "a blueprint to carry out our co-equal goals and a framework about which we can revise the RVNAF attitude toward the conduct of the war." Abrams added that the task of improving the South Vietnamese armed forces was no longer just an advisory responsibility, but was "everybody's job." More combined operations were necessary in which "the ARVN commander feels he is running the show," and he warned his fellow generals that if American military leaders continued to distrust and avoid the South Vietnamese combat commanders, then "our cause here is helpless."[30]

Meeting with General Vien the next day, Westmoreland repeated what he had said at the National Press Club, explaining the need to "phase out" American forces as the South Vietnamese took over more of the war effort. The Joint General Staff chief agreed, and Westmoreland set the MACV staff working on yet another study of the South Vietnamese military structure, with instructions to come up with "a force capable of operating with only minimal U.S. support." He asked for detailed estimates on American combat support currently being furnished to the South Vietnamese and for the best ways of having South Vietnamese units provide that support. He was especially concerned with helicopter and artillery elements.[31]

A variety of assumptions, sometimes conflicting, formed the basis of much of the new planning that was now under way in Saigon. On the one hand, Westmoreland seemed to be formulating a new policy, one that would give Saigon a larger role, in anticipation of some sort of negotiated settlement. He told Wheeler of his hopes for a "gradual transfer of responsibilities" to the South Vietnamese military at some future date when, "as a result of negotiations or of reaching the stage where our basic objectives have been accomplished," it would become possible to withdraw American troops. But given a choice, Westmoreland preferred to pursue American objectives in Vietnam through military operations. A battlefield victory remained his primary objective. Uncomfortable with any type of ceasefire arrangement, the MACV commander "very strongly" urged his military superiors to "resist the imposition of any truce terms which would compel friendly forces, particularly RVNAF, to accept a freeze or stand-in-place agreement during negotiations." The prerequisite to any truce was Saigon's ability "to fully occupy and control the country." Any cessation of combat should be preceded by a complete North Vietnamese withdrawal—an eventuality, Westmoreland believed, that could come about only as a result of the enemy's complete defeat on the battlefield.[32]

Both political and military considerations influenced much of Westmoreland's thinking at this point. Too many optimistic reports on his part might encourage an unwarranted American withdrawal—while the reverse might have just about the same effect. President Johnson's sensitivity to public opinion polls and his aspirations for a second presidential term were well known. Responding to the needs of his superiors, Westmoreland's formal reports thus continued to be optimistic, depicting progress and improvement, and most of the MACV reporting systems had been geared to present the same kind of picture.[33] But the MACV commander's more personal evaluations of Saigon were often less san-

[30] MFR, Kaufman, 2 Jan 68, sub: MACV Commanders Conference, 3 December 1967, History file 26–A6, Westmoreland Papers, HRB, CMH.

[31] MFR, Westmoreland, 18 Dec 67, sub: Meeting With General Vien, 4 December, 1500 Hours, History file 26–8; Ltr, Westmoreland to Weyand, 5 Dec 67, COMUSMACV Signature file, 1967. Both in Westmoreland Papers, HRB, CMH.

[32] Msg, Westmoreland MAC 12397 to Wheeler (Info Sharp), 20 Dec 67, COMUSMACV Message file, Westmoreland Papers, HRB, CMH.

[33] For example, see Msg, Westmoreland MAC 8073 to Wheeler, 25 Aug 67, sub: Assessment of Progress by CTZ, History file 21–A11, Westmoreland Papers, HRB, CMH.

guine, differing little from the more critical press reports. He felt no hesitation, for example, in clearly explaining to Washington that "leadership problems still plague the ARVN (although everyone is working very hard on this one, as you know), corruption is everywhere, night fighting requires further improvement, weekends off are far too common, and a number of advisors have difficulty in getting their opposite number to take advice."[34] Such caveats were also commonplace in Westmoreland's reports and, for those who read them, they continued to reveal the MACV commander's strong misgivings regarding South Vietnamese military capabilities and revealed the vast number of problems that had to be overcome before Saigon could accept complete responsibility for the defense of South Vietnam.

Support for Saigon

The more tangible aspects of improving the South Vietnamese armed forces, the provision of new materiel and equipment, was not without its own peculiarities. Even though the North Vietnamese had not yet introduced tanks, artillery, guided missiles, planes, or ships into the southern battlefields, their lightweight small arms and antitank missile launchers were of recent design and had proved highly successful in combat. In contrast, South Vietnamese infantry, both regulars and territorials, were still using World War II–vintage American weapons. The enemy, Westmoreland charged, had "designed and produced a formidable arsenal of weapons" for the sole purpose of waging "his so-called wars of national liberation." The South Vietnamese "are undergunned and they know it," and "the aggressiveness normally associated with confidence in their equipment is lost." Saigon's soldiers needed modern rifles, machine guns, and rocket and grenade launchers as soon as possible. Current production and delivery schedules were, he complained, "inadequate" and had to be accelerated rapidly. The message was clear. If the South Vietnamese were performing poorly on the battlefield, Westmoreland placed part of the blame on the unwillingness of the Defense Department to supply them with better weapons.[35]

Central to MACV commander's complaint was the delay in providing the Colt M16 automatic rifle to the South Vietnamese forces.[36] An experimental version of the M16 (the XM16 E1) had been used by American units in South Vietnam as early as 1965, and had proved highly successful. The new rifle was not only ideal for the smaller Vietnamese soldier, because of its light weight and small size, but also an excellent weapon for jungle warfare, having a higher rate of fire than the heavier Russian-designed AK47 used by the enemy. In the fall of 1965, when Westmoreland had initially requested 170,000 rifles to equip all American, South

[34] Msg, Westmoreland MAC 8875 to McConnell, acting JCS chairman, 20 Sep 67, History file 22-A16, Westmoreland Papers, HRB, CMH.
[35] Msg, Westmoreland to Sharp, 28 Feb 68, sub: Weaponry for RVNAF, COMUSMACV Message file, Westmoreland Papers, HRB, CMH.
[36] For background, see Materiel I & M: M16 Rifle file, SEAB, CMH, especially Memo, Director, FPAO, to General Johnson, 7 Nov 66, sub: Findings of Small Arms Weapons Systems (SAWS); and Thomas L. McNaugher, *The M16 Controversies* (New York: Praeger, 1984).

Korean, and South Vietnamese infantry battalions (including South Vietnamese ranger and airborne units but not the territorials), the Joint Chiefs of Staff had agreed to only 100,000 M16s, stipulating that American combat forces in South Vietnam be equipped first. At the time the MACV commander replied that 100,000 rifles would "solve immediate problems," but raised his overall request to 179,641, of which 115,436 were for the South Vietnamese units.[37]

Although the Defense Department ultimately approved the 179,641 request, several factors delayed the delivery of M16s to the South Vietnamese troops during 1966 and 1967. First, the steady buildup of American combat forces in South Vietnam increased Westmoreland's requirements for M16s proportionally. A second factor was the limited production of the new rifle. Contributing causes were incremental orders, the manufacturing capability of Colt Industries,[38] the increased expense of either subcontracting production or purchasing the Colt patent, and the desire of the Defense Department to keep costs as low as possible. To these considerations must be added the lower priority given to modernizing the South Vietnamese armed forces due to the evolving strategy that assigned American forces primary responsibility for offensive combat operations.

In November 1966 the Joint Chiefs revised the M16 distribution plan, giving priority to U.S. combat and divisional support units in South Vietnam, and McNamara himself deferred the issue of the rifles to South Vietnamese units indefinitely. Only at the personal request of Westmoreland and Admiral Sharp in early 1967 did the Defense Department finally approve the distribution of about 8,000 M16s to the South Vietnamese airborne (3,000) and marines (5,000). The first rifles arrived in April and the remainder by the end of May.

In both April and July 1967 Westmoreland restated his requirement for 115,436 M16 rifles for the South Vietnamese, and in August, at the request of the Joint Chiefs, resubmitted it once again, adding 3,000 more for newly created units. Pointing to improvements in "combat effectiveness, morale and aggressiveness" by those South Vietnamese units that had received M16s, he asked that the remainder be given the weapon as soon as possible. According to General Abrams, the MACV commander continued to give the South Vietnamese high priority in September but did an about-face in October, requesting that all American combat support units be equipped with the new weapon (amounting to about 100,000 more M16s) before giving any more to Saigon. Perhaps he feared a public relations disaster if all American units were not equipped first. In October the Joint Chiefs approved an immediate delivery of 5,000 more M16s to the South Vietnamese and in early November finally agreed to honor the total South Vietnamese request, with delivery of the balance scheduled during the first eight months of 1968.[39]

[37] Msg, COMUSMACV MAC 42787 to CINCPAC, 6 Dec 65, History file 2–G2, Westmoreland Papers, HRB, CMH.
[38] In December 1966 Colt's maximum manufacturing capacity was about 25,000 rifles per month.
[39] Msg, COMUSMACV to CINCPAC, 21 Oct 67, sub: Modernization of ARVN Weapons, SEAB, CMH. See also Msg, COMUSMACV MAC 32534 to CINCPAC, 4 Oct 67, sub: M16A1 Rifle Priorities, COMUSMACV Signature file, 1967, Westmoreland Papers, HRB, CMH; Msgs, Johnson WDC 12935 to Abrams, 290324 Sep 67, and Abrams MAC 9179 to Beach (CINCUSARPAC), 301134 Sep 67, Abrams Papers, HRB, CMH.

Efforts to modernize South Vietnamese field communications encountered similar delays.[40] In October 1966 MACV prepared plans to improve communications within the South Vietnamese infantry battalions by replacing the older MAP-supplied AN/PRC-10 radios with the more powerful AN/PRC-25s. Westmoreland expected about 3,000 new sets by June 1967 and 28,000 more over the following five years. Saigon agreed to distribute the older models to the Regional Forces and the revolutionary development teams. But the effort lagged. Most new radios went to American troops, and only 2,321 reached the South Vietnamese by November 1967. However, in 1968, after the United States had placed a higher priority on modernizing the South Vietnamese forces, the Defense Department delivered 6,000 new radios in a matter of weeks.

This pattern was repeated for other items of equipment, such as armored vehicles, trucks, artillery, and aircraft. In almost every case MACV had requested moderate quantities of new equipment as early as 1965, but McNamara had repeatedly put off the requests and given priority to American combat units. South Vietnamese requirements, Abrams acknowledged, had "not been handled with the urgency and vigor that characterizes what we do for U.S. needs." Saigon had simply been shortchanged by everyone's reliance on American military might.[41]

Only in late 1967, with the spotlight again fixed on the image and capabilities of the South Vietnamese, did Washington approve the old requests. The only truly new orders were for about 2,500 M60 machine guns and 800 M29 81-mm. mortars to replace similar weapons of World War II–vintage. MACV asked for these items on 21 October, Admiral Sharp's headquarters endorsed the requests on 8 November, and McNamara gave his approval the following February, promising delivery by the end of 1968. As with the M16s, MACV contended that the new machine guns and mortars were lighter, and thus more suitable for the smaller South Vietnamese soldier; would increase his confidence; and, at the same time, demonstrate American concern and support for the Saigon regime.[42] But only Washington's decision to halt further U.S. troop deployments to South Vietnam made the approvals possible.

The South Vietnamese Air Force, Marine Corps, and Navy had similar problems obtaining new equipment. Serious personnel, logistical, and maintenance problems still beset the air and naval components, and their modernization was understandably slow. On 24 October 1967 MACV finally authorized the U.S. Naval Advisory Group to convert the remaining South Vietnamese Marine Corps 75-mm. pack howitzer battery to a six-gun 105-mm. unit (giving them one artillery battalion of six 105-mm. batteries). At about the same time the South Vietnamese Air Force finally converted one of its propeller-driven fighter-bomber (A-1 "Skyraider") squadrons to F-5 jet fighters, and a slightly augmented South Vietnamese Navy coastal command began integrated operations with U.S. Navy vessels. But Saigon's navy still remained largely a collection of riverine craft,

---

[40] For details of early plans to modernize the South Vietnamese armed forces, see Materiel I & M file and I & M Pre-1968 file, SEAB, CMH.

[41] Msg, Abrams MAC 5307 to Johnson, 040950 Jun 67, Abrams Papers, HRB, CMH.

[42] Msg, COMUSMACV to CINCPAC, 21 Oct 67, sub: Modernization of ARVN Weapons, SEAB, CMH.

coastal junks, and cargo-carrying landing craft, and its air force was woefully short of helicopters. The old American H–34 helicopters used by the South Vietnamese Air Force were no longer in production, loss rates were high, and replacements were scarce. Of 105 helicopters authorized, only 72 were in service in August 1967 and that number was not expected to exceed 77 until January 1969.[43]

Anxious to accomplish some equipment modernization as soon as possible, MACV began to "lend" equipment to the South Vietnamese army. General Johnson had suggested the practice in June 1967, to overcome Saigon's severe shortage of wheeled vehicles and to make use of the large numbers of excess trucks in local U.S. Army depots. Westmoreland and Vien agreed to the idea, and in July MACV turned over 250 jeeps and 76 trucks to the South Vietnamese. Although at first regarding the measure as a temporary expedient, Westmoreland expanded the practice by ordering American units to turn in excess vehicles, logistics personnel to scour depots for spare trucks and parts, and maintenance shops to restore damaged machines as quickly as possible for transfer. By the end of the year American military units had loaned nearly 1,500 trucks to the South Vietnamese army, and MACV was considering transferring 935 more trucks and extending the procedure to tanks and armored personnel carriers. At this juncture, however, the practice came to a sudden halt. Westmoreland and his USARV deputy, Lt. Gen. Bruce Palmer, Jr., determined that the "temporary loan" concept was becoming a substitute for the Military Assistance Program.[44] Most of the items on loan would probably not be returned, and American stocks had become dangerously low. The proper course of action, according to Westmoreland and Palmer, was to speed up equipment deliveries and end the drain on the U.S. Army supply system.[45]

In October 1967, to systematize his various requests and proposals to modernize the South Vietnamese armed forces, Westmoreland consolidated all of them into a special five-year Military Assistance Plan, encompassing weapons, communications, and ground, water and air transportation.[46] In November he boiled down his outstanding requests into a special ten-point package—which included the new rifles, machine guns, mortars, and radios, plus 1,702 trucks, 4,183 M79 40-mm. grenade launchers, artillery, and artillery ammunition—with suggested delivery dates. In early February 1968, in the midst of the Tet offensive, he recommended accelerating delivery of all requests and added a new requirement for 234 armored personnel carriers and 27 helicopters. Later in the month he reiterated his previous requests and added another for 10,000 M72 (LAW) 66-mm. antitank rockets and, for the territorials, 268,000 M16 rifles and 11,200 M79 grenade launchers.

---

[43] USMACV, "Command History, 1967," 1:207–13, HRB, CMH.

[44] The Army component command in Vietnam supervised the transfer process.

[45] For summary, see Msgs, Palmer ARV 191 to Beach, 27 Jan 68, and Beach HWA 0384 to Palmer, 2 Feb 68, subs: Loan of Equipment to ARVN, COMUSMACV Message file; Msg, Palmer to Westmoreland, 26 Jan 68, sub: Loan of Equipment to VNAF, COMUSMACV Signature file, 1968. All in Westmoreland Papers, HRB, CMH. At the time Saigon was short 1,525 ¼-ton jeeps and 1,672 2½-ton trucks.

[46] Msg, Pearson, MACV J–3, to Deputy, SACSA, JCS, 25 Oct 67, sub: Optimum RVNAF Force Structure, History file 24–A29, Westmoreland Papers, HRB, CMH.

Washington now gave these requests immediate attention. The U.S. Air Force and Coast Guard, for example, turned in about 20,000 M16s for shipment to South Vietnam, and the Defense Department airlifted some 1,000 M60 machine guns and 25 M29 mortars to Saigon. All were earmarked for the South Vietnamese armed forces. But by then even more equipment was needed to replace that lost in the heavy fighting that was taking place, and MACV began working on a much larger modernization effort for its hitherto neglected ally. Meanwhile, the major enemy offensive in progress made it apparent that the deeper questions involving the image of Saigon's fighting forces would be decided on the battlefield and not in Washington or in the American press.[47]

[47] For details, see USMACV, "Command History, 1968," 1:262–68, and documents in RVNAF materiel files, SEAB, CMH.

American Leaders Charting a New Course

PART FOUR

Reevaluating the Effort
(1968)

16

A Year of Planning

The first six months of 1968 promised to bring about major changes in the American approach to the war in Southeast Asia. The enemy's countrywide Tet offensive began on the night of 29–30 January and lasted through the following month. Fierce fighting occurred throughout South Vietnam as American and South Vietnamese forces gradually pushed the attackers back into their jungle bases. At the end of the offensive the Viet Cong ranks had been decimated, with little to show for their efforts. On the battlefield, they had been beaten. However, the Tet attacks also had a great impact outside of South Vietnam. In the United States optimistic reports on the progress of the war had lulled both the American public and U.S. political leaders into a false sense of security. The offensive came as a shock. If the enemy was still capable of attacking in force, an end to the war was a long way off.

The immediate American response was the emergency deployment of the 3d Brigade, 82d Airborne Division, and a U.S. Marine Corps regiment to South Vietnam on 13 February. Later in the month General Wheeler visited South Vietnam to assess the situation. Upon returning he submitted a request for 206,000 additional American troops, ostensibly to exploit the enemy's setbacks at Tet, but also to reconstitute the strategic reserves in the United States.[1] Before Clark Clifford, who had replaced McNamara as secretary of defense on 1 March, could evaluate the request, it was leaked to the press and became a matter of public debate. To some it appeared that Westmoreland needed more troops to stave off defeat; to others the additional forces represented the continuation of a bankrupt strategy that offered no hope of victory.

The magnitude of the troop request stunned many Americans, and their increasing disillusionment with the war soon became evident. Senator Eugene McCarthy nearly upset President Johnson in the New Hampshire Democratic presidential primary on 10 March, and three days later Senator Robert F. Kennedy, a more powerful contender, entered the presidential race. Both senators

---

[1] See extracts of "Report of the Chairman, Joint Chiefs of Staff, Gen. Earle G. Wheeler, on the Situation in Vietnam," 27 Feb 68, in Porter, *Vietnam*, 2:501–04; Westmoreland, *Soldier Reports*, pp. 350–60.

Secretary of Defense Clark Clifford Holding a Press Briefing *in Saigon, with General Abrams and Brig. Gen. Winant Sidle, the MACV information officer, in the background*

made the war the central issue of their campaigns, advocating an immediate halt to the bombing of North Vietnam and a negotiated settlement. All these breaking events helped mold President Johnson's televised announcment on the thirty-first that he would not stand for reelection; that Westmoreland would receive only a token increase of 13,500 troops; and that, to hasten the start of negotiations, he had greatly curtailed the air campaign against North Vietnam. Several days later, on 3 April, Hanoi agreed to begin truce talks and an end to the war in the near future seemed possible.[2]

The prospect of an early ceasefire or truce agreement, possibly involving mutual American and North Vietnamese troop withdrawals, gave a new impetus to improving the South Vietnamese armed forces. If Saigon was to stand alone, much had to be done. After four years as the MACV commander, Westmoreland left in June, and his successor, General Abrams, inherited the responsibility for this immense task. But the MACV commander's military and political superiors in Washington were to scrutinize this effort much more closely than they had ever done in the past.

[2] For a detailed treatment, see Herbert Y. Schandler, "Making a Decision: Tet 1968" (Ph.d. diss., Harvard University, 1974).

292

The Tet Expansion

Before the Tet offensive, General Westmoreland had sought to increase the size of the South Vietnamese armed forces and to modernize their equipment gradually. In 1967 he had won approval for a force level of 685,739 and planned to increase that to 763,954 by June 1969 (an increase of 78,215). By early January 1968, before Tet, the MACV staff was thinking in terms of raising the supported strength to 777,884 by 1970 (a total increase of 92,145) and 799,742 by 1971 (a grand total increase of 114,003). Most of the increases were slated for regular and territorial infantry. Westmoreland's immediate reaction to the Tet offensive was to accelerate this projected growth as rapidly as possible. At the time he estimated that Saigon had about 647,000 men on the military rolls and, despite serious losses through casualties and desertions, that the size of its armed forces would reach about 685,000 soldiers in June, 751,000 by the end of 1968, and 777,000 by mid-1969. Although the figures were only estimates for planning purposes, they appeared realistic in light of the new mobilization measures taken by President Thieu in response to the Tet crisis.[3]

On 9 March 1968 the MACV staff completed a detailed two-year plan for an enlarged, modernized South Vietnamese armed forces of 779,154 men in 1969 and 801,215 in 1970. The plan divided the strength increases almost evenly between regulars and territorials, but recommended no changes in organization. The increases were to "round-out" and "balance" the existing force structure so that Saigon could "make significant" progress toward a "self-sustaining RVNAF." To MACV, "balancing" the force structure meant completing earlier efforts to give each infantry division three infantry regiments and one 155-mm. howitzer battalion, and each regiment, four infantry battalions, one reconnaissance company, and one supporting 105-mm. howitzer battalion. Symmetry for the sake of simplicity. The plan also added two more armored cavalry squadrons, "to increase ARVN mobile forces and to improve . . . [their] capability to open and secure highways"; enlarged the marine corps force into a light division; and provided the air force with eight new helicopter squadrons. To create a self-sufficient logistical system, the plan proposed adding eight truck companies (seven light and one medium), five boat companies (four medium and one heavy), four engineer construction battalions, and the equivalent of four military police battalions,[4] and increased the size of engineer, medical, and port commands. Westmoreland also added 31,475 "pipeline," or excess, spaces to carry personnel in training, in hospitals, or in other categories so that they would not be counted against unit operational strengths. At the time he felt that the major limiting factor in the expansion was, not the lack of competent leaders or the danger of inflation, but Saigon's ability to mobilize the necessary manpower.[5]

On 15 March Westmoreland requested that the 31,475 pipeline spaces be approved immediately to allow the South Vietnamese to expand their draft calls

---

[3] For background, see RVNAF I & M Origins, 1968, files, SEAB, and USMACV, "Command History, 1968," 1:249–61, HRB. Both in CMH.

[4] Military police personnel were used for security, traffic control, and prisoner-of-war camps.

[5] Quoted words from USMACV, "Command History, 1968," 1:249–50, HRB. See also Msg, COM-USMACV MAC 06882 to CINCPAC, 091250 Mar 68, SEAB. Both in CMH.

and begin training as many men as they could. Once replacements had made up the heavy infantry losses experienced during the Tet fighting, the spaces could be used to accommodate officers, noncommissioned officers, and air, naval and army technicians for the more demanding training programs that the expansion entailed. He also wanted the Regional Forces companies organized into battalions and planned to activate 177 battalion headquarters as soon as possible.[6]

General Creighton W. Abrams, Jr.

Wheeler and Clifford quickly endorsed Westmoreland's request, and in late May the secretary of defense also approved 84,000 more spaces to expand Saigon's training capacity. With this increase the American leaders had raised the authorized strength of the South Vietnamese armed forces to about 801,000 two years earlier than initially planned.[7]

The May Plan

In April additional guidance began to arrive in Saigon from Washington regarding the withdrawal of American forces. Wheeler informed Westmoreland that a partial or total withdrawal of American forces might occur in the near future. The Joint Chiefs chairman was under the impression that the MACV plans to modernize and expand the South Vietnamese military had made no provisions for this. Wheeler was concerned about Saigon's ability to provide adequate air and artillery fire support, air transportation, and logistics—areas in which the South Vietnamese were now receiving considerable direct support from American units. As a possible solution, he suggested attaching Vietnamese to American support units for training and eventually transferring the American equipment directly to the South Vietnamese crews. He also advised Westmoreland to begin providing Saigon with more arms and equipment as quietly as possible "in an effort to get under the wire on any potential freeze on force strength, armament or composition which might develop in negotiations"; to

[6] Msg, COMUSMACV MAC 07327 to CINCPAC, 150106 Mar 68, sub: RVNAF Force Levels, SEAB; Action Memo 68–57, CofS, MACV, 29 Mar 68, sub: Command/Staff Conference [With Vien], no file, Westmoreland Papers, HRB. Both in CMH.

[7] Msg, JCS to CINCPAC, 060058 Apr 68, sub: RVNAF Force Level; Msg, JCS 6703 to CINCPAC, 172116 Apr 68, sub: RVNAF Improvement and Modernization; Memo, JCSM-233–68 to SecDef, 15 Apr 68, sub: Accelerated Expansion of RVNAF; Memo, SecDef (Nitze) to Chairman, JCS, 24 May 68, sub: Accelerated Expansion of RVNAF. All in SEAB, CMH.

review the South Vietnamese military force structure once again to determine its "optimum organization within the 801,000 manpower ceiling"; and to study expedients for preparing Vietnamese units during the next six months to take over American equipment that might be left behind in South Vietnam. He added that MACV might have as little as one month to come up with suitable programs.[8]

On 17 April Secretary Clifford elaborated on Wheeler's earlier guidance and directed that the new force structure had to include "adequate" support units "for or within" the South Vietnamese armed forces, with "the ultimate goal of self-sufficiency vis-a-vis the NLF/NVA." American units could make up serious deficiencies during a transition period. Clifford also suggested that these plans be presented to Saigon in terms of helping it strengthen its forces, rather than preparing it to continue the war alone. Although Clifford was unable to give Westmoreland any guidelines concerning the timing of an American troop withdrawal, he spoke of the "urgency" of strengthening the South Vietnamese armed forces "as quickly as possible" and "as soon as possibile" with "time-phased goals." On the other hand, he also emphasized the need "of gradually shifting the burden of the war to [the] GVN forces," to concentrate on those actions most likely to provide immediate substantial improvements, and to avoid "attempting to do everything at once." Clifford wanted the MACV plans completed by 6 May.[9]

In developing what became known as the May Plan, MACV planners assumed that, following a ceasefire and a mutual U.S.–North Vietnamese troop withdrawal, it would take six months for North Vietnam and the United States to withdraw the bulk of their combat troops from South Vietnam. They also proposed a five-year period (1968–73) to organize an "optimum" South Vietnamese military structure; during that period a "residual" U.S. force would supply supplemental combat and logistical support. With this assistance, the planners felt that the South Vietnamese could deal with the Viet Cong and any limited incursions by regular North Vietnamese forces. They assumed that North Vietnam would continue supporting the Viet Cong with materiel and personnel, enabling the insurgents to field an army of 177,000 to 267,000 troops of all types.[10]

The MACV May Plan specified no major changes in the organization of the armed forces but incorporated only the increases that Westmoreland had already agreed on in March. It proposed activating most of the new combat units during the first year of the plan (1968–69). The only new additions called for were 3 more transportation companies, 3 battalions of heavy 8-inch howitzers, and 3 companies of M48 main battle tanks. MACV expected South Vietnamese ground strength

[8] Msg, Wheeler JCS 04005 to Westmoreland and Sharp, 121700 Apr 68, sub: RVNAF Expansion and Modernization, SEAB, CMH.

[9] Msg, JCS 6703 to CINCPAC, 172116 Apr 68, sub: RVNAF Improvement and Modernization (repeats text of Memo, SecDef to Chairman, JCS, 16 Apr 68, sub: RVNAF Improvement and Modernization), SEAB, CMH.

[10] For details, see Fact Sheet, MACJ–311, sub: Modernization and Improvement of RVNAF, in COMUSMACV Fact Book, 1968, vol. 1, Westmoreland Papers, HRB, CMH. See also Msg, COMUSMACV MAC 11948 to CINCPAC, 271422 Apr 68, sub: RVNAF Improvement and Modernization; Msg, MAC 12540, 030610 May 68; Msg, MAC [no. ?], 082027 May 68; Msg, MAC 13650, 132103 May 68. All in SEAB, CMH.

to peak in 1969–70, after which it planned to deactivate several infantry units and use the manpower spaces to form the new air and naval forces. Manned by personnel who had undergone three to five years of intensive training, these later additions consisted of several new oceangoing ships, 120 more river patrol craft, 12 new helicopter squadrons (for a total of 17, as opposed to a total of 13 called for earlier), a second F–5 jet fighter squadron, 4 more subsonic A–37 Dragonfly ground support squadrons (adding to the existing three), 3 new (fixed-wing) gunship squadrons (added to the existing one), and several air defense units.

The compensatory reduction in ground units projected between 1969 and 1973 was significant. MACV wanted to delete an entire infantry division by June 1972 and to reduce the number of infantry battalions in the remaining divisions from 12 to 9 (returning to 3 battalions per regiment). Although the reduction would eliminate about 24 battalion headquarters, it would strengthen the remaining ones by adding a fourth rifle company (as in U.S. infantry battalions). Also slated for deactivation were 32 Regional Forces companies (out of 1,196) and 253 Popular Forces platoons (out of 4,861). The total reduction would amount to 8,700 for the army regulars and 11,800 for the territorials.

Assuming a negotiated withdrawal of American and North Vietnamese forces beginning 1 July 1968, MACV planners also proposed a large U.S. residual force. Starting in June 1969 with 61,512 personnel, this force was to decline gradually to under 20,000 by June 1973. U.S. Air Force personnel made up the bulk of the projected residual force—31,000 in June 1969 and 17,000 by June 1973—with the number of U.S Army personnel declining sharply from about 24,500 to zero during the same period. MACV, however, saw a continuing need for a residual force of 16,693 (15,076 Air Force and 1,617 Navy) after 1973 to perform tasks that the South Vietnamese would still be unable to accomplish. This secondary residual force would have been even larger but for MACV's assumption that the complex U.S. Army communications system within South Vietnam could be run by civilian contractors.

Based on the five-year May Plan, MACV drew up supporting equipment delivery schedules that showed the extent of the modernization contemplated. Included were more M16 rifles (677,600 added to the 123,600 expected to have arrived by June 1968); M60 machine guns (9,800 added to the existing 5,700); M79 grenade launchers (19,300 added to the existing 15,500); M29 81-mm. mortars (1,147 added to the existing 265); and AN/PRC–25 field radios (30,900 added to the existing 5,900). Increases in artillery included 301 more 105-mm. howitzers (added to the existing 510);[11] 187 heavy 155-mm. howitzers (added to the existing 130); and 39 heavy 8-inch artillery pieces. South Vietnam's transport and armor forces were also to be updated with over 18,000 jeeps; 10,800 late-model trucks; 110 more armored cars (300 already in service);[12] and 65 M48 tanks (none currently in service).

---

[11] Including 72 lightweight M102 pieces for the airborne, marine, and the delta-based artillery battalions.
[12] Armored cars equipped Regional Forces mechanized platoons and served as convoy escorts. For a full listing of materiel, see Msg, COMUSMACV MAC 11512 to CINCPAC, 240205 Apr 68, sub: RVNAF Improvement and Modernization, SEAB, CMH.

M16 Training Exercise for South Vietnamese Soldiers

V-100 Armored Car

New Guidance

As the Joint Chiefs of Staff and the Office of the Secretary of Defense considered the May Plan, they became increasingly convinced that negotiations would be drawn out, with no immediate settlement of the war. This realization led to a rather sudden change in their priorities in June. For domestic political reasons, President Johnson, seconded by Secretary Clifford, demanded that Saigon's visibility in the fighting effort be increased. Both officials wanted MACV's plans to incorporate the possibility of unilateral U.S. troop withdrawals and hoped that MACV could at least make some sort of symbolic substitution of American with South Vietnamese ground combat units as quickly as possible. Any measures that could reduce American casualties and muffle domestic criticism of the war effort were critical in a presidential election year. While visiting Saigon in July, Clifford personally communicated these views to General Abrams. The secretary's immediate concern was increasing the number of South Vietnamese ground combat units—"maximizing foxhole strength"—rather than making the South Vietnamese self-sufficient by creating more support units. Abrams agreed to study Clifford's ideas, taking into consideration the combat situation, and suggested only that some U.S. armor or artillery units might be replaced "as a transition step."[13]

Meanwhile, on 25 June, Paul Nitze, the deputy secretary of defense, approved those portions of the May Plan providing new equipment for the existing military force and activating the new combat units called for by the plan during 1969 and 1970.[14] In line with Clifford's guidance he temporarily tabled the question of additional support forces and asked the Joint Chiefs to review the remainder of the May Plan in light of the military situation in Southeast Asia and the prospect of lengthy negotiations. Nitze suggested revising the plan to address two contingencies. First, he wanted a "Phase I" plan that provided "maximum possible GVN ground combat capability, assuming continued U.S. participation in the war at presently approved levels," especially direct American logistical support so that the South Vietnamese could undertake a larger share of the ground fighting. Second, he recommended drawing up a parallel "Phase II" plan that would support the development of a self-sufficient South Vietnamese force structure "capable of meeting insurgency requirements that could remain if North Vietnam and U.S. forces withdrew." In this respect, the rationale behind Phase II was identical to that of the original May Plan. But in neither the May Plan nor in Nitze's new guidance did American leaders consider creating a South Vietnamese force that would be capable of countering a major North Vietnamese offensive by itself. Phase I enhanced South Vietnamese combat strength while relying on continued American participation in the ground war; Phase II grafted a thin veneer of support units on to the existing structure, but left Saigon's forces capable of coping with only an indigenous insurgency. Neither addressed the

---

[13] Memo, Col R. B. McRae, SACSA, JCS, to DePuy, 26 Jul 68, sub: SecDef Trip Report, SEAB, CMH.
[14] This included 1 infantry regiment, 9 infantry companies, 1 ranger group headquarters, 1 cavalry squadron, 4 105-mm. and 2 155-mm. artillery battalions, 12 reconnaissance companies, 9 Special Forces detachments, 143 Regional Forces companies, and 300 Popular Forces platoons, and reequipping two helicopter squadrons with UH-1 aircraft.

Presidents Johnson and Thieu Meeting Again in Honolulu *to discuss war requirements*

prospect of a unilateral American withdrawal that would leave South Vietnam facing a combined Viet Cong and North Vietnamese Army threat.[15]

Plan Six

Independent of American planning, the South Vietnamese drew up their own modernization program,[16] which Defense Minister Vy presented to General Wheeler in Honolulu on 19 July. Dubbed Plan Six, the Vietnamese program was more ambitious than the earlier American proposals and went much further toward creating a self-sufficient military power in the South. Plan Six called for a balanced armed forces, 816,655 strong. The proposed logistical structure was roughly similar to the May Plan, but other areas were markedly different. Saigon wanted no reductions in regular or territorial infantry, and placed greater emphasis on armor, artillery, and communications, proposing four new armored brigades (with three tank and eight mechanized infantry battalions), three more

[15] Memo, Nitze to Chairman, JCS, 25 Jun 68, sub: RVNAF Improvement and Modernization, SEAB, CMH. The Phase I plan was to be ready by 15 September 1968, and the Phase II plan by 1 November 1968, later changed to 30 September and 15 November, respectively.
[16] The following section is based on Draft Memo, Wheeler to SecDef, circa July 1968, sub: Republic of Vietnam's Ministry of Defense Plan Six, SEAB, CMH.

armored cavalry squadrons, and fifteen more artillery battalions (including five with 105-mm. self-propelled artillery). The Vietnamese also suggested doubling the number of oceangoing warships, significantly increasing the number of amphibious craft, and adding three more riverine groups. In the air, Plan Six called for the latest American high-performance jet aircraft, 36 F–4D Phantom fighter-bombers and 127 A–7 Corsair attack bombers, as well as one AH–1G Cobra attack helicopter squadron and four battalions of Hawk surface-to-air missiles.

Saigon's plan also contained proposals to improve military living standards. It recommended free food for regular and territorial soldiers and their dependents; increased pay for the Popular Forces; better military commissaries; and expanded assistance to war veterans. Overall, Plan Six was thus expensive; the cost of new equipment alone ran about $1,714 million, compared to $1,040 million for the U.S. May Plan. But for the money, Saigon could have deployed a potentially powerful air-sea-land mobile striking force, and the increased food and financial support for soldiers and dependents might have helped free the regular combat units of their parochial area orientation.

The American reception to Plan Six was cool. Wheeler viewed it as "overambitious"—the new aircraft, armor, ships, and tanks would require a much larger logistics and training system than that proposed, and the equipment needed would seriously weaken U.S. military forces worldwide. He might also have been concerned that such a force, even if feasible, might encourage Saigon to widen the war. Wheeler thus promised only that Plan Six would be considered in the development of current plans.

The Improvement and Modernization Plans

In the months that followed, events began to overtake what had now become known as the Phase I and Phase II RVNAF Improvement and Modernization Plans. In mid-July Abrams requested that Washington reconsider deferring the creation of the Vietnamese logistical units and authorized the immediate activation of seventy-five support units as the "absolute minimum essential requirements" to support the combat activations already taking place. The new MACV commander also reminded the Joint Chiefs that American units could not provide more logistical or combat support for the South Vietnamese without reducing their support of U.S. combat forces. American logistical units were already "fully committed," and because no American force increases were anticipated, he could not increase the support being given to the South Vietnamese except in the event of a dire emergency.[17]

More modifications soon followed. By October MACV realized that Saigon's mobilization measures would soon push its armed forces over the 801,000 mark. Eager to use all the men available, General Bolton, head of the MACV military

---

[17] First quotation from Memo, JCSM–455–68 to SecDef, 19 Jul 68, sub: RVNAF Improvement and Modernization. The additions included three transportation companies, three ordnance companies, and an engineer battalion. Second quotation from Msg, Abrams MAC 21928 to CINCPAC (Info JCS), 290859 Jul 68, sub: RVNAF Improvement and Modernization. Both in SEAB, CMH.

assistance staff, suggested that the Phase I force level be increased to 810,000 and the Phase II to 825,000. Abrams agreed and requested an immediate increase of the American-supported force structure to 851,000 men. As explained by his civilian deputy, Robert Komer, these increases could always be used for territorial infantry and, at the very least, would deny recruits to the Viet Cong. Komer also successfully resisted Bolton's efforts to increase the size of the South Vietnamese Navy and Air Force at the expense of the territorials and turned aside other proposals to withdraw the regular army from its pacification security role. South Vietnam needed all the security forces it could muster, he argued, to launch its Accelerated Pacification Campaign,[18] a large American-sponsored effort to expand Saigon's control of the countryside. Both Komer and Abrams still expected some sort of ceasefire in early 1969 and wanted as much territory under control as possible. With these endorsements, Deputy Defense Secretary Nitze approved the increase on 1 November 1968.[19]

Again, events overtook American planning. On 9 November General Abrams proposed abandoning the distinctions between Phase I and II and making an immediate transition, or "acceleration," to Phase II, with a total force structure of 877,090 personnel. By beginning Phase II as quickly as possible, Abrams contended, he could cut as much as two years off the planned 1973 completion date and, by using materiel from American units scheduled to be phased out, greatly reduce the cost of the plan. Initially, he earmarked the equipment of four U.S. artillery battalions, two engineer battalions, and six transportation companies for the South Vietnamese.[20] Washington again agreed and on 18 December Defense Secretary Clifford approved most of the provisions of what became known as the Accelerated Phase II Improvement and Modernization Plan.

The improvement and modernization plans were all similar to the original MACV May Plan. All were five-year plans that retained and built upon the existing force structure and the increases already scheduled for 1969–70. Despite the nomenclature, they were neither "phases"—that is, meant to follow one another—nor "plans." More correctly, they were personnel and equipment programs. The Phase II plan in its original form would have transferred about 10,000 infantry spaces (2,651 from the regulars and 7,295 from the territorials) to the air force and navy and replaced four ranger battalions with four 155-mm. howitzer battalions. Other unspecified deactivations were to supply personnel for two more engineer battalions, one signal battalion, and eight transportation companies, and for two special brigade headquarters to control armored cavalry squadrons operating in concert. The improvement and modernization plans were also more conservative than the May Plan and dropped the proposals for 8-inch howitzers, M48 tanks, and air defense units. As long as Saigon's primary mission remained area security, American planners felt that a simpler force structure was more appropriate.

---

[18] For discussion, see Hunt, *Pacification*, forthcoming.

[19] Memo, Bolton to CofS, MACV, 31 Aug 68, sub: RVNAF Force Structure Phase II; Msg, COMUSMACV MAC 29424 to CINCPAC, 041215 Oct 68, sub: RVNAF Improvement and Modernization; Memo, Komer to Berger, 22 Oct 68. All in SEAB, CMH.

[20] Msg, Abrams MAC 34325 to CINCPAC, 090515 Nov 68, sub: Implementation of Phase II for RVNAF Improvement and Modernization, SEAB, CMH. MACV did not intend to "redeploy" these units from Vietnam, but to deactivate them and use their allotted manpower spaces elsewhere.

While Americans agreed that the projected expansion of the South Vietnamese military should allow it to deal only with an internal insurgency, they failed to arrive at a consensus defining the precise nature of that threat. The Joint Chiefs of Staff held that any mutual cessation of hostilities ought to include an effective ceasefire; a verified withdrawal of all North Vietnamese military personnel, including those in Cambodia and Laos; an end to infiltration from North Vietnam; a substantial reduction in terrorism; the repatriation of U.S. prisoners; an observed demilitarized zone between North and South Vietnam; preservation of South Vietnamese sovereignty; and continued U.S. assistance to Saigon to cope with the residual insurgency. They recognized that many of these conditions might not be possible, but neither they nor MACV thought it practical to consider developing a more powerful, more mobile army along the lines of Plan Six.[21]

T-Day Plans

In July 1968 the American staffs also began work on contingency plans for the withdrawal of U.S. forces from South Vietnam.[22] These withdrawal, or "T-Day" (termination of hostilities day), plans were general in nature and only slightly related to the improvement and modernization plans. They assumed that a hypothetical ceasefire agreement reached on T-Day would be accompanied by the conditions previously outlined by the Joint Chiefs. The planners outlined five possible withdrawal "scenarios," or cases, following a ceasefire: 1) a major American redeployment within six months; or 2) within twelve months, both leaving behind a residual military assistance advisory group (MAAG); 3) a twelve-month redeployment, leaving behind a MAAG and a corps-size balanced residual force of at least two combat divisions and support units; or 4) a twelve-month redeployment, leaving behind a MAAG and a smaller residual force of combat and support units that would make up on a "one-to-one" basis deficiencies in the improvement and modernization program (with a peak of 15,240 U.S. personnel); and 5) a mutual American–North Vietnamese withdrawal under the provisions of the Manila Communique (which essentially resembled the first case). Nitze later suggested a sixth, or "worst," case—a complete and unilateral U.S. withdrawal, including advisers within six months—but Westmoreland, in his new post as Army chief of staff, strongly opposed even the consideration of such an alternative.[23]

---

[21] See Col. J. A. Wickham, SACSA, JCS, "Background Paper for the Chairman, JCS, for a Meeting With the Secretary of Defense, 23 December 1968," 20 Dec 68; and MACV threat analysis in Msg, COMUSMACV MAC 29815 to CINCPAC, 080425 Oct 68, sub: RVNAF Improvement and Modernization, Phase II. Both in SEAB, CMH.

[22] For details, see Withdrawal Planning files, SEAB, CMH, especially Msg, JCS 6359 to CINCPAC, 031450 Aug 68, sub: T-Day Planning; Memo, Col Eugene M. Perry, G–3, USARV, 6 Dec 68, sub: T-Day Planning Conference; and SACSA, JCS, T-Day Planning Briefing to LTG DePuy, AVCSA, 25 Mar 69.

[23] Quoted work in Memo, Nitze to JCS, 17 Oct 68, sub: T-Day Planning. See also Memo, Westmoreland to SecArmy, 19 Nov 68, sub: T-Day Planning; Memo, Und SecArmy David E. McGiffert to SecArmy, 4 Dec 68, sub: Post-Hostilities Planning. All in SEAB, CMH.

In each instance the time between T-Day and the commencement of the withdrawal period was six months. Thus, the minimum withdrawal time was one year, and in no scenario did the planners envision a complete withdrawal. They interpreted the terms of the Manila Communique of October 1966, which had called for reciprocal withdrawals, as exempting American advisers and any other support forces that might be necessary to offset South Vietnamese military weaknesses. Most senior planners leaned toward case four, the most conservative scenario, which envisioned the retention of a residual force of 88,517 combat and 38,934 support troops, grouped in two air mobile divisions, one armored cavalry squadron, three air cavalry squadrons, an Australian–New Zealand task force of two battalions, one Korean regiment, one Thai battalion, some locally based naval and air units, and a logistical support brigade. Equally significant, MACV planners foresaw American redeployments occurring in "slices" of balanced combat and combat support units, rather than reducing combat strength and increasing the proportion of U.S. combat support available to Saigon.

General Abrams viewed the T-Day planning in Washington with trepidation, perceiving a lack of coordination between plans for the troop withdrawal and the plans for South Vietnamese modernization. Accelerating the Phase II plan making the South Vietnamese self-sufficient as quickly as possible would help close the gap. Both he and Wheeler agreed that a withdrawal in six months, as suggested by the Manila declaration, was physically impossible and would seriously disrupt the modernization plans. Abrams also argued that each T-Day scenario should specify not only a ceasefire but also the complete withdrawal of all North Vietnamese forces from both South Vietnam and their border sanctuaries in Laos and Cambodia. In their current form, the existing T-Day plans appeared to ignore all such military factors, stipulating only the withdrawal of American forces, and were thus incompatible with the major assumptions of MACV's modernization plans.[24]

Wheeler admitted that the modernization and withdrawal planning had not been properly tied together in Washington. As a partial remedy, he ordered his staff to produce some sort of equivalency formula between similar American and South Vietnamese units so that Americans units could be withdrawn as equivalent South Vietnamese units were activated. For example, his staff theorized that one U.S. infantry battalion was equal in combat effectiveness to three South Vietnamese battalions. Thus the activation of one South Vietnamese regular infantry battalion and, for example, six to eight Regional Forces companies might allow one American infantry battalion to come home. If tied to the activation of new South Vietnamese units, such a formula could serve as a rationale for specific American withdrawals.[25]

Despite the significance of the planning for Saigon's military future, U.S. planners rarely consulted with South Vietnamese staffs and, at best, brought

---

[24] Msg, Abrams MAC 12903 to McCain, 240445 Sep 68; Msg, Wheeler JCS 11349 to Abrams, 042225 Oct 68; Msg, Abrams MAC 14387 to McCain (Info Wheeler), 251034 Oct 68; Msg, Wheeler JCS 12997 to Abrams, 082311 Nov 68; Msg, Abrams MAC 16245 to Wheeler, 260819 Nov 68. All in Abrams Papers, HRB, CMH.

[25] Msg, Wheeler JCS 14412 to Abrams, 092319 Dec 68, Abrams Papers, HRB. See also SACSA Project Trade-off file, SEAB. Both in CMH.

only the highest Vietnamese political and military leaders into their discussions. American leaders in both Saigon and Washington were concerned that the South Vietnamese might interpret the withdrawal plans as a precursor to outright abandonment. In any case, the various ceasefire contingencies being studied by the planners would probably have made little sense to the South Vietnamese. To them the North Vietnamese Army and the Viet Cong were indistinguishable. If the enemy withdrew, the war would end.[26]

The T-Day plans formulated during 1968 were planning exercises only. None of the plans was ever implemented and, without a clearer idea of the type of settlement that would emerge from the negotiations, none of them could have been put into effect. But the plans tell much about the assumptions and intentions of American military planners. The establishment of phased withdrawal schedules militated against any precipitious "retreat" from South Vietnam, as did the decision to retain some kind of military residual force indefinitely. The Army T-Day planning chief, Col. John O. Shoemaker, recommended against "adopting or nominating to OSD other alternates which would shorten redeployment or phasedown times, or decrease the size of [the] approved OSD residual forces." In effect, the T-Day plans also assumed that a total U.S. withdrawal from South Vietnam would not occur in the foreseeable future and rejected any unilateral American withdrawals. With these assumptions, there was less incentive to make the various South Vietnamese improvement and modernization plans more comprehensive or to prepare the South Vietnamese to handle the war by themselves. Nitze himself suggested at the year's end that the Phase II force structure provided too much conventional combat power to the South Vietnamese and that a different type of army might be needed to cope with the smaller internal insurgency remaining after a mutual American–North Vietnamese military withdrawal. To this end, he recommended developing plans for a posthostilities "Phase III" force structure, orienting the South Vietnamese even more towards territorial security than the current Phase II plan.[27]

An Assessment

In Saigon, American officials were not as optimistic. Ambassador Bunker felt that it was in Hanoi's interest to begin serious peace talks as quickly as possible. Open negotiations would allow its leaders to propose a ceasefire and some type of mutual withdrawal almost immediately. American public opinion, Bunker felt, would force the United States to accept any reasonable terms. Although no longer a candidate for reelection, President Johnson was eager to end his term of office with some sort of agreement that might promise an end to the war. Bunker thought that the North Vietnamese would be willing to compromise if

---

[26] For Vietnamese comments on withdrawal planning, see MFR, Maj C. M. Cooke, Jr. (USAF), OSD, 14 Nov 68, sub: Trip Report, SEAB, CMH.

[27] Quoted words from MFR, Shoemaker, 5 Feb 69, sub: N and T-Day Costing Scenarios. See also Memo, Nitze to Chairman, JCS, 18 Dec 68, sub: RVNAF Phase II Force Structure. Both in SEAB, CMH.

the withdrawal of American troops could be assured. But neither he nor Abrams believed that Hanoi would seriously honor the spirit of any agreement and expected that it would, at the very least, continue to support the war in the South with men, materiel, and leadership. Bunker conveyed his concerns repeatedly, both to his superiors in Washington and to the Vietnamese in Saigon.[28] However, for reasons American officials were unable to discern, North Vietnamese leaders made no effort to take advantage of the difficult American political situation and little progress was made toward a ceasefire or a negotiated withdrawal.

Once the shock of the Tet attack had worn off, and once the expectation of an immediate peace agreement had disappeared, military planners found it difficult to sustain the urgency that had characterized American planning in March and April. On the military side, Abrams began to make his own planning adjustments with more deliberation. The new combined campaign plan drawn up in 1968 for the following year gave identical combat missions to both American and regular South Vietnamese combat troops. It relieved South Vietnamese regulars from their security mission and assigned them conventional combat missions closely coordinated with those of American units. It also planned more advisory support for the territorials while grouping them into larger battalion-size units.[29]

However, the new campaign plan suggested no changes in command relations or strategy. Both Abrams and Westmoreland, prior to the latter's departure, again rejected any kind of combined or unified military command. Westmoreland, in particular, continued to view any NATO- or SEATO-type multinational command as being "too cumbersome," a "waste in personnel assets," and riddled with language and security problems. Besides, he added, "it is doubtful if there is sufficient RVNAF professionalism to fill the additional positions of a combined staff." Reflecting on the last three years, he again asserted that "joint planning and operational relationships between U.S. MACV and JGS are such that COMUSMACV does, for all practical purposes, exercise adequate operational control of RVNAF" and that, "within the capabilities of RVNAF, . . . General Vien and the JGS have been receptive to our suggestions and act accordingly." No alterations in command and control or in the advisory system were necessary.[30]

Thus, despite the many different plans, proposals, and contingencies studied by American officials during 1968, a major change in U.S. policy toward the war seemed unlikely. Although the possibility of a mutual withdrawal had existed since the Manila Conference of 1966, no one in Hanoi, Saigon, or Washington believed that such an agreement could be easily negotiated or fairly implemented. But in revamping Saigon's armaments, the Americans were doing little more than pouring new wine into old bottles. Much more important were Amer-

---

[28] See especially Msg, AmEmbassy SGN 42463 to SecState, 120410 Nov 68, sub: An Interpretation of Hanoi's Future Strategy; Msg, State 241183 to AmEmbassy, Saigon, 19 Sep 68, sub: Consultations With Thieu on Cease-fire and Joint Commission. Both in Bunker Papers, DS.

[29] JGS-MACV, Combined Campaign Plan 1969, AB 144, 30 Sep 68, pp. 6–8, SEAB, CMH; Fact Sheet, MACJ–321, 1968, sub: Increased Responsibility for RVNAF, MICRO 3/2190, RG 334, WNRC.

[30] Msg, COMUSMACV MAC 05123 to CINCPAC, 191132 Feb 68, sub: Command Relationships, COMUSMACV Message file, Westmoreland Papers, HRB, CMH. Defense Department officials continued to be interested in some kind of multinational "joint command." See *U.S.-Vietnam Relations*, 7:sec. IV. C. 6. (c), p. 56 (refers to Draft Memo, DOD to President, 4 Mar 68, copy in SEAB, CMH).

ican judgments on the condition of those bottles. If all the positive statements made by MACV in 1967 about its Asian ally were just so much propaganda, then all the new equipment and recruits meant little, the war had arrived at a stalemate, and any plans for reducing U.S. participation were fraught with danger.

17

Saigon Takes Action

On 20 January 1968, about one week before the enemy launched its first major offensive of the war, Maj. Gen. George I. Forsythe, the assistant CORDS director, sat down with President Thieu for an informal discussion of the future of the military effort in South Vietnam. The newly installed president laid out some of his major plans and hopes for the new year. At the outset he outlined a "pinch out" strategy that he and Westmoreland had supposedly discussed. First he wanted to clear the delta region, now reinforced by the U.S. 9th Infantry Division and the South Vietnamese Marines. Once the territorials were able to assume the security mission there, he intended to move his regular troops north, first to the Saigon area and then to the two northern corps zones. In this way the allied forces would slowly squeeze the enemy from the bottom up. The process, he assured Forsythe, would even permit some American combat troops to return home in the near future.

To ensure the success of this concept, Thieu wanted to take the South Vietnamese corps and division commanders out of the area security chain of command and have the forty-four province chiefs report directly to the central government in Saigon. Once the corps commanders relinquished their area security responsibilities, he felt that they could focus on mobile combat operations, making it easier for the United States to redeploy its combat forces. In the process, many of the more ineffective or corrupt South Vietnamese senior officers would be replaced by more able and professional military leaders. But the pace of the entire process, Thieu cautioned, would be extremely slow and methodical, something he feared the Americans would neither understand nor accept. As he explained his plans, Forsythe felt that the 1963–65 coup period weighed heavily on the president's mind. Judging a wholesale purge of South Vietnamese officers as simply impossible, Thieu warned that each major command change would have to be carefully planned and orchestrated. The army could not be removed from politics overnight. The military establishment had been and still was his major political supporter and the only cohesive force holding the country together. His American advisers would have to be patient.[1]

---

[1] MFR, Forsythe, 21 Jan 68, sub: Visit With President Thieu, 20 January 1968, SEAB, CMH.

Thieu's presentation reflected some of the discontinuities and ambiguities in allied strategy. In terms of "operational strategy"—the deployment and employment of American and South Vietnamese military forces within the borders of South Vietnam—the two allies appeared far apart. For almost a year now General Westmoreland had been building up his forces, not in the Delta, but in the I Corps Tactical Zone at the opposite end of South Vietnam. At this very moment his attention was riveted on the siege of one of his northernmost outposts, Khe Sanh, where U.S. Marine Corps units were repelling heavy enemy assaults. Perhaps understandably, Thieu's major interests lay elsewhere. His analysis of the current situation pointed out how much of the entire pacification campaign—from the assignment of roles and missions to the establishment of a more effective national government—depended, not on battlefield successes, but on the reform and reorganization efforts within the South Vietnamese armed forces and government. Thieu even tied U.S. troop withdrawals to progress in these areas. But however perspicacious his observations, Thieu, as well as most of his high-level American advisers, failed to deal with some of the broader aspects of allied military strategy and specifically with the current and future intentions of North Vietnam. Would the heavy losses being suffered by the North Vietnamese during the current offensive force them out of the struggle? How would the allies deal with the enemy's military sanctuaries just across the South Vietnamese borders in Laos and Cambodia? Perhaps the South Vietnamese president viewed such matters as American affairs, and certainly his American advisers had not encouraged him otherwise. Nevertheless, when all was said and done, Saigon's leaders had at least begun to consider their future actions in the war without American prodding.

Changes in Command

Whatever its impact in the United States, the general offensive launched by the enemy during the Tet (lunar new year) holiday galvanized the Vietnamese leaders into action and made them much more receptive to American advice. On 14 February, in the midst of the fighting, Westmoreland urged Thieu and Vien to make several controversial command changes under the cloak of military necessity. They tentatively agreed to replace all four corps commanders, removing two, Vinh Loc in the Highlands (II CTZ) and Nguyen Van Manh in the Delta (IV CTZ), immediately. For the moment Thieu agreed to retain General Lam, who had proven his loyalty during the Buddhist crisis in 1966, as I Corps commander and General Khang, a Ky supporter, in his III Corps post. However, he wanted to separate the Capital Military District command from Khang's control and this provoked the most discussion. Day-to-day operations in the Capital Military District were the responsibility of Col. Nguyen Van Giam, Khang's deputy. Although highly praised by his American advisers in 1967, Giam had performed poorly during the Tet fighting. Westmoreland wanted him replaced by Colonel Hai, a Thieu supporter who was currently heading the Ranger Command, but Vien thought it politic to discuss the matter with Khang first, and

Thieu, who had other plans for Hai, refused to heed Westmoreland's advice.[2] Whatever Khang's political ties, Thieu respected his military abilities and appeared reluctant to dispense with his services just yet. Khang, when consulted, suggested Chinh, Ky's old friend and Hunnicutt's former nemesis, for the job, but for the meantime nothing was decided.[3]

Whether Thieu could actually push through any of these changes without a major revolt was another question. The whole matter of military appointments remained extremely political. A repetition of the Thi affair, or worse, in the middle of the Tet fighting would have been a disaster for both Saigon and MACV. However, the politico-military mix in South Vietnam had changed since 1966. The elections had greatly increased Thieu's prestige and authority, and his American support was secure. Moreover, the heavy fighting had temporarily diverted the attention of the generals from politics to purely military concerns. With this in mind, Thieu dismissed both Vinh Loc and Manh on 23 February. Neither general had shown much leadership during the enemy offensive, and the forces under their control had been badly mauled. Thieu's action thus appeared to be based primarily on military necessity. The other army leaders accepted the dismissals without fuss, and the two generals left quietly, each appointed to minor posts: Vinh Loc, as the Central Training Command director; and Manh, as inspector general.

The demise of Vinh Loc was a victory for both Thieu and Westmoreland. The II Corps commander had ruled the Central Highlands as a personal fief since 1965 and was the last of the old, independent general-warlords who had habitually defied the central government in Saigon. To Americans, he was a "mercurial, unstable opportunist"—more of a politician than a general and more effective as a governor than a fighter.[4] But Loc's successor, General Lu Mong Lan, was not necessarily an improvement. As commander of the 25th, 23d, and 18th Infantry Divisions between 1962 and 1966, Lu Lan had received poor ratings from almost all of his American advisers, and, since September 1966, had served as the deputy chief of staff for training and director of the Central Training Command.[5] He was, however, an ardent Thieu supporter and could be expected to follow the dictates of the Saigon government more closely than his predecessor.

Nguyen Van Manh, heading the IV Corps Tactical Zone at the beginning of the year, was also a Thieu supporter, but the poor performance of his regular and territorial units in the Delta during Tet made him more of a liability than an asset to the new president. His replacement, surprisingly, was none other than Nguyen Duc Thang, the former revolutionary development minister and close

[2] MFR, Westmoreland, 15 Feb 68, sub: Meeting With President Thieu and General Vien, 1700 H, 14 February, Personal Correspondence file, Westmoreland Papers, HRB, CMH. Bunker used the same tactic. See Msg, Bunker SGN 18699 to President, 9 Feb 68, Bunker Papers, DS.

[3] Telecon, Westmoreland to Weyand, 15 Feb 68, sub: Appointment of MG Chinh, Fonecon file, Westmoreland Papers, HRB, CMH.

[4] For comments, see Msg (source of quotation), Westmoreland MAC 2812 to Wheeler, 091345 Apr 66, COMUSMACV Message file; Notes of 16 Feb 68, p. 9, History file 29–1; MFR, Westmoreland, 13 Nov 67, sub: Signing of Combined Campaign Plans . . . , History file 24–A22. All in Westmoreland Papers, HRB, CMH. See also Don Oberdorfer, *Tet!* (Garden City, N.Y.: Doubleday, 1971), pp. 130–31.

[5] See comments in MFR, Accousti, 25 Dec 65, sub: COMUSMACV Visit . . . , History file 3–A2, Westmoreland Papers, HRB, CMH; Briefing Book for SECDEF Honolulu Conference, 20–21 Nov 63, box 2, accession no. 69A702, RG 334, WNRC.

associate of Ky. Thang was a favorite of the Americans, a thorn in the side of the senior generals, and no friend of Thieu. As revolutionary development minister, he had been habitually frustrated over Saigon's unwillingness to replace corrupt or ineffective officials and had complained loud and often about its neglect of area security.[6] Now as a corps commander, he had authority to clean up the Delta. Westmoreland was extremely pleased by the move, calling it "the most important single appointment that has been made in the last year," and for the next few months Thang proved himself an able military leader as well as a competent civil administrator.[7]

Meanwhile, Thieu began a wide purge of his political enemies. Many suspected opponents of the regime were arrested, including political, union, and religious leaders, and doctors, lawyers, professors, and students. Most prominent were Truong Dinh Dzu, the peace candidate who had taken second place in the presidential elections, and Thich Tri Quang, the rebellious Buddhist political leader. Although most were eventually released, Dzu languished in prison many years. More dangerous to Thieu were those Ky-appointed officials who still owed their loyalty to the vice-president. On 1 March Thieu issued a decree transferring responsibility for the appointment of province chiefs from the four corps commanders to himself and, shortly thereafter, dismissed eleven province chiefs for alleged corruption and incompetence.

Thieu's actions provoked immediate internal rumblings within his administration. On 31 March Vice-President Ky met with a number of senior generals—including Lam, Khang, Thang (three of the four current corps commanders), and Joint General Staff Chief Vien. All were concerned with Thieu's failure to consult with the Military Council prior to the recent command changes, feeling the threat of further unilateral dismissals jeopardized the stability of the armed forces as well as their own futures. Current rumors held that Thieu had asked General Tran Thien Khiem, his former mentor and patron, to return from his post as ambassador to Taiwan and replace Vien as head of the armed forces. Other gossip had Thieu recalling General Do Cao Tri, the ambassador to South Korea, to replace Khang as III Corps commander. Replacements were also rumored for National Police Director Loan and Col. Van Van Cua, mayor of Saigon. All were allies of Ky. Moreover, Thang complained that Thieu was bypassing his corps headquarters, dealing directly with the division commanders in the IV Corps zone, and was planning to replace several province chiefs with more of his own supporters. According to Thang, Thieu had never designated him as the government delegate to the corps and thus he had no authority over province and district chiefs. Ky and the other generals vowed to resign if such practices continued. They demanded that Thieu dismiss his chief political adviser,

---

[6] Msg, CIA Intelligence Rpt, DAIN 050342, 7 Jan 68, sub: Major General Thang's Reasons for Resigning, and Rejection of This Resignation by Senior Generals and President Thieu, SEAB, CMH.
[7] Notes of 2 May 68 (source of quotation), History file 30–A, and Telecon, Westmoreland to Bunker, 2 May 68, sub: Visit to IV Corps and Press Matters, Fonecon file. Both in Westmoreland Papers, HRB, CMH. See also Msgs, Bunker SGN 16225 to President, 171115 Jan 68; Bunker SGN 16515 to SecState, 210650 Jan 68; and Bunker to Rostow, 170907 Dec 67. All in Bunker Papers, DS. Bunker, who perceived Thang as pushy and temperamental, claimed that Ky, Vien, and Edward Lansdale, the influential CIA official, had talked Thang into accepting the corps command.

Nguyen Van Huong, and honor his promise made the previous July to consult closely with the senior generals on all important matters.[8]

As a sign of his independence, Thieu chose not to attend the meeting called by Ky and, despite the threat of mass resignations, continued to reorganize his government and the army. On 18 April he made his minister of planning, General Quang, who in 1966 had been dismissed as the IV Corps commander for corruption, his special assistant for military affairs and security. In May he replaced Prime Minister Nguyen Van Loc, another long-time Ky associate, with Tran Van Huong, a well-known opponent of the vice-president, and brought General Khiem back from Taiwan to be his minister of the Interior.

Both Bunker and Komer wanted Thieu to use the Tet emergency to justify a more far-reaching overhaul of the central administration. While Bunker admitted that "these changes involve very complicated relationships among the leaders here, especially in the military," and cautioned against allowing "our eagerness for change to outweigh the overall objectives of maintaining unity of leadership," he judged Thieu "overly cautious and reluctant to move on such matters" and in need of continuous pressure. Thieu had blamed some of his difficulties on Nguyen Van Loc, Ky's prime minister, but Bunker felt that Thieu, Loc, and Vien just "seemed to have 'complexes' about relieving people" and were reluctant to act alone. Again, the ambassador wanted Thieu to move faster and further, noting that the worst corruption was centered around the police and customs officials at the docks and airports; he wanted Loan dismissed, Huong to clean up the administration, and Vien to do the same with the army. Judging Vien as honest but soft on corruption because of his family's financial involvements, Thieu promised that Huong would move as quickly as possible. The president again explained that no one wished to be responsible for firing officials, noting that Diem had dealt with such matters personally in the early 1960s and had taken all the criticism. Thieu wanted this responsibility shared between all the higher Vietnamese leaders.[9]

In April and May Westmoreland became involved in an acrimonious debate over the selection of a new commander for the politically sensitive Capital Military District. Because the Tet offensive had temporarily made Saigon itself a critical battleground, the MACV chief deemed the appointment significant. Khang still retained control of the district through his deputy, Colonel Giam, but this arrangement had stretched Khang's span of control too far. Westmoreland now suggested that General Pham Van Dong, an old warhorse, be brought out of retirement for the job. Dong had served with French forces during World War II and the Indochina conflict, and had survived Dien Bien Phu to command

---

[8] Msg, CIA Intelligence Rpt, DAIN 630833, 31 May 68, sub: Possible Resignations of Senior Military Officers, SEAB, CMH. According to Bunker, Thang, upon his appointment as corps commander, had espoused the direct election of province chiefs, refused to join the Military Council, and intended to ask Thieu that he *not* be the government delegate (see Msg, Bunker SGN 16515 to SecState, 210650 Jan 68, Bunker Papers, DS); however, the ambassador later told Westmoreland that Thang had changed his mind (see Telecon, Westmoreland to Bunker, 2 Mar 68, Fonecon file, Westmoreland Papers, HRB, CMH).

[9] First, second, and third quotations from Msg, AmEmbassy SGN 21733 to State 111142 Mar 68. Fourth quotation from Msg, Bunker SGN 22386 to SecState, 181200 Mar 68. See also Msg, Bunker SGN 26727 to SecState, 081125 May 68, sub: Thieu's Plans for New Government; Msg, Bunker SGN 27359 to SecState, 151125 May 68. All in Bunker Papers, DS.

a division of Nung tribesmen in the new army of South Vietnam. Among Americans he had the reputation of being an aggressive commander who was accused of "bloodthirstiness in his pursuit of enemy forces,"[10] but had been forced to retire in early 1965 over personal differences with General Nguyen Khanh, then heading the military junta. Dong, however, remained out of work. Despite his close ties with both Thieu and Loan, the Vietnamese leaders still had a healthy fear of older generals like Dong, whom they regarded as too "political"—that is, having political ambitions and loyalties not necessarily identical with those of their own. The "biggest problem," Westmoreland concluded, was still "finding a good man who is also politically acceptable."[11] Thieu agreed but once again seemed willing to stick with Khang and Giam. Appearing to both fear and respect Khang, he admitted to Bunker that "unfortunately we do not have many real generals who know how to command more than a division," including, he added, himself.[12]

At the same time several unforeseen events worked to Thieu's advantage. Loan was severely wounded in combat on 5 May and unable to return to duty. One month later, on 2 June, a rocket fired by a U.S. helicopter wounded Colonel Cua and killed several other Ky supporters in Cholon.[13] Shortly thereafter, an angry General Khang resigned his corps command over the affair. Although there was no evidence that the incident was other than accidental, Khang and many other Vietnamese tended to see the conspiratorial hand of their seemingly all-powerful American allies behind every such event. Had they not, after all, engineered the fall of Diem that had originally propelled the military into politics, and were they not now giving their full support the President Thieu? If so, perhaps it was wiser to step aside and let them have their way. General Thang, apparently of the same mind and frustrated over his inability to control local promotions and appointments, hung on a big longer but finally quit in early July.

In the ensuing weeks Thieu moved quickly. He placed General Nguyen Van Minh, the commander of the 21st Infantry Division in the Delta and a nephew of

---

[10] Intelligence Memorandum 69–43, Directorate of Intelligence, CIA, October 1969, sub: Key Appointees to the South Vietnamese Cabinet, p. 11, copy in SEAB, CMH.

[11] For a running account, see Telecon, Westmoreland to Bunker, 27 Apr 68 (source of quotation), sub: CMD and Thieu; Telecon, Westmoreland to Weyand, 6 May 68, sub: Update. Both in Fonecon file, Westmoreland Papers, HRB, CMH. On Giam, see Msg, CG, II FFV, HOA 1539 to Westmoreland, 21 Oct 67, sub: ARVN Officers Evaluation, COMUSMACV Message file; MFR, Westmoreland, 15 Feb 68, sub: Meeting With President Thieu and General Vien, 1700 H, 14 February, History file 29–56. Both in Westmoreland Papers, HRB, CMH. On Dong, see MFR, Vann, 16 Mar 68, sub: Conversation on 8 March With Retired Major General Pham Van Dong, SEAB, CMH; Intelligence Memorandum CRM 69–43, October 1969, Directorate of Intelligence, CIA, sub: Key Appointees to the South Vietnamese Cabinet, pp. 9–11, copy in SEAB, CMH; Msg, Bunker SGN 25561 to SecState, 241215 Apr 68, sub: Meeting With Thieu, Bunker Papers, DS.

[12] Msg, Bunker SGN 27359 to SecState, 151125 May 68, Bunker Papers, DS.

[13] Msg, COMUSMACV to JCS, 080817 Jun 68, sub: Report of Investigation Concerning the Death of Senior Vietnamese Officials, History file 33–16, Westmoreland Papers, HRB, CMH; Interv, Frank et al. with Khang, 30 Sep 75, pp. 45–48, U.S. Marine Corps Oral History Collection, MCHC; Memo, Col Robert M. Cook, IG, MACV, to COMUSMACV, 29 Jun 68, sub: Combined Investigation of U.S. Helicopter Incident of 2 Jun 68, in Rpt, Inspector General, MACV, sub: Forwarding DF's on Reports of Investigations and Inquiries, 1967 Thru June 1968, annex 1, vol. 1, accession no. 77/0074, RG 334, WNRC. Wounded were Giam; Cua, the mayor of Saigon; and the National Police chief of staff. Killed were the Saigon military police chief, the commander of the 5th Ranger Group, two other high police officials, the Saigon port director, and Ky's brother-in-law.

Tran Van Huong (Thieu's prime minister), in charge of the Capital Military District; replaced Thang in the IV Corps with General Thanh, commander of the 7th Infantry Division; and, as predicted, brought Do Cao Tri back from South Korea to head the III Corps zone. Colonel Hai, whom Westmoreland had previously nominated to head the Capital Military District, replaced Loan as director of the National Police, and the long-time Ky associate finally dropped out of Saigon politics. Khang somehow made his peace with the president and managed to salvage his Marine Corps Command. Thieu also kept Vien as head of the Joint General Staff, although some Vietnamese generals believed that he continued to hold the job only because of Thieu's reluctance to name a stronger man to the post.[14]

Most of the new appointees had the double virtue of being friends of the president and fairly well thought of by their American advisers. They, in turn, quickly began to purge Ky adherents from their own staffs and commands. With his base of power eroding almost daily, Vice-President Ky went into semiretirement at the coastal town of Nha Trang. Thieu, skittish by nature and uncertain of Ky's intentions, called three coup alerts between April and October 1968, but his caution proved needless. He had outmaneuvered Ky and his supporters, and the new president's leadership of the government and the armed forces went unchallenged.[15]

Mobilization

Thieu also exploited the military crisis to force the government to institute the manpower mobilization measures ardently wished for by General Westmoreland.[16] He did this slowly, gradually overcoming the objections of the national legislature, which had refused to recognize the earlier mobilization decrees issued by the Directory. In January 1968 Thieu temporarily suspended almost all military discharges and, on 10 February, in response to the Tet offensive, recalled fifteen thousand reservists to active duty.[17] At the same time, he began another amnesty program for deserters and draft-dodgers and, to make up combat losses as quickly as possible, returned battlefield laborers (convicted deserters) to active duty status.

Westmoreland and Bunker felt that this was only a beginning. Both urged lowering the draft age to eighteen and recalling older reservists, measures that Americans had long believed necessary if Saigon was to expand its armed forces. Westmoreland was also worried that Thieu might try to obtain extra manpower by drawing men from the various draft-exempt paramilitary organizations being supported by the United States—the police, various types of propaganda and refugee teams, the revolutionary development cadre, and the South Vietnamese Kit Carson Scout force assigned to U.S. combat units—and lobbied successfully

---

[14] Hinh and Tho, *South Vietnamese Society*, pp. 144–45.
[15] Msg, Bunker SGN 32385 to President, 11 Jul 68; Msg, AmEmbassy SGN 39970 to SecState, 10 Oct 68, sub: Talk With President Thieu on Latest Coup Rumors. Both in Bunker Papers, DS.
[16] On mobilization, see USMACV, "Command History, 1968," 1:270–75, HRB, CMH.
[17] Those 18- to 33-year-olds with less than five years of service.

to have such personnel retain their draft-exempt status. The MACV commander also remained opposed to a civilian mobilization, that is, militarizing the civilian work force, on the grounds that the government was too weak and inexperienced to carry out the extensive planning and administrative supervision needed.

Between April and June 1968 Thieu and the South Vietnamese legislature dickered back and forth over the details of a mobilization bill. Both houses rejected Thieu's request for broad authority in this area, but could not agree on a more specific legislation. Finally, a joint session of the legislature agreed on a compromise measure, which was promulgated on 19 June. The bill lowered the military draft age from twenty to eighteen and allowed the government to conscript males between the ages of eighteen and thirty-eight for service in either the regulars or the territorials. The term of service was made indefinite, or as long as the war lasted. In addition, the legislation specified that youths of seventeen and men between the ages of thirty-nine and forty-three could be conscripted for noncombat military service, and all other males between sixteen and fifty were to serve in a new paramilitary organization, the People's Self-Defense Force, a part-time hamlet militia.

In the meantime, Saigon had sponsored a vigorous recruiting campaign to replace combat casualties and bring the armed forces up to their authorized 1968 strength of 712,000. By 30 June 1968 Saigon claimed to have 765,000 servicemen in uniform, representing a temporary overstrength of 48,000 and a substantial headstart on the goals envisioned by the various improvement and modernization programs currently under consideration. American advisers were exceedingly pleased, and General Abrams released funds for an additional 34,000 spaces on 1 July and the remainder by October. When it appeared that the South Vietnamese would soon reach their new 801,000 force ceiling, the Joint General Staff proposed suspending the general recruiting effort. Not wishing to see the momentum of the mobilization halted, Abrams obtained approval to raise the authorized force level of the armed forces to 850,000, and recruiting and training continued at the same pace. Army planners felt that they could ensure delivery of almost all new equipment requested by Westmoreland and Abrams by mid-1969. The only bottleneck to activating new units was in training personnel for those forces using complex war materiel, such as aircraft, ships, and the more sophisticated electronic equipment.[18]

Sustained recruiting was necessary for another reason. Whatever the cause—influx of new recruits, heavy combat, dilution of good leadership—the desertion rate, which had fallen in 1967, steadily rose throughout 1968. Starting in February in the midst of the Tet offensive, desertions in the armed forces doubled from 4,000–5,000 per month to 10,000–12,000, reaching a peak of 15,060 during October and 139,670 for the entire year. During this period the monthly desertion rate (monthly deserters per 1,000 troops) rose from the 10–11 per 1,000 of 1967 to 15–16, without, however, reaching the high levels of 1965 and 1966 (*see Tables 3 and 11*). The losses were slightly higher for the regular army (58 percent), but advis-

---

[18] MACV Briefing for Secretary of Defense, 15 Jul 68, pp. 34–36, SEAB, CMH; Fact Book, MACV, December 1968 (updated), MICRO 1/1968, RG 334, WNRC.

New Recruits Entering an Induction Center

ers felt that many of them simply reenlisted in territorial units closer to home. Some 23,633 deserters returned to service during the year, but the bulk of these came back in February, March, and April (4,599, 7,484, 2,719), perhaps reflecting the confusion of the Tet fighting and the general amnesty that ended on 15 March. American leaders could only press the South Vietnamese to improve their desertion apprehension programs throughout the year. Vien, for his part, established monthly desertion quotas—acceptable maximum desertion rates for all commands—in September, and in October liberalized the army's restrictive leave policies and ordered district headquarters to provide lodging, transportation, and messing for military transients. Many deserters, he felt, were simply average soldiers trying to go home for a few days. Apprehension of deserters was the responsibility of the National Police, and in this realm Vien could only urge them to be more vigilant—and more honest—in issuing and checking identification cards and to hasten completion of the fingerprint identification system for the armed forces. Between March 1968 and April 1969, Saigon tried over 20,000 soldiers for desertion and sentenced over 11,000 to battlefield labor units.[19]

[19] USMACV, "Command History, 1968," 1:275–80, HRB, CMH; Fact Sheet, MACJ–14, 28 May 69, sub: RVNAF Desertions, MICRO 3/1751, RG 334, WNRC; Fact Sheet, MACJ–14, sub: RVNAF Deserter Trials (as of 30 Apr 69), SEAB, CMH.

TABLE 15—SELECTED ANNUAL PROMOTIONS FOR CALENDAR YEAR 1969

Grade	Number Considered	Number Recommended	Goal	Percent Goal/Recommended
Colonel	182	55	357	15.4
Lieutenant Colonel	1,080	598	903	66.2
Major	4,321	1,647	2,362	69.7
Captain	6,642	6,642	8,528	77.9
Total	12,225	8,942	12,150	73.6

Source: Fact Sheet, MACJ-14, 31 Jan 69, sub: RVNAF Promotions, MICRO 1/2265, RG 334, WNRC.

The Reform Effort

The Tet fighting and the ensuing expansion of the armed forces further de-layed adoption of the administrative reforms advocated by MACV. Progress in liberalizing promotions was unsatisfactory, and career advancement for offi-cers remained hamstrung by rigid promotion rules, favoritism, and politics.[20] There was no mandatory retirement for officers, and many battalions were still commanded by senior captains and regiments by senior majors, with little hope of promotion. The number of senior noncommissioned officers entering the officer corps numbered 1,337 during the first half of the year but fell to a few hundred during the second half, while battlefield commissions awarded to non-commissioned officers remained insignificant—less than 100—and the lack of the required academic degrees prevented their further advancement.[21] Of 6,840 offi-cer promotions in the first half of 1968, 2,895 were automatic advancements at company-grade level (aspirant to second lieutenant, second to first lieutenant); 2,193 were special promotions; 1,282 were annual merit promotions; and 110 were battlefield promotions. Under American impetus, the Joint General Staff began a forced three-year promotion program in September to fill 90 percent of the officer positions at the authorized grade level. This entailed promoting large numbers of company-grade officers, lieutenants and captains, into the field-grade ranks and greatly expanding the number of colonels and generals. Not surprisingly, MACV expectations were once again too optimistic. Vien's promo-tion boards ruled on special and annual promotions to captain, major, lieutenant colonel, and colonel, and President Thieu himself controlled all general officer advancements. Both proved extremely parsimonious. When the number of spe-cial promotions began to fall off at the end of 1968, the Joint General Staff raised the annual promotion quota, and when the number of annual promotions proved too small, Vien reconvened the board to reconsider all candidates who had been turned down. The results were again disappointing (*Table 15*). Thieu proved equally cautious and, for example, approved only two of fifteen colonels recommended by the board for promotion to brigadier general. Thus at the end of 1968 the regular forces were short three-quarters of their general officers, one-

[20] A 9 May 1968 decree made attendance at the staff school a requirement for promotion above captain. See Fact Book, MACV, December 1968, MICRO 1/2193, RG 334, WNRC.
[21] In contrast, during World War II the American Army relied heavily on direct commissions from enlisted ranks to make up for heavy company-grade officer casualties.

TABLE 16—SOUTH VIETNAMESE OFFICER STRENGTH, REGULAR FORCES,[a]
DECEMBER 1968

Grade	Authorized	Available	Shortage
Generals			
Five-star	1	0	1
Four-star	2	1	1
Three-star	19	9	10
Two-star	61	19	42
One-star	104	14	90
Total generals	187	43	144
Colonels	591	43	548
Lieutenant Colonels	1,774	737	1,037
Majors	4,215	2,483	1,732
Total field grade	6,580	3,263	3,317
Captains	11,349	6,900	4,449
1st Lieutenants, 2d Lieutenants, Aspirants	23,509	25,869	(+2,360) [b]
Total company grade	34,858	32,769	2,089
Grand total	41,625	36,075	5,550

[a] Army, navy, air force, marine corps.

[b] In excess of authorized.

Source: Fact Sheet, MACJ–14, 28 May 69, sub: RVNAF Officer and NCO Strength, MICRO 3/1763, RG 334, WNRC. Total RVNAF officer and NCO strength figures are provided in Appendix B of this volume.

half of their field-grade officers, and 4,449 out of 11,349 authorized captains, leaving about 26,000 junior-grade officers to take up the slack (Table 16).[22]

The heavy demand for combat replacements, the suspension of some training programs, and the surge of new recruits severely strained the South Vietnamese training system. Most schools and training camps were shut down during the Tet fighting from a few days to several months, and many were heavily damaged. The Vietnamese put most of these installations back into operation quickly and during 1968 expanded them to make room for the great influx of recruits and advanced trainees. In April the Central Training Command raised the official capacity of its camps and centers from 48,500 to an emergency level of 67,700 and in the remaining months of the year pushed 168,355 regular army and Regional Forces recruits and 22,483 Popular Forces recruits through abbreviated training courses. In addition, the command arranged unit training for 13 new infantry battalions and 176 new Regional Forces companies, and refresher training for 13 infantry battalions and 89 Regional Forces companies. It also supervised training for 44 new Regional Forces heavy weapons platoons and for 588 new and 656 existing Popular Forces platoons. The Joint General Staff also reduced the number of Popular Forces training camps from thirty-seven to nineteen and placed the camps under the Central Training Command. Only the ten division training

[22] Fact Sheet, MACJ–14, 31 Jan 69, sub: RVNAF Promotions, MICRO 1/2265; Fact Sheet, MACJ–14, 28 May 69, sub: RVNAF Officer and NCO Strength, MICRO 3/1763; MACV J–1, Briefing on ARVN Promotion System, circa 1968–69, MICRO 74/1191. All in RG 334, WNRC. See also USMACV, "Command History, 1968," 1:284–288, and "1969," 2:IV–53 to IV–62, HRB, CMH.

centers remained independent. One result of the heavy demands placed on the command was the decline in the quality of training. Individual training temporarily fell from twelve to nine weeks (compared to sixteen weeks for an American soldier), and desertion rates among trainees were unusually high.[23]

Saigon's military schools experienced similar strains. In transition from a two- to four-year institute, the Da Lat Military Academy graduated no officers in 1968, but by reducing the officer candidate course from thirty-six to twenty-four weeks, the Central Training Command was able to expand the capacity of the Thu Duc School from 3,800 to 6,000 cadets. Over 12,000 new candidates began training in 1968, and over 19,000 cadets graduated from Thu Duc and the smaller officer schools during the year. The capacity of the Noncommissioned Officers Academy at Nha Trang also expanded from 2,750 to 5,000, but the school replaced its long sixteen-week course by one nine-week program, attended by over 13,000 students during the year. The academy also ran an officer candidate course for about a 1,700 students who could not be accommodated at Thu Duc. Although the South Vietnamese language school had been almostly completely destroyed in the Tet fighting, the Central Training Command quickly rebuilt it, increasing its capacity from 1,000 to 5,000 students.[24]

Programs to improve amenities for South Vietnamese soldiers, veterans, and dependents continued to lag. In January 1968 MACV took on the advisory mission to Saigon's Ministry of Veterans Affairs from State Department agencies, and Westmoreland established a separate veterans advisory activity in his J–1 (Personnel) section and, later in the year, expanded the activity into a Mobilization and War Veterans Advisory Branch. At the same time, Thieu merged the Ministry of Veterans Affairs with the Ministry of Defense, which became the Ministry of Defense and War Veterans. Despite the organizational changes, progress was slow. The Cat Lai project providing vocational training to disabled servicemen was supposed to handle 1,200 annually but graduated only 95 soldiers in 1967 and 191 in 1968. Finding employment proved even more difficult. MACV could do little but request that American and Vietnamese officials expedite security clearances for veterans seeking work, and the ministry made plans to use 1,000 physically handicapped soldiers as security guards, replacing Popular Forces troops. At the urgings of the MACV staff, Saigon also began establishing state factories producing simple military items (operational rations, clothing, small arms ammunition, and so forth) to provide jobs for veterans, and constructed nursing homes for unemployable disabled servicemen. However, a preliminary survey indicated that at least 8,000 physically handicapped servicemen were still on military rolls, showing that much more had to be done.[25]

While military pay rates remained unchanged in 1968, inflation continued to shrink the purchasing power of the piaster. To provide more assistance in this area, commissary outlets increased from 134 to 190 in 1968, and by the end of the year MACV had transferred the financing entirely to Saigon. Although the Joint

[23] USMACV, "Command History, 1968," 1:296–300, HRB, CMH. Fact Sheet, MACT, 3 Apr 68, sub: Training Status of RVNAF, MICRO 3/2290, RG 334, WNRC.
[24] For status of the other schools, see Fact Book, MACV, December 1968 (updated August 1969), MICRO 1/2193, RG 334, WNRC.
[25] USMACV, "Command History, 1968," 1:291–94, HRB, CMH.

Red Cross Representatives at Phu Quoc Island POW Facility

General Staff had spent or committed the $42 million American grant provided by MACV in 1967, the South Vietnamese government contributed $43 million more in foreign exchange credits for further purchases. Revenues from commissary food sales increased from $1 million in 1967 to $25 million in 1968, half of which was used to purchase new commodities. After the funding transfer, MACV closely monitored commissary finances, and General Abrams intervened personally to ensure that the Saigon administration exempted commissary imports from taxation and duties, thereby keeping retail prices low. MACV was also successful in bringing about a more liberal distribution of field rations to Vietnamese combat troops, but was unable to convince Saigon to establish a system of regular unit messes. South Vietnamese military policy limited regular messes to units with thirty or more bachelors assigned, and, even if the means to support a larger effort could have been found, it would have proved extremely difficult to break the Vietnamese soldiers' habit of eating with dependents. Another program supplementing troop rations of units with territorial security missions also fell by the wayside, and U.S. corps, division, and province advisers were even unaware of the $3.56-million program's existence.[26] American control

[26] CORDS Field Evaluation Rpt, Maj Ralph F. Willard and Lt Col L. M. Lopez, 11 Aug 68, sub: Evaluation Report: RVNAF Ration Supplement Program for RVNAF Battalions and RF Companies in Direct Support of Revolutionary Development, SEAB; USMACV, "Command History, 1968," 1:294–96, HRB. Both in CMH.

and direction of such matters could simply not be extended beyond a certain level.

Dependent housing programs again constituted the greatest disappointment of the year. The self-help construction project, approved back in December 1966 and supported by American building material, was a complete failure. Few of the planned units were ever built, and General Abrams could only comment laconically that at the current rate of construction it would take fourteen years to finish even this minor effort. The United States also supplied half of the funds for the South Vietnamese regulars' dependent housing program and building material for a similar Popular Forces effort. But the Vietnamese completed only 4,912 units for the regulars in 1968, scheduled only about 5,000 more to be built in 1969, and had made no preparations for the planned 79,000 units for the Popular Forces.[27]

The construction of prisoner-of-war (POW) facilities was more successful. In 1968 the Joint General Staff expanded the camps in each zone and, at Westmoreland's insistence, constructed a new central facility on Phu Quoc Island. Total capacity for the mainland camps was about 10,000, with room for another 12,000–13,000 on Phu Quoc. International Red Cross representatives regularly inspected the camps to ensure compliance with the Geneva Conventions. The disposition of prisoners, however, remained an area of concern. Many captured Viet Cong adherents, especially those in nonmilitary positions, became political prisoners, incarcerated in mainland jails and prisons or in the infamous island facility of Con Son off the southern coast of South Vietnam. Thousand of others, however, who had supposedly surrendered voluntarily, went to *Chieu Hoi* ("Open Arms") reindoctrination centers. Although the *Chieu Hoi* effort inevitably included many who had only marginal affiliations with the Viet Cong, it also included high-ranking leaders and, in several instances, entire enemy units whose personnel were obviously not given POW status (and it is doubtful that they desired it). Of the 18,171 former Viet Cong released from these centers in 1968, many joined the American Kit Carson Scout program, Saigon's propaganda teams, or the South Vietnamese armed forces. The number of such "returnees" also showed that Saigon's army was not the only one with a serious desertion problem.[28]

---

[27] Msg, Abrams MAC 5878 to Weyand, 040943 May 68, Abrams Papers, HRB, CMH; Fact Book, MACV, December 1968 (updated), MICRO 1/1968, RG 334, WNRC; MFR, Col George E. Dexter, SACSA, JCS, 28 Aug 69, sub: Trip Report, SEAB, CMH.

[28] USMACV, "Command History, 1968," 1:549–51 and 2:851–59, HRB; Msg, COMUSMACV MAC 13366 to CINCPAC, 110550 May 68, sub: Vietnamese Prisoners of War, SEAB. Both in CMH.

18

Progress or Stagnation?

In 1968 the American field advisory network was beginning to adjust to the renewed emphasis on South Vietnamese performance. MACV created about two thousand more field advisory positions during the year for newly activated regular units and raised the number of advisory cells (MATs and MALTs) working with territorials to 353. However, the strength and responsibilities of the regular army advisory teams remained the same, as did the preparation for advisory duty and the general philosophy behind the entire effort.[1] The regimental and battalion teams still consisted of only two to four advisers, making it extremely difficult to operate physically on a 24-hour basis or to do more than act as fire support coordinators and liaison teams.[2] Many of the battalion advisers, lieutenants and junior captains, lacked the experience to do much more. The Special Forces units advising the CIDG program were not much better off. But the mid-level advisers at regimental, division, and province headquarters and on Special Forces B and C teams were now seasoned veterans, many serving their second and even third tour in South Vietnam. It was in these officers that the heart of the field advisory effort now resided.

Advising on the Ground

The precise mission of an individual adviser was still subject to much disagreement due, for the most part, to the different circumstances each adviser found himself. In mid-1968, for example, Maj. Charles C. Pritchett, a field historian and former adviser himself, interviewed many tactical advisory team members to ascertain their actual role while on operations. As others before him,

[1] See O.W. Hammond, *Role of the Advisor* (Control Data Corp., 1969). Hammond observed that American Foreign Service officers, in contrast, received ten months of language instruction before beginning overseas tours that normally lasted at least two years.
[2] For example, see comments in Intervs, Maj Charles C. Pritchett, CO, 20th Military History Detachment, with Maj Paul J. Kennedy, Jr., Senior Adviser, 43d Regt, 18th Div, 16 Jul 68, VNIT 197; with Lt Col George G. Hines, Senior Adviser, 9th Div, 21 Sep 68, VNIT 291; with Maj Richard W. Pfeiffer, Senior Adviser, 3d Airborne Bde, Airborne Div (Team 168), 10 Jun 68, VNIT 167; and with Maj Joseph R. Lanthrom, Senior Adviser, 9th Regt, 5th Div, 4 Sep 68, VNIT 258. All in HRB, CMH.

he concluded that their "prime responsibility" was not advising, but acting as liaison officers and providing American combat support. In the field their role "was characterized by the continued coordinating with U.S. units operating in the vicinity, obtaining and controlling light fire teams [heavily armed helicopters], U.S. Air Force tactical airstrikes, US artillery support and helicopters for general use."[3] Lt. Col. Evan F. Riley, an adviser in the III Corps area, explained that, when not on operations, he served primarily as "an expediter," pushing the Vietnamese into doing a variety of chores that they already knew how to accomplish but tended to put off until the last minute.[4] Yet another judgment was rendered by the IV Corps logistics adviser, Lt. Col. William E. Schiller, who related that he and his staff section were "totally immersed" in supporting the subordinate advisory teams in the corps zone and that he rarely if ever acted in an advisory capacity within the corps headquarters.[5]

Others saw their role differently. Maj. Joseph R. Lanthrom, a senior adviser in the nearby 9th Regiment, 5th Infantry Division, took strong exception to the idea that American advisers were primarily fire support coordinators. In his view, "ARVN couldn't get through a normal day without our support" and "wouldn't last two weeks" if the advisers left. There were too many chores, he complained, "that these people are either incapable, incompetent, or too lazy to do." While describing his relationships with the Vietnamese as excellent and while enjoying his work, he was "sure" that, if alone, the regimental commanders "would plan operations where they could not make contact" and "absolutely sure" that the battalion commanders would do the same. Only by constantly nagging and cajoling their counterparts were the advisers able to make the South Vietnamese carry out their assigned tasks. The Vietnamese, he went on, "can't or they won't plan in advance," and their entire approach to the war was lackadaisical. It had taken ten months of work, for example, to persuade his counterpart to conduct night operations. "If we had Vietnamese that were as concerned about their plight as we are," he concluded, "our efforts to help them—the advisory duty—wouldn't have been any problem at all." Lanthrom, however, was optimistic. Despite his misgivings, he believed that the combat performance of the South Vietnamese had improved since his first tour as an adviser in 1965 and, looking back on his experiences as an adviser in the South Korean Army, predicted that the Saigon army would continue to do so through sustained advisory tutelage.[6]

Lanthrom's views were also common in the field, but they hardly reflected the conventional wisdom at MACV headquarters. In recognition of the changing "advisory" status in some units, MACV contemplated further reductions in the

---

[3] Quoted words from Rpt, Pritchett, 3 Jun 68, sub: The Saigon Offensive, 5–12 May 1968, VNIT 140, HRB, CMH. See also Memo, Maj John A. Cash, Historian, CMH, to Charles MacDonald, Chief, Current History Branch, CMH, 29 May 68, VNIT 131, HRB, CMH, which noted that the then Office of the Chief of Military History had requested military history detachments in Vietnam to examine the role of advisers and that the field historians found "that in most instances the advisor really plays a liaison rather than an advisory role."

[4] Interv, Maj Lawrence D. Sylvan, 45th Military History Detachment, with Riley (hereafter cited as Riley Interv), 3 Jul 69, VNI 437, HRB, CMH.

[5] Interv, Pritchett with Schiller, Advisory Team 96, 20 Oct 68, VNIT 290, HRB, CMH.

[6] Interv, Pritchett with Lanthrom, 4 Sep 68, VNIT 258, HRB, CMH.

size of the combat advisory teams and once again debated the merits of changing their official mission from advice to "combat support coordination." At the suggestion of Lt. Gen. William R. Peers, the U.S. I Field Force commander, MACV experimentally reduced the advisory contingent of the South Vietnamese 22d Infantry Division in late 1968 to an austere combat assistance team (CAT). But MACV discovered that eliminating too many positions made it impossible for the advisory teams to carry out their liaison functions, and subsequent investigations by the MACV Office of the Inspector General also revealed that many of the field teams were still understrength and desperately short of critical equipment, especially tactical radios. In some cases, nearby American units had loaned officers, noncom-

Advising Vietnamese Trainees on M60 Firing Techniques

missioned officers, and communications equipment to the detachments so that they could put at least one adviser with each South Vietnamese combat battalion.[7] Nevertheless, MACV declared the CAT reduction concept sound and planned to reduce all division and corps advisory teams during 1969.[8]

Westmoreland also wanted to divest MACV and the 5th Special Forces Group of the valuable but troublesome CIDG program. The United States, he observed, could not support the effort "ad infinitum" and something had to be done "to get us out of the picture." Attempts to convert CIDG units to territorials had failed in 1966 and 1967, but he felt that the current mobilization efforts of Saigon offered a new chance and advised Ambassador Bunker that "if we don't take advantage of this opportunity that general mobilization affords us, [it] may be a long time before we can solve this problem again." However, with no improvement in relations between the Vietnamese and Montagnards since 1966, conversion efforts had little success. MACV managed to transform only three CIDG camps into Regional Forces during the year. On the other hand, the American corps-level commanders made extensive use of the various MIKE Force reaction units throughout the year, and, despite several cases of combat exhaustion, their

---

[7] DFs, MACIG–INSP to Asst CofS, J–5, MACV, 17 Sep 68, sub: Special Inspection of the 9th Infantry Division Detachment, Advisory Team 60, and 25 Aug 68, sub: Special Inspection of the 1st Infantry Division Advisory Detachment, Advisory Team 3, SEAB, CMH. Both reports noted the absence of any record of previous IG inspections of the teams.

[8] Fact Sheet, MACMA–PP, 13 Aug 69, sub: Combat Assistance Team (CAT), MICRO 40/0983, RG 334, WNRC. See also Msg, Peers NHT 875 to Abrams, 261120 Jun 68; Msg, Peers NHT 896 to Abrams, 301225 Jun 68; and Msg, Peers to Abrams, 051153 Oct 68. All in Abrams Papers, HRB, CMH.

Adviser in II Corps Checking Weapon of a Popular Forces Soldier

continued employment as fire brigades in the remote border regions seemed assured.[9]

Evaluating the South Vietnamese

To sharpen the evaluation reports submitted by the field advisers, MACV adopted an entirely new reporting system early in 1968. Dubbed the System for Evaluating the Effectiveness of RVNAF (Republic of Vietnam Armed Forces), or SEER,[10] the revision entailed the preparation of quarterly reports that were more detailed but less time consuming than the old monthly evaluations. To reduce adviser bias and subjectivity, SEER used a standard format for all tactical advisers. In general, it addressed three areas: military performance, personnel

[9] Quoted words from Telecon, Westmoreland to Bunker, 5 May 68, Fonecon file, Westmoreland Papers. See also USMACV, "Command History, 1968," 1:344; Msg, Kerwin HOA 2194 to Abrams, 141030 Dec 68, Abrams Papers. All in HRB, CMH. By December 1968 the CIDG program was 42,000 strong in fifty-three camps with 231 regular companies, 43 MIKE Force companies, and 123 reconnaissance platoons. The ethnic composition of the force was now 42 percent Montagnard, 44 percent Vietnamese (mostly religious sects), and 14 percent other nationalities. See Fact Book, MACV, December 1968, MICRO 1/1968, and especially 2062, RG 334, WNRC.

[10] For details, see MACV Directive 335–13, 1 Jan 68, sub: System for Evaluating the Effectiveness of RVNAF (SEER), SEAB; USMACV, "Command History, 1967," 1:191–93, HRB; Fact Sheet, MACJ–341, 8 Jan 68, sub: MACV System for Evaluating the Effectiveness of RVNAF (SEER), SEAB. All in CMH.

324

and materiel status, and long-term historical trends. The basic feeder report was a multiple-choice questionnaire with 157 topics. Subject areas included counterpart relations, composition and employment of units, unit capabilities and effectiveness, leadership, discipline and morale, training, equipment, combat support, and staff operations. Advisers were asked to judge, for example, whether their counterparts accepted advice "always," "frequently," "occasionally," "rarely," or "never"; if staff work was "effective," "fairly effective," or "ineffective"; and whether fire support could be provided in five, ten, twenty, or thirty minutes. In many cases advisers had to grade their units by using both Vietnamese and American standards in such areas as leadership, operations, training, and fire support. One regimental adviser, Maj. Paul J. Kennedy, Jr., described it as "a multiple guess-type report which requires about 3 hours," with another day or so spent reviewing the submissions of his subordinate battalion advisers."[11] With some modification MACV adopted the same system for evaluating the South Vietnamese Marines, Air Force, Navy, and Territorial Forces.

Advisers also continued to submit monthly statistical reports on the activities of each South Vietnamese unit. Elaborate in scope, these reports detailed the size (battalion, company, platoon) and duration of each operation, the unit mission (search and destroy or security, directly supporting or not directly supporting the area security campaign), and the results (enemy and friendly losses in men and materiel). They broke down combat casualties into eight categories (mines, artillery, sniper fire, and so forth), operations into eleven, and enemy-initiated actions into eighteen. The MACV staff placed this data, together with the SEER submissions, on computer data cards for further analysis. With this information MACV analysts felt that they could better assess the status and performance of each South Vietnamese unit, and U.S. agencies in Saigon and Washington used such information, along with that generated by American units, to measure the progress in the war effort on the battlefield.[12]

The reliability of MACV's methodology was open to question. Despite the wealth of statistical data on Vietnamese units, it often fell far short of reporting what actually was taking place in the field. Preliminary advisory judgments of South Vietnamese performance during the Tet offensive ran the gamut from excellent to poor. Many small outposts were overrun and some territorial units refused to fight; many others, regulars and territorials alike, defended their bases and homes tenaciously and acts of self-sacrifice were common. Westmoreland estimated South Vietnamese combat losses at about 2,000 dead during the first two weeks of the offensive, compared to 1,000 American soldiers killed and over 31,000 enemy claimed dead. At Hue the South Vietnamese 1st Infantry Division clung tenaciously to its command post in the old citadel and, assisted primarily by South Vietnamese ranger, airborne, and marine units, managed to clear the city after taking about 2,000 casualties (357 dead, 1,830 wounded, 42 missing),

---

[11] Interv, Pritchett with Kennedy, 16 Jul 68, VNIT 197, HRB, CMH.

[12] For a discussion on the use of the statistical evidence, see Thomas C. Thayer, "How To Analyze a War Without Fronts: Vietnam, 1965–72," *Journal of Defense Research*, Series B: Tactical Warfare Analysis of Vietnam Data, 7B, no. 3 (Fall 1975). During the period 1966–72 Thayer was director of the Southeast Asia Office, Office of the Assistant Secretary of Defense for Systems Analysis, which published the periodic *Southeast Asia Analysis Report*.

Fighting To Hold Saigon. *A South Vietnamese Marine grenadier (top left) prepares for action, while rangers (top right) clear a side street and dismounted cavalry (bottom) carry a wounded comrade to safety.*

and claiming 2,642 enemy killed (681 individual weapons and 129 crew-served weapons captured).[13] A more serious problem was the reluctance of South Vietnamese units to pursue enemy forces after overcoming their initial attacks. Except for some of the marine, airborne, and other select troops, most units were more concerned with their own immediate safety and with that of their dependents. As the offensive developed, many Vietnamese corps and division commanders and province chiefs pulled their units out of the countryside to defend towns, cities, key installations (such as airfields and bridges), and their own bases. Westmoreland and Abrams wanted them back out in the field as quickly as possible performing security tasks. But too often the Vietnamese commanders relied on aggressive American commanders or excessive American firepower to destroy enemy forces that had entrenched themselves in many urban areas. For example, at Can Tho, the capital of the delta region, South Vietnamese troops refused to attack the Viet Cong forces occupying the local university and the latter finally had to be rooted out by massive air attacks. A "very bad show" and a "very lousy job," said Westmoreland. Both he and Abrams were also concerned over the South Vietnamese propensity for looting, which General Abrams described as "extensive and systematic," especially in the urban areas. Several days later, however, Westmoreland rationalized that "looting has always been a problem for commanders in all wars," that "this war is no exception," and that "it will be ever thus." Although his reports to Washington understandably omitted the worst South Vietnamese debacles, they were also openly critical of Saigon's military leadership.[14]

Despite some notable exceptions, Westmoreland felt that the various Vietnamese military components had performed creditably during Tet. Their units had held together and had repulsed numerous enemy attacks in almost every province, and there had been no popular uprising or mass defection as predicted by enemy leaders. More important, he estimated that total enemy losses had been staggering—35,000 to 45,000—while combined American–South Vietnamese fatalities numbered about 6,000.[15] Westmoreland interpreted the 1:7 kill ratio in favor of Saigon as "one of the best indicators" of South Vietnamese military progress.[16] But until the new SEER system could be implemented, MACV had only the vaguest notion of what had actually occurred. The high enemy losses might be the product of massive American air and artillery support or faulty enemy tactics, or perhaps figments of someone's imagination. The impressionis-

---

[13] For studies highlighting South Vietnamese operations during this period, see Joint General Staff J-5, *The Viet Cong "Tet" Offensive (1968)*, ed. Pham Van Son and trans. Robert J. Parr et al. (Saigon, circa 1969); Hoang Ngoc Lung, *The General Offensives of 1968–69*, Indochina Monographs (Washington, D.C.: U.S. Army Center of Military History, 1981). On combat losses, see USMACV, "Command History, 1968," 2:906, HRB, CMH; Historical Summary, Advisory Teams 3 and 4, "The Battle of Hue, 31 Jan–25 Feb 68," Peter E. Kelly Papers, MHI.

[14] First and second quotations from Telecon, Westmoreland to Eckhardt, 6 Feb 68, Fonecon file. Third quotation from Msg, Abrams PHB 202 to Westmoreland, 020330 Mar 68, COMUSMACV Message file. Remaining quotations from Msg, Westmoreland MAC 3630 to Wheeler, 160515 Mar 68, sub: Performance of ARVN During Battle of Hue, COMUSMACV Message file. All in Westmoreland Papers, HRB, CMH.

[15] For various figures, see USMACV, "Command History, 1968," 1:131, HRB, CMH; Pacific Command, *Report on the War in Vietnam*, p. 161.

[16] COMUSMACV Fact Book, 1968, vol. 1, p. J–1–B, Westmoreland Papers, HRB, CMH.

tic advisory reports and evaluations that first arrived at Westmoreland's desk could not provide him the objective data needed to assess South Vietnamese leadership, tactics, staff work, logistics, and other performance areas during the heavy fighting.

As the smoke cleared in early March, General Wheeler requested a detailed assessment of South Vietnamese military performance and current status. In his preliminary response Westmoreland noted that Vietnamese battle casualties numbered 9,754 and unit replacements 14,428, but he had no estimates on what he believed to be "significant losses" from desertion, disease, and accidents. Of the 155 regular South Vietnamese maneuver battalions (regular infantry battalions of all types and cavalry squadrons), his advisers had rated 57 "combat ineffective" on 19 February but only 37 by 1 March. Although advisory evaluations of South Vietnamese combat effectiveness were still incomplete, Westmoreland judged that "overall reports" indicated a generally "satisfactory performance." Saigon's logistical system was operating "satisfactorily," and, except for minor interruptions to local cable and wire services, its communications system was intact.[17]

On 13 March Wheeler passed Westmoreland's judgments on to the secretary of defense, adding updated statistics and his own comments based upon his recent visit. He explained that, by MACV yardsticks, Vietnamese units were "combat ineffective" when combat losses and desertions reduced them to less than 60 percent of their authorized strength (54 percent for airborne units). A massive influx of replacements during February had restored many units to a "combat effective" status. In terms of "the standard indicators of the effectiveness of a military force"—"kill ratio, number of combat operations, casualties and weapon losses"—Wheeler felt that Saigon's forces were "functioning in a satisfactory manner." Appended statistics backed this up, showing the South Vietnamese kill ratio had risen from 2.92:1 in January to about 6:1 in March; the average number of weekly search-and-destroy operations had increased from 50 to 80; and the number of weapons captured compared to the number lost had remained at about 3:1 in favor of Saigon. He conceded that the record was not "unblemished." There were "instances of poor individual and unit performance," and many units were "tired and on the defensive." But he emphasized that "RVNAF fought and continues to fight in spite of being the primary enemy target and suffering heavy casualties," and "there were no unit and relatively few individual defections." Wheeler added that most American officers were "pleasantly surprised" at the South Vietnamese performance, and he predicted "increased effectiveness" from the South Vietnamese once mobilization and modernization measures were fully instituted.[18]

On 21 March Westmoreland submitted a more comprehensive and generally optimistic staff report.[19] The Tet offensive, it concluded, had "had [a] less serious effect on the RVNAF personnel situation than was initially anticipated"; South

---

[17] Msg, Westmoreland MAC 03023 to Wheeler, 3 Mar 68, sub: Present Status of RVNAF, COMUS-MACV Message file, Westmoreland Papers, HRB, CMH.

[18] Memo, Wheeler to SecDef, 13 Mar 68, sub: RVNAF Effectiveness, SEAB, CMH.

[19] Quoted words in this and the following two paragraphs from Rpt, MACJ-341, 21 Mar 68, sub: Report-Assessment of RVNAF Status, SEAB, CMH.

Vietnamese morale and esprit were good, "and, in fact, seem to be higher than before the Tet offensive [had] begun." Although pointing out several weaknesses, the report emphasized that they were being thoroughly addressed. Its harshest words were reserved for the Territorial Forces—"treachery on the part of individual RF/PF soldiers or small groups, many watch towers and outposts abandoned without significant contact with the enemy"—and noted a major "degradation" of the territorials in twenty of the forty-four South Vietnamese provinces. But even for these units, the evaluation was positive: "RF/PF unit performance was generally better than expected by most advisors" and, in general, the territorials "stood and fought."

Although giving the impression of a complete survey, Westmoreland's March study had little to say on South Vietnamese logistics, performance in combat (as opposed to results), and leadership. The report rated units as "combat effective" if they had the "capability" of accomplishing "assigned missions," but also gave overall ratings of either "satisfactory," "average," "marginal," or "unsatisfactory" to each unit. Interpretations of these categories were left up to the reader and contributed to certain anomalies in evaluating unit status. For example, the report graded the 9th Infantry Division headquarters and the three infantry regiments and one artillery battalion assigned to the division all "marginal," because of low strengths and poor leadership, but it described the "overall combat effectiveness" of the division as "satisfactory." On the other hand, it gave low marks to the 1st Division, a unit that had performed exceedingly well during Tet, because of heavy casualties, while, at the same time, also awarding it the overall rating of "satisfactory."

The sections treating the South Vietnamese Navy and Air Force were more simplistic. The report described the sea service as having "met and exceeded all operational commitments," rated its performance as "excellent," and cited improvements in both morale and leadership. It described the marine battalions as "highly effective" and the performance and leadership of the air force as "exemplary," "exceptional," "excellent," "courageous," and "outstanding." Air Force personnel had performed with "unparalleled zeal and dedication"; their morale had steadily improved; and strike sorties, flare drops, and supply missions had greatly increased. It gave similar treatments to the training and school centers, the logistical system, and communications network. Although Westmoreland's assessment contained enough critical comments to give it a veneer of objectivity and truth, too much of it was simply public relations–oriented and uncritical. Without any interpretation of the rating categories, it had little value and its primary use was to reassure Washington that all was well.

An internal analysis of the March report by General Davis, the MACV J-1, found the lack of consistency and numerous contradictions in ratings disturbing. Davis had a manual cross-check done of recent surveys of South Vietnamese military leaders and discovered that a previous survey had recommended eight South Vietnamese commanders for immediate relief, while the March report rated one of these officers as "outstanding," three as "excellent," and four as "satisfactory." The latter also rated fifty-seven other officers—mostly captains, majors, and lieutenant colonels—as "unsatisfactory," of which only three had been noted as deficient in any previous reports. Davis also saw little correlation between the March report and a new assessment prepared by MACV in April. Of the fifty-seven commanders rated "unsatisfactory" by the April survey, none of their units or staffs had been cited for leadership problems in the March report; conversely, none of the units cited by the March report for leadership deficiencies had their commanders appear on the new survey's unsatisfactory list. He admitted that changes in advisers or changes in tactical situations explained some of the contradictions, but not all of them. General Abrams was also uneasy, noting that "the preponderance of outstanding ratings throughout the RVNAF . . . appears inconsistent with on-the-ground observations and results," and recommended "a closer look at the evaluation process."[20]

The SEER report instituted in January was unable to resolve the confusion. Despite claims of objectivity, the SEER questionnaire was inherently subjective, and much of the resulting data was incompatible with earlier reports, making the identification of long-term trends difficult. Differences in mission, enemy activity, terrain, weather, and combat support, and the inability to tie quarterly evaluations and ratings with specific goals, made it impossible for SEER analysts to arrive at meaningful comparisons of units or realistic estimates of progress.[21] The cumulative data received through SEER (for example, 20 percent of the advisers felt that their counterparts "frequently seek advice"), they admitted, served only to provide MACV with "general indicators of progress or regression."[22] The assessment of individual units still depended on the weight that evaluators assigned to each subject area.

Compounding the confusion in evaluating South Vietnamese units was the tendency of some MACV analysts to ascribe improved combat effectiveness to the arrival of new equipment, especially the M16 rifles.[23] In the light of favorable feedback from the field, the new M16s seemed responsible for higher Vietnamese kill ratios and for a general increase in morale, esprit de corps, and aggressiveness. Undoubtedly, the South Vietnamese soldiers were pleased with the new "Big Black Gun." If anything, one adviser felt, they cleaned and oiled their new rifles too much, feeling that "if a little bit of oil is good, then a whole bunch of oil" is better.[24] However, although the lightweight automatic rifles were a boon to the South Vietnamese soldier, initial claims of improved combat effectiveness were skewed by a distribution policy that favored better units like the airborne and marines. More time was needed for more balanced judgments.

Faced with continued irregularities and contradictions between SEER and other evaluations, MACV revised the feeder reports in midyear. To provide greater perspective, the third SEER evaluation for the quarter ending in Septem-

---

[20] Quoted words from Ltr, Abrams to Weyand, 23 May 68, sub: Evaluation Reporting. See also DF, MACJ–14, to CofS, MACV, circa April 1968, sub: RVNAF Evaluation. Both in SEAB, CMH.

[21] SEER Evaluation, January–March 1968, MICRO 135, RG 334, WNRC, noted these factors and warned that "a comparison of the unit scores or the operational results of units facing different environments should be approached with caution."

[22] DF, Maj Gen Elias C. Townsend, MACV J–3, 19 Sep 68, sub: SEER Follow-on, Regressive Trends, SEAB, CMH.

[23] See Talking Paper, MACJ–341, circa 1968, sub: Evaluation of the Impact of Arming the Vietnamese Army with the M–16 Rifle, MICRO 3/1907, RG 334, WNRC; and studies in RVNAF I & M: M–16 files, SEAB, CMH.

[24] Interv, Pritchett with Lanthrom, 4 Sep 68, VNIT 258, HRB, CMH.

ber 1968 called for comments from senior advisers to clarify and supplement the raw data. The results revealed many long-standing problems that had not registered on previous surveys: the tendency of security missions to "reduce the effectiveness of ARVN units through [the] development of complacency and erosion of initiative"; the close tie between poor dependent housing and low troop morale; the unwillingness of commanders to delegate authority, and thereby develop leadership and initiative in subordinates; the lack of any effective career management program; and the general belief that combat operations obviated the need for training. The new evaluation also pointed out the inability of MACV to show any correlation between the rate of desertion, the number of new recruits, the level of combat activity, leadership, or morale. In one case it noted that a unit's declining statistical performance was probably the result of enemy withdrawals from its area of operation; in another it pointed out that lower ratings were possibly due to a 75-percent turnover in battalion advisers, because "new advisers are known to make more severe assessments."[25]

Although the MACV staff considered SEER a "valid" report, the military analysts recognized that much of the data on unit performance would have to remain "uncorrelated." The task of converting the individual responses to computer data cards was "excessively error-prone and time-consuming." Comparisons of unit effectiveness were possible only when similar units were opposing enemy forces of equal size, composition, and mission. Kill ratios told little by themselves. Advisers found the application of both American and Vietnamese standards highly confusing, and their evaluations were hampered by the short terms they spent advising any particular unit. And, as in the past, responses to questions involving the relationship between advisers and counterparts were often more favorable than warranted because the advisers were, in effect, grading themselves.[26]

Roles and Missions

American advisers in the field were also running up against some of the same old problems involving leadership and roles and missions. In the II Corps Highlands General Peers, Lu Lan, and the two Vietnamese infantry division commanders fretted over the poor quality of the South Vietnamese regimental and battalion-level commanders, and their inability to replace them without the approval of Saigon. The 23d Division, based in the remote interior, was regarded as a "backwater" and could not seem to attract good officers; the 22d, nestled in coastal Binh Dinh Province, was a more popular unit but seemed permanently attached to its static security missions.[27]

In February 1968 Lt. Col. William A. Donald (USMC), a MACV CORDS evaluator, made a detailed examination of one of the 22d's regiments providing

[25] SEER Evaluation, July–September 1968, MICRO 135, RG 334, WNRC.
[26] Rockett et al., *SEER Revision*, Document no. ASDIRS 2650, Pentagon Library.
[27] Msg, Peers NHT 742 to Abrams, 050204 Jun 68; Msg, Peers NHT 835 to Abrams, 150530 Sep 68. Both in Abrams Papers, HRB, CMH.

area security. His findings were curious. The Marine Corps officer described the regimental commander as "astute," with "an impressive grasp of VC/NVA tactics and the military significance of terrain," but also as "politically motivated" and "a supreme practitioner of caution." His subordinate battalion commanders were capable, but lacked aggressiveness and imagination. There were few company- or platoon-level operations, he noted, and leadership at the lower levels and on the staffs was minimal. Donald pointed out that almost all operations were planned by the regimental commander, with little assistance from his nominal staff who appeared to serve primarily as bodyguards and aides. Both the regimental and battalion commanders acted as their own intelligence officers, even operating spy networks with their personal funds and friends. He also reported that unit commanders habitually employed internal informants, enforced discipline through whippings or confining soldiers to makeshift "tiger cages" for military infractions, and used prisoners and Viet Cong suspects as laborers. The American advisers interviewed by Donald held that the entire unit was run by an inside clique of favorites, "armed with an uncanny flair for mediocrity," who, despite spending their nights at home when their troops were in the field, were decorated "with awesome regularity." Not surprisingly, Donald reported that the unit was deficient in almost all military activities, allowing the local Viet Cong to dominate the countryside, especially during the hours of darkness. He also noted that the division commander had not visited the regiment or the battalions in several months, and no one appeared concerned over what the unit did or did not accomplish.[28]

The situation described by Donald obviously reflected larger problems at the division and corps levels. In fact, the role of the 22d Division had become a tug-of-war between Peers, who favored employing the unit in mobile operations along the border, and Ambassador Komer, the MACV CORDS deputy, who wanted the South Vietnamese regulars to concentrate on providing security in populated areas. Peers strongly objected to outside intruders like Donald and felt that Komer was clearly interfering with his command prerogatives. Angry, he urged Abrams to do away with the CORDS dual chain of command, arguing that it was the primary culprit behind the inconsistent evaluations that disturbed MACV. One result was a formal complaint lodged by the MACV inspector general against the CORDS staff, criticizing the unilateral evaluations made by CORDS personnel and recommending their replacement by combined inspection teams more understanding of local situations. But Peers' complaints and the entire evaluation problem only reflected the persistent indecision at MACV over the roles and mission of South Vietnamese combat forces and the formulation of allied strategy. By this time even Komer admitted that the practice of putting the South Vietnamese regular units into the population security business "did not work well in practice" and had been originally done only "as a means of getting ARVN to pay some attention to pacification, i.e., protection of the people." Still, he remained reluctant to replace the regulars with territorials and, like Abrams and Bunker, felt that the possibility of an imminent ceasefire made territorial

---

[28] CORDS Field Evaluation Rpt, Donald, 16 Feb 68, sub: Evaluation Report: 41st Regiment, 22d ARVN Division in Support of Pacification, SEAB, CMH.

security a continued high priority. General Peers would just have to learn to get along with the CORDS system.[29]

Similar problems occurred in General Thanh's IV Corps Tactical Zone. Col. Sidney Berry, senior adviser to the South Vietnamese 7th Infantry Division in 1965, had described Thanh as an "aggressive" commander with "sound tactical sense" who "knows when to commit his reserve" and "has a deep understanding of the war and his division."[30] Westmoreland called him the "best division commander in country" in 1967 and "one of my favorite division commanders" in 1968.[31] But Komer's CORDS advisers differed and in 1967 found "his personal cautiousness and reluctance to push the battalions [those in securing missions] into more offensive activities . . . difficult to understand," claiming that he discouraged the initiative and aggressiveness of his subordinates.[32] Komer agreed and in 1968 described Thanh as unaggressive, unimaginative, and "rather a xenophobe."[33] Komer's assistants noted worsening command and control problems at the lower tactical levels and a general confusion over the division's roles and missions. Tactical advisers, they reported, claimed that the army units contributed little more that their "presence" to local security; were idle most of the time; and, when aroused, were content with "merely chasing the VC and showing the flag." Despite all the revolutionary development training, the regular troops were also back in the old "chicken-stealing business," foraging for food and living off the local peasantry.[34]

The differences of opinion may again have only mirrored the confusion in the American and South Vietnamese high commands over what was expected of the Vietnamese units. But in other cases, the matter of roles and missions seemed superfluous. For example, a battalion of the 9th Regiment, 5th Division, assigned to the security campaign had the daily mission of clearing a section of Route 13, a major artery north of Saigon. In March 1968 the division commander withdrew the unit from the area security program, but the battalion continued to perform the task of clearing the same stretch of road each day. Although the category of the mission assigned to the unit had changed, its mission remained the same, and who could say that its work did not contribute to several missions—or to none?[35]

In the III Corps Tactical Zone Lt. Gen. Walter T. Kerwin, Jr., the senior American adviser and the American ground commander as of 1 September, had other problems. He was pleased with General Do Cao Tri's aggressiveness as the new

[29] Quoted words from Memo, Komer to COMUSMACV, 2 Sep 68, sub: ARVN Bn in DS of RD, SEAB, CMH. See also Msg, Peers NHT 1329 to Abrams, 150539 Sep 68, Abrams Papers, HRB, CMH; Memo, Colby to CofS, MACV, 15 Apr 68, sub: Evaluation of ARVN Battalions in Support of RD, SEAB, CMH; Hunt, *Pacification*, forthcoming.

[30] As recorded in MFR, Bird, 24 Dec 65, sub: Conference at Can Tho on 23 Dec 65, History file 3–A1, Westmoreland Papers, HRB, CMH.

[31] Notes of 14 Mar 67, History file 13–C; Notes of 13 Jan 68, History file 28–A. Both in Westmoreland Papers, HRB, CMH.

[32] CORDS Field Evaluation Rpt, Hurd and Deford, 2 Sep 67, sub: The ARVN 7th Division in Support of RD, SEAB, CMH.

[33] Ltr, Komer to Vann, 2 Jul 68, Vann Papers, 1968, MHI.

[34] CORDS Field Evaluation Rpt, Sidney A. Chernenkoff, 12 Dec 68, sub: Evaluation of ARVN Support of Pacification in IV Corps, SEAB, CMH.

[35] Interv, Pritchett with Lanthrom, 4 Sep 68, VNIT 258, HRB, CMH.

corps commander, but confided to General Abrams that "we may have a bear by the tail." Tri, in violation of MACV's rules of engagement prohibiting operations in Cambodia, showed signs of mounting operations across the border against retreating enemy forces. An international incident with neutral Cambodia seemed possible.[36] However, the Vietnamese general also had his hands full. His territorial security responsibilities kept his artillery spread out in two-gun platoons and his armored vehicles guarding roads and bridges; his distrust of Khang's marines, who were based within his zone, forced him to maintain a separate command post for Thieu in case the president should be driven out of Saigon by an attempted coup; and the ineptness of his subordinates, especially General Giai commanding the 18th Division and General Thuan of the 5th, continually frustrated him. Tri had even relieved one Vietnamese marine commander, only to have him reinstated personally by Vien, and another had allegedly engineered an assassination attempt against his American marine adviser.[37] Kerwin and the division advisers sided completely with Tri, noting that the 18th was even a "laughing stock" to the Vietnamese and that the 5th had "withdrawn into a shell" and was doing nothing constructive.[38] Minor incidents, like the 5th Division commander's daily pot shots at birds from the second story balcony of his home and the subsequent accidental wounding of his intelligence adviser, were not uncommon and at times trivialized and mocked the entire war effort. Kerwin appealed to Abrams for help, and the MACV commander reportedly "raised hell" with Thieu over the matter.[39] But Thieu, perhaps feeling safer with old friends like Giai around the capital to keep a watch on Khang and the ambitious and popular Tri, did nothing.[40]

Where leadership was better and where units, whatever their mission, were more aggressive, American evaluations were positive.[41] Many of the better Vietnamese commanders continued to crop up in the northern zone, far away from the Saigon political arena. There American advisers had consistently praised General Truong, whose 1st Division had performed well during the recapture of Hue City, and credited Col. Truong Tan Thuc with turning around the independent 51st Infantry Regiment, whose former commander had led the rebel troops in the 1966 Buddhist crises. Lt. Col. W. Ray Bradley, the experienced senior adviser to the 51st, described Thuc as the most effective commander he had ever known. According to Bradley, the problem of gaining "rapport" with his counterpart had never surfaced, and Thuc personally sought his advice on everything from tactics to administration and logistics. Although they disagreed at times,

---

[36] Quoted words from Msg, Kerwin HOA 0997 to Abrams, 061100 Aug 68. See also Msg, Kerwin HOA 1444 to Abrams, 030250 Sep 68. Both in Abrams Papers, HRB, CMH.

[37] Interv, Pritchett with S Sgt Norman S. Coop, Adviser, 5th Armored Cavalry Squadron, circa June 1968, VNIT 140, HRB, CMH. See also Msg, Kerwin HOA 1205 to Abrams, 020729 Sep 68; Msg, Kerwin HOA 2194 to Abrams, 141030 Dec 68; and Msg, Kerwin HOA 1358 to Abrams, 21 Sep 68. All in Abrams Papers, HRB, CMH.

[38] Quoted words from Msg, Kerwin HOA 1947 to Abrams, 180910 Nov 68. See also Msg, Kerwin HOA 2299 to Abrams, 241030 Dec 68. Both in Abrams Papers, HRB, CMH.

[39] Comments of Lt. Gen. William E. Potts on draft manuscript "Advice and Support: The Final Years," 12 Apr 84, SEAB, CMH.

[40] Msg, Abrams MAC 17004 to Wheeler, 120729 Dec 69, Abrams Papers, HRB, CMH.

[41] For example, see Intervs, Pritchett with Pfeiffer, 10 Jun 68, VNIT 167, and with Capt Joseph W. Kinzer, Liaison Officer, 3d Bde, Airborne Div, 27 Jan 68, VNIT 101, HRB, CMH.

often it was Thuc who tactfully brought Bradley over to his point of view. The Vietnamese commander, Bradley believed, cared for his troops, rewarding those who performed well in combat with cash from his own pocket or special privileges. Bradley's major job was coordinating American air and artillery support, and he felt that the unit really didn't need any "advisers." Because Thuc and his major staff officers spoke excellent English, Bradley considered himself to be "the luckiest advisor in the country" and his job to be relatively easy and enjoyable. His operations noncommissioned officer, Sfc. Adolf Sierra, agreed. Sierra, a sixteen-year Army veteran who had been with the regiment two years, stressed the improvements he had seen take place in leadership and morale, explaining that the troops had "more pride . . . and behave quite a bit different than they used to." Sierra expected to stay with the unit at least another year by requesting further tour extensions and felt that, with continued American air support, the 51st "should be able to take most of the [ground combat] load" on its own.[42]

Conflicting Assessments

Despite SEER's questionable validity and the persistence of leadership and political problems in the South Vietnamese armed forces, MACV and the Joint Chiefs of Staff believed that Saigon's credible performance during Tet, together with the manpower gains being made through mobilization and the addition of large quantities of new equipment, provided the foundation for a future South Vietnamese military force able to stand alone. However, in December 1968 the Central Intelligence Agency (CIA) reached different conclusions in a sobering appraisal of Saigon's military capabilities.[43] Eschewing the positive tenor of MACV reports that emphasized "progress," the CIA study focused on perennial South Vietnamese military problems, such as poor leadership, dependence on American combat support, desertions, low morale, corruption, and other negative factors. It attributed South Vietnamese successes during the Tet offensive to increased U.S. fire support and other American assistance, without which "the South Vietnamese military establishment would crumble rapidly under a heavy Communist assault." Saigon's inability to take over a greater share of the combat burden stemmed from "the long-standing lack of effective leadership, an inequitable selection and promotion system, poor training, inadequate fire power, and an antiquated logistical system," aggravated further by "low pay scales and . . . widespread corruption, political favoritism, and privilege-seeking that are rife within the military establishment." The story of woe was now quite old.

The assessment noted that the "statistical indicators of performance" showed that the South Vietnamese had gained valuable battlefield experience, but criti-

---

[42] Quoted words from Interv, Maj Lamar F. Peyton with Bradley and Sierra, 6 Aug 68, VNIT 240. For similar comments from 1st Division advisers, see ibid., with Maj Jose L. Morales et al., 20 Jul 68, VNIT 243. Both in HRB, CMH.
[43] Information, to include quoted matter, in this and the following two paragraphs from Intelligence Memorandum 68–152, Directorate of Intelligence, CIA, December 1968, sub: South Vietnam's Military Establishment: Prospects for Going It Alone, copy in SEAB, CMH.

cized their reliance on American firepower and tactics—pulling back and waiting for air strikes and artillery support after sighting enemy forces. The evaluation of Vietnamese military performance during Tet was also highly critical, claiming that the figures that implied an increase in effectiveness tended "to submerge certain qualitative factors that are essential for an adequate assessment." MACV statistics, the CIA analysis charged, did not differentiate between enemy losses by American fire support and those caused directly by South Vietnamese combat action. The study also pointed out, as many MACV advisers had also noted, that many South Vietnamese commanders had refused to take the initiative after the enemy's Tet offensive had ended and had remained in defensive positions.

The CIA study then went through the standard laundry list of South Vietnamese deficiencies: the highly restrictive promotion system, the poor quality of training, low pay scales (when compared to Vietnamese civilian salaries), and the faltering dependent housing program. Political and cultural factors, often ignored by MACV, undermined military effectiveness and prevented cooperation between commanders. Saigon still made key military appointments on the basis of loyalty rather than ability. Widespread corruption prevailed among political and military leaders. Despite American pressures for change, Saigon stubbornly clung to an officer procurement policy that excluded nearly all candidates who had not passed through Vietnam's rigid and highly expensive educational system. Given the current "social and psychological environment" in South Vietnam, the Central Intelligence Agency believed that little positive change could be expected and that Saigon would be unable to assume a greater share of combat operations.

Abrams attacked what he termed the CIA's "distorted picture" of the military situation in South Vietnam. None of the modernization programs was designed to let the South Vietnamese "go it alone," he pointed out, and the balanced Phase II force structure only allowed Saigon to cope with an "internal threat" by itself. The CIA analysts were pummeling straw men by implying that more was expected. Abrams denied that U.S. artillery or air support to the South Vietnamese had ever been "heavy," that their logistical system was "antiquated," or that their pay scales were too low. He admitted, as Westmoreland had often done, that "[poor] leadership, corruption, desertion, and political favoritism are problems endemic to South Vietnam" and, like Westmoreland, asserted that MACV was "working on them and progress is being made." He praised the South Vietnamese for not lowering their educational standards for officers and held that substantial improvements were being made in most of the other areas criticized by the Central Intelligence Agency. Abrams did not specify how he intended to improve leadership or stem corruption, but emphasized the benefits derived from desertion control measures and the current modernization program.[44]

Again, the differences in the evaluations lay in their balance—one side stressing optimistic statistics and programs that seemed easy to measure and quantify,

[44] Quoted words from Msg, Wheeler JCS 14581 to Abrams, 122217 Dec 68, sub: RVNAF Capabilities. See also Msg, Abrams MAC 17134 to Wheeler, 151112 Dec 68. Both in Abrams Papers, HRB, CMH.

and the other making pessimistic generalizations that were difficult to document. Where the truth lay, no one could tell. Perhaps the greatest barrier to an accurate appraisal was the lack of standards or goals, which was tied to the general confusion about where the war was going in the long run. Because of this, the future role of the South Vietnamese armed forces and how best to prepare them for it eluded any consensus of opinion in either Washington or Saigon.

Vietnamization Becomes Policy

PART FIVE

A New Direction
(1969–1970)

19

Vietnamization

In the spring of 1969 President Richard M. Nixon initiated his new policy of "Vietnamization." Vietnamization had two distinct elements: first, the unilateral withdrawal of American troops from South Vietnam; and, second, the assumption of greater military responsibilities by the South Vietnamese armed forces to make up for that loss. Military planners had based previous withdrawal plans on a reduction in enemy forces. T-Day planning had assumed that negotiations would lead to mutual troop withdrawals, and perhaps to some kind of armistice. The strength and condition of Saigon's military forces was not critical. The Accelerated Phase II Improvement and Modernization Plan, the most recent and most extensive program for the expansion of the South Vietnamese armed forces, also premised a mutual withdrawal, but with no armistice and varying degrees of projected North Vietnamese support for a "residual" Viet Cong insurgency. Vietnamization, in contrast, was a policy, rather than a plan, and rested on the twin assumptions that the combatants would not reach any political settlement, or understanding, and that the fighting in the South would continue with no voluntary reduction in enemy force levels. Although in theory the subsequent withdrawal of American troops depended on improvements in South Vietnamese military capabilities and the level of combat activity, in practice the timing and size of the withdrawals were highly political decisions made in the United States.

National Security Study Memorandum 1

Prior to the promulgation of Vietnamization, the new administration undertook a complete review of the situation in Southeast Asia. In mid-December 1968 President-elect Nixon examined the Central Intelligence Agency's critical evaluation of the South Vietnamese armed forces, undoubtedly raising many questions in his mind regarding the direction of future American policy.[1] Upon taking office the following month, he directed all agencies involved with the war to review the CIA study and prepare detailed estimates of the current military

[1] Msg, Wheeler JCS 14581 to Abrams, 122217 Dec 68, sub: RVNAF Capabilities, Abrams Papers, HRB, CMH.

and political situation in South Vietnam. Major respondents were to include MACV, the U.S. Embassy in Saigon, the Joint Chiefs of Staff, the Department of Defense, the Department of State, and the Central Intelligence Agency.

The Nixon request, embodied in National Security Study Memorandum 1 (NSSM 1), or "the 29 Questions," covered six broad subject areas: negotiations (questions 1–4), the enemy situation (5–10), the state of the South Vietnamese armed forces (11–13), the status of pacification (14–20), politics in South Vietnam (21–23), and American objectives (24–29). The questions were quite specific and made reference to divergent views. Those pertaining to the improvement of the South Vietnamese military, for example, asked respondents to note any "differences of opinion" and present evidence for each viewpoint, as well as to comment on the discrepancies between the CIA's December study and contemporary MACV evaluations. Comments were solicited on the effectiveness of South Vietnamese "mobile, offensive operations," the "level of 'genuine' small unit actions and night actions," the officer selection and promotion systems, the quality of leadership "as distinct from changes in paper programs," and the continuing high desertion rates. NSSM 1 also requested estimates of South Vietnamese capabilities against a combined Viet Cong–North Vietnamese Army threat in the event of a unilateral U.S. troop withdrawal. Finally, it demanded specific recommendations to improve Saigon's military leadership, organization, training, and logistical support to enable the South Vietnamese to handle either an independent Viet Cong or a combined enemy threat.[2]

In Vietnam General Abrams passed the White House's request down to each of his corps senior advisers for reply.[3] Lt. Gen. Richard G. Stilwell, representing the I Corps Tactical Zone in the north, cited "unanimity" among his field advisers "that significant strides have been made in the improvement of ARVN forces [during 1968]." The responses from the II and IV Corps zones were more predictable, stressing statistical improvements in South Vietnamese combat performance and the value of increased U.S. combat support. Only General Kerwin, the III Corps senior adviser, noted "considerable differences of opinion concerning the extent of RVNAF improvement" in his area.[4] Most of his field advisers saw improvements in the units they advised, but Kerwin felt that many of them

---

[2] Quoted words from Msg, Vice-Adm Johnson JCS 972 to Nazzar, acting CINCPAC, Info Abrams, 23 Jan 69, sub: Situation in Vietnam, Abrams Papers, HRB, CMH. For agency responses, see NSSM 1 files in SEAB, CMH; fldrs 13, 20, 134, and 136 of Thomas C. Thayer Papers, HRB, CMH; U.S. Congress, House, *Congressional Record*, 92d Cong., 2d sess., 10 May 72, vol. 118, pt. 13, pp. 16749–16836; and summarization in Henry Kissinger, *White House Years* (Boston: Little, Brown, 1979), pp. 238–39. For Kissinger's pessimistic views, see Memo, Kissinger to President, 10 Sep 69, sub: Our Present Course in Vietnam, reproduced in ibid., pp. 1480–82.

[3] None of the U.S. corps senior advisers appeared to have had access to the CIA study. The II Field Force commander noted the lack, and the other responses made no mention of it. For the corps-level responses, see Msg, Kerwin (III CTZ) HOA 252 to Corcoran, CofS, MACV, 251545 Jan 69, MICRO 1/379; Ltr, HQ, IFFV (II CTZ), to COMUSMACV, 27 Jan 69, MICRO 1/414; Ltr, HQ, III MAF (I CTZ), to COMUSMACV (sent by Stilwell, temporarily in command), sub: Situation in Vietnam, with enclosure "Answers to Twenty Questions," MICRO 1/451. All in RG 334, WNRC. See also Ltr, HQ, U.S. Army Advisory Group, IV CTZ, 26 Jan 69, sub: Situation in Vietnam, SEAB, CMH. Unless otherwise specified, information in this and the following three paragraphs, to include respective quotations of the senior advisers, are from the above-cited documents.

[4] Stilwell headed the U.S. Army XXIV Corps and was acting commanding general of the III Marine Amphibious Force (III MAF). (The XXIV Corps was a subordinate command of III MAF, *(Continued)*

lacked the objectivity and experience to make valid judgments. He himself saw "no marked improvement" during 1968 in two of the three South Vietnamese divisions in the III Corps zone and rated one-third of the South Vietnamese maneuver battalions in the zone as "effective," one-third as "ineffective," and the remaining one-third as "unsatisfactory." "Taken as a whole," he concluded, "ARVN units are much less effective than similar US units and achieve minimal results." He did note, however, "substantial" improvement in the Territorial Forces caused by better weapons, logistics, and administration, and the assistance provided by U.S. mobile advisory teams.

Remarks on various aspects of Saigon's military condition varied from zone to zone. All senior advisers found little improvement in South Vietnam's

Maj. Gen. Richard G. Stilwell and General Ngo Quang Truong *in I Corps*

officer selection and promotion systems, and, while some discussed slight improvements in leadership, all agreed that this remained a serious problem. The submissions from the I and III Corps zones were especially critical of small unit leadership and tactics. The II Corps zone (I Field Force) report held "that RVNAF is improving steadily under current programs and that much progress can be expected in the future as current and planned programs move forward," but noted several dissenting opinions on which it chose not to elaborate. Stilwell, in the northern I Corps zone, praised the efforts of General Truong, the 1st Infantry Division commander, in improving leadership; but Kerwin in the III Corps area around Saigon was extremely critical, gloomily concluding that South Vietnamese officers continued to be "urban oriented, basically alienated toward the rural population, unfamiliar with the terrain and countryside, and . . . [to experience] difficulty in communicating with their peasant or lower class urban soldiers."

In the opinion of all advisers, efforts to control desertions had failed because of a lack of command attention and poor leadership at all levels. Other contributing causes were the increased fighting, restrictive leave policies, the larger pro-

(Continued) created opposite the DMZ area during the Tet offensive.) Kerwin was the II Field Force (III CTZ) commander. As the ranking American tactical commanders in their respective zones, each was also the corps senior adviser and supervised all subordinate American advisers. The responses from the I, II, and IV Corps zones were staff studies, while Kerwin sent a personal message that allowed him to be more candid.

portion of draftees, overcrowded training centers, the assignment of soldiers outside of their home areas, and the failure of South Vietnamese leaders to regard desertion a serious crime.

To the key question of South Vietnam's ability to handle either a Viet Cong or combined Viet Cong–North Vietnamese Army threat with various degrees of American support, the answers by the corps senior advisers were almost unanimous. With the successful completion of the current expansion program, they agreed that South Vietnam would be able to "contain" the Viet Cong threat, except in the III Corps Tactical Zone where, in Kerwin's opinion, continued American air and artillery support would be needed. Against a combined threat, however, all doubted that the South Vietnamese could do little more than hold their own and judged their offensive capabilities marginal at best. Although they made no recommendations as to how the South Vietnamese could deal with either a Viet Cong or a combined threat, and suggested no major changes in their military organization or strategy, all saw a pressing need for more air, artillery, and logistical support, and more attention to training and retraining. They also saw the elimination of corrupt or ineffective leaders at all levels as necessary, but had no suggestions on how this could be done. Kerwin stressed greater political unity, appointments and promotions based on merit, and greater use of women in the armed services, and suggested a massive effort to transfer military personnel to units based in their native provinces as one way to reduce desertions and identify the army with the people. He reckoned it would take five years to make such changes and recommended that, in the interim, American ground forces be slowly withdrawn, with MACV retaining its aviation, artillery, and "mobility assets" until the South Vietnamese became self-sufficient in these areas. Stilwell proposed a similar transition, but recommended that, instead of withdrawing American ground units, American and South Vietnamese forces conduct more combined operations to acquaint the Vietnamese with the kind of mobile offensive tactics practiced by U.S. units. The four senior advisers were hopeful that the South Vietnamese could eventually deal with the insurgency by themselves, but none felt that they could ever handle a conventional North Vietnamese threat or a combined Viet Cong–North Vietnamese Army opponent. In summary, the advisers doubted Saigon's ability to survive alone, and most of the measures suggested to improve South Vietnamese capabilities were similar to those that MACV had been pursuing for years.

At MACV headquarters General Abrams' staff incorporated the judgments of the corps senior advisers into its response to NSSM 1,[5] but left out many of the adverse comments or noted them briefly without elaboration. Much of Kerwin's critical appraisal of the state of the infantry divisions in the III Corps Tactical Zone, for example, was omitted, and favorable remarks were given more play. Moreover, the MACV staff claimed to be "in no position to detail the extent of differences of opinions concerning the extent of the RVNAF improvement" or to "determine the basis from which other opinions [that is, those in the CIA study] are developed." Abrams intended MACV to speak with one voice. In truth, the

---

[5] Quoted words in this and the following two paragraphs from Msg, Abrams to Johnson, sub: Situation in Vietnam, MICRO 1/0104, RG 334, WNRC.

command had been asked to evaluate its own work, and like the individual U.S. advisers in the field, Abrams and his staff emphasized accomplishments rather than shortcomings.

Most of MACV's response rehashed the now familiar statistical indicators of progress. Steady or slightly rising kill and weapons-captured ratios were billed as significant, as were the rising percentage of days (35.1 to 44.7) the average infantry-type battalion spent on offensive operations. Statistical variations were explained by changing combat conditions (for example, declining enemy activity after the Tet offensive; the unwillingness of the North Vietnamese to undertake large-scale operations or fight major engagements, and so forth). Promotions and appointments were presented in the same fashion. The rising desertion rates could not be ignored, but MACV glibly explained that "prior to 1968, the RVNAF was a relatively stable force filled primarily with mature, trained individuals" and that the younger draftees and conscripts produced by the 1968 mobilization were more prone to desert.

Despite the picture of steady progress portrayed by MACV in all current programs, the command's outlook for the future was not optimistic. Without extensive U.S. military support, MACV also concluded that the South Vietnamese could not handle the Viet Cong and, without both U.S. ground and support forces, could not cope with the North Vietnamese Army. In this aspect Abrams accurately reflected the convictions of his senior subordinates. Current MACV estimates of enemy strength in South Vietnam put the Viet Cong in the neighborhood of 150,000 men and North Vietnamese forces at about 125,000. By 1972, the report continued, existing modernization efforts (the Accelerated Phase II Improvement and Modernization Plan) would allow the South Vietnamese to deal successfully with the Viet Cong insurgency without direct American ground support, but American materiel and advisory support "would be required indefinitely to maintain an effective force," as would lower desertion rates and better leadership. MACV recommended no changes in command or organization and no new materiel programs. The current modernization program was the most that Saigon could sustain. But this program would *not* allow the South Vietnamese to deal with the North Vietnamese military threat because "the RVNAF simply are not capable of attaining the level of self-sufficiency and overwhelming force superiority that would be required to counter combined Viet Cong insurgency and North Vietnamese Army main force offensives." According to Abrams, nothing could be done.

In analyzing South Vietnamese military capabilities, the NSSM 1 responses of the U.S. Commander-in-Chief, Pacific, the Joint Chiefs of Staff, the U.S. Embassy in Saigon, and the State Department generally endorsed the MACV reply.[6] All of these respondents agreed that the problems identified by MACV were not new, and most focused their attention on the desertion rate. The embassy report pointed out that the rate had fallen from a high of 18.3 (per 1,000 troops per month) in October 1968 to 12.6 in December, although this was still higher than

---

[6] The following discussion of NSSM 1 responses, to include quoted matter, may be found in U.S. Congress, House, *Congressional Record*, 92d Cong, 2d sess., 10 May 72, vol. 118, pt. 13, pp. 16750–54 for summary; pp. 16754–92 for State and U.S. Embassy; and pp. 16792–836 for Office of the Secretary of Defense, all with comments on JCS, MACV, and CIA submissions.

the average 10–11 per 1,000 rate in 1967. It also noted that, without accurate personnel records and other data sources, it was impossible to pinpoint why desertion rates rose or fell from one month to the next. The State Department agreed with MACV and the embassy that mobilization had pushed desertion rates up, but noted that those combat units with high desertion rates in 1967 also had the worst rates in 1968, suggesting that "chronically inferior leadership" was a "significant factor."

The Defense Department and the Central Intelligence Agency offered the most pessimistic replies to NSSM 1 and were especially critical of Saigon's military capabilities. Both agencies felt that recent improvements in strength, equipment, and performance failed to offset continuing problems in leadership, motivation, and desertion. The basic weaknesses remained uncorrected. In their opinion the officer corps needed to be completely reformed by removing favoritism from appointments and promotions, by ending corruption, and by separating the army from the political process. MACV's favorable statistical indicators of performance, they contended, were misleading. The South Vietnamese depended too much on American fire support in battle. Without full American assistance, the Defense Department held that Saigon could not be expected to contain even the Viet Cong, let alone a combined enemy threat.

Decision for Withdrawal

American and South Vietnamese leaders in Saigon had considered the matter of unilateral American troop withdrawals for some time. Westmoreland had suggested the possibility in his November 1967 press briefing, and in April and July 1968 Thieu had publicly voiced the possibility of withdrawing substantial American forces in late 1968 and 1969. The Washington-originated T-Day planning in 1968 also alerted MACV to such an eventuality, as did the continuous press statements of Vietnamese leaders, starting in September, that constantly predicted imminent U.S. troop withdrawals.[7]

On 17 January 1969 General Abrams and Ambassador Bunker formally discussed the possibility of American troop redeployments with President Thieu. Reminding Bunker and Thieu that MACV had not recommended any withdrawal and that "the time is [not] yet right for [a] withdrawal of major [American] combat units," Abrams nevertheless proposed having South Vietnamese marine units replace U.S. 9th Division forces in the Delta, making it possible to send some American troops home by midyear. He also suggested having American units train similar newly activated South Vietnamese units and turn over their equipment to them intact upon their redeployment to the United States. Thieu

---

[7] Rpt, MACJ–303, sub: Force Planning Synopsis for General Abrams (hereafter cited as Force Planning Synopsis), pp. 2–4, SEAB, CMH, which traces the sequence of withdrawal planning. On Vietnamese comments, see Msg, Bunker SGN 845 to SecState, 151410 Jan 69; and Thieu's news conference of 2 Apr 68 cited in Telg, AmEmbassy SGN 23738 to SecState, 2 Apr 68. Both in Bunker Papers, DS.

agreed but, to Abrams' chagrin, made the discussion public, announcing the following day that American withdrawals would soon begin.[8]

On 20 January General Wheeler informed Abrams that the "continuation of US-GVN discussion in Saigon addressing US troop reductions in conjunction with increasing GVN capabilities is approved," but asked him to "quietly put the damper on" any public discussion of the matter by American or South Vietnamese leaders.[9] Abrams subsequently relayed the request to his field and component commanders and to the Vietnamese leaders, but was unable to halt Saigon's speculations in the press.

During February both the Joint General Staff and the South Korean military command pressed MACV for details on American withdrawal planning. Abrams had nothing to offer. While awaiting more guidance from Washington, he had his staff identify specific indicators bearing on the feasibility of reductions, but took no further action. These indicators, or conditions, included the enemy threat, progress in pacification, and the rate and extent of South Vietnamese military improvement. Abrams later insisted that all withdrawals be tied to these three factors.

On 5 March Melvin R. Laird, Nixon's new secretary of defense, visited Saigon, accompanied by General Wheeler. Briefed by MACV on the situation in Vietnam, Laird declared his satisfaction with the progress that had been made, both in the war effort and the South Vietnamese armed forces, and instructed Abrams to accelerate all programs turning over the war to Saigon. He also accepted Abrams' three withdrawal conditions but wanted to firm up redeployment planning with hard numbers and dates as soon as possible. Laird advised Abrams to use the figure of 44,000 men for planning purposes. Citing political pressures at home, the defense secretary requested specific plans "before the time given to the new administration runs out, be it three, six, or nine months, but probably with[in] the next three or four months."[10]

Laird returned to Washington determined to take action. Despite the critical responses of his own staff to NSSM 1, he was convinced that the South Vietnamese could eventually defend themselves without American ground troops. Nixon had suggested the existence of a "secret plan" to end the war during his presidential campaign, but had yet to come up with any alternatives to the application of greater military force, and the secretary felt that he had a better idea. On 13 March he reported the results of his Saigon visit to the president. Although the enemy had been beaten on the battlefield, Laird related that Abrams believed that an American military victory was impossible, "considering the restrictions with which we are compelled to operate." He also pointed out that MACV had no program to reduce the American military commitment in Vietnam and felt that "the development of such a program should receive our first priority." He disagreed strongly with MACV's assumption that successful American troop

---

[8] Quoted words from Force Planning Synopsis, pp. 4–5, SEAB, CMH. See also Msg, Abrams MAC 766 to Wheeler, 171342 Jan 69, file VIET 37002, box 18, accession no. 75103, RG 330, WNRC.
[9] Force Planning Synopsis, p. 6, SEAB, CMH.
[10] Quoted words from Force Planning Synopsis, p. 10, SEAB, CMH. See Interv (transcribed), Col William D. Johnson and Lt Col James C. Ferguson with Gen Andrew J. Goodpastor (hereafter cited as Goodpastor Interv), 1976, sec. 4, pp. 53–54, Andrew J. Goodpastor Papers, Senior Officers Debriefing Program, MHI. Goodpastor served as the deputy MACV commander from July 1968 to April 1969.

withdrawals had to be tied to similar North Vietnamese reductions and argued that the large American military presence stifled South Vietnamese initiative. The "orientation" of American military leaders in Vietnam, Laird contended, "seems to be more on operations than on assisting the South Vietnamese to acquire the means to defend themselves," and this might explain why MACV continued to tolerate such things as Saigon's high military desertion rates and marginal military leadership. In summation, he recommended withdrawing 50,000–70,000 American troops in 1969 and initiating a more comprehensive withdrawal plan as soon as possible.[11]

On 14 March Wheeler informed Abrams of Laird's report to the president and the higher withdrawal figures being discussed. He also warned MACV of the confusion in Washington between the earlier T-Day planning based on a mutual withdrawal and the possibility of a unilateral withdrawal as the current South Vietnamese improvement and modernization plans were realized. Abrams apparently was not surprised by the news, having correctly appraised Laird's intentions during his visit to Saigon. On 23 March he approved tentative planning for the withdrawal of a two-division-size force (50,000 men) in 1969 and, on the thirtieth, hinted to Wheeler that more cross-border air strikes would help justify the withdrawal from a military point of view. The MACV chief also repeated his personal opposition to unilateral U.S. troop withdrawals and his insistence that all withdrawals depend on his assessment of the military situation in Vietnam.[12]

Laird's determination to effect a major change in American policy toward the war in Vietnam remained fixed. In subsequent discussions with Nixon, Henry A. Kissinger, the president's special assistant for national security, and the Joint Chiefs of Staff, he pursued this goal vigorously, finally persuading the president to embark on a policy of what he termed *Vietnamization*—turning the ground war over to the South Vietnamese. On 10 April Kissinger, with the approval of the president, issued National Security Study Memorandum 36 (NSSM 36), directing Laird to prepare "a specific timetable for Vietnamizing the war." The plan was to cover "all aspects of US military, para-military, and civilian involvement in Vietnam, including combat and combat support forces, advisory personnel, and all forms of equipment." Its objective was "the progressive transfer . . . of the fighting effort" from American to South Vietnamese forces. Neither a further expansion of the South Vietnamese armed forces nor the withdrawal of the North Vietnamese Army was envisioned. Instead, through phased troop withdrawals, the American military presence in South Vietnam was to be reduced to a support and advisory mission. Troop withdrawals were to begin 1 July 1969, with alternative completion dates of December 1970 (eighteen months), June 1971 (twenty-four months), December 1971 (thirty months), and December 1972 (forty-two months). Kissinger requested a tentative plan—an "initial overall report outline"—by 1 June. Thus, despite the divergent views of the major U.S. agencies involved in the war effort and despite the unanimous opinion of these same agencies that the South Vietnamese could never deal with a combined Viet

---

[11] Memo, Laird to President, 13 Mar 69, sub: Trip to Vietnam and CINCPAC, 5–12 March 1969, file VIET 333 LAIRD, box 96, accession no. 75089, RG 330, WNRC.

[12] Quoted words from Msg, Wheeler JCS 03218 to Abrams, 140044 Mar 69. See also Msg, Abrams MAC 4036 to Wheeler, 301218 Mar 69. Both in Abrams Papers, HRB, CMH.

Cong–North Vietnamese Army threat, the new administration had instructed the American military command to develop plans for turning over almost the entire ground war effort to the forces of Saigon.[13]

Withdrawal Planning

In the weeks ahead the Office of the Secretary of Defense and the American military staffs examined what they felt were the critical elements of the new policy: the size, composition, and rate of the American withdrawals; and, a part of the same question, the size and composition of the forces to remain.[14] MACV and the Joint Chiefs favored gradual withdrawals of balanced (combat and support forces) increments. They also argued that U.S. forces supporting the war in South Vietnam from other areas, Thailand, for example, should not be included in the withdrawals and that such forces should be considered "support," rather than "combat," elements. The Office of the Secretary of Defense, in contrast, held that the air interdiction forces based outside of South Vietnam had been ineffective, could therefore be reduced without great loss, and should be part of any withdrawal schedule. In addition, Defense Department officials wanted a more rapid reduction of U.S. maneuver units (infantry and armor), arguing that this would allow MACV to render more American air, artillery, and logistical support to the South Vietnamese. Battlefield statistics seemed to show that this was the best means of increasing South Vietnamese military effectiveness. The Joint Chiefs countered that, despite current increases in American combat support, South Vietnamese statistical effectiveness was actually declining in relationship to that of U.S. troops in combat, adding that "there remains considerable doubt as to the accuracy of the body count method in providing realistic kill data." They did, however, admit that the South Vietnamese were receiving less combat support than American troops (15 percent of the helicopter, 10 percent of the air transport, and 32 of the percent air and artillery fire support given to U.S. forces) and that the Saigon forces should improve if more support were made available.[15]

While Washington debated the new policy, General Abrams at MACV headquarters questioned the size and pace of the withdrawals. On two separate

[13] Quoted words from NSSM 36, Kissinger to SecState, SecDef, and Director of Central Intelligence, 10 Apr 69, sub: Vietnamizing the War, copy in SEAB, CMH. See also Goodpastor Interv, 1976, sec. 4, pp. 53–54, Goodpastor Papers, Senior Officers Debriefing Program, MHI; Kissinger, *White House Years*, pp. 271–72; Richard M. Nixon, *The Memoirs of Richard Nixon* (New York: Grosset and Dunlap, 1978), p. 392; Historical Division, Joint Secretariat, U.S. Joint Chiefs of Staff, "The Joint Chiefs of Staff and the War in Vietnam, 1969–1970" (hereafter cited as "Joint Chiefs of Staff in Vietnam, 1969–1970"), The History of the Joint Chiefs of Staff (Washington, D.C., 1976), pp. 102–04, HRB, CMH.

[14] Force Planning Synopsis, pp. 20–72, SEAB, CMH.

[15] Arguments noted in JCS, J–5 TP 26–9, 31 May 69, Talking Paper for the Chairman, JCS, for a Meeting With the Secretary of Defense, 31 May 69, sub: NSSM 36—Vietnamizing the War, SEAB. See also "Joint Chiefs of Staff in Vietnam, 1969–1970," pp. 106–09, HRB. But in Msgs, Moorer JCS 06688 to McCain, 292331 May 69, and Moorer JCS 06267 to McCain, 222314 May 69, Abrams Papers, HRB, the OSD and JCS positions on the composition of withdrawal increments seem to be reversed. All in CMH.

occasions Wheeler reassured Abrams that any American redeployments would take into consideration the military situation in South Vietnam and that the 1 July date set by Kissinger was only for planning purposes. But Abrams knew better and his concern proved justified. Only a few days after Wheeler's second communique, he received notice that withdrawals might come sooner than expected and to prepare alternate plans for the redeployment of 50,000 and 100,000 troops.[16]

As the withdrawal plans took shape, significant ambiguities in Kissinger's initial guidance became apparent.[17] A major assumption by all military planners was the retention of a large American residual support force of approximately 275,000 troops in South Vietnam following the withdrawal of most combat forces. The residual force was to consist of 215,300 Army personnel in five categories: command and control (4,900); combat forces (50,200, including two combat divisions and two combat brigades); combat support forces (54,900, including twenty-eight artillery, four engineer, and nine signal battalions, forty-seven helicopter companies, sixteen fixed-wing aircraft companies, and four armored cavalry squadrons); combat service support forces (88,700, including fourteen engineer construction and nineteen signal battalions); and military advisers (16,600).[18] The mission of these forces would remain unchanged, and the residual logistical component would generally support American combat units alone. Of the engineer battalions that remained, ten would continue work on the South Vietnamese road network to reduce Saigon's future dependence on aerial resupply; and the twenty-eight signal battalions would continue to operate the existing sophisticated communications systems until other alternatives were found.

During the withdrawal MACV wanted to turn over its major bases and port operations to the South Vietnamese and redeploy American forces in "slices" of combat units and "all elements that supported them." In addition, MACV planned to speed up the current South Vietnamese expansion programs by having departing U.S. units turn their equipment directly over to newly activated Vietnamese forces. But the core of Vietnamization planning was the large residual support force, which constituted the principal response of American military leaders to what seemed to be an impossible order. Whether such a force could be reconciled with the spirit of Kissinger's Vietnamization directive was highly questionable. Nevertheless, the final MACV Vietnamization plan incorporated all of the above elements into a single package.[19]

The MACV Vietnamization "plan" was actually neither a plan nor a program but, at best, a procedural document, with only general guidelines regarding the size, composition, and timing of the future American troop reductions. It recognized that Washington would determine the size and date of these reductions,

---

[16] Msgs, Wheeler JCS 04800 to Abrams, 192113 Apr 60; Wheeler JCS 05386 to Abrams, 021455 May 69; and McConnell (acting JCS chairman) JCS 05630 to Abrams, 072132 May 69. All in Abrams Papers, HRB, CMH.

[17] Talking Paper, AVHGC–P, USARV, 17 Jul 69, sub: NSSM 36—Vietnamization, SEAB, CMH.

[18] For example, see Msg, Abrams MAC 6685 to McCain, Info Johnson, 252322 May 69, summarized in Force Planning Synopsis, pp. 37–38, SEAB, CMH, citing Abrams' contention that NSSM 36 intended a large U.S. residual combat force to support Saigon.

[19] U.S. Embassy (Saigon) and MACV, Vietnamizing the War: A Mission Coordinated Plan, 20 Jul 69, SEAB, CMH.

and General Abrams their specific composition based on his estimate of the military situation at the time. At the insistence of Laird, the first redeployment increment of 25,000 troops in July 1969 consisted primarily of combat troops (the U.S. 9th Infantry Division less one brigade and a Marine Corps regiment), but succeeding drawdowns contained proportional shares of combat and support forces.[20] Because no agreement was possible on the size and timing of the withdrawals, Nixon, Laird, and Abrams adopted a flexible "cut-and-try" approach without any fixed timetable (*see Appendix C*). But within Vietnam Abrams' basic redeployment philosophy was to retain "a balanced combat capability and as much capability for as long as possible."[21]

A Self-Sufficient Saigon

On 8 June 1969 Presidents Nixon and Thieu met at Midway Island to discuss Vietnamization. Although Vietnamese officials had not been involved in the Vietnamization planning process, Saigon accepted American withdrawals as a political necessity. But the Vietnamese leaders were concerned over their own future military capabilities.[22] Thieu pointed out that the current MACV expansion and modernization programs allowed Saigon to deal only with a residual insurgency. To fight both the Viet Cong and the North Vietnamese Army a more extensive program was needed, and Thieu presented a Vietnamese plan addressing that concern. His proposals were similar to Plan Six of the preceding year. The Vietnamese wanted their manpower ceiling of 875,780 raised to 1,014,762; two more armored brigade headquarters (for the II and III Corps Tactical Zones, in addition to the one in the I Corps); and three more armored cavalry squadrons. They also proposed exchanging their gasoline-powered M113 armored personnel carriers for diesel models and replacing their old M41 light tanks with Sheridan missile tanks or M48 main battle tanks. These changes would give the South Vietnamese the means to deal with North Vietnamese armor attacks across the Demilitarized Zone and in the western border areas.

To free their division and corps artillery for mobile operations, the Vietnamese recommended establishing a new territorial artillery branch, with sixty-five 105-

[20] Msg, Abrams MAC 7021 to Wheeler, 021053 Jun 69, cited in Force Planning Synopsis, pp. 51–52, SEAB, CMH, notes Abrams' intention to "lead off with first rate US combat units to make the reduction credible" (p. 51), but the "Joint Chiefs of Staff in Vietnam, 1969–1970," pp. 110–13, HRB, CMH, makes it clear that this was done at Laird's insistence. In subsequent withdrawals MACV "phased out," or disestablished, units in South Vietnam, using their personnel as replacements for units in-country, while the military services in Washington reduced the replacement flow from the United States accordingly.

[21] Quoted words from Talking Paper, AVHGC–P, USARV, 17 Jul 68, sub: NSSM 36—Vietnamization, SEAB. See also Msgs, Wheeler JCS 05242 to Abrams and McCain, 161849 Apr 70, and Wheeler JCS 6730 to Abrams and McCain, 312204 May 69, Abrams Papers, HRB. All in CMH.

[22] The Joint Chiefs of Staff authorized combined planning with the Vietnamese in mid-July. See Msg, Abrams MAC 11579 to Wheeler, 050744 Sep 69, sub: Combined Planning. For the opinion of Vietnamese leaders, see Msg, Abrams MAC 9093 to Major Subordinate Commands, 150305 Jul 69, asking for such information and the subsequent responses. Both in Abrams Papers, HRB, CMH. Unless otherwise noted, the discussion that follows on the Vietnamese plan is based on Planning Paper, Joint General Staff, 8 Jun 69, sub: RVNAF Improvement Program, SEAB, CMH.

mm. (390 pieces) and eighteen 155-mm. (108 pieces) howitzer batteries, to provide fixed area fire support for territorial security forces. To further strengthen the regular forces, they asked for eight new corps artillery battalions (one 8-inch and one 105-mm. self-propelled battalion per corps headquarters) to provide mobile support for the armored brigades. For air defense, they requested eleven air defense artillery battalions, one for each division, and, to augment the two F–4 squadrons (thirty-six fighters) already included in MACV's current modernization plans, eight radar stations and two Hawk missile batteries. Other recommendations included replacing their older C–47 and C–119 transport aircraft with the larger C–130 models; enlarging the South Vietnamese Marine Corps to a division-size force by activating three more infantry battalions (for a total of nine) and a third artillery battalion; and creating three new air units, one each for search and rescue (forty-one aircraft), coastal and river surveillance (forty-six aircraft), and commando operations (eight aircraft). For the territorials the Vietnamese requested over 100,000 Popular Forces spaces (for 2,869 platoons) and about 23,000 Regional Forces slots (for forty-six Regional Forces companies and the conversion of CIDG units into Regional Forces), thus freeing more regular forces from their area security missions.

Finally, the Vietnamese plan proposed a massive injection of American financial aid to improve the living standards of South Vietnamese servicemen. Included were pay increases for territorials, free messing for all servicemen, free rice issue for all soldiers and their dependents, doubling the number of combat rations (one to two million monthly), and more working capital for the commissary system. In part, the expenditures involved would be covered by increasing joint support funds from 14.8 billion piasters to 49.5 billion, which, in turn, meant supplementing the proceeds of the Commercial Import Program and other USAID programs with direct American financial assistance.

Thieu pointed out that American support for Saigon's defense budget had remained relatively static since 1967, while the budget itself had steadily risen. From 1967 military expenditures had grown from 45.6 billion piasters to 100.4 billion in 1969, out of a total national budget of 150 billion. In contrast, the amount of joint support funds during those years had fallen from 18.3 billion to 14.8. Despite increased revenues in 1969, some 50 billion piasters had to be provided through deficit financing, further increasing the rate of inflation. Without more U.S. financial assistance, this trend threatened to continue and become worse as military expenditures mounted.[23]

Following the Midway meeting and the public announcement of the Vietnamization-withdrawal policy, Defense Secretary Laird asked Abrams to examine and comment on the South Vietnamese proposals. Abrams' reply weeks later was basically negative. MACV had already approved some of the requests, such as increases in the navy and marine forces, and was awaiting the approval of the Joint Chiefs of Staff. Abrams had also recommended increases for the territorials,

---

[23] Rpt, Joint General Staff, circa June 1969, sub: Summary of Financial Requirements Needed To Support the RVNAF, SEAB, CMH. The same trend is noted in Irving Heymont, *Resource Allocations in Support of the RVN Army, Regional Forces, and Popular Forces: FY68*, RAC–TP–368 (McLean, Va.: Research Analysis Corp., 1969), p. 3.

although his staff had held the Popular Forces expansion to 58,500. However, he flatly disapproved the requests for new air, armor, and artillery units and equipment in their entirety. Abrams felt that American aircraft operating in and around South Vietnam obviated the need for air defense artillery and that the currently authorized seventeen armored cavalry squadrons were adequate to handle the armor threat. He also declared all of the special air squadrons and the new naval, armor, and artillery equipment requested by Saigon unnecessary, agreeing only to add three towed artillery battalions (two 105-mm. and one 155-mm.). He considered the requests for additional financial support also unnecessary, and too expensive and too complex for the South Vietnamese to manage by themselves. Support for military dependents "was [an] internal South Vietnamese problem," and he argued that "MACV should not address increase[s] of [the] standard of living for one segment of [the] GVN population." He also felt that all of the financial proposals were inflationary, serving only to "extend and perpetuate the country's dependence on imports."[24]

General Abrams did support a general force structure increase of 117,047 and a 30,000 increase in the National Police, which, when approved, would raise the overall strength of the armed forces to 992,837 and the National Police to 122,200 by 1972. Like Westmoreland before him, he considered himself to be on much safer ground recommending increases in what were essentially light infantry, easily trained and cheaply equipped. But even here Abrams was cautious. He insisted that none of the "spaces" be released until he deemed the South Vietnamese able to recruit, train, equip, and maintain new forces without slighting existing units. He further advised Washington that no new weapons be added to Saigon's arsenal until the South Vietnamese were able to provide trained personnel to maintain and operate them. He intended to have his command conduct a quarterly review beginning in 1971 to determine the advisability of any further changes in the South Vietnamese military organization.

Both Admiral John S. McCain, Jr., the new Commander-in-Chief, Pacific, and the Joint Chiefs of Staff supported MACV's recommendations. The Joint Chiefs pointed out that existing South Vietnamese equipment "appeared adequate in terms of current requirements and the limited Vietnamese technical capability," but added that "as these capabilities improve and if operational needs change, more sophisticated weapons systems should be considered for introduction into the RVNAF." They doubted that the South Vietnamese could sustain a force structure greater than 875,790, but agreed that the safest course was to activate more light infantry units that required less cadre, training, and equipment. However, the Joint Chiefs also recognized that Saigon had to prepare for more than just a residual insurgency and noted that the ambitious Midway proposals of the Vietnamese did not address what American advisers considered key South Vietnamese military weaknesses—poor leadership and high desertion rates.[25]

On 18 August 1969 Secretary Laird approved the force structure increases recommended by Abrams, agreeing that MACV had final authority over their

---

[24] USMACV, "Command History, 1969," 2:VI–4 to VI–15, HRB, CMH.
[25] Quoted words from ibid., VI–12. See also Msg, Wheeler JCS 09112 to Abrams, 231308 Jul 69, Abrams Papers. Both in HRB, CMH.

release. Collectively they became known as the Midway increase. In the interest of economy, he also directed that funding be provided by reprogramming internal U.S. service budgets and that equipment be provided from existing service stocks and redeploying American units. The action served notice to the services that greater financial and materiel support for Saigon would come out of their own budgets and resources. Laird also asked the Joint Chiefs and the services to again review all current efforts for improving the Vietnamese armed forces and, modifying earlier guidelines, to put together a new program that would enable the South Vietnamese to deal successfully with a combined Viet Cong–North Vietnamese threat. The review was to consider not only changes in force structure and additional equipment but also new ways to improve leadership, to reduce desertions, and to develop strategy and tactics best suited to South Vietnamese capabilities.[26]

On 2 September MACV responded to Laird's request, repeating what everyone by now already knew. The current modernization and improvement program, even with the new Midway increase, did not permit the South Vietnamese to handle the current combined enemy threat (about 232,000 troops) without direct U.S. combat assistance. According to MACV, Saigon's armed forces could not be expanded beyond the presently authorized manpower ceiling of 993,000, nor could they be improved qualitatively to the extent necessary to deal with a combined threat. What the secretary wanted simply could not be done.[27]

MACV again enumerated the many actions being taken to remedy South Vietnam's military defects. Poor leadership, it asserted, was more serious among company-grade officers (aspirant to captain) and noncommissioned officers. As a cure, MACV promised that American advisers would continue to emphasize merit promotions and leadership training. To improve morale and reduce desertions, MACV would continue supporting South Vietnamese desertion control campaigns, more liberal awards and leave policies, political indoctrination programs, and completion of the fingerprint identification system. It made no mention of corruption or poor leadership at higher levels, but noted the increased number of combined operations and the ongoing MACV programs to improve South Vietnamese intelligence and logistical operations. Yet neither Abrams nor his staff was able to suggest any changes in Saigon's military organization, strategy, or tactics that would enable the South Vietnamese to deal with a combined enemy threat. The quantitative and qualitative increases needed to realize such an objective were not feasible. Saigon's current policy of improving area security with more and better Territorial Forces, thereby freeing regular units for mobile operations, was all that could be accomplished.

While endorsing the MACV analysis, Admiral McCain stressed the danger of overtaxing Saigon's manpower and training capacity by any further expansion. The Accelerated Phase II Improvement and Modernization Plan, together with the Midway increase, was already "extremely ambitious" and, he warned, "further acceleration could prove self-defeating."[28]

---

[26] USMACV, "Command History, 1969," 2:VI–14 to VI–15, HRB, CMH.
[27] Ibid., VI–127 to VI–128, HRB, CMH.
[28] Ibid., VI–131 to VI–132, HRB, CMH.

Laird refused to take no for an answer. On 10 November he directed the Joint Chiefs of Staff to come up with a new plan, a Phase III plan, that would, one way or another, create a South Vietnamese military force that could "maintain at least current levels of security." The secretary stipulated that the new plan take into consideration unilateral U.S. withdrawals that would reduce American military strength first to a "support force" of 190,000–260,000 troops by July 1971 and then to a much smaller advisory force by July 1973. Laird's instructions not only ordered the services, for the third time, to come up with a more suitable Vietnamization plan but also put them on notice that a large residual support force was not in the offing.[29]

Awaiting the military's response, Laird's staff hoped for a more comprehensive program that would address the "critical problems of corruption, leadership, motivation and morale." The situation called for "an imaginative structure tailored to the real needs of the RVNAF (not merely to what present U.S. functions they can handle)," and some Defense Department officials feared that "a narrow, conventional Phase III force could have far reaching negative implications."[30]

This time the response was more positive. In their revised, more optimistic estimates MACV planners assumed continued success of the current South Vietnamese expansion programs—due to be completed in July 1970—and continued progress in the area security effort. With more people under direct Saigon control, both recruiting and desertion control programs could be made more efficient. A reduced Viet Cong threat would also free more troops, staffs, and materiel from local security responsibilities; open up more land supply lines; and boost troop morale. MACV planners also assumed a declining North Vietnamese Army threat within South Vietnam, continued U.S. materiel and financial support for Saigon, and no reduction in U.S. support activities in neighboring areas. If Hanoi's forces based just outside the borders of South Vietnam were ignored, then Laird's request could be met within the context of existing political and economic constraints.[31]

MACV submitted its specific recommendations at the end of December and the Joint Chiefs incorporated them into a Phase III RVNAF Improvement and Modernization Plan one month later. Phase III raised South Vietnamese military strength to 1,061,505 over a three-year period (mid-1970 to mid-1973) and created new support units to replace departing American forces. Included were ten new field artillery battalions, twenty-four truck companies, and five or six more helicopter squadrons for the regulars, and more Popular Forces units and seventy heavy (4.2-inch) mortar platoons for the territorials. To ease the impact of these increases, which amounted to about 70,000 spaces, the plan also projected the

[29] Quoted words from Memo, Laird to Chairman, JCS, 10 Nov 69, sub: Vietnamization—RVNAF Improvement and Modernization Aspects and Related US Planning, SEAB. See also Msgs, Wheeler JCS 14113 to Abrams, 131416 Nov 69, sub: Vietnamization—The Consolidation Phase, and CINCPAC OKA 1840 to Abrams, 181020 Nov 69, sub: Vietnamization, Abrams Papers, HRB. All in CMH.
[30] Memo, Asst SecDef to SecDef, 15 Dec 69, sub: Vietnamization Progress, file VIET 385, box 18, accession no. 75103, RG 330, WNRC.
[31] USMACV, "Command History, 1969," 2:VI–151 to VI–157, HRB, and planning documents in CRIMP, 1969, file, SEAB. Both in CMH. On 12 November 1969 General Bolton, now the deputy director of operations in the Office of the Deputy Chief of Staff for Military Operations, was designated to direct efforts within the Army Staff to support the Vietnamization effort and ease coordination between the military staffs in Saigon and Washington.

gradual elimination of some 50,000 paramilitary slots by reducing the number of Vietnamese revolutionary development cadre and by closing down the Civilian Irregular Defense Group, the Provincial Reconnaissance Unit, and the Kit Carson Scout programs. But Laird's staff also noted that the Joint Chiefs had tied their proposals to the existence of a large American residual support force, and suspected that the military was still trying to use its evaluations of South Vietnamese military capabilities to stall the withdrawal process.[32]

In mid-February 1970 Laird visited Saigon a second time to talk the whole matter over again with Abrams and Thieu. Abrams declared that success in Vietnamization "depends in a large measure on the availability of sound GVN leadership," noted that Thieu regularly solicited his views on the subject, and explained that he and Thieu were focusing on the replacement of three or four inept division commanders. The secretary of defense apparently made no suggestions, but communicated his disappointment with the lack of any new or fresh concepts. He also thought that Abrams and Bunker were more worried about the possibility of a North Vietnamese ceasefire proposal and still mystified over Hanoi's failure to make such overtures earlier. When Laird met separately with the South Vietnamese leaders, he found them more concerned with the Phase III plan. They made, in fact, a direct appeal to the secretary for more support, requesting 175-mm. artillery pieces to counter enemy long-range artillery opposite the Demilitarized Zone, field artillery instead of mortars for the territorials, and air defense artillery to protect military units and airfields, and again asked for direct financial assistance to improve the living standards of South Vietnamese military personnel.[33]

Upon returning to Washington, Laird ordered the military to reevaluate the proposed Phase III plan and the Vietnamese requests, and to come up with an even stronger program. Two months later, after considering the recent Vietnamese requests, the Joint Chiefs submitted a revised version entitled the Consolidated RVNAF Improvement and Modernization Plan, or CRIMP, which covered the 1970–72 fiscal years and raised the total supported South Vietnamese military force structure to an even 1.1 million. The new plan added two long-range (175-mm.) artillery battalions, replaced the projected territorial mortar units with 176 two-gun (105-mm.) territorial artillery platoons, and provided an air defense force of two antiaircraft battalions (40-mm. and 50 cal.) and an intercepter squadron. At the request of the South Vietnamese, it also included separate ration supplement and dependent housing support programs. Laird endorsed the first two years of the three-year program in early June, but deferred approval of the remainder until he had a better idea of the long-range military situation in South Vietnam and the financial situation in the United States.[34]

---

[32] USMACV, "Command History, 1969," 2:VI–151 to VI–157, HRB, and planning documents in CRIMP, 1969, file, SEAB. Both in CMH. See also Memo, Asst SecDef for SA to SecDef, 31 Jan 70, sub: RVNAF Phase III, file VIET 333 LAIRD, 28 Feb 70, box 13, accession no. 76076, RG 330, WNRC.

[33] Draft Memo, Laird to President, 14 Feb 70, sub: Trip to Vietnam and CINCPAC [with General Wheeler], 10–14 February 1970, file VIET 333 LAIRD, 15 Feb 70, which includes resumes of talks with Thieu, Ky, Khiem and Vy; Briefing for SECDEF and CJCS, in Briefing Book no. 2, file VIET 333 LAIRD, 11 Feb 70. Both in box 13, accession no. 76076, RG 330, WNRC.

[34] USMACV, "Command History, 1970," 2:VII–4 to VII–16, HRB, and planning documents in CRIMP, 1969, file, SEAB. Both in CMH.

Secretary of Defense Melvin R. Laird's Second Trip to Saigon. *Escorting the secretary are Ambassador Bunker and Prime Minister Tran Thien Khiem (right).*

Washington Takes Control

Despite the haggle over the final improvement and modernization program, both the American military and civilian leaders were more concerned with the timing and impact of the projected U.S. troop withdrawals. In these matters Washington's civilian leaders had clearly taken control, and the concept of retaining a large American residual support force in Vietnam never had much of a chance. But Abrams and Laird both realized that the ability of the remaining allied forces to maintain "current levels of security" depended more on enemy inactivity than anything else. Ignoring the North Vietnamese Army units in Cambodia, Laos, and southern North Vietnam did not make them go away. Nor did ignoring those inept or corrupt South Vietnamese leaders who seemed to crop up in any discussion of Vietnamization. Perhaps they would have agreed with John Paul Vann who told one assistant secretary of defense visiting the Delta in 1969 that the United States had to acquire a veto power over South Vietnamese military appointments as it had over the South Korean Army during the Korean conflict; it was "either that, or just wait until they lose many lives and then they

357

will do it right." Abrams obviously chose the latter course, as Westmoreland had done before.[35]

Throughout the evolution of the new Vietnamization policy, American leaders in Washington harbored no illusions as to Saigon's strengths and weaknesses. Despite the plethora of optimistic, or at least hopeful, official plans and reports, they remained well informed regarding the situation in South Vietnam. The responses to NSSM 1 only assembled and made more authoritative much information that was already known, at least to those officials who were willing to read and learn.[36]

In December 1969, for example, a report from Kissinger's staff brought the entire matter of South Vietnamese leadership to his personal attention. Citing the notoriously incompetent commanders of the 5th, 18th, and 25th Infantry Divisions around Saigon, the report maintained that "the Allies are not following through on their verbal insistence that gross incompetents and crooks in the Republic of Vietnam's Armed Forces (RVNAF) be removed from positions of responsibility and that known men of reasonable honesty and effectiveness be promoted in their place." Noting the importance of the senior military officers who served as both troop commanders and political leaders, it held that "the continued US tolerance of inordinately incompetent and corrupt officers in senior positions debases US credibility and makes a sham of hopes for significant progress in Vietnamization." To the Vietnamese, American tolerance of such men was equivalent to American approval. "Senior US officials in Saigon and Washington," the report charged,

are generally accorded no credibility in Vietnam when they assert that they have pressed hard for certain major personnel changes, when they cite corroborating statistics on new province chiefs, etc., or when they assert that such desirable changes cannot be implemented by President Thieu because of the risks of precipitating a military coup.

It concluded that such personnel changes were critical to the Vietnamization effort, could not be made by Thieu alone, and required American presidential action, making improved leadership the condition of continued American support.[37]

Such suggestions also revealed the great differences between political realities in Washington and Saigon. The objectives of American leaders in the two capitals appeared to be widening daily. Behind the new policy of Vietnamization was the recognition that the United States could no longer support an open-ended military commitment in Southeast Asia. Americans wanted less, not more, in-

[35] MFR, Asst SecDef for SA, 26 Nov 69, sub: Trip Report, file VIET 333 SELIN, box 18, accession no. 75103, RG 330, WNRC.

[36] For example, see Memo, SecArmy Stanley R. Resor to SecDef, 6 Oct 69, sub: Secretary of the Army Trip Report, 20–28 August 1969, file VIET 333 (ALPHA) 1969, box 96, accession no. 75089, RG 330, WNRC; Draft Memo, Laird to President, 14 Feb 70, sub: Trip to Vietnam and CINCPAC [with General Wheeler], 10–14 February 1970, file VIET 333 LAIRD, 15 Feb 70, box 13, accession no. 76076, RG 330, WNRC. For Abrams on South Vietnamese leadership, see Msg, Abrams MAC 13589 to McCain and Wheeler, Info Kissinger, Helms, Weyand (in Paris), Laird, and SecState William P. Rogers, 191120 Oct 69, sub: Assessment of the Situation in Vietnam, Abrams Papers, HRB, CMH.

[37] Memo, Sven Kraemer, thru John Holdridge, to Kissinger, 22 Dec 69, sub: RVNAF Leadership and US Responsibility (Excerpt From My Trip Report Submitted September 12, 1969), SEAB, CMH. Holdridge headed the East Asia desk of the National Security Council.

volvement in Vietnam. Secretary Laird called Vietnamization "a critical test case for the Nixon Doctrine," the thrust of which was on assistance programs that could be accomplished by indigenous governments with minimal American involvement.[38] His continued insistence on a plan for a completely self-sufficient South Vietnamese armed forces swept aside any notion of a residual support force, as did the retention of troop withdrawal decisions at the presidential level. MACV could determine the composition of the withdrawal increments, but not their size or timing. Whether Abrams and MACV could successfully Vietnamize the war within these parameters remained to be seen. Like Westmoreland, Abrams would have preferred to have the struggle determined on the battlefield, where his overwhelming military power could be brought to bear. Instead, the success of American policy seemed to depend increasingly on the actions of the South Vietnamese themselves. Nevertheless, Abrams was resolved to keep as much American combat strength in South Vietnam as his superiors would allow and continued to expect some sort of negotiated settlement that would have major ramifications on all his current plans. Any agreements in this area that called for a rapid withdrawal could undercut the entire Vietnamization effort as well as MACV's improvement and modernization programs. Such considerations kept Abrams looking over his shoulder, always keeping his rapid (T-Day) withdrawal planning current should a sudden breakthrough in Paris precipitate a major change in U.S. policy.[39]

---

[38] Memo, Laird to Asst SecDef for ISA, 27 Aug 70, sub: Southeast Asia Strategy Alternatives, file VIET 381, 4 Dec 70, box 13, accession no. 76076, RG 330, WNRC. President Nixon had outlined this policy publicly during his visit to Guam in July 1969. See Nixon, *Memoirs of Richard Nixon*, pp. 394–95.

[39] For a treatment of the continued T-Day planning in South Vietnam, see interviews with planners in Ltr, Maj Ronald W. Schuette, CO, 23d Military History Detachment, to the Office of the Chief of Military History, 5 May 69, VNIT 394, HRB, CMH.

20

Spotlight on Saigon

The first two years of the Nixon administration were critical in determining the final form of the South Vietnamese armed forces. Outside factors were favorable for growth and reform. Enemy activity remained light, and the government of South Vietnam appeared strong. In Saigon President Thieu further strengthened his position in August 1969 by appointing a close ally, General Khiem, as prime minister, and Khiem, in turn, was able to form a loyal government of soldiers, civil servants, and technicians, and, through persuasion and coercion, to bring the elected legislature into line. In the United States the new policy of Vietnamization and American troop redeployments muffled domestic criticism of the war and, more important, gave General Abrams firm guidance on what was to be expected of Saigon's military forces. MACV was to prepare the South Vietnamese armed forces to face a combined Viet Cong–North Vietnamese Army threat by 1973, or sooner, without direct American ground combat support. Abrams and his generals had to accomplish what they had previously judged as impossible.

One War, One Strategy

In many ways General Creighton Abrams was the opposite of his predecessor. In contrast to Westmoreland's aura of spit-and-polish formalism, Abrams, according to one associate, habitually had a "tough, noisy, abrasive," no-nonsense air about him, and at times seemed to cultivate the image of the rugged cigar-smoking combat leader who had once been one of General George S. Patton's top tank commanders in World War II. In private, however, his well-known fondness for classical music and his after-hours congeniality belied these surface impressions. More pragmatic and perhaps less reflective than Westmoreland, Abrams rarely engaged in speculation, focusing his energies on those problems he felt were solvable within the confines of his military responsibilities. Saigon's growing political stability allowed him to leave South Vietnamese national politics, for the most part, in the hands of Ambassador Bunker, with whom he had a close personal relationship. Abrams' major task was improving

Abrams Discussing His Strategy in I Corps

the South Vietnamese armed forces. But, although his tenure as Westmoreland's deputy for over a year had given him a close look at his Vietnamese allies, he had no magic solutions for their endemic military problems.[1]

In September 1968 Abrams promulgated his "one war" operational strategy. By formally ending the division of roles and missions between American and South Vietnamese combat forces, he eliminated the tacit existence of two separate military strategies, attrition and pacification. Henceforth, American and Vietnamese military forces would carry out the three military pacification tasks of search and destroy, clearing, and security simultaneously.[2] He directed that all allied forces, including American and South Vietnamese ground troops, tactical air units and B–52 bombers, territorial and police forces, and the CIDG, attack in concert enemy main and local forces, guerrillas, and political cadre "across the broad spectrum of the conflict."[3] All units and commands were to emphasize

[1] Quoted words from Interv, Lt Cols James Tussing and William D. Wilson with Lt Gen Joseph M. Heiser, Jr., CG, 1st Logistical Command (1968–69), March 1976, sess. 2, pp. 21-27, and sess. 3, p. 68, Senior Officers Debriefing Program, Joseph M. Heiser Papers, MHI. See also Intervs, author with Col James Anderson (hereafter cited as Anderson Interv), 23 Jun 83, and with Maj Gen James N. Ellis (hereafter cited as Ellis Interv), 29 Jun 83, SEAB, CMH. Anderson and Ellis were former aides to General Abrams.

[2] For public relations reasons, MACV had replaced the term *search and destroy* with *reconnaissance-in-force* ("Rif") and, in mid-1969, with *preemptive operations*.

[3] USMACV, "Command History, 1969," 1:II–3, HRB, CMH.

pacification security. Westmoreland had already outlined this new orientation in January, when the Tet offensive had suddenly upset his plans.[4] Abrams now intended to put his predecessor's proposals into effect.

In 1969, while undertaking this operational reorientation, Abrams acquired a second and coequal objective, Vietnamization—supervising the withdrawal of U.S. ground combat troops and fostering the growth of South Vietnamese military capabilities. In assessing his plans and programs for both tasks Abrams also had to constantly analyze enemy strength and intentions, as well as any diplomatic progress in the Paris peace talks that might bring his efforts in South Vietnam to a sudden halt.[5] Fortunately for the Americans, the enemy commanders continued to keep their main forces on the opposite side of the South Vietnamese borders, in their Cambodian, Laotian, and North Vietnamese sanctuaries, appearing to fall back into the Phase II, or guerrilla warfare, stage of their war strategy. This, in turn, made Abrams' new emphasis on pacification possible, even though in reality the American combat forces often had little else to do.[6]

New Generals, New Leadership

In January 1969 the ailments of the South Vietnamese armed forces were practically identical to those existing in 1965. Although MACV had reequipped almost the entire military apparatus and doubled its size, the old maladies remained: corruption, poor leadership, high desertion rates, a sluggish supply system, and problems in morale, pay, dependent care, and so forth. The responses to NSSM 1 only confirmed this. Progress had been made and duly recorded, but how much progress and was it enough? Would the South Vietnamese military structure be able to hold together under pressure or, once American troops had withdrawn, would it crumble under attack or perhaps collapse from its own weight? General Abrams, in a now familiar refrain, declared that Saigon's military expansion was now "virtually complete" and vowed that "from this time forward, qualitative improvement is the primary basis for advances in effectiveness."[7] Whether he could keep this promise depended on how well MACV could plan for the eventual departure of U.S. forces and whether the South Vietnamese generals would be more responsive to American advice.

[4] See Memo, Chapman to President, 2 Feb 68, sub: Strategy for the Conduct of the War in SEASIA, box 127, Johnson Papers, MHI. Chapman noted that Westmoreland's new strategy was "in consonance with the Marine Corps view that the Pacification Program is the key to ultimate victory" and that "the major battles which may result are not designed with the sole object of killing VC or NVA."
[5] For example, Msg, Bunker SGN 17150 to SecState, 251445 Aug 69, sub: Contingency Planning for PRG/DRV Cease-Fire Proposal, Bunker Papers, DS.
[6] In Msg, Abrams MAC 13589 to McCain and Wheeler, 191120 Oct 69, sub: Assessment of the Situation in Vietnam, Abrams Papers, HRB, CMH, Abrams also noted that the enemy still had the strategic initiative and could increase the level of combat simply by crossing the border in force.
[7] Ibid.

One positive sign was the large number of command changes made in 1969 and 1970,[8] as President Thieu continued to replace many Ky-appointees and independents with men more loyal to himself. Although American field advisers had recommended many of the replaced commanders for cashiering, their influence on these changes is impossible to measure. In the northern zone General Lam continued to head the I Corps, while Generals Truong and Toan retained command of the South Vietnamese 1st and 2d Infantry Divisions, respectively, both highly rated units. In August 1970 Thieu promoted Truong, whom Americans regarded as Saigon's best fighting general, and gave the 1st Division to General Pham Van Phu. Phu, an older professional with a career stretching back to Dien Bien Phu, had served with both the 1st and 2d Divisions, the 44th Special Tactical Zone, and, since January, as head of the *LLDB* (Vietnamese Special Forces), replacing the somewhat notorious Doan Van Quang who had commanded the component since 1964.[9]

In the II Corps Tactical Zone Thieu kept General Vo Vanh Canh, who had taken over the 23d Infantry Division in 1968 when the previous commander was killed, in office, but replaced the 22d Infantry Division commander, General Nguyen Van Hieu, in 1969 with General Le Ngoc Trien, the Quang Trung Training Center commandant. Finally, in August 1970, the president removed Lu Lan as corps commander and selected General Ngo Dzu, another senior officer with a long service record, as his replacement. American advisers rated all three of the new commanders highly.

Around Saigon, the III Corps commander, General Do Cao Tri, finally engineered the replacement of two of his weak division commanders in August 1969, replacing Thuan of the 5th Infantry Division with Hieu from the 22d Division and Giai of the 18th Infantry Division with Tho from the Thu Duc Infantry School. Both departing commanders had been political generals, and after years of frustration with their performance, the American advisers were glad to see them leave. However, the American officials had major reservations about the incoming commanders, regarding neither Hieu nor Tho as a dynamic leader. In the 25th Infantry Division General Thinh, who had replaced the timorous Chinh back in January 1968, remained in command.

In the IV Corps Tactical Zone the three current division commanders had relieved political generals of mixed abilities in mid-1968. Since then the 9th and 21st Infantry Divisions had done fairly well according to MACV statistical evaluations, but the 7th Infantry Division had gone steadily downhill after the neighboring U.S. 9th Infantry Division had redeployed from Vietnam in July 1969.

---

[8] For command changes and personalities, see MACDP Roster of RVNAF Personalities files; Braddock Political file; and South Vietnamese officer dossiers. In addition, the CIA intelligence information cables contain much gossip on military appointments and personalities. All in SEAB, CMH.

[9] According to American embassy records, Doan Van Quang, a former Co supporter, had been heavily involved in the opium-diamond trade and was being blackmailed by National Police Director Loan to support Ky. Quang (not to be confused with the deposed IV Corps commander, Dang Van Quang) now became inspector general, but it was Phu who remained in favor and later commanded the II Corps during the 1975 Highlands disaster.

Thieu and General Thanh, the corps commander, tried to rectify the situation in January 1970 by sending Col. Nguyen Khoa Nam, an airborne brigade commander, to head the 7th Division and by making Col. Vo Huu Hanh, the Hau Nghia Province chief, Phu's replacement in the 44th Special Tactical Zone. Nam had earned a good military reputation in the airborne force, while American advisers considered Hanh a much better combat commander than administrator.[10] The South Vietnamese president, however, was forced to make a more drastic change in mid-1970, when Thanh was killed in action. Thieu replaced Thanh, first with Ngo Dzu and then, after moving Dzu to the II Corps, with General Truong from the 1st Division. Although the untimely death of the experienced Thanh was a blow, the elevation of Truong and others appeared to pave the way for a new generation of professional soldiers.

By the end of 1970 just about all of the junta generals that had put together the original Directory had passed from power. With them went many of their deputies, staff officers, and other aides, as well as many South Vietnamese mid-level commanders, a second-echelon turnover marked by over thirty regimental command changes in 1969 and 1970. Of the old guard, there was only General Khang of the marines, General Dong of the airborne, and the ubiquitous General Minh of the still sensitive Capital Military District.

Although Abrams hoped that the new South Vietnamese corps and division commanders would set a quicker pace for the rest of the armed forces, his evaluations of these men and their subordinates was suspect. Official MACV judgments still remained skewed by an overreliance on statistical evidence, an emphasis on positive reporting, and the suppression of adverse information. In addition, the low level of enemy activity and the vast amount of American combat support available precluded any real test of South Vietnamese combat performance during 1969. As a result, staff evaluations at MACV based on statistical indicators continued to exhibit marked differences from those of individual advisers in the field.[11] For example, General Toan's 2d Division had the highest ratings in leadership and performance during 1969, yet one year earlier American advisers had recommended Toan's dismissal for incompetence and his involvement in smuggling activities.[12] In a more pointed case, one MACV evaluation described the new commander of the 18th Division as a "highly respected and admired general," while another judged him to be a "coward and military incompetent." Americans could not even agree on the dynamic General Tri who had taken over the III Corps. While his field advisers lauded his energy and decisiveness, General Abrams himself remained skeptical of his abilities, feeling that he

---

[10] Ltr, Vann to Berger, 13 Jan 70, sub: Response to Your Telegraphic Inquiry of 1600 Hours, 13 January 1970, SEAB, CMH.

[11] For example, Thayer, "How To Analyze a War Without Fronts," pp. 813–15; Memo, Kraemer to Kissinger, 22 Dec 69, sub: RVNAF Leadership and US Responsibility (Excerpt From My Trip Report Submitted September 12, 1969); Ltr, SecArmy Stanley Resor to Abrams, 25 Oct 69, with attached trip report. Documents in SEAB, CMH.

[12] Whether the improved ratings were the result of Toan's leadership, or the extensive aid given to the 2d Division by the U.S. 23d Infantry Division on 1969 (see Chapter 21), or for some other reason, is difficult to determine.

was too independent, too critical of his own government and his fellow officers, and "not a team player."[13]

John Paul Vann, the highly respected American adviser who had worked extensively with South Vietnamese leaders since 1962, felt that the high ratings awarded by MACV to certain Vietnamese commanders in the IV Corps Tactical Zone were extremely misleading. In January 1970, at the request of Ambassador Bunker, he produced his own evaluations, which differed markedly from the official judgments of MACV. Vann recommended all three division commanders and the special zone commander for relief. In this case, Thieu incidentally relieved the 7th Division commander three weeks later,

General Nguyen Van Toan

but kept the 9th and 21st Division commanders in office and named the officer heading the special zone as the next commander of the 1st Division. Vann also recommended ten colonels for advancement (four later took over significant combat commands, and three others headed the key Provinces of Bien Hoa, Gia Dinh, and Chuong Thien). Yet none of them had received favorable ratings in the evaluation reports of the field advisers. Clearly MACV was still having serious problems developing a consensus on the worth of South Vietnamese leaders and especially identifying those who failed to perform well.[14]

During the second half of 1970 the Office of the Secretary of Defense also took another look at the matter of South Vietnamese leadership. Secretary Laird's staff pointed out the lack of "a systematic and continuous MACV effort to have the GVN replace poor combat commanders with good ones." All were impressed by the system established by Komer for replacing ineffective province and district officials. As explained by Ambassador William E. Colby, who succeeded Komer in November 1968, the procedure depended more on a flow of information from CORDS officials to Thieu and Khiem than on any special relationships or leverage. In response, Laird asked the Joint Chiefs of Staff and MACV to reassess their efforts to put the best South Vietnamese leaders in key posts. He reminded them of the high priority he had given to improving South Vietnamese leadership.

[13] First and second quotation from Thayer, "How To Analyze a War Without Fronts," p. 814. Third quotation from Msg, Abrams MAC 5960 to Wheeler and McCain, 031017 May 70, Abrams Papers, HRB, CMH, which also contains evaluations of other senior South Vietnamese generals prepared by Lt. Gen. William E. Potts, Abrams' J–2. See comments of Potts on draft manuscript "Advice and Support: The Final Years," SEAB, CMH.

[14] Ltr, Vann to Berger, 13 Jan 70, sub: Response to Your Telegraphic Inquiry of 1600 Hours, 13 January 1970. For other views, see Rpt, MACC–IV, 19 Feb 70, sub: Evaluation of ARVN Commanders; Komer, 11 Aug 70, sub: Vietnam Trip Report, 8–17 July 1970, p. 10; Fact Sheet, Kraft, 10 Feb 70, sub: Assessment of ARVN/VNMC Organizations. All in SEAB, CMH.

Citing the remarkable progress of the 7th Division after Thieu had installed a strong commander, he asked whether Komer's methods could be used to effect changes in Vietnamese military commands.[15]

The Joint Chiefs of Staff, now under the chairmanship of Admiral Thomas H. Moorer,[16] felt that there was no need for concern. MACV had always given a high priority to placing the best South Vietnamese officers in combat commands, and field advisers had always supplied MACV with regular assessments of Vietnamese combat leaders down to the battalion level. The Joint Chiefs in their reply noted the many command changes that had taken place since 1968, intimating that MACV recommendations had played a key role in this process. They held that MACV considered only one of the eleven division commanders as "unsatisfactory" (Hieu of the 5th Division, who was recommended for relief) and rated only one other division commander and just two of the thirty-three regimental commanders as "marginal" and subject to further "monitoring." In such cases, they explained, field advisers assembled supporting evidence for adverse recommendations, which were then forwarded to the appropriate echelon for action. In the case of general officers and senior colonels, General Abrams or the American ambassador handled the matter personally. As they had done many times in the past, the Joint Chiefs reminded the defense secretary that the replacement of senior South Vietnamese military personnel was a "sensitive matter" that had to be "handled with great care" and pursued "at a pace that is acceptable to the GVN and President Thieu."[17]

Another facet of Saigon's leadership problem was the fate of the relieved officers. Few actually left military service, and most continued to move over to district or province posts, to higher-level staffs, or to the establishments of the Central Training Command. This was especially true of generals and senior colonels, who continued to jam the upper echelons of the officer corps and prevented the rapid advancement of their sometimes more competent juniors. For example, General Nguyen Thanh Hoang, relieved from his command of the 7th Division, went on to attend the new National Defense College and returned to the IV Corps the following year to become deputy commander; General Thuan, the retired 5th Division chief, moved over to head the Thu Duc Infantry School and later became the III Corps commander; General Giai, fired from the neighboring 18th Division, took over a major training center and later headed the Ranger Command; and General Lu Lan, dispossessed of his II Corps command, became inspector general of the armed forces and later commandant of the National Defense College. These lateral moves enabled Thieu to placate the outgoing generals and reduce any friction caused by the loss of positions that carried extensive military and political power. Generally, charges of corruption went uninvestigated and unpunished. MACV held that such matters were internal South Vietnamese affairs and, officially, professed ignorance of any legal

---

[15] Quoted words from Memo, Office of Asst SecDef for SA to SecDef, 17 Sep 70, sub: RVNAF Leadership. See also MFR, Colby, 17 Jun 70, sub: Removal of Corrupt or Ineffective Officials; Memo, Laird to JCS, 13 Oct 70, sub: RVNAF Leadership. All in SEAB, CMH.

[16] Moorer replaced General Wheeler in July 1970, after the latter had completed his sixth year as JCS chairman.

[17] Memo, JCSM–558–70 to SecDef, 3 Dec 70, sub: Republic of Vietnam Armed Forces Leadership (based on Msg, CINCPAC to JCS, 21 Nov 70, sub: RVNAF Leadership), SEAB, CMH.

proceedings taken by Saigon against any military officers.[18] The main task of MACV was still to provide advice and assistance to the South Vietnamese, and General Abrams, following the policies of his predecessor, refused to police an army that, in his opinion, had to learn to take care of itself.

The Advisers

Despite the new policy of Vietnamization, the philosophy and organization of the advisory effort remained unchanged.[19] General Abrams and his major tactical commanders continued to act as the principal American advisers, while the combat teams performed primarily liaison and support functions. Province and district teams remained strong and, with the general lull in combat operations, had more to do. Yet Abrams himself was concerned over the quality of his senior tactical advisers, charging that, in selecting such officers, his staff was "often 'hung up' on quality criteria such as 'must be a War College or C & GSC [U.S. Army Command and General Staff College] graduate,' 'must have command experience,' etc." Instead, he demanded "guys who can lead/influence . . . the business of pacification," officers who "feel empathy toward the Vietnamese, . . . appreciate their good points and understand their weaknesses." While noting that "fighting" was "still important," he wanted advisers who "have a sensitivity to humans" and "who can pull ideas and actions out of the Vietnamese" in the pursuit of two major goals: "pacification and upgrading the RVNAF."[20]

But in the field, advisers at all levels began to think in terms of "working themselves out of a job."[21] Seeing the end of the U.S. involvement growing closer, some became tougher and more demanding. Lt. Gen. Arthur S. Collins, Jr., the often outspoken II Corps senior adviser, announced that he was fed up with "buttering up" the Vietnamese and "telling them how great they are," pointing out that "we've been doing that for about ten years and it hasn't been very effective."[22] He ordered his subordinate advisers not to play "that ball game" any longer and to demand better results. But even the feisty Collins later admitted that his own, more direct advisory style had had little positive effect.[23]

In January 1969 MACV instituted the combat assistance team (CAT) concept throughout Vietnam, reducing the number of tactical advisers to the absolute minimum and officially changing their mission "from advising to combat support coordination." Because the experimental reduction of the 22d Division advi-

[18] Msg, SecDef to AmEmbassy, Saigon, DAIN 403641, 9 Jan 69, sub: Sparkman Letter ("JGS refuses to release such information to MACV"), SEAB, CMH.

[19] For example, see USMACV, "Command History, 1970," 2:VII–62 to VII–63, "COMUSMACV's Guidance on Selecting Advisors," HRB, CMH.

[20] MFR, Brig Gen Albert H. Smith, Jr., MACV J–1, 15 Dec 69, sub: General Abrams' Guidance on Selecting Advisors, SEAB, CMH.

[21] For example, Interv, Maj Edward J. Jasaitis, CO, 20th Military History Detachment, with Lt Col Ferdinand H. Hauser, Senior Adviser, 2d Regt, 1st Div (hereafter cited as Hauser Interv), 24 Sep 69, VNIT 476, HRB, CMH.

[22] Transmittal Ltr, U.S. Army Advisory Group, II CTZ, 16 Jul 70 (transcript of presentations at Senior Advisers Conference, 28 Jun 70), Seibert Papers, MHI.

[23] Ltr, Collins to Ngo Dzu, 6 Dec 70, Arthur S. Collins Papers, MHI.

TABLE 17—ADVISORY TEAM PERSONNEL REDUCTIONS, SEPTEMBER 1969

Unit	Strength Reduction
I Corps Headquarters	58
1st Infantry Division	18
2d Infantry Division	22
II Corps Headquarters	140
22d Infantry Division	40
23d Infantry Division	35
III Corps Headquarters	?
5th and 18th Infantry Divisions	? [a]
25th Infantry Division	25[b]
IV Corps Headquarters	?
7th Infantry Division	50
9th Infantry Division	70
21st Infantry Division	70
Airborne Division	46
Marine Division	?

[a] Under study.
[b] Eleven more planned.
Source: Fact Sheet, MACMA–PP, 13 Aug 69, sub: Combat Assistance Team (CAT), MICRO 40/0983, RG 334, WNRC.

sory team had proved too drastic, MACV decided to leave the small regimental and battalion teams intact and reduced the size of only the larger division and corps detachments, allowing the teams enough strength to continue to provide American tactical commands with necessary operational and intelligence information. The ensuing reductions differed from unit to unit, and depended on MACV's assessment of the problems facing each advisory team (*Table 17*). In the Highlands, for example, the 22d Division advisory team lost forty spaces; the 23d Division's team, thirty-five; and the busy 24th Special Tactical Zone team in Kontum Province, none. MACV reduced the II Corps team, however, by a hefty 140 men and made similar cuts in the other zones. These reductions continued throughout 1970 and 1971, although at times MACV and the corps senior advisers had to beef up those teams supporting Vietnamese units in heavy combat by temporarily withdrawing advisers from units or staffs in quieter areas.[24]

In December 1969 Secretary Laird asked the service secretaries to take a closer look at the field advisory program, pointing out that the Vietnamization program was making this effort increasingly important. While directing them "to eliminate as many advisors as possible," he also recommended that "only the most highly qualified" soldiers be assigned to the job. Impressed with the Army's success in improving the quality of the CORDS advisers through special programs and incentives, he asked if something similar could be done to upgrade the rest of the advisory effort.[25]

[24] Fact Sheet, MACMA–PP, 13 Aug 69, sub: Combat Assistance Team (CAT), MICRO 40/0983, RG 334, WNRC. Henceforth, division advisory teams became "D-cats"; regimental teams, "R-cats"; and battalion teams, "B-cats."
[25] Memo, Laird to Service Secretaries, 16 Dec 69, sub: Quantity and Quality of US Advisors in Vietnam, SEAB, CMH.

Advisers' Living Conditions, *which varied from the Spartanism of a district compound at Cai Lai to the amenities of a corps advisory headquarters (bottom) at Pleiku*

The Army staff mulled over the matter for about a month. Admittedly, the Army's advisory assignment policies had many shortcomings. Officers considered U.S. troop assignments more desirable for career advancement than advisory duty, too few volunteered for the task, and MACV often "diverted" those that had received advisory training to other positions. Even in MACV's Training Directorate, supposedly one of the focal points of the advisory effort, the director and his staff rotated often and few had any extensive training experience.[26] In addition, the Army had little data on those officers who had served tours as advisers—whether they were young or old, black or white; what their level of education, source of commission, or

Teaching Through Demonstration

branch specialty was; or how successful they had been.[27] Preparation for advisory duty was unchanged, and the six-week military advisory course at Fort Bragg, North Carolina, remained weak.[28] One adviser, who already had a strong background in the Vietnamese language, felt that the language instruction offered at Fort Bragg was worthless and complained that the course work "didn't teach you how to be an adviser in any capacity."[29] The preparation for advisory duty had obviously not improved since 1965.

The Army Staff considered many remedies, such as revised selection procedures, materiel incentives, and more extensive training, but failed to agree on any clear-cut solution. General Abrams himself was more concerned with just filling the ranks of his advisory teams with personnel at their authorized grade level (that is, lieutenant colonels in positions calling for lieutenant colonels, and so forth), and thereby reducing the number of low-ranking advisers with little or no military experience. Admiral McCain passed on this concern to Washington, recommending that the Army accept more grade imbalances elsewhere to satisfy

[26] Office of the Secretary of Defense, Selected Items from SEA and Korea Trip Report [of] D. R. Cotter, Director, Overseas Defense Research, ARPA, circa 1970, SEAB, CMH.

[27] For the Army's response, see Memo, Resor to SecDef, 2 Feb 70, sub: Quantity and Quality of Advisors in Vietnam; and supporting internal studies in file on advisers (1969). Both in SEAB, CMH.

[28] HQ, CONARC, "Study of the U.S.A. Institute of Military Assistance, Ft. Bragg, N.C.," circa 1970, Newton Papers, MHI, which briefly notes problems in the faculty and the instructional program. The many interviews taken by U.S. Army military history detachments in the field with American advisers in 1969–70 also point out the almost universal opinion that the MATA course was of limited use.

[29] Interv, Maj Lawrence D. Sylvan, CO, 45th Military History Detachment, with Capt Gil Trevino, Senior Adviser, 32d Ranger Bn (44th Special Tactical Zone), 26 Sep 69, VNIT 494, HRB, CMH. Trevino had attended a thirty-seven week course on the North Vietnamese dialect as part of his intelligence training and had been in Vietnam as an adviser since June 1968.

Vietnam's personnel requirements. But he also warned that too many "compensating incentives" might only confirm the undesirability of advisory duty in the minds of many officers.[30]

Despite the obvious need for change, the reply of Secretary of the Army Stanley R. Resor on 2 February 1970 was superficial, stressing minor improvements in advisory assignments and promising unspecified actions that would somehow make advisory duty more attractive. The Army Staff would continue to study the matter, he promised, but longer tours were out of the question. The Army was already losing too many officers because of long and frequent family separations; junior officers with young families were especially sensitive to repeated unaccompanied overseas assignments. Instead, he hoped that MACV could improve advisory quality by reassigning experienced officers from departing American units and reducing the size of the various advisory detachments wherever possible. General Kerwin, now the Army's deputy chief of staff for personnel, was more pessimistic, and confided to Abrams that there were simply not enough captains, majors, and lieutenant colonels to go around without abandoning the twelve-month tour policy. Already the possibility of a third tour after returning home for about one year was causing too many resignations. The need to provide advisers for new units and strengthen the province and district teams only made the personnel situation worse. Despite the CAT reductions, the overall strength of the field advisory teams actually increased from about 7,000 to 11,900 during 1969 and then to 14,332 in 1970 *(Table 18)*.[31] The problem seemed unsolvable.

Internal Reform

Given the weaknesses of the lower advisory echelons in experience and leverage, the senior American advisers at MACV were understandably more comfortable dealing with broad administrative programs. Indigenous South Vietnamese efforts to improve overall unit effectiveness centered on Saigon's low-key New Horizons campaign, initiated in 1967 on a test basis and formally adopted in 1969. New Horizons was essentially an effort to improve leadership, logistics, and administration in small units by sending teams from the Political Warfare Department to regular and territorial elements that had performed poorly. The teams were to investigate problem areas in morale, attitude of commanders toward troops, status of military dependents, relationships

---

[30] Quoted words from Msg, CINCPAC to JCS, DAIN 259341, 112253 Jan 70, sub: U.S. Advisors in Vietnam, SEAB. See also Msgs, Abrams MAC 1285 to Wheeler and McCain, 280305 Jan 70, sub: Assessment of the Situation in Vietnam, and Eckhardt CTO 810 to Abrams, 250235 May 65, Abrams Papers, HRB. Both in CMH.

[31] Memo, Resor to SecDef, 2 Feb 70, sub: Quality and Quantity of Advisers in Vietnam, SEAB, CMH; Tab 9 ("Quantity and Quality of Advisors") of Secretary Laird's Trip to Vietnam, 9–13 February 1970, file VIET 333 LAIRD, 9 Feb 70, box 13, accession no. 76076, RG 330, WNRC; Msg, Kerwin WDC 04323 to Abrams, 071910 Mar 70, sub: 100 Percent Personnel for MACV, SEAB, CMH; Fact Book, MACV, December 1968 (updated August 1969), MICRO 1/1293, RG 334, WNRC; USMACV, "Command History, 1970," 2:VII–63 to VII–79, HRB, CMH.

TABLE 18—APPROXIMATE FIELD ADVISORY STRENGTH, 1969–1970

Type	I CTZ	II CTZ	III CTZ	IV CTZ	Total
Combat Advisers					
Corps	203	272	372	312	1,159
Division [a]	194	136	261	227	818
Regiment [a]	24	24	27	27	102
Armored Cavalry Regiment	?	44	35	24	103
Infantry Battalion [a]	82	86	144	126	438
Marine Battalion	36	. . .	. . .	. . .	36
Ranger Battalion	?	12	39	25	76
Other commands [b]	21	46	85	92	244
Total	560	620	963	833	2,976
Support Advisers					
Logistics	. . .	. . .	. . .	. . .	390
School/Training	. . .	. . .	. . .	. . .	1,524
Total	. . .	. . .	. . .	. . .	1,914
CORDS Advisers					
CORDS	736	1,516	1,455	1,976	5,683
Mobile Training Teams	275	622	619	789	2,305
Total	1,011	2,138	2,074	2,765	7,988
Component Advisers					
Air Force Advisory Group	. . .	. . .	. . .	. . .	494
Naval Advisory Group	. . .	. . .	. . .	. . .	960
Total	. . .	. . .	. . .	. . .	1,454
Grand total					14,332

[a] Includes airborne units.

[b] Quang Da Special Zone (I CTZ), 24th Special Tactical Zone (II CTZ), Capital Military District (III CTZ), and 44th Special Tactical Zone (IV CTZ).

Sources: Fact Book, MACV, December 1968 (updated August 1969), MICRO 1/2193, RG 334, WNRC; USMACV, "Command History, 1970," 2:VII–63 to VII–79, HRB, CMH.

with the local population, the availability of a variety of amenities from entertainment to medical care, and the administration of military justice, and to offer guidance for improvement. However, the program continued to bog down in the preparatory stage throughout 1969 and 1970, while the political warfare teams underwent more training. The Joint General Staff also formed committees in each corps zone to supervise the effort, but, despite much publicity, little was done.[32]

Saigon made only slightly more progress in those areas monitored and pushed directly by Americans. Although MACV continued to keep close watch on South Vietnamese military promotions,[33] the Joint General Staff refused to drop its time-in-grade requirements for advancement and continued to base

[32] USMACV, "Command History, 1969," 2:VI–139 to VI–145, HRB, CMH.

[33] The following discussion on South Vietnamese military promotions is based on ibid., 2:VI–53 to VI–66, and "1970," 2:VII–26 to VII–28, HRB, and on MACV monthly reports on RVNAF officer strength and promotions, SEAB. Both in CMH.

promotions on longevity rather than on merit or responsibility. Accordingly, the MACV-sponsored three-year promotion program designed to close the gap between actual and authorized grades was far behind its goals. As a partial remedy, MACV persuaded the Vietnamese to reconvene the previous year's annual officer promotion board in May 1969 and to hold another officer promotion board in August. These actions resulted in 3,000 additional promotions but were unable to put the program back on track.

By the end of 1969 the officer corps, now 41,625 strong in the regular army, was still badly unbalanced. With only about one-third of its authorized strength in full colonels and a little over one-half of its lieutenant colonels, majors, and captains, most of the gaps had to be filled with aspirants and lieutenants. When the Joint General Staff announced the findings of the 1969 annual promotion board in February 1970, the results were again disappointing. Of 7,000 officer "promotions," only about 700 were actual grade changes, the remainder being conversions from temporary to permanent grades. A special promotion board in May yielded 1,347 actual promotions, Thieu advanced 21 high-ranking officers in August, and a special measure at the end of the year produced 577 more officer grade advancements. These final promotions were perhaps the most significant because they included battalion, company, and platoon commanders whose positions ought to have made them candidates for possible advancement regardless of time-in-grade or other factors.

Despite these measures, Saigon was unable to meet its promotion goals in 1970. Eligibility was still a problem, and MACV was still unable to convince the South Vietnamese high command to drop its time-in-grade or educational qualifications for either officer or noncommissioned officer promotions. The policy made sense in the technical branches and in the air force and navy, where training, experience, and technical knowledge were more critical, but it continued to militate against the selection and advancement of the most able leaders in the army. Although MACV had pushed Saigon into making more promotions than it had in the past, American advisers had no idea whether the right people had been promoted fast enough to improve overall leadership. Finally, the steady increase in the size of the armed forces—over 8,000 officer positions added in 1969 alone—and the continuing drain of able personnel into nonmilitary positions at corps, province, and district levels—over 6,800 officers performing duties with various civilian agencies as of December 1969—tended to dilute any progress in improving the grade structure within the army proper.

The enlisted ranks benefited more from the institution of a formal program. In 1968 MACV and the Joint General Staff had established quarterly enlisted promotion quotas by grade for each corps tactical zone. Although MACV was disappointed that the South Vietnamese used only about 40 percent of their allocation during 1969, that percentage represented over 17,000 enlisted promotions in an area where almost no progress had been made in the past.

Progress in other areas lagged. Enlisted personnel accounting continued to be chaotic, eternally hamstrung by the high desertion rates that made it almost impossible to match individual skills and training with assignments. The South Vietnamese military postal system also remained ineffective. Service was irregular and undependable. Many soldiers were insufficiently literate to make use of the mails, and those that were hesitated to trust their monthly paychecks to its care. Saigon's officer rotation program, acclaimed in past MACV reports, was another total failure. Many officers continued to homestead on rear staffs and training centers, while others never left combat units. For almost all soldiers, leaving combat units, even for a few days, was difficult. American field and staff advisers urged South Vietnamese commanders to keep 5 to 10 percent of their personnel on leave at any one time and to grant leave in large enough blocks to allow soldiers time to travel home and return. But Vietnamese commanders continued to grant military leave sparingly, preferring to give soldiers only three or four days at a time. American-inspired directives from the Joint General Staff to be more liberal had little effect. The South Vietnamese commissary system, revitalized by MACV in 1967, also ran into difficulty when the Ministry of Finance refused to release sufficient import credits to replenish exhausted stocks. Low military pay was also a constant headache and continued to foster corruption and moonlighting by all members of the armed forces. Despite the increased number of promotions and a general pay increase of about 19 percent in October 1970, MACV could not stem the steady erosion in the buying power of the piaster and local inflation continued to reduce real military wages. Thus, when prostitutes, laundresses, and barkeeps catering to the comparatively wealthy American troop units could make more money in two or three weeks than a division commander or a province chief could in an entire year, a certain amount of corruption seemed necessary, if only to redress the economic balance of Vietnamese society.[34]

Helping somewhat at the lower levels were improvements in South Vietnamese operational rations. The Joint General Staff ended all restrictions on their use in August 1968, and MACV began transferring about one million individual rations a month to Saigon. In late 1969 the Joint General Staff followed up Thieu's Midway Island requests for additional support in this area by proposing a direct American grant of rice, sugar, and canned food, amounting to about 300 pounds of foodstuffs per man per year. MACV, with the approval of the Department of Defense, opted for a modified plan that included both regulars and territorials, and both officers and enlisted ranks, but limited the supplement to about 100 pounds per man annually and required Saigon to prepare a detailed distribution plan to ensure that the food would not somehow end up on the black market or in private storerooms. The result was an elaborate system of monthly ration cards and supply accountability that, starting in 1970, was closely watched by American field advisers throughout the South Vietnamese logistical chain of command. However, field advisers continued to report that existing

---

[34] Interv, author with Lt Col Theodore D. Risch, Senior Adviser, 41st Regt, and G–1 Adviser, II CTZ (November 1968–November 1969), 26 Feb 76, SEAB, CMH. The South Vietnamese had tried to adopt the U.S. Army's complex military occupational specialty (MOS) system, assigning each soldier permanent and temporary skill designations based on a four-digit code; see Khuyen, *The RVNAF*, pp. 50–51. See also ibid., pp. 123–27; USMACV, "Command History, 1969," 2:VI–53, VI–63 to VI–64, VI–76 to VI–77, and "1970," 2:VII–91 to VII–95, HRB, CMH; Msg, CINCPAC to JCS and SecDef, DAIN 505047, 29 Jul 70, sub: Tango 17 for Admin CINCPAC Congressional Hearing, SEAB, CMH.

ration supplement programs were a shambles, and thus the prognosis for the new effort was not favorable. One adviser noted that even when unit messes and operational rations were available, the Vietnamese soldiers, almost by force of habit, continually scavenged for food: chickens, vegetables, rats, monkeys, snakes, or whatever could be found and eaten.[35]

During this same period the MACV staff made renewed attempts to spark the military dependent housing program. The effort had fallen by the wayside in 1968, and the separate American-funded self-help building program made little progress until 1969, when the South Vietnamese finally completed a few thousand units. In early 1970 a joint MACV–Joint General Staff dependent shelter program group loosely estimated that 240,000 shelters were still needed for regular and Regional Forces dependents. As a solution, the group recommended that, over an eight-year period (1970–77), Saigon house 40,000 families in vacated American facilities and construct 200,000 new units. It fixed American support for the new program at $6 million per year, while the South Vietnamese share was to begin at $5 million and rise to $13.2 million, and include the additional funds necessary for the purchase of real estate and the construction of community facilities (schools, wells, roads, and so forth). As before, dependent housing was to be cheap and efficient, consisting of ten-unit, one-story tenements of wood with corrugated steel roofs on a cement base with a porch, family room, sleeping loft, and outside cooking shelter.[36]

Again, the program got off to a slow start. Saigon's dependence on a rigid annual budget hampered the purchase of building material in advance of each fiscal year, and by the end of 1970 the South Vietnamese had completed only about half of the 16,000 shelters planned. But at least something had been done, and MACV was again optimistic. President Thieu was solidly behind the program, and, at Thieu's personal request, President Nixon agreed to double American financial support. Thieu, for his part, promised to commit the equivalent of four South Vietnamese engineer construction groups to the project in 1971. With this boost, MACV and the Joint General Staff hoped to cut construction time in half and complete the program in four years.

MACV also felt that it had solved its prisoner-of-war problem. By 1970 the five mainland camps and the larger facility on Phu Quoc Island held 37,000 prisoners of war, of which about 8,000 were North Vietnamese Army soldiers and the remainder Viet Cong. Approximately 40 percent of the total had been captured by American forces. While MACV transferred custody of these prisoners to Saigon, U.S. military police advisers closely monitored the facilities and International Red Cross representatives visited frequently. Abrams and Bunker both realized that the treatment of prisoners was a political issue in the United States,

---

[35] USMACV, "Command History, 1970," 2:IX–85 to IX–89, HRB, CMH; Fact Book, MACV, December 1968 (updated), MICRO 1/1968, RG 334, WNRC; CORDS Field Evaluation Rpt, Lt Col Nicholas Terzopoulos, 15 May 70, sub: RD Ration Supplement Program, SEAB, CMH; Interv, author with Lt Col Richard O. Brunkow (hereafter cited as Brunkow Interv), Senior Adviser, 42d Ranger Group, IV CTZ (circa 1970–71), 26 Feb 76, SEAB, CMH.

[36] USMACV, "Command History, 1969," 2:VI–64, and "1970," 2:IX–54 to IX–63, HRB, CMH; Fact Book, MACV, December 1968 (updated August 1969), MICRO 1/1968, RG 334, WNRC; file on ARVN dependent housing, SEAB, CMH.

underlined in 1970 by the public revelation of harsh maximum security conditions, the "Tiger Cages," in the nonmilitary island prison facility of Con Son.[37]

The incident also highlighted another related concern—the arrest and imprisonment of Viet Cong who could not be classified as military personnel. In this area the process of classification, detention, trial, and sentencing still remained chaotic. Between 1969 and 1971 Saigon had about 40,000–50,000 nonmilitary prisoners in fifty detention centers, thirty-seven province jails, four mainland prisons, and the central prison on Con Son. MACV estimated that about 65 percent were Viet Cong, including most of the Con Son inmates, as well as several thousand that were released each year after serving short sentences. The situation upset American civilian officials who felt that Saigon failed to keep adequate administrative control over the process, especially at the local level, and released or improperly sentenced many Viet Cong leaders. Vietnamese province chiefs, they complained, often sentenced civilians with only tenuous Viet Cong connections to long jail terms and even summarily executed some defendants, while other Vietnamese officials routinely accepted bribes to destroy Viet Cong dossiers or release key Viet Cong cadre. American civilian CORDS advisers, however, were less concerned with legal niceties than with the reluctance of Vietnamese officials to act against Viet Cong cadre, feeling that many Saigon administrators feared future reprisals should some sort of ceasefire agreement suddenly recognize the legitimacy of the Viet Cong political apparatus.[38]

Organization and Training

The brightest side of the advisory effort was now the physical growth and formal training of the South Vietnamese military forces. Since the advent of general mobilization in 1968, Saigon had managed to draft the manpower needed to feed the American-advised training camps and military school system, which subsequently produced the personnel for newly activated units. MACV, for the most part, was able to provide equipment for new units in a timely fashion from normal U.S. production or, when convenient, from redeploying U.S. units or from excess military stocks. To improve training, MACV established a quarterly evaluation program similar to the SEER and HES systems and greatly increased the number of Vietnamese students attending military service schools in the United States.

MACV reported military instruction to be "generally satisfactory" in service schools and "adequate" in training centers, although some of the old problems

---

[37] USMACV, "Command History, 1970," 2:X–4 and X–37 to X–66, HRB, CMH; Msg, AmEmbassy SGN 10622 to SecState, 151000 Jul 70, sub: Vietnamese Press Reaction to Disclosures, Con Son, file Con Son Island and Tiger Cages, Bunker Papers, DS. The Con Son facility also housed twenty-nine POWs who had been convicted of capital offenses while in regular prisoner-of-war camps.

[38] See documents in file on detainees, prisons, VCI processing, SEAB, CMH. On Con Son, the Provincial Reconnaissance Units, and the controversial Phoenix program, see William Colby (with Peter Forbath), *Honorable Men: My Life in the CIA* (New York: Simon and Schuster, 1978), especially pp. 266–80. See also Memo, Resor to SecDef, 6 Oct 69, sub: Secretary of the Army Trip Report, 20–28 August 1969, file VIET 333 (ALPHA) 1969, box 96, accession no. 75089, RG 330, WNRC.

still remained. One experienced training adviser, Lt. Col. Norman M. Stevens, felt that the Vietnamese were still "overly dependent on lectures" and paid "only lip service to practical training." On the positive side, he judged Vietnamese recruits as well prepared for combat as American soliders and also noted that, contrary to his expectations, the Vietnamese were now conducting extensive amounts of night training, a measure American advisers had encouraged for several years. Stevens further observed that the effectiveness of all unit training was "directly dependent upon the quality of the leadership" displayed by the unit's commander; the better leaders worked closely with their troops during refresher training, while those with a "lackadaisical attitude" saw their feelings reflected by both the troops and the local instructors. According to Stevens, problems in training had their roots in poor leadership rather than in the content or quality of the instruction itself.[39]

Brig. Gen. Stanley L. McClellan, the MACV training director as of June 1971, was more confident. Noting the higher quality of advisers being assigned to his staff and the school and training centers, the systematic revision of all South Vietnamese training programs, and the improved ability of the Central Training Command to forecast and plan future training requirements, he believed that Saigon's military training apparatus was steadily improving. However, McClellan also labeled the ubiquitous Chinh, who had replaced Vinh Loc as the Training Command director in April 1970, as "a dynamic prime-mover in the training business" and noted the judgment of General Abrams that Chinh "has no equal in the matter of training leadership."[40] If so, Chinh had turned over a new leaf, or, more likely, American evaluations were once again becoming too optimistic.

More significant was the absence of any major changes in the basic deployment or organization of the South Vietnamese armed forces.[41] Saigon's chain of command and its balance of military forces, or force structure, remained essentially the same. After so many years of development, MACV was still adding on to, or rounding out, what had been built before—fine-tuning the existing structure to make it self-sufficient in the area of logistics, communications, and fire support. In many respects, what remained the same was more significant than what was added to the mix.

Abrams appeared satisfied with Saigon's command organization and recommended no major changes in this area. Vy remained minister of defense and Vien continued to head the Joint General Staff. Both generals acted as coequals under President Thieu, and each had his own area of authority. Vice-President Ky had little power, and most of his close supporters were no longer in office. Vien's staff still served as the administrative headquarters for all the military

---

[39] First and second quotations from USMACV, "Command History, 1970," 2:VII–34. Remaining quotations from Interv, Maj Lawrence D. Sylvan with Stevens, Senior Adviser, Chi Lang National Training Center, circa September 1969, VNIT 494. Stevens had completed training assignments with both the Iranian and Taiwanese armed forces. For a broad overview of training, see USMACV, "Command History, 1970," 2:VII–33 to VII–60. All in HRB, CMH.

[40] Memo, McClellan to Maj Gen Howard H. Cooksey, DEPCOMUSSAG, 2 Aug 73, sub: Official Army History of the Vietnam War, SEAB, CMH.

[41] On organization, see USMACV, "Command History, 1970," 2:VII–3 to VII–21, and files on RVNAF force structure, SEAB, CMH.

services, retaining more or less direct control of the airborne and marine forces, a few support units, the base depots, and the training centers and military schools. The four corps commanders continued to control the bulk of the regular and territorial forces and to combine military duties with political responsibilities.

By the end of 1970 the force structure of the armed forces appeared to have finally settled down. After two years little had changed. Each of the 9 regular divisions had 3 infantry regiments, and each regiment had its fourth infantry battalion, completing the expansion that Westmoreland had begun back in 1965. With 9 infantry divisions, the airborne and marine divisions, 2 independent regiments, and the extra "DMZ" regiment assigned to the South Vietnamese 1st Division, the regular army could marshal about 120 infantry battalions, plus 20 ranger, 9 airborne, and 9 marine battalions of roughly similar size and capability. Both the airborne and marine forces had their own division- and regimental-level command structures, while the ranger battalions were apportioned between five group (regimental-level) headquarters. Saigon's 17 armored cavalry squadrons (also battalion-size units) were assigned either to the regular infantry divisions or to the newly activated armor brigades in each zone. Of the 43 medium (105-mm.) and 15 heavy (155-mm.) artillery battalions, forty-six belonged to the divisions and the remainder to the corps. Infantry divisions, ranger groups, armor brigades, corps artillery, and independent regiments, together with local Vietnamese Special Forces units, signal and engineer groups, and supporting area logistical commands, also worked directly for the corps commanders. Only the airborne and marines acted as a national reserve. By 1970 MACV had equipped almost all of these forces with the new weapons and equipment specified in the improvement and modernization programs, an immense task made possible only by a vast increase in direct U.S. military aid to Saigon since 1968 (*see Table 19*). MACV also enlarged the South Vietnamese Navy and Air Force with more bases, machines, and personnel; but, like the army units, their missions, deployments, and organizations remained unchanged.[42]

MACV also strengthened other Vietnamese military organizations. The size of the territorials rose to over half a million men, while the police put about 100,000 uniformed men in the cities, towns, and villages. To further beef up internal security, American and South Vietnamese civilian officials created the Provincial Reconnaissance Unit (PRU) program in April 1969.[43] The PRUs were platoon-size paramilitary units assigned to provincial headquarters to operate against local Viet Cong political cadre. As such they constituted the spearhead of the CORDS/CIA-sponsored PHOENIX program, Saigon's effort to eliminate the political infrastructure of the insurgency. Recruits were generally former Viet Cong soldiers. Although falling under the authority of the National Police, the PRUs were led by South Vietnamese army officers, assisted by about one hundred MACV advisers,

---

[42] Fact Book, MACV, December 1968 (updated August 1969), MICRO 1/2193, RG 334, WNRC. The M16 rifle completely replaced the carbines, M1 rifles, BARs (Browning automatic rifles), and various types of shotguns and submachine guns. The airborne forces received special lightweight 105-mm. howitzers that were easier to move by air.

[43] For background on the controversial PRUs, see Blaufarb, *Counterinsurgency Era*, pp. 209–12 and 245–48; Hunt, *Pacification*, forthcoming.

TABLE 19—COST OF SOUTH VIETNAMESE ARMY AND TERRITORIAL FORCES

Fiscal Year	Total Cost [a]	U.S. Share	Direct U.S. Support	MAP/MASF [b]
1959	231	189 (82%)	151 (80%)	38 (20%)
1960	251	206 (82%)	143 (70%)	63 (30%)
1961	258	201 (78%)	165 (72%)	36 (28%)
1962	314	247 (79%)	123.5 (50%)	123.5 (50%)
1963	292	207 (71%)	103.5 (50%)	103.5 (50%)
1964	364	216 (59%)	104 (48%)	112 (52%)
1965	559	361 (65%)	116 (32%)	245 (78%)
1966	738	434 (59%)	148 (34%)	286 (66%)
1967	746	429 (58%)	149 (44%)	280 (56%)
1968	832	533 (64%)	101 (19%)	432 (81%)
1969	1,645	1,072 (65%)	70 (7%)	1,002 (93%)

[a] In millions of U.S. dollars. Costs do not include the South Vietnamese Air Force, Navy, or Marine Corps, and include the territorials only for the 1962–69 period.

[b] Military Assistance Program/Military Assistance Service Funded

Source: Table computed from figures presented in Heymont, *Resource Allocations in Support of the RVN Army, Regional Forces, and Popular Forces: FY68*, pp. 3–5; ibid., *Resource Allocations for the RVN Army, Regional Force, and Popular Force: FY69*, RAC–TP–401 (McLean, Va.: Research Analysis Corp., 1970), pp. 4–5.

and were under the overall supervision of the Central Intelligence Agency. General Abrams accepted the need for such politico-military units, but was uneasy about MACV's association with them, feeling that he had responsibility for the program with little or no control over it. In fact, the PRUs soon acquired a reputation as assassination squads, leading Abrams to order his advisers not to participate in their field operations or to sanction torture or any other illegal practices. He hoped that American military personnel could be withdrawn from the program as soon as possible.[44] MACV had too many other problems to worry about.

The following year Abrams was finally able to pull MACV out of another troublesome effort, the CIDG program. Like Westmoreland, he had hoped to convert these forces into territorial units, preferably Regional Forces, but by mid-1970 had managed to transfer only about thirty of one hundred camps in this manner. As an alternative, he and Vien agreed in June to consolidate the remaining camps into "ranger border defense battalions," enabling the minority units to retain their special identity and, at the same time, become an official part of the armed forces. With enemy activity on the borders light, the conversions took place in about six months, and by the end of the year the U.S. 5th Special Forces Group had officially ended its long-standing program. In its place were thirty-seven new ranger battalions (*Table 20*), each about 400 men strong, and totaling about 14,500 troops out of a goal of 17,000. Saigon agreed to give each soldier Vietnamese citizenship, the Vietnamese Special Forces and rangers provided cadre, and MACV supplied regular field advisory teams to the units. As in many other areas, American recommendations had thus been greatly modified by local circumstances. The final solution to the CIDG effort only confirmed its status as

---

[44] Msg, Abrams MAC 15636 to Moorer (acting JCS chairman), 031058 Dec 69, sub: PRU, Abrams Papers, HRB, CMH.

TABLE 20—CIDG CONVERSIONS, DECEMBER 1970

Administrative Area	Camps	Ranger Border Defense Battalions	Closed
I Corps Tactical Zone	11	8	3
II Corps Tactical Zone	15	12	3
III Corps Tactical Zone	12	9	3
IV Corps Tactical Zone	11	8	3
Total	49	37	12

Source: Kelly, *U.S. Army Special Forces,* pp. 152–53.

a special army, albeit without American involvement, and many of the old problems, such as racial and religious hostility, remained unresolved.[45]

What the individual CIDG soldier thought about the solution was unrecorded. According to one MIKE Force adviser, the troopers were tired. Many had been in the program since the early 1960s and, in their eyes, little had been accomplished. The fighting along the border, if anything, had become tougher, and many were "just wondering if it's all worth dying for, because the Vietnamese government means little or nothing to them . . . and it has shown them hardly anything at all." Nevertheless, Americans leaders felt that minority groups like the Montagnards had little choice but to turn to Saigon. Ambassador Bunker noted that the *FULRO* movement had apparently collapsed in February 1969, when several thousand members tramped out of the Cambodia forests and turned themselves in at Ban Me Thuot, and Col. Harold R. Aaron, the American Special Forces group commander in 1969, concluded that the performance of the *LLDB* was slowly improving, especially in the central and northern border areas. If anything, the transition to Vietnamese control was long overdue.[46]

Like Westmoreland before him, Abrams was reluctant to support any truly significant changes in the existing South Vietnamese force structure or command organization. MACV's ambiguous attitude toward the conversion of the CIDG to territorial units was but one example. In July 1969, when Maj. Gen. Roderick Wetherill, the IV Corps senior adviser, suggested yanking elements of the South Vietnamese 18th Division out of the placid Saigon area and into the delta border regions where they might pick up some useful combat experience, Lt. Gen. Julian J. Ewell, the U.S. II Field Force commander (and III Corps senior adviser), treated the proposal as a joke—"the 18th couldn't hit the ground with their [sic] hat in Delta terrain against the VC"—and insisted they stay at home, out of harm's way. Abrams apparently agreed and let the matter drop.[47]

[45] Msg, Abrams MAC 1617 to Peers, 060137 Feb 69, Abrams Papers, HRB, CMH; Kelly, *U.S. Army Special Forces,* pp. 151–59 and 182–93; Davis Interv, 27 Feb 76, SEAB, CMH (Colonel Davis was a Special Forces adviser, November 1966–September 1967, and senior adviser to the Ranger Command, June 1970–January 1971, and to the Ranger Training Command, January–June 1971); USMACV, "Command History, 1970," 2:XIV–1 to XIV–5, HRB, CMH; After-Action Rpt, HQ, 5th Special Forces Group (Airborne), 1st Special Forces, 28 Feb 71, sub: Keystone Robin C, SEAB, CMH.

[46] Quoted words from Interv, Maj Roy S. Barnard with Specialist Dennis McFall, FO, 5th Mobile Strike Force, circa 1970, VNIT 677, II, 218, HRB, CMH. See also Msg, Bunker SGN 3381 to President, 220355 Feb 69, Bunker Papers, DS; Transmittal Ltr, Aaron, HQ, 5th Special Forces Group (Airborne), 1st Special Forces, 24 May 69, sub: Vietnamese Special Forces (VNSF), SEAB, CMH.

[47] Msg, Wetherill CTO 1093 to Abrams, Info Ewell, 051450 Jul 69; and for source of quotation, Msg, Ewell HOA 2036 to Abrams, 060105 Jul 69. Both in Abrams Papers, HRB, CMH.

Six months later Maj. Gen. Melvin Zais, commanding the U.S. Army XXIV Corps in the northern zone, proposed breaking up the large South Vietnamese 1st Division (with four regiments and about nineteen combat battalions) into two divisions controlled by a "light corps" headquarters responsible for the defense of the DMZ area. But his immediate superior, Lt. Gen. Herman Nickerson, Jr. (USMC), commanding the III Marine Amphibious Force (and the I Corps senior adviser), and General Lam, the local Vietnamese corps commander, both vetoed the idea, citing the lack of enough experienced Vietnamese officers to staff a new command.[48]

To his later regret, Abrams again did not pursue the matter, and the problem of further strengthening the DMZ area remained unaddressed for the time being. The MACV commander, in fact, went on record against any major changes in South Vietnam's military organization, deployment, or strategy. Abrams declared that any major alterations in these areas would upset existing "personal power relationships" and "institutional balance," divert "executive attention" and "resources" from more basic concerns, and, in general, cause confusion and loss of momentum. Historically, he noted, military reorganizations were always exceedingly difficult, and he felt that, for the time being, "US/GVN energies should be devoted to improving the functioning of [the] present structure." Admiral McCain was in complete agreement, and thus MACV continued to support the status quo.[49]

The Vietnamese leaders were not so complacent. In January 1970, at the request of Thieu, Abrams and Bunker met with the Vietnamese president, Prime Minister Khiem, Defense Minister Vy, and General Vien to discuss Vietnamization and the U.S. troop drawdown. General Abrams explained to the group that MACV's projected American residual support force could not remain indefinitely and would eventually be reduced to a small advisory contingent. To allay fears that the United States might abandon Saigon, he promised that all American withdrawals would be tied closely to the military situation, the growth of South Vietnamese military capabilities, and any agreements that might be reached in Paris with Hanoi. The Saigon generals disagreed, feeling that the American pullout was being undertaken without any regard for these factors. Addressing what they felt were the political and military realities in Saigon and Washington, the Vietnamese proposed a radically different deployment strategy: regrouping all American and other foreign troops along the coast in a reserve role, turning area security missions completely over to the territorials, and outposting the borders with ranger and CIDG forces. The South Vietnamese regulars, with increased American air, artillery, and logistical support, would undertake most of the conventional fighting. To do this, they again asked for more armor and artillery—field pieces for the territorials and self-propelled guns for the regulars—the latest American jet fighters for air defense and direct air support, sixty-

---

[48] Msg, CG, III MAF, to COMUSMACV, 081416 Dec 69, sub: Creation of Small Tactical ARVN Corps With the 11th DTA. For another example, see Msgs, McGown CTO 1211 to Abrams, 160310 Nov 70, and Abrams MAC 15103 to McGown, 240505 Nov 70, sub: Deployment of Marine Division Headquarters in Cambodia. All in Abrams Papers, HRB, CMH.

[49] Quoted words from Msg, Abrams MAC 4336 to McCain, 061020 Apr 69. See also Msg, McCain HWA ? to Wheeler, 122222 Apr 69. Both in Abrams Papers, HRB, CMH.

four battalion-level headquarters for the territorials, and an increase of over one hundred thousand personnel. Also tacked on once again were free food for servicemen and more building material for dependent housing.[50]

Abrams was unimpressed. He passed on the new requests to his superiors, but, as usual, without his endorsement. In two or three years, "when US forces might be reduced to a MAAG," he felt that it might be appropriate to ask the Vietnamese to reevaluate their needs. But any planning for such an eventuality at this point, he held, would be a grave error, convincing Saigon that the United States was pulling out of Vietnam on a fixed timetable regardless of the military situation.[51] He could not support any major changes in U.S. operational strategy or deployments within South Vietnam. Perhaps Abrams still hoped for some kind of residual support force and recognized that planning for a total U.S. military withdrawal only made a complete withdrawal more likely to occur.

Several months later, National Security Decision Memorandum (NSDM) 36 brought up the matter of South Vietnamese military capabilities and deployments again. NSDM 36 proposed the possibility of an immediate ceasefire.[52] General Abrams' response was predictable. He came down vehemently against any such arrangement. Distrusting any promises or agreements that North Vietnam might make, he predicted that the enemy would return in force once American forces finally left and "the effects would be disastrous." To his surprise, the South Vietnamese leaders, including both Thieu and Ky, appeared strongly in favor. Worried, the MACV commander promised to discourage them, feeling that they had not thought out the consequences. Bunker, however, regarded the public position of the Vietnamese leaders simply as good politics, but little more. Local CIA reports, he noted, indicated that most of the senior South Vietnamese officers regarded a ceasefire as "tantamount to surrender" and would probably "support a coup d'etat under these circumstances."[53]

Nevertheless, on orders from Washington, Abrams pursued the matter during the year and found his own major subordinates more optimistic.[54] Most felt that even the withdrawal of all American advisers and air support would not be critical in the event of a ceasefire and would cause problems only for some of the new support units and the more technical training programs. General Collins bluntly explained the thinking of many of the senior tactical commanders to Abrams. The presence or absence of advisers, he contended, meant little. Most

---

[50] Msg, Abrams MAC 555 to McCain, 131100 Jan 70, sub: RVNAF Force Planning, Abrams Papers, HRB, CMH. The discussions took place after the Joint Chiefs had submitted the Phase III Improvement and Modernization Plan, but before Laird's visit to Vietnam and the preparation of CRIMP.

[51] Msg, Abrams MAC 808 to McCain and Wheeler, 190526 Jan 70, sub: RVNAF Force Planning, Abrams Papers, HRB, CMH.

[52] See files on VSSG—Cease Fire—1970, SEAB, and on VSSG Ceasefire, fldr 5, Thayer Papers, HRB. Both in CMH.

[53] First quotation from Msg, Abrams MAC 14426 to McCain, 170432 Nov 70, sub: Cease-Fire Study, Abrams Papers, HRB, CMH. Second and third quotations from Msg, Bunker SGN 12017 to SecState, 271045 Jul 70, sub: Thieu's Public Statements on Ceasefire, bk. 17, Bunker Papers, DS. See also Msgs, Abrams MAC 3120 to Wheeler, 100454 Mar 70, sub: NSDM 36: Cease-Fire, and Abrams MAC 3472 to McCain, 161251 Mar 70, sub: Cease-Fire, Abrams Papers, HRB, CMH; Intelligence Information Cable, CIA, 8 Nov 69, sub: Views of JGS Officers on Senator Don, General Duong Van Minh, and on a Cease-Fire, SEAB, CMH.

[54] See incoming messages in Abrams Papers, HRB, CMH, for November 1970 on the ceasefire study and VNAF air support.

of the military advisory effort provided only a channel to funnel American combat and logistical support to the South Vietnamese; if U.S. military forces withdrew, that channel would no longer be needed. The Vietnamese, he reminded Abrams, "do not need more advice" and "it is only laziness and failure on the part of the chain of command to get out and do their job that prevents their forces from becoming more effective." According to Collins, they could win the war in three months if they had "the desire or the will and this is something that advisers cannot provide."[55]

But South Vietnamese leaders also hesitated to make any changes in their military structure or strategy of their own volition. Although Abrams believed that Thieu was in "full control" of the military, the South Vietnamese president was not as confident. In July 1970 he tried to pave the way for the separation of military and political powers by replacing the term *corps tactical zone* with *military region*, by strengthening the office of the deputy corps commander for security, and by taking the division commanders out of the area security chain of command. But the changes were ineffective. Corps commanders continued to act as military governors of their zones (or regions) and retained all their area responsibilities; division commanders and staffs were still heavily involved in the territorial chain of command through their area security missions. As before, the separation of the army tactical units from province and district affairs depended on Saigon pulling the corps and divisions completely out of the security business and making province chiefs rely totally on territorials and police. That, in turn, meant assigning South Vietnamese regulars a greater role in the conventional war effort.[56]

Manpower

Changes in South Vietnamese deployments and operational strategies would have necessitated changes in Saigon's manpower procurement policies. Its recruiting and induction system, monitored carefully by the MACV J–1 staff and American personnel advisers at corps, division, and province levels, remained territorially oriented.[57] Aided by the 1968 mobilization decrees, Saigon continued to fill its ranks with volunteers. Voluntary enlistments supplied most recruits for the air force, navy, marines, and territorials, and over half of the new manpower for the regular army came from the same source. Most units continued to run local recruiting campaigns within their operational areas, and the proximity of units to the friends and families of prospective soldiers was a major selling point. Vietnamese corps and division personnel officers also took pains to see that conscripts were assigned, whenever possible, to units close to their homes.

---

[55] Msg, Collins NHT 2128 to Abrams, 040845 Nov 70, Abrams Papers, HRB, CMH.

[56] Quoted words from Msg, Bunker SGN 9884 to SecState, 230300 Jun 70, sub: Meeting With President Thieu on June 19—Political Situation, Bunker Papers, DS. See also DF, MACJ–312 to Asst CofS, CORDS, 30 Jun 70, sub: Reorganization of RVNAF, SEAB, CMH; USMACV, "Command History, 1970," 2:VII–16 to VII–20, HRB, CMH; Tran Dinh Tho, *Pacification*, Indochina Monographs (Washington, D.C.: U.S. Army Center of Military History, 1980), pp. 37–38.

[57] See Ltr, MACJ–14, 8 Sep 69, sub: Division Recruiting System, SEAB; USMACV, "Command History, 1969," 2:VI–50 to VI–51, and "1970," 2:VII–21, HRB. Both in CMH.

Both MACV and the Joint General Staff continued to feel that this policy increased morale and deterred desertion, although no evidence existed for either. For the same reasons, dependent quarters were almost always located near the bases of the soldiers using them, greatly complicating the responsibilities of the unit commander, but making military life more socially and economically attractive for the individual soldier.

Of course, as MACV pointed out from time to time, it was easier for soldiers to desert when they were close to home, and units in the heavily populated areas continued to have the highest desertion rates. A solution to the desertion problem remained, in fact, elusive.[58] Despite the best efforts of MACV and the Joint General Staff, Saigon lost 139,670 men in 1968 through desertions. General Abrams, however, maintained that the desertion control measures adopted by Saigon were adequate. Judging that the problem was in the field where unit commanders were not enforcing the desertion policies, he ordered all American advisers to take "aggressive positive action" to ensure that these regulations were carried out.[59] Abrams wanted the Vietnamese desertion control committees at corps, division, and province levels to focus their attention on new recruits, who, in his opinion, were the most prone to desert. By the end of 1969 net desertion rates had fallen from the October 1968 high of 17.2 per 1,000 troops to a monthly average of about 12, with the Territorial Forces, as usual, having about half the rate of the regular ground forces. MACV attributed the lower rates to improved leave policies, more awards and decorations, better indoctrination of servicemen, and more efficient draft apprehension methods, but offered no proof of any casual relationship. Despite the lower figures, the number of deserters, some 123,363 in 1969, still appeared too high.

In the course of 1969 MACV's analysis of South Vietnamese desertions revealed a significant anomaly. Without any apparent reason, units in the Delta had the highest desertion rates in the country, even though enemy activity and strength in the region were low; the tempo of operations was slow; and such factors as pay, housing, commissaries, leave, and transportation compared favorably to that elsewhere. Puzzled, the MACV staff asked the IV Corps advisers for an explanation. The response was direct. Advisers felt that the primary cause of the higher rates was poor leadership. Other causative factors were the high proportion of peasant soldiers with little education, the ease with which deserters could disappear and change identities in the crowded Delta, and the slightly higher casualty rate in the zone. MACV's own desertion control committee suggested a contributing problem: the high illiteracy rate among Vietnamese servicemen. Written regulations, forms, and notices concerning pay, leave, and other matters that affected their lives were often incomprehensible without visual and audio assistance, and, for the same reason, written communications between soldiers and dependents were poor. Again, MACV could only insist that

---

[58] For general information on desertions for the 1969–70 period, see USMACV, "Command History, 1969," 2:VI–68 to VI–76, and "1970," 2:VII–28 to VII–31, HRB; DF, MACV J–14 to CofS, MACV, 12 Jun 69, sub: RVNAF Desertion Control Activities, SEAB. Both in CMH. Unless otherwise stated, the following discussion on military desertions is based on these sources.

[59] Abrams' message of 6 Feb 69 to advisers cited in USMACV, "Command History, 1969," 2:VI–68, HRB, CMH.

field advisers urge local unit commanders to give more attention to all aspects of the problem.

Despite statistical evidence of improved military amenities, Saigon's military desertion rate again began to rise during 1970. Again perplexed, both MACV and the Joint General Staff commissioned more comprehensive studies on the causes of desertion. MACV concluded that the problem was socio-economic rather than military; that the predominant cause was family concerns; and that cowardice, or fear of death or danger, was not a major factor. Interviews with convicted deserters appeared to support this view and also indicated that most deserters were experienced soldiers and not raw recruits—a finding that was contrary to MACV's long-held assumption that deserters were primarily new, bewildered inductees who deserted while in training or in transit to assigned units. However, because the survey interviewed only 520 soldiers, the results were not conclusive.

According to a general MACV survey of field advisers in 1970, "protracted operations" and "isolated location" led "poor leadership" as the three primary *military* causes for desertion.[60] Referring to its previous analysis, MACV noted that the two leading military causes also had socioeconomic roots; both entailed the separation of soldier and family. Thus when analyzing the rise in desertions during the heavier fighting of 1970, MACV concluded that the culprit was family separation rather than poor leadership. The American staff also reasoned that the relationship between pay and desertions was negligible because the lowest paid units, the Popular Forces, had the lowest desertion rates. The Popular Forces, recruited from the hamlets and villages they protected, were also the least isolated units and the least likely to conduct protracted combat operations.

On the surface, MACV's deductions seemed logical. However, the utility of its evaluation is questionable, for most armies can hardly be effective if they are unable to wage war away from the populated areas they are supposed to protect. More to the point were the conclusions of the Joint General Staff and the South Vietnamese desertion control committees, which emphasized that commanders at the lower military echelons showed too little concern for the welfare and morale of the individual soldier and failed to understand that such matters were command responsibilities that demanded their attention. Here, the circle came back again to leadership, or the lack thereof.

In the field other problems appeared that had never been uncovered by the formal MACV staff surveys. John Paul Vann noted that above and beyond the problems of desertions was the equally old nemesis of "ghost" soldiers or "in-service deferments." The practice of excusing soldiers from military duty for bribes or other favors was now deeply ingrained in the armed forces. Vann felt that about 20 percent of the army fell into this category and doubted if even the Vietnamese generals knew the full extent of it. As an example, Brig. Gen. John H. Cushman, the deputy IV Corps senior adviser, made a personal spot check of one South Vietnamese battalion in July 1970. Cushman found that the unit had an authorized strength of 665, an assigned strength of 396, and a present-for-duty strength that day of only 296. Checking closer, he noted that the Vietnam-

[60] USMACV, "Command History, 1970," 1:VII–31, HRB, CMH.

ese battalion commander lined up 281 men for a combat operation; but when advisers made a second check in the field a few hours later, less than 200 men were present. The battalion had melted down to an oversize company. Where the other soldiers had gone, or if they had ever even existed, remained a mystery.[61]

Evaluating Saigon

The bottom line of all evaluations of South Vietnamese military effectiveness was performance. Was the military getting the job done, and was its performance actually improving? The response to both these questions by official reports and evaluations throughout 1969 and 1970 was positive—and this may explain, in part, why the desertion, leadership, and other endemic problems of the Saigon military forces did not appear so forbidding.[62] Begun in 1968, SEER, the System for Evaluating the Effectiveness of RVNAF, continued to produce a wealth of statistical data and subjective evaluations in digestible formats.[63] The more detailed statistical inputs now allowed MACV to make absolute comparisons with past performances and between different units. As before, the subjective responses were more limited and generally used to supplement and clarify the statistical information. In June 1969 Defense Secretary Laird called SEER "a major step toward improved measuring and reporting on the effectiveness of RVNAF" and requested that the raw data be forwarded directly to his own staff for analysis.[64] The following month, General Wheeler, equally impressed by SEER-based statistics during a visit to Vietnam, used them to justify recommending withdrawal of a second increment of 25,000 American troops.[65] Thus by 1970 SEER had become a major tool for gauging the success of Vietnamization.

SEER was, in fact, much abused. Despite its title, it had never been designed to compute the "effectiveness" of the South Vietnamese military, and was no more than a limited management tool. Although SEER and its sister evaluation systems, HES and TFES,[66] brought together a large number of recurring statistical reports used to keep track of the war, each had major limitations. SEER, for example, could not match unit performance with unit missions or, more important, with the level and type of enemy activity. This task belonged to the various analysts at MACV, the Joint Chiefs of Staff, the Central Intelligence Agency, and

[61] Related in Memo, Vann to Jacobson, 13 Aug 70, sub: Inquiry From Ambassador Bunker About "Ghosts on the Payroll," Vann Papers, MHI.

[62] The MACV submissions were based on the monthly Operational Statistical Report and the quarterly Effectiveness Report, supplemented in 1970 by a quarterly Problem Area Letter (the latter dealt with difficulties that the adviser could not solve at his echelon). See MACV Directive 335–13, Change 2, 10 Feb 70, sub: Reports and Statistics: System for Evaluating the Effectiveness of RVNAF (SEER), SEAB, CMH.

[63] See quarterly USMACV SEER evaluations, SEAB, CMH, published approximately two months after the end of each reporting period.

[64] Memo, Laird to Chairman, JCS, 12 Jan 69, sub: Reports of RVNAF Effectiveness, and Attached Documents, SEAB, CMH.

[65] Msg, Wheeler JCS 09112 to Abrams, 231308 Jul 69, Abrams Papers, HRB, CMH.

[66] TFES (Territorial Forces Evaluation System) was similar to SEER and dealt with Regional and Popular Forces; HES (Hamlet Evaluation System) tried to measure the pacification status of individual hamlets.

the Office of the Secretary of Defense. But both analysts and managers generally had a preference for statistical, rather than anecdotal, evidence and often let the raw data stand by itself.

By itself, the raw data was impressive. SEER inputs showed that the South Vietnamese kill ratio (ratio of enemy killed to friendly killed or missing-in-action) had reached a high of 5.2 during the first quarter of 1969, had leveled off at about 3.6 to 3.7 by midyear, had finished at 5.4 during the last quarter, and then had steadily risen in 1970 from 6.1 to 7.3, 7.6, and 9.3.[67] Overall, enemy losses to the South Vietnamese, the weapons captured to weapons lost ratios, and the amount of weapons and supplies found in caches (hidden enemy supply points) followed a somewhat different pattern, starting out at a relative high rate during the first half of 1969 and then leveling off at two-thirds to one-half of that amount for the remainder of the period, with the exception of the second quarter of 1970, when operations in Cambodia pushed these statistics up. The data seemed to indicate that the South Vietnamese were improving both in "effectiveness" (that is, results) and in "efficiency" (that is, results compared to their own output and losses).

The quarterly subjective evaluations submitted by American field advisers, also as a part of SEER, were more ambiguous, even when transformed into numerical values by MACV analysts. For example, the advisory assessment of South Vietnamese operational effectiveness sought to determine how well units performed combat tasks, irrespective of results achieved. Theoretically, it appeared possible to divorce how a unit went about performing its mission from the nature or difficulty of the task. The results over the eight quarters of 1969 and 1970 failed to show any discernible trends. Although reports on individual units pointed out major differences in such things as leadership and staff work, countrywide assessments showed no marked variations or patterns.

Military analysts made much use of the raw SEER data. At MACV they ranked the various South Vietnamese ground combat units (infantry, ranger, airborne, and so forth) against one another using a variety of statistical measurements, especially ratios that allowed for differences in combat activity (for example, the ratio of enemy killed per hour of actual combat).[68] While producing no absolute judgments of military capabilities, the practice allowed MACV to pinpoint weak units and target them for remedial action. Other SEER analysts tried to show correlations between leadership ratings and desertion rates, or between these elements and enemy "density" or even weather and combat results. Casualties due to mines and boobytraps were separated from those suffered in firefights with enemy units. The availability and type of combat support, the amount of training and recuperation time available, and the ability of staffs to plan operations were other factors that, from time to time, entered into explanations of why specific South Vietnamese units performed in a satisfactory or unsatisfactory manner. But, in general, once the raw data had been presented, there were simply too many variables to make any broad generalizations. An aggressive unit like the South Vietnamese 1st Division might have a low kill ratio

---

[67] Figures from pt. 1 of USMACV SEER Evaluation, October–December 1970, SEAB, CMH.
[68] For example, see quarterly USMACV SEER evaluations, SEAB, CMH.

due to higher mine and boobytrap casualties. Airborne and marine units might receive top ratings in leadership and, at the same time, lead the military in desertions, perhaps because of the many sustained operations undertaken by these units far from home areas. The civilian analysts at the Office of the Secretary of Defense and the Central Intelligence Agency could do no better. Too often progress, if any, had to be measured in fractions of percentage points that meant little, given the generally low level of combat activity in South Vietnam during this period.[69]

Official MACV assessments of the South Vietnamese military were based primarily on raw SEER data. As in the past, such reports were dry and made greater use of objective or numerical data than of the more subjective evaluations. Presentations were uniform, stressed statistics that showed improvements, and tempered problem areas (such as desertions, leadership, and grade imbalances) with discussions of causes and remedial actions, or countered them with more optimistic data. With the decreasing support for the war in the United States, General Abrams' superiors encouraged such submissions, and General Wheeler himself pressed MACV for more official reports highlighting South Vietnamese progress that could "give us ammunition to use in our contacts with the press here"—and, he might have added, with his civilian chiefs as well.[70]

The report of Brig. Gen. William R. Kraft, Jr., the acting MACV J–3, was typical. In discussing leadership, Kraft noted that advisers placed almost 60 percent of the South Vietnamese combat commanders (divisions, regiments, and battalions) in the category "above average" and suggested that only a few ineffective officers remained in command "partially due to the limited depth and unknown quality of potential replacements." He judged the general combat capability of South Vietnamese units as "good and increasing"—advisers rated 46 percent as "excellent" and only 9 percent as "poor," 70 percent as "improving" in capability and only 4 percent as "regressing." He also described most units as "combat tested," although only a few had seen sustained combat. Kraft went on to analyze individual units and commanders in these terms, painting an overall picture of an extremely capable military force, with but a few weak commanders and a desertion problem that was being rapidly brought under control by more command attention to the morale and welfare of the individual soldier.[71]

In a personal assessment of the war to Wheeler in January 1970, Abrams presented an identical analysis. While noting that "serious deficiencies still hamper its overall performance," he felt that the South Vietnamese military showed "improvement in combat effectiveness, increased confidence in its own ability, and improved flexibility in combat operations." Abrams noted that almost all statistical indicators of combat performance had risen and that Saigon's "share of results" had also increased. The data, he pointed out, reflected the increased participation of the South Vietnamese in the war and the success of Vietnamization. The only "serious deficiencies" noted by Abrams were the "dilution" of available leadership and skills caused by the continued expansion of the armed

---

[69] For example, see the monthly *Southeast Asia Analysis Report.* Copies in HRB, CMH.
[70] Msg, Wheeler CJCS 09507 to Abrams, 041858 Aug 69. Response in Msg, Abrams MAC 10252 to Wheeler, 080252 Aug 69. Both in Abrams Papers, HRB, CMH.
[71] Fact Sheet, Kraft, 10 Feb 70, sub: Assessment of ARVN/VNMC Organizations, SEAB, CMH.

forces and the low operating strengths of many units caused by desertions. His ensuing zone-by-zone analysis of the military situation emphasized kill ratios and other combat statistics. He saved most of this criticism for the areas of combat support, logistics, and communications, where shortages in equipment and trained personnel would not be corrected until the current improvement and modernization program had been completed. The only long-range difficulties he foresaw was continued shortages of artillery and tactical airlift.[72]

The Central Intelligence Agency, known for its more pessimistic evaluations of South Vietnamese military progress, had little to add. Its analysis, also written in January 1970, viewed the situation as "murky" and made no predictions. Based on battlefield statistics and the quarterly SEER reports, the CIA analysts arrived at about the same conclusions as MACV: Performance was up, although problems in leadership, promotions, desertions, and dependent housing remained. Some South Vietnamese units had done well in 1969 and some had done poorly, but most units were simply untested. Time, the CIA study held, was on the side of Saigon, which could be expected to continue to improve its military forces as long as enemy activity remained light.[73]

All these judgments differed little from those made during General Westmoreland's tenure of office, and, in fact, a great deal of their content, including the emphasis on progress, had become so much bureaucratic ritual. As in the past, the inclusion of a few problem areas, such as desertions, gave the evaluations an aura of authenticity because it implied a balanced treatment. However, the optimism generated by the SEER data cannot be entirely reconciled with the pessimistic reports Abrams had made regarding the ability of the South Vietnamese to handle the war by themselves. The military's own responses to NSSM 1 had made this abundantly clear to everyone in Washington. In truth, SEER and its companion systems could not measure objective progress, only relative progress—that is, gains made by one unit over another, or over past performance. To produce more meaningful progress reports, MACV would have to establish standards or goals in each measured area. In addition, SEER would have to make allowances for changing levels of combat activity, weather, and terrain—all vital factors in the performance of combat missions. The verdict on South Vietnam's supposedly improved military performance and on MACV's Vietnamization efforts had yet to be heard.

[72] Quoted words from Msg, Abrams to Wheeler, 22 Jan 70. See also Msg, Abrams MAC 1285 to Wheeler and McCain, 280305 Jan 70, sub: Assessment of the Situation in Vietnam. Both in Abrams Papers, HRB, CMH.
[73] Intelligence Memorandum, Directorate of Intelligence, CIA, 23 Jan 70, sub: Vietnamization: Progress and Prospects, copy in SEAB, CMH.

21

One War: The Highlands

General Abrams realized that it would take more than increases in manpower and equipment to bring the South Vietnamese military out of its slump. What the Central Intelligence Agency had termed paper programs, even if realized, were not enough. His Combined Campaign Plan for 1969, drawn up in mid-1968, suggested one answer. The plan formally ended the division of missions between American and South Vietnamese combat forces, specifying that the "RVNAF must participate fully within its capabilities in all types of operations . . . to prepare for the time when it must assume the entire responsibility." American military forces were to share the task of engaging enemy units with their less mobile Saigon allies. The plan emphasized the importance of combined operations, to include the integration of planning, combat support, and intelligence. In the Korean conflict hastily formed South Korean units had fought side by side with American forces and had done well. Troops had learned to fight by fighting. Now that the political machinery of Saigon had settled down, perhaps the same thing would work here.[1]

Up to 1968 American and South Vietnamese units had operated side by side but rarely in close cooperation. Various Vietnamese units, from regulars to territorials, CIDG, and militia, often served as adjuncts to American search-and-destroy operations, normally performing secondary missions, such as dealing with the enemy's local and guerrilla forces that American combat commanders had neither the time nor the patience to ferret out. Combined endeavors, like the Marine Combined Action Program (CAP) and Operation FAIRFAX, were exceptions. But following the Tet offensive in early 1968, many American commanders began to reexamine the combined operations concept. The nature of the Tet fighting had forced closer cooperation between the two national forces, and guidance from Washington had already driven home the necessity of forcing the South Vietnamese back in the forefront of the war effort. Upon replacing West-

---

[1] Quoted words from JGS-MACV, Combined Campaign Plan 1969, AB 144, 30 Sep 68, p. 8, SEAB, CMH. See also p. 12. For background on Korea, see CMH's United States Army in the Korean War series and Robert K. Sawyer, *Military Advisors in Korea: KMAG in Peace and War*, ed. Walter G. Hermes (Washington, D.C.: Office of the Chief of Military History, 1962), especially pp. 147–48. The adoption of the KATUSA (Korean Augmentation to the United States Army) program, which had integrated thousands of South Korean soldiers into U.S. Army units, was never seriously considered for South Vietnam.

moreland in mid-1968, General Abrams had encouraged even closer cooperation between allied and South Vietnamese units, and combined operations appeared implicit in his new "one war" policy. However, he left the nature of these efforts up to the discretion of his senior commanders.

In the past, MACV had generally found it difficult to successfully encourage combined operations in the field. The lack of a unified allied military command continued to be a major deterrent, and language and cultural barriers between the Vietnamese and Americans remained strong, and severely limited cooperation and coordination between the two armies. American combat commanders were generally reluctant to operate with South Vietnamese units. Too often they regarded them as no more than "an additional burden" that had to be taken in tow, more "apt to cause problems . . . than be helpful."[2] Without helicopter support, field operations conducted by the South Vietnamese were normally limited to the amount of water they could carry—about three days at most—with ammunition resupply and medical evacuation being additional restraints. Most Americans also believed that the Vietnamese commanders and units could not perform psychologically or physically at the same pace as their American counterparts; their staff work was inadequate and their counterintelligence abilities suspect, making Americans hesitant to bring them into the planning process.[3] Many of their concerns were justified. After years of providing decentralized territorial security, Vietnamese division and regimental staffs had become lethargic; their tactical logistical systems immobile; and their primary fire support element, the artillery, inured to static area defense. Nevertheless, when General Abrams and his subordinates embarked on their new "one war" campaign, they had high hopes that American units might serve as models for Saigon's soldiers by integrating the operations of the two national forces more closely.[4]

Combined Operations: I CTZ

The relations between American and South Vietnamese forces already differed greatly from zone to zone.[5] In the I Corps Tactical Zone Lt. Gen. Robert E. Cushman, Jr. (USMC), commanding the III Marine Amphibious Force since mid-1967, and his principal subordinate, General Stilwell, heading the XXIV Corps, felt that the South Vietnamese 1st Infantry Division was equal to any

[2] Truong, *RVNAF and US Operational Cooperation and Coordination*, p. 162.

[3] For example, see Msg, Walt to Westmoreland, 261345 Aug 65, COMUSMACV Message file, Westmoreland Papers, HRB, CMH. On the lack of secure communications in RVNAF, see Fact Sheet, HQ, II FFV, circa 1969, sub: Security of Operations and Communications, SEAB, CMH

[4] For treatments of combined operations, see Truong, *RVNAF and US Operational Cooperation and Coordination*; ibid., *Territorial Forces*, pp. 116–24; and Clarke, "The Role of USARV Units in Vietnamization," CMH Monograph 192M.

[5] Unless otherwise noted, the following section is based on CORDS Field Evaluation Rpt, Pacification Studies Group, 28 Apr 69, sub: Study of 1st Infantry Division (ARVN) Support of Pacification in Quang Tri and Thua Thien Provinces, SEAB, CMH; Ltr, III MAF to COMUSMACV, circa 1969, sub: Situation in Vietnam, MICRO 1/451, RG 334, WNRC; and Charles R. Smith, "U.S. Marines in Vietnam, 1969: High Mobility and Stand-down" (Washington, D.C.: U.S. Marine Corps History and Museums Division, 1986); Truong, *RVNAF and US Operational Cooperation and Coordination*, pp. 93–118. For a ground-level evaluation, see Hauser Interv, 24 Sep 69, VNIT 476, HRB, CMH.

American unit and had full confidence in its commander, General Truong. Truong's division had been operating closely with the U.S. 3d Marine Division, the 101st Airborne Division (Airmobile), and the 1st Brigade of the 5th Infantry Division (Mechanized) in Quang Tri and Thua Thien Provinces, and remained the showpiece of the South Vietnamese Army. Local security was for the most part in the hands of the Territorial Forces, with rear-echelon Vietnamese, U.S. Army, and U.S. Marine Corps forces contributing. In Quang Nam Province the U.S. 1st Marine Division defended the Da Nang area, working when necessary with the South Vietnamese Quang Da Special Zone and its 51st Infantry Regiment, as well as with the South Korean Marine Brigade (*see Map 4*). In the southern half of the zone the U.S. 23d Infantry Division ("American") paired itself with the weaker South Vietnamese 2d Infantry Division in Quang Tin and Quang Ngai. Since 1968 the subordinate brigades and regiments of the two units had shared common operational areas and conducted a series of intensive combined operations.[6] Although encountering little sizeable enemy resistance, Cushman judged the endeavor a success and continued it in 1969. Abrams, in turn, felt so confident of allied capabilities in the northern zone that he moved the U.S. 1st Cavalry Division south at the end of 1968 and sent home one of the two American marine divisions there the following year.

During 1969, in compliance with MACV guidance, Cushman and Stilwell reoriented American combat forces in the zone toward area security, tying their operations more closely with those of the local territorial and police forces. During this transition the Marines intensified their Combined Action Program; the 101st Airborne Division formed eighteen mobile training teams to work with outlying territorials; and the American Division began its own CAP-like effort with local militia, supported closely by American combat battalions. Larger operations, however, especially those in the mountainous interior, continued to be carried out in a unilateral fashion, with multinational efforts, such as the final assault on Hamburger Hill in May 1969, being the exception rather than the rule.

Combined Operations: II CTZ

In the II Corps Tactical Zone American and South Vietnamese commanders pushed multinational operations with more vigor, although ultimately with less success. As in the northern corps zone, the effort in the Highlands had begun well before MACV had formally published Abrams' one-war campaign directive. In March 1968 General Peers took command of the I Field Force, the American corps-level headquarters in the Highlands, and, at about the same time, General Lu Lan replaced Vinh Loc as the South Vietnamese II Corps commander. Peers had commanded the U.S. 4th Infantry Division there in 1967, and was thus thoroughly familiar with the zone. Lu Lan, a native of Binh Dinh Province and a former commander of one of the local divisions, was equally at home in the area. Peers described him as "a highly competent officer and an

---

[6] A U.S. Army division normally had three infantry brigades, each roughly similar in size to a South Vietnamese infantry regiment.

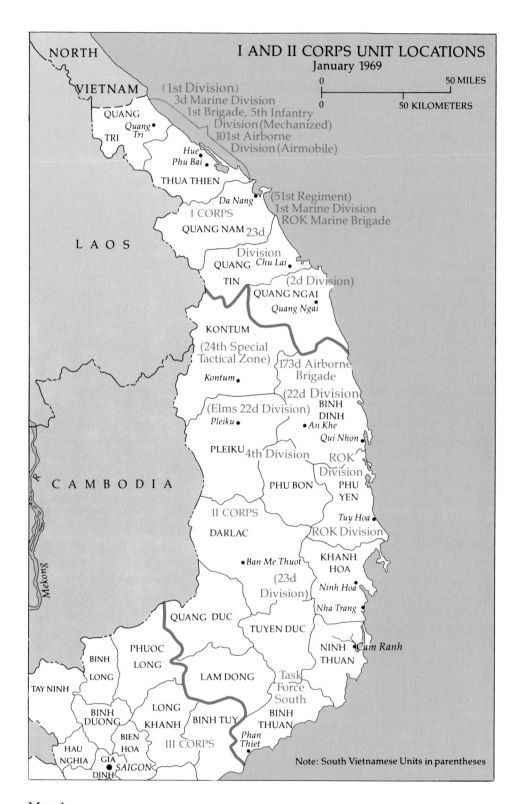

I AND II CORPS UNIT LOCATIONS
January 1969

0   50 MILES

0   50 KILOMETERS

NORTH

VIETNAM

(1st Division)
3d Marine Division
1st Brigade, 5th Infantry
Division (Mechanized)
101st Airborne
Division (Airmobile)

QUANG
Quang
Tri

TRI

Hue
Phu Bai

THUA THIEN

Da Nang

(51st Regiment)
1st Marine Division
ROK Marine Brigade

I CORPS

QUANG NAM 23d

Division

QUANG Chu Lai

TIN

(2d Division)

QUANG NGAI

Quang Ngai

LAOS

KONTUM

(24th Special
Tactical Zone)

Kontum

173d Airborne
Brigade

(22d Division

(Elms 22d Division) BINH
DINH

Pleiku •An Khe

Qui Nhon

PLEIKU 4th Division

ROK
Division

CAMBODIA

PHU BON

PHU
YEN

II CORPS

Tuy Hoa

DARLAC

ROK Division

•Ban Me Thuot

KHANH
HOA

(23d
Division)

Ninh Hoa

Nha Trang

QUANG DUC

TUYEN DUC

NINH •Cam Ranh

THUAN

PHUOC
LONG

BINH

LONG

Task
Force
South

LONG

TAY NINH

LAM DONG

BINH
DUONG

LONG
KHANH BINH TUY

BINH
THUAN

BIEN
HOA

Phan
Thiet

HAU
NGHIA GIA
DINH •SAIGON

III CORPS

Note: South Vietnamese Units in parentheses

MAP 4

Maj. Gen. William R. Peers *(center) shortly before taking command of I Field Force*

excellent tactician, with exceptional knowledge of the terrain and the people."
Although later evaluators would be more critical, he appeared to be a marked
improvement over Vinh Loc. After the Tet offensive had begun to subside, Peers
and Lu Lan reevaluated the situation in the zone and began to put the pieces of a
new campaign together.[7]

Due to the marginal effectiveness of the South Vietnamese military units in
the zone, the two generals had much to do. Initially, both commanders reorganized their military forces. Peers grouped his 4th Division in the mountainous
western Highlands of Darlac, Pleiku, and Kontum Provinces, where it could
serve as a shield for the flat farming areas on the coast. There the U.S. 173d
Airborne Brigade, two South Korean divisions, and the bulk of Lu Lan's territorial units remained strung out along the coastal lowlands, providing security for
the zone's most populated areas. Lu Lan also split his regular forces, deploying 2
infantry regiments in the Highlands and another 4 on the coast; guarded his
east-west supply routes with two cavalry squadrons; and kept his three ranger
battalions in reserve. In the ensuing months he also supervised the training of
selected infantry battalions for security duty and the activation of several new

[7] Quoted words from Peers' briefing to the Army Policy Council, "Presentation to the APC, Lieutenant General W. R. Peers, 28 May 1969" (hereafter cited as Peers APC Briefing), pp. 2–3, SEAB. See
also Senior Officer Debriefing Rpt, Peers (hereafter cited as Peers Debriefing Rpt), 23 Jun 69, HRB;
Senior Officer Debriefing Rpt, Lt Gen Arthur S. Collins (hereafter cited as Collins Debriefing Rpt), 7
Jan 71, HRB. All in CMH.

regular infantry battalions, 240 territorial companies, and 1,060 territorial platoons. With the entire U.S. 4th Division and two of the better South Vietnamese regular regiments holding the enemy at bay along the border, Peers and Lu Lan planned to concentrate on restoring and expanding Saigon's control of the coastal population, especially in traditionally hostile Binh Dinh and Phu Yen Provinces.

Amid this reshuffling and buildup, the two commanders began a series of monthly command meetings that cemented their close relationship. During these meetings Lu Lan proposed a series of combined operations between his regulars and selected U.S. units along the coast.[8] General Peers tentatively agreed, pointing out that some of his regular combat commands were already in the process of training a number of Vietnamese long-range patrol units, and suggested that Brig. Gen. Richard J. Allen's 173d Airborne Brigade operate with Lu Lan's territorials in Binh Dinh, Phu Yen, and Phu Bon Provinces in an effort similar to Operation FAIRFAX. According to Peers, Generals Westmoreland, Abrams, and Vien strongly supported the concept, and Allen and General Hieu, commanding the South Vietnamese 22d Infantry Division, had already begun establishing a small territorial leadership course at An Khe that could serve as a foundation for the endeavor. Lu Lan, however, insisted that it was his regulars that needed the assistance and wanted the 173d to develop its relationship exclusively with the 22d Division rather than the territorials. He proposed that the two combat units begin a combined drive against the regular Viet Cong forces remaining in and around Binh Dinh as soon as possible. Although preferring a more locally oriented effort, Peers finally agreed. He ordered Allen to begin what Americans later called the "pair-off" program, and for the next twelve months one of Allen's airborne battalions operated with each of Hieu's regiments.[9]

The Binh Dinh pair-off between the units of the 173d and the 22d proved almost a replica of FAIRFAX. The participating American units brought substantial air, artillery, engineer, and other support to the combined endeavor from their parent units, and American and Vietnamese commanders generally colocated command posts, shared a common area of operation, and planned and carried out operations together. In the process the American officers tried to increase pressure on local enemy forces through intensive patrolling and to encourage South Vietnamese battalion-, company-, and platoon-level leadership through longer, more decentralized operations. Vietnamization, as later conceived in 1969, was not an objective, and, in fact, the entire effort represented a return to

---

[8] For memoranda of thirteen successive conferences, entitled "First (Second, Third, etc.) Senior Commanders Conference," see I FFV G–3 records, box 1, accession no. 70A1783, RG 334, WNRC, especially Encl 4 to Third Senior Commanders Conference. In the same location see I FFV Quarterly Summary Reports for CYs 68 and 69 and the II Corps adviser Quarterly Review. See also Senior Officer Debriefing Rpt, Brig Gen John W. Barnes, 15 Dec 68, and Senior Officer Debriefing Rpt, Brig Gen J. S. Timothy (hereafter cited as Timothy Debriefing Rpt), 2 Dec 69, HRB, CMH.

[9] The American 2d Bn (Airborne), 503d Infantry (or 2–503d Abn), with the South Vietnamese 40th Regt in Binh Dinh from Landing Zone English; the 4–503d Abn with the South Vietnamese 47th Regt in nearby Phu Yen; and the 1–503d Abn and the 1st Bn (Mechanized), 50th Infantry, with the South Vietnamese 41st Regt in the Soui Cai Valley. See the ORLLs of the 173d Airborne Bde, July 1968–July 1969, HRB, CMH. Although each of the 22d Division's regiments had four infantry battalions, all were understrength and several were always in training, "standing down" (resting), or under the operational control of province or district chiefs, and thus the strengths of the two "paired-off" units were approximately equal.

the old strategy of pacification, with American combat operations now tied much closer to the overall task of local security.

Encouraged by General Abrams, Peers attempted to extend the pair-off program throughout the zone. In the western Highlands he instructed the U.S. 4th Division to support the South Vietnamese 24th Special Tactical Zone (with the three-battalion 42d Infantry Regiment) and the South Vietnamese 23d Infantry Division in the Ban Me Thuot area (site of the division headquarters and its 45th Regiment). He also directed Allen to organize a Task Force South with his remaining two airborne infantry battalions, "pairing up" these units with several Vietnamese ranger battalions and the remaining regiments of the 23d Division (44th and 53d) south of Binh Dinh. Peers also encouraged similar efforts between American and South Vietnamese infantry units in the Highlands and artillery, reconnaissance, and logistical support units throughout the corps.

The success of the program varied greatly from unit to unit. In the interior Highlands the pair-off program of the U.S. 4th Division was undeveloped. The three powerful brigades of the American division spent most of their time in what might be termed conventional antiguerrilla, or jungle, operations: backing up CIDG border camps, and serving as a blocking force in order to keep enemy units in Cambodia and Laos from the populated coastal regions to the east. Their relations with the CIDG, the 24th Special Tactical Zone, and the South Vietnamese 23d Division were cordial, and operations were conducted on a coordinated basis, but were rarely combined or integrated.[10]

Along the coast, the programs of the 173d and Task Force South were more effective. In general, it appeared easier for American units to assume the traditional South Vietnamese area security missions than to have Saigon's combat units undertake the more mobile conventional operations normally pursued by the Americans. Yet even here some participating American commanders were disappointed, pointing to the stubborn reluctance of many Vietnamese officers to relinquish any authority to their subordinates, especially the lowly company commanders and the platoon leaders.[11] Nevertheless, Generals Peers and Lu Lan continued to hope that such soldier-to-soldier efforts, together with the delivery of M16 rifles and other new equipment, would give the South Vietnamese small-unit leaders the confidence and ability to operate with minimum supervision. At the very least, they believed that the program greatly increased the military and police pressure on the local insurgents, reflecting MACV's renewed emphasis on territorial security.

I Field Force's associate battery program, an artillery combined operations endeavor, was less effective. Like the infantry pair-off program, the effort had no

---

[10] The ORLLs of the 4th Infantry Division make no mention of any pair-off or combined operations programs in 1968 or 1969. The debriefing report of the unit's commander between 5 January and 30 November 1968, Maj. Gen. Charles P. Stone, 15 Nov 68, p. 4, HRB, CMH, notes the emphasis on the "one war concept," and the corollary of combined operations to "instill new confidence in ARVN," but gives no specifics as to what was done. The HQ, I FFV, Briefing for General Johnson, Spring 1968, box 1, accession no. 70A1783, RG 334, WNRC, sketches the program and notes the division's association with the South Vietnamese 45th Regiment (23d Division) at Ban Me Thuot, which it later supported during the Duc Lap battles of July–August 1968.

[11] For example, see COAAR, HQ, 3d Bn (Airborne), 506th Infantry (or 3–506th Abn), 31 Apr 69, sub: HANCOCK EAGLE; ORLL, HQ, I FFV, October 1969, p. 66; and ORLLs of the 3–503d and the 3–506th Abn for 1968–69. All in HRB, CMH.

specific goals and depended largely on the initiative of local unit commanders. Peers and Lu Lan made no effort to pull the six indigenous South Vietnamese artillery battalions out of their scattered static defensive positions, preferring to rely on the seventeen U.S. artillery battalions in the zone for mobile operations. Participating American artillery units thus concentrated on smaller tasks to improve their counterparts—integrating communications nets, exchanging target and intelligence information, providing training teams or any other support needed, and so forth. Some American commanders limited their "programs" to ceremonial social visits, and others merely augmented the existing advisory effort. While the temporary provision of training teams, weather data, building and barrier material, firing

South Vietnamese 23d Infantry Division Troops *firing a 155-mm. howitzer*

charts and other paper supplies, and perhaps an occasional helicopter ride or a free meal, bolstered South Vietnamese morale, neither Peers nor Lu Lan had any larger program for freeing the Vietnamese artillerymen from their static support role, grouping them into larger units, and giving them offensive combat support missions.[12]

Even less successful was the long-range reconnaissance patrol (LRRP) training program for South Vietnamese reconnaissance company troops. In 1968 and 1969 some 421 students completed on-the-job training with elements of the U.S. 20th, 58th, and 74th Infantry ranger detachments in the II Corps area. However, American instructors complained that the students tended to be marginal and that the training was not compatible with South Vietnamese methods of operation. Without the communications and air mobility of their American counterparts, South Vietnamese reconnaissance companies normally operated only under the direct control of their regimental or division commanders. These commanders, they explained, used the "reconnaissance" units as security, mobile reaction, or ambush forces and rarely broke them down into the small decentralized scout patrols employed by the Americans. Unless the Vietnamese changed some of their basic operational procedures, the training was largely a waste.[13]

---

[12] See Ott, *Field Artillery*, pp. 190–94, and, for details, ORLLs of I FFV Artillery; 5th Bn, 27th Artillery (or 5-27th Arty), 6-32d Arty, 41st Artillery Group, 7-15th Arty, 2-17th Arty, 7-13th Arty, 52d Artillery Group, 3-6th Arty, 5-22d Arty, 6-14th Arty, 1-92d Arty, 4th Infantry Div, and 173d Airborne Bde for 1968–69; and Senior Officer Debriefing Rpt, Brig Gen Winant Sidle (hereafter cited as Sidle Debriefing Rpt), 10 Sep 69, p. C–I–3. All in HRB, CMH.

[13] For details, see ORLLs of HQ, I FFV, 4th Infantry Div, and 173d Airborne Bde for the concerned period, and Timothy Debriefing Rpt, 2 Dec 69, annex A, pp. 14–15. All in HRB, CMH.

Peers also tried the combined approach against another persistent South Vietnamese program, dependent housing. In December 1968 he directed his subordinate commands to provide both construction materials and technical assistance for local South Vietnamese dependent housing projects and formed his own dependent housing council to push the effort. By distributing building material directly to the South Vietnamese units, he hoped to bypass the bureaucracy in Saigon and get the job done quickly, instructing his units to make "maximum use of scrap and salvage materiel."[14] However, progress was abysmally slow. Although American units prepared building plans and construction schedules for their "sister" units, the shortage of construction supplies, especially cement, continually impeded the effort. When materials were available, labor was scarce. As in the earlier self-help projects, Americans soon discovered that Vietnamese units were too busy during the "dry" season to organize construction efforts and too wet during the long monsoon season to perform them, as the rains tended to halt all such work throughout the zone.[15] Later, in late 1969, drastic cuts in the shipment of building materials to Vietnam led I Field Force to first reduce and then to terminate the program. In the end, less than fifty ten-family housing units were completed, a fraction of what was actually needed. Worried by the poor showing, the deputy I Field Force commander instructed subordinate units to modify their programs so that "the revised I FFORCEV goal for Phase I will consist of the total of family units under construction and completed." Such bureaucratic practices only dismayed staff officers trying to keep the program moving, and they began to lose heart.[16]

Despite these setbacks, Vietnamization began ahead of schedule when, in January 1969, Peers and Lu Lan agreed to replace one brigade of the U.S. 4th Division in Kontum Province with the military forces of the South Vietnamese 24th Special Tactical Zone. Peers regarded the zone's organic infantry unit, the (nondivisional) 42d Regiment, as well led, familiar with the land, and accustomed to using American fire support when needed. Based in a sparsely populated border area, the 42d had developed a higher degree of combat expertise than its pacification-bound sisters along the coast, and, with II Corps armor and ranger reinforcements, its American advisers felt that the regiment could hold the northern Highlands. The new realignment left two American brigades and two Vietnamese regiments along the border, with the dangerous coverture task thus divided about equally between the two armies.[17]

Elsewhere in the II Corps zone, progress was less dramatic. Reflecting the increasing American interest in area security, Peers had ordered his pair-off programs expanded in July 1968 to include all Territorial Forces within the vicinity of each American unit, and by mid-1969 a variety of programs catering to the territorials had replaced most of the original effort. Brig. Gen. John W. Barnes, who had succeeded Allen as commander of the 173d Airborne Brigade in De-

---

[14] ORLL, HQ, I FFV, January 1969, pp. 28–29, HRB, CMH.

[15] See ORLLs of 4th Infantry Div and 173d Airborne Bde, HRB, CMH.

[16] Quoted words from ORLL, HQ, 4th Infantry Div, October 1969, pp. 41–42, HRB. See also Memo, Brig Gen Gordon J. Duquemin, Deputy Senior Adviser, II CTZ, to Collins, 25 Jun 70, sub: Conference on Vietnamization and Pacification, SEAB. Both in CMH.

[17] The redeployed U.S. brigade moved to the coast and one regiment of the South Vietnamese 23d Division continued to operate along the southern II Corps border area in Darlac Province.

399

cember 1968, officially ended the unit's pair-off program in April 1969 and replaced it with Operation WASHINGTON GREEN, an intensive area security effort with territorial and paramilitary forces in Binh Dinh Province. In essence, WASHINGTON GREEN was a second Operation FAIRFAX, but without the presence of South Vietnamese regulars.[18]

WASHINGTON GREEN proved to be the final American campaign in Binh Dinh Province, and its greatest achievement may have been in training an impressive number of territorial and paramilitary forces. However, in the long run the operation appeared no more successful than FAIRFAX's efforts to clean up Gia Dinh Province around Saigon prior to the Tet offensive. Binh Dinh was not easily pacified by military action alone. American and Vietnamese local intelligence was poor, the area was a traditional enemy stronghold, and province and district officials were never able to eliminate the local Viet Cong infrastructure. General Barnes admitted that "there is not a favor throughout the brigade to do this thing," explaining that many of his combat commanders found themselves frustrated by the lack of traditional fighting and measureable results. As Peers' successor in March 1969, Lt. Gen. Charles A. Corcoran, reflected, "Barnes may have just been keeping the lid on the situation." After the brigade finally left Vietnam in 1971, the greater portion of the province reverted to Viet Cong control.[19]

Generals Peers' artillery assistance programs also began leaning towards the territorials. In late 1968 he began establishing combined fire support coordination centers in each province; placing all territorial outposts under American, Korean, or South Vietnamese artillery fans; and streamlining fire request and clearance procedures. But the new centers did little to increase territorial aggressiveness or free South Vietnamese artillery of its heavy area security responsibilities.[20]

Although these combined activities were more thoroughly planned than those in the I Corps zone, it was difficult to measure their effect on the ground. American advisers continued to rate the South Vietnamese 22d and 23d Divisions considerably lower than their northern sisters (the 1st and 2d Divisions), and the two units remained comparably weaker in strength and battlefield experience. General Peers seemed confused as to whether he should concentrate on developing the regulars or improving the territorials, and complained about the lack of guidance from MACV. Despite "a considerable effort toward the development of a 'One War' concept at MACV-Saigon level," he felt that "it was extremely difficult for Headquarters, I FFV to pull together its several functions into a unified effort." If the goal was pacification, then the greater emphasis on territorial security made sense; if the objective was Vietnamization, then other measures and arrangements were called for. At the end of his tour Peers recommended that Washington come up with a more structured plan, outlining con-

[18] See ORLLs of 173d Airborne Bde, 1968–71, HRB, CMH. Barnes had been the deputy corps senior adviser. The April, July, and October 1969 ORLLs of the 3–503d and the 3–506th Abn, HRB, CMH, indicate that these units continued to conduct combined operations with the newly formed South Vietnamese 54th Regiment, the third and last of the 23d Division's infantry regiments.

[19] First quotation from comments of Barnes in CORDS Field Evaluation Rpt, Pacification Studies Group, 28 Jul 69, sub: 173d Airborne Brigade Participation in Pacification in Northern Binh Dinh Province, p. 10. Second quotation from comments of Corcoran in Memo, Maj John B. Walker to CofS, MACV, 15 Apr 69, sub: CG Visit, 14 Apr 69. Both in SEAB, CMH.

[20] See artillery ORLLs for details; and Sidle Debriefing Rpt, 10 Sep 69, pp. 5–7. All in HRB, CMH.

crete military objectives, matching them with political goals, and suggesting specific methods to achieve both. Although optimistic, he admitted that all was not well: The 22d Division, "potentially the best division in II Corps," just sits "in the cities and towns and outlying areas for weeks on end . . . [with a] continual tendency to revert back to the territorial function." The 23d was a bit better but had also done poorly in 1968, and, in several actions, despite substantial American air and artillery support, had been saved only by the prompt intervention of American units.[21]

The following year General Corcoran, the new I Field Force commander, witnessed both the strengths and weaknesses of Peers' efforts. From May to June 1969 North Vietnamese Army elements pushed east from the "Tri-border" area into the Ben Het–Dak To region of western Kontum Province, and, in October through November, launched similar attacks to the south in the vicinity of Duc Lap and Bu Prang, southwest of Ban Me Thuot. In general, South Vietnamese forces along the border repelled these frontier assaults and held their advanced bases without American ground assistance. However, losses on both sides were heavy and post-battle autopsies revealed serious problems. South Vietnamese forces survived only through the massive intervention of American fire support and logistical assistance. Neither the Vietnamese commanders nor their staffs were accustomed to operating under stress and around-the-clock, coordination among commands was intermittent, and staff work was poor—or, more often, nonexistent. In the 24th Special Tactical Zone, the South Vietnamese 42d Regiment fought well, but lost most of its leaders and received few replacements. Participating CIDG elements had also done well at times, but were neither equipped nor trained for sustained combat. In both clashes Lu Lan and the Vietnamese corps headquarters had done little, leaving the tactical commanders to sink or swim on their own. The limitations of Vietnamese air and artillery were well known, and Corcoran was not surprised that strong U.S. military support was necessary. Nevertheless, advisers felt that their counterparts tended to avoid maneuver, shy away from the offense, and fight from fixed positions, where they could use massive U.S. artillery and tactical air support to destroy the attacking forces with minimum loss to themselves. Once the attackers began to withdraw, they showed little desire to pursue the enemy.[22]

During 1970 Vietnamization pursued its inexorable course. As the U.S. 4th Division left Vietnam, the South Vietnamese 22d Division moved into Pleiku with its 47th Regiment, taking responsibility for the 24th Special Tactical Zone and the defense of the northern Highlands, scene of many major American battles. Lu Lan's Vietnamese forces now had almost complete responsibility for the western borders. His new adviser, Lt. Gen. Arthur S. Collins, Jr., was troubled about the future. Upon reviewing some of the more optimistic portions of Peers' debriefing report, he questioned the existence of any discernible progress

[21] First and second quotations from Peers Debriefing Rpt, 23 Jun 69, p. 17, HRB. Third quotation from Peers APC Briefing, 28 May 69, pp. 5–6, SEAB. See also, for example, ORLL, HQ, I FFV Artillery, October 1968, pp. 3–4, HRB. All in CMH.
[22] COAAR, HQ, I FFV, 24 Jun 69, sub: ARVN Operation DAN QUYEN, 24 Apr–5 Jun 69; USMACV, "Command History, 1969," 3:annex H ("The ARVN Ben Het–Dak To Campaign"). Both in HRB, CMH. See also studies located in file 228–03, Vietnamization as It Pertains to II CTZ, fldr 66, box 22, accession no. 72A403, RG 319, WNRC.

during the past two years. "Frankly," Collins observed, "I do not know what happened between 1968–1970," believing that "if the ARVN combat units had improved as much as indicated by General Peers, somewhere along the line they had again slipped back a long way." Upon his arrival in February 1970, Collins judged that the local Vietnamese forces were "woefully weak because of lack of leadership at the regimental and battalion level," and he exhibited little of Peers' optimism.[23]

Brig. Gen. Gordon J. Duquemin, Collins' deputy senior adviser, agreed. As an example, he cited one battalion of the 53d Regiment (23d Division). The unit "sat in Dalat during all of 1969 and killed only ten enemy while suffering just two of its members killed

Lt. Gen. Arthur S. Collins, Jr.

in action," a record, he pointed out, that "can hardly justify the cost of its existence." In the opinion of Duquemin, most South Vietnamese commanders "would rather avoid the enemy than . . . fight him." He felt that it was "patently ridiculous" for American advisers to give an experienced Vietnamese commander any tactical advice because, in most cases, they were just "attempting to force him to do something he does not want to do." But given the existing situation, Duquemin felt that such "prodding constitutes our major contribution to the Vietnamization process" and lamented on American inability to have incompetent South Vietnamese commanders promptly removed. The "basic problem," he concluded, "is their officer personnel system," and, until it can be completely overhauled, "we can't expect to do anything substantive." Many of Collins' other subordinates seconded these judgments, although the II Corps CORDS representative pointed out that the major thrust of U.S. policy during the last two years was on upgrading the territorials—and thus largely ignoring the regulars.[24]

In perspective, Collins and his subordinates may have been too hard on their predecessors. Progress in almost all aspects of the Vietnam War had always been relative at best, at least from the viewpoint of MACV. However poor Collins found his allies in 1970, the days when the Highlands had been run as a political fief of General Vinh Loc while Americans did all the heavy fighting were cer-

[23] Collins Debriefing Rpt, 7 Jan 71, p. 6, HRB, CMH. See also Truong's critical treatment in *RVNAF and US Operational Cooperation and Coordination*, pp. 135–41.

[24] Quoted words from Memo, Duquemin to Collins, 25 Jun 70, sub: Conference on Vietnamization and Pacification. See also Memo, Willard E. Chambers, DEPCORDS, II CTZ, to Collins, 26 Jun 70, sub: Advisory Effort; Memo, Col Donald A. Seibert, G3, I FFV, to Collins, 25 Jun 70, sub: Comments on I Field Force Vietnam Involvement in Pacification. All in SEAB, CMH. Chambers, Seibert, and Duquemin were all responding to questions by Collins on these topics.

tainly over. Now it was the American units providing the territorial security and the Vietnamese regulars arrayed along the Highland borders. Progress had indeed come to the II Corps Tactical Zone under the advisership of General Peers and his compatriots. Whether that progress was enough to meet the goals of Vietnamization remained to be seen.

22

One War: Cambodia

The southern half of South Vietnam was always more critical than the sparsely populated north. Here was the essence of the southern republic, its capital, its people, and, with the delta waterways, most of its natural wealth. The French had administered the area, what they called Cochinchina, as a separate entity and had held on to this final portion of their Southeast Asian empire as long as they could; the South Vietnamese government had divided it into two corps tactical zones, twenty-six provinces, and a number of special areas; and the Viet Cong had treated it as one general administrative region, Nam Bo, directly under the Central Office South Vietnam. In its personality the warm, fertile delta and hill country was clearly distinct from the mountains of central and northern South Vietnam, and certainly different from the chilly, harsh, and, to many Westerners, Prussian atmosphere of its sister state in the North. If the southerners were ever to discover their national identity, they would have to draw upon the delta wellsprings for their culture and strength.

Combined Operations: IV CTZ

A successful program of combined operations was vital to the allied cause in the III and IV Corps Tactical Zones. Although almost all of the larger enemy units had pulled back into their Cambodian sanctuaries by the end of 1968, they could return at any time, and the local Viet Cong insurgents were still strong in many provinces. The combined North Vietnamese–Viet Cong threat was still too much for the South Vietnamese forces. American advisers had almost consistently given the six local Vietnamese divisions low ratings, considered those closest to Saigon the worst, and regarded the area's ranger and territorial units as no better. Static security missions and high living costs had steadily eroded troop morale, and military appointments still depended more upon political loyalties than fighting ability. For many years primary responsibility for defense of the region had thus fallen on the shoulders of II Field Force, the American corps-level command, and its four divisions.[1] American commanders had arranged these forces in an outer defensive ring, or arc, protecting Saigon, within which were three South Vietnamese divisions and a host of territorial units. Three other South Vietnamese divisions and even more territorials garrisoned the Mekong Delta rice basin south of the capital (*Map 5*).

Because of the importance of this area, the selection of the U.S. 9th Infantry Division for redeployment came as a surprise. Arriving in 1967 with the mission of cleaning out persistent enemy strongholds along the coastal waterways, the division had operated only sparingly with territorial units and elements of the South Vietnamese 9th Infantry Division. Its departure left only light American support forces south of Saigon and gave the South Vietnamese IV Corps head-quarters complete responsibility for the heavily populated Mekong Delta. In part, the decision was political, emphasizing the new policy of Vietnamization as well as the U.S. administration's commitment to bring home combat troops rather than just support personnel. In addition, enemy forces in the Delta were much weaker than at any other time; the area remained at the end of Hanoi's logistical pipeline; and, should trouble arise, General Abrams could easily rein-force the Delta with American units from the III Corps zone.[2]

The redeployment of the American unit was rapid. Elements of the 9th began standing down on 18 June 1969, and the division had left by the end of August (leaving one brigade behind in the III Corps zone). Filling in behind it was the South Vietnamese 7th Infantry Division, a marginal unit that had done little serious campaigning. At the time, five of its twelve infantry battalions were under the direct control of various province chiefs, and most of the remainder were scattered about performing static security missions. As these troops hastily occupied the evacuated American facilities at Dong Tam and elsewhere, they had little opportunity to familiarize themselves with the local enemy and terrain. Because of delays in the formation of new territorial units, the corps commander also continued to hold the division responsible for its existing area security missions. Thus, despite additional aviation support and the rapid activation of thirty-four new Regional Forces companies, the 7th Division was spread ex-tremely thin, and its offensive capability dropped accordingly. Throughout the rest of the year its advisory ratings steadily fell, and only the arrival of a new division commander in January 1970 halted the perceived decline.[3]

---

[1] Major American ground combat forces in the delta area consisted of the 1st, 25th, and 9th Infantry Divisions, and, since 1968, the 1st Cavalry Division and three brigade-size units, the U.S. 199th Light Infantry Brigade, the 11th Armored Cavalry Regiment, and the 3d Brigade of the 82d Airborne Division. Only the 9th Division operated in the IV Corps Tactical Zone.

[2] For a discussion of the U.S. 9th Division operations, see Intervs, Pritchett with Maj Walter R. Bishop, Adviser, Kien Hoa Province, 2 Oct 68, VNIT 278, and with Hines, 21 Sep 68, VNIT 291, HRB, CMH; Julian J. Ewell and Ira A. Hunt, Jr., *Sharpening the Combat Edge*, Vietnam Studies (Washington, D.C.: Department of the Army, 1974). Ewell commanded the 9th Division from February 1968 to April 1969.

[3] For an analysis of the 7th Division during this period, see Memo, JCSM–558–70 to SecDef, 3 Dec 70, sub: Republic of Vietnam Armed Forces Leadership, SEAB, CMH.

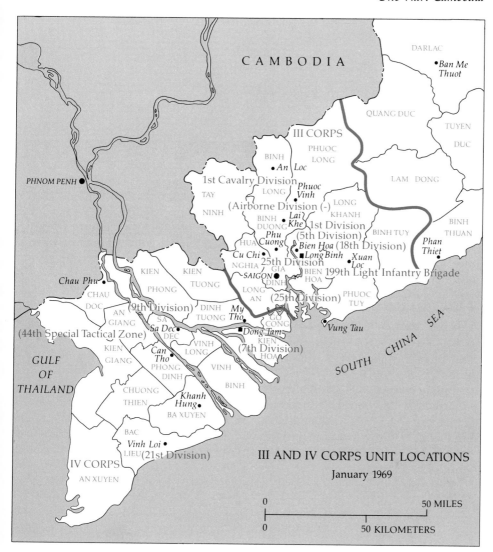

MAP 5

Fortunately for Saigon, enemy activity remained low in the Delta during late 1969 and 1970, as it did throughout South Vietnam, and the ineffectiveness of the 7th Division had no immediate repercussions. American corps-level advisers believed that its shortcomings could be easily remedied or, at least for the time being, balanced by the increasing mobility of the neighboring South Vietnamese 9th Division, which General Thanh, the IV Corps commander, had withdrawn from its area security missions and was now using as the corps reaction force. Reinforcing South Vietnamese marine units also helped, although American

CORDS evaluators felt that the relationships of the marines with the rural population left much to be desired.[4]

Combined Operations: III CTZ

Americans made determined efforts to ensure that redeployments in the III Corps Tactical Zone were planned with greater care. In December 1968 Col. Robert E. Hayes, the assistant deputy senior adviser, summarized local South Vietnamese military weaknesses. Unit commanders were inexperienced, and over half of the critical infantry battalion commanders had been in command less than six months. Only one infantry regiment, one infantry battalion, and 10 percent of the rifle companies had commanding officers at their authorized grade level. Battalion and regimental staffs were poor, and command and staff procedures overcentralized. Battalion commanders ran most operations in person, leadership at company and platoon levels was marginal, and the number of small unit operations remained limited. As in the Highlands, the Vietnamese artillery battalions were dispensed throughout the zone in two-gun platoons providing area fire support. Although the corps had begun to consolidate several of its gun platoons and could count on the activation of two new artillery battalions in 1969, Vietnamese artillery units were too scattered to support mobile operations now or in the immediate future. Hayes also pointed out that the desertion rate, though declining, was still higher than in 1967 and that, despite the activation of hundreds of new territorial units in the zone, American advisers had been unable to pry the South Vietnamese regulars from their area security missions. The number of infantry battalions performing area security duties had remained the same, leaving most of the South Vietnamese regular forces in the area still closely grouped around Saigon.[5]

Vietnamese hopes in the zone centered on the new III Corps commander, General Do Cao Tri. To Americans Tri appeared as a short, stocky, handsome Vietnamese who, like Ky, affected a certain military flamboyance with his dress and manner. The general spoke fluent French, reflecting a long military career that stretched back to the first Indochina War. After taking part in the November 1963 overthrow of President Diem, he was exiled to Saigon's embassy in South Korea and, upon his return to South Vietnam in 1967, resumed his military service, becoming III Corps commander in August 1968. Despite popular rumors that he had used his position to further his family's financial interests, his reputa-

---

[4] Tab D ("IV Corps-RVNAF Performance and Recent Activities") of Notebook Complied for SD Vietnam Trip, 9–14 Feb 70, VIET 333 LAIRD, box 13, accession no. 76076, RG 330, WNRC; CORDS Field Evaluation Rpt, Terzopoulus, 26 Mar 70, sub: The Vietnamese Marine Brigade Bravo in Kien Hoa Province, SEAB, CMH (U.S. Marine Corps advisers blamed troop discipline problems on combat fatigue). For difficulties on the IV Corps border, see Interv, Sylvan with Trevino, Operations Adviser, 44th Special Tactical Zone, 22 Oct 69, VNIT 494, HRB, CMH.

[5] Briefing, Hayes, 28 Dec 68, sub: Problems in ARVN Units; Msg, HQ, U.S. Army Advisory Group, III CTZ, to CG, II FFV, 16 Jul 69, sub: Combined Campaign Plan 1970, AB 145. Both in SEAB, CMH. See also Ott, *Field Artillery*, pp. 198–200.

tion as a capable, energetic military leader had earned him the respect of both his American advisers and his own troops.[6]

Tri's American counterpart in April 1969 was the former commander of the U.S. 9th Division, General Ewell. As II Field Force commander, the aggressive Ewell now focused his attention on broader concerns. On 16 April Abrams informed him that he could expect no further U.S. reinforcements and would somehow have to get the three local South Vietnamese divisions moving "despite their commanders." Four days later, at the MACV Commanders Conference, Abrams repeated this guidance, instructing Ewell to devote his main efforts to "the less glamorous areas" of population security and "upgrading RVNAF." As long as the enemy main force units remained in Cambodia, these were to be his major concerns.[7]

Impressed with the success of combined operations in the I Corps Tactical Zone, Ewell decided to sponsor a similar program in the III Corps area. Drawing on his experiences in the U.S. 9th Division, he believed that successful counterinsurgency operations were predicated on the availability of helicopter support. However, simply attaching American aviation units to Vietnamese units was an unsatisfactory proposition, because the principal Vietnamese commanders and staffs lacked the experience and, in his opinion, the will to effectively employ such expensive "resources." Instead, he wanted each major Vietnamese unit in the zone married to a similar American force that would funnel the necessary aviation, artillery, and communications support needed to put the Vietnamese ground combat forces back on their feet again. General Tri agreed with the concept, admitting that "the major problem of II FFV is the improvement of the three ARVN Divisions," and together they set about creating a "buddy system" that would "superimpose" one major U.S. unit on each of Tri's divisions.[8]

Unlike General Peers, the I Field Force commander who had pioneered the pair-off program in the Highlands, Ewell wanted to supervise the combined operations program closely, especially at its inception. Too often in the past, similar efforts had become disorganized and gone astray. On 22 June he formally announced his intention to "buddy up US and ARVN units to conduct combined operations [that would] . . . maximize the effectiveness of both forces [and] achieve in 2, 3, or 4 months a quantum jump in ARVN and RF/PF performance." Shortly thereafter, on the twenty-sixth, he and Tri jointly proclaimed the new *Dong Tien* (or "Progress Together") Program, calling for the "close and continuous association of [American and South Vietnamese] units . . . to effect a significant increase in the efficiency of utilizing critical combat support elements, particularly [U.S.] Army aviation assets." The official objective of *Dong Tien* was training "ARVN and US forces which can take over the complete responsibility for an area [of the other] on short notice." The program was to commence on

---

[6] See Ewell, "Impressions of a Field Force Commander in Vietnam," 15 Apr 70, p. 1, SEAB, CMH. In Senior Officer Debriefing Rpt, Brig Gen Dennis P. McAuliffe, 26 Nov 70, p. 15, HRB, CMH, McAuliffe believed that the corruption charge was false and politically motivated, explaining that Tri's wealth was inherited and based on his family's extensive landholdings in Bien Hoa Province.

[7] First quotation from Msg, Abrams MAC 4813 to Ewell, 161036 Apr 69, Abrams Papers, HRB. Remaining quotations from MFR, Ewell, 26 Apr 69, sub: General Comments at the MACV Commanders Conference, 20 April 1969, SEAB. Both in CMH.

[8] Msg, CG, II FFV (Ewell sends), to COMUSMACV, 13 Jun 69, SEAB, CMH.

1 July 1969 and encompass the entire corps zone.[9]

Initially Ewell and Tri created eight *Dong Tien* zones, each consisting of one or more of the eleven provinces in the III Corps area. In each zone a "senior area coordinator" was responsible for coordinating all military operations, allowing "critical assets, particularly Army aviation support," to be allocated on an area, rather than on a unit, basis. American combat support, especially rotary-wing aviation, would thus be funneled through this senior area coordinator, normally a U.S. division or brigade commander, and not through the South Vietnamese division or regimental headquarters. The program directive also made no mention of withdrawals or the need to put the South Vietnamese units into fighting shape, and affirmed "that

**General Do Cao Tri and
Lt. Gen. Julian J. Ewell**

ARVN and U.S. commanders each retain their full command responsibilities."[10]

Ewell's immediate goal was to breath some life into the Vietnamese infantry battalions and have half of their rifle companies in the field, day and night.[11] But he did not want his own commanders taking control of the Vietnamese units involved, reminded them that "this is not, repeat, not the intent of the exercise," and explained his wishes in more detail:

In planning and conducting combined operations, ARVN units are to remain under the operational control of their own commanders. Combined ARVN and US planning should be conducted. ARVN Forces [should] operate in close co-ordination with US forces and the ARVN commander is advised and coached by the US commander, but it is essential that ARVN commanders at all echelons continue to exercise operational control of their own units during these operations. . . . The whole purpose of the DONG TIEN . . . Program is to have the ARVN units take over their own independent operations as rapidly as possible. To accomplish this, insure that the ARVN commanders at all echelons control their own units.[12]

General Tri was equally explicit to his subordinates. In a command letter he emphasized that the the program would make more air and artillery support available to the Vietnamese ground combat commanders and urged them to make the most of it. The Vietnamese general also demanded that his field com-

---

[9] First quotation from MFR, HQ, II FFV, 29 Jun 69, sub: Commanders Conference, 22 June 1969, p. 5. Remaining quotations from Circular no. 525-1, HQ, II FFV, 26 Jun 69, sub: Military Operations: Operation Dong Tien ("Progress Together"). Both in SEAB, CMH.

[10] Circular no. 525-1, HQ, II FFV, 26 Jun 69, sub: Military Operations: Operation Dong Tien ("Progress Together"), SEAB, CMH.

[11] MFR, HQ, II FFV, 15 Jun 69, sub: II FFV Commanders Conference, SEAB, CMH.

[12] Msg, CG, II FFV, to Subordinate Units, 25 Jun 69, sub: Combined Operations, SEAB, CMH.

manders correct specific shortcomings in intelligence, staff work, leadership, and morale; endorsed Ewell's goal of putting half of the Vietnamese rifle companies in the field; and required that the number of South Vietnamese combat operations be increased irrespective of the statistical results. He wanted maximum pressure placed on all enemy forces.[13]

To set the stage, Ewell moved almost all of his combat units out of the Saigon area and turned over the defense of the capital to the Vietnamese. He transformed the U.S. Capital Military Assistance Command, a small tactical headquarters in Saigon, into an advisory organization for the South Vietnamese Capital Military District, and charged it with transferring local American sensor and ground radar installations to the South Vietnamese. Ewell also relieved the U.S. Bien Hoa Tactical Area Command, east of Saigon, of its tactical responsibilities and fashioned it into an advisory and liaison agency to the South Vietnamese Long Binh Special Zone headquarters, a local area command. To ease the transition, the II Field Force Artillery headquarters supervised on-the-job training for special zone artillery personnel. All these changes were essentially administrative and encountered few difficulties.[14]

Meanwhile, the main *Dong Tien* operations began almost immediately.[15] East of Saigon, the U.S. 199th Light Infantry Brigade moved to Xuan Loc, headquarters of the South Vietnamese 18th Infantry Division, and began a series of combined operations with what was still considered one of the worst units in South Vietnam. To the west, in marshy Long An Province, the U.S. 3d Brigade, 9th Infantry Division, began a similar effort with elements of the South Vietnamese 46th and 50th Regiments (25th Infantry Division). Later, in 1970, when the participating South Vietnamese regulars turned their attention to Cambodia, the two American brigades worked closely with the Territorial Forces that remained.

Northwest of Saigon, the U.S. 25th Infantry Division, commanded by Maj. Gen. Ellis W. Williamson, attempted to massage some life into the rest of the South Vietnamese 25th Division. Still based chiefly in southern Hau Nghia, between the American division's rear at Cu Chi and Saigon city, the Vietnamese unit had improved under General Thinh, but was still a mediocre division even by South Vietnamese standards. In mid-1969 Williamson moved an entire U.S. brigade south to the Cu Chi area to work with Thinh's 49th and 50th Regiments, an endeavor that his successor in September, Maj. Gen. Harris W. Hollis, continued and later supplemented with similar efforts between armor and engineer units of the two divisions.[16]

In Hau Nghia, most of the *Dong Tien* units directed their combat efforts against enemy units of Sub-Region 1 in the upper Saigon River area. In October 1969 the *Dong Tien* forces established an integrated fire support base in the

[13] Memo, III CTZ (Lt Gen Tri) to Subordinate Commanders, 17 Jul 69, sub: Improving Methods of Operations, SEAB, CMH.
[14] ORLL, HQ, II FFV, January 1970, p. 23, and April 1970, p. 21, HRB, CMH.
[15] For information, see ORLLs of participating units. All in HRB, CMH.
[16] See appropriate ORLLs of the U.S. 25th Infantry Div and Senior Officer Debriefing Rpt, Hollis, 1 Apr 70, HRB, CMH. Williamson commanded the 25th from July 1968 to September 1969, when he was succeeded by Hollis, who had briefly headed the 9th Division prior to the unit's redeployment from South Vietnam.

"Citadel" region east of Cu Chi, and in February of the following year the South Vietnamese assumed area responsibility for most of northern Hau Nghia Province, including traditional enemy base areas like the Ho Bo and Boi Loi Woods. During this period most of the combined operations were small-scale affairs—routine patrols, night ambushes, and an occasional skirmish with enemy local units that had stayed behind trying to keep the Viet Cong political infrastructure alive. As in the other programs, there were no pitched battles with Vietnamese and American units fighting side by side, and thus no hard testing of the Vietnamese unit. In addition, American efforts had focused on the South Vietnamese infantry battalions, largely ignoring the regimental and division elements. Nevertheless, Hollis judged the program a success and, although moving the participating brigade back to the border region early in 1970, encouraged similar efforts with South Vietnamese airborne, territorial, and CIDG forces around Tay Ninh city. In many respects the entire program of the American 25th was thus no more than a limited training exercise for a variety of South Vietnamese units, but it was an exercise that was desperately needed and long overdue.

The 5th Division

T he most important *Dong Tien* operation took place directly above Saigon between the South Vietnamese 5th Infantry Division and the U.S. 1st Infantry Division.[17] Both units stood astride Route 13, the major artery connecting the capital region with the Cambodian border and, conversely, a primary avenue to Saigon for enemy units infiltrating south. Since 1965 the American division had worked the area, driving the regular enemy units across the Cambodian border and slowly rooting out his larger local forces. During the same period the 5th Division, under General Thuan, had generally performed what at best could be described as securing missions in central and southern Binh Duong Province. In 1968 South Vietnamese intelligence estimated that seventeen thousand enemy troops were active in the division's theoretical area of responsibility. But out of almost two thousand combat operations supposedly conducted by one of the 5th Division's regiments that year, only thirty-six had led to engagements with enemy forces, and these resulted in only seventeen enemy reportedly killed and five captured, at a cost of fourteen soldiers killed and three weapons lost.[18] Such poor track records reflected what Americans derisively called Saigon's "search and avoid" tactics, and were patently unacceptable to Ewell and Tri.

Up to 1969, overriding political concerns had forced MACV to live with the marginal performance of the 5th Division. The close friendship between Presi-

---

[17] Unless otherwise cited, the following section is based on COAARs, 17th Military History Detachment, 1st Infantry Div, 25 Oct 69, sub: Operation Dong Tien, pt. 1, fldr 26, box 4, accession no. 70A4868, and 3 Jan 70, sub: Operation Dong Tien, pt. 2, fldrs 19, 19A, 19B, box 2, accession no. 71A2312. Both in RG 319, WNRC.

[18] CORDS Field Evaluation Rpt, Capt Gregory D. Tillitt, 25 Feb 69, sub: Effectiveness of the 1st Battalion, 7th Regiment, 5th ARVN Division, SEAB, CMH. The 17,000-strength estimate was undoubtedly too high, and may have included Viet Cong cadre and sympathizers, or the tabulators may have simply padded the figures for political purposes.

dent Thieu and General Thuan was well known, as was the political role of the 5th in stabilizing the old military regime.[19] However, by mid-1969 the political as well as the military situation around the capital had changed, and the threat of a military coup was remote. At the same time, the projected redeployment of U.S. forces from South Vietnam made it all the more necessary that Saigon bring units like the 5th back into the mainstream of the war effort as soon as possible.

In August 1969 General Tri, with Thieu's approval, replaced Thuan with General Hieu. His appointment paralleled the arrival of a new commander of the U.S. 1st Division, Maj. Gen. Albert E. Milloy. Both had had extensive experience with the problem-riddled 5th. Hieu had led the division briefly during the 1964 coup period, then served as chief of staff in the II Corps headquarters (under Tri), and, since June 1966, commanded the South Vietnamese 22d Infantry Division. Advisory reports had been favorable, and he had the confidence of his immediate superiors.[20] Milloy, in turn, had served as the 5th Division's senior adviser back in 1965, and had subsequently headed a nearby brigade of the U.S. 1st Division until July 1966. Together they had much to do in what turned out to be a relatively short period of time.

The *Dong Tien* operation between the two units lasted from July 1969 until the departure of the American division from South Vietnam in March 1970. During this period infantry battalions of the 5th Division's 7th Regiment worked extensively with those of the U.S. 1st Division's 2d Brigade in central Binh Duong Province, while similar units of the the 5th Division's 8th Regiment operated with battalions of the 1st Division's 1st and 3d Brigades in the northern Binh Duong jungles.[21]

In practice, the methods employed were simple. In each case, American and South Vietnamese infantry battalions shared common fire support bases and patrolled a common operational area in the dense forests surrounding these strongpoints.[22] The two battalion commanders planned and commanded the operations jointly, with the Americans providing the helicopter support for troop movements and resupply. With the extra push of working with American commanders, staffs, and troops, the lethargic Vietnamese battalions began to wake up. As in the earlier pair-off program, decentralized operations meant that small-unit leaders learned to make decisions on their own, while battalion commanders and staffs learned to control airmobile operations and troop actions over a wider area. Marginal officers were identified and often replaced, and, perhaps most important, Vietnamese morale began to climb. As explained by one participating American battalion commander, once the Vietnamese found out that they could "go out in the jungle, operate and not be swallowed up by big cracks in the ground or overcome by vast groups of enemy, . . . [they gained] a

---

[19] For example, see Msgs, Ewell HOA 1159 to Abrams, 211020 Apr 69, and Ewell HOA 1941 to Abrams, 291320 Jun 69, Abrams Papers, HRB, CMH.

[20] For example, see comments in History file 6–B4; Msg, Rosson NT 1289 to Westmoreland, 21 Oct 67, COMUSMACV Message file. Both in Westmoreland Papers, HRB, CMH.

[21] The third regiment of the 5th Division, the 9th, and the divisional armored cavalry squadron continued to operate in the northern part of the III Corps zone and were not included in the program.

[22] Fire support bases were temporary defensive positions with artillery, communications, and supply units located within a circular ring of earthenwork emplacements.

***Dong Tien* Infantry Operations,** *during which U.S. commanders coached their South Vietnamese counterparts*

certain kind of confidence."[23] And it was this confidence, born of successful experience, that the units of the 5th Division needed so badly.

Drawbacks to the 1st Division's *Dong Tien* operation were primarily in the areas of scope and duration. Periodically the Vietnamese regimental commanders rotated participating infantry battalions, but only two were active in the program at any one time, and neither the regimental nor the division headquarters became closely involved in the effort. Later, as the program progressed, Hieu brought a few of his artillery batteries into the endeavor, and approved liaison and training between various 1st and 5th Division support units. But only two Vietnamese artillery batteries ever participated, the involvement of other 5th Division elements remained minimal, and the 5th's 9th Regiment took no part in the effort. Almost all helicopter and most artillery support were American. Another significant factor, one that was both helpful and seductive, was the inactivity of enemy military forces, and thus, as in the other *Dong Tien* operations, there was no real test of South Vietnamese effectiveness in heavy fighting. However, when the program terminated in March 1970, it had pried the 5th Division out of

[23] Interv, author with Lt Col John Radcliffe, CO, 1st Bn, 26th Infantry, 28 Aug 69, p. 3, in Ltr, 17th Military History Detachment to Office of the Chief of Military History, circa September 1969, sub: After-Action Interview Report on Operations To Upgrade Units in Phu Giao District, fldr 26, box 4, accession no. 70A4868, RG 319, WNRC.

its safe havens in southern Binh Duong and oriented its soldiers away from the political and economic concerns of the Saigon metropolitan area. As the U.S. 1st Division began its redeployment in early 1970, Hieu moved his division headquarters north and, with the help of adjacent American units, gradually took over responsibility for the 1st Division's former operational area without incident. Whether the 5th was ready or not, a major milestone in Vietnamization had taken place.

The Airborne

A final *Dong Tien* operation took place between units of the U.S. 1st Cavalry Division (Airmobile) and the South Vietnamese airborne force.[24] The airborne, now a complete nine-battalion division with three regimental and one division headquarters, artillery and supporting services, was still part of the general reserves under the supervision of the Joint General Staff. Saigon had never employed the force as an entire division and was still parceling it out in small multibattalion task forces that continued to suffer more than their share of wear and tear.[25] In contrast, other elements of the airborne force, including the division headquarters and many of the support units, had seen little action in the field, rarely moving from their Tan Son Nhut base camp just northwest of Saigon. Something had to be done to revitalize this key unit that would someday have to serve as the mobile reserve force for the entire country, and in October 1969 General Ewell nominated the U.S. 1st Cavalry Division for the task.

Since its arrival in late 1968, the U.S. 1st Cavalry Division had been operating along the sparsely populated Cambodian border, engaging regular enemy forces that ventured south across the frontier. Although the division had conducted a number of minor combined operations with assorted South Vietnamese units, it had remained aloof from the main *Dong Tien* Program. However, the reduced amount of enemy activity along the border during the second half of 1969 enabled Ewell to expand the missions of the airmobile unit. In October and November representatives of II Field Force and III Corps met in a series of meetings at General Tri's Bien Hoa headquarters, and laid out the ground rules for the Cavalry-Airborne *Dong Tien* operation. Tri emphasized the need for close coordination of commands and staffs at the division and brigade/regimental levels, but felt that integrated operations at the battalion level were unnecessary. Presumably the Vietnamese airborne battalions were experienced enough to take care of themselves, but the airborne brigade and division staffs needed much work. The American air cavalry unit would have to make helicopters available and supply certain airmobile and communications equipment that the Vietnamese lacked.

---

[24] Unless otherwise noted, the following section is based on ORLLs of HQ, II FFV, and 1st Cavalry Div for 1969–70, HRB, CMH.

[25] For example, see Msg, Kerwin HOA 704 to Abrams, 10 Feb 69, Abrams Papers, HRB, CMH, describing the ambush of one airborne battalion, resulting in 47 killed and 90 wounded for 68 claimed enemy dead.

With these exceptions, the Vietnamese were to be in charge of their own operations, including their logistical needs. Tri also wanted the Airborne Division to establish a forward headquarters with a full tactical operations center alongside the U.S. division headquarters.

Almost immediately the South Vietnamese 2d Airborne Brigade moved into War Zone C along the Cambodian border for combined operations with the cavalry division's 1st Brigade. Operating from Tay Ninh city, the two brigade commanders opened fire support bases across War Zone C for the three participating airborne battalions. The South Vietnamese bases, each housing one airborne battalion and a supporting artillery battery, were staggered between 1st Brigade fire bases, making American artillery support readily available. Initially, the commanders matched each airborne battalion with a cavalry unit, and cavalry personnel gave airborne troops and their advisers elementary instruction in combat air assaults, extractions, and resupply. But the American cavalry units had relatively little to do with the day-to-day ground operations of the airborne. Each airborne battalion had its own area of operation and, supported by helicopters of the U.S. 11th Combat Aviation Group, constantly patrolled their jungle zones. In December the American division's 2d Brigade began a similar program with the South Vietnamese 1st Airborne Brigade east of War Zone C, in the Phuoc Binh border area.

General Ewell reinforced the Vietnamese and advisory communications systems with American forward observers, special liaison teams, and extra radios. This assistance, together with the overlapping artillery support and the close proximity of American airmobile infantry battalions, ensured that he could quickly aid the Vietnamese units should strong enemy forces be encountered. But despite Ewell's concern, such occasions never arose, and the airborne operations were relatively uneventful. After several months in the field, General Tri rotated other airborne units through the 1st Cavalry Division's "training area" until the program ended in April 1970.

The effort was a mixed success. As in similar programs, American air, communications, and logistical support enabled the South Vietnamese units to run extended operations well beyond their normal supply and support capabilities. However, the airborne force never operated as an entire division. Because the division commander, General Dong, failed to establish a tactical command post and rarely took to the field, his staff and support units benefited little. Americans still considered Dong a problem child and felt that the airborne force unit had significant weaknesses that *Dong Tien* had been unable to address. Nevertheless, the combined effort set the stage for more ambitious undertakings in Cambodia one month later.

Ewell also encouraged other elements under his command to stage more operations with South Vietnamese units of all types. American armor generally worked with the Territorial Forces, rather than with similar South Vietnamese units. Despite great differences in organization and equipment, the two types of forces had much in common. Both were scattered throughout the corps area; most of their bases were located along the growing road network; and, up to a point, the two complemented one another—the armored cavalry supplying fire-power, mobility, and communications; and the territorials providing foot troops as well as local intelligence.[26] Artillery *Dong Tien* operations begun in early November 1969 were less successful. Nearly identical to the effort General Peers had run earlier in the Highlands, they failed to integrate the artillery into the "infantry" *Dong Tien* effort, and, with few exceptions, American and South Vietnamese artillery units were not combined in any fashion. Thus in April 1970 the III Corps still lacked a mobile artillery force, and its offensive operations relied heavily on American fire support.

In summary, the *Dong Tien* Program benefited the participating infantry, airborne, and territorial tactical units, but did little for their higher commands and staffs, or for their support units. Although easing the transfer of significant territorial and base responsibilities from American to South Vietnamese units, the program did little to reduce General Tri's area security responsibilities throughout the zone. As long as American units supplied most of the command and control and the intelligence, logistical, and fire support, the South Vietnamese corps commander found it difficult to force his own divisions and regiments to become more involved in these matters. In fact, the early Vietnamization of the Capital Military District and the Bien Hoa Tactical Area Command, as well as the American redeployments from the III and IV Corps Tactical Zones during the year, had the same effect. The old problem of roles and missions had never really disappeared.

Dong Tien ought to have had more ambitious objectives. A comprehensive plan for increasing the security responsibilities of the territorials and allowing the regulars to regroup into more mobile offensive configurations was urgent. But the area security tasks of Tri's regulars appeared to rise, rather than diminish, as American units moved elsewhere or redeployed from South Vietnam. As in the II Corps zone, more direction from MACV or Washington was needed. If the South Vietnamese regulars were to be trained to fight a war of attrition—with continued American air and advisory support as suggested by NSSM 36—then they had to be completely disentangled from the area security mission as quickly as possible. But without such instructions, Ewell and his division commanders had to gear their efforts to more limited short-term goals. Although American combat commanders, staff officers, and even enlisted personnel became advisers during the process, they had even less guidance and training than those serving with the MACV advisory teams, who now slipped further into the role of liaison officers. In general, American commanders also continued to view such tasks with distaste, regarding them as secondary duties that consumed valuable time and resources and that duplicated the efforts of the advisory teams. And in the end, their ability to influence the Vietnamese was no greater than that of the individual adviser. Without a combined (or multinational) command, perhaps nothing more could have been expected. Yet the American withdrawal had just begun, and there was still much time for modifications and experiments with this type of approach.

[26] See ORLLs of the 11th Armored Cavalry Regt and the 1st and 25th Infantry Divs, late 1969–early 1970. All in HRB, CMH.

417

Cambodia: A Test

The performance of the South Vietnamese forces in Cambodia was the first major test in many years of their true combat capabilities. The Cambodian "invasion" was actually a series of multibattalion cross-border attacks, begun in late April and early May of 1970 by several American and South Vietnamese task forces in the II, III, and IV Corps zones.[27] The attacking forces generally operated independently from one another. In some cases the initial assaults turned into long-term occupations of Cambodian territory, and staging bases for further assistance to the new Cambodian regime of General Lon Nol; in other cases the operations were no more than raids into enemy bases close to the border, followed by rapid withdrawals back into South Vietnam (*Map 6*).

In general, South Vietnamese units performed well. Although there was little serious opposition, several things were immediately apparent. First, the South Vietnamese had the capability to plan and conduct mobile operations far from their home bases. The area security tasks of the departed units were easily assumed by territorial and police forces. Second, the South Vietnamese were able to do so without direct American combat intervention. American cross-border forays were largely independent of the South Vietnamese advances. Third, as the operations began to lengthen out, it also became evident that the South Vietnamese were able to supply and support these endeavors with minimal American assistance. Advisers with the troops in Cambodia also noticed a marked increase in South Vietnamese morale; Vietnamese soldiers appeared elated that the war was finally being taken out of South Vietnam and into enemy "home" areas, leaving their own bases secure. Although the South Vietnamese operations were accompanied by high desertion rates, they did not seem to have any relationship to the enthusiasm of the Vietnamese troops, and the periodic rotation of units from Cambodia ameliorated the effect of these losses. Unfortunately for MACV, the rising Vietnamese esprit de corps was the type of improvement that would never show up on the American SEER statistical reports.

Other peculiarities of the campaign also failed to register on the SEER reports and SEER-based analyses. In almost every case the attacking South Vietnamese forces consisted of regimental-size task forces, usually a combination of armor and light infantry, controlled by a small provisional headquarters. In both the III and IV Corps zones, where the bulk of the operations took place, the Vietnamese corps commanders personally directed the attacks, while the division headquarters remained immobile and, aside from administrative support, played almost no role in the operations. South Vietnamese advances were focused along major road networks, and resupply was accomplished almost entirely by road. Truck units from South Vietnamese area logistics commands hauled supplies from the coastal depots to small field dumps along the border and from there delivered them to units in the field. Enemy forces made no attempt to interdict these lines.

---

[27] For details, see COAARs of involved U.S. units and advisory teams, as well as the appropriate sections of USMACV, "Command History, 1970." All in HRB, CMH. See also Tran Dinh Tho, *The Cambodian Incursion*, Indochina Monographs (Washington, D.C.: U.S. Army Center of Military History, 1979).

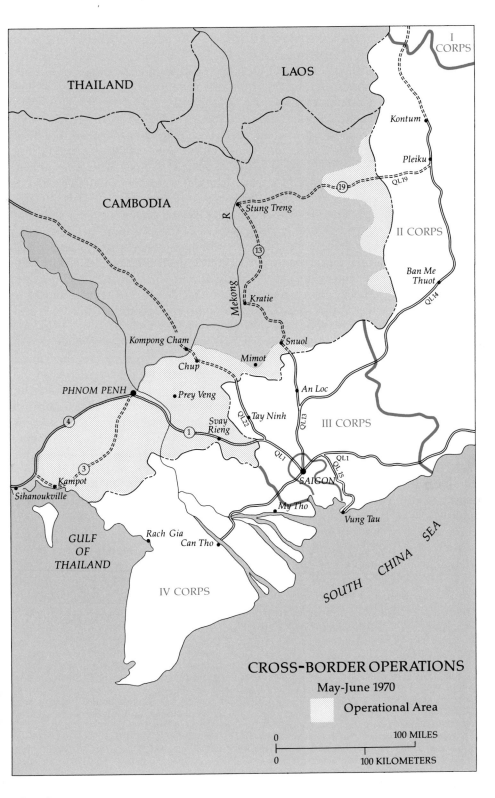

THAILAND

LAOS

I
CORPS

Kontum

CAMBODIA

Pleiku

QL 19

19

R

Stung Treng

Mekong

II CORPS

13

*Ban Me
Thuot*

QL 14

Kratie

Kompong Cham

Snuol

Chup

Mimot

PHNOM PENH

Prey Veng

An Loc

4

*Svay
Rieng*

QL 22

Tay Ninh

QL 13

III CORPS

1

Kampot

3

QL 1

SAIGON

QL 1

QL 15

Sihanoukville

My Tho

Vung Tau

GULF
OF
THAILAND

Rach Gia

Can Tho

SOUTH CHINA SEA

IV CORPS

CROSS-BORDER OPERATIONS

May–June 1970

Operational Area

| 0 | | 100 MILES |
| 0 | | 100 KILOMETERS |

MAP 6

American support was still vital in certain areas. Vietnamese airborne units that air assaulted into the jungle areas north of the "Fishhook" required extensive U.S. helicopter assistance, and all South Vietnamese offensive operations supplemented their own supporting fires with extensive American tactical air strikes and heavy artillery bombardments.

Problem areas included poor field and depot vehicle maintenance, the slow replacement of damaged equipment, and weak tactical intelligence, but they were not significant. The thousands of prisoners of war, Viet Cong suspects, and refugees swamped South Vietnamese intelligence personnel, who were unable to put together a clear picture of enemy activities after the initial attacks were over. Actually, Viet Cong and North Vietnamese military forces, in partial disarray, withdrew deeper into the Cambodian jungles and offered little resistance to the attackers. Perhaps Saigon's greatest setback of the entire campaign was the loss of two of its best leaders, the III Corps commander, General Tri, and the IV Corps commander, General Thanh, both killed in helicopter accidents after personally leading their forces throughout the battles.

Profound differences also remained within the South Vietnamese and U.S. high commands over the purpose of the Cambodian intervention. In March and early April American leaders had viewed initial South Vietnamese incursions into Cambodia by the aggressive General Tri with trepidation and made strong efforts to disassociate U.S. personnel from these attacks.[28] Fearing that the United States would be accused of widening the war, Ambassador Bunker discussed the matter repeatedly with President Thieu and Prime Minister Khiem, emphasizing the need to keep Cambodia neutral and the danger of any ground assistance to Phnom Penh, even if requested by the Cambodian government.[29] But once Communist military forces seriously threatened the new Cambodian government, General Abrams and his immediate superior, Admiral McCain, quickly changed their minds and came out strongly in favor of South Vietnamese military intervention with American combat support. Then, on 25 April, the Joint Chiefs of Staff passed down orders from President Nixon to move both South Vietnamese and American ground combat forces into Cambodia to aid beleaguered Phnom Penh and "get the job done using whatever is necessary." General Wheeler himself now urged Abrams to push his slower and presumably more timid Vietnamese counterparts to move at a quicker pace.[30]

In early May, however, as domestic American criticism of the incursion into Cambodia mounted, the American leaders again changed direction. Wheeler ordered the MACV commander to finish his sweeps of the border sanctuaries, end the affair, and publicly stress that his forces were not "bogged down" in

---

[28] For example, see Msgs, Abrams MAC 4229 to McCain, 311446 Mar 70; Abrams MAC 4530 to Wheeler, 061506 Apr 70; and Moorer JCS 04681 to McCain and Abrams, 062154 Apr 70. All in Abrams Papers, HRB, CMH. See also Kissinger, *White House Years*, pp. 488–89.

[29] Msg, Bunker SGN 4725 to Asst Sec Green, 301220 Mar 70, sub: Cross-Border Operations and Relations With Cambodia, bk. 16, Bunker Papers, DS. For a discussion of JCS rules of engagement restricting cross-border operations, see USMACV, "Command History, 1968," 1:371–75, HRB, CMH.

[30] Quoted words from Msg, Moorer to Abrams and McCain, 250015 Apr 70. See also Msgs, McCain to Wheeler, 220435 Apr 70, sub: Cambodian Assessment; Abrams MAC 5336 to McCain, 220517 Apr 70; Moorer JCS 05634 to McCain and Abrams, 232355 Apr 70; and Wheeler JCS 0571 to Abrams, 251802 Apr 70. All in Abrams Papers, HRB, CMH.

South Vietnamese Troops En Route to Cambodia

Cambodia. Abrams, in turn, passed this guidance on to President Thieu, urging him "to clean up and get out of the [Cambodian] base areas all the supplies and equipment we could and then come back into South Vietnam and proceed on an expeditious basis with the pacification program in South Vietnam." Defense Secretary Laird was of the same mind. Worried that the South Vietnamese, "wandering all over Cambodia," would sooner or later be badly mauled by their opponents, he also insisted on their return to South Vietnam "so that they could continue with their normal functions." But Thieu had other ideas. The Vietnamese president saw the survival of the Lon Nol regime as vital to Saigon; recommended throwing even more Vietnamese troops across the border; and even transferred General Chinh, Tri's deputy, to the Central Training Command so that Ky's old ally would not be commanding troops in the Saigon area while Tri was away in Cambodia. Thus, despite the subsequent withdrawal of American combat forces from Cambodia, including U.S. advisers, and the limitations placed on American support there, South Vietnamese forces continued to hold these border areas and operate deep inside Cambodia for the remainder of the conflict.[31]

[31] First quotation from Msg, Wheeler JCS 06139 to McCain and Abrams, 042139 May 70, Abrams Papers. Second quotation from Msg, Abrams MAC 6403 to Wheeler and McCain, 11 May 70, Abrams Papers. Third and fourth quotations from MFR, Odeen, Office of the Asst SecDef for SA, 15 May 70, sub: Meeting With Secretary Laird on Vietnam, fldr 75, Thayer Papers. See also Msg, Abrams MAC 7169 to Wheeler, 261135 May 70, sub: General Haig Visit, Abrams Papers. All in HRB, CMH.

Cambodian War Booty

Despite the success of the Cambodian experience, American field commanders were still pessimistic. In the I Corps Tactical Zone, where no cross-border operations had occurred, Lt. Gen. James W. Sutherland, Jr., the U.S. Army XXIV Corps commander since June 1970, reported that the South Vietnamese leaders from corps and battalion were good to excellent but "still not ready to stand on their own," and were hampered by the "lack of competent small unit leaders."[32] Other continuing problem areas were the inability of existing engineer units to maintain roads and bases, a shortage of aerial resupply support, poor equipment maintenance, and a sluggish resupply system that still made units reluctant to turn in inoperative equipment.

In the II Corps area General Collins was also dubious of South Vietnamese capabilities. The dissolution of the 24th Special Tactical Zone headquarters along the Laotian border and the transfer of its responsibilities to the South Vietnamese 22d Division had not brought any noticeable improvement to the Highlands.[33] Local American and South Vietnamese cross-border incursions there had amounted to only minor raids. The South Vietnamese 42d Infantry Regiment had continued its decline begun during the Ben Het battles of 1969, and neither the 42d nor the 22d's 47th Regiment had done well during the struggle for the

---

[32] Msg, Sutherland to Rosson, DEPCOMUSMACV, 10 Aug 70, SEAB, CMH.
[33] JGS Memo 1167, 11 Apr 70, sub: Disbanding of 24th STZ of the 22d DTA, SEAB, CMH.

border outpost of Dak Seang in April 1970.[34] Collins regarded the other five South Vietnamese regiments in the zone as acceptable, but saw their "lack of aggressiveness" as a "persistent" and "fatal weakness."[35] "We need more fighters and fewer shadow boxers," Collins opined, reckoning that "we have perhaps overadvised them to the point where some of the lack of initiative . . . might be traced to overactive advisors."[36] In his opinion, South Vietnamese units were "no match" for their North Vietnamese opponents, and South Vietnamese commanders relied too heavily on American air and artillery support now that it was available in quantity. In combat, they were simply unwilling to close with enemy forces. "The failure is one of leadership . . . and one of will." But, Collins had to conclude, "the one thing that can be said is that ARVN soldiers are doing the fighting and taking the casualties."[37]

Some of Collins' subordinate advisers emerging from the Dak Seang campaign seconded his views, and contrasted American air superiority with North Vietnamese "bunker superiority." One, an eight-month veteran adviser, concluded that the primary Vietnamese problem was still poor leadership: "The only time they fight is when they are cornered and have to fight." He predicted that "in the end, when the American forces do pull out, the NVA will move back in" and that, judging by the punishment the enemy had already taken from American firepower and survived, "the South Vietnamese will not be able to stop them."[38]

Even in the III and IV Corps Tactical Zones, American enthusiasm for the Cambodian experience and its beneficial influence of the South Vietnamese had begun to wane by the end of 1970. Although advisers continued to admire the uncharacteristic dynamism exhibited by Generals Tri and Thanh, the two corps commanders, they also began to focus their attention on perennial South Vietnamese shortcomings. Near Saigon, advisers described Chinh's replacement, General Phan Dinh Thu (alias Lam Son), as a "drunkard" and a "playboy," and certainly a poor second for the aggressive Tri.[39] In the Delta General Cushman pointed out continued grave deficiencies in leadership, training, maintenance, and personnel management, and was especially critical of local South Vietnamese artillery units. Admitting that the war in the Delta was a Vietnamese affair—

[34] Prior to the Dak Seang battle, the 47th Regiment replaced the U.S. 3d Brigade, 4th Infantry Division, at Pleiku and the South Vietnamese 22d Division assumed responsibility for the northern Highlands with both the 42d and 47th Regiments (later reinforced by the 45th Regiment, 23d Division, out of Ban Me Thuot). In the ensuing struggle the South Vietnamese suffered 1,625 casualties (216 killed, 1,281 wounded, 128 missing) and claimed 1,697 enemy dead.

[35] Quoted words from Ltr, Collins to Dzu, 6 Dec 70. See also MFR, Collins, 28 Dec 70, sub: Talks With Colonel Ba (Phu Yen Province Chief) and Captain Caligori (Australian Army), RF/PF Training Adviser. Both in Collins Papers, MHI.

[36] Quoted words from Msg, Collins to Rosson, 9 Aug 70. See also Interv, Col Chandler Robbins III with Collins, 1981, pp. 360–62, Senior Officers Oral History Program. Both in Collins Papers, MHI.

[37] Quoted words from Msg, Collins to Abrams, 23 Apr 70. See also Msg, Collins to Duquemin, 19 Apr 70. Both in Collins Papers, MHI.

[38] Interv, Barnard with Sfc David Butler, Senior Adviser, 2d Bn, 42d Regt, n.d., 2d sess., p. 319, VNIT 677, HRB, CMH. For similar comments from other advisers associated with the Dak Seang battle, see ibid., pp. 298–99, 305–06, 345–347, 388–89. For more optimistic views, see ibid., 1st sess., pp. 14, 32–33, 47–50.

[39] MFR, Vann, 21 May 70, sub: Conversation With General Pham Van Dong, Minister of Veterans Affairs, on Thanh's Replacement in the IV CTZ, Vann Papers, MHI.

"not having had much in the way of U.S. combat forces to start with, there had not been a reliance by ARVN on the U.S. to do most of the fighting"—he was concerned over the lack of improvement in leadership and the lack of motivation in individual soldiers. The net result was a "greater reliance on air and artillery support and a greater reluctance to close with the enemy by fire and manuever." Too much of the Vietnamization program, he felt, was devoted to sophisticated equipment, and it was "increasingly evident" that this emphasis tended to "inhibit the [South] Vietnamese from responding with the more primitive means available to them to cope with infiltration and the problem of locating the enemy (such means as night ambushes and patrols)."[40]

Cushman's comments once again revealed the continuing confusion in roles and missions and American strategy. Were the South Vietnamese regulars to continue their territorial security orientation (pacification), or were they to engage the larger enemy forces in mobile offensive operations (attrition)? Were the Vietnamese to follow American prescriptions against crossing into Cambodia and Laos? Or should they pull their own artillery out of static security missions to support such endeavors? Why did aggressive commanders like Tri and Thanh make Abrams nervous? American military leaders may have been confused by the entire matter of Vietnamization, which was a method of pulling American troops out of the war but not a strategy for fighting it. If the South Vietnamese simply could not fight well enough, then these questions were academic. But American leaders in Saigon and Washington chose to ignore such troubling matters. Most were more intent on showing how the Cambodian incursion had weakened the enemy and thus justified further troop withdrawals, paying more attention to what the American public thought of the episode than to what the operation showed about South Vietnamese military strengths and weaknesses. What now passed for American strategy in Vietnam was dependent on a variety of factors that appeared to have little relationship to what was occurring in Southeast Asia.

Hereafter, MACV was to label almost every South Vietnamese combat action, in fact almost every activity, as another "test" of Vietnamization. However, few American generals had favorable predictions to make regarding Saigon's ability to stand alone. At this stage senior American advisers may have become too pessimistic in their evaluations, reacting perhaps to the many overly optimistic reports of progress in the past. Almost all of them continued to complain about poor South Vietnamese leadership; but, like the weather, no one did anything about it. General Westmoreland himself, visiting Vietnam in July 1970 as the Army chief of staff, saw "a need to clean house in the senior ranks of the Vietnamese Army"; pointed out to Thieu and Vien that there were "many young colonels capable of assuming general officer responsibilities and eager to do so"; and recommended "forced retirements" for those who had proved wanting.[41] Yet, American leaders still hesitated to push the Vietnamese generals on such matters. Saigon's stubborn resistance to even the most well-meaning foreign interference in its affairs had become gospel among American officials: If the

---

[40] Msg, Cushman to Rosson, 10 Aug 70, SEAB, CMH.
[41] Memo, Westmoreland to SecDef, SecArmy, Chairman JCS, 4 Aug 70, sub: Trip Report (7–21 July 1970), COMUSMACV Message file, Westmoreland Papers, HRB, CMH.

Vietnamese leaders demanded complete authority in this area, then let them have it. Washington may have also felt that such personnel changes were not that critical, and that if the Vietnamese generals could keep enemy forces bottled up in their cross-border sanctuaries, then the war was close to being won. But little more than a dozen South Vietnamese battalions had been involved in Cambodia at any one time, and the enemy response had been negligible. The real testing was still to come.

23

Vietnamizing Military Support

MACV stopped far short of Vietnamizing the battlefield through combined operations, relying more on persuasion, American troop withdrawals, and enemy inactivity to slowly increase the responsibilities of South Vietnamese combat units. Could the same approach work with the military support apparatus that was fueling the entire war effort? The scope of these seemingly secondary activities was vast. Each day the U.S. Army port commands at Saigon and Cam Ranh Bay supervised the unloading of huge seagoing ships filled with fuel, supplies, and equipment; arranged for their temporary storage; and then waved them on through an internal sea, land, and air transportation network to a variety of depots, large and small, scattered throughout the country. There, war materiel was carefully stored, catalogued, maintained, and ultimately disbursed to lesser storage areas and to the users themselves—an endless process without which no military operations could have been planned or undertaken. Other units kept the system moving, building and repairing roads, waterways, and airfields; repairing worn or damaged equipment; and operating the communications-electronics network that kept the whole process functioning smoothly from the most remote outpost in the Central Highlands to the hundreds of civilian industries back in the United States.

Many of the support units belonged to the U.S. Army's 1st Logistical Command at Long Binh, just outside of Saigon, or to one of its subordinate area support commands; others, smaller units, were integral components of the units they supported (for example, divisional support commands); while still others, like engineer, signal, and aviation forces, had separate command and logistical organizations of their own. Prior to 1969 these units had been preoccupied with satisfying the needs of U.S. combat forces and, despite the fact that many of them operated from fixed locations, close to similar South Vietnamese units and installations, their missions and activities had remained separate. This arrangement suited General Abrams, who indicated in late 1968 that he did not intend to use American support units and technical personnel to train Vietnamese forces

427

unless absolutely necessary.[1] MACV's concern over South Vietnamese support capabilities was not yet paramount.

Early Planning

The administration's decision to Vietnamize the war caught MACV by surprise. Although Kissinger's original directive, NSSM 36, provided for continued U.S. military support of Saigon's combat units, MACV's decision to redeploy American support units along with combat troops made it necessary to plan for the Vietnamization of all support activities as quickly as possible. Neither the T-Day nor the current improvement and modernization plans foresaw Saigon facing a combined Viet Cong–North Vietnamese Army threat alone. Instead, each sought to assure South Vietnam a measure of logistical self-sufficiency in a less demanding situation—either a ceasefire or a continuing American military ground presence. Thus MACV had to develop new programs, allowing Saigon to assume all military support functions, from harbor operations to maintenance of the large microwave and tropospheric scatter communications system. Despite Abrams' earlier hesitation, American support units quickly became involved.

MACV at first hoped to speed up Vietnamization by having redeploying U.S. units turn over their equipment directly to similar newly activated South Vietnamese units. The earlier T-Day plans had tried to schedule possible redeployment and activation dates to allow such transfers. Dubbed "Switchback" by American staffs,[2] they seemed the quickest way of building up South Vietnamese support capabilities should a rapid American troop withdrawal be necessary. But without any redeployment master plan, such turnovers proved difficult to implement. In March and April 1969, for example, two American artillery battalions turned over their equipment to two new South Vietnamese units, but MACV was unable to match activation and redeployment dates, and there was thus little interaction between the losing and gaining units.[3] MACV also rejected the Switchback concept for the activation of two South Vietnamese ordnance companies, two engineer battalions, and one engineer heavy equipment company during the second half of 1969. Rather than use unit-to-unit equipment turnovers, MACV outfitted the new South Vietnamese formations with excess equip-

---

[1] Msg, COMUSMACV to CINCPAC, Info JCS, DAIN 387793, 26 Dec 68, sub: RVNAF Improvement and Modernization—Phase II, SEAB, CMH.

[2] See ORLL, 1st Logistical Command, April 1969, p. 51, HRB, and the file on Vietnamization turnovers, SEAB. Both in CMH. (Switchback turnovers should not be confused with the earlier effort to turn over control of the CIDG program from the CIA to the Special Forces that was also codenamed Switchback.)

[3] U.S. 6th Bn, 77th Artillery (105-mm.) to South Vietnamese 213th Artillery Bn and U.S. 6th Bn, 84th Artillery (155-mm.) to South Vietnamese 45th Artillery Bn, noted in ORLL, HQ, II FFV, October 1969; ORLL, 9th Infantry Div Artillery, April 1969, p. 2; ORLL, HQ, I FFV, April 1969, p. 42; and ORLL, 41st Artillery Group, April 1969, pp. 14–15. All in HRB, CMH. MACV actually phased these units out of the local U.S. Army force structure and did not redeploy them. Because the men were reassigned to other units, there was no drop in American troop strength.

ment from U.S. Army depot stocks.[4] Again, without firm U.S. redeployment dates, MACV's ability to match activations and redeployments was limited. MACV's Vietnamization plan, published in July 1969, was grounded in a flexible "cut-and-dry" philosophy that militated against Switchback becoming a major redeployment tool. Only in the case of several water transportation and aviation unit turnovers in late 1969 and 1970 was the original Switchback concept realized.

On their own initiative American support units began to turn over portions of the war effort to their South Vietnamese counterparts well in advance of the formal Vietnamization plan. In September 1968 Maj. Gen. Joseph M. Heiser, Jr., commanding the 1st Logistical Command, initiated Op-

Lt. Gen. Joseph M. Heiser, Jr.
(1969 photograph)

eration BUDDY "as a means of improving ARVN's logistical forces in order to insure their readiness to assume responsibilities connected with T-Day planning and MACV-RVNAF improvement and modernization programs." Key to General Heiser's BUDDY concept was a "transitional training program" based on his Korean War experience. He intended to attach Vietnamese soldiers, and even entire units, to appropriate American logistical units for extensive training. He wanted formal and on-the-job instruction followed by combined operations, and finally the gradual turnover of selected U.S. logistical functions and installations in Saigon. To make the program work, Heiser asked MACV to assign the logistical advisers directly to the 1st Logistical Command to help plan training programs with U.S. and Vietnamese logistical staffs. Switchback operations were to be an integral part of the overall BUDDY program.[5]

Preparations for the endeavor took up most of October, and early the following month Heiser sent a rough plan to MACV and USARV, the Army component command, for approval. At the same time he directed his four subordinate support commands to coordinate with local American logistical advisers and submit supporting plans for the project. Shortly thereafter, a USARV-sponsored conference established a working committee with representatives from the 1st Logistical Command, USARV, and MACV to "conduct initial negotiations with overall objectives of the (Buddy) operation."[6] Based on this groundwork, the

---

[4] ORLL, 18th Engineer Bde, October 1969, pp. 7–8; ORLLs, 29th General Support Group, July 1969, p. 3, and October 1969, p. 8. All in HRB, CMH.
[5] Quoted words from ORLL, 1st Logistical Command, January 1969, p. 49, HRB, CMH. For relevant correspondence on the 1st Logistical Command's efforts to assist Saigon during this period, see fldr 8 (lst Log Cmd—Misc Documents), box 13, accession no. 70A6868, RG 319, WNRC.
[6] Ibid.

logistical command produced a detailed operational plan and appeared ready to implement an organized program.

Heiser's program quickly ran into trouble in early 1969. Aside from a few local on-the-job training (OJT) arrangements, the Vietnamese proved unresponsive. His staff reported that MACV had advised South Vietnamese commanders against taking part in anything more elaborate.[7] Heiser was puzzled. Finally, on 12 May Maj. Gen. Raymond C. Conroy, the MACV J–4, notified USARV that the assignment of South Vietnamese units or personnel to U.S. units as conceived by Heiser was not "feasible or desirable." He elaborated:

The concept of a U.S. unit training an ARVN unit, attached for rations and quarters only, is considered suitable for use in support of T-Day training requirements when limited time will be available to train and turnover equipment. It is not planned to use this concept for training ARVN units under other than T-Day conditions (i.e., rapid withdrawal).[8]

Conroy recommended that Heiser's units sponsor only those OJT programs requested specifically by South Vietnamese commanders and their advisers. He promised that MACV would try to determine South Vietnamese logistical support needs with more precision. But until the Vietnamization and the final improvement and modernization plans were complete, MACV authorized the 1st Logistical Command only to provide "supply maintenance, and technical assistance" for the existing Phase II Improvement and Modernization Plan.[9]

As Defense Secretary Laird and General Abrams began to sort out differences in the Vietnamization effort, Conroy became more interested in Heiser's ideas. In April he started putting together his own special staff branch to handle American on-the-job training for the Vietnamese, and in early July held an OJT conference to discuss current programs and future efforts. But 1st Logistical Command representatives still found the attitude of MACV and the Joint General Staff disappointing, complaining that "ARVN is not pushing an OJT training effort . . . , that the OJT training programs will be utilized only when the requirement cannot be filled by service school training," and that "the approach being taken by the MACV J–4 does not appear to have a true sense of urgency."[10] Col. Hubert S. Cunningham, the MACV training director, later tried to clarify the command's position and explained that, although the OJT effort was "an integral part of the overall training process," it would not be "controlled or require authorization at the MACV level."[11] In other words, on-the-job training was to be a policy rather than a plan or a program, and without central direction the more comprehensive OJT effort envisioned by Heiser was reduced to a variety of widespread but uncoordinated programs run by lesser staffs and support units.

---

[7] For discussion, see DF, HQ, USARV, G–3, 31 Mar 69, sub: General Heiser's Letter Concerning 'Operation BUDDY,' in file 206–02.1 ARVN Modernization, Mar–Apr 69, SEAB, CMH.

[8] Ltr, Conroy to CG, USARV, 12 May 69, sub: Project Buddy, fldr 8, box 13, accession no. 70A6868, RG 319, WNRC.

[9] Quoted words from ORLL, 1st Logistical Command, July 1969, annex F. See also ibid. for April 1969, p. 51; July 1969, annex F; and October 1969, annex F. All in HRB, CMH.

[10] Quoted words from Rpt, Lt Col A. E. Ferguson and Capt E. L. Bischoff, 3 Jul 69, sub: Trip Report to MACV OJT Training Meeting, fldr 8, box 13, accession no. 70A6868, RG 319, WNRC. For another criticism, see Study, Earl I. Jones and Henry M. Parsons, 15 Aug 70, sub: Improvement of RVNAF Training Through Applied Research and Technology, SEAB, CMH.

[11] Ltr, Cunningham to CofS, MACV, 10 Aug 69, sub: AAR, SEAB, CMH.

Instruct and Advise Team Member at South Vietnamese Logistical Depot

The effort to improve Vietnamese storage and maintenance capabilities was typical. In July 1969 the U.S. Army Support Command, Saigon, an element of the 1st Logistical Command, sent out a highly skilled six-man training team to work with Vietnamese base depot personnel, and by the end of the year cells were working with each of the five South Vietnamese area logistics commands. Called instruct and advise teams, they operated like the mobile advisory teams that assisted the Territorial Forces but never became part of the official advisory network. Although successful in making the marginal system work better, they lacked the muscle to tackle the basic shortcomings of the Vietnamese depots—corruption, a transient work force, and limited facilities—and could not begin to address related logistical problems, such as poor unit maintenance, the absence of liaison between depots and field support units, and the reluctance of units to turn in inoperable equipment. American ordnance advisers in the III Corps zone noted that many of these difficulties began to sort themselves out during the Cambodian operations of 1970, which gave an air of immediacy to all logistical endeavors. Perhaps the pressure of combat was the only sure way of forcing the South Vietnamese to solve their logistical problems.[12]

[12] See ORLLs, 1st Logistical Command, July 1969, annex F, October 1969, annex F, and January 1970, p. 31; ORLL, Saigon Support Command, October 1969, p. 16, and later ORLLs. See also Intervs, 2d Lt Barry Clendenin with Lt Col Donald Y. Hiatt, Senior Ordnance Adviser, 3d Area Logistics Command, 5 Dec 70, pp. 11–13, VNIT 819, and with Capt Claude P. L. Kugel, MACV Advisory Team 9, Ordnance Section, 16 Dec 70, p. 11, VNIT 817. All in HRB, CMH.

The Ports

During the latter half of 1969 MACV began a concerted effort to Vietnamize the port system in South Vietnam.[13] On 12 August 1969 General Abrams approved the creation of "local joint committees" of American and South Vietnamese port operators, local logistical commanders, and American port advisers "to promote the takeover or joint utilization by ARVN of selected US military port operations." To assist with overall coordination, he created a combined MACV–Joint General Staff committee, with participation of USARV and 1st Logistical Command staff officers, and directed that priority be given to the complete "ARVNization" of the Binh Thuy–Can Tho port area in the IV Corps Tactical Zone, the "joint utilization" of the Saigon commercial port, and the expansion of South Vietnamese military responsibilities at other ports.[14]

The Saigon Support Command, the logistical headquarters for both the III and IV Corps areas, supervised the most extensive port ARVNization. The effort depended heavily on Switchback and OJT programs, and much had already been done prior to the Abrams directive. In February 1969 the command had ordered its subordinate units, the 4th Transportation Command and the 29th General Support Group, to begin "BUDDY (OJT)" programs that expanded past assistance to South Vietnamese forces "to encompass the capability to assume functions and missions as US units are phased out."[15] Thus, even before Vietnamization became an official policy, U.S. Army port units were giving practical classes to their Vietnamese counterparts in marine maintenance; landing craft, crane, tugboat, petroleum, and convoy operations; and harbor-master procedures (at the Saigon, Newport, Cat Lai, Dong Tam, and Binh Thuy ports). But at the same time, the command warned that more was needed and recommended a "consolidated training program" and a "theatre level" language program to aid "the successful completion of T-Day Plans."[16]

The Saigon Support Command tied the port ARVNization effort closely to the transfer (Switchback) of marine cargo craft to newly activated South Vietnamese Army water transportation units. In two cases U.S. Army marine transportation and maintenance units gave extensive technical training to key Vietnamese personnel, and new Vietnamese crews trained with departing American crews for about four months before the South Vietnamese units, the 203d and 305th Transportation Groups, were allowed to operate alone. Less successful was Project Switch 1097, the transfer of boats belonging to the U.S. 1097th Transportation Company at the small delta port of Dong Tam. The American unit had left South Vietnam with the U.S. 9th Infantry Division in July 1969, and it was not until the following year that personnel from a new South Vietnamese trans-

---

[13] For more details, see ORLLs of the 1st Logistical Command's subordinate support commands (at Saigon, Cam Ranh Bay, Qui Nhon, and Da Nang), HRB, CMH.

[14] ORLL, 1st Logistical Command, October 1969, annex F, HRB, CMH. Later ORLLs survey the countrywide port turnover program during each reporting period. The term *ARVNization* also became commonplace and a substitute in many official documents for the term *Vietnamization*.

[15] Msg, Saigon Support Command to Subordinate Units, 17 Feb 69, sub: BUDDY OPS, SEAB, CMH.

[16] ORLL, Saigon Support Command, July 1969, p. 19, HRB, CMH.

portation group were ready to begin operations. With no one to perform mainte-nance the equipment deteriorated rapidly, and it was several weeks before the U.S. 544th Transportation Company, 4th Transportation Command, could recon-dition it.[17]

As these transfers occurred, American harbor commands accelerated efforts to train and expand South Vietnamese military port units, especially in the III and IV Corps Tactical Zones. Here the large Saigon commercial port and the delta riverways were able to supply the Vietnamese military with experienced personnel for harbor and riverine units, easing their expansion and training. In October 1969 the Vietnamese assumed partial control of the small Binh Thuy–Can Tho port complex in the Delta with equipment lent by the U.S. 159th Trans-portation Battalion and, one year later, acquired complete responsibility for the entire harbor operation there. In the III Corps area Col. John E. Murray, com-manding officer of the U.S. 4th Transportation Command, and the commander of the South Vietnamese Saigon Terminal Transportation Command signed a thirty-day test agreement "outlining the responsibilities for the administration, coordination, and control and movement of cargo and the joint US-RVNAF Operation of the Saigon Port."[18] Shortly thereafter, the South Vietnamese unit began operating several of the major shipping piers and by 1970 had taken responsibility for almost all harbor operations handling USAID and defense-related shipments in the Saigon Port, leaving only the Newport area just south of Bien Hoa to the U.S. 4th Transportation Command for American military ship-ping. Also in 1970, the Vietnamese assumed control of Dong Tam and Vung Tau, another small port nearby, and, after a long OJT period with American crews, took over five tugboat detachments that served the Saigon area.

North of Saigon, where American support units had constructed and oper-ated the major military ports by themselves, Vietnamization proceeded at a slower pace. Cam Ranh Bay in south-central II Corps remained an American facility throughout 1970, but the U.S. Army Support Command, Cam Ranh Bay, established BUDDY and Switchback programs to enable the South Vietnamese 5th Area Logistics Command to assume harbor and depot responsibility for the small port of Nha Trang, a few miles north. After long negotiations, the 5th and the U.S. 124th Transportation Command signed a local turnover agreement on 1 August 1969. Cam Ranh Bay remained the main receiving area for overseas shipments in the II Corps Tactical Zone, and Nha Trang handled shallow-draft operations. Deep-draft Vietnamese cargo was first offloaded at Cam Ranh Bay and then forwarded to Nha Trang on lighters. American supplies arriving at Nha Trang traveled by road to Cam Ranh Bay depots. Later, on 27 October, MACV and the Joint General Staff formally approved the agreement, and the Nha Trang Port officially became a South Vietnamese activity.

[17] See ORLLs of Saigon Support Command and subordinate units for 1969–70, especially for the 4th Transportation Command and the 159th Transportation Bn, HRB, CMH.
[18] Quoted words from ORLL, 4th Transportation Command, October 1969, p. 8, HRB, CMH. See also Interv, 1st Lt David Wigdor, 15th Military History Detachment, with Maj James Piner and Col Paul A. Pencola, Advisory Team 10, 4th Area Logistics Command, Can Tho, 26 Oct 69, fldr 8, box 13, accession no. 70A6868, RG 319, WNRC.

Training South Vietnamese in Harbor Operations

The U.S. Army Support Command, Qui Nhon, in the northern II Corps Tactical Zone also made an early start, beginning a BUDDY program in March 1969 "to develop ARVN logistical support capability within the USA SUPCOM, QN area of responsibility through on-the-job training programs designed to satisfy current and future needs evolving from the modernization programs and eventual transfer of logistical responsibilities." Progress was initially slow, and the command complained in April 1970 that the Vietnamese were not taking the training programs seriously. Perhaps the initial impetus of the Vietnamization program had begun to weaken. Vietnamese complacency soon changed in June when the U.S. 5th Transportation Command at Qui Nhon moved north to replace redeploying U.S. Marine Corps support units at Da Nang, leaving a small provisional terminal transportation company to supervise what now had become a South Vietnamese operation (by the 201st Terminal Service Company and elements of the 203d Transportation Group). Suddenly the Vietnamese took a greater interest in the BUDDY programs, the ARVNization of the Qui Nhon Port became an "oversized training project," and the transfer of responsibility was accomplished quickly.[19]

---

[19] First quotation from ORLL, 45th General Support Group, April 1969, p. 4. Second quotation from ORLL, 4th Transportation Command, April 1970, p. 8. Both in HRB, CMH.

Vietnamization by Function

Throughout 1969 and 1970 the 1st Logistical Command's general support groups continued to strengthen the five South Vietnamese area logistics commands through small low-level OJT programs between transportation, quartermaster, ordnance, and other support units. Similar assistance activities existed in the fields of aviation, engineers, communications, psychological operations, and intelligence. In the intelligence area Americans and South Vietnamese had worked closely together for several years.[20] Since 1966 the Joint General Staff had assigned South Vietnamese military intelligence detachments to almost all U.S. corps-level, division, and separate brigade headquarters. These thirty-man teams received what amounted to on-the-job training in intelligence operations and, as U.S. units departed, supplied experienced personnel to new South Vietnamese units. At the national level the MACV J–2 (Intelligence) staff continued to oversee the three combined intelligence centers (interrogating prisoners, analyzing captured documents, and examining captured war materiel) and the larger combined intelligence center, which acted as a theater clearinghouse for information with a staff of about five hundred American and one hundred South Vietnamese servicemen. As American participation in the war wound down between 1969 and 1972, Lt. Gen. William E. Potts, Abrams' J–2, gradually transferred the centers to the Vietnamese.[21]

Vietnamization brought comparatively few changes to the South Vietnamese tactical intelligence community. Redeploying American units normally turned over their current intelligence files to units replacing them, but there seemed little need to organize special training because Saigon's problems stemmed from its inability to act on, rather than acquire, information. The U.S. 135th Military Intelligence Group (Counterintelligence) sent only a liaison team in a fruitless attempt to wean the South Vietnamese Military Security Service away from its "counter-coup" mentality, and the U.S. 1st Military Intelligence Battalion (Air Reconnaissance Support) temporarily integrated American and South Vietnamese operations. Another effort in this category, Operation TIGHT JAW, began in November 1968 to create "a combined U.S. and RVNAF border surveillance program, which . . . [could] be turned over to the RVNAF for unilateral operation, at an appropriate time." TIGHT JAW was concerned mainly with the turnover of selected U.S. ground sensor fields to South Vietnamese commands as American users redeployed. Such transferals usually involved classroom and on-the-job training by special mobile training teams and U.S. sensor control and management platoons (SCAMPs). Finally, General Abrams sought to boost Saigon's cross-border intelligence capabilities by strengthening the South Vietnamese Strategic Technical Directorate, the counterpart of the MACV Studies and Observation Group (SOG). Abrams felt that the Vietnamese office was hampered by the extremely marginal cadre assigned, the lack of aircraft to support cross-

---

[20] For details, see Lung, *Intelligence*, pp. 79–128; McChristian, *Role of Military Intelligence*, pp. 21–93; Msg, McCain to Lt Gen Bennett, Director, DIA, 242218 Sep 70, sub: Interagency Intelligence Vietnamization Committee, Abrams Papers, HRB, CMH.

[21] Potts Interv, 12 Apr 84, SEAB, CMH.

border intelligence missions, and the continued use of mercenary field detachments. The South Vietnamese also had more serious problems in the intelligence arena. These included the absence of an effective national-level intelligence body, the continued multiplicity of military and civilian intelligence agencies, and the lack of attention given to intelligence by South Vietnamese commanders in the field.[22]

The U.S. 4th Psychological Operations Group also undertook several combined activities to support Vietnamization. Beginning in 1969, the group sponsored combined psychological operations (PSYOPS) development centers in each corps zone, staffed by local PSYOPS personnel (from U.S. PSYOPS and South Vietnamese political warfare battalions) with representatives from MACV, the Saigon government (*Chieu Hoi* Ministry and Vietnamese Information Service), and the local American and South Vietnamese corps-level headquarters. In May 1970 the group established a theater-level combined U.S.-Vietnamese psychological operations center to unify all such activities and phase out the American operational role.[23]

The experience of the twenty-seven nondivisional U.S. engineer battalions in Vietnamization was considerably different. These battalions normally gave most of their support to American units and bases, providing only occasional training for South Vietnamese engineers and engaging in few combined projects.[24] In the latter half of 1969 General Abrams reaffirmed their limited role and decided against directly committing them to any large-scale Vietnamization effort. Instead, he wanted U.S. Army engineers to concentrate on finishing critical construction projects, especially the road-building program, prior to their redeployment. Abrams expected the growing road network to make up for the declining amount of aviation transport available as American units departed. Once constructed, South Vietnamese military engineers and civilian contractors would have only the relatively easy task of maintaining it.[25]

American engineer units continued to support their South Vietnamese counterparts with several smaller efforts. Through local OJT programs they trained several Vietnamese engineer units, activated with inexperienced personnel, in quarry blasting and rock crushing; asphalt production and paving; water distribution; and the operation and maintenance of earthmoving and grading equip-

[22] Quoted words from MACV OPLAN 103–69, "TIGHT JAW," 17 Apr 69. See also ORLL, 525th Military Intelligence Group, April 1970, encl. 1; ORLLs, 1st Military Intelligence Bn, October 1969, pp. 3–4, January 1970, p. 4, July 1970, pp. 1–2, and October 1970, p. 4; Msg, Abrams MAC 2339 to Wheeler, 200327 Feb 70, sub: RVNAF Cross-Border Capability, Abrams Papers; SOG annexes to MACV command histories. All in HRB, CMH. See conclusions of Lung, *Intelligence*, pp. 232–40.

[23] ORLL, HQ, XXIV Corps, July 1970, p. 23; ORLL, 4th Psychological Operations Group, April 1969, pp. 1–2. Both in HRB, CMH. For further details, see ORLLs of 6th, 7th, 8th, and 10th Psychological Operations Bns, HRB, CMH, and PSYOPS documents in fldr 3, box 2, accession no. 70A4136, RG 319, WNRC.

[24] For example, see ORLL, 35th Engineer Group, October 1967, p. 6; ORLL, 34th Engineer Group, January 1968, pp. 13 and 19–20; ORLL, 79th Engineer Group, January 1968, p. 11 and encl. 18 ("AAR-ARVN Refresher Training"). All in HRB, CMH. See also Robert R. Ploger, *U.S. Army Engineers, 1965–1970*, Vietnam Studies (Washington, D.C.: Department of the Army, 1974), pp. 167–75.

[25] See MFR, Maj David F. Nidever, Plans Officer, USARV, 24 Jun 70, sub: Vietnamization of LOC Program, SEAB, CMH, which notes that the LOC (lines of communications), or road network, program was to be finished by the end of 1971.

Transporting Supplies on Upgraded Roads in the Delta. *More and better roads reduced dependence on aerial resupply.*

ment, generators, cranes, arc welders, air compressors, mixers, and so forth.[26] These endeavors reached a peak in 1970 and then slowly faded as U.S. engineer units redeployed from Vietnam. MACV also used U.S. Army engineer equipment to create new Vietnamese engineer units in 1970, but as before there was little interaction between losing and gaining units. One major exception was the organization and training of four South Vietnamese land-clearing (plow) companies in 1970 by the U.S. 62d Engineer Battalion.[27] Plow units had been critical for the Americans in Vietnam. American engineers used the D–7E "Rome Plow" bulldozers (made in Rome, Georgia), rather than chemical defoliants, to keep roadsides and base perimeters clear of fast-growing jungle vegetation, eliminating potential ambush sites. South Vietnamese engineers asked for more in 1971, but Abrams turned down their request because of their inability to maintain the

[26] For example, see Draft Study, JGS, June 1970, sub: Examples of Improvement and Modernization of the 6th ARVN Engineer Group, SEAB. For the 18th Engineer Bde's ARVN Affiliation Program, see ORLLs of 35th, 45th, and 937th Engineer Groups, 1969–70, HRB. For the 20th Engineer Bde's Buddy Program, see ORLLs of 34th, 79th, and 159th Engineer Groups, 1969–70; ORLLs of subordinate engineer battalions; and Interv, Capt Curt E. Schlautterback, CO, 26th Military History Detachment, with Lt Col Lewis Armintillo, Senior Engineer Adviser, II Corps, 22 Nov 69, VNI 717, HRB. All in CMH.

[27] See ORLL, 62d Engineer Bn (LC), April 1970, pp. 2–5 and encl. 16 ("OPLAN 1–70, 25 Mar 70, OPERATION SWITCHBLADE II"), and subsequent ORLLs, HRB, CMH.

existing equipment.[28] In this case, the hurried training program had obviously been unsuccessful.

Another aspect of engineer Vietnamization was the increasing use of indigenous private contractors and, for unskilled labor, the direct hiring of Vietnamese civilians. Early in 1969, as an experiment, MACV "civilianized" six U.S. Army engineer battalions by replacing lower enlisted ranks with Vietnamese workers. However, the need to keep the Army units mobile and the marginal performance of the civilians led the engineers to abandon the practice. More successful was an agreement in 1970 to have a private American contractor provide extensive training for Vietnamese engineer and ordnance personnel in various mechanical skills. In this way, Vietnamization could proceed without diverting American engineer units from their primary construction tasks.[29]

The Vietnamization of the fixed communications system involved extremely complex equipment that made careful planning a necessity. By 1969 the U.S. Army was operating three types of communications systems in South Vietnam: the Combat, the Corps (Regional) Area, and the Defense Communications Systems. The last, renamed the Integrated Communications System, Southeast Asia (ICS, SEA), included a large fixed-station wideband communications net, an undersea cable system, and several extremely sophisticated line-of-sight and tropospheric scatter facilities serving all of Southeast Asia. The U.S. 1st Signal Brigade operated that portion of the ICS within South Vietnam, as well as most of the 220 corps area installations and about 70 local telephone networks.[30]

Since 1966 the 1st Signal Brigade had encouraged ad hoc BUDDY-type relationships between U.S. signal battalions and their local South Vietnamese counterparts. In part a public relations policy, the practice also ensured that American communications units kept track of Vietnamese signal activities. At times, U.S. commanders developed close personal relationships by having their units run special training programs for Vietnamese signal personnel; make "loans" of excess supplies or equipment; and, on occasion, perform certain repair work that was beyond local Vietnamese capabilities.[31] But up to 1969 U.S. signal units had their hands full with American communications needs, and assistance to the South Vietnamese was minor.

During 1969 this situation began to change in two ways. First, the 1st Signal Brigade encouraged direct assistance to South Vietnamese units through existing BUDDY relationships. Second, the brigade began to make substantial preparations for the eventual turnover of the entire fixed communications system. In late 1969 it drew up plans for an intensified BUDDY effort with the South Vietnamese Signal Directorate, which MACV and the Joint General Staff subsequently ap-

---

[28] Msg, Abrams MAC 11251 to Major Subordinates, 300421 Nov 71, sub: Land Clearing Companies, Abrams Papers, HRB, CMH. The bulldozers were normally used in populated areas and on dryer level terrain.

[29] See ORLL, HQ, USARV, July 1969, pp. 41–42; ORLL, 815th Engineer Bn (Construction), April 1969, pp. 10 and 13. Similar programs for U.S. Army aviation units were turned down. See ORLL, 269th Combat Aviation Bn, July 1968, pp. 9–10 ("Program 6"). See also USMACV, "Command History, 1970," 2:VII–89. All in HRB, CMH.

[30] Bergen, *Military Communications*, pp. 291–343.

[31] For example, see ORLL, 52d Signal Bn, October 1969, p. 10; ORLL, 73d Signal Bn, July 1968, p. 3; and ORLL, 69th Signal Bn, January 1968, p. 2. All in HRB, CMH.

proved. The American signal command then published a procedural regulation on 26 March 1970, requiring subordinate signal units down to company level to establish "RVNAF mission essential training . . . objectives and perpetuate an effective (BUDDY) program." The new program, called *Cung Than Thien* ("Buddy's Together"), matched American and South Vietnamese signal units operating in similar geographical areas for training and other assistance. In 1970 and 1971 these activities, although small, trained several hundred Vietnamese signalmen in various highly technical communications specialities.[32] The 1st Signal Brigade also tasked subordinate units to conduct "surveys by combined teams of all communications facilities and sites within each CTZ where 1st Signal Brigade and ARVN Signal Directorate elements were providing dual support" in order "to determine where integration can take place and a single facility or system replace existing dual operations." Whenever possible, South Vietnamese units were to assume sole responsibility for such sites, and American operators were to turn over their equipment to the new users. An 8-kilometer "short-haul" microwave link between Dong Tam and My Tho in the IV Corps Tactical Zone was the first of many facilities to be turned over to the South Vietnamese in this manner.[33]

The Vietnamization of local ICS centers, the Dial Telephone Exchange System (DTE), and other complex communications installations was more elaborate.[34] In April 1969, at the request of the Department of the Army, the 1st Signal Brigade presented a draft plan for turning over the ICS and "associated systems" (that is, selected terminal equipment, such as dial and manual telephone switchboards). The plan depended on extensive training programs for the Vietnamese by U.S. Army signal schools and private contractors. As in the case of the engineers, these measures allowed Vietnamization to proceed independent of the continuing U.S. drawdown.[35]

While the U.S. Departments of Defense and the Army considered the merits of the plan, the 1st Signal Brigade went ahead with its own effort to integrate selected Vietnamese personnel into the existing system. Under the supervision of the U.S. Army Regional Communications Group, Vietnam, and the 361st and 369th Signal Battalions, an Army signal instruction team began training selected Vietnamese in the more complex communications managerial and repair skills at the South Vietnamese Signal School at Vung Tau.[36] Eight weeks of formal instruction were followed by six to nine months of on-the-job training with American

[32] For examples, see ORLLs of U.S. Army signal units for April and July 1970, HRB, CMH.

[33] First quotation from ORLL, 1st Signal Bde, April 1970, p. 8, HRB, CMH. Second and third quotations from Rpt, Maj Richard J. Myer, Jr., Plans Officer, 1st Signal Bde, 23 Jan 70, sub: USARV Communications and Electronics Signal Conference Briefing, p. 4, fldr 24 (Training of ARVN Signal Corps by 1st Signal Bde, Jan–Feb 70), box 4, accession no. 71A6879, RG 319, WNRC. See also ORLL, 2d Signal Group, January 1970, pp. 13–14; ORLL, 369th Signal Bn, January 1970, pp. 1–2. Both in HRB, CMH.

[34] For general coverage, see the background briefings found in fldr 24, box 4, accession no. 71A6879, RG 319, WNRC.

[35] Study, 1st Signal Bde, April 1969, sub: Training Plan for ARVN and RTA To Operate and Maintain the ICS, DTE and Tandem Switch System in VN and Thailand, SEAB, CMH.

[36] See ORLLs, 1st Signal Bde, January 1970, p. 8, and July 1970, p. 6; ORLLs, 361st Signal Bn, July 1969, p. 1, and October 1969, p. 2. See also ORLLs of USASTRATCOM, Signal Support Agency, Saigon; U.S. Army Regional Communications Group, Vietnam; and 369th Signal Bn for the period 1969–70. All in HRB, CMH.

operators at selected ICS sites. The best pupils returned to Vung Tau to become instructors. To support the effort, the Joint General Staff created an extension of the South Vietnamese English Language School at Vung Tau and, in late 1969, sent over five hundred students through a six-month crash English-language course to ease their future training by American instructors. By early 1970 the Vung Tau school had graduated about one hundred technical controllers and had enough Vietnamese instructors to replace the U.S. training teams. The brigade had also begun similar programs in other communications specialities (microwave repair, fixed station carrier, and DTE equipment repair), with the additional objective of Vietnamizing the instructional process as quickly as possible. But the overall program was not nearly large enough. American signal officers had reservations about its progress, pointing out that "if the current rate continues, it will take sixteen years to staff the system (ICS, SEA) with Vietnamese." According to brigade planners, the South Vietnamese lacked "the broad scientific and technical education base to provide sufficient input of students to allow take over of the ICS in [a] short time frame." Neither qualified students nor qualified instructors existed. As a minimum, the brigade estimated that it would take four years after the establishment of a suitable training facility before the South Vietnamese could assume control of the ICS facilities in South Vietnam, and "a period of eight to ten years would be even more realistic."[37]

Despite this pessimism, planning continued, and in November 1969 a combined USARV-MACV-JCS survey outlined specific communications sites and equipment to be turned over to the South Vietnamese. With this guidance, MACV drew up a more detailed signal Vietnamization plan, based on the 1st Signal Brigade's original training concept, and forwarded it to the Joint Chiefs of Staff as part of the Phase III Improvement and Modernization Plan. In January 1970 Secretary of the Army Resor endorsed the concept and requested that detailed planning be initiated immediately. By that time, however, American unit withdrawals made it increasingly difficult for the 1st Signal Brigade to participate in any long-range training programs. Instead, MACV was forced to rely heavily on outside assistance to carry out the ICS transfer. Final plans directed that civilian contractors assume initial operational and maintenance responsibility for communications sites scheduled to be turned over to Saigon. These contractors would also establish and operate an ICS signal school in South Vietnam and, after a three-year training period, turn over both the school and the communications sites to Saigon. The residual network was named the Single Integrated Telecommunications System, or SITS. Vietnamese personnel undergoing on-the-job training with American signal units in South Vietnam or training in the United States would be integrated into SITS by the contractor as they became available, and the U.S. Army would have only a general supervisory responsibility for the effort.

After much planning and negotiation the Department of Defense sent out bids in 1970 and awarded the training contract to the Federal Electric Company, a subsidiary of International Telephone and Telegraph.[38] In this way, the concept of

---

[37] First quotation from ORLL, 361st Signal Bn, October 1969, p. 2. Second and third quotations from ORLL, 1st Signal Bde, October 1969, pp. 18–19. Both in HRB, CMH.
[38] See USMACV, "Command History, 1970," 2:IX–91 to IX–94, HRB, CMH.

close Vietnamese-American cooperation remained, but U.S. Army signal units were not committed to a major training mission that would have tied down large numbers of highly skilled personnel for long periods of time and, in the event of a rapid withdrawal, might have caused considerable confusion.

Rotary-wing Aviation

The Vietnamization of rotary-wing (helicopter) operations in South Vietnam was one of MACV's most carefully controlled efforts.[39] In 1967 the South Vietnamese Air Force (VNAF) had five rotary-wing aircraft squadrons, each equipped with about twenty relatively slow, bulbous CH–34 "Choctaw" helicopters. In contrast, the U.S. Army operated the equivalent of almost fifty helicopter squadrons and several thousand machines in South Vietnam. Tentative MACV modernization plans for the VNAF only envisioned modernizing four of the existing squadrons with modern Bell UH–1 helicopters ("Slicks") sometime between 1969 and 1973, at a rate of about one squadron each year.

In December 1967 General William W. ("Spike") Momyer, the MACV deputy for air and the commander of Seventh Air Force, recommended that eight more helicopter squadrons be added to the VNAF, that the number of machines in each squadron be increased, and that helicopter gunships be added to the South Vietnamese inventory. He also wanted the CH–34s replaced by more modern aircraft in the process. Because training would consume at least eighteen months for each individual pilot, Momyer requested that the expansion be approved as soon as possible. Such a growth would "provide the VNAF with the capability to assume complete support of the ARVN." However, the Army deputy component commander, General Palmer, strongly opposed the measure, feeling that the Army had no machines to spare for the South Vietnamese, and the matter was temporarily dropped.[40]

In 1968 the various expansion plans called for between eight and twelve new VNAF helicopter squadrons, and the Army chief of staff, General Johnson, even recommended that four additional squadrons be given to the army for an air cavalry squadron in each corps zone. Abrams and Palmer disagreed, pointing out the difficulties Saigon would have operating separate aviation elements in the army and introducing the complex AH–1G "Cobra" gunship into their inventory. At the time, Abrams had good reason to regard Johnson's suggestion as unrealistic, for helicopters were still in extremely short supply. By the end of 1968 the U.S. Army had made only nine new helicopters available to the VNAF and an expected delivery rate of three machines per month made even the modernization of the existing squadrons questionable.[41]

[39] For details, see files on Vietnamization—Helicopters, SEAB, CMH.
[40] Quoted words from Ltr, U.S. Air Force Advisory Group (Momyer) to COMUSMACV, 1 Jan 69, with draft study "VNAF Airlift Support of ARVN." See also Ltr, Palmer to Cdr, Seventh Air Force, 3 Jan 68, sub: VNAF Airlift Support of ARVN. Both in SEAB, CMH.
[41] Msgs, Johnson WDC 7637 to Abrams, 242206 May 68; Palmer ARV 1423 to Abrams, 261005 May 68; Abrams MAC 7056 to Johnson, 290847 May 68; Abrams MAC 16521 to McCain, 020330 Dec 68. All in Abrams Papers, HRB, CMH. Like Westmoreland, Abrams retained command of the Army component headquarters (USARV), while his deputy, General Palmer, actually supervised the large staff.

The decision to Vietnamize the war forced the U.S. Army to change its priorities. In February 1969 General Westmoreland, who had replaced Johnson as the Army chief of staff, agreed to divert helicopters scheduled for Army units in Europe, Korea, and the United States to VNAF, and the delivery rate to Saigon increased dramatically.[42] By the end 1969 MACV had reequipped four of the five existing VNAF rotary-wing squadrons with the new UH–1 machines and had increased the number of aircraft per squadron from twenty to thirty-one. In addition, the secretary of defense approved the earlier 1967 U.S. Air Force expansion proposals and incorporated them into the Phase III Improvement and Modernization Plan. By 1971 VNAF was to have eight new UH–1 squadrons and one support squadron equipped with the larger Boeing-Vertol CH–47 ("Hook") supply helicopter, for a total of fourteen squadrons. Bell production lines had supplied machines for the four converted squadrons, but aircraft for the nine new formations would have to come from other sources if the units were to be activated on schedule. The only other source of helicopters was from redeploying American units.

The entire matter of helicopters was complicated by the involvement of two U.S. military services—the U.S. Army, which controlled most rotary-wing aviation units in the American armed forces, and the U.S. Air Force, which advised the Vietnamese air component. The fact that VNAF helicopter units and crews had worked closely with U.S. Army aviation units for many years eased a potentially difficult situation. Most South Vietnamese helicopter pilots had trained at U.S. Army installations in the United States and had received further instruction by U.S. Army aviation battalions in South Vietnam before being assigned to their units. When Saigon had activated two of its first CH–34 squadrons (VNAF 211th and 217th Helicopter Squadrons) in the Delta, MACV assigned U.S. Army advisers to the U.S. Air Force advisory team working with the squadrons and gave the U.S. Army 164th Combat Aviation Group the mission of training the new units in airmobile tactics and techniques. After the completion of the training, the group continued to supervise the operations of the two VNAF units through 1969 and integrated South Vietnamese airmobile operations with those of nearby American air units (13th Combat Aviation Battalion and the 7th Squadron, 1st Cavalry). Similar relationships existed between local American aviation units and the VNAF 215th Helicopter Squadron at Nha Trang (II CTZ) and the VNAF 213th Helicopter Squadron at Da Nang (I CTZ). American helicopter units also normally supplied all command and control and gunship support to their South Vietnamese counterparts.[43]

Preparations for expanding VNAF helicopter strength with nine additional squadrons involved even closer coordination between the South Vietnamese Air Force; the U.S. Army component command, which was responsible for delivering the machines; the U.S. Seventh Air Force, supervising the Air Force advisers; the U.S. 1st Aviation Brigade, the parent headquarters of all U.S. Army non-

---

[42] Msg, Westmoreland WDC 1896 to Abrams, 032242 Feb 69, Abrams Papers, HRB, CMH.

[43] For details, see appropriate ORLLs of 1st Aviation Bde, especially April 1970, pp. 5–7, and July 1970, pp. 8–9, as well as those of subordinate units—for example, 145th Combat Aviation Bn, January 1967, p. 7; 214th Combat Aviation Bn, July 1968, pp. 8–9; and 13th Combat Aviation Bn, October 1970, p. 1. All in HRB, CMH.

442

divisional aviation units in South Vietnam; and U.S. Army training installations in the United States. In April 1969 the Department of the Army approved a MACV proposal to train 1,475 VNAF pilots and 1,875 VNAF mechanics during 1969 and 1970, to include an elaborate English-language instructional program for all trainees. All technical training would take place at Forts Wolters, Rucker, and Eustis, and the program was to be completed by the end of 1970.

This timetable proved ambitious, and the final MACV rotary-wing Vietnamization plan scheduled the activation of all the new VNAF squadrons between September 1970 and March 1971.[44] The procedures used were complex but effective. South Vietnamese pilot candidates and maintenance trainees, after graduating from English-language courses at Vung Tau and attending aviation training schools in the United States, served with U.S. Army aviation units in South Vietnam for on-the-job training. Saigon's nine new squadrons received aircraft from redeploying U.S. Army helicopter companies, which conducted ninety days of flight training for the pilots and about thirty days of maintenance training for the new VNAF mechanics prior to the turnover date. For another ninety days after each unit activation, the 1st Aviation Brigade provided an Army training team and a small maintenance cadre to each squadron. Whenever possible, these teams were composed of personnel from the departing American units who were familiar with the Vietnamese airmen, but the new U.S. Air Force advisory team chief supervised this final stage.

During 1970 and 1971 MACV completed its planned helicopter turnover and activation program on schedule. Given the unusual number of organizations and headquarters involved, the Vietnamization of rotary-wing support was a model effort due primarily to the American ability to define objectives early and plan accordingly. In all, twelve U.S. Army helicopter companies trained almost 250 VNAF pilots and several hundred support personnel. The unique training process undoubtedly curtailed helicopter support to U.S. Army combat units. In order to activate the VNAF CH–47 squadron, an entire U.S. CH–47 company completely halted all operations in August 1970, and for one month its personnel did nothing but train the new Vietnamese unit. However, if U.S. military leaders believed that it was imperative to increase Saigon's tactical air mobility, making it possible for the South Vietnamese to duplicate American military tactics, then these measures were necessary investments.

An Assessment

MACV pursued Vietnamization of support operations in several different ways. In most cases, General Abrams depended on his subordinate commands to accomplish the actual planning and implementation. As in the pair-off and *Dong Tien* programs, regular U.S. Army units, headquarters, and installa-

---

[44] MACV, RVNAF/AFGP/USARV I & M Helicopter Augmentation Plan 70–51, May 1970, SEAB. For details of the plan and its execution, see ORLLs of 1st Aviation Bde, April 1970, pp. 5–7, and July 1970, pp. 8–9, as well as those of subordinate units—for example, 13th Combat Aviation Bn, October 1970, p. 1, HRB. All in CMH.

tions became heavily involved in what was essentially an advisory effort. In those areas that had been thoroughly planned, as in the case of rotary-wing aviation, the degree of participation was large and Vietnamization encountered few problems once American military leaders made the decision to go ahead. Of course, the expansion of the South Vietnamese Air Force was also dependent on both the U.S. military drawdown and the heavy commitment of U.S. Army training installations in the United States. But MACV instituted no analogous program in the equally complex area of communications-electronics, and private contractors were needed to bridge the gap between withdrawal and Vietnamization. In a somewhat similar approach, the U.S. Army engineers concentrated on completing a fixed number of projects so that the Vietnamese would be left with only the task of maintaining them.

Because American logistical commands had begun the Vietnamization of the port supply system early, the process that expanded existing South Vietnamese capabilities through on-the-job training and equipment turnovers proved to be a relatively easy administrative task. But in many other areas—transportation, quartermaster, ordnance, tactical communications, and depot maintenance, for example—Vietnamization lacked central direction, and the training process was never seriously analyzed or evaluated.[45] On paper, some of the OJT results were impressive. During 1970, for example, the U.S. 1st Cavalry Division noted that it had given 281 South Vietnamese soldiers 24 hours of weapons training each, yielding an impressive 6,744 man-hours of instruction; and, using similar arithmetic logic, MACV claimed that American units had trained a grand total of 47,000 Vietnamese servicemen during the year.[46] But such statistics were deceptive and reflected only a broad, uncoordinated effort by American commands to assist South Vietnamese units when suitable opportunities arose. The lack of any overall planning, supervision, or analysis made these kinds of measurements useless, and such practices may only have hidden deeper Vietnamese problems in supply and support. Theoretically, by May 1970 Saigon had the capability of satisfying 100 percent of its land, 80 percent of its water (coastal), and 30 percent of its air transportation, and 74 percent of its harbor operations needs.[47] Yet the performance of the South Vietnamese in such areas as supply management and control had always been marginal, and they had little practice in orchestrating all their new logistical and communications resources to support intensified combat operations. MACV had established a supporting framework for Saigon's ground combat forces, but the new support system would have to be continuously improved if it was to handle this aspect of the war effort alone.

[45] See H. Wallace Sinaiko et al., *Operating and Maintaining Complex Military Equipment: A Study of Training Problems in the Republic of Vietnam,* IDA Research Paper P-501 (Arlington, Va.: Institute for Defense Analyses, 1969), especially on on-the-job training (pp. 38–39), training aids, English-language instruction, and the relationship between training and the introduction of new equipment in underdeveloped nations.
[46] USMACV, "Command History, 1970," 2:VII–42; ORLL, 1st Cavalry Div, July 1970, tab G–2. Both in HRB, CMH.
[47] Msg, CINCPAC to JCS, 10 May 70. For a general overview, see General Accounting Office, Report to the Congress by the Comptroller General of the United States, "Logistics Aspects of Vietnamization, 1969–72," no. B–159451, circa 1973. Both in SEAB, CMH.

The ever-present specter of renewed large-scale fighting continued to cast a shadow over the entire Vietnamization effort. MACV had molded the South Vietnamese logistical system into an area support configuration most suitable for a low-intensity counterinsurgency campaign. The attention it had paid to South Vietnam's fixed area communications, tactical aviation, low-level intelligence, improved local road nets, and decentralized supply system all pointed in this direction. The state of the South Vietnamese Air Force was the best example of this policy. The United States had committed much time and money expanding Saigon's air strength and capabilities. The new helicopter squadrons greatly increased the potential of the South Vietnamese Army in an antiguerrilla campaign, but might be highly vulnerable against a more conventional enemy employing sophisticated air defense weapons. The expensive helicopter fleet gave the ground army a great deal of tactical mobility, but at the expense of strategic mobility that a larger number of fixed-wing transports would have supplied. Other types of Vietnamese air units were purposely provided with low-performance short-range A–37 and F–5 fighter-bombers, with no sophisticated fire control systems or electronic warfare equipment. According to General Momyer, American military leaders feared that possession of more advanced aircraft might tempt Saigon to broaden the conflict and provoke even stronger North Vietnamese retaliation. Momyer believed that limiting South Vietnamese capabilities in the air—and perhaps elsewhere as well—"enhanced . . . the potential for keeping the fighting at a relatively low level" and "increased . . . the outlook for a political settlement.[48] Whether Hanoi would appreciate such thoughtfulness on the part of its enemy was questionable.

[48] Quoted words from William W. Momyer, *The Vietnamese Air Force, 1951–1975: An Analysis of Its Role in Combat*, USAF Southeast Asia Monograph, vol. 3, no. 4 (Washington, D.C.: Government Printing Office, 1977), pp. 54–55. See also Ray L. Bowers, *Tactical Airlift*, The United States Air Force in Southeast Asia (Washington, D.C.: Office of Air Force History, 1983), p. 639.

U.S. Advisers: The First To Come and the Last To Leave

PART SIX

Successes and Failures
(1971–1973)

24

The Last Buildup

The withdrawal of U.S. military forces from South Vietnam continued throughout 1971 and 1972 almost without a break in stride (*see Appendix C*). American
military strength passed through the so-called residual support phase sometime
in 1971, and in April of the following year MACV began contingency planning for
a total U.S. withdrawal as early as 1 November 1972.[1] As American troops redeployed, Vietnamization, the expansion of South Vietnamese military responsibilities, marched speedily forward. The period was marked by heavy combat.
South Vietnamese cross-border operations into Cambodia and Laos during 1971
met with stiff opposition, and in early 1972 were countered by the massive North
Vietnamese "Easter" offensive into South Vietnam. Fighting was intense, casualties and equipment losses were high, and the nature of the combat was increasingly conventional. Guerrilla activity behind South Vietnamese lines was
negligible, while the employment of tanks, long-range artillery, and sophisticated missiles became commonplace. Major political landmarks included the
South Vietnamese presidential elections in 1971 and the U.S. presidential elections in 1972. The latter year saw not only the reelection of President Nixon but
also an intensive U.S. air and naval campaign against North Vietnam, followed
by a final accord between the United States, South Vietnam, and North Vietnam
that provided for a military truce, the return of American prisoners of war, and
the termination of all U.S. military activities in Vietnam by the end of March
1973.

The Advisory Drawdown

Throughout 1971 and 1972 American advisers in the field and at MACV headquarters continued to serve primarily in a liaison capacity, monitoring the
status of South Vietnamese units and staffs and coordinating direct U.S. materiel
assistance and combat support. While U.S. advisers at all levels continued to
provide advice, only those at the very highest echelons, at the corps and theater

[1] Msg, Abrams MAC 03113 to Major Component Cdrs, 070446 Apr 72, sub: Vietnamization Joint
Planning, Abrams Papers, HRB, CMH.

449

(MACV) levels, had the prestige, power, and experience needed to push specific programs and policies. But even here they continued to use leverage sparingly and with great restraint if at all. In the field the quality of the average adviser actually improved during this period as MACV transferred soldiers with at least some field experience from departing U.S. combat units directly to advisory teams for the remainder of their tours. What the advisory effort gained in expertise, however, was often offset by the shorter length of time the newly assigned advisers spent with the Vietnamese units before rotating back to the United States.

As U.S. combat units left South Vietnam and the South Vietnamese assumed total responsibility for the war, many advisers found their work load increasing. In September 1971 General Abrams directed that the current advisory effort focus primarily on management support programs and revolutionary development. The South Vietnamese regulars, he felt, were performing fairly well in the field and needed little operational advice. Assistance was most needed in the areas of command and control, personnel, logistics, training, communications-electronics, and intelligence, and, on the civilian side, in local self-defense, self-government, and economic self-development. He also pointed out that the advisory effort was not being slighted. By the end of the year 66 percent of the U.S. military forces would have left South Vietnam, while the total advisory effort would have declined by only 22 percent, primarily by reducing the size and number of the tactical detachments.[2]

Nevertheless, compared to the gradual establishment of the advisory system, the reductions were swift and relentless. At the end of 1971 Abrams dissolved the MACV Office of the Assistant Chief of Staff for Military Assistance, one of the two focal points for all military support to South Vietnam and turned most of its functions over to his personnel (J–1), operations (J–3), and logistics (J–4) staff sections. The MACV Training Directorate inherited the task of managing the Military Assistance Program and several other functions, such as budgeting assistance, that other special staff sections had performed. Abrams had also intended to move the logistics advisers over to the Training Directorate; but, in order to better supervise the increased flow of materiel into South Vietnam, they remained under the MACV J–4.

Early in 1972, when the remaining U.S. combat forces in Vietnam amounted to about one brigade, a larger reorganization transformed the MACV headquarters from a joint operational command into a country advisory group.[3] Although still called the U.S. Military Assistance Command, Vietnam, or MACV, the new organization had three service advisory groups (Army, Navy, Air Force), supported by three service component commands and four smaller organizations for air intelligence, counterintelligence, and naval gunfire support. The U.S. Army Advisory Group consisted primarily of the former MACV Training Directorate,

---

[2] General information on the advisory reorganization may be found in USMACV, "Command History, 1971," 2 vols. (Saigon, 1970), 1:VIII–72 to VIII–83, and "1972–1973," 1:annex C, HRB, CMH.
[3] Msg, Abrams MAC 02304 to Major Subordinates, 140537 Mar 72, sub: Reorganization of Military Assistance Command, Vietnam, Abrams Papers, HRB, CMH.

Transferring an American Base to Saigon. *Left to right: General Nguyen Van Minh, the III Corps commander, and Lt. Gen. Frank T. Mildren, the USARV deputy commander, complete the formal transfer.*

plus the hitherto independent airborne and Strategic Technical Directorate advisory teams and the technical and special branch (for example, engineers, rangers, armor) advisers. Abrams retained direct control of the remaining field advisory teams through the four U.S. corps-level commands.

In the field Abrams had pared down the U.S. corps-level headquarters and combined them with the local corps advisory groups to form regional assistance commands. The U.S. Army XXIV Corps and I Corps Advisory Group became the First Regional Assistance Command;[4] I Field Force and II Corps Advisory Group, the Second Regional Assistance Group; II Field Force and III Corps Advisory Group, the Third Regional Assistance Command; and the Delta Military Assistance Command and IV Corps Advisory Group, the Delta Regional Assistance Command. The commander of each regional assistance command represented MACV and acted as the senior adviser to the South Vietnamese corps commander. The only exception was in the II Corps area, where Abrams named John Paul Vann to head of the Second Regional Assistance Group in April

---

[4] Upon the departure of the III Marine Amphibious Force in 1971, the XXIV Corps became the controlling U.S. military headquarters in the I Corps zone.

1971. As a civilian, Vann had a general officer serving as his deputy and exercising legal "command" over the remaining U.S. military units there.[5]

The combat assistance teams in the field began disappearing even earlier. With the exception of the airborne advisers and some teams in the northern corps, MACV closed out all of the battalion teams by 30 June 1971 and began phasing out the regimental teams in September. By the end of the year the U.S. Army tactical advisory strength had fallen from 5,416 (4,811 authorized) to 3,888 (5,003 authorized) and the MACV staff advisory strength from 1,894 (1,622 authorized) to 1,395 (1,261 authorized), and many were military cadre from departing American units trying to complete their twelve-month overseas tours.

The province, district, school, training center, and other advisory elements felt the same ax. The mobile advisory team school at Di An closed its doors in September 1971, and by the end of the year the number of MATs working with the Territorial Forces had shrunk from 487 to 66. The strength of the CORDS personnel at MACV, corps, provinces, and districts fell by over half during 1971 (6,147 to 2,682) and continued to decline throughout 1972. In the schools and training centers many of the advisory teams faded away as incumbent advisers finished their tours without replacements; the teams at the military police, quartermaster, adjutant general, and administrative and finance schools closed shop in 1971 and the others soon followed. However, the U.S. Air Force and U.S. Naval Advisory Groups, mostly technical personnel, lost few advisers in 1971 and remained strong until the final departure. The only other additions were about fifteen special training teams thrown together in 1972 to help rebuild some damaged units and to provide instruction for some of the more sophisticated war materiel that had only recently arrived.[6]

During 1972 General Abrams, and his successor in June, General Frederick C. Weyand, threw the weight of the advisory effort into a succession of materiel supply projects that enabled the South Vietnamese to complete existing modernization programs; to make up heavy combat losses; to create new units; and to fill their depots with munitions, fuel, spare parts, and other supplies. These projects can be summarized briefly. Project 981, begun in the spring of 1971, was an effort to identify and correct all major equipment shortages in the armed forces. Project 982, started that August, was a complementary program to raise the stockage of parts in army depots to a one- to three-year supply rate level. Following the North Vietnamese Easter offensive in March 1972, MACV also supervised a massive resupply operation to replace all South Vietnamese equipment lost in combat.[7] Washington supplemented this effort in May with Project

[5] The command relationships are spelled out in Ltr, Abrams to Vann, 15 May 71, Vann Papers, MHI. Vann had "coordinating authority and supervision over the function of the deputies" (that is, the senior U.S. military commander in the II Corps zone); could inspect and monitor their activities, require coordination, but not compel action; and was to appeal differences in the military sphere to Abrams himself.

[6] During 1972 authorized advisory strength for both organizations rose slightly, but the assigned strength of the U.S. Naval Advisory Group fell from 3,288 to 2,912 and the U.S. Air Force Advisory Group from 1,011 to 904. On the Cambodian training effort, see Stanton, *Green Berets at War*, pp. 285–91.

[7] Including 67,801 individual and 3,166 crew-served weapons, 382 artillery pieces, 622 tracked and 2,035 wheeled vehicles, and 11,599 major communications items. See USMACV, "Command History, 1972–1973," 2:E–3 to E–4, HRB, CMH.

ENHANCE, which supplied the equipment for new armor, artillery, and air units. Also in May MACV established Project VER, another effort to sort out problems in the South Vietnamese logistical system that had resulted in a critical shortage of spare parts. Finally, in October Washington initiated Project ENHANCE PLUS to expedite delivery of all items due from previous projects, "plus" other materiel that the United States might not be able to send once a ceasefire had taken effect. The result was a massive sea- and airlift between 23 October and 12 December 1972 that brought over 105,000 major items of equipment to South Vietnam, about 5,000 tons by air and the rest by sea.

Inside South Vietnam MACV logistics advisers concentrated on centralizing supply and support activities and on organizing them along functional lines. In 1971 and 1972 they helped established a National Materiel Management Agency under the Central Logistics Command, which began a centralized accounting system for all supplies and equipment in the armed forces. During the same period logistics advisers supervised completion of the depot upgrade program started in 1969, helped combine the four army base depots in Saigon into one organization (the South Vietnamese 1st Associated Depot at Long Binh), and assisted the transfer of depot overhaul scheduling to the new Materiel Management Agency. The Joint General Staff partially remedied civilian labor shortages by allowing the depots to hire 15-, 16-, and 17-year-olds, pushing them through intensive training courses and, at the age of eighteen, enrolling them in a special military reserve corps that exempted them from the draft.[8] The Logistics Command also took over general management of land, sea, and air transportation units, while a new communications agency under the Joint General Staff J–6 (Signal) oversaw both radio and telephone communication networks. MACV estimated that by 1973 these systems could adequately support the combat arms, although several agencies operating more complex equipment would need the assistance of U.S. civilian employees and outside contractors for several years.

In the field of supply the most critical and the most costly item in the South Vietnamese inventory was ammunition. In 1972, under MACV guidance, the Central Logistics Command established a more detailed system to monitor the status of all munitions: base, field, and unit depot stockage; unit expenditures; and ammunition maintenance. Unused ammunition was subject to rapid deterioration and had to be examined periodically and, if necessary, reconditioned or destroyed. Stockage levels in each ammunition category were critical. Munitions stocks increased from 79,000 short tons in January 1969 to 146,900 in January 1972 and 165,700 in January 1973. However, a normal monthly expenditure rate of 30,000 short tons, which could rise to over 100,000 short tons per month in periods of intense combat, made continued resupply from the United States vital. Another potential problem was the vulnerability of ammunition dumps; the enemy had destroyed over 24,000 short tons of depot ammunition during the

[8] USMACV, "Command History, 1972–1973," 2:E–7 to E–8, HRB, CMH; Khuyen, *RVNAF Logistics*, pp. 110–11. Prior to 1970 government workers had to be eighteen years of age or older.

Project ENHANCE PLUS Equipment. *Much of the project equipment, such as the F–5 fighters (top) and the M48 tanks (below), had to be stored until the South Vietnamese could be trained to use it at some later date.*

Easter offensive alone. The South Vietnamese would have to maintain, protect, and ration their existing stocks as carefully as possible.[9]

A Final Military Expansion

The South Vietnamese armed forces changed little during 1971–72. Consisting of about one million men, divided equally between the Territorial Forces (Regional Forces and Popular Forces) and the ground, air, and sea components of the regular army, this force was deployed throughout the country in a bewildering number of hierarchical, fixed area commands. Neither MACV nor the Joint General Staff had seriously supported efforts to reduce or end the area responsibilities of the corps and division headquarters, and these elements thus continued to be administrative rather than tactical commands.[10] The successive improvement and modernization plans updated the equipment of this force, moderately increased the combat support available for it (more artillery, armored personnel carriers, and helicopters), and gave it the capability to sustain itself (logistics, maintenance, communications) within South Vietnam. But they did not change its mission, operational strategy, or deployment. Simply stated, the mission of the armed forces was to preserve the government of South Vietnam through defensive firepower and territorial security—a combination of the old strategies of attrition and pacification. Because MACV envisioned no geographical expansion of the ground war, Saigon's forces remained organizationally and psychologically defensive. Although Vietnamization implied continued American air and logistical support, American leaders in Washington had not clearly defined the extent and duration of that support, nor had they addressed the future of the war in Southeast Asia outside the borders of South Vietnam.

Both MACV and the Joint General Staff continued to make minor adjustments in the South Vietnamese military force structure. In early 1971 Abrams agreed to reduce the number of battalions in each South Vietnamese infantry regiment from four to three and to raise the number of rifle companies per battalion from three to four, thus eliminating thirty-four battalion headquarters and enlarging the remaining battalions. He also approved more military police forces and a nineteenth armored cavalry squadron; more Regional Forces battalion headquarters for better territorial command and control; thirteen coastal radar stations to make up for the projected absence of U.S. sea patrol aircraft; and signal, engineer, and amphibious support battalions for the Vietnamese Marine Division, enabling it to operate as an entire unit. In order to remain within the 1.1 million strength ceiling fixed in 1969, MACV made compensating cuts in Saigon's Popu-

[9] For a general background in ammunition logistics, see Khuyen, *RVNAF Logistics*, pp. 163–75 and 218; USMACV, "Command History, 1972–1973," 2:E–16 to E–18, HRB, CMH; Fact Book, MACV, December 1968 (updated), MICRO 1/1968, RG 334, WNRC; Joseph M. Heiser, Jr., *Logistic Support*, Vietman Studies (Washington, D.C.: Department of the Army, 1974), pp. 106–33.
[10] Vien and Khuyen, *Reflections on the Vietnam War*, pp. 93–94, 107, 153.

lar Forces strength. The reductions were minor and did not signify any changes in strategy or deployment.[11]

In April 1971, after seeing his forces handled roughly in Laos, General Vien again submitted his own proposals to MACV for new equipment and new units. First he wanted his light M41 tanks replaced by M48 battle tanks and his recoilless rifles replaced by antitank missiles. He also requested three new M48 tank battalions, four self-propelled 155-mm. howitzer battalions, and four armored infantry battalions. To deal with enemy long-range artillery, he felt that four new target acquisition (ground radar) battalions were needed, as well as five new artillery group headquarters to centralize his own guns. Vien was again thinking ahead to future conventional battles. But General Abrams described almost all of his requests as nonessential and promised only to consider activating one M48 battalion, three 155-mm. self-propelled artillery battalions, and one artillery group in the northern zone, where encounters with well-equipped enemy units were most likely.[12]

While Vien was submitting his proposals in Saigon, Nixon and Kissinger asked Laird to have the U.S. military leaders again reevaluate future South Vietnamese needs.[13] For this purpose, Abrams could assume continued American air support and a U.S troop redeployment rate averaging 12,500 per month, allowing MACV to evolve gradually into an advisory group. In his reply Abrams pointed out that recent South Vietnamese experiences in Laos showed that Saigon "cannot sustain large scale major cross border operations . . . without external support," and he affirmed that "the present goal of developing a RVNAF that can counter an enemy within South Vietnam, with the inherent capability to conduct limited cross border operations, should not be changed." Further clarifying his viewpoint, he maintained that "it is neither desirable nor possible to give RVNAF the capability to conduct independent major cross border operations." He believed that on the ground "no major changes in organization [were] required," that in the air the "VNAF at the present rate of development will be capable of supporting RVNAF in containing the in-country threat," and that the development of an air cavalry force was "too sophisticated and complex for RVNAF to attempt now." He judged the Vietnamese army's level of maintenance as "excellent," noting the soldiers now "appreciate the fact that they must make their equipment last and there have been significant improvements in this area over the last few years." With a MAAG strength of 40,000–50,000 ("based on the assumption that the U.S intelligence community will remain in Vietnam in the planned strength as long as required") and continued American air support at its current level (averaging 8,000–10,000 tactical air and 1,000 B-52 sorties per month, figures suggested by Kissinger), he felt that it was "reasonable . . . to assume that the RVNAF will be able to provide an adequate degree of security."[14]

[11] For organizational changes, see USMACV, "Command History, 1971," 1:VIII–2 to VIII–27, and "1972–1973," 1:C–12, HRB, CMH.

[12] Ibid., "1971," 1:VIII–9 to VIII–11, HRB, CMH.

[13] Memo, Kissinger to SecDef, 1 Apr 71, sub: Improvement and Modernization of South Vietnamese Armed Forces (RVNAF), SEAB, CMH. The memo is based on the meeting of 26 March 1971 between President Nixon, Admiral Moorer, and Deputy Secretary of Defense David Packard.

[14] Msg, COMUSMACV to JCS, 031015 Apr 71, sub: Vietnamization, SEAB, CMH.

Armor Engine Maintenance Class for the New M48 Tank

But South Vietnamese leaders obviously disagreed with MACV on these issues. In July 1971 Vien began pressing Abrams for the tanks, missiles, and artillery he had requested. Abrams still hesitated and, after studying the proposal for several more months, agreed only to approve the activation of a single M48 tank battalion. At this late stage he wished to avoid introducing new weapons into the South Vietnamese inventory or creating new units that required highly trained, experienced personnel. In September, however, Vien persuaded him to go along with another Vietnamese proposal, activating a new infantry division in the northern tactical zone. The forces for the new division were to come from existing units: the fourth "DMZ" regiment of the 1st Division; the fourth battalion of the other infantry regiments in the I Corps area; some of the better regional forces units; and the extra artillery battalions assigned to the I Corps headquarters. By the end of the year the South Vietnamese, assisted by special MACV training teams, had actually formed these two new units, the 3d Infantry Division and the 20th Tank Battalion, and stationed them opposite the North Vietnamese border to help fill in the gap left by departing American units.

MACV again considered reorganizing the entire ranger structure. In September 1971 Lt. Gen. Welborn G. Dolvin, commanding the XXIV Corps in the I Corps area, recommended assigning the corps ranger groups as well as the newly constituted "border defense ranger battalions" (ex-CIDG units) to the South Vietnamese divisions. Vann, in the Highlands, disagreed and pointed out that in his zone the former CIDG units were still 90-percent Montagnard; they were not mobile and could not be controlled properly by the regular divisions. If necessary, Vann thought it preferable to assign the eight border defense battalions in the I Corps zone and the twelve in the II Corps zone to the province chiefs. Maj. Gen. John H. Cushman, heading the Delta Military Assistance Command in the IV Corps area, went along with Vann, noting that all the ranger units in the south were under the 44th Special Tactical Zone while the divisions worked the interior and coastal areas. Abrams also agreed, but was still wary of giving the Ranger Command in Saigon operational control of the field battalions. On 29 September he finally approved a Joint General Staff proposal standardizing the regular ranger battalion force at twenty-one battalions and seven groups, leaving one three-battalion group with each corps commander and allowing Vien to place the remaining three groups under his direct control. The reorganization would add nine battalions to Saigon's weak general reserve force. To support the realignment, Abrams authorized activation of a seventh ranger group headquarters and Vien upgraded one of the eight border defense ranger battalions in the Delta into a mobile unit. The Vietnamese, however, were still unsatisfied. In early 1972 they began organizing another division in the northern I Corps zone, composed of local ranger and armored elements under General Toan, but the Easter offensive began before the unit could be fully activated.[15]

In October 1971 Admiral McCain also became more concerned with future South Vietnamese capabilities and asked MACV to consider providing Saigon with an interdiction capability, developing an air cavalry force, and creating self-propelled artillery units.[16] Based on this request, Abrams decided to activate three seagoing cutters, an air attack squadron (armed C–47 cargo planes), and eight additional naval patrol aircraft to bolster mid-range interdiction forces. He again vetoed the adoption of self-propelled artillery and canceled the five squadrons of short-take-off-and-landing air transports approved by Washington.

Following the Easter offensive of 1972, MACV and the Joint Chiefs of Staff suddenly decided that further additions had to be made. These included two more M48 tank battalions; two additional air defense and three more 175-mm. self-propelled artillery battalions; crews for one hundred sophisticated antitank (TOW) missiles launchers; and, for the South Vietnamese Air Force, thirteen aviation squadrons. The new air units represented a major expansion and included aircraft for two more squadrons of heavy CH–47 helicopters, three of A–37 jet fighter-bombers, two of large C–130 transports, and five of F–5 jet fighters. Perhaps anticipating some kind of agreement in Paris, the Department of Defense agreed to ship this materiel to South Vietnam as soon as possible under the

[15] Msg, Cowles (CofS, MACV) MAC 08535 to SRAG, TRAC, DRAC, 041110 Sep 71, sub: Ranger Command Situation; Msg, Vann NHT 1767 to Cowles, TRAC, DRAC, 081100 Sep 71, sub: Ranger Command Structure; Msg, Cushman CTO 984 to Cowles, 072155 Sep 71; Msg, Carley (MACV J–3) MAC 11132 to Cushman, 250740 Nov 71, sub: Ranger Conversion Action. All in John H. Cushman Papers, MHI. See also Msg, Abrams MAC 09307 to Dolvin, 270532 Sep 71, sub: Ranger Command Structure, Abrams Papers, HRB, and McGushin (Staff and Senior Adviser, Ranger Command, JGS, January–November 1972) Interv, 27 Feb 76, SEAB. Both in CMH. Toan had stepped down as commander of the nearby 2d Division to take over the Saigon Armored Command in January 1972, but subsequently returned to the field.

[16] This and the following paragraph are based on USMACV, "Command History, 1972–1973," 1:C–12, HRB, CMH.

code name Project ENHANCE and to raise and train units and crews at some later date.[17] At the same time, in order to strengthen the territorials, MACV authorized more Regional Forces battalions and enlarged province tactical staffs to provide better command and control. To create these new units without violating the 1.1 million strength ceiling, MACV and the Joint General Staff again made compensatory reductions in Popular Forces strength.

As in 1971, American officials contemplated no changes in South Vietnamese strategy or deployments for 1972. The discussions that preceded this decision again emphasized the purely defensive orientation of Saigon's armed forces. Their job, according to the Joint Chiefs of Staff, was "to eject the enemy's main forces from GVN territory . . . , prevent their reentry, and provide territorial forces adequate to deal with the local insurgents. . . ." The new units would only fill gaps that had appeared in the South Vietnamese defenses during the Easter offensive: better tanks and antitank weapons to counter enemy armor; long-range artillery to combat Russian-made 122- and 130-mm. pieces; and more Northrop F–5 supersonic fighters to bolster South Vietnam's weak air defenses. Neither the F–5 nor the subsonic Cessna A–37, the mainstays of Saigon's fighter-bomber force, had the range or electronic equipment to venture far from its home bases. During these discussions Abrams even suggested adding high performance attack fighters (F–4, A–4, or A–7) and laser-guided bombs for South Vietnam, but the Joint Chiefs of Staff felt that the request was too exorbitant and too late. Pilots and air crew could not be trained for several years, and the cost of maintaining such equipment was too high. Time and money had just about run out. Air interdiction would have to be performed by U.S. air elements in the foreseeable future.[18]

As the extent of the American disengagement become more apparent, U.S. officials in Washington also began having second thoughts about their allies. In July 1972 Nixon and Kissinger asked Laird to reconsider two matters, the size of the South Vietnamese general reserves and the composition of the air force. Kissinger pointed out the need for ground forces that "can fight outside their traditional (i.e., recruitment) areas," forces that would be "nationally recruited and mobile reserve units similar to the Marines and airborne." Manpower could be made available by deactivating units that were no longer needed. He also suggested that the South Vietnamese be given additional and more sophisticated aircraft to make up for the future absence of American airpower.[19]

Laird understood some of the rationale behind Kissinger's proposals.[20] Traditionally, he admitted, only South Vietnamese airborne and the marine units could be employed throughout the country. Other regular army units had strong

[17] For details, see NSDM 168 file, SEAB, CMH. The U.S. 175-mm. artillery pieces were mounted on self-propelled but unarmored tracked chassis and were not normally used in direct support of tactical combat operations.

[18] For quotation and discussion, see Memo, JCSCM-1900-72, 2 Jun 72, sub: Military Assistance to the RVN, p. 5, SEAB, CMH.

[19] Quoted words from Memo, Kissinger to SecDef, 12 Jul 72, sub: Military Assistance to the RVN, SEAB, CMH. See also Kissinger, *White House Years*, p. 989.

[20] This and the following paragraph, to include quotations, are based on Memo, Laird to Asst to the President for NSA, 4 Aug 72, sub: Reserve Forces for the RVNAF. See also feeder reports in files on RVNAF assessment, 1972–73. All in SEAB, CMH.

territorial bonds due to Saigon's local recruiting and stationing policies. Any interzone movement of army troops had serious sociological and psychological drawbacks. Troops, and even officers, had deserted in large numbers when moved to another zone; officers were reluctant to work under new commanders, and troops despaired for families and property left behind. The importance that the average South Vietnamese soldier attached to the physical proximity of family and friends was also well known, as were the inadequacies of the army's postal and banking facilities. In the past, Laird observed, these factors had made it almost impossible to move army units about at will and their piecemeal deployment made them vulnerable to being defeated in detail. Without American air power to compensate for local inferiority, the South Vietnamese defenses could be isolated and destroyed zone by zone.

But the secretary of defense held that these limitations were no longer valid. The cross-border operations had shown that South Vietnamese ground units could operate effectively outside of their traditional boundaries for extended periods of time. The recent movement of the 21st Infantry Division and a regiment of the 9th Infantry Division from the IV to the III Corps Tactical Zone during the Easter offensive and the employment of ranger groups throughout South Vietnam were examples of this new mobility. Continued improvements in the Territorial Forces, especially the creation of more Regional Forces battalions and larger province headquarters, would further ease the interzone employment of the regulars. Like Abrams, he also argued that any major reorganization of the armed forces as suggested by Kissinger would threaten Saigon's stability during a critical period. The creation of new reserve units would stretch South Vietnamese manpower and financial resources even further and, because of the "counter-coup" role played by the general reserves in the past, would have major political ramifications. Instead, Laird emphasized the "evolutionary" development of the existing force structure in order to increase the psychological and sociological mobility of the regular army. Radical surgery was too costly and too dangerous.

Three weeks later Laird suddenly revised these judgments, apparently deciding that the South Vietnamese divisions were not as mobile as he had thought. Citing the unique national recruiting and centralized administrative policies of the airborne, marine, and reserve ranger forces, he blithely instructed Admiral Moorer, chairman of the Joint Chiefs of Staff, to "urge the JGS to review this matter and to initiate corrective action." As a rationale for his second thoughts, he cited information provided by Moorer that "usefully described the obstacles which existing RVNAF pay and recruitment procedures create for nationwide deployment of most ARVN units." But, at best, his suggestion was a bit late, as was Kissinger's original inquiry. Perhaps Laird, like so many other American officials, had been focusing too long on what was coming out of Vietnam and not what was left in, and was now trying to cover his tracks.[21]

The defense secretary's original reply of 4 August reflected the conventional wisdom of most U.S. civilian and military leaders. On paper the size and

---

[21] Memo, Laird to Chairman, JCS, 26 Aug 72, sub: Reserve Forces for the RVNAF. In Memo, Laird to Asst to the President for NSA, 26 Aug 72, sub: Reserve Forces for the RVNAF, Laird indicated that he included supposedly new information, but the text only reiterated what he had presented in the 4 August memo. Both in SEAB, CMH.

strength of the South Vietnamese armed forces in mid-1972 was formidable, totaling 574,020 regulars (464,838 army, 49,454 air force, 42,842 navy, and 16,886 marines) and 528,596 territorials (300,646 Regional Forces and 227,950 Popular Forces), or about 1.1 million troops and another 2 or 3 million in the local People's Self-Defense Force (PSDF) militia. The four corps headquarters (now called regional commands), still with political as well as military responsibilities, controlled regular army units and local security forces (Territorial Forces, police, PSDF) within their respective zones. In the regular army each of the now eleven infantry divisions had nine infantry and four artillery battalions and an armored cavalry squadron.[22] Between them, the four corps commanders also had four ranger groups (of three battalions each); three new M48 tank battalions (two still in training); four armored brigade headquarters (each with two nondivisional armored cavalry squadrons); four air defense battalions (one in training and two being formed); fourteen (five 105-mm., four 155-mm., and five 175-mm.) nondivisional artillery battalions; thirty-three border defense ranger battalions (former CIDG forces); and, in territorial support, over two hundred 105-mm. two-gun artillery platoons. The one airborne and one marine division and the three ranger groups of the general reserve, as well as the special 81st Airborne Ranger force completed the regular ground combat forces.[23]

The strength of the South Vietnamese Air Force was equally impressive, although many units had not yet been activated. At the time of the U.S. withdrawal thirty-nine squadrons were fully operational, twelve more in training, and fifteen more scheduled for activation as pilots and maintenance crews became available. The final total would give the air component nineteen fighter squadrons (three of A–1 propeller-driver fighter bombers, ten of A–37 jet fighter-bombers, and six of F–5 jet fighters), three ground support squadrons (C–47 and C–119 transports armed as "gunships"), twenty-five helicopter squadrons (twenty-one of UH–1 transports and four of CH–47 heavy cargo aircraft), three reconnaissance squadrons (modified C–47 and C–119 transports), two training and eight liaison squadrons, one Special Air Mission Squadron, and five transport squadrons (C–130 and C–7 "Caribou"). The two squadrons of the larger C–130A cargo aircraft had replaced five squadrons of smaller C–119 and C–123 transports, more than doubling South Vietnamese airlift capability. Final strength totaled 1,099 fixed-wing aircraft and 1,098 helicopters, making Saigon's air force one of the largest in the world.[24]

The South Vietnamese Navy had about 1,500 vessels. Approximately 400 were coastal or seagoing vessels charged with halting the infiltration of men and supplies by sea from North Vietnam. Assisting them were sixteen coastal radar stations manned by naval personnel. Another 700 craft operated on the inland waterways, especially in the Delta, controlling supply routes and supporting

[22] The 1st and 22d Infantry Divisions had taken over the two remaining independent regiments, giving each division twelve battalions (for a total of 105 infantry battalions in the army). Each division also had three 105-mm. and one 155-mm. artillery battalions and one armored cavalry squadron (still composed of M41 light tanks and M113 armored personnel carriers).

[23] USMACV, "Command History, 1972–1973," 1:C–12 to C–22, HRB, CMH.

[24] USMACV, "Command History, 1972–1973," 1:C–11 to C–22 and C–72 to C–84, HRB, CMH. Jack S. Ballard, *Development and Employment of Fixed-Wing Gunships, 1962–1972*, The United States Air Force in Southeast Asia (Washington, D.C.: Office of Air Force History, 1982), pp. 251–54.

ground operations. Others were logistical craft serving the harbor and coastal water transportation networks, including 11 large landing ships and 161 medium landing craft that gave the navy an "over-the-beach" supply and transport capability.[25]

The air force had the most noticeable significant weaknesses. Most of the new aircraft that arrived in South Vietnam during 1972, including 300 helicopters and 200 jet fighters, had neither pilots nor crews. Although Abrams and Weyand kept the U.S. Air Force Advisory Group as large as possible, and supplemented it with special mobile training teams, little could be done to speed up the recruitment and training of personnel in these highly skilled occupations. The Vietnamese had to integrate many new types of aircraft into their logistical system and take over several large air bases vacated by the U.S. Air Force. MACV estimated that the full 66-squadron air fleet could not be put into operation until 1974. But this depended entirely on Saigon's future ability to train enough personnel, especially middle management and logistical specialists, to support the enlarged force.

The U.S. Naval Advisory Group was more satisfied with the status of the South Vietnamese Navy. Like the air force, the navy needed highly trained technical personnel to operate and maintain complex equipment. However, most of the naval expansion had taken place prior to 1972, and there was no last minute influx of materiel. During 1972 U.S. Navy advisers concentrated on specific problem areas, such as overhaul scheduling, supply and parts requisitions, and repair capabilities. When they left Vietnam, the navy needed U.S. civilian contractor support in only a few areas.

Morale in both technical services also appeared good. Since 1965 neither the air force nor the navy had been involved in politics at the local or national levels. Professionalism had increased, and desertion rates were negligible. As in other armed forces, interservice rivalry and cooperation between the different services in the field presented certain problems. Air and naval units, including helicopter squadrons and riverine forces, supported but were not directly controlled by army division and corps commanders. In many cases, service component commanders were often unfamiliar with the capabilities and limitations of the other, and differences in the field had to be resolved at the Joint General Staff level if at all. However, given the ambiance of the different services—the heavy involvement of the army in politics and its scattered deployment, and the need to centralize the command and logistical elements of the navy and air force—these difficulties were probably unavoidable.[26]

The cost of the South Vietnamese military expansion was high. Between 1968 and 1972 almost all portions of the South Vietnamese defense budget moved steadily up (*Table 21*). From a projected calendar year 1968 budget of about $530 million (not counting MAP/Military Assistance Service Funded costs), annual South Vietnamese military expenditures rose to $787 million during fiscal year

[25] USMACV, "Command History, 1971," 2:VIII–15 to VIII–16, and "1972–1973," 1:C–20 and C–51 to C–70, HRB, CMH.

[26] For a discussion of the air-ground coordination problem, see Interv, Maj Dillard, Military History Branch, MACV, with Maj Gen John R. McGiffert, DepCdr, TRAC (hereafter cited as McGiffert Interv), 10 Oct 72, MACV History Branch Interviews, MHI.

TABLE 21—SOUTH VIETNAMESE DEFENSE BUDGET

	FY 69	FY 70	FY 71	FY 72
U.S. Dollar-Piaster Conversion Rate	1:118	1:118	1:118	1:400
Total Defense Budget [a]	2,107.6	2,528.7	2,763.8	2,228.1
Source				
MAP/MASF [b]	1,320.3	1,437.8	1,415.6	1,695.0
USAID Programs	84.6	99.5	79.5	50.5
RVN Funds	702.7	991.4	1,268.7	482.6
Distribution				
Ammunition	532.5	770.0	654.2	731.6
Pay	663.5	946.3	1,112.5	437.3
Materiel	827.7	595.8	707.5	941.9
Other	83.9	216.6	289.6	117.3
Distribution by Force				
Army	1,233.8	1,337.3	1,411.8	1,126.9
Navy	85.7	209.7	226.1	149.3
Air Force	227.3	221.7	408.5	542.8
Regional Forces	285.1	392.9	349.6	227.4
Popular Forces	119.3	170.6	179.7	99.8
Paramilitary [c]	156.4	196.5	188.1	81.9

[a] In millions of U.S. dollars.
[b] Military Assistance Program/Military Assistance Service Funded
[c] Police, revolutionary development cadre, People's Self-Defense Force.

Sources: Based on data presented in the MACV command histories, and especially on Heymont, *Resource Allocations for the RVN Army, Regional Force and Popular Force:* FY69, pp. 1–7; Heymont et al., *Resource Allocations for the RVN Security System:* FY70–FY71, RAC-TP-452 (McLean, Va., Research Analysis Corp., 1972), pp. 1–4; Heymont, *Resource Allocations and Costs for the Republic of Vietnam Security System: FY72 (Final Report),* OAD–CR–3 (McLean, Va.: General Research Corp., 1973), pp. xiii–xvii. Due to changes in methodology in determining costs, this table is not comparable to Table 19 based on earlier RAC studies that addressed only the South Vietnamese Army and Territorial Forces.

(FY) 1969 and $1,348 million in FY 1971, and increased another 32 percent in FY 1972 (although in 1972 the new piaster conversion rate made it appear less when expressed in U.S. dollars).[27] Direct U.S. materiel assistance to the armed forces exhibited the same trend, rising gradually from an estimated $300 million in FY 1965 and to $600 million in FY 1968 and then jumping to $1,320 million in FY 1969 and nearly $1,700 million in FY 1972. High ammunition costs in FYs 1970, 1971, and 1972 reflected the Cambodian, Laotian, and Easter offensives, and ominously showed what might be expected in the future; the increased air force support during FY 1972 was due to the large number of aircraft shipped to Vietnam before the ceasefire agreement, and underlined the high cost of replacing this type of equipment should significant combat losses occur. The rising

[27] USMACV, "Command History, 1967," 2:1058, HRB, CMH, notes a proposed defense budget for CY 1968 of VN$62.6 billion, of which VN$17.5 billion were joint support funds. In billions of piasters, the calendar defense budget went from about 30.4 in 1965 to 45.6 in 1967, 121.5 in 1970, and about 200 in 1972. See ibid., "1970," 2:IX–115, "1971," 1:VIII–86, and "1972–1973," 2:F–4; Fact Sheet, MACCO, 23 May 68, sub: Growth of the Republic of Vietnam Defense Budget During the Period 1964–1968, in COMUSMACV Fact Book, vol. 2, Westmoreland Papers. All in HRB, CMH. The different methods used to account for expenditures and the multiple changes in official exchange rates (*see* Table 22) made it difficult to arrive at precise figures, but those presented are accurate for comparative purposes.

budget also contributed to inflation in South Vietnam, to the steady decline in the local value of the piaster, and to the parallel erosion in the purchasing power of military salaries. The withdrawal of the U.S. ground troops, whose money had also contributed heavily to the Vietnamese economy, if not to Vietnamese society, was another hidden cost of Vietnamization that struck at the same time.

The Failure of Reform

As the MACV staff devoted increasing attention to introducing new equipment and building up South Vietnamese military support organizations, other programs fell by the wayside. The new dependent housing program begun in 1970 was an example. The original MACV plan had called for 20,000 shelters to be built each year between 1970 and 1975, for a total of 120,000 units. A joint U.S.-South Vietnamese fund was to cover costs, with South Vietnamese Army engineers performing the construction. The effort barely got off the ground in 1970, but Saigon completed 15,280 units in 1971 and began construction of 4,140 more. Then, under the press of events, the program fell apart in 1972; only 1,690 more shelters were completed that year, leaving a shortage of at least 100,000 units. Other problems remained. Of about 50,000 shelters constructed prior to 1970, many were in disrepair; most housing was still located around division and regimental base camps; and many dependents continued to live within tactical military installations. The new mobility of the armed forces cited by Laird was sometimes hard to find.[28]

Saigon's treatment of Montagnard dependents was even worse. The Thieu regime resumed the practice of forcibly relocating the tribes from their traditional homelands, generating some 52,000 Montagnard "relocatees," or refugees, in 1970–71. General Dzu, the II Corps commander, felt that the action was necessary because of his inability to provide security for the scattered Highlander villages and his conviction that many were aiding the Viet Cong.[29] In early 1971 Gerald Hickey, the noted Rand Corporation sociologist, visited some of the relocated villages, reported the resettlement effort badly mismanaged, and attempted unsuccessfully to halt or slow down the movements.[30] In March the matter came to the attention of the secretary of the Army, and in April it was aired by Senator Ted Kennedy's Senate Judiciary Subcommittee on Refugees.[31]

---

[28] USMACV, "Command History, 1972–1973," 2:E–33 to E–34, HRB, CMH.

[29] MFR, Brownback, CORDS, II CTZ, 4 Feb 71, sub: Meeting With General Dzu, 3 February 1971, SEAB, CMH.

[30] MFR, Hickey, 13 Feb 71, sub: Unlearned Lessons of History: Relocation of Montagnards; Ltr, Hickey to Colby, 22 Feb 71; Memo, Tart to DEPCORDS, 26 Feb 71, sub: Meeting With General Dzu on 26 February (Thieu had read Hickey's MFR and had ordered Dzu to meet with the American scholar). All in SEAB, CMH.

[31] Memo, Lt Col Richard G. Cardillo, OPS/IA/SO(CA), DA, 19 Mar 71, sub: Information for Secretary of the Army; MFR, Lt Col Peter P. Petro, Plans and Operations Div, OCLL, 22 Apr 71, sub: Report of Hearing, Senate Judiciary Subcommittee on Refugees, Senator Kennedy, Chairman. Both in SEAB, CMH.

Appearing before the subcommittee on the twenty-second, William Colby, Komer's successor as the MACV CORDS director, defended the resettlement effort on the grounds of security and, while admitting that "some relocations were handled badly," maintained that "most of them were handled effectively."[32] However, a study conducted by his staff the following month concluded that the movements had been "ill-planned, ill-conceived, and ill-executed," citing one case where three hundred of nineteen hundred Montagnards died at one relocation site and adding that "countless other thousands are literally wards of the highland province social welfare services and various volunteer agencies."[33] Under pressure from MACV and the U.S. Embassy, Saigon subsequently ordered the practice abandoned, declaring that the tribes should remain in their home areas and pointing out to II Corps officials that the North Vietnamese had never been successful in enlisting Montagnard support for their cause.[34] Nevertheless, the damage was done. American ranger advisers called the resettlements "a disgrace" that only worsened relationships between South Vietnamese officers and the ethnic minority soldiers of the border defense ranger battalions.[35] Already the American presence in the Highlands was sorely missed.

Although most Vietnamese were better off than their Montagnard neighbors, food was a constant concern of soldiers and their dependents. Massive inflation and the disruption of the economy caused by the fighting had continued to drive up the price of rice. With over seven hundred outlets by the end of 1972, the commissary distribution system proved effective, but its prices were only about 6 to 10 percent below market. The three-year American canned food program was also beneficial, but ended in 1972. Saigon replaced it with an expanded military farming program, using excess military-owned land and, as laborers, dependents and off-duty and disabled soldiers. Supervised by the South Vietnamese Quartermaster Corps, the program proved to be a marked success. However, under pressure from politicians and businessmen who feared military competition in the marketplace, Saigon suspended the program in late 1972 and later completely abandoned it. In the field and in most base camps, units continued to eat informally, with soldiers buying snacks on the local market, pooling their money to purchase bulk items for the evening meal, or simply eating with their dependents. With the internal insurgency weaker, and combat more sporadic,

---

[32] As related in MFR, Petro, 22 Apr 71, sub: Report of Hearing, Senate Judiciary Subcommittee on Refugees, Senator Kennedy, Chairman, SEAB, CMH.

[33] Quoted words from CORDS Field Evaluation Rpt, Pacification Studies Group, 12 May 71, sub: Highland Resettlement: Lessons Learned. See also ibid., 15 Apr 71, sub: Montagnard Resettlement. Both in SEAB, CMH.

[34] MFR, Johnson, Central Pacification and Development Council, Development Center Liaison Group, 4 May 71, sub: Action Taken by CPDC/CC To Resolve the Problems Concerning the Relocations of Both Montagnards and Vietnamese (March–April), which notes that 54,788 people had been relocated in II Corps, about 10,000 more in southern I Corps, and 38,252 had been scheduled to be moved over the next several months; Transmittal Ltr no. 0366, Steward, Director, War Victims Directorate, CORDS, to Subordinate Offices, 20 May 71, sub: CPDC Communique 1412 on Relocation of Civilians. Both in SEAB, CMH.

[35] Interv, author with Lt Col Charles D. Burnette, Senior Adviser, Ranger Command, II CTZ (January–December 1971), 27 Feb 76, SEAB; USMACV, "Command History, 1971," 1:VII–41, HRB, says little, but the author's monograph, "The Refugee Problem in South Vietnam, 1960–1972," SEAB, is a brief introduction to the large quantity of material available at CMH on this subject.

such arrangements appeared acceptable to advisers as long as the units stayed close to home.[36]

Difficulties in recruiting manpower also recurred.[37] Province chiefs tended to funnel conscripts into their own Territorial Forces and other local security agencies like the police and the People's Self-Defense Force. As a result, regular force (army, navy, air force, and marine corps) accessions during 1971 were below expectations. The regulars took in about 96 percent of their quota in volunteers, about 160,000 men, but only a little over 50 percent of their conscript quota of 66,900. As usual, the air force, navy, and army support and headquarters units had no trouble filling their ranks, while the combat units, especially the infantry battalions, went hungry. With few conscripts and volunteers, combat battalions were mustering only 65 percent of their authorized strength toward the end of 1971, whereas other army units averaged 96 to 121 percent.

In August 1971 General Abrams demanded that the Joint General Staff take immediate action to correct the problem. The South Vietnamese response was slow. Vien counted on the reorganization of the infantry regiments (eliminating the headquarters and headquarters company of each fourth battalion) to provide extra manpower and, as an interim measure, ordered all army headquarters elements reduced to 90–95 percent of their authorized strength. Saigon also proferred a small bonus to all new recruits, volunteers and conscripts alike, who were assigned to combat battalions. As before, American advisers at MACV and in the field prodded the Vietnamese to enforce existing manpower policies: meeting recruiting quotas, prosecuting draft-dodgers, reducing desertions, tightening up deferments, and so forth. MACV estimated that about 100,000 PSDF members had joined the militia illegally, probably through bribery or falsifying records, to avoid conscription and thus urged that its ranks be investigated. The advice again went unheeded. As a result, in March 1972, on the eve of the Easter offensive, the assigned strength the South Vietnamese infantry battalions remained unchanged, and MACV felt that many could put less than half of their authorized strength in the field.

The heavy fighting of 1972 spurred Saigon into action. On 9 April Vien reduced individual training from twelve to nine weeks; on the twelfth, granted amnesty to deserters and draft-dodgers who either returned to duty or reported for conscription before the end of May; and on the twenty-fourth, awarded pardons to military convicts serving in labor units. The first measure increased the weekly recruit output from 5,600 to 9,500, the second returned about 11,500 men to service, and the third saw most of the 15,800 military laborers rejoin their units. Vien also authorized his corps commanders to draft Territorial Forces personnel or entire territorial units into the regular army.

---

[36] See Khuyen, *RVNAF Logistics*, pp. 120–25. Vietnamese units still had no formal messes and were only authorized to organize informal "cooking services" from personnel at hand. A good Vietnamese treatment is Social Behavior Division, Combat Development and Test Center–Vietnam, JGS, *Report of the Study on Living Standards, Republic of Vietnam Armed Forces (Army)*, English translation (Saigon, 1969), especially pp. 79–86, copy in SEAB, CMH. For examples, see Interv no. 183, Maj Kenneth J. Necessary, Senior Adviser, 7th Armored Cavalry Regiment (1970–71), May 1974, Fort Knox Armor School Interviews, MHI.

[37] The discussion on manpower is based on USMACV, "Command History, 1971," 1:VIII–5 to VIII–9, and "1972–1973," 2:C–16 to C–19, HRB; and studies in files on manpower, SEAB. All in CMH.

As the battlefield situation worsened in May, Thieu swallowed more American advice, agreeing to draft 17- and 39- to 43-year-olds, to tighten academic deferments, and to establish corps and provincial manpower committees, which reported daily to a joint Vietnamese-American committee in Saigon. Constant pushing by both the American and South Vietnamese high commands finally produced results. It was almost a repeat of the mobilization efforts taken after the Tet attacks in 1968. From May to August 1972 the provinces shoveled about 150,000 new recruits into the training camps, and this influx, coupled with the earlier measures taken in April, slowly pushed up at least the paper strength of the combat units. By July the average assigned strength of the infantry battalions had risen to 88 percent, and the 3d Division, virtually destroyed in the early fighting, was again operational. Six months later, on the eve of the final American withdrawal, most South Vietnamese units had achieved almost 100 percent of their fill. Reassured, MACV breathed a sigh of relief. There was, however, a cost to be paid. The quality of the "fill" was questionable—pardoned deserters, draft-dodgers, quickly trained recruits, and overworked veterans did not make the stuff of good fighting units. Moreover, wide gaps still existed between the assigned strength of the infantry battalions and the number of men actually in the field.[38] The improvements of assigned strength figures sought after by MACV did not necessarily signify improvements in combat effectiveness. As long as the South Vietnamese depended on a mixed bag of transients to fill up their fighting forces, even these statistics had little meaning.

The Vietnamese generals continued to uphold the secondary school educational prerequisities for entrance into the officer and noncommissioned officer corps. MACV apparently gave up its efforts to change this policy, perhaps agreeing with General Dong Van Khuyen, head of the Central Logistics Command, that increases in the availability of secondary education made the matter less significant.[39] But an analysis of Saigon's educational system shows that Khuyen was wrong. In 1970–72 the number of Vietnamese students enrolled in secondary schools hovered around 20–25 percent of those eligible, a marked increase from the 3 percent of 1954–55 and the 11–16 percent of 1960–65, but hardly a social revolution. Furthermore, most of the schools were located in the cities and larger towns; about two-thirds of the students were enrolled in private schools, many with high tuition rates; and less than half of the students entering secondary schools ever graduated.[40] The class bias of the South Vietnamese officer corps thus continued, and even the lower officer ranks of the armed forces remained populated largely by the wealthier, educated urban Vietnamese.[41] The continued

---

[38] For example, see Chart, "Divisional Status," in COMUSMACV Special Talking Papers (General Abrams Visit, 18–24 Oct 72), tab 7, encl. 1, SEAB, CMH.

[39] Khuyen, *The RVNAF*, pp. 76–77 and 209.

[40] See Table, "Education Statistics, Form–VN/ED 12–10–68," in "USAID/Vietnam Office of Education Briefing Materials, 1969," copy of pamphlet in SEAB, CMH, which indicates that less than half of the students completing the school cycle (the equivalent of American grades 6–9) received a baccalaureate I (grade 11), making them eligible for the noncommissioned officer corps, and less received a baccalaureate II (grade 12), making them eligible for the officer corps.

[41] For statistical data, see Viet-Nam Info Series no. 36, "Secondary Education in Viet-Nam, *Viet-Nam Bulletin* (weekly publication of the Embassy of Viet-Nam in Washington, D.C., circa 1970), copy in SEAB; USMACV, "Command History, 1971," 1:VII–42 to VII–43, and "1972–1973," 1:D–41, HRB. All in CMH.

domination of both the officer corps and the civil administration by the "educated urban petty bourgeoisie," as later explained by another South Vietnamese general, made it difficult for military leaders to identify with the peasantry who made up 80 percent of the population and most of the armed forces. The resulting situation, he felt, was "a major cause for ineffective leadership."[42]

Promotions also continued to be a sore point.[43] The program begun in 1968 to bring the armed forces up to 90 percent of the authorized grade levels in each rank by 1970 had failed, and an amended goal of 85 percent for 1971 proved equally unattainable. On the insistence of MACV, the Joint General Staff relaxed some of its standards in September 1971, boosting total promotions that year to 4,107 mid-grade (captain through lieutenant colonel) officers and 46,640 noncommissioned officers, of which 859 officers and 16,172 noncommissioned officer advancements were based on performance in battle. However, the problem of grade imbalance remained acute, especially in combat battalions. For example, each infantry battalion ought to have been commanded by a lieutenant colonel, but in November 1971 fifty were still commanded by captains, two by lieutenants, and most of the rest by majors, and about one half of all the commanders had been in command less than a year.

The following year saw little improvement, and officer promotions continued to lag. Neither promotion quotas nor overall goals were met. In May 1972 forty-three infantry battalions were commanded by captains and two by lieutenants. The performance of many South Vietnamese officers during the Easter offensive resulted in many promotion recommendations, but the Joint General Staff refused to relax its rigid time-in-grade advancement criteria and turned most of them down. In an armed forces officer corps of 72,277 (83,738 authorized), only 4,352 received promotions in 1972 out of a target goal of 9,253, and of these only 762 received battlefield promotions out of a goal of 2,755.

In October 1972 President Thieu approved measures that increased time-in-grade requirements for most promotions. Experience, rather than merit, was the primary factor in advancement. The officer corps thus remained unbalanced with about 51,816 second lieutenants, 12,609 captains (of 23,348 authorized), 7,728 field-grade officers (of 13,707 authorized), and 79 general officers (of 264 authorized). Thieu did, however, liberalize enlisted promotions during the Easter offensive, which resulted in 59,066 battlefield promotions, mostly in the lower grades. Altogether, there were almost 100,000 enlisted promotions in 1972, a quarter of which were noncommissioned officer advancements, and the enlisted ranks, especially the noncommissioned officer corps, came much closer to matching the authorized grade structure.

The desertion problem also went unsolved, and was most critical in ground combat units.[44] The underlying causes were well known. The problem started

---

[42] Tho, *Pacification*, p. 193.

[43] The discussion on promotions is based on USMACV, "Command History, 1971," 1:VIII–29 to VIII–32, and "1972–1973," 1:C–28 to C–29, HRB; Memo, JCSM–363–72 to SecDef, 12 Aug 72, sub: Situation in the RVN Short-Range Improvement in the Republic of Vietnam Armed Forces, pp. A–5 to A–6, SEAB; and files on RVNAF promotions, SEAB. All in CMH.

[44] The discussion on desertions is based on USMACV, "Command History, 1971," 1:VIII–29 to VIII–37, and "1972–1973," 1:C–28 to C–30, HRB, CMH; files on RVNAF desertions, SEAB, CMH; and Truong, *Territorial Forces*, p. 136.

with the lowest private and wound its way up to the highest levels of government. For example, in 1971 Prime Minister Khiem ordered General Truong, the IV Corps commander, to halt his campaigns against "ghost" and "ornamental" soldiers, deserters, and draft-dodgers in the IV Corps zone, claiming that his efforts were upsetting the delta rice harvest. Truong questioned Khiem's motives, but obeyed. With only lukewarm backing from Saigon, many of the antidesertion programs thus came to naught. Gross desertions rose from 150,469 (126,753 net) in 1970 to 168,997 (140,277 net) in 1971, while the average monthly desertion rate (deserters per 1,000 troops) increased from 12.3 to 13.4, reaching a high of 15.5 during periods of heavy combat activity.[45] In contrast, combat losses (killed in action) totaled 7,512 in 1970 and 7,862 in 1971. As usual, desertion rates were highest in ground combat units. The army rate (including support units) rose to 23.0, the marine corps (with fewer support units) to 59.7, and some of the army infantry battalions went even higher. The air force and navy had no significant losses. On the recommendation of MACV, the Joint General Staff approved incentive pay for those serving in combat units (about $7.00 per month), and both considered but rejected dropping or modifying the indefinite term of service.

According to MACV, Saigon's personnel situation grew worse in 1972. Combat losses more than doubled, totaling 16,086 killed and thousands more seriously wounded. Moreover, gross desertions jumped to 190,000 (160,000 net), for an average monthly rate of 16.5 (13.2 net). Starting at 10 in January, the monthly rate rose to 16 during the Easter offensive and continued to rise throughout the second half of the year, averaging 19.8 (16.7 net) and reaching a high of 21.9 (19.3 net) in December. Although the Joint General Staff replaced these losses with new recruits, the resulting high personnel turnover severely damaged unit morale and cohesion. MACV felt that desertions would clearly be one of Saigon's most serious military problems for many years to come.

Americans viewed the failure of many of their military reform efforts with perplexity and perhaps indifference. They could always place the blame on South Vietnamese ineptitude and their unwillingness to take American advice. On the other hand, the sacrifice of so much American flesh and blood demanded that some accounting be made. Yet it was always easier to take the more optimistic view that the glass was half full and that American materiel aid and assistance had at last given Saigon the means to defend itself. On the surface, the bureaucratic programs pushed by so many minor MACV staff officers seemed relatively insignificant. In most American minds the tanks, helicopters, artillery, and all the other war paraphernalia in the hands of Saigon far outweighed the construction of a few thousand dependent shelters or the establishment of military farms. Perhaps it was too difficult for urban-oriented Americans to see the relationship between such programs and increased military effectiveness. For a clearer assessment, most turned to the battlefield, for it was here and not in Saigon that the fate of South Vietnam was being decided.

---

[45] Net desertions were determined by subtracting the number of deserters who returned "voluntarily" from the number of gross desertions.

25

A Matter of Leadership

By 1971 the war in the field had changed a great deal. The heavy manpower losses suffered by the Viet Cong during the Tet offensive of 1968 and the intensive pacification security programs implemented or advised by MACV had broken the back of the once strong internal insurgency. The North Vietnamese attempted to keep the war behind their enemy's lines alive by the continued infiltration of small combat teams ("sapper" units and small rocket artillery detachments), but could do little more. The Viet Cong that remained spent most of their time merely surviving, blending in with the civilian population or hiding in remote jungle bases. General Abrams and his staff were circumspect, wary of claiming pacification a success too early but soothed by the statistical indicators that told them that overt Viet Cong activity among the population had been drastically reduced. Nevertheless, the greatly diminished American ground combat capabilities made them exceedingly nervous. As always, the North Vietnamese could increase the tempo of the war at any time simply by crossing the border and attacking. But they could ill-afford the expected combat losses and, in view of the continuing American withdrawals, probably saw little need for immediate action.[1]

In South Vietnam, Saigon's military forces had responded to the changing situation in a variety of ways. Some commanders began to lie back and relax, like one armored squadron commander who told his adviser that his mission was simply "to rest."[2] Others, under the impetus of aggressive generals like Tri, Thanh, and Truong, kept busy, usually operating in regimental-size combined arms task forces similar to the mobile groups employed earlier by the French. Even without their American advisers, such units continued to operate with relative impunity in Cambodia, and, if the South Vietnamese appeared to rely too heavily on artillery and air power to destroy their opponents, their tactics did not differ greatly from those of neighboring American forces. But as yet the enemy had not stood and fought, and there had been no thorough test of South Vietnamese leadership or fighting abilities.

[1] USMACV, "Command History, 1971," 1:I-8 to I-9, HRB, CMH.
[2] Interv no. 183, Necessary, May 1974, Fort Knox Armor School Interviews, MHI.

South Vietnamese Soldiers Pushing Through the Laotian Jungle

LAM SON 719

More ambitious undertakings were already in the works. In December 1970 the Joint Chiefs of Staff asked MACV to prepare contingency plans for South Vietnamese cross-border campaigns into Cambodia, Laos, and North Vietnam, supported by heavy American air and naval forces.[3] Based on this guidance, MACV and the Joint General Staff sent strong South Vietnamese forces into Cambodia and Laos the following year. The Cambodian offensive, actually a continuation of the previous year's occupation, met with stiff resistance. In April 1971 attacking South Vietnamese forces ran into trouble around the Cambodian town of Snuol, due north of Saigon, about 8 kilometers over the border. The heavy ground cover enabled the North Vietnamese to bring up strong forces, including field and antiaircraft artillery, on the South Vietnamese flanks and rear. By the end of May the enemy had isolated the South Vietnamese and, after a

---

[3] Msg, McCain to Abrams, 062132 Dec 70, Abrams Papers, HRB, CMH. According to Kissinger, Abrams himself suggested the Laotian operation and President Nixon approved the concept officially on 18 January 1971. See Kissinger, *White House Years*, pp. 987–96; Hoang Ngoc Lung, *Strategy and Tactics*, Indochina Monographs (Washington, D.C.: U.S. Army Center of Military History, 1980), p. 73.

relief force from the south had suffered heavy losses, forced them to withdraw under the cover of massive U.S. air strikes.[4] In September the North Vietnamese tried similar tactics west of Snuol, but here the open terrain worked against them. After taking heavy losses from reinforced South Vietnamese infantry and armor units supported by air and artillery, it was the North Vietnamese who were forced to withdraw.

In many ways LAM SON 719, the South Vietnamese offensive into Laos in February 1971, was similar to the Snuol operation. This time the attacking South Vietnamese sent in their best units, the 1st Infantry Division, the Airborne Division, selected ranger and armored units, and later the Marine Division. General Lam, the I Corps commander, struck west across northern South Vietnam, through Khe Sanh, and deep into Laos. Tchepone, about 40 kilometers inside the Laotian border, was his ground objective, but the purpose of LAM SON 719 was to cut the north-south flow of supplies along the Ho Chi Minh trail and destroy enemy supply depots (*see Map 7*). American military forces secured staging areas just inside the border of South Vietnam and provided artillery and air support. No advisers or other American personnel accompanied the attacking troops.

Evaluating LAM SON 719 is difficult. Many official reports described the operation as a rapid raid into hostile territory and declared it a success. Enemy losses were heavy in both men and materiel, and the attacking forces simply pulled back after completing their mission. Other evaluations told a different story.[5] Abrams reported gloomily that the episode confirmed that Saigon "cannot sustain large scale major cross border operations . . . without external support."[6] The South Vietnamese encountered much stiffer opposition than expected, and the operation had to be ended in haste. Helicopter-borne troops spearheaded the initial South Vietnamese advance, but supplies depended on a narrow jungle road leading back into South Vietnam. The rugged terrain confined armored units to the roadway secured by a series of isolated fire support bases on both flanks. The North Vietnamese response was rapid. Apparently they had been preparing for such an attack, stockpiling weapons and ammunition and building defensive positions along possible routes of attack, helicopter landing zones, and fire support base locations. As a result, they were able to surround South Vietnamese support bases with well dug-in antiaircraft, mortar, and artillery positions; isolate them; and overrun several with mass infantry assaults supported by armor. Their 152-mm. howitzers and 130-mm. guns outranged the South Vietnamese 105-mm. and 155-mm. pieces, and were difficult to locate; their use

[4] MFR, HQ, 3d Armored Bde Advisory Detachment, TRAC, 7 Sep 71, sub: Snuol, Relief of Task Force 8, MICRO 110 (no frame no.), RG 334, WNRC. The operation is also covered in Interv, Gen Michael S. Davison, Senior Officers Debriefing Program, Michael S. Davison Papers, MHI.
[5] USMACV, "Command History, 1971," 2: E–15 to E–48, HRB, CMH; Vien and Khuyen, *Reflections on the Vietnam War*, pp. 99–103; Msg, Bunker SGN 4630 to President, 300805 Mar 71, bk. 17, Bunker Papers, DS; Nguyen Duy Hinh, *Lam Son 719*, Indochina Monographs (Washington, D.C.: U.S. Army Center of Military History, 1979). In Msg, Bunker SGN 4508 to SecState, 280935 Mar 71, bk. 17, Bunker Papers, DS, the ambassador blames the American press corps for doubts raised over the operation's success.
[6] Msg, COMUSMACV to JCS, 031015 Apr 71, sub: Vietnamization, SEAB, CMH.

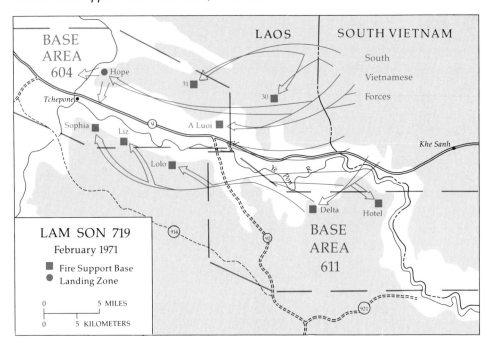

MAP 7

of armor was another unwelcome surprise. In short, the North Vietnamese re-acted by massing their forces for a decisive battle, which, in the end, the South Vietnamese chose to decline.

In general, the South Vietnamese troops fought hard, even in retreat, forcing the enemy to take heavy losses. Operational difficulties centered around poor reporting by subordinate commanders, overdependence on helicopters, lack of ground mobility, and piecemeal use of reserves. Neither the airborne nor the marines had operated in divisional strength before, and their divisional staffs were weak, unable to handle the vast amount of coordination necessary with attached and supporting forces not to mention their own subordinate brigades and battalions.[7] Unlike Cambodia, the geography of southern Laos, mountain-ous and heavily forested, made it difficult for the South Vietnamese to gain maximum advantage from their superior ground and air mobility. Thus the battle quickly boiled down to a contest of will and fighting ability. Approximately 45 percent of the 17,000 South Vietnamese troops committed during the heaviest fighting were casualties, including about 1,500 dead or missing compared to 13,000 claimed enemy dead. In addition, over 100 helicopters were lost, together with 96 artillery pieces and 141 armored vehicles, many of which were destroyed by their own crews to prevent capture.[8] The Airborne and 1st Divisions had the

---

[7] For example, see Interv no. 183, Necessary, Fort Knox Armor School Interviews, MHI.
[8] Hinh, *Lam Son 719*, pp. 126–40; Msg, Sutherland QTR 0539 to Abrams, 261130 Mar 71, Abrams Papers, HRB, CMH.

most success but suffered the most losses, and General Sutherland, the local American ground commander, felt that their casualties might have been reduced by a least half if U.S. advisers had been present to help direct the large amounts of tactical air, helicopter, B–52, and artillery support available.[9] Sutherland was also dismayed by the vast quantities of supplies left behind, even when there was plenty of time to save them, and, as an example, cited the return of one South Vietnamese force to an abandoned base at the insistence of its adviser to retrieve 170 truckloads of materiel.[10] General Abrams was also disappointed over the inability of the South Vietnamese to use American combat support more effectively and, as a "remedial action," ordered his corps senior advisers to put together mobile support groups to work directly with South Vietnamese corps commanders in future large-scale field operations.[11] To assist, he assigned an additional senior Army officer as "air-mobile adviser" in each corps zone to help coordinate U.S. helicopter support to South Vietnamese field units.[12]

More serious was the confusion and bickering within the South Vietnamese high command itself. Both Abrams and Sutherland wanted the South Vietnamese to remain in Laos, reinforce the embattled units, and fight a major battle then and there.[13] General Alexander Haig, Nixon's personal military adviser, visited Sutherland in the field and noted Washington's agreement on this point.[14] American fire support might not be available in some later battle. But the Vietnamese were hesitant. Alarmed by the heavy casualties taken by the airborne troops, President Thieu wanted to replace them as soon as possible with Khang's marines. Lam, the operational commander, opposed the switch, regarding the move to be politically motivated, but he himself refused to commit his remaining infantry division, the 2d, into the fray.[15] Vien told Abrams he would personally order Lam to throw in the 2d if the Americans agreed to commit two U.S. ground combat brigades across the border, and this Abrams refused to do. Rather than gamble by increasing the stakes, the Vietnamese thus chose to break off and withdraw. Perhaps this was best, for by 24 March, as their forces pulled back across the border, Sutherland reported serious squabbling between Lam, Dong (still the airborne commander), Khang (the marine commander), and Vien, and felt that Lam had lost control over his major subordinates.[16] Vien, in turn, later claimed that Thieu had begun to direct portions of the battle personally from

[9] Msg, Sutherland QTR 0566 to Abrams, 281110 Mar 71, sub: AAR on LAM SON 719 by 3 Div SA's, Abrams Papers, HRB, CMH.
[10] Msg, Sutherland DNG 1280 to Abrams, 030145 May 71, sub: ARVN Supply Discipline, Abrams Papers, HRB, CMH.
[11] Msg, Abrams MAC 03942 to Major Subordinates, 18 Apr 71, Abrams Papers, HRB, CMH.
[12] Msg, Abrams MAC 11252 to Major Subordinates, 300448 Nov 71, sub: VNAF/RVNAF Helicopter Operations, Abrams Papers, HRB, CMH. See also, in same papers, subsequent messages on this subject.
[13] Msg, Sutherland QTR 0251 to Abrams, 060344 Mar 71, sub: ARVN Reinforcement of Lam Son 719; Msg, Abrams MAC 02372 to Sutherland, 061014 Mar 71. Both in Abrams Papers, HRB, CMH.
[14] Msg, Sutherland DNG 0843 to Abrams, 181425 Mar 71, Abrams Papers, HRB, CMH; Kissinger, *White House Years*, pp. 1008–09.
[15] Msg, Sutherland QTR 0174 to Abrams, 281410 Feb 71; Msg, Sutherland QTR 0237 to Abrams, 051155 Mar 71. Both in Abrams Papers, HRB, CMH.
[16] Msg, Sutherland QTR 0503 to Abrams, 241446 Mar 71; Msg, Sutherland QTR 0515 to Abrams, 250430 Mar 71. Both in Abrams Papers, HRB, CMH.

Saigon, ignoring both his general staff and the local corps commander.[17] The final battle, if there was to be one, would be fought elsewhere.

Leadership Changes

Whatever their shortcomings, the Laotian and Cambodian attacks put the enemy on the defensive and gave General Abrams and his counterparts time to take stock of the ongoing Vietnamization effort. While the more formal administrative and logistics improvement programs continued, progress in other areas remained more difficult to measure. In July 1971 Abrams noted that MACV's role in South Vietnam would soon be reduced to military assistance and that Saigon's major weaknesses continued to be poor leadership and its inability to use the increasing amount of American fire support now becoming available. American "re-inforcement" in these two areas was critical.[18] Concerning military deployments, Abrams remained conservative. Rather than move one of the South Vietnamese delta-based divisions north, as recommended by General Cushman, the IV Corps senior adviser, he went along with Vien's decision to create the new 3d Infantry Division from existing regular and territorial elements in the I Corps zone.[19] He also vetoed proposals to prolong the life of the remaining U.S. combat units in South Vietnam by augmenting them with Vietnamese personnel.[20] The MACV commander still wished to avoid any radical changes and improve the existing structure as much as possible.

Leadership changes were critical during this interim period. General Dolvin, who succeeded Sutherland as the I Corps senior adviser in September 1971, seemed satisfied with the South Vietnamese commanders there. Lam remained corps commander; Phu stayed on in the 1st Division;[21] and General Vu Van Giai, Phu's deputy, who had perfomed well during the Laotian operation, moved over to head the new 3d Division. Dolvin was disturbed only by Toan, the 2d Division commander who, although a good combat leader, continued to get himself into personal difficulties and was replaced by the less competent but more placid Col. Phan Hoa Hiep the following January. However, the American advisers could not have been too happy with the new deputy corps commander, General Hieu, who had just been booted out of the 5th Infantry Division near Saigon.[22]

In the Central Highlands the new senior adviser of the II Corps Tactical Zone, John Paul Vann, was less confident. Officially named "director" of the Second

[17] Freund Briefing Notes to Westmoreland, circa July 1971 (based on conversations with Vien in June and July 1971), Presidential Meetings file, 1971, Westmoreland Papers, HRB, CMH.

[18] Msg, Abrams MAC 06474 to Major Subordinates, 050611 Jul 71, Abrams Papers, HRB, CMH.

[19] See Msg, Cushman CTO 0756 to Abrams, 170645 Jul 71, sub: Redeployment of 9th ARVN Division, Abrams Papers, HRB, CMH.

[20] See Msg, Lt Gen McCaffrey (DCG, USARV) ARV 1427 to Abrams, sub: 196th Bde and Bde/1st Cav; Msg, Abrams MAC 04980 to McCaffrey, 290957 May 72, sub: Redeployment of the 196th Inf Bde. Both in Abrams Papers, HRB, CMH.

[21] Phu was later in charge of the ill-fated retreat from the Highlands in 1975.

[22] See Msgs, Dolvin DNG 2692 to Abrams, 171600 Sep 71, sub: Security Assessment, and Dolvin DNG 0045 to Abrams, 061150 Jan 72, sub: Personnel Changes in MR-1, Abrams Papers. For an evaluation of Hiep, see Senior Officer Debriefing Rpt, Col James R. Henslick, 27 Jan 73. All in HRB, CMH.

Regional Assistance Group, Vann was the only civilian to occupy such a post during the war, but his past military experience and his deep knowledge of Vietnamese affairs made him a good choice for the job. His evaluations were always to the point and more candid than those of his fellow advisers in uniform. Vann's counterpart, General Ngo Dzu, was something of an unknown, a pre-Directory division commander who had served well on the Joint General Staff until suddenly nominated to take over the IV Corps Tactical Zone upon the death of General Thanh in May 1970 and then the II Corps following the dismissal of Lu Lan in August. Vann judged Dzu as capable and hardworking, but with a tendency to overreact and a habit of depending too much on his American

John Paul Vann

advisers rather than his own staff. Yet the two worked reasonably well together, their common difficulties stemming from the poor quality of Dzu's subordinates, especially his two infantry division commanders. General Trien, commanding the 22d, had repeatedly expressed his aversion to the post and threatened to hospitalize himself if he was not transferred.[23] General Canh, heading the 23d, was little better. General Collins, Vann's predecessor, had already recommended his relief and Vann seconded the judgment.[24] However, Thieu refused to replace either officer, and Dzu, not known as a strong supporter of the president, speculated that Thieu was trying to undermine his command in order to engineer his own dismissal.[25]

Vann also noted other problems: accommodations between the territorials and the local Viet Cong; continued mistrust between the Vietnamese and Montagnards; poor South Vietnamese leadership at the battalion and company levels; and a general lack of military discipline—he estimated that between 10 and 30 percent of the Viet Cong terrorist incidents in the zone were actually the result of South Vietnamese "banditry," which he attributed mostly to the continued high inflation rate. But, on balance, he noted significant improvements in almost all areas and felt that, by juggling command relationships, units, and staff per-

---

[23] Msg, Vann no. 0147 to Abrams, 041140 Feb 72, sub: Replacement of 22nd ARVN Division Commander. See also Msg, Vann NHT 0680 to Abrams, 201109 Sep 71, sub: RVNAF Leadership. Both in Abrams Papers, HRB, CMH.

[24] Msg, Collins NHT 0012 to Abrams, 020845 Jan 71; Msg, Vann PKU 0991 to Abrams, 141130 Dec 71, sub: Divisional Leaderships in II Corps. Both in Abrams Papers, HRB, CMH.

[25] See Msgs, Vann NHT 0428 to Abrams, 171210 Jul 71, sub: Conversations With General Dzu, and Vann PKU 0243 to Abrams, 190405 Feb 72, Abrams Papers, HRB, CMH.

sonnel, Dzu was doing the best he could with what he had and was prepared well enough for the expected enemy offensives in 1972.[26]

In the III Corps Tactical Zone close to Saigon the South Vietnamese leadership situation was worse. The American senior advisers, Lt. Gen. Michael S. Davison, commanding the II Field Force, and his successor in June 1970, Maj. Gen. Jack J. Wagstaff, heading the Third Regional Assistance Command, agreed on this issue. The death of Do Cao Tri had been a blow to the corps and his replacement, General Nguyen Van Minh, could not fill his shoes. Minh had commanded the 21st Infantry Division in the Delta from 1965 to 1968 and the senior U.S. officer there, Maj. Gen. George S. Eckhardt, had recommended his dismissal, noting that he was "very temperamental and has frequently requested relief when under stress or when at odds with [the] corps commander."[27] But Minh's close friendship with President Thieu brought him command of the Capital Military District in 1968, and he now held what was the most important South Vietnamese field command in the war. American evaluations, however, remained unchanged. Davison described him as "burned out" and "desperate"; Wagstaff reported that he was "over worked" and "highly emotional" ("as is well known") and that his decisions were "colored largely by his sensing of the moment."[28]

Of the three infantry division commanders in III Corps, Davison named General Thinh, heading the 25th, as the best—capable and self-confident, but "inscrutable," "most oriental," and "cautious and conservative."[29] For his own reasons Thieu replaced him in January 1972 by a newcomer, Le Van Tu, a general highly recommended by Vann. In the 18th Division Thieu had relieved Do Ke Giai (not to be confused with Vu Van Giai heading the 3d Division) in 1969, but replaced him with General Tho, who turned out equally bad in the eyes of his advisers.[30] Worst of the lot was the 5th Division commander, General Hieu. Hieu's forces had been badly handled during the Snuol operation, and his troops, according to Davison, were close to mutiny.[31] Pushed by both Abrams and Minh to relieve him, Thieu finally acceded and in April 1971 brought Col. Le Van Hung up from Phong Dinh Province to take over the battered 5th. Unfortunately, Hung was the one South Vietnamese officer whose candidacy American advisers had specifically recommended against.[32] Thus, like Dzu, Minh had to make do by manipulating command relationships and, like Tri before him, ended up employing regimental-size task forces in the field commanded by a few

[26] Msg, Vann NHT 0670 to Abrams, 171424 Sep 71, sub: Security Assessment, Abrams Papers, HRB, CMH.

[27] Msg, Eckhardt to Westmoreland, 290305 Feb 67, sub: Relief of General Minh, 21st Div ARVN, COMUSMACV Message file, Westmoreland Papers, HRB, CMH.

[28] Interv, Davison, p. 28, Senior Officers Debriefing Program, Davison Papers, MHI. Msg, Wagstaff HOA 1830 to Abrams, 171510 Sep 71, sub: Security Assessment (see also Msg, Funkhauser (acting Senior Adviser, TRAC) HOA 1658 to Abrams, 231350 Aug 71, sub: Discussion With General Minh), both in Abrams Papers, HRB, CMH. Minh was the nephew of Thieu's ex-prime minister, Tran Van Huong.

[29] Msg, Davison HOA 0203 to Abrams, 030230 Feb 71, Abrams Papers, HRB, CMH.

[30] SACSA Evaluation Sheet, 1969; Memo, DA, DCSOPS, Bennett to Bolton, 31 Jan 70, sub: Assessment of BG Tho, ARVN. Both in SEAB, CMH.

[31] Msg, Davison HOA 0761 to Abrams, 150750 Apr 71, Abrams Papers, HRB, CMH.

[32] See Msg, Abrams MAC 05552 to Milloy, Vann, Wagstaff, and Cushman, 050546 Jun 71, Abrams Papers, HRB, CMH, asking for nominees to replace Hieu and their subsequent responses.

of his better field-grade officers and leaving his marginal division commanders and their staffs out of the action.

The IV Corps Tactical Zone seemed in better shape. South Vietnam's best general, Ngo Quang Truong, had taken command in August 1970 and his senior adviser, General Cushman, was satisfied with his performance.[33] After Thanh's death, General Tran Van Hai, the former ranger commander who headed the 44th Special Tactical Zone, had assumed control of all local cross-border operations, and Cushman felt that Hai's two subordinates, Col. Pham Duy Tat, who commanded the corps ranger group, and Col. Vu Quoc Gia, who headed the 4th Armored Brigade, were able leaders.[34] But as in the other corps, the division headquarters did little, and Truong and Hai used Gia's two cavalry squadrons, Tat's rangers, and some divisional regiments in small tasks forces along and across the border.[35]

If MACV or the corps senior advisers had any influence over the South Vietnamese command changes and internal reorganizations, it was indeed well hidden. The army had never been able to divorce itself from politics and military professionalism was still at a premium. Despite the trappings of democracy, military officers continued to rule the country, and family relationships, personal loyalties, and regional, school, and business ties still determined entree into the upper levels of the officer corps.[36] In October 1971 Thieu won the presidential election for his second term, receiving about 92 percent of the ballots cast. But there was no opposition. Thieu's candidacy went uncontested despite the best efforts of the U.S. Embassy to come up with an alternate. Both Ky and Duong Van Minh ("Big Minh"), the senior retired general who had led the coup against Diem back in 1963, dropped out of contention; and Truong Dinh Dzu, the popular "peace" candidate of the 1967 election, remained jailed, as did Deputy Tran Ngoc Chau, one of Thieu's prominent critics, despite his legislative immunity and the decision of the South Vietnamese supreme court overturning the results of his questionable trial.[37] No organized opposition groups appeared in the legislature or in the population at large, and the once militant An Quang Buddhist sect remained quiet. Thieu's close friend, General Khiem, continued to serve as prime minister, directing the central administration in Saigon, while the army kept its monopoly of political appointments at the corps, province, and district levels. The army's control of the political administration ensured political stability

[33] Msg, Cushman CTO 1022 to Abrams, 171440 Sep 71, Abrams Papers, HRB, CMH.
[34] Msg, Cushman CTO 1146 to Cowles, 260300 Oct 71, sub: Fortnightly Cambodian Report, Cushman Papers, MHI. For favorable comments on Hai, see Notes of 5 Apr 66, History file 5-D; MFR, Westmoreland, 15 Feb 68, sub: Meeting With President Thieu and General Vien, 1700, 14 February, History file 29–56. Both in Westmoreland Papers, HRB, CMH. For negative comments on Gia, see Evaluation, MACCORDS IV CTZ, February 1970, MICRO 3/1450, RG 334, WNRC.
[35] See also Msg, Cushman CTO 767 to Cowles, 191200 Jul 71, sub: Fortnightly Cambodian Report, Cushman Papers, MHI.
[36] For example, see Rpt, DOD, ISA (Vietnam Task Force), 27 Aug 71, sub: Daily Highlights of Vietnamization and Pacification: An Assessment of the RVNAF Officer Corps (based on a study prepared by the U.S. Embassy, Saigon), copy in SEAB, CMH.
[37] See case study folders on the Chau case, SEAB, CMH. In Bunker Papers, DS, the ambassador's regular messages to Washington show that embassy officials tried hard to keep Ky and Minh in the race, feeling they were weaker candidates who posed no threat to Thieu, and that they were wary of stronger civilians contenders like Chau and Dzu. Chau had been arrested, convicted, and sentenced for supposed liaisons with his brother, an enemy officer, between 1965 and 1968.

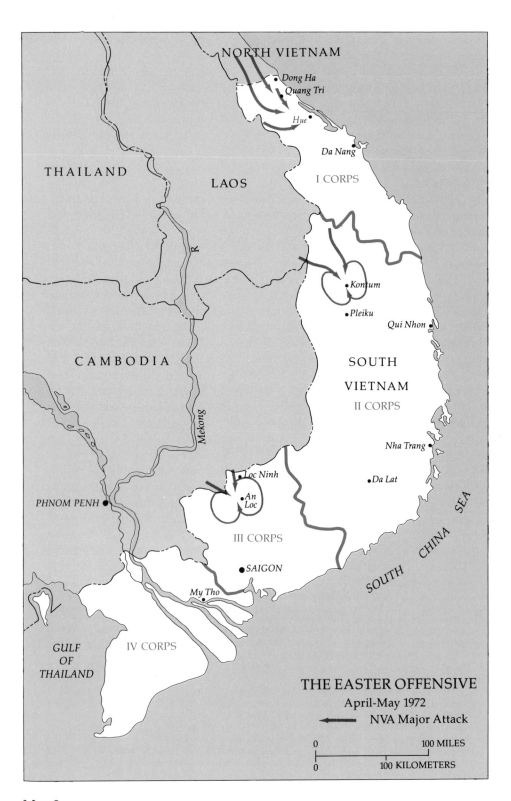

NORTH VIETNAM

Dong Ha
Quang Tri

Hue

Da Nang

I CORPS

THAILAND

LAOS

R

Kontum

Pleiku

Qui Nhon

CAMBODIA

SOUTH

VIETNAM

II CORPS

Nha Trang

Mekong

Da Lat

Loc Ninh

An
Loc

PHNOM PENH

III CORPS

SOUTH CHINA SEA

SAIGON

My Tho

GULF
OF
THAILAND

IV CORPS

THE EASTER OFFENSIVE
April-May 1972

◄──── NVA Major Attack

0   100 MILES
0   100 KILOMETERS

MAP 8

but did not translate into popular support for the regime, and the military voters, the so-called Khaki Party, were not a cohesive social or political force.[38] Meanwhile, despite the apparent consolidation of Thieu's power, widespread administrative corruption remained a major problem, and Ambassador Bunker spent much of his time urging Thieu to clamp down on the worst abuses, especially the large-scale narcotics and smuggling activities in Saigon.[39]

The Easter Offensive

It took almost one year for the North Vietnamese to rebuild their strength and launch their own major offensive. On 30 March 1972 three North Vietnamese Army divisions crossed the Demilitarized Zone in northern I Corps, overrunning advance bases of the new South Vietnamese 3d Division; three days later, three more enemy divisions headed south across the Cambodian border toward Saigon, surrounding positions held by the 5th Division in the III Corps Tactical Zone; and two weeks after that, two other divisions attacked the 22d Infantry Division in the Highlands, while smaller units struck at towns in Binh Dinh Province along the coast. Because of the timing of the attacks, they were quickly dubbed the "Easter offensive"(*Map 8*).[40]

The Easter offensive represented a radical departure from past North Vietnamese strategy and tactics. The attacks were characterized by massive coordinated assaults against South Vietnamese defensive positions with infantry, armor, and heavy artillery. The North Vietnamese committed almost their entire conventional combat force in an effort to seize selected population centers of South Vietnam for political purposes. In the northern zone, after weeks of heavy fighting, they overran both the South Vietnamese 3d Division and the 20th Tank Battalion and the city of Quang Tri; in the Highlands, they badly mauled the 22d Division and threatened to capture Kontum city; and above Saigon, they seized Loc Ninh, destroyed the 5th Division's 9th Regiment, and surrounded the remainder of the division at An Loc, about halfway down the road to Saigon. Following these powerful thrusts, the North Vietnamese tried to consolidate their gains while besieging An Loc and Kontum. Possession of either of these cities, along with Quang Tri, would greatly enhance the prestige and legitimacy of the Viet Cong, and the capture of An Loc would open the door to Saigon.

The lull that followed the initial drives gave the South Vietnamese time to recover. In the northern zone South Vietnamese ranger and marine units arrived to help the 1st Division defend Hue, while in the Highlands the bulk of the

---

[38] Intelligence Memorandum 2107/71, Directorate of Intelligence, CIA, 21 Dec 71, sub: South Vietnamese Political Stability Prospects in the Wake of President Thieu's Reelection, copy in SEAB, CMH.

[39] For example, see Msg, Bunker SGN 1515 to SecState, 311040 Jan 70, sub: Discussion With President Thieu January 30—Corruption; and especially Msg, Bunker SGN 6694 to SecState, 031159 May 71, sub: Drugs and Smuggling. Both in Bunker Papers, DS.

[40] For details, see USMACV, "Command History, 1972–1973," 2:annexes J, K, I, HRB, CMH; Ngo Quang Truong, *The Easter Offensive of 1972*, Indochina Monographs (Washington, D.C.: U.S. Army Center of Military History, 1980); and G. H. Turley, *The Easter Offensive, Vietnam, 1972* (Novato, Calif.: Presidio Press, 1985).

South Vietnamese 3d Infantry Division and 20th Tank Battalion Soldiers
positioned near the city of Quang Tri

airborne and the 23d Infantry Division reinforced Kontum. In the III Corps area the Joint General Staff threw both ranger and airborne units into An Loc and brought the 21st Division out of the Delta to protect Saigon. This risky move, successfully transferring an army division from one zone to another, was unprecedented and reflected Saigon's increasing anxiety over the outcome of the battle.

Heavy fighting continued throughout the summer. The South Vietnamese found their light M41 tanks outclassed by the Russian-made battle tanks employed by North Vietnam and had to rely on air support and short-range rockets and missiles to destroy enemy armor; the North Vietnamese, in turn, had to weather the terrific American air bombardments because of their decision to wage positional warfare. Defenders were often well entrenched and the attacking forces on both sides suffered heavy losses. In the end, stiff South Vietnamese defense at An Loc and Kontum; fierce counterattacks by airborne and marine units around Quang Tri; and heavy U.S. air support, including massive numbers of B–52 "arc light" bomber strikes, directed by the remaining field advisers slowly wore out Hanoi's forces. By mid-June they abandoned the sieges of Kontum city and An Loc, and on 16 September South Vietnamese troops finally reoccupied Quang Tri city, or what was left of it. The North Vietnamese had won only two district towns, Loc Ninh, near the Cambodian border, and Dong Ha, opposite the Demilitarized Zone, a small showing for the heavy prices paid.

Although public MACV reports lauded the bravery of the South Vietnamese defenders and stressed the overall failure of the offensive, they did not reveal just how close the outcome of the battle had been. Initially before the extent of the offensive had fully developed, General Abrams exuded confidence. On 24 April he reported that the morale of the South Vietnamese was high and their leadership good, even "outstanding" in the northern zone. Saigon had been able to move reserve units from zone to zone with ease, and its logistical system was operating effectively. Heavy U.S. support in the movement of troops, equipment, and supplies was necessary and the presence of American advisers directing air and naval fire support critical, but this had been expected.[41]

Seven days later the situation had changed drastically, and the MACV commander's optimism evaporated. In the north Dong Ha, Quang Tri city, and the 3d Division had fallen and Hue was in danger; in the Highlands the 22d Division had collapsed and Kontum city was under siege; and above Saigon the 5th Division was isolated at An Loc and dependent on air resupply. General Abrams claimed that the enemy had been hurt, but the extent of the damage was unknown. In his opinion, American air power, and not South Vietnamese arms, had caused most of his losses. Internal "dissension" in the two northern zones had crippled field operations and was beginning to become a factor in the critical III Corps area. Only the delta region was relatively quiet. The South Vietnamese had used up all of their reserves, and Abrams doubted whether they could hold Hue or Kontum. He warned Washington that "the senior [South Vietnamese] military leadership had begun to bend and in some cases to break, . . . [was] losing its will, and cannot be depended on to take the measures necessary to stand and fight."[42]

What had happened? What had caused the turnabout and Abrams' subsequent dismay? Was the enemy simply too powerful? Or too cunning? The answer lay in the South Vietnamese themselves. Saigon had once again failed to solve its leadership problems.[43] At Quang Tri, Giai and his troops had fought hard for nearly three weeks without respite. Reinforcements arrived, but the 3d Division commander found it almost impossible to control them. At one point he had nine brigades of ground combat troops under his authority, and, as in LAM SON 719, many of the reinforcing reserve units refused to take orders from the local commander, in this case Giai, making a coordinated defense difficult and a counterattack impossible. One of his regiments surrendered after only token resistance.[44] Lam, the corps commander and Giai's immediate superior, refused to lend a hand and rarely visited the front line, choosing to monitor the progress of the battle through periodic reports back in Da Nang. General Toan's new division of ranger and armored units had never been put together, for Toan

---

[41] Msg, Abrams MAC 03757 to Laird, 241111 Apr 72, sub: Personal Assessment of the Situation in RVN as of 24 April 1972, Abrams Papers, HRB, CMH.

[42] Quoted words from Msg, Abrams MAC 04021 to Laird, 011601 May 72, sub: Personal Assessment of the Situation in RVN as of 1 May 1972, Abrams Papers, HRB, CMH. See also Nixon, *Memoirs of Richard Nixon*, pp. 544–95.

[43] In Vien and Khuyen, *Reflections on the Vietnam War*, p. 105, the Vietnamese generals agree.

[44] Memo, Lt Col William C. Camper, Senior Adviser, 2d Regt, and Maj Joseph Brown, Jr., Deputy Senior Adviser, 2d Regt, to Senior Adviser, MACV Advisory Team 155, 3d Div, 13 Apr 72, sub: Surrender at Camp Carroll, SEAB, CMH.

himself was needed elsewhere. Also as in LAM SON 719, President Thieu began directing the field commanders personally from Saigon, contributing to the confusion and making an orderly withdrawal from Quang Tri impossible.[45] According to Maj. Gen. Frederick J. Kroesen, Jr., the I Corps senior adviser and commander of the First Regional Assistance Command, several of Giai's subordinate commanders threatened to abandoned their positions, with or without orders, and then went on to carry out their threat.[46] Order was restored only when President Thieu removed both Lam and his deputy, Hieu, and brought up General Truong to sort out the situation. Lam received a vague "special assistant" post to the Ministry of Defense; Hieu was out of work, but only for a while; and Giai, placed temporarily under arrest in Saigon, became the scapegoat for the debacle.

In the II Corps Tactical Zone Dzu and Vann finally got two new division commanders just before the attacks began, but neither commander had had much time to shape up his unit. The 22d Division was split between the Highlands and the coast, where it still had area security missions, and was more or less chopped up in detail. The division headquarters was overrun at Tan Canh. Dzu blamed himself for the initial defeats, lost heart, and was replaced by General Toan.[47] At the time that Abrams made his pessimistic report to Washington, Kontum city, key to the Highlands, was defended by a mixed bag of airborne, ranger, territorial, and armored forces, and one regiment of the 23d Division. Vann suggested putting Dzu's deputy, General Phong, in charge of the defense, but Phong's sister-in-law, the wife of Prime Minister Khiem, intervened and vetoed the job as too dangerous. Instead the task went to Col. Ly Tong Ba, the new commander of the 23d Division. Ba, like Giai in the north, found it impossible to control the nondivisional elements supposedly under his command, and Vann himself reported on 2 May that the airborne and ranger commanders at Kontum were "in almost open rebellion" and later, on the eighth, noted the start of several Montagnard mutinies. The situation was precarious. Realizing their survival depended on American support, South Vietnamese officers even threatened to forcibly prevent any advisory evacuation of Kontum. However, the North Vietnamese attackers took their time investing the city, giving the defenders a chance to reorganize. At Vann's suggestion, the corps commander replaced the airborne and ranger units with the other two regiments of the 23d, and with his entire division on line, Colonel Ba was able to hold out against repeated enemy attacks. Vann committed himself totally to the struggle, constantly pushing and cajoling South Vietnamese commanders and staffs into action and offering monetary rewards to any soldier who destroyed an enemy tank. But the hardworking American senior adviser did not live to see the outcome. Shuttling in and out of the battle areas almost daily, day and night, Vann, who had vowed to remain in Vietnam until the end, died on the night of 9–10 June, when his helicopter

[45] See Truong, *Easter Offensive*, pp. 31–47.
[46] Msg, Kroesen DNG 1144 to Abrams, 021325 May 72, sub: General Assessment MR I, Abrams Papers, HRB, CMH.
[47] See Msg, Vann PKU 0707 to Abrams, 070728 May 72, Abrams Papers, HRB, CMH. Toan, a Thieu supporter and commander of the 2d Division in the I Corps Tactical Zone for many years, had taken a staff job in January 1972; but because of the Easter offensive, he returned as corps operations officer for Lam and then Truong, and on 10 May took over the II Corps.

Col. Tran Van Nhut (left) and Maj. Gen. James F. Hollingsworth *(right) reflecting on the defense of An Loc with Robert Thompson, the British counterinsurgency expert*

crashed near Kontum. In Vann's death, the southern republic lost one of its staunchest supporters. Brig. Gen. Michael D. Healy replaced him, and the group was redesignated the Second Regional Assistance Command.[48]

In the III Corps Tactical Zone Maj. Gen. James F. Hollingsworth played the same role that Vann had in the Highlands. His advisers found Minh, the South Vietnamese corps commander, "wanting"; related that Hung, commanding the 5th Division, "choked" and "didn't do a damn thing"; and threatened (privately) to shoot his deputy division commander at An Loc.[49] Despite the presence of four divisions and strong ranger and airborne reinforcements, the South Vietnamese leaders failed to break the siege of An Loc by force of arms. As elsewhere, a stubborn defense and heavy U.S. Air Force support finally wore down the attackers and forced them to break off. But South Vietnamese losses were

[48] Quoted words from Msg, Vann PKU 0667 to Abrams, 020310 May 72, sub: Daily Evaluation, Abrams Papers, HRB, CMH. In same papers, see Msgs, Vann PKU 0713 to Abrams, 080313 May 72, and Vann PKU 0769 to Abrams, 141200 May 72, sub: AIK Fund To Reward Soldiers Who Destroy an Enemy Tank With an M72. See also Interv, author with Maj John R. Finch, Advisory Team 33, 23d Div (1972), 11 Jul 85, SEAB, CMH.

[49] See McGiffert Interv, 10 Oct 72, MACV History Branch Interviews, MHI; Interv, author with Lt Col Benjamin L. Abramowitz, Senior Adviser, 8th Regt, 5th Div (June 1971–April 1972), 26 Feb 76, SEAB, CMH.

heavy, and, for example, the 5th division's 8th Regiment, which had returned from Snoul in 1971 with five hundred men, walked out of An Loc with about two hundred.

According to Brig. Gen. John R. McGiffert II, Hollingsworth's deputy, An Loc would never have held out without the handful of American advisers directing the air strikes and shoring up the local leadership.[50] Some of the few South Vietnamese leaders to stand out were Col. Le Quang Luong, an airborne brigade commander, and Col. Tran Van Nhut, the local province chief and former highly rated protege of Do Cao Tri. Following the heavy fighting, Thieu replaced almost all of the division commanders in the zone: Hung of the 5th and General Nguyen Vinh Nghi of the 21st by airborne officers, and Tho of the 18th by Col. Le Minh Dao, another officer recommended by Vann in 1971. Later, in August, he also moved Nhut, who had performed well in the defense of An Loc, up to the northern zone to command the 2d Division, which had suddenly fallen apart in the Que Son Valley under General Hiep. But, as in the past, the displaced commanders continued to serve in key positions. Hung moved up to be deputy III Corps commander; Tho took over the Da Lat Military Academy; and Nghi became the new IV Corps commander, replacing Truong when he went north. In addition, General Minh remained in overall command of the zone despite continued American insistence that he be replaced.[51] A large turnover among regimental and battalion commanders also occurred, but few if any Americans could say whether the end results were positive or negative.[52]

General Abrams never doubted the cause of all these difficulties—poor South Vietnamese military leadership. He passed this judgment directly to President Thieu, Ambassador Bunker, and Defense Secretary Laird, clearly discouraged and feeling that his power to rectify the situation was limited.[53] Initially, he had insisted that certain sophisticated weapons arriving from the United States dur-

---

[50] McGiffert Interv, 10 Oct 72, MACV History Branch Interviews, MHI.

[51] On key South Vietnamese leaders, see South Vietnamese officer dossiers and also comments of Donald P. Gregg in copy of Rpt, CIA, 6 May 72, sub: MR 3 Monthly Operations Report, April 1972. All in SEAB, CMH. Nghi had actually left prior to the deployment of the 21st Division in the fighting along Route 13. Col. Tran Quoc Lich took over the 5th and General Tu kept his command of the 25th; however, Thieu dismissed both in 1973, according to Vien (*Leadership*, p. 213), for "corruption involving 'ghost and ornamental soldiers,' bribery for promotions, contribution of money to unit commanders, and illicit use of military vehicles and construction materials." Tu and Lich were "subsequently arrested and prosecuted by a military court." Thieu finally replaced Minh as III Corps commander in August 1973 with General Thuan, the president's old ally who had led the 5th Division from 1965 to 1969 despite continuous American efforts to bring about his relief for incompetence; Le Nguyen Vy, who had done well in the U.S. 1st Infantry Division's *Dong Tien* operation, but poorly as the deputy division commander at An Loc, took over the 5th at about the same time; and General Hiep spent a few months at the National Defense College in Saigon, before heading the South Vietnamese delegation to the Joint Military Commission from 1973 to 1975. On Minh, see Msg, Bunker to Kissinger, 9 Oct 72, Presidential Message file, Bunker Papers, DS, describing Minh as a problem "we have had . . . for a long time and have repeatedly brought to Thieu's attention."

[52] For mixed opinions on the turnover, see Transmittal Ltr, DAAG, 12 Apr 73, sub: Senior Officer Debriefing Reports; Senior Advisor, ARVN, 1st, 3rd, 5th, 9th, 25th and 18th Infantry Divisions, Period Ending February 1973, SEAB, CMH.

[53] Msg, Abrams MAC 04039 to Laird, 020443 May 72, Abrams Papers, HRB, CMH, which details his meeting with Bunker and Thieu; Kissinger, *White House Years*, pp. 1111–12. In SEAB, CMH, see also Potts Interv, 12 Apr 84; Anderson Interv, 23 Jun 83; Ellis Interv, 29 Jun 83, and Interv, author with Gen William B. Rosson (hereafter cited as Rosson Interv), former DEPCOMUSMACV, 1969–70, 16 Mar 84, all of which attest to Abrams' private discouragement.

ing the battles be given only to those troops that had performed well in combat, and specifically excluded some of the airborne units, but a few days later agreed to defer the matter to the South Vietnamese commanders.[54] After all, it was their war from now on. When the Vice-President Spiro Agnew, visiting South Vietnam in mid-May, asked him about the reportedly high number of "inadequate" South Vietnamese general officers, Abrams claimed that Thieu had changed commanders "in each case where inadequate performance had been brought to his attention" and that the real problem was the lack of experienced leaders to promote.[55] But, in fact, he was still hesitant to tell the South Vietnamese who to fire and hire. Frustrated and dissatisfied with South Vietnamese military leadership, Abrams could only shrug his shoulders to General Rosson when the subject came up, saying, "We've done what we can."[56]

During the rest of 1972 Thieu did what he could to improve military leadership, shuffling around his senior commanders and, in November, creating twenty-nine new generals.[57] He also cashiered three remaining stalwarts: Nguyen Van Vy, minister of defense since 1967; Du Quoc Dong, the airborne commander since September 1964; and Le Nguyen Khang, the marine corps commander since February 1964. In the case of Vy, Thieu was forced to take action against him, and seven other officers, over a corruption scandal involving the mandatory Soldiers Saving Fund.[58] He replaced him with Khiem, who also continued to serve as prime minister. The other two generals had been political, rather than combat, officers. Dong, the long-term Thieu associate, moved over to head the Capital Military District, while Khang received a nebulous "special assistant" post under Vien on the Joint General Staff. Of the two, Americans considered Khang the better commander, but his past alliance with Ky proved a major liability. Luong, who had performed well during the siege of An Loc, took over the Airborne Division and General Bai The Lan, an experienced marine officer, assumed command of the marine component. By this time most American military advisers appreciated that good fighters were not necessarily good administrators. Some made better province chiefs than combat commanders; others, who had perhaps "burned out" after long years in combat units, were due for stints at training centers, schools, or high-level staffs. Given the cultural heritage of Vietnam, and the confused social and political milieu of the times, recurrent instances of corruption were not necessarily signs of poor military or administrative ability. In any case, MACV influence in these matters continued to be minimal. Americans remained unhappy with South Vietnamese military lead-

[54] Msg, Abrams MAC 04267 to McCaffrey and Kroesen, 081002 May 72, sub: AT Weapons Systems; Msg, Abrams MAC 04384 to Kroesen, 110705 May 72. Both in Abrams Papers, HRB, CMH.
[55] Msg, Abrams MAC 04600 to Agnew, 171034 May 72, sub: MEMCON of Meeting at TSN Base Operations VIP Lounge, Abrams Papers, HRB, CMH.
[56] Rosson Interv, 16 Mar 84, SEAB, CMH.
[57] Msg, AmEmbassy SGN 16147 to SecState, 1410027 Nov 72, sub: Thieu Selects Generals Promoted; Two New Division Commanders Named, SEAB. For specific changes, see USMACV, "Command History, 1971," 1:VIII–27 to VIII–29, and "1972–1973," 1:C–25 to C–28, HRB; and South Vietnamese officer dossiers, SEAB. All in CMH.
[58] The Soldiers Saving Fund was a pension fund supported by automatic deductions from military paychecks. See Memo, OSD, Downing to Marshall, 29 Sep 72, sub: The Future of the Advisory Effort in SVN, SEAB, CMH.

ership, but had to be satisfied with Vietnamese promises to clean house once the military situation was in hand.[59]

U.S. leaders in Washington seemed satisfied with the situation and asked only how they could help. To bolster the "will and backbone" of the South Vietnamese, Defense Secretary Laird promised to send a special Department of Defense logistics team "as visible and positive evidence" of continued U.S. support and urged General Abrams to pass the message that Washington would not let Saigon down in this area.[60] General Palmer, now the Army vice chief of staff, was more specific and suggested immediate replacement of all South Vietnamese light M41 tanks with the larger M48s, equipping the infantry with the new TOW antitank missiles, and sending counterbattery and helicopter advisers and technicians.[61] General Abrams was more amenable to such requests for the South Vietnamese than he had been in the past, and so the vast materiel programs to replace their lost or damaged supplies and equipment and also to fill in perceived gaps in their weapons and capabilities began in earnest (see Chapter 24). However, the MACV commander's superiors were neither naive nor complacent, and Secretary Laird himself reminded President Nixon that recent South Vietnamese problems on the battlefield "were not due to shortcomings in weapons or organization, but rather were caused by deficiencies in leadership and will."[62]

South Vietnamese success in repulsing the offensive, and in quickly rebuilding and reequipping badly damaged forces, was a surprise to many American advisers and to the North Vietnamese as well. But postmortems of the offensive raised many questions. How critical was the role of U.S. air power? What sort of logistics or air support could be expected from the United States in the future? Would South Vietnamese military strategy and dispositions remain essentially defensive or, with the North Vietnamese forces now shattered, would they move across the border? An extensive appraisal done by a special Department of Defense task force in mid-1972 answered some of these questions. The final report emphasized two elements: the failure of the enemy Easter offensive to disrupt any aspects of the Vietnamization process, and the vigor and effectiveness shown by the South Vietnamese military forces. What alarmed the task force was the complete absence of any long-range military planning by either the Joint General Staff or MACV. Military commands and staffs at all levels were completely absorbed in short-range operational plans to block local enemy offensives and regain parcels of lost territory; no one was considering the ramifications of a change in U.S. administration or a congressional decision to cut off assistance to

---

[59] See discussion in Msg, Bunker SGN 10678 to SecState, 19 Jul 72, Bunker Papers, DS.

[60] Msg, SecDef OSD 04321 to Bunker and Abrams, 031617 May 72, sub: Bolstering GVN and RVNAF Leadership, Abrams Papers, HRB, CMH.

[61] Msg, McCaffrey ARV 1166 to Abrams, 050100 May 72 (relaying Palmer proposals), and reply in Msg, Abrams MAC 04371 to McCaffrey, 101725 May 72, sub: Operational Assistance. Both in Abrams Papers, HRB, CMH.

[62] Memo, Laird to President, 12 Jun 72, sub: Military Assistance to the RVN. The sentiment was also conveyed to Ambassador Bui Diem in Memo of Conversation, 8 Jun 72, sub: Vietnamese Ambassador Diem's Farewell Call on Secretary Laird (11:20–12:15, 2 Jun 72), prepared by Dennis J. Doolin and G. Warren Nutter. Both in SEAB, CMH. Nutter was the assistant secretary of defense for international security affairs.

Saigon. Continued American support to make up the difference between South Vietnam's massive financial needs and her limited resources was an "explicit assumption" by everyone. Other serious problems also remained. Corruption, the report stated, was "pervasive" and "grossly exceeds traditional oriental patterns"; corrupt, ineffective leaders were "still moved over and up to even more rewarding opportunities for corruption." Although applauding the recent changes in corps and division commanders, the task force concluded that "the ability of US personnel to identify real [South Vietnamese] leaders and to influence their placement had not markedly improved." The investigators predicted continued improvements over the next six months, but were worried about Saigon's long-term prospects. In their opinion, continued social injustice, open political chicanery, and economic dependence on the United States would ultimately give the people little to fight for against an opponent whose determination appeared unshaken.[63]

In August Defense Secretary Laird asked the Joint Chiefs of Staff to review the status of the advisory effort. Despite the critical role of the advisers in repelling the recent North Vietnamese offensive, the secretary wanted their number reduced as quickly as possible. Replying in early October, the Joint Chiefs pointed out not only the temporary shift in the field advisory effort from management to tactical assistance but also the constant readjustments that MACV had made to provide special teams to beleaguered South Vietnamese units, as well as training teams for badly damaged formations and those receiving new Project ENHANCE equipment. The reply also noted that MACV was phasing down advisory teams assigned to tactical units faster than those supporting provinces and districts, but discerned no trends in those units and headquarters where advisory teams had been phased out. It underlined the continued need for battalion-level advisers in the marine and airborne forces, units that were bearing the brunt of the remaining fighting, and also the general weakness of all South Vietnamese forces in conventional ground tactics. Although the Joint Chiefs were reticent to recommend any specific cutbacks, they highlighted the scheduled elimination of about 1,700 more advisory positions; the reduction in the average size of the division advisory teams from 36 to 15; the retention of advisers throughout the revolutionary development support system (that is, down to the district level); the heavy training work load of the Air Force Advisory Group, especially after a 50-percent strength reduction in 1972; and the long-term need for advisory assistance in the area of logistics. In a separate internal study Defense Department planners recommended a 2,500-man advisory force for 1973, including 380 tactical advisers (20 per division and 50 each for the Air Force and Navy), 500 staff advisers (20 per corps, 100 each for the Air Force and Navy, and 220 for the South Vietnamese Joint General Staff), and over 1,600 for the revolutionary development support effort. They thus projected an even smaller role for the Army

---

[63] Rpt, Col Donald S. Marshall and Col David E. Farnham, n.d., sub: Appraisal of the Situation in Vietnam, SEAB, CMH. Marshall and Farnham visited South Vietnam between 10 June and 20 July 1972, during which time they conducted extensive interviews with key MACV, American embassy, and U.S. field advisory personnel.

ground combat advisers and a renewed emphasis on territorial security and staff management.[64]

Ceasefire

The ceasefire agreement of 23 January 1973 marked an end to the American policy of Vietnamization. The agreement specified the complete withdrawal of all American military forces from South Vietnam, including advisers, and the cessation of all U.S. military actions in support of Saigon. The North Vietnamese, in turn, agreed to a ceasefire in place, the return of American prisoners of war, and an end to infiltration into the South. The accord caught many American generals by surprise, including General Abrams, the new Army chief of staff,[65] who had felt that the United States would end up with some type of permanent ground and air commitment similar to that in South Korea.[66] Instead, there was to be no residual support force, not even an advisory mission, and, in theory, the Viet Cong and Saigon governments were to settle their political differences at some later date. Whether the agreement was only a device to ease the disengagement of the United States from Southeast Asia, or whether it gave the Vietnamese a realistic opportunity to settle their own differences, remains an open question.[67]

Henry Kissinger, who led the American negotiating team in Paris, saw a major breakthrough in the long, arduous, and often bizarre process on 8 October 1972. After a series of fruitless morning and afternoon sessions, Le Duc Tho, Hanoi's chief representative, suddenly suggested separating the military and political aspects of the war and reaching an accord to end the fighting as soon as possible. The North Vietnamese dropped their objections to continued American military aid to Saigon and agreed to cease their own infiltration of troops into the South. In the ensuing days the two parties worked out the details of the agreement, producing a draft on the twelfth. At the same time Kissinger informed Ambassador Bunker what was in the works and urged that Saigon try to hold on to as much territory as possible.[68]

Nixon, Haig, Laird, and Abrams endorsed the agreement, but both Nixon and Bunker felt that Thieu's acquiescence might be difficult. The Vietnamese

---

[64] Memo, Laird to Chairman, JCS, 26 Aug 72, sub: US Advisors in the Republic of Vietnam; Memo, JCSM–445–72 [to SecDef], 6 Oct 72, sub: US Adviser in the RVN; Memo, Maj Downing, Office of the SecDef, to Col Marshall, 29 Sep 72, sub: The Future of the Advisory Effort in SVN. All in SEAB, CMH.

[65] Abrams stepped down as MACV commander on 28 June 1972 to replace Westmoreland as the Army chief of staff, and the U.S. Senate confirmed the appointment on 12 October.

[66] Rosson Interv, 16 May 84, SEAB, CMH. Rosson was the U.S. Army Pacific component commander at the time.

[67] The subject is treated in almost all of the Vietnamese-authored Indochina Monographs. A good introduction to the evolution of the peace talks is Allan E. Goodman's *The Lost Peace: America's Search for a Negotiated Settlement of the Vietnam War* (Stanford, Calif.: Hoover Institution Press, 1978).

[68] For a day-by-day treatment, see Kissinger, *White House Years*, pp. 1342–58; Nixon, *Memoirs of Richard Nixon*, pp. 690–707.

chief of state had recently rejected all proposals that allowed North Vietnamese troops to remain on South Vietnamese soil and had given no indication that his position had changed. In consultations between Kissinger, Bunker, and Abrams in Saigon during 19–23 October, this proved to be the case. Despite Kissinger's assurance of American military intervention should North Vietnam violate the agreement, and despite Abrams' presentation of the ENHANCE PLUS military equipment delivery program, Thieu remained intransigent. A subsequent meeting between Haig and the Vietnamese president proved equally unproductive. Thieu contended that American estimates placing North Vietnamese military strength in the South at 140,000 were "imaginary and misleading" and suggested that the actual figure was not less than 300,000.[69] Kissinger, however, determined that the basic problem was Thieu's lack of confidence in his own military forces, together with his psychological dependence on American assistance, and Bunker reported that most of the other Vietnamese military and civilian leaders did not share Thieu's pessimism.[70]

On 15 November Nixon, having brought his second presidential election campaign to a successful conclusion, dealt with Thieu directly. Although agreeing to have Kissinger suggest minor changes in the draft text to Hanoi, he felt that substantive changes were unnecessary. The critical factor, he told Thieu, was "our own firm determination to see to it that the agreement works and our vigilance with respect to the prospect of its violation." "It is unrealistic," he went on, "to assume that we will be able to secure the absolute assurances which you would hope to have on the [NVA] troop issue." "Far more important than what we say in the agreement," Nixon held, "is what we do in the event the enemy renews its aggression." Should that occur, the American president gave Thieu his "absolute assurance that . . . it is my intention to take swift and severe retaliatory action." But he warned the South Vietnamese leader that Washington's ability to take such action depended on the support of Congress and the American public. If Saigon failed to support the draft peace agreement and appeared "as the obstacle to a peace which American public opinion universally desires," then, he concluded, "I would, with great reluctance, be forced to consider other [unilateral] alternatives." Again he gave Thieu his "personal assurances that the United States will react *very* strongly and rapidly to any violation of the agreement."[71]

Several days later, on the eve of the resumption of the Paris talks, Nixon sent a series of even more strongly worded messages to Saigon through Ambassador Bunker. Reiterating his promise "to take massive action against North Viet-Nam in the event they break the agreement," Nixon declared that "the time for deci-

---

[69] Quoted words from Msg, Bunker to Kissinger, 3 Nov 72. For MACV estimates, see Memo, Weyand to Bunker, sub: Comparison of MACV and JGS Enemy Strength Estimates, which were essentially the same, although Bunker's COMUSMACV Fact Sheet, circa December 1972, sub: Enemy and RVNAF Force Strength, shows that MACV estimated that all North Vietnamese Army units were at half strength and that Hanoi probably could have brought them up to their full complement in a short period of time. All documents in Bunker Papers, DS.

[70] Kissinger, *White House Years*, p. 1375; Msg, Bunker SGN 0280 to Kissinger, 260615 Nov 72, Bunker Papers, DS. Kissinger also pointed out that Thieu's stand enhanced his own bargaining position (pp. 1379–80).

[71] Ltr, Nixon to Thieu, 15 Nov 72, Bunker Papers, DS.

President Richard M. Nixon (left) and Henry A. Kissinger *(right) conferring on the ceasefire negotiations*

sion has come" and Thieu must now decide, "whether he trusts me and signs what I have determined is the best agreement we can get or we have to go it alone. . . ." The president explained that "even with [the] massive mandate I personally received in the election," Congress would not support a continuation of the war in the light of Hanoi's recent peace offers. The leading American senators who still strongly supported the administration's policy on Vietnam "were not only unanimous but vehement in stating their conclusion that, if Saigon is the only roadblock for reaching agreement on this basis, they will personally lead the fight when the new Congress reconvenes on January 3 to cut off all military and economic assistance to Saigon." A continuation of the war in its present form was impossible, he emphasized, explaining that "the door has been slammed shut hard and fast by the long time supporters of my policies in Viet-Nam in the House and Senate who control the purse strings." Nixon warned that further delays on Thieu's part were dangerous and gravely damaged the administration's ability to support him, instructing Kissinger to "tell him that the fat is on the fire" and "it is time to fish or cut bait." In the end, Thieu had no option but to comply.[72]

---

[72] Msg, Kissinger WHS 2257 to Bunker, 260510 Nov 72, Bunker Papers, DS, which repeated two memos from Nixon to Kissinger on the matter and Nixon's instructions to pass both memos to Thieu.

492

The Last Assessment

Ironically, it was the North Vietnamese who proved recalcitrant when talks resumed in late November 1972, signing the agreement only after one of the most intensive American air offensives of the war. Meanwhile, in Vietnam, intermittent fighting continued. But neither MACV nor the Joint General Staff seriously considered military operations into Laos or North Vietnam after LAM SON 719. Such excursions appeared too ambitious and the specter of defeat too alarming. After the dust of the Easter offensive had begun to settle, American and South Vietnamese commands focused their attention on the continued U.S. withdrawal, the final buildup of the South Vietnamese military forces, and the prospects of a ceasefire in place. From October 1972 to January 1973 military activity degenerated into small-scale actions as each side sought to station troops inside the "territory" of the other. The South Vietnamese armed forces, although temporarily stronger than those of North Vietnam, tried to occupy and hold as much ground as possible, and Saigon's defensive strategy prevented them from undertaking anything more ambitious. Strategically, the initiative on the ground war still belonged to the enemy.

In a final assessment of the military situation in Vietnam General Weyand, the last MACV commander, was cautious.[73] He declared Saigon's military forces "capable of defending the South Vietnamese from any but a major power supported attack of massive proportions." The North Vietnamese, he held, had been forced to make "a reassessment . . . of their . . . reliance on force as the primary means to political ends"; the Saigon regime was a "visible, viable alternative to the political system and way of life sponsored by Hanoi"; and current South Vietnamese attitudes "hold promise of an eventual end to the pervasive corruption that undermines governmental effectiveness. . . ." If the ceasefire provisions were honored, Weyand felt that the armed conflict would gradually fade away. If not, he predicted that "we will be faced with the difficult decision of US reinvolvement and the inevitable questioning of the validity of our past involvement."

Weyand expected that enemy troops would remain in the South for what he called a "mid-term period," 1974 to 1978, and would concentrate in the northern I Corps Tactical Zone and the border areas above Saigon. Noting the large-scale movement of enemy tanks, artillery, air defense weapons, and troop replacements into South Vietnam, he felt that North Vietnam would be capable of launching a major offensive in the I and III Corps areas by 1974. South Vietnamese ability to meet this threat hinged on Thieu's skill in attracting domestic and international support, reducing internal corruption, and improving military leadership, as well as on "the continuation of adequate levels of U.S. military and economic assistance."

To improve South Vietnamese military capabilities Weyand recommended the continued use of ranger forces on the borders, strengthening them whenever possible, and also better employment and training of the corps armored bri-

---

[73] Unless otherwise stated, the following discussion is based on Msg, COMUSMACV MAC 39933 to JCS, 070930 Mar 73, sub: Assessment of RVNAF, SEAB, CMH. All quotations are from this source.

gades. South Vietnamese artillery was "outgunned" by the longer-range North Vietnamese pieces, and South Vietnamese air power would have to make up for this grave deficiency.[74] He deemed the South Vietnamese Air Force able to supply adequate fire support, tactical and strategic mobility, air defense, and air reconnaissance if it could maintain its equipment without direct American assistance. Weyand also discussed Vietnamese capabilities in administration, training, communications, logistics, and intelligence, but saved his greatest concern for the area of maintenance, feeling that the Vietnamese still needed to be convinced that it "deserves top and unrelenting priority." Despite years of advice and assistance, and the vast logistical materiel support programs recently comp-

General Frederick C. Weyand

leted, he was disappointed, noting that "few ARVN units have an adequate maintenance program" and that "a lack of trained personnel at all levels" was still evident. Because of a "chronic" shortage of spare parts, unit requisitioning procedures had become "haphazard, unsupervised and, as a result, uncertain and unreliable," leading to "extensive, uncontrolled cannibalization at all levels...." What had happened since Abrams' more optimistic report on South Vietnamese logistics in April 1971 is difficult to say.

On the key question of South Vietnamese strategic mobility, the interzone movement of locally recruited units, the answer was the same. The South Vietnamese possessed the sea- and airlift capabilities to move major units, and any problems in this regard had been due "to inadequate leadership, poor discipline or general combat effectiveness of the unit prior to movement." The "mobility question" revolved around "whether the key leader of the unit being deployed can see a clear cut need for such a deployment." If a "serious threat either to his nation or his home . . . can be easily seen . . . and can be easily communicated by the leader to his subordinates," Weyand believed that troop movements into combat areas would become more routine and hoped that, with the American withdrawal, "RVNAF leadership will perceive a more 'personal' threat and will be more inclined to adjust forces country wide to meet changing threats."

In the area of leadership Weyand considered the four corps commanders "patriotic, well motivated, competent, and reasonably considerate of the welfare

---

[74] The U.S.-supplied 175-mm. pieces were too inaccurate and slow firing to combat the North Vietnamese Army's 122-mm. and 130-mm. guns effectively, and counter-battery radars had not worked well.

of their men," but felt that the combined burdens of political and military responsibilities overtaxed their time and abilities. At the division level, commanders were "generally well grounded in fundamental tactics and fully capable of performing their assigned mission," but the quality of their staffs and subordinate commanders "varies widely"; most failed to understand "the need for improved maintenance and logistics discipline." Province and district leadership also varied considerably, but here he noted that Saigon was making an ever-increasing number of assignments on the basis of demonstrated administrative and military ability rather than on political considerations.

Weyand was thus hopeful and wary at the same time. In his eyes much depended on Thieu and his senior military leaders. Major problem areas, such as maintenance and tactical mobility, were directly dependent on South Vietnamese leadership. They had the means to defend themselves, but had they the will?

Weyand chose not to elaborate on Saigon's obvious continued need for American assistance, a political question over which he had little say or influence. Significantly, he also omitted any discussion of strategy, noting only that South Vietnamese ground forces "are totally committed and deployed to meet the enemy threat with no available reserve." For the time being, their emphasis on territorial defense, a carryover of the old pacification strategy, made it impossible for the South Vietnamese to adopt a more offensive military posture. Technically, Saigon's ground forces were highly mobile, but as long as the South Vietnamese leaders deployed them in area security missions throughout the country, their combat power could not be concentrated for conventional battles. In short, they were no more mobile than they had been in 1965 and were thus vulnerable to the military and psychological disabilities of fighting a static defensive war.

The ceasefire began at 8 o'clock Sunday, 28 January 1973, and the war ground to at least a temporary halt. In the sixty days that followed, slightly over 58,000 foreign troops departed South Vietnam, including about 23,000 Americans, 25,000 Koreans, and a few hundred assorted Thais, Filipinos, and Nationalist Chinese. Their exodus left about 550,000 South Vietnamese regulars and another 525,000 territorials to face a regular North Vietnamese Army that Americans estimated at 500,000–600,000 troops, of which about 220,000 were in South Vietnam and the rest close by. The final U.S. withdrawals were timed to match the release of American prisoners of war by North Vietnam. MACV headquarters dissolved on 29 March, and three new agencies took over its remaining functions. Largest was the U.S. Support Activities Group, a new joint command under General John W. Vogt, Jr. (USAF), located at Nakhon Phanom Air Base in Thailand. The mission of the group was to plan for the possible resumption of the air war in Southeast Asia and to maintain liaison with both the South Vietnamese Air Force and nearby U.S. air combat units. Second was the U.S. Defense Attache Office in Saigon under Maj. Gen. John E. Murray. Operating from the capital and field locations, the office was to monitor South Vietnamese military activities, providing technical assistance in such areas as communications and intelligence but, in accordance with the ceasefire agreement, giving no advice on military operations or tactics. Third was the U.S. delegation to the Four-Party Joint Military Commission, whose job it was to assist in implementing the ceasefire.[75] U.S. Army advice and assistance to South Vietnam thus would continue, but in a much more remote and indirect manner. With the ceasefire, another stage in the long struggle for Southeast Asia ended and a new one began.

[75] USMACV, "Command History, 1972–1973," 2:annexes G and H, HRB, CMH; William E. LeGro, *Vietnam from Cease-Fire to Capitulation* (Washington, D.C.: Government Printing Office, 1981), pp. 18–19 and 30–31; Nguyen Duy Hinh, *Vietnamization and the Cease-Fire*, Indochina Monographs (Washington, D.C.: U.S. Army Center of Military History, 1980). For a detailed political treatment, see Walter Scott Dillard, *Sixty Days to Peace: Implementing the Paris Peace Accords, Vietnam 1973* (Washington, D.C.: National Defense University, 1982).

26

Trojan Horses

What can be said about the American advisory effort in South Vietnam? Beginning almost unnoticed with a few hundred individuals in 1954, it had grown to about ten thousand a decade or so later, representing the largest such commitment in the history of warfare. By the end of the U.S. involvement in 1973 countless American military personnel had spent endless hours studying, discussing, and administering to the various components of the South Vietnamese armed forces. Vast quantities of war materiel had been injected to make Saigon's military machine stronger, and a multitude of regular American combat units had come to give it the respite needed to heal and to grow. But how had the patient fared? What was the prognosis? Had it been merely a matter of physical healing and increasing the strength of its body, or was there a mental health problem that could not be cured by greater physical fitness alone? Or, as many critics of the war seemed to suggest, was the patient some sort of laboratory freak, only temporarily animated by the marvels of modern military technology and fated to collapse when disconnected from its American power source? Sooner or later the questions to be asked boiled down to the very nature of warfare and the relationship of numbers and weaponry with the old intangibles of leadership, will, and purpose.

Roles and Missions

American leaders made several critical decisions in 1965 that conditioned the entire war in Vietnam. All had a direct impact on the development of the South Vietnamese armed forces as well as on the U.S. advisory effort. One was the decision to limit the ground war to the borders of South Vietnam. This policy forced American and South Vietnamese military leaders to fight a defensive war, leaving the strategic initiative on the ground to the Viet Cong and North Vietnamese. Another was the decision to wage a war of manpower attrition against Hanoi. Although the strategy of attrition appeared to complement the strategy of pacification, U.S. officials tended to regard the former as a separate endeavor, believing that vastly superior American firepower would force the North to cease its support of the southern insurgency. The decision to retain separate American and South Vietnamese military chains of command was also crucial. Made by the U.S. military commander in South Vietnam for local political reasons, it greatly complicated the tactical operations of the various allied combat units in Vietnam and made it impossible to remedy inherent weaknesses in the existing advisory system.

Several of these decisions merely continued existing policies that had evolved prior to the commitment of American ground combat troops. Restricting the ground war to South Vietnam kept allied military objectives limited. The United States never seriously considered expanding the battlefield into Laos, Cambodia, or North Vietnam for fear of turning the conflict into a major war. In a manner of speaking, Hanoi reciprocated by refusing to acknowledge the presence of its troops in the South. Almost as if returning the favor, American officials shied away from a combined command, preferring to maintain the illusion that U.S. troops were merely assisting Saigon on a temporary basis.

Reserving the attrition mission for American combat units had the effect of relegating almost the entire South Vietnamese armed forces to static security missions. The existence of two military commands, each pursuing different strategies and each with different roles and missions, also made it easier for American military leaders and their superiors to regard both pacification and the advisory effort as secondary activities and the pursuit of the strategy of attrition as the major task. The ensuring confusion between the two strategies was reflected throughout the advisory effort, especially in the tactical advisory teams and the Special Forces detachments. In the South Vietnamese army, military commanders were also unable to sort out their political and military responsibilities, often to the detriment of both. The nature of the war, the absence of a strong political administration in Saigon, and the relative inexperience of the South Vietnamese officer corps in dealing with political, social, and economic problems greatly exacerbated the situation. American efforts to end these problems by creating a strong popular government in the South, separating the military and political responsibilities of the South Vietnamese generals, and bringing the South Vietnamese armed forces back into the more conventional war effort were ultimately unsuccessful.

Political leaders in Washington clearly made the decision to Vietnamize the war. Begun in 1969, Vietnamization was not a strategy for fighting or winning the war, or even for achieving America's limited objectives in South Vietnam. At best, it was a political strategy for continuing U.S. support for a domestically unpopular conflict and, at worst, a face-saving abandonment of a commitment that American leaders felt they could or should no longer honor.

The individual views of both American and South Vietnamese leaders on Vietnamization vary greatly. Addressing a military audience in 1980, General Stilwell declared that "mainly we were looking for a quick exit."[1] In his memoirs General Westmoreland notes only "the mood of the American people and the Congress" and President Nixon's ensuing conclusion "that if he could bring the

---

[1] Richard G. Stilwell, "Commentary: A Soldier's Viewpoint," in *The American Military and the Far East: Proceedings of the Ninth Military History Symposium, U.S.A.F. Academy, 1–3 October 1980* (Washington D.C.: U.S. Air Force Academy, 1980), p. 68.

prisoners of war home, he could end the American involvement."[2] In Vietnam Abrams' evaluations of the policy appeared to depend greatly on the changing military situation, and, although worried, he rarely speculated on its long-term implications. Lt. Gen. Ralph E. Haines, the U.S. Army component commander in the Pacific (1968–70), called Vietnamization "a race against time," adding that, "although each passing day works in our favor," he feared "that we might give away the farm precipitiously."[3] Abrams probably would have agreed. Kissinger also referred to Vietnamization as "a race," and both he and Nixon considered the withdrawals to be an "irreversible" process.[4]

The South Vietnamese generals, for their part, emphasized that Vietnamization never meant an end to their need for American financial and materiel assistance and that the continuation of extensive military aid was originally an integral part of the program.[5] Several felt that "U.S. leaders had imposed American strategic limitations upon Saigon," and ultimately ensured the defeat of its army.[6] Vien, at the time, believed that more was necessary. He wanted more heavy equipment and proposed invading the southern portion of North Vietnam; but, like Westmoreland, he never had any hope that Washington would support such an operation.[7] In Saigon neither MACV nor the Joint General Staff ever came up with any new military strategy, both preferring to stay with what they were familiar, and in Washington civilian leaders continued their almost total abdication of their military responsibilities. Although suggestions on military operations, tactics, and techniques were plentiful in the U.S. capital, few political leaders in positions of authority were willing to make a hard reappraisal of U.S. objectives in Southeast Asia or issue more useful guidelines to their military subordinates.[8]

The ceasefire agreement reached at the end of 1972 was the last major decision affecting the advisory effort. It, too, was a political decision made by America's political leaders over the objections of their military subordinates who, nonetheless, expected it at the same time. The day it went into effect was the day Vietnamization ended, because it called for the termination of all direct military support to Saigon. Although its ramifications are beyond the scope of this work, several significant factors relating to its implementation were immediately evident. None of the U.S. military commands or civilian agencies had adequately prepared the Vietnamese for such an eventuality. Until the end, Saigon remained

[2] Westmoreland, *Soldier Reports*, p. 395.

[3] Ltr, Haines to Lt Gen Melvin Zais, CG, XXIV Corps, circa 1969–70, Ralph E. Haines Papers, MHI.

[4] Kissinger, *White House Years*, pp. 272; Nixon, *Memoirs of Richard Nixon*, p. 392.

[5] For example, Hinh, *Vietnamization and the Cease-Fire*, pp. 184–86 and 190–91.

[6] Lung, *Strategy and Tactics*, p. 135. See also Vien and Khuyen, *Reflections on the War in Vietnam*, pp. 114–15. In *On Strategy: The Vietnam War in Context* (Carlisle Barracks, Pa.: Strategic Studies Institute, U.S Army War College, 1981), Harry G. Summers, Jr.'s unusual contention that MACV gave too much attention to counterinsurgency operations in the 1965–68 period may indeed have application to the South Vietnamese army during 1970–75, a point which he later alludes to in "Principles of War and Low-Intensity Conflict," *Military Review* 65 (March 1985): 47.

[7] Cao Van Vien, "The Strategy of Isolation," *Military Review* 52 (April 1972): 22–30.

[8] For a critical introduction to the organization of the war effort at the Washington level, see Robert W. Komer's *Bureaucracy Does Its Thing: Institutional Constraints on U.S.-GVN Performance in Vietnam* (Santa Monica, Calif.: Rand Corp., 1972), especially chap. 6, "Lack of Unified Management"; and also Geoffrey Piller's interesting "DOD's Office of International Security Affairs: The Brief Ascendancy of an Advisory System," *Political Science Quarterly* 98 (Spring 1981): 59–78.

an American protectorate in terms of foreign policy and military strategy. American planning had simply been inadequate. Perhaps U.S. leaders still felt that Saigon had no real hope of standing alone, and the tons of ENHANCE PLUS war materiel shipped to Vietnam during the final months were no more than a bribe to bring Thieu to the negotiating table and sooth any guilt feelings American military and civilian leaders had about abandoning their former wartime ally. They may have also feared that many of the earlier Vietnamese requests for more assistance might come back to haunt them as they had during the Easter offensive. Yet young nations have met worse crises and survived. The South Vietnamese were still better equipped than their opponents and, for the moment, had the upper hand, given the exhaustion of enemy forces following Hanoi's latest offensive. Certainly Saigon's generals ought to have known by now how to fight a war and how to handle their American benefactors. With the foreigners at last departed, their survival depended solely on their own wits and on their own political and military skills. The next few years would tell who occupied the Trojan horses that the peace accords had left behind.

The Political Dimension

The situation facing General Westmoreland in 1965 was not completely unique. As wartime military advisers to underdeveloped countries, General Otto Liman von Sanders in Turkey during World War I and General Joseph W. Stilwell in China during World War II had faced similar problems.[9] During the First World War Sanders had headed the German advisory mission assisting the primitive Ottoman army in a minor but potentially critical theater of war; Stilwell, Chiang Kai-shek's military adviser, found himself in an analogous situation on the Asian mainland during the Second World War. Like Westmoreland, both represented powerful industrial nations and directed military advice and assistance programs to weaker wartime allies, with little guidance from their home governments. All three had to deal with inefficient authoritarian governments ruling premodern societies dominated by hereditary elites. In each of the three countries political affairs were almost inseparable from military matters, and even minor changes in military leadership, organization, or employment had deep political ramifications. There were, however, significant differences. Unlike his predecessors, General Westmoreland commanded large bodies of his own military forces that shared the same battlefield with the indigenous troops being advised. In this respect, the situation in South Vietnam was more analogous to the American experience in the Korean conflict in the early 1950s. As in the case of South Vietnam, the U.S. Army provided military advisers throughout the local armed forces. But in South Korea, the American commander-in-chief, General of the Army Douglas MacArthur, not only advised but commanded all allied forces—and, in fact, delegated command of the South Korean Army to

[9] See Otto Liman von Sanders, *Five Years in Turkey*, trans. Carl Reichmann (Annapolis, Md.: U.S. Naval Institute, 1927); and Barbara W. Tuchman, *Stilwell and the American Experience in China, 1911–45* (New York: Macmillan, 1971).

local U.S. ground commanders like General Matthew B. Ridgway. With the strong support of South Korean President Syngman Rhee, Ridgway had a great deal of control over all aspects of the Korean armed forces and was able to relieve, promptly and without fuss, any Korean officer whose performance was lacking.[10]

Ridgway was later puzzled over Westmoreland's refusal to insist on a similar arrangement with the Saigon regime, but the political situations were not comparable. In South Korea the power and personality of President Rhee were decisive. A courageous and forceful man, Rhee ruled with an iron hand and tolerated no opposition; Saigon, in contrast, produced no strong civilian leader after the death of Diem and faced a widespread internal insurgency. Since November 1963 the country had been run by a coterie of relatively inexperienced and competing military officers who, despite the establishment of the presidential system of government, were never able to extract themselves from the political administration or to provide the leadership needed to run the country. For Westmoreland then, control over the South Vietnamese army meant control over the South Vietnamese government as well. Such a relationship would have revived charges of American colonialism; thrown into question the legitimacy of the Saigon regime; and, he believed, undercut the faltering counterinsurgency program. For these reasons Westmoreland felt that it was necessary to forego the advantages of a combined command and concentrate on creating a stable government in Saigon while having American troops deal with the more immediate threat posed by the growing number of conventional enemy forces.

General Westmoreland's concern over the stability of the Saigon regime was well founded. The I Corps Tactical Zone revolt in early 1966 showed just how close the patchwork government was to falling apart. Continued armed confrontations between South Vietnamese combat units, and even between American and South Vietnamese units, spelled disaster for the entire war effort. Had American officials taken direct control over the Saigon government, the situation might have been much worse. As it was, the resolution of the I Corps fracas was a very near thing, and the ensuing truce between the military cliques and the establishment of a stable government an altogether risky business. Considering the size of the American involvement, the influence of MACV and the U.S. Embassy was surprisingly minimal. Yet, Westmoreland and his associates made it abundantly clear to South Vietnamese leaders like Thieu and Ky that the proviso for continued American support was political stability: A return to the coup period of 1964–65 would not be tolerated. In this matter American officials took a firm stand, and the South Vietnamese fell into line comparatively quickly.

Whether American policy in this regard was fully successful is a matter of conjecture. The entire process of putting together a stable government proved agonizingly slow. With guidance from the U.S. Embassy and MACV, the South Vietnamese leaders tried to fashion a constitutional democratic regime in the space of two short years. It simply could not be done. The authoritarian traditions handed down to the Vietnamese had prepared them poorly for the task. The consensus type of government that had evolved in the West, with its empha-

---

[10] For Ridgway's comments, see interview in *Southeast Asia Analysis Report*, October 1969, pp. 44–63, HRB, CMH.

sis on participation and compromise, was alien to Vietnamese culture and politics. The result, a cross between a presidential and parliamentary system of government, served only as a facade for the continuation of military rule. Without any political party system, the military candidate became president, and the president appointed the prime minister from outside a legislature that had little power. In the process, it was only natural for conservative Americans like Ambassador Bunker to prefer the "cautious and methodical" Thieu over the "decisive but impulsive and sometimes irresponsible" Ky. But, as even Bunker admitted, Thieu was simply not a good leader and failed to pull the army out of the political arena.[11] Stability was achieved, but the division between military and civil authority never occurred. In a way, the whole adventure seemed a show for world, and especially for American, public opinion. But perhaps the expectation that a working democratic republic could be established in the midst of a civil war was too great, and the system that was created did at least provide the basis for such a government once peace had returned.

Continuing military rule had two direct effects. First, it limited the amount of popular support that Americans hoped the new government would garner from a participatory electoral process. Second, it made it extremely difficult to reform military leadership from above. Without any grass roots party system, the presidential and legislative elections served only to rubberstamp candidates put forward by the Saigon generals. Those same generals continued to monopolize political appointments at the province and district levels, military commanders continued to have political responsibilities, and senior officers continued to dominate the political bureaucracy in Saigon. Once elected president, Thieu tried to place his own supporters, or officers who were at least favorably disposed to his new regime, in positions of authority whenever the opportunity arose. Incumbents he gently eased into lesser posts. Although some of his appointees were able military leaders, too many others had little to recommend them aside from their loyalty to the president. The process was slow and stretched out over many years. In general, Thieu made significant changes only during periods of extreme national emergency, such as the Tet attacks of 1968 and the Easter offensive of 1972, when he could justify politically sensitive moves by military necessity. While the U.S. Embassy and MACV were often pleased when such changes occurred, they had little influence on their frequency or scope. At no time did Generals Westmoreland or Abrams, or any other American leaders, make such changes a prerequisite to continued American support.[12] As a result, a great many South Vietnamese officers whom Americans considered incompetent occupied important command and staff positions for years on end, and it was such men who frustrated American field advisers and often set the tone for the rest of the South Vietnamese army.

The entire matter of corruption in the military complicated the problem of leadership. American observers had no way of gauging official malfeasance other

---

[11] Msg, Bunker SGN 1474 to SecState, circa late 1968, Bunker Papers, DS.

[12] See Vien et al., *U.S. Adviser*, pp. 39–40; and Allan E. Goodman, "Dynamics of the U.S.–South Vietnamese Alliance: What Went Wrong" (Paper delivered at Vietnam War Conference sponsored by the Woodrow Wilson Center's International Security Studies Program and the *Wilson Quarterly*, Washington, D.C., January 7–8, 1983).

TABLE 22—OFFICIAL PIASTER EXCHANGE

Calendar Year	Piasters per U.S. Dollar
1964	35
1966	80
1967	118
1970	285
1972	420
1974	560
1975	700

Source: Compiled by author from information in South Vietnamese Inflation file, SEAB, CMH.

than through the accumulation of rumors and secondhand stories. Advisers generally knew only what their counterparts chose to tell them, and that was usually next to nothing. If corruption was, in fact, common, it was not systematic and varied greatly from area to area according to the mores of local commanders and the opportunities available. How much of it was unique to South Vietnam, or even the Far East, was another question mark. Certainly the same type of activities had and still existed throughout the world, and their occurrence in South Vietnam was in no way unusual.[13] However, official corruption was especially debilitating in South Vietnam for several reasons. First, the government was at war, a civil war at that, and desperately needed the respect and loyalty of the people who were being asked to defend and support it. Second, the lack of separation between civil and military authority made it nearly impossible for the army to distance itself from the opportunities for graft, favoritism, and other forms of abuse that normally came hand in hand with political responsibility. From the beginning, the fledgling army was too weak and divided to impose any kind of apolitical military professionalism on the political structure of South Vietnam. Instead of bringing reform to the civil administration, the army was corrupted by the temptations of political power. Although MACV could not often tie corruption per se with poor military leadership, the system of pervasive corruption clearly made it more difficult for Saigon to identify, promote, and use its most able leaders.

Low pay, inflation, American opulence, and a cultural inheritance that condoned such practices all contributed to the spread of bureaucratic corruption. Between 1964 and 1972 consumer prices in South Vietnam rose 900 percent and the price of rice 1400 percent, while incomes rose only about 300 percent for officers and, at most, 500 percent for enlisted men. During the same period the official dollar-piaster exchange rate increased from VN$35 to VN$420, was continuing to rise, and was also undercut by a black-market rate that was considerably higher *(Table 22)*. As a result, a full colonel in the South Vietnamese Army saw his monthly salary shrink from about US$400 to US$85; an army captain, from US$287 to US$61; and a private, from US$77 to US$30 *(see Table 23)*.[14] Limited pay increases, a complex allotment system, an expanded post exchange and commissary, and at times free rice and more combat rations were not enough

---

[13] Stephen B. Engberg, "A Framework for Understanding Corruption," SAAFO–SRA–1974, p. 1, SEAB, CMH, points out that the problem was also considered major in North Vietnam.

[14] Khuyen, *The RVNAF*, pp. 252–53.

TABLE 23—COMPARATIVE ESTIMATES OF ANNUAL MILITARY BASE PAY [a]

Rank	South Vietnamese Army [b]		U.S. Army [b]
	1964	1970	1968
Enlisted			
Private	377	328	1,361
Private First Class	411	337	1,652
Corporal	446	345	2,282
Corporal First Class	477	358	. . . . . [c]
Sergeant	521	400	2,714
Staff Sergeant	. . . [d]	. . . [d]	3,143
Sergeant First Class	608	413	3,647
Master Sergeant	694	421	5,803 [e]
Master Sergeant First Class	781	442	6,916 [f]
Officer			
Aspirant	955	526	. . . . . [c]
2d Lieutenant	1,389	611	4,118
1st Lieutenant	1,606	686	4,792
Captain	1,909	779	5,980
Major	2,300	901	6,433
Lieutenant Colonel	2,690	985	7,624
Colonel	3,124	1,154	8,446
Brigadier General	4,209	1,322	11,398
Major General	4,339	1,406	13,720
Lieutenant General	4,773	1,575	17,100
General	5,207	1,743	19,292

[a] In. U.S. dollars.

[b] The Vietnamese figures represent piasters converted to U.S. dollars using the official exchange rates of US$1:VN$35 for 1964 and US$1:VN$285 for 1970. The South Vietnamese Army had five to eight pay echelons, or steps, within each enlisted grade, three to five steps for company and field pay grades, but none for general officers. The step increases were minor, amounting to about 2–4 percent of the base pay. The American figures are also for base salaries and do not include substantial two-year step increases based on time in service and not time in grade (with about fifteen steps per grade). The step increases would raise American salaries by about one-third in the senior officer grades. Family and other allowances are found in both armies for this period, but they would not change the comparative estimates significantly.

[c] No U.S. equivalent.

[d] No Vietnamese equivalent.

[e] Over eight years of service.

[f] Over ten years of service.

Sources: U.S. Army Register, 1969, vol. 1, p.468; Khuyen, The RVNAF, p. 221.

to satisfy consumer demands over the long run. To make ends meet, an increasing number of soldiers and their dependents took on a variety of odd jobs and part-time work, and the use of military positions, military transport, military labor, and perhaps what appeared to be excess military supplies to make a few extra piasters here and there did not seem so wrong. Of course, the higher the rank and the greater the authority, the greater the opportunities and the temptations.[15]

MACV and the U.S. Embassy were on the right track in trying to replace the Directory with a constitutional nonmilitary government, but the job was never done. Military men remained entrenched in all echelons of the government. South Vietnamese Army officers continued to monopolize province and district posts; military units continued to have territorial police responsibilities; and

[15] For an excellent and candid overview of the corruption problem, see ibid., pp. 341–78.

corps commanders continued to act as regional governors. American advisers urged internal reform, but their efforts were naive, and, rather than attacking the root of the problem, consisted mainly of lecturing counterparts on the value of virtuous behavior. Those who heeded such advice were assuredly less wealthy, though not necessarily more effective leaders than those who did not.

The American Military Commanders

It is almost impossible to generalize about the American advisory system in South Vietnam. In one respect, there was only one adviser who counted, the MACV commander. He was both chief of the U.S. combat forces in Vietnam and senior adviser to the Vietnamese generals; he headed the Army component command and the U.S. Army advisory detachments, including the U.S. Army Special Forces units. While other senior American officers made recommendations regarding the Saigon military establishment from time to time, it was the MACV commander who determined what action would be taken. As the chief American military representative in South Vietnam, he served as a kind of head physician, ruling on the health of his Vietnamese patient, prescribing various medicines, diets, and physical therapies, and determining the advisability of surgery. Of course, even the MACV commander was not omnipotent. Nothing, for example, could be done without the consent of the patient, and nothing could be done if the necessary medicines were unavailable. The MACV commander was also answerable to his political and military superiors in Washington and, in many politico-military matters, had to work closely with the U.S. ambassador in Saigon. However, in almost every case, his opinion on the status of the South Vietnamese armed forces was accepted by his superiors, his requests for supplies and monies were met as quickly as possible, and his treatment of the patient went unchallenged. In many ways then the entire advice and assistance effort depended almost totally on the man who occupied this key post.

In style the two principal MACV commanders, General Westmoreland and Abrams, were markedly different. In the media and to the casual onlooker, Westmoreland appeared as the aloof, autocratic general—the far-seeing strategist, forever "peering through the fog of battle to distant vistas"—while Abrams seemed the tougher, more earthy soldier's soldier, "a slumbering volcano" who might erupt at any time if inadvertently disturbed.[16]

But neither image was accurate, for the events that engulfed both commanders greatly circumscribed their actions. Westmoreland, in the Vietnam driver's seat since 1964, had more political and military leeway than Abrams was ever to even hope for. Westmoreland either made or was a major contributor to all of the decisions affecting the advisory effort between 1965 and 1968. He gambled on an American military victory on the battlefield and political stability in Sai-

---

[16] On Westmoreland, as related in Joseph Kraft, "Jurists Shouldn't Use Westmoreland Case To Generalize Law," *The Star Ledger*, 2 Dec 84, sec. 3. On Abrams, as related in Palmer, *The 25-Year War*, p. 26. See also George C. Wilson, "Creighton Abrams: From Agawan to Chief of Staff," *The Washington Post*, 5 Sep 74, D–4; and, on Westmoreland, "Man of the Year," *Time*, 7 Jun 66, pp. 15–21.

gon, and probably came as close to succeeding as anyone could have. His arduous effort to create a stable government in Saigon was a major achievement of military statesmanship. Whether he could have applied more American force against North Vietnam without abandoning America's limited objectives is doubtful. Other alternatives eluded him. His continued reluctance to establish a multinational command deeply undercut his own efforts to direct the war and foster greater American support for it. Despite his protestations to the contrary, he did not encourage the South Vietnamese to take part in the offensive American combat operations, assigned them the secondary task of providing static territorial security, and failed to give his field and staff advisory effort any sense of immediacy.

The relationship between Westmoreland and his military and civilian superiors is controversial. Somewhere along the line, American leaders began to equate the abstract statistical evaluations of South Vietnamese military performance, both on and off the battlefield, with actual improvements in military capabilities. Yet somewhere along that same line, more realistic evaluations of those capabilities were too often sidetracked by military careerism, bureaucratic optimism, political propaganda, and either the unwillingness or the inability of so many American leaders, in Washington as well as in Saigon, to take a hard look at what was occurring even when all the facts—good and bad—were available. To be both fair and accurate, the official bureaucratic "party line" stretched from the smallest advisory detachment, up the chain of command to MACV, and thence across the Pacific to Hawaii and on to Washington, and to the Pentagon and the White House. Too often all parties reassured one another that all was well with Saigon's heterogeneous collection of military forces. Most tended to accept only that information that they wanted to hear, and America's civilian political leaders were surely the worst offenders. There were always ways of ignoring the warnings of officials like Taylor, or the more critical assessments of John Paul Vann. But too many official military evaluations of the South Vietnamese armed forces were also misleading, if not inaccurate, and smacked of a public relations effort that had little to do with military professionalism. Perhaps Westmoreland had simply given up trying to explain his difficulties to Washington. President Johnson's manipulation of the bombing campaign and the press, Wheeler's proposal to put American battalions into Saigon proper, General Johnson's views on the Special Forces, McNamara's insistence on more statistics, and the many ill-conceived suggestions that seemed to flow from Washington undoubtedly had worn Westmoreland thin, as they would his successor. Westmoreland's superiors seemed unable to understand the complexity of the task they had ordered him to fulfill.

The enemy's Tet offensive in 1968 forced all participants to lay their cards on the table. North Vietnam had sent thousands of young men to their death for unattainable military objectives, while the stalemate that Westmoreland had finally forced on the battlefield did not bring him the military victory he so ardently desired. Although he had attempted to increase South Vietnamese participation in the conventional war effort during 1967, he also requested several hundred thousand additional American troops in early 1968, which, had they been sent, would have certainly delayed for many years any plans he may have entertained to Vietnamize the war.[17] Without any new strategy, direction, or guidelines, Westmoreland had reached a dead end, and, without suitable targets, Abrams and the huge American expeditionary force in South Vietnam would soon be forced to sit on their bayonets.[18]

The mission and role of General Abrams in South Vietnam was narrower, or at least much more circumscribed by his superiors in Washington. Kissinger thought the new MACV commander was "doomed to a rearguard action," explaining that "the purpose of his command would increasingly become logistic redeployment and not success in battle" and that Abrams "could not possibly achieve the victory that had eluded us at full strength while [U.S. military] forces were constantly dwindling."[19] In actuality, Abrams had the tough and less rewarding task of getting the South Vietnamese to fight. Unlike Westmoreland, he ought to have had a clear understanding of what was to be done and the time it had to be done in. The establishment of a stable government in Saigon, the strengthening of the American pacification support effort under Komer and his successors, and an enemy that had almost abandoned large-scale offensive operations were further advantages that Westmoreland had never enjoyed. Abrams also found another asset in Ambassador Bunker who, if lacking the analytical mind of Taylor, proved more astute than the excitable Lodge whom President Johnson had foisted on Westmoreland for his own political reasons. Bunker made a good match for the congenial Abrams, and took many South Vietnamese political problems off the back of the MACV commander.

Abrams himself was no stranger to the political arena. Although associated in the public mind with his World War II service under General Patton, he also was eminently successful as the commander of federalized troops at the University of Mississippi in 1962, and in Birmingham the following year, becoming much admired by the Kennedys. Later, as the Army vice chief of staff (1964–67) and Army chief of staff (1972–74), he proved extremely adept in dealing with the U.S. Congress and was a primary candidate for the chairmanship of the Joint Chiefs of Staff before his untimely death in September 1974. However, as an adviser, he lacked the bull-headed persistence of someone like "Blowtorch" Komer or even of Westmoreland, once he set himself on a particular problem. Like his predecessor, Abrams recognized that the essential problem of Saigon was military leadership, but he was unwilling to take a hard line on the matter or to associate with those who did, even when the problem was obviously more critical than it had been in the past. Perhaps even more than Westmoreland, he was a team player until the end and never sought to challenge the many political and military restrictions that his command had inherited from previous regimes. Frustrated by South Vietnamese military politics and his inability to influence South Vietnamese actions, Abrams felt that he and his fellow senior advisers had much less power and influence over their counterparts than anyone in Washington believed

---

[17] The same point is made in Msg, SecState (Rusk) STATE 124584 to AmEmbassy, Saigon, 5 Mar 68, History file 30–A9, Westmoreland Papers, HRB, CMH.

[18] Paraphrasing Napoleon's alleged comments on the guerrilla war in Spain, "You can do anything with bayonets but sit on them."

[19] Kissinger, *White House Years*, pp. 272–73.

possible.[20] The long efforts of Nixon and Kissinger to gain Thieu's acquiescence to the ceasefire agreement was a case in point. It was doubtful whether Abrams or Bunker could have done it on their own, for Thieu had proved equally stubborn on other matters that would have clearly improved the military position of Saigon.

Abram's efforts to prepare Saigon to carry on the war effort alone had many shortcomings. In most cases, his plans depended on what he perceived Saigon was able to do and not on what it needed to do to survive. The most glaring example was the great quantity of war materiel that the United States literally dumped into South Vietnam between 1971 and 1972. Ironically, many of the items proved to be the same materiel previously requested by the Joint General Staff but rejected by American leaders. If more heavy equipment was necessary, MACV and the Department of Defense should have made plans for it much earlier. Abrams also made no serious efforts to have the South Vietnamese withdraw their regular units from their area security roles, which, as the Cambodian and Laotian incursions showed, could have been assumed entirely by Territorial Forces by 1970 if not earlier. It was only at the insistence of Laird that MACV came up with a program for freeing South Vietnamese divisional artillery from its static security missions by activating territorial 105-mm. artillery platoons. Although Laird and Kissinger's sudden and late concern over the mobility of the South Vietnamese divisions may have been self-serving, they did have a point. If the 500,000 territorials, aided by 2–3 million PSDF militiamen, could not allow the regulars to regroup and serve as a reserve force, what good were they? In the same vein, if the vast amount of American air power needed to support Saigon was too expensive and only gave the enemy more hostages to bargain with, how useful was it? Perhaps as Kissinger hinted, Abrams and his subordinate commanders had never really changed their NSSM 1 assessments and regarded Vietnamization as an unfortunate policy that had to be carried out, rather than as a challenge to be met. Thus, as General Weyand, the last MACV commander, left, many questions involving South Vietnamese leadership, strategy, and the roles and missions of the various components of Saigon's armed forces remained unresolved.

The Advisers

Despite a great deal of rhetoric to the contrary, the MACV commanders did not expect their field and staff advisers to play a major role in the improvement of the South Vietnamese military forces. As liaison teams attached to almost every South Vietnamese headquarters, training camp, school, airfield, or port, they kept adjacent and higher American commanders abreast of what their allies were doing and where and when they were doing it. In the absence of a unified command or separate areas of operation, these teams provided an indispensable link between a variety of units sharing the same battlefield; the same

---

[20] Anderson Interv, 23 Jun 83, SEAB, CMH.

roads, bases, and air waves; and the same enemy. Had the U.S. advisory network not existed prior to the arrival of American ground troops in 1965, it—or something very similar to it—would have had to have been created. The great expansion of U.S. military power in South Vietnam after 1965 also increased the combat assistance tasks of the teams. Only these cellular units, with their radios and interpreters, had the ability to make the vast amounts of American firepower available to the South Vietnamese on the battlefield, immediately when and where it was most needed. Again, had the advisory teams not been in place prior to 1965, some sort of similar organization would have been needed.

Many American leaders, however, still had a general belief that the advisory teams would have a direct, personal effect on the thousands of Vietnamese commanders being advised. Perhaps it appeared almost self-evident that the U.S. field and staff advisers ought to have some sort of long-term impact on Vietnamese military leadership, if only through sheer weight of numbers. And perhaps it also seemed self-evident that that impact should be positive, given the high quality of American military personnel, almost all officers and noncommissioned officers, assigned as advisers. American military professionalism would hopefully be passed from adviser to advisee as they lived and worked together; in the process the latter would somehow assimilate all manner of American military know-how, to include everything from U.S. Army combat, training, and management techniques to its apolitical concepts of service, duty, and national loyalty. To this end both Westmoreland and Abrams urged the field advisers to befriend their counterparts, establish close "rapport" with them, and convert them to the American military way of thinking and doing. But neither commander ever went beyond this limited concept, or seriously considered adopting alternative means of improving South Vietnamese leadership similar to that developed by Ambassador Komer to relieve incompetent Vietnamese province chiefs. Most advisers had little influence over South Vietnamese military leadership, and many found that, as one adviser later phrased it, "getting someone relieved or replaced was like getting a politician out of office."[21] Thoroughly frustrated, many of the better advisers resorted to questionable practices to improve performance, even contributing cash from their own pockets to encourage the South Vietnamese to fight.[22]

What exactly went on between the thousands of advisers and their counterparts at the grass roots level can never be completely reconstructed. Experiences varied widely. Some became close friends and others bitter adversaries, and still others had little personal interaction. Some advisers lived in plush, secure compounds with all the amenities of home, while others survived in primitive jungle bases with only the barest necessities. Some, based close to Saigon, ate well; others scrounged what they could from nearby American units and post exchanges; and still others adjusted their diet to the local foods as best they could. For some advisers, tours meant long, boring stints at some out-of-the-way district

---

[21] Brunkow Interv, 26 Feb 76, SEAB, CMH.

[22] For example, Msg, Vann PKU 0769 to Abrams, 141200 May 72, sub: AIK Fund To Reward Soldiers Who Destroy an Enemy Tank With an M72, Abrams Papers; Vossen Interv, 19 Jul 68. Both in HRB, CMH. See also Corson, *The Betrayal*, p. 193. Khuyen, *The RVNAF*, p. 321, notes that Saigon also adopted the practice of cash inducements in 1972.

headquarters; for others, they brought danger and exhaustion from endless combat patrols—and perhaps a sudden death on some lonely jungle trail. Most, especially those at the lower levels, merely monitored the actions of their counterparts or directed the heavy volume of American firepower that was almost always available to extricate their one-year allies out of trouble. Yet, there were many others, often unheralded, like General Hollingsworth, the legendary Vann, and the many Special Forces advisers, who often provided the South Vietnamese with the leadership that they so sadly lacked.

A few generalizations can be made. Preparation for advisory duty was minimal. Few advisers had any kind of useful Vietnamese-language training, and the short preparatory MATA course at Fort Bragg provided only an introduction to the problems of working in a foreign culture. Many advisers were newly appointed lieutenants, captains, and majors with comparatively little experience, even with American units. Almost all had to overcome the acute cultural shock from being dropped into a completely alien environment before they could begin to become effective. Verbal communication with their counterparts was dependent on the ability of their Vietnamese interpreters, and the rest had to be picked up while "on-the-job." The "job," or tour, rarely lasted more than six months with any one unit, as advisers moved back and forth from field to staff positions within their division, corps, or province advisory detachments. Only personnel slated for posts with province and district advisory teams received additional training within South Vietnam, and only prospective province senior advisers had more formal instruction in the United States and longer tours in South Vietnam. Other key personnel, such as the MACV staff section chiefs and the corps senior advisers, had longer tours by virtue of their general officer status, but their advisory duties were often performed by deputies. Very few advisers thus had the time to become well acquainted with their counterparts, and most rotated back to the United States just when they were beginning to know their way around. They did, however, feel they knew enough to give their charges consistently low marks in leadership, and this alone suggests that the advisers had strong misgivings regarding the benefits their presence conveyed. In fact, during the final years of the American involvement, many speculated that the South Vietnamese actually depended too much on the air and artillery support brought by the advisers and that they may have been stifling, rather than encouraging, South Vietnamese initiative.[23]

The quality of the field advisers was a matter to which MACV and the Department of the Army gave only peripheral attention. In terms of rank and military education, the advisory system was rich. Prior to 1965, many of the better advisers were also volunteers who had perhaps been attracted to one of the few assignments that offered some measure of actual combat experience. The arrival of American ground combat forces quickly changed all that. American unit commands became the most coveted assignments, and Westmoreland understandably demanded the best officers for these posts. While the Army later established elaborate programs, including monetary incentives, to attract better CORDS ad-

---

[23] For example, see Truong, *RVNAF and US Operational Cooperation and Coordination*, pp. 163–68; David H. Hackworth, "Our Advisors Must Pass the Ball," *Army* 21 (May 1971): 61–62.

visers, it did nothing similar for the rest of the advisory effort. Westmoreland's promise that Army promotion boards would treat advisory duty equal to command assignments was misleading. Promotion boards were subject to only general guidance from the outside, and there was no agreement within the Army that command and advisory assignments were in any way comparable. The two jobs were, in fact, incredibly different, and even officers who had served in the highly rated province senior adviser program later exhibited a low selection rate for promotion.[24] In a different context, Westmoreland also asserted that good combat commanders did not necessarily have the qualities of good advisers, but the special qualities desirable for advisory duty remained unknown. In the end American officers were expected to adjust to the needs of the job, and the selection of advisers depended solely on the availability of personnel for short overseas tours over and above the needs of regular U.S. units in South Vietnam. Given the limited power of the field advisers, and their brief training and short stints in any one position, the value of possessing a special aptitude for the job was probably unimportant.

Advising From the Top

Both Generals Westmoreland and Abrams enjoyed almost complete control over South Vietnamese military expenditures. The MACV staff undertook nearly all planning and programming, and the Joint General Staff and the Central Logistics Command contributed little in this area.[25] The Saigon defense budget continued to cover only salaries and minor operating expenses, while direct U.S. military appropriations in Washington took care of the rising cost of equipment and supplies. The overall South Vietnamese budget also continued to depend heavily on direct and indirect U.S. aid programs. But MACV's use of this potential leverage never went beyond dictating the size and composition of the South Vietnamese military establishment. For other areas, the MACV commanders relied on their own personal influence and that of their major subordinates.

Employing U.S. unit commanders as ad hoc advisers through combined operations was another approach that was never really given much of a chance. In general, American commanders were reluctant to participate in combined endeavors and preferred to perform what they considered their primary missions without such added burdens. The assignment of different responsibilities to American and South Vietnamese units enforced the natural separation of the multinational allied forces, as did the absence of a combined command. Only at the corps level did the senior American officer serve as both adviser and commander. But even here a delineation of responsibilities was evident. The American force commander was concerned primarily with the mobile offensive operations of his divisions and brigades, and his South Vietnamese counterpart

---

[24] Memo, SecArmy Robert F. Froehlke to SecDef, 15 Aug 72, sub: Province Senior Advisors, SEAB, CMH.
[25] Khuyen, *RVNAF Logistics*, pp. 96–97.

511

was absorbed in territorial security and political matters. The U.S. corps-level advisory team was separate and distinct from the much larger U.S. field force staff in terms of organization, personnel, equipment, and physical location. While the prospect of Vietnamization spurred MACV to encourage more combined operations as part of the advisory effort to improve Saigon's military forces, it never formulated any overall plan or program, and thus, except in the more technical areas, the advisory effort was decentralized and extremely haphazard.

MACV's attention to statistical evidence went beyond the demands of McNamara's "whiz kid" defense analysts or his civilian business management techniques that had been taken over by a cost-conscious military bureaucracy. The great postwar controversy between CBS News, a major American media organization, and General Westmoreland himself showed that the obsession with statistical data, however irrelevant, was not limited to the American armed forces or to the federal government, but may be one of the many phenomena of modern industrial society. Americans, from the president on down, constantly demanded a statistical accounting for the war, almost always eschewing the more complicated explications of events in Southeast Asia for the simpler, more easily digestible ones based on numerical evidence, which was to many the "bottom line."[26]

Nevertheless, there can be no question that senior military and civilian leaders systematically misused the detailed reports submitted by field advisers. Although continuously revised, the reports carried essentially two types of information to the MACV staff and higher commands. First, and most useful, was the objective data covering South Vietnamese military strength, location, equipment, and operations. Even this information could not be taken completely at face value. Unit strength figures were complicated by differences in authorized, assigned, present-for-duty, and actual operational strengths; enemy losses were prone to exaggeration; and equipment tallies gave no indication of condition, use, or location. Second were the subjective reports with the opinions of individual American advisers on the performance of the units or staffs being advised. At best, this information was supposed to make it possible to compare the relative status of similar South Vietnamese units and to identify specific problem areas within each unit. Instead, military and civilian analysts in Saigon and Washington often used the data to assign absolute values to South Vietnamese units in order to show that progress was being made. In many cases, MACV reports emphasized only data that reflected favorably on the state of the South Vietnamese armed forces and played down or ignored negative information. Not surprisingly, ratings in most categories steadily improved, if only by fractions of percentage points, and slips were explained by command changes or combat losses beyond the "control" of MACV. Such thinking was highly deceptive. Understrength battalions that had acquitted themselves fairly well on the battlefield might receive a "marginal" rating, while others, with nothing more than static security responsibilities, might be deemed "satisfactory." Yet, there were

[26] Former CIA Vietnam station chief John Limond Hart makes the same point in "The Statistics Trap in Vietnam," *The Washington Post*, 6 Jan 85, C-7.

enough critical situation reports coming out of MACV from 1965 to 1973 to show that the optimism generated by such data was unwarranted. In too many cases the so-called indicators of progress used by MACV, JCS, and DOD statisticians were just so much interagency propaganda.[27]

The same obsession to show measurable progress also affected the programs pursued at the MACV level. High strength levels disguised the fact that MACV efforts to have the Joint General Staff establish a centralized recruiting system never got very far off the ground. As long as the MACV commanders continued to push the expansion of the South Vietnamese regular and territorial forces, manpower remained a critical problem, especially considering the heavy drain from desertions and combat casualties. To keep the expanding South Vietnamese military structure filled, MACV found it expedient to retain the existing decentralized recruitment and induction system. Local recruiting by provinces and regular units thus continued, and, after short two- to four-month training periods at local camps, most new trainees returned to their inducting headquarters. While this type of local unit recruiting, training, and stationing kept voluntary enlistments high, it reinforced the parochialism endemic to the entire armed forces. Again, MACV fully realized the side effects of these practices, but felt that the gains made in recruitment were worth the risk.

MACV also backed away from pushing the Joint General Staff into adopting any kind of personnel rotation system. Soldiers, officers and enlisted alike, normally spent their entire service in one unit and in one geographical area, again strengthening local ties at the expense of broader loyalties. Lack of mobility in the armed services had other undesirable effects. For example, South Vietnamese commanders remained reluctant to free their better officers for advanced schooling, making it impossible to use military schooling as a prerequisite for advancement—the wrong people would have been promoted—and forcing the Joint General Staff to ignore it as a criterion.[28]

The absence of any rotation system between the classroom and the field meant that South Vietnamese cadre at training camps and schools tended to stagnate. American advisers continuously complained about their marginal quality, but nothing was ever done. MACV was concerned primarily with the statistical totals: training camp and school capacity and fill, number of courses offered, and hours of instruction completed. Deficiencies in instruction were remedied by graduating more students or offering more advanced courses to graduates. The language barrier minimized direct American influence in the classroom. Only a relatively small number of Vietnamese could be given the extensive English-language training necessary to attend military schools in the United States, and U.S. advisers at the Vietnamese camps could do little but monitor the volume of training and perhaps offer a few suggestions regarding instructional techniques. Here as elsewhere, concern for statistical results tended to mask underlying and more serious problems.

More disappointing was the failure of MACV to end the class bias of South Vietnam's officer selection and promotion system. As long as admittance to the

[27] For a discussion of "sanitizing" reports, see Richard McMahon, "Saigon '75: The Inevitable Collapse," *The Retired Officer*, April 1985, pp. 18–22.
[28] Khuyen, *The RVNAF*, pp. 95 and 212.

officer and noncommissioned officer candidate programs depended on high school–level diplomas, the average Vietnamese peasant or city worker was effectively excluded from the military command structure—and, for that matter, from the entire governmental administration. The American position on the issue was ambivalent, on the one hand, recognizing the value of having an educated military cadre and, on the other, aware that the practice excluded most of the South Vietnamese population from the civil and military bureaucracy. As a result, MACV ended up nagging the Joint General Staff about the educational restrictions but backed away from taking forceful action. If leaders could not be inducted into the officer corps, then the officers would be made into leaders. To this end MACV had the South Vietnamese Central Training Command establish a variety of leadership courses throughout the military school system and comforted itself by tallying the number of students exposed and the number of classes and hours taught. In the meantime, few enlisted personnel were ever commissioned, battlefield officer appointments quotas were ignored, and the indigenous peasant leaders who had neither the time nor the funds for education remained in the lower enlisted ranks.

MACV efforts to accelerate South Vietnamese officer promotions also met with repeated failure, and annual appointment goals in almost all officer ranks went unsatisfied. Although MACV had helped the Joint General Staff develop personnel accounting and promotion systems modeled after those used by the U.S. Army, the MACV commanders were unable to persuade the Vietnamese leaders to abandon their rigid time-in-grade promotion requirements. General Thieu and a few of his associates personally handled colonel and general officer promotions; annual promotion boards, which emphasized seniority, decided on those for lieutenant colonels and below. Few officers retired—how could they make a living?—and few were dismissed. The South Vietnamese practice of transferring, rather than cashiering, incompetent commanders weighed down the officer corps still further. MACV repeatedly bought and resold the standard South Vietnamese arguments for the status quo: Inexperienced officers should not be promoted until fully tested over several years, and experienced officers were too rare to be dismissed whatever their faults in one particular job. The actual basis for Vietnamese intransigence lay in the political role of the officer corps and the desire of the senior generals to control its composition. Rapid promotions would destroy the existing network of local ties and personal loyalties that not only provided the current leaders with their political power but also formed the economic and social underpinnings of the Saigon regime. As explained by Thomas C. Thayer, a leading Department of Defense analyst, "The steady expansion in the size of the RVNAF overtook army policies in the sense that the need for more senior officers—and hence promotions—outstripped the capacity of the RVNAF political system to sanction such promotions."[29] In the interest of political stability, MACV stayed its hand.

Unwilling to push for radical change in these and other areas, U.S. military leaders in South Vietnam found themselves endlessly tinkering with the existing

---

[29] Thayer, "How To Analyze a War Without Fronts," p. 816.

military structure to make it work better. Complex pay scales, military commissaries and post exchanges, dependent housing, unit messes, a military medical system, more generous leave policies, more awards and decorations, veterans benefits, and even such things as military farms were all minor ingredients that were supposed to make military life more palatable to the Vietnamese soldier. They were never intended as a substitute for good military leadership, organization, and strategy. That some of these programs were successful is beside the point. Indeed, their very success may have obscured the need for a general overhaul of the entire military system. Considered together with the expanding size of the force, the greater quantities of modern arms and equipment provided, and the elaborate military educational and training system established, they gave the impression that great progress had been made in revitalizing and improving South Vietnam's military forces, when many of these measures were only props intended to shore up a flawed piece of architecture. MACV always considered a complete overhaul as too risky, too dangerous, too liable to upset the delicate political structure in Saigon, and such changes were beyond its responsibility. Why, after all, should Americans force changes down the throats of the Vietnamese generals who, by 1968, ought to have known what was possible and what was necessary to ensure the survival of South Vietnam?

This tendency to "shore up" can best be seen in the organization of the South Vietnamese armed forces. Ostensibly American military leaders exercised absolute control in this area, for all elements of the Vietnamese military had to be approved by MACV in order to receive materiel support and advisory teams. In practice, however, MACV exercised very little positive direction. From the very beginning of the U.S. advisory effort in the 1950s, American military leaders had sought to strengthen the South Vietnamese armed forces by steadily enlarging it. These increases came about in three ways: the expansion of existing elements, the creation of new ones, or the "legalization" of those which the South Vietnamese had created on their own. The result was a highly eclectic hodgepodge of military units and commands. To face a conventional enemy, corps and divisions existed; to fight an unconventional war, ranger and Special Forces units and a network of tactical zones appeared; and to provide internal security, province and district headquarters and the territorials constantly expanded. As new needs came to light, new units and often entirely new military organizations were created to answer them. This pattern repeated itself again and again. Rather than make the regular army units more mobile, the South Vietnamese, with MACV approval, expanded their tiny airborne and marine forces. These general reserve units retained their separate service identity with their own command structure, administration, supply depots, and training centers. However, no real need existed for an independent parachute corps or a separate amphibious warfare branch. The CIDG program was an example of an almost autonomous army with its own recruiting, training, and administration services; its own command structure; and its own regular, territorial, and general reserve forces, not to mention the Greek-letter elements run by the U.S. Army Special Forces or the 81st Airborne Ranger unit. The Territorial Forces were another army unto themselves. Smaller examples abound: the extra armored cavalry squadrons for each corps headquarters; the territorial armor, artillery, and boat units; the large, independent tactical air and riverine forces; the "reconnaissance" companies for each infantry regiment; and the various paramilitary forces, such as the Field Force Police, the armed revolutionary development cadre, the Provincial Reconnaissance Units, and the huge People's Self-Defense Force that numbered 2–3 million part-time personnel by the end of 1972.

Senior American officers had approved each of the above elements to satisfy specific and, by themselves, justifiable needs. However, during this process no individual or organization—neither MACV nor the Joint General Staff—bothered to analyze the armed forces as a living organism and gauge the effect that all these additions would have on the other components. In many cases these separate elements competed with, rather than complemented, the others. From the beginning, the politicization of the army encouraged the habit of building onto the armed forces in this piecemeal fashion. Corps-controlled ranger and armored units balanced divisional infantry battalions; the marine and airborne brigades anchored military factions in Saigon; the air force and navy were separate power centers; and each individual province chief had almost a personal army with his own province and district operational centers, intelligence networks, Regional and Popular Forces rifle units, mortar batteries, administration and supply companies, training camps, recruiting centers, and paramilitary forces. Much the same was true of the CIDG program representing the Montagnard tribes and other South Vietnamese minorities that had been hostile or indifferent to the Saigon regime. This intricate system of checks and balances gave the country a degree of political stability but did nothing for military effectiveness. The South Vietnamese military was surely one of the most complex and intricate armies that the modern world had ever seen, with too many overlapping layers of command and a scattered focus of power and responsibility.

During this process of growth some consolidation had been accomplished, usually for political, rather than military, reasons. Following the fall of President Diem, for example, the Saigon generals placed the South Vietnamese Special Forces and ranger units directly under the corps commanders; with the withdrawal of U.S. Special Forces, MACV and the Joint General Staff agreed to disband the CIDG program, and many of its constituent parts were absorbed into the regular army. Again, the Saigon government's decision to disestablish what had become a separate and potentially hostile Montagnard army is understandable, but even here the thirty or so border defense ranger battalions created from former CIDG units retained a separate status. The successive improvement and modernization programs after 1968 resupplied the armed forces with better weapons and equipment, especially the armor, artillery, engineer, signal, ordnance, air, and naval components, but no general reorganization occurred. Nor did the Joint General Staff or MACV make any plans for such a reorganization in the future. The few studies done of this nature concerned the establishment of a smaller, less expensive "post-hostilities" army, a situation that remained only a remote possibility.

After 1968 the old patterns repeated themselves. When North Vietnamese armor made its appearance, the MACV–Joint General Staff response was to create more new units, armored brigades, and heavy tank battalions, with no thought given to strengthening the existing armored cavalry squadrons. When the South Vietnamese decided in 1971 that more regular troops were needed in the northern zone, the Joint General Staff, with MACV approval, raised a new division there, rather than transferring one of the more idle divisions from the southern Delta to the north. The bulk of the armed forces was still too regionally oriented to be moved back and forth between tactical zones.

The mobility problem had always existed and was recognized by all. As early as 1967 the MACV commander had asked the Joint General Staff to relieve the regular South Vietnamese infantry battalions of their territorial security responsibilities, and in 1968 and 1969 the American–South Vietnamese combined plans had talked about the need to create "mobile divisions" and relieve Vietnamese corps and division commanders of their area security tasks. MACV itself had contended in 1972 that the successful cross-border operations had shown that the territorials could easily cope with internal security in the absence of the regular troops. But nothing was done. In American eyes the territorials remained what one adviser called "our reluctant dragons," whose combat capabilities remained, for the most part, untested.[30] The departure of the American troops and advisers in 1973 found the organization and disposition of the South Vietnamese armed forces just about what it had been in 1965: the bulk of the ground combat forces, regulars and territorials alike, committed to local security; and mobile defense left to a small and diverse general reserve.[31] As before, South Vietnamese superiority in numbers and equipment was again offset by inferiority in operational and strategic mobility. American leaders regarded the South Vietnamese cross-border incursions as highly dangerous and daring undertakings, calculated risks rather than military necessities, and insisted that Saigon's military strategy and posture remain purely defensive. Thus, South Vietnamese military plans and operations were not coordinated with the great American air and sea power that was brought to bear against North Vietnam in the closing months of the year. The Hanoi regime, in contrast, remained totally committed to the mobile offensive throughout Southeast Asia and thus continued to retain the initiative on the South Vietnamese battlefield.

Why did MACV allow Saigon to retain such a passive military posture? Did the American military leaders truly expect the South Vietnamese to survive without continued American air and naval support? Again, the answer may lie in the initial response of the U.S. military leaders to National Security Study Memorandum 1. The presidential memo had ordered MACV to assess the current and future capability of South Vietnam to deal with a combined Viet Cong–North Vietnamese Army threat. The response of the American generals had been unanimous. While the South Vietnamese were fully capable of handling the internal "Viet Cong" insurgency, they lacked the ability to deal with the North Vietnamese Army at present and in the foreseeable future. Despite all the optimistic statistics and all the reports of increasing South Vietnamese battlefield effectiveness, this was the final judgment of the top American advisers—Saigon flatly

---

[30] Riley Interv, 3 Jul 69, VNI 437, HRB, CMH.
[31] For example, see comments in Tho, *Pacification*, p. 167.

could not get the job done alone. Neither MACV nor any of the responding corps senior advisers offered any remedy. MACV thus designed and carried out the subsequent Vietnamization program with the unwritten proviso that South Vietnamese survival depended on continued American combat and materiel support. The possibility that this support might be greatly reduced, or altogether eliminated in the future, was something that neither MACV nor the Joint General Staff considered. Nor did they take into consideration the military effects of a temporary ceasefire or the likelihood of renewed U.S. combat assistance once that assistance had been withdrawn. The question of how the South Vietnamese were to continue the war alone was completely sidestepped.

If MACV let some matters slip by, it gave others too much attention. The U.S. command worried incessantly about the South Vietnamese desertion problem. The matter appears repeatedly in all types of status reports, resulting in a continuous flow of remedial advice to the field and detailed explanations to higher commands. The volume of attention alone indicated the importance MACV attached to the problem. American reports drew all sorts of conclusions from changing South Vietnamese desertion rates; high rates were testaments to poor leadership and declining rates to improving leadership, never mind the high percentage of desertions in the well-led general reserve units. They could also be taken to measure the popularity of the war effort, the regime, or just about anything associated with the military. High rates could signify low unit morale, leading to low unit strengths and rapid personnel turnover, all of which could explain South Vietnamese ineffectiveness in combat. The inability of MACV to correlate high desertion rates with low operational results was always a puzzle. Regardless, MACV and the entire U.S. advisory effort devoted much time and money trying to "solve" the desertion problem by sponsoring a variety of expensive programs to make military life more acceptable to the average soldier and by acquiescing to a unit stationing policy that virtually destroyed the potential mobility of Saigon's army.

But MACV may have exaggerated the significance of the desertion problem. A monthly South Vietnamese desertion rate of 10 (deserters per 1,000 troops) meant that about 10,000 men were deserting monthly, or 120,000 annually, from an armed force of roughly 1 million. The annual desertion rate in this case would have been 120, but would be perhaps doubled or tripled in line infantry units. Such counts were typical of the South Vietnamese armed forces throughout this period. In comparison, the annual desertion rates of the U.S. Army in World War II, Korea, and Vietnam were much lower and the high U.S. Army rate of 73.5 per 1,000 in 1971 was unusual. However, in these cases U.S. combat units were located abroad, in areas where it was exceedingly difficult to survive far from a soldier's home unit. Where was a deserter to go? A fairer comparison might be made with U.S. desertion rates during the American Civil War. As might be expected, the practice was much more common when home was just around the corner. Federal desertion rates totaled over 150 deserters per 1,000 troops in 1862 and 1863 and soared to 280 in 1864 and 450 in 1865. Viet Cong desertion rates were equally high, reaching 200 per 1,000 in 1969 and leveling off at about 100 in 1970 and 1971. Admittedly, differences in desertion criteria and general circumstances make accurate comparisons difficult. In addition, it was common for deserters to reenlist in other units, making a true desertion loss count impossible. Seen in this light, the South Vietnamese figures appear less surprising and less unusual. Historically, high desertion rates were common in civil wars and were not necessarily decisive factors on the battlefield.[32]

MACV concern over low South Vietnamese unit strengths was also misplaced. The high visibility of these figures may have tended to exaggerate their importance. Both Westmoreland and Abrams responded to the problem by simply declaring a moratorium on the activation of new South Vietnamese units until the existing ones had been brought up to strength. This simple tactic proved effective. As an interim measure, Westmoreland established an assigned strength goal of about 70 percent (470 men) for all South Vietnamese infantry battalions, and he and his successors worked hard to keep these indicators as high as possible. After 1968 unit strength figures became major barometers of South Vietnamese military vitality, and the entire progress of the Vietnamization program depended on keeping training centers, schools, and units filled with personnel before new units could be established. The 90-percent strength level reached by most South Vietnamese units on the eve of the American departure was a major achievement of MACV and the Joint General Staff. Yet, what exactly did such figures measure? The larger (900 +) U.S. infantry battalions could rarely put more than about 500 men in the field,[33] and, if anything, personnel turbulence was greater in American units because of the standard one-year tour length. As MACV considered the U.S. units to be at least twice as effective as their Vietnamese equivalents, there seemed to be no correlation between unit performance and unit strengths of 50 percent and higher. South Vietnamese recruiting and training centers may have been simply shoveling men into units willy-nilly, with little thought to quality or unit cohesion. Unit strength was only one of many factors contributing to unit effectiveness and, by itself, did not warrant the comparatively large amount of attention it received. The matter constantly diverted American attention away from more serious problems, such as leadership, and gave everyone a false sense of optimism as the advisory effort drew to a close.

MACV recognized that a comprehensive unit refresher training program could mend much of the damage caused by the high personnel turnover in most South Vietnamese ground combat units. Periodic retraining would have given unit commanders the opportunity to build unit cohesion without the pressure of constant operational requirements, and in this area American advisory teams might have played a significant role. To this end MACV had the Joint General

---

[32] On the U.S. Army wartime desertion rates, see Paul L. Savage and Richard Gabriel, "Cohesion and Disintegration in the American Army: An Alternative Perspective," *Armed Forces and Society* 2 (Spring 1976): 347–48. The authors do not clarify whether these figures apply to the entire U.S. Army or only to those elements abroad. On Federal desertion rates during the American Civil War, see Monograph, "A Study of Desertion," circa 1935, p. 6, file HRC 251.2, HRB, CMH. On Viet Cong desertion rates, see J. A. Koch, *The Chieu Hoi Program in South Vietnam, 1963–1971* (Santa Monica, Calif.: Rand Corp., 1973), fig. 4., p. 11. The figures include only Viet Cong military deserters. Adding political cadre deserters would have raised the rate by about one-third and inclusion of the North Vietnamese Army deserters would have halved it.

[33] Roughly four rifle companies of 110 men each, and about 60 more for the reconnaissance platoon and support and headquarters elements.

Staff schedule each South Vietnamese infantry and ranger battalion for such training over a three-year period. But the effort continually coughed and sputtered without going very far. Operational commitments, especially during the South Vietnamese cross-border incursions and the North Vietnamese Army offensives, constantly interrupted the training schedule, and MACV failed to put out the extra effort needed to keep the program on track. Moreover, the whole thing was unpopular. South Vietnamese corps and division commanders were reluctant to release organic units, and soldiers were reluctant to go. The large training centers were often in "foreign" provinces, far from friends, family, and familiar places. In-place training had few adherents, and few South Vietnamese officers saw any point in training for something that was already going on. Practical experience was more important than formal instruction. MACV simply was unable to "sell" the concept of training to the South Vietnamese. What were the units to be trained for? Had not everyone been doing the same thing—the patrols, ambushes, and guard duty—for decades? What point was there in training for a conflict that was already taking place? American units had undertaken no training exercises in Vietnam, so why should the South Vietnamese? Without any new goal or vision, the participants lacked enthusiasm for the program. The passive military policies of Saigon tended to drain inspiration and hope from even the best South Vietnamese leaders. The failure of the retraining effort led back to the territorial orientation of the armed forces and the emphasis on the defense.

During the early years of the war, the nature of the fighting justified a defensive territorial strategy. Up to 1964 the military threat to the Saigon regime came from an internal insurgency, aided by the inability of the South Vietnamese themselves to establish an effective government. After 1964 the "outside" military threat from North Vietnam increased steadily but was countered by the rapid buildup of American military power. The enemy's major offensive in early 1968 was a watershed in the struggle. Thereafter, a strong and relatively stable regime ruled Saigon and the internal insurgency grew steadily weaker. At this juncture a major overhaul of the South Vietnamese military was possible, one that would have made the regular forces an instrument of national, rather than local, power. The slow U.S. troop withdrawals that followed ought to have made this clear and, at the same time, buffered the transition. Instead, American military leaders believed that such a transition was impossible and that the South Vietnamese would never be able to deal with the North Vietnamese Army by themselves. American military support would be needed as long as the war continued. MACV tailored the South Vietnamese military force structure accordingly—to fight a defensive war of attrition similar to that which had been waged by the withdrawing American forces, with local deficiencies being made up for by U.S. air and sea power. This partnership had worked fairly well during the North Vietnamese Easter offensive in 1972, and the successive U.S. air-sea offensive against the North Vietnamese had appeared equally effective. The South Vietnamese leaders, for their part, accepted these arrangements, confident that American firepower would be made available if necessary. No one, neither South Vietnamese nor American leaders, had bothered to seriously contemplate alternative situations that might necessitate radical changes in South Vietnamese military policy, strategy, and organization.

The American advisory effort in Vietnam was ultimately unsuccessful, and the military defeat of Saigon in 1975, barely two years after the final American departure, was dramatic in its swiftness. However, this is not to suggest that had the effort been handled otherwise that the outcome would have been any different. Each major decision in either Saigon or Washington took into account many factors that were not readily apparent to outside observers (and obviously ignored many that were). Vietnamese political instability made a combined command impractical. American desires to limit the conflict forced MACV to adopt a defensive strategy, and Saigon's military weaknesses forced the South Vietnamese to take a back seat in the war effort. Such constraints may have made American objectives in South Vietnam hopeless from the start. But above all, the determination of the North Vietnamese and the Viet Cong to persevere through all hazards and see the war through to its ultimate conclusion proved decisive, once again illustrating most of British military historian J. F. C. Fuller's four maxims of modern warfare: political authority, economic self-sufficiency, national discipline, and machine weapons.

However, if the final judgment must be that it was beyond the capacity of one power to reform and reshape the society of another, nevertheless many insights may still be drawn from the experience. Foreign advisory duty, for example, was much more complicated than it appeared, and, if more was expected, advisers should have been better prepared for their assignments and given longer tours. Greater guidance was also needed at all levels so that advisers had specific goals and the capability of fulfilling them. For those occupying critical positions and who, like Westmoreland, found themselves acting as political as well as military counselors, the need for such assistance was by far the greatest. Their experiences showed that superiority in materiel could not compensate for the lack of a unified command, nor could sophisticated plans and programs make up for the absence of more cohesive military and political objectives. As always, political and military leadership was critical throughout the war, and an understanding of the inextricable nature of political and military affairs was basic to any analysis of the conflict by those who occupied positions of authority. Finally, if men and materiel are not to be wasted needlessly, American leaders, military and civilian alike, must continually struggle against the bureaucratic careerism endemic to modern governments that distort and confuse the underpinnings of policy and strategy, and ultimately bring ruin to those institutions that allow it to flourish. The cult of optimism fostered in Saigon and Washington was self-defeating and, in the end, only encouraged the continuation of policies and practices that had little hope of success. These are but a few of the lessons of the war in Vietnam. And given the intensely political nature of that struggle, and the key role played by American civilian leaders in the United States, it would be a serious error if the author has given the impression that the search for understanding should stop here. From the dirt trails and rice paddies of Vietnam, the trail inevitably leads back to the halls of the Pentagon, the Capitol, and the White House, and the rest of the American heartland, all of which had a part in producing the calamitous events of this strange period in the history of the United States.[34]

[34] Bibliographies of the Vietnam War era include Richard Dean Burns and Milton Leitenberg, *The Wars in Vietnam, Cambodia and Laos, 1945–1985*, War/Peace Bibliography Series, no. 18 (Santa Barbara, Calif.: ABC-Clio Information Services, 1984), listing six thousand entries; Christopher L. Sugnet and John T. Hickey, *Vietnam War Bibliography* (Lexington, Mass.: Lexington Books, 1983), noting some four thousand items; and Louis A. Peake's new *The United States in the Vietnam War, 1954–1975: A Selected, Annotated Bibliography* (New York: Garland, 1986). For further discussion of primary material, see Ronald H. Spector, *Researching the Vietnam Experience*, Historical Analysis Series (Washington, D.C.: U.S. Army Center of Military History, 1984), and the bibliographical essay that follows.

Appendixes

A—U.S. ARMY ADVISORY BUILDUP [1]

Assigned Area	1956	1957	1958	1959	1960	1961	1962	1963	1964	1965	1966
Corps	0	1	2	3	3	3	4	4	4	4	4
	0	5	10	15	15	100	380	380	384	571	942
Division	10	10	10	7	7	8	9	9	9	10	10
	30	30	30	35	35	35	162	360	432	520	725
Regiment	31	31	31	22	22	25	31	31	31	31	31
	35	35	31	26	26	29	155	134	66	93	93
Infantry Battalion .	..	..	..	..	69	96	97	97	97	124	128
	0	0	0	0	0	672	286	291	485	620	640
Airborne Battalion	0	0	0	0	0	0	0	6	6	6	8
	0	0	0	0	0	0	0	18	30	18	24
Ranger Company/ Battalion	0	0	0	0	7Cos	35Cos	72Cos	11Bns	20Bns	20Bns	20Bns
	0	0	0	0	7	18	36	33	60	100	100
Province	0	0	0	0	0	39	39	36	42	43	44
	0	0	0	0	0	39	117	235	390	882	862
District	0	0	0	0	0	0	0	0	113	151	206
	0	0	0	0	0	0	0	0	565	725	1171

[1] The figures above the lines represent the number of units; the figures below the lines represent the total number of advisers. The latter figures do not include 20 officers and 22 enlisted personnel, USMC, assigned to field units; 30 officers and 8 enlisted personnel, USMC, assigned to advise the Vietnamese Marine Corps; and 100 advisers, primarily specialists in jungle warfare, provided by Australia. In addition, six civilians from the United Kingdom constituted a British Advisory Mission to the Vietnamese National Police.

Source: Talking Paper, Schandler, 23 Jul 67, sub: MACV Advisory Structure, tab A, SEAB, CMH.

B—South Vietnamese Armed Forces Officer and NCO Strength, December 1968

Organization	Authorized	Available	Shortage
Regular Forces			
Officers	41,625	36,075	5,550
NCOs	113,381	96,310	17,071
Total	155,006	132,385	22,621
Territorial Forces			
Officers	18,152	17,398	754
NCOs	48,316	41,876	6,440
Total	66,468	59,274	7,194
Total RVNAF			
Officers	59,777	53,473	6,304
NCOs	161,697	138,186	23,511
Total	221,474	191,659	29,815

Source: Fact Sheet, MACJ-14, 28 May 69, sub: RVNAF Officer and NCO Strength, MICRO 3/1763, RG 334, WNRC.

C—U.S. Troop Redeployments

Increment	Date	Army Reduction	Air Force Reduction	Navy Reduction	Marine Corps Reduction	Total Reduction	Remaining (549,500) [1]
I.....	Jul–Aug 69	15,712	(+321)	1,222	8,387	25,000	524,500
II	Sep–Dec 69	14,092	2,532	5,412	18,464	40,500	484,000
III....	Feb–Apr 70	29,396	5,614	2,110	12,880	50,000	434,000
IV ...	Jul–Oct 70	15,932	7,362	9,666	17,040	50,000	384,000
V	Oct–Dec 70	38,054	613	1,328	5	40,000	344,000
VI ...	Jan–Apr 71	41,848	1,194	5,600	11,358	60,000	284,000
VII...	May–Jun 71	15,030	164	516	13,590	29,300	254,700
VIII ..	Jul–Sep 71	21,769	5,700	1,122	109	28,700	226,000
IX....	Sep–Nov 71	35,000	5,600	1,400	0	42,000	184,000
X	Dec 71–Jan 72	36,718	6,265	2,017	0	45,000	139,000
XI....	Feb–Apr 72	58,096	8,765	4,032	(+893)	70,000	69,000
XII...	May–Jun 72	14,552	4,884	526	38	20,000	49,000
XIII ..	Jul–Aug 72	8,484	1,354	155	7	10,000	39,000
XIV...	Sep–Nov 72	7,282	3,208	603	907	12,000	27,000
Total		351,965	52,934	35,709	81,892	552,500	

[1] Highest authorized U.S. military strength, 1968–69.
Source: Army Activities Report:SE Asia, 8 Nov 72, pp. 4–5, HRB, CMH.

Bibliographical Note

Because the American advisory effort in South Vietnam was an integral part of the missions of so many diverse agencies, headquarters, staff sections, units, and detachments during 1965–73, almost all information on advisory activities must be culled from a great quantity of archival material. Much of this material is currently in the custody of the U.S. Army Center of Military History (CMH) in Washington, D.C. At the center and in the field U.S. Army historians became record managers and archivists during the Vietnam War, soliciting key documents that, in their judgment, the government's complex recordskeeping systems would never file or retire. Historians in other agencies played similar roles. Thus, despite the absence of any centralized system to preserve and order the vasts amounts of paperwork generated by the war, much of the critical historical documentation has survived intact.

The quality of the documentation varies greatly from agency to agency. In the Army, experience showed that commanders and staff officers tended to retain important documents in their own possession, where they were most readily available for reference. Many higher-level commands and staffs also tended to ignore records management regulations, and often records managers and file clerks at all levels were too inexperienced to properly comply with the detailed recordskeeping procedures. At the small advisory detachments, typewriters and file cabinets were generally lacking and the diary-type journal files mandated by MACV regulations never kept. Understandably, such units retired few, if any, records, and the historian can piece together only a small portion of their activities through interviews and an occasional special report preserved by some higher-level headquarters for its own purposes. The eventual assignment of U.S. Army military history detachments to support corps advisory teams and the 5th Special Forces Group (Airborne) alleviated this situation somewhat. As a result, interview reports and supplementary documents sometimes make it possible to reconstruct at least the type of problems that small unit advisers faced and to correlate their work with programs and policies pursued at higher levels. At the upper echelons the advisory record is more complete, and for the historian the problem is one of focus because of the plethora of material available and the inextricability of the broader advisory effort from almost all American military and political activities in South Vietnam. In Washington the same constraints apply, although they are of a lesser nature due to the fact that the guidance and direction to South Vietnam was funneled through relatively formal communications channels and meetings that can be more easily reconstructed. Although the opening of the Richard M. Nixon Papers in the future will undoubtedly shed more light on Washington decision-making, it will not alter the nature of the official guidance received by General Abrams and Ambassador Bunker concerning American policy.

Military Records

During the Vietnam War the Army used a functional file system, known as TAFFS (The Army Functional File System), to organize the steadily mounting masses of paperwork generated by its commands and staffs. Although not an Army command, MACV adopted a records system similar to TAFFS. Replacing an older decimal file system in the early 1960s, TAFFS established separate recordskeeping systems for different types of organizations and assigned different retention periods for different categories of records, designating only a few categories in each subsystem as permanent. Under the provisions of TAFFS, Army commands and staffs reviewed their files annually and forwarded older records in permanent and semipermanent TAFFS categories to intermediate records holding areas, where they were stored and further sorted and ultimately—under the records management authority of the Army's Office of the Adjutant General (TAG)—shipped to the Washington National Records Center (WNRC), National Archives and Records Administration, Suitland, Maryland. But the entire process was detailed and time-consuming, involving both the preparation of transmittal slips that described the contents of each folder and compliance with complex security procedures for handling classified documents. At times, as many as ten years or more elapsed before the retired records arrived at Suitland, often without their original transmittal slips or with only the most general indication of their contents.[1]

An Army investigation of its records management system in 1969–70 revealed serious problems. Army organizations in Vietnam, especially combat units, were not complying with TAFFS by failing to maintain and retire key historical records, such as military plans and even daily journals. Lack of command interest, the exigencies of an operational environment, and the absence of trained administrative personnel were the primary causes. Normally, headquarters retired only a portion of their own internal records and, in the interest of expediency, as few as possible, particularly in the case of classified documents whose processing was extraordinarily elaborate. The complexity of recordskeeping procedures, the Army's emphasis on statistical data, and the reluctance of many officers to commit

---

[1] Author's discussions with Dr. John Hatcher, Chief, Records Management Division, TAG, and Paul Taborn, TAG, during 1972–85; and author's own experience with records management in the field during 1969–70. TAFFS—which is detailed in Army Regulation 345–215, Records Management: TOE Units of the Active Army and the Army Reserve, 1 November 1962; in Army Regulations 340–18–1 through 340–18–16, Office Management: The Army Functional File System, 14 August 1969; and in Army Regulation 340–2, Office Management: Maintenance and Disposition of Records in TOE Units of the Active Army and the Army Reserve, 30 September 1969—is being replaced by the subject-oriented MARKS, or the Modern Army Recordkeeping System. For a short history, see Vincent H. Demma's "Military History and Army Records," in *A Guide to the Study and Use of Military History*, ed. John E. Jessup, Jr. and Robert W. Coakley (Washington, D.C.: U.S. Army Center of Military History, 1979), pp. 381–91.

potentially controversial information and decisions to paper were contributing factors that also adversely affected the quality of the documents that were retired. As a result, key working papers—especially rough drafts and interoffice memorandums; impromptu studies, reports, and estimates; and the submissions of subordinate commands—often ended up in unmarked folders stored in nameless desks, file cabinets, and safes, where they could be retrieved by the immediate users. Periodically such collections grew too bulky to store and too large to retire, and overworked records managers simply destroyed them. In other cases, primarily at the upper echelons, commanders regarded their military messages, orders, memorandums, and letters as personal correspondence and retained them for their own use.

To rectify this situation, TAG and CMH pursued two different courses of action. During the period 1969–71 TAG sent a series of records management teams to South Vietnam, to ensure that Army commands reemphasized the need to adhere to the TAFFS recordskeeping procedures and to physically supervise the retiring of key records. As a further measure, TAG declared an indefinite moratorium on the destruction of all records retired from Army commands in South Vietnam.[2] CMH (then the Office of the Chief of Military History) took a slightly different approach. With the support of the chiefs of military history, Brig. Gens. Hal C. Pattison and James L. Collins, Jr., and Charles B. MacDonald, chief of the Current History Branch (which later became the Southeast Asia Branch), Army historians made concerted efforts to preserve historical records pertaining to the war by directly soliciting documents and, indirectly, by having field historians assist records managers with placing documents of historical interest under the proper TAFFS control. In Vietnam the MACV and USARV historical offices and the twenty-seven U.S. Army military history detachments in the field also assisted by supervising the preparation of various command historical reports and by preparing their own reports and interviews on those aspects of the war that they felt were not covered adequately in the official records. These field historians funneled their own interviews and reports, together with copies of other key documents, directly back to CMH or to its archival repository, the Military History Research Collection (MHRC; later the Military History Institute, or MHI) at Carlisle Barracks, Pennsylvania. In the United States, historians at CMH and Carlisle Barracks also began a massive effort to acquire personal papers and document collections of key individuals and offices associated with the war. These records included the personal papers of Generals Westmoreland and Abrams, of Ambassadors Komer and Colby, and of many American corps-level commanders, as well as the reports of major Army combat units and key staff agencies, such as the Office of the Special Assistant for Counterinsurgency and Special Activities (SACSA) in the Joint Chiefs of Staff and the Department of Defense's Office of the Assistant Secretary of Defense for Systems Analysis. Although the original copies of most of these records ought to have been retired by the originating agency, much of the documentation is un-

---

[2] These included reports in semipermanent files. The catalyst for these actions was the inability of the Peers Investigating Committee to locate certain records of the 23d Infantry Division involving the massacre at My Lai. Author's discussions with Seymour Pomerance and Ollon McCool, TAG representatives who visited South Vietnam, 1970, and with Waldemar Anderson, TAG, 23 Jan 85.

doubtedly unique, and constitutes an indispensable source for the historian of the Vietnam War.[3]

In the mid-1970s TAG initiated a large-scale effort to centralize Army records returned under TAFFS and temporarily stored in intermediate records-holding areas throughout the world. Under its supervision almost all known retired Army and MACV records pertaining to the Vietnam War were subsequently relocated to WNRC, where they came under TAG's records management authority. In 1981 TAG began a long-range project to bring these holdings, consisting of some 50,000 linear feet of textual files, under better archival control. Preliminary surveys have indicated that approximately 65 percent of these records could be disposed of as "ephemeral," and the remainder reorganized to improve researcher accessibility. Pending the transfer of these holdings to the Modern Military Field Branch of the National Archives, TAG will continue its projected reorganization, as well as accessioning new material that occasionally comes to light.[4]

The ensuing sections describe the various sources of information used in the preparation of this volume, both as a more complete explanation of the citations found in the text and as a guide for future researchers. However, much of the source material pertaining to the Vietnam War is still in a state of flux and its final organization and disposition unsettled.

Unpublished Primary Source Material

Washington National Records Center

As of 1985 the official Department of Defense (DOD) records pertaining to the war in Vietnam are stored at WNRC in Suitland, Maryland, just outside of the District of Columbia. There TAG has assigned specific record group (RG) numbers to files in its custody. Most useful for the Vietnam era are RGs 319 (Records of the Army Staff), 334 (Records of Interservice Agencies, such as MACV), 335 (Records of the Office of the Secretary of the Army), and 338 (Records of U.S. Army Commands, 1942–), although RGs 153 (Records of the Office of the Judge Advocate General, Army) and 159 (Records of the Office of the Inspector General) also contain useful material. The records of the secretary of defense are organized similarly, but are not under the control of TAG. Although transmittal, or accession, forms outlining the contents of these holdings are normally available at Suitland, permission to view the actual documents must be obtained from the retiring agency.

Currently, individual accession forms are the only guide to retired records and often give only the most general idea of their contents. For Army records these forms generally note only the retiring headquarters, the numerical TAFFS subject file, and a brief subject heading (for example, OPLANS or Miscellaneous Documents), and many are still under security control. Aside from a portion of those retired by the MACV headquarters, most of these records detail the activi-

---

[3] For further discussion, see Spector, *Researching the Vietnam Experience.*
[4] Author's discussion with Hatcher, 3 Apr 65.

ties of major U.S. units and commands, and few have any direct bearing on the advisory effort. In many cases, the author was the first individual to open and examine these documents in the early 1970s, often making photocopies of those deemed most valuable. All of these records, including retired MACV documents and those placed in storage by CMH, are under the control of TAG. Ultimately, TAG will transfer these records to the Modern Military Field Branch of the National Archives for permanent organization and storage.

TAG also has custody of a large collection of documents on approximately 150 rolls of microfilm, originally assembled by the MACV historical office. Many of these records, dating from 1964 to 1972, were used in preparing the annual MACV command histories and thereafter retained in a large backup information file. Prior to the American withdrawal in 1973, the MACV historian had the entire collection microfilmed and returned to the United States. While awaiting the arrival of retired records from intermediate records-holding areas, the author made extensive use of this important source, and it is apparent now that much of its contents are unique. A computer printout of the collection is available at the WNRC and CMH, but the program, which at one time correlated the documents to specific subject areas, has been lost. Aside from the security classification, the order of presentation in each roll appears to be random.

U.S. Army Center of Military History

Individual documents in the custody of CMH in Washington, D.C., consist of studies, reports, briefings, memorandums, letters, messages, and similar unpublished primary source material. As a rule, the writing historians have organized such records into broad topical areas and, when appropriate, broken them down further by years, corps zones, or other subcategories. Documents with information pertaining to multiple categories were usually duplicated and copies placed in both subject areas. These collections are maintained in the working files of the Southeast Asia Branch (SEAB), the research files of the Historical Records Branch (HRB), or in CMH's storage files within RG 319 at WNRC. Most of the documents cited in this volume may be found in SEAB in the following file categories established by the author: RVNAF Organization, RVNAF Assessments, Vietnamization, Combined Operations, Advisers, South Vietnamese Military Politics, RD Support, T-Day Planning, and Withdrawal Planning. Others, such as those pertaining to the Chinh-Hunnicutt affair and the Tran Ngoc Chau case, are in special case study folders retained in SEAB or stored at WNRC. Upon completion of the U.S. Army in Vietnam series, all document collections will be transferred to the Modern Military Field Branch of the National Archives.

Document collections of a single individual or office have generally been kept intact. The largest and most important are the William C. Westmoreland Papers, an extensive group of approximately 18 linear feet of papers assembled and maintained by General Westmoreland and his personal staff during his tenure as MACV commander. Most significant is his diary, or history, contained in about thirty loosely bound volumes detailing his daily activities and decisions, and often the thoughts behind the decisions. Appended to the entries are copies of pertinent incoming and outgoing messages, memorandums, reports, and other documents that Westmoreland considered important at the time the entries were made. The history is supplemented by several collections, most of which are described below, and the papers assembled by his aide, Col. Paul L. Miles, Jr. The original Westmoreland Papers used by the author have now been transferred to the Lyndon Baines Johnson Library, Austin, Texas, at the request of General Westmoreland, with photocopies of the collection retained at HRB, CMH, and at MHI. Citations in this volume refer to some of the following collections within the Westmoreland Papers: History file, 1964–68 (Westmoreland's notations in his diary, made generally on a daily basis, with documents appended in tabs); MACV Commander (COMUSMACV) Message file, 1964–68 (backchannel radio message traffic to or from Westmoreland, as opposed to routine message traffic to or from COMUSMACV); COMUSMACV Signature file (correspondence signed by Westmoreland); Fonecon file (records of telephone conversations between Westmoreland and other American military and civilian leaders in South Vietnam); Personal Correspondence file (in general, correspondence not relating to operational activities); Deputy MACV Commander (DEPCOMUSMACV) Message file, 1967–68 (backchannel messages to or from Abrams while serving as Westmoreland's deputy); DEPCOMUSMACV Signature file (correspondence signed by Abrams); Chief of Staff Message file (backchannel messages to or from Westmoreland's chief of staff); Chief of Staff Signature file (correspondence signed by the MACV chief of staff); Chief of Staff Correspondence file (various documents to and from the MACV chief of staff); Embtel/Deptel Message file (copies of messages to or from agencies in the U.S. Embassy, Saigon, which were passed to MACV); and Presidential Meetings file (documents relating to Westmoreland's tenure as Army chief of staff and member of the Joint Chiefs of Staff, 1968–72).

Other collections at HRB, CMH, include the papers of Creighton W. Abrams, Jr.; Arthur S. Collins, Jr.; Michael S. Davison; Welborn G. Dolvin; James F. Hollingsworth; John E. Murray; Bruce Palmer, Jr.; William R. Peers; James W. Sutherland, Jr.; and Jack J. Wagstaff. Of these, the most extensive and the most useful are the Abrams Papers, consisting of incoming and outgoing backchannel messages during his service in Vietnam (1967–72).

The papers of Thomas C. Thayer, HRB, CMH, constitute a reference collection assembled by the former director of the Southeast Asia Office in the Office of the Assistant Secretary of Defense for Systems Analysis. Generally covering the 1967–75 period, the papers are eclectic but contain a great variety of valuable statistical information, trip reports, and significant DOD internal correspondence. Key subject areas are NSSM 1, Vietnamization, South Vietnamese leadership and assessments, negotiations, refugees, and the Viet Cong–North Vietnamese enemy threat. A finding aid prepared by HRB is useful.

The DEPCORDS (MACV Deputy for Civil Operations and Revolutionary Development Support) and Pacification files, SEAB, CMH, include the personal papers of Ambassadors Robert W. Komer and William E. Colby, and other pacification-related material collected by two branch historians, Drs. Richard A. Hunt and Thomas W. Scoville. Of particular interest to this study are the Revolutionary Development Support files, addressing the role of South Vietnamese regular military forces in providing area security, and the topical collections dealing with political problems and corruption. Related collections at CMH are a nearly complete set of province senior adviser reports (in SEAB) and the papers of Richard A. Gard, an official with the U.S. Embassy, Saigon (in HRB). Also useful are the Donald S. Marshall Papers, a collection of documents and other papers assembled by Colonel Marshall who served on the Army Staff and then with MACV's Strategic Plans Office during the tenure of General Abrams. Although the Marshall Papers are now in the custody of TAG, many items were duplicated and integrated into SEAB holdings.

CMH also houses a large collection of interviews. In HRB are over one thousand interview reports, identified by VNI or VNIT numbers. Each report generally consists of one or more taped oral interviews conducted by U.S. Army military history detachments in Vietnam with field- and company-grade officers and senior enlisted personnel, to include a significant number of advisers, starting in 1968. Most are lengthy discussions of the activities and problems of mid-level commanders and staffs, and many include extensive backup documentation. Although few have been transcribed, almost all have summaries prepared by the interviewers, and the branch's finding guides allow researchers to identify interviews by name, date, and unit.

In SEAB are the interviews conducted by the author with the following individuals: Lt. Col. Benjamin L. Abramowitz, Senior Adviser, 8th Regiment, June 1971–April 1972 (26 Feb 76); Samuel Adams, former CIA analyst (April and May 1975); Col. James Anderson, aide to General Abrams (23 Jun 83); Lt. Col. Leon L. Anderson, Senior Adviser, 32d Regiment, October 1967–June 1968, and 10th Regiment, December 1971–June 1972 (26 Feb 76); Lt. Col. Richard O. Brunkow, Senior Adviser, 42d Ranger Group, IV CTZ, circa 1970–71 (26 Feb 76); Lt. Col. Charles D. Burnette, Adviser, Chi Lang National Training Center, August 1963–January 1964, Battalion Adviser, 33d Regiment, January–May 1964, aide to General Paul Harkins, June–August 1964, and Senior Adviser, Ranger Command, II CTZ, January–December 1971 (27 Feb 76); Lt. Col. Medley M. Davis, Special Forces A Detachment, Khe Sanh, and S–3, Special Forces C Detachment, Da Nang, I CTZ, November 1966–September 1967, Senior Adviser, Ranger Command, JGS, June 1970–January 1971, and Ranger Training Command, January–June 1971 (27 Feb 76); Maj. Gen. James N. Ellis, aide to General Abrams (29 Jun 83); Maj. John R. Finch, Advisory Team 33, 23d Division, 1972 (11 Jul 85); Maj. Gen. John F. Freund, various assignments in Vietnam, 1964–67 (25–26 May 72); Donald P. Gregg, former CIA field officer, III CTZ, 1972 (19 Mar 83); Allan E. Goodman, former Rand Corporation analyst (15 Mar 83); Col. Archelaus L. Hamblen, Jr., Deputy Senior Adviser, I CTZ, March–June 1966 (January 1979); Lt. Col. Lawrence W. Hoffman, Battalion, S–1/S–4, and S–2/S–3 Adviser, Airborne Division, January–December 1966 (25 Mar 75); Maj. James E. Mace, Battalion Adviser, Airborne Division, February 1966–February 1967 (25 Mar 75); Maj. George McGuillen, Battalion Adviser, Civil Guard and 7th Division, 1962–63 (26 Feb 76); Lt. Col. Edward F. McGushin, Battalion and Staff Adviser, Airborne Division, August 1966–June 1967, Staff and Senior Adviser, Ranger Command, JGS, January–November 1972 (27 Feb 76); Col. Rod Paschall, Special Forces Adviser, 1962–63 (15 Oct 84, 25 Apr 85, 19 Aug 86); Lt. Gen. William E. Potts, MACV J–2, 1969–72 (12 Apr 84); Lt. Col. Theodore D. Risch, Senior Adviser, 41st Regiment, and G–1 Adviser, II CTZ, November 1968–November 1969 (26 Feb 76); General William B. Rossen, Chief of Staff, MACV, July 1965–August 1967, DEPCOMUSMACV, May 1969–September 1970, CG, USARPAC, October 1970–January 1973; Lt. Col. Donald G. Wells, Battalion and Staff Adviser, Airborne Division, August 1965–August 1966 (25 Mar 75); and author's own conversations when his unit, the 17th Military History Detachment, was attached to Advisory Team 95 (III CTZ) in 1970.

Other CMH collections that proved useful are as follows: stored at WNRC, an almost complete set of the quarterly unit operational reports/lessons learned (ORLLs), prepared by all major Army units in Vietnam, and an extensive collection of unit combat operations after-action reports (COAARs); in HRB, the monthly *Southeast Asia Analysis Report* (January 1967–January 1972, plus index), prepared by the Office of the Assistant Secretary of Defense for Systems Analysis,[5] the weekly *Army Buildup Progress Report* (11 Aug 65–20 Dec 72), prepared by the Office of the Chief of Staff of the Army (and which became the *Army Activities Report: SE Asia* on 26 Mar 69), a good but incomplete collection of senior officer debriefing reports, the MACV command histories, the JCS histories, and the RNVAF quarterly assessments, prepared by the Defense Attache Office in Saigon; and in SEAB, complete sets of the JGS-MACV annual campaign plans AB 141 through 147 for 1966–72. Also available, either in SEAB, CMH, or stored at WNRC, are a variety of studies prepared by the twenty-seven U.S. Army military history detachments that served in Vietnam, together with other studies and documents of historical interest that the detachments passed directly back to CMH. While CMH records also include large numbers of contract reports and published government studies pertaining to the war in Vietnam, the holdings of the Pentagon Library are much larger and more complete in this area, and additional listings are available from the Defense Technical Information Center (DTIC; formerly the Defense Documentation Center, or DDC) and the Department of Commerce's National Technical Information Service (NTIS).[6]

U.S. Army Military History Institute

Located at the U.S. Army War College, Carlisle Barracks, Pennsylvania, the U.S. Army Military Institute (MHI) contains valuable reference facilities, special collections, and document archives relating to the war in Vietnam. Document holdings consist of approximately 128 linear feet of records and several hundred reels of microfilm, much of which is duplicated in CMH and TAG/WNRC holdings. There are also seventy-five private collections of retired senior Army officers who played prominent roles in the Vietnam War. These collections have often been supplemented by extensive transcribed interviews, conducted by U.S.

[5] Thomas C. Thayer, "A Systems Analysis View of the Vietnam War, 1965–1972," February 1965, Document no. ADA–051610, Defense Technical Information Center, Alexandria, Va., reproduces in twelve volumes all of the articles in the 52-issue series *Southeast Asia Analysis Report*.

[6] TAG has declassified approximately thirty-five hundred Vietnam operational, after-action, and debriefing reports, and has made them available for sale to the public through NTIS.

Army War College students during the past ten years (as part of a larger Senior Officers Debriefing Program sponsored by the MHI oral history office). The principal collections examined by the author are the papers of Creighton W. Abrams, Jr. (generally confined to his service on the Army staff, with little on his duties in Vietnam); Arthur S. Collins, Jr. (an excellent oral interview); John H. Cushman (backchannel messages); Michael S. Davison; Julian J. Ewell (oral interview); Andrew J. Goodpastor (extensive oral history); Ralph E. Haines (oral history and logistics information); Joseph M. Heiser, Jr. (oral history); Harold K. Johnson (oral history and a large collection of documents and personal papers); Peter E. Kelly; Henry C. Newton; Donald A. Seibert (draft memoirs); John Paul Vann (small but useful); and Melvin Zais.

In addition, MHI has custody of several separate oral history collections. One group includes 18 untranscribed interviews taken in Vietnam during 1972 by MACV and CMH historians (cited as MACV History Branch Interviews), a number of them with such key senior U.S. Army advisers as Brig. Gen. John R. McGiffert II, deputy commander of the Third Regional Assistance Command (III CTZ), and Col. Donald J. Metcalf, who advised the South Vietnamese 3d Division. Another group consists of approximately 250 untranscribed interviews, taken in 1973–74 at Fort Knox, Kentucky (cited as Fort Knox Armor School Interviews), with armor officers and noncommissioned officers who had served in Vietnam, many as advisers with South Vietnamese armored units and commands. Although the quality of this second group varies, there is much useful low-level information.

U.S. Department of State

In addition to its own large archival holdings, the U.S. Department of State (DS) currently has custody of the personal and official papers of Ellsworth Bunker, the former U.S. ambassador to South Vietnam, 1967–73 (located in boxes 294 and 295, RG 74D417). This material consists primarily of his regular situation reports to the president, but includes other documents, such as correspondence and memorandums authored by Lodge, Kissinger, and Nixon. The author obtained permission to use the papers from Ambassador Bunker prior to his death in 1984.

Published Primary Sources

Document Collections

The most well-known collection of published documents is the Pentagon Papers, a document history of the U.S. involvement in the war in Vietnam up to early 1968 prepared by the Department of Defense. The declassified version printed for the House Committee on Armed Services (U.S. Department of Defense, *United States–Vietnam Relations, 1945–1967*, 12 vols. [Washington, D.C.: Government Printing Office, 1971]) is the most extensive and is supplemented by the Senator Gravel edition (*The Pentagon Papers: The Defense Department History of United States Decisionmaking on Vietnam*, 4 vols. [Boston: Beacon Press, 1971]). A privately assembled companion collection, Gareth Porter, ed., *Vietnam: The Definitive Documentation of Human Decisions*, 2 vols. (Standfordville, N.Y.: Coleman, 1979), has difficulty living up to its title, but contains many critical declassified documents that supplement those presented in the Pentagon Papers.

Memoirs and Firsthand Accounts

Autobiographical material is often difficult to analyze out of its historical context. While valuable, the personal testimonies of early military advisers, such as Otto Liman von Sanders, *Five Years in Turkey*, trans. Carl Reichmann (Annapolis, Md.: U.S. Naval Institute, 1927), and Joseph W. Stilwell, *The Stilwell Papers*, ed. Theodore White (New York: Sloane, 1948), fall into this category, just as Bernard Fall's popular *Street Without Joy: Indochina as War, 1946–54* (Harrisburg, Pa.: Stackpole, 1961), must be complemented by Mao Tse-tung's revolutionary primers like *Basic Tactics*, trans. Stuart R. Schram (New York: Praeger, 1966); *Selected Military Writings of Mao Tse-tung* (Peking: Foreign Languages Press, 1963); or *Selected Works*, 4 vols. (Peking: Foreign Languages Press, 1961–65). In this respect, General Westmoreland's *A Soldier Reports* (Garden City, N.Y.: Doubleday, 1976), written with the assistance of Charles B. MacDonald, is more comprehensive. Although assembled well after the events in Vietnam had reached their final conclusion, it is based on the MACV commander's voluminous personal papers and is seconded by the Vietnam Studies series cited below. Marine Corps commander Lewis W. Walt's *Strange War, Strange Strategy: A General's Report on Vietnam* (New York: Funk and Wagnalls, 1970) and Admiral U. S. G. Sharp's *Strategy for Defeat* (San Rafael, Calif.: Presidio Press, 1978) are less revealing, and General William B. Rosson's "Nine Steps Into the Maelstrom," *Army* 34 (July 1984): 24–36, (August 1984): 42–55, (September 1984): 30–39, is too brief. More studies like General Bruce Palmer, Jr.'s *The 25-Year War: America's Military Role in Vietnam* (Lexington, Ky.: University Press of Kentucky, 1984) are needed to flesh out those brief glimpses into American military workings, best illustrated by pieces such as General Richard G. Stilwell's short "Commentary: A Soldier's Viewpoint," in *The American Military and the Far East: Proceedings of the Ninth Military History Symposium, U.S.A.F. Academy, 1–3 October 1980* (Washington, D.C.: U.S. Air Force Academy, 1980), pp. 65–68. Meanwhile, from the bottom up, Samuel Adams' "Vietnam Cover-up: Playing War With Numbers," *Harper's*, May 1975, pp. 41–44, laid the basis for a major public controversy, with records and testimony from both sides of the Westmoreland-CBS lawsuit currently winding their way to public archival institutions. The controversy was recently detailed in Bob Brewin and Sydney Shaw's *Vietnam on Trial: Westmoreland vs. CBS* (New York: Atheneum, 1987).

On the political side, the published coverage is just as sparse, further underlining the importance of the Pentagon Papers. Ambassadors Henry Cabot Lodge's *The Storm Has Many Eyes* (New York: Norton, 1973) and Maxwell D. Taylor's *Swords and Plowshares* (New York: Norton, 1972) have little on the post-

1965 period, while Ellsworth Bunker never finished his projected memoirs. William Colby (with Peter Forbath), *Honorable Men: My Life in the CIA* (New York: Simon and Schuster, 1978), and Komer's special studies do better treating the mid-level managers in South Vietnam, but Lyndon B. Johnson's sketchy *The Vantage Point: Perspectives of the Presidency, 1963-1969* (New York: Holt, Rinehart and Winston, 1971); Richard M. Nixon's *The Memoirs of Richard Nixon* (New York: Grosset and Dunlap, 1978); and Henry Kissinger's *White House Years* (Boston: Little, Brown, 1979) give only cursory treatment to key questions, and the secretaries of defense for both American presidents have remained mute. Perhaps they had little to say.

For the South Vietnamese, Nguyen Cao Ky's *Twenty Years and Twenty Days* (New York: Stein and Day, 1976) and Tran Van Don's *Our Endless War: Inside Vietnam* (San Rafael, Calif.: Presidio Press, 1978) are eclectic but useful. Together with the CMH Indochina Monographs, these books are just about all that is available in English from the side of Saigon, much of which was summed up earlier in Cao Van Vien's "The Strategy of Isolation," *Military Review* 52 (April 1972): 22-30.

The Department of the Army's Vietnam Studies also fall into the autobiographical category, although many were actually prepared by supporting staffs and only incidentally reflect the primary author's personal experiences and outlook. The series began in 1970 when, at the suggestion of Charles MacDonald, General Westmoreland, in his capacity as the Army chief of staff, asked several active and retired U.S. Army officers who had occupied key posts in Vietnam to prepare short monographs on areas relevant to their particular expertise and experience. The results were mixed. Some assigned subordinates to do the actual writing, while others readily took pen in hand to accomplish the task. Those authored, for example, by General Ewell and Colonel Kelly bear the strong stamp of their assigned author, while others merely chronicle the activities of particular branches of service. All, however, are useful, and the resulting twenty-two studies add much to an understanding of how the Army approached the often neglected areas of intelligence, logistical support, base development, riverine operations, and tactical communications. William M. Momyer's *The Vietnamese Air Force, 1951-1975: An Analysis of Its Role in Combat*, USAF Southeast Asia Monograph, vol. 3, no. 4 (Washington, D.C.: Government Printing Office, 1977), is a similar work, but all too brief. The ten Army Vietnam Studies cited in the text are noted below.

Collins, James Lawton, Jr. *The Development and Training of the South Vietnamese Army, 1950-1972*. Washington, D.C., 1975.

Ewell, Julian J., and Hunt, Ira A., Jr. *Sharpening the Combat Edge*. Washington, D.C., 1974.

Hay, John H., Jr. *Tactical and Materiel Innovations*. Washington, D.C., 1974.

Heiser, Joseph M., Jr. *Logistic Support*. Washington, D.C., 1974.

Kelly, Francis J. *U.S. Army Special Forces, 1961-1971*. Washington, D.C., 1973.

Larsen, Stanley Robert, and Collins, James Lawton, Jr. *Allied Participation in Vietnam*. Washington, D.C., 1975.

McChristian, Joseph A. *The Role of Military Intelligence, 1965–1967.* Washington, D.C., 1974.
Ott, David Ewing. *Field Artillery, 1954–1973.* Washington, D.C., 1975.
Ploger, Robert R. *U.S. Army Engineers, 1965–1970.* Washington, D.C., 1974.
Starry, Donn A. *Mounted Combat in Vietnam.* Washington, D.C., 1978.

The CMH Indochina Monographs are more useful. Prepared by prominent leaders of the former armed forces of South Vietnam, Laos, and Cambodia who fled Southeast Asia in 1975, they give an interesting look from "the other side of the hill." Under the supervision of General William E. Potts (USA, Ret.) and the staff of the General Research Corporation (GRC), a private research firm, these officers prepared the twenty monographs based on a contract between GRC and CMH. Although the authors attempted, in many cases, to present definitive histories of particular areas of interests based on records made available to them, there are enough personal commentaries within each of the studies to make them extremely valuable, if used with care. Although only one, Cao Van Vien, *The Final Collapse* (Washington, D.C.: U.S. Army Center of Military History, 1983), received a wide publication distribution, all were published by CMH in a more informal format and are available at service and government depository libraries. Those by Vien and Ngo Quang Truong are especially noteworthy. William E. LeGro, *Vietnam From Cease-Fire to Capitulation* (Washington, D.C.: Government Printing Office, 1981), written by the former intelligence officer of the Defense Attache Office, Saigon, is a related work that also borders on being a memoir. The sixteen Indochina Monographs cited in the text are noted below.

Hinh, Nguyen Duy. *Lam Son 719.* Washington, D.C., 1979.
——. *Vietnamization and the Cease-Fire.* Washington, D.C., 1980.
——, and Tho, Tran Dinh. *The South Vietnamese Society.* Washington, D.C., 1980.
Khuyen, Dong Van. *The RVNAF.* Washington, D.C., 1980.
——. *RVNAF Logistics.* Washington, D.C., 1980.
Lung, Hoang Ngoc. *The General Offensives of 1968–69.* Washington, D.C., 1981.
——. *Intelligence.* Washington, D.C., 1982.
——. *Strategy and Tactics.* Washington, D.C. 1980.
Tho, Tran Dinh. *The Cambodian Incursion.* Washington, D.C., 1979.
——. *Pacification.* Washington, D.C., 1980.
Truong, Ngo Quang. *The Easter Offensive of 1972.* Washington, D.C., 1980.
——. *RVNAF and US Operational Cooperation and Coordination.* Washington, D.C., 1981.
——. *Territorial Forces.* Washington, D.C., 1981.
Vien, Cao Van. *Leadership.* Washington, D.C., 1981.
——, and Khuyen, Dong Van. *Reflections on the Vietnam War.* Washington, D.C., 1980.
——; Truong, Ngo Quang; Khuyen, Dong Van; Hinh, Nguyen Duy; Tho, Tran Dinh; Lung, Hoang Ngoc; and Vien, Chu Xuan. *The U.S. Adviser.* Washington, D.C., 1980.

Official Publications

Official Department of the Army publications include regulations, manuals, pamphlets, and other documents that detail military doctrine, procedures, organization, tactics, and equipment. Most are organized according to subject area and amended almost continuously. Others, like the *U.S. Army Register* that lists all regular and reserve officers serving on active duty by name, noting rank, age, place of birth, education, source of commission, and branch, are published annually. (Similar aids exist for the U.S. Navy, Marine Corps, and Air Force.) Good collections are maintained by many Army libraries, and the holdings at MHI are among the most complete.

Of more immediate value are the histories and historical reports prepared by military units and commands in the field. These include ORLLs, after-action reports, annual historical summaries, and other analagous studies that are normally classified and receive a limited distribution. For this volume, the most useful are the MACV command histories, actually a massive seminarrative staff study that was assembled annually by the MACV historical office. The quality varies greatly according to the candor and completeness of individual staff submissions, but the large amounts of raw historical data filling each volume make the series an invaluable source. Less useful in this regard are the Pacific Command's *Report on the War in Vietnam* and the Joint Chiefs of Staff histories, all of which contain more interpretive and less raw material. These and the historical reports of smaller units and commands can be found at CMH, MHI, and WNRC. Complete citations for the three larger histories are noted below.

Historical Division, Joint Secretariat, U.S. Joint Chiefs of Staff. "The Joint Chiefs of Staff and the War in Vietnam, 1960–1968." Parts 1–3. The History of the Joint Chiefs of Staff. Washington, D.C., 1970.

——. "The Joint Chiefs of Staff and the War in Vietnam, 1969–1970." The History of the Joint Chiefs of Staff. Washington, D.C., 1976.

——. "The Joint Chiefs of Staff and the War in Vietnam, 1971–1973." The History of the Joint Chiefs of Staff. Washington, D.C., 1979.

Military History Branch, Headquarters, United States Military Assistance Command, Vietnam. "Command History, 1964." Saigon, 1965.

——. "Command History, 1965." Saigon, 1966.

——. "Command History, 1966." Saigon, 1967.

——. "Command History, 1967." Volumes 1–3. Saigon, 1968.

——. "Command History, 1968." Volumes 1–2. Saigon, 1969.

——. "Command History, 1969." Volumes 1–3. Saigon, 1970.

——. "Command History, 1970." Volumes 1–4. Saigon, 1971.

——. "Command History, 1971." Volumes 1–2. Saigon, 1972.

——. "Command History, 1972–1973." Volumes 1–2. Saigon, 1973.

(Most of the MACV command histories are supplemented by a special annex treating the operations of the Studies and Observation Group (SOG) and other highly classified intelligence areas. Each annex was published and distributed separately.)

U.S. Pacific Command. *Report on the War in Vietnam (as of 30 June 1968): Section I, Report on Air and Naval Campaigns Against North Vietnam and Pacific Command-wide Support of the War, June–July 1968* (by Admiral U. S. G. Sharp); *Section II, Report on Operations in South Vietnam, January 1964–June 1968* (by General William C. Westmoreland). Washington, D.C.: Government Printing Office, 1969.

Secondary Sources

Special Studies

The author also consulted a wide variety of special studies, reports, and research papers on the Vietnam War prepared by a variety of government offices, contract firms, and private scholars. Although most are either unpublished or received extremely limited distribution, many are available at CMH, MHI, DTIC, NTIS, and various Army libraries. Those noted in the text are cited below.

Andreacchio, Nicholas A. "An Historical Analysis of ARVN Armor Operations From Conception to the Present, Focusing on the Two Northern Provinces." Circa 1969. Copy in SEAB, CMH.

Bergerud, Eric M. "The War in Hau Nghia Province, Republic of Vietnam, 1963–1973." Ph.D. diss., University of California, Berkeley, 1981.

Bowman, Stephen Lee. "The U.S. Army and Counterinsurgency Warfare: The Making of Doctrine, 1946–1964." M.A. thesis, Duke University, 1981.

Bredo, William; Shreve, Robert O.; Seeley, Donn E.; Edwards, Morris O.; Tater William J.; Aylward, Michael J.; Slawson, Paul S.; and Goshe, Frederick. *Land Reform in Vietnam,* SRI Project no. IU–6797. Menlo Park, Calif.: Stanford Research Institute, 1968.

Bullard, Monte R. "Political Cadre Systems in the Military." Student paper written at U.S. Army Command and General Staff College, Fort Leavenworth, Kans., June 1970.

Central Intelligence Agency. National Intelligence Survey 43D. "South Vietnam: General Survey." April 1965. Copy in SEAB, CMH.

Clarke, Jeffrey J. "The Role of USARV Units in Vietnamization." CMH Monograph 192M. Washington, D.C.: U.S. Army Center of Military History, 1974.

Ello, Paul S.; Joyce, Richard P.; Williams, Robert H.; and Woodworth, William. *U.S. Army Special Forces and Similar Internal Defense Advisory Operations in Mainland Southeast Asia, 1961–1967.* McLean, Va.: Research Analysis Corp., 1969.

Goodman, Allan E. *An Institutional Profile of the South Vietnamese Officer Corps.* Santa Monica, Calif.: Rand Corp., 1970.

———. "A Social and Political Profile of the Republic of South Vietnam's Officer Corps." Internal Rand study (and a forerunner for the published report noted above), September 1968. Copy in SEAB, CMH.

——. "Who Was on First?: The Political Structure of the RVNAF Officer Corps." Internal Rand study (and a forerunner for the published report noted above), May 1968. Copy in SEAB, CMH.

Government Accounting Office. Report to the Congress by the Comptroller General of the United States. "Logistics Aspects of Vietnamization, 1969–72." No. B–159451, circa 1973. Copy in SEAB, CMH.

Hammond, O. W. *Role of the Advisor*. Control Data Corp., 1969.

Heymont, Irving; Emery, Ronald B.; and Phillips, John G. (?) "Cost Analysis of Land Combat Counterinsurgency Operations: Vietnam, [1957–1964]." Draft working paper of the Preliminary Report. Research Analysis Corp., McLean, Va., n.d. Copy in SEAB, CMH.

Heymont, Irving. *Resource Allocations for the RVN Army, Regional Forces, Popular Forces, and U.S. Army Advisory Program: FY65–FY67*. RAC–TP–333. McLean, Va.: Research Analysis Corp., 1968.

——. *Resource Allocations in Support of RVN Army, Regional Forces, and Popular Forces: FY68*. RAC–TP–368. McLean, Va.: Research Analysis Corp., 1969.

——. *Resource Allocations for the RVN Army, Regional Force, and Popular Force: FY69*. RAC–TP–401. McLean, Va.: Research Analysis Corp., 1970.

——; Bennett, Walter H.; Downing, David A.; and Ray, Dorothy L. *Resource Allocations for the RVN Security System: FY70–FY71*. RAC–TP–452. McLean, Va.: Research Analysis Corp., 1972.

——. *Resource Allocations and Costs for the Republic of Vietnam Security System: FY72 (Final Report)*. OAD–CR–3. McLean, Va.: General Research Corp., 1973.

Hickey, Gerald Cannon. *The American Military Advisor and His Foreign Counterpart: The Case of Vietnam*. Santa Monica, Calif.: Rand Corp., 1965.

——. *The Highland People of South Vietnam: Social and Economic Development*. Santa Monica, Calif.: Rand Corp., 1967.

Janicik, Edward E. "Evolution of Missions for US Land Forces, March 1965–July 1966." Study of the Institute for Defense Analyses, Arlington, Va., 1968. Copy in SEAB, CMH.

Joint General Staff J–5. *The Viet Cong "Tet" Offensive (1968)*. Edited by Pham Van Son. Translated by Robert J. Parr et al. Saigon, circa 1969.

Koch, J. A. *The Chieu Hoi Program in South Vietnam, 1963–1971*. Santa Monica, Calif.: Rand Corp., 1973.

Komer, Robert W. *Bureaucracy Does Its Thing: Institutional Constraints on U.S.-GVN Performance in Vietnam*. Santa Monica, Calif.: Rand Corp., 1972.

Military History Branch, MACV. "The March-June Political Crisis in South Vietnam and Its Effect on Military Operations." December 1966. Copy in SEAB, CMH.

Moss, Molton; Shivar, Richard S.; Moser, John O.; Voynitch, Alexander, Jr.; and Ehrlich, Eugene A. "U.S. Preparedness for Future Enemy Prisoner of War/Detainee Operations." Study prepared under the auspices of the Engineer Studies Group, 1977. Copy in U.S. Army Corps of Engineers Library.

Office of the Provost Marshal, MACV. "Provost Marshal History, 1964–1973." Copy in SEAB, CMH.

Palmer, Bruce, Jr. *US Intelligence and Vietnam*. Special issue of the CIA's *Studies in Intelligence*. Vol. 28, no. 5, 1984 (TE–SINT 84–005).

Rockett, Frederick C.; Fiman, Byron G.; and Fox, Wyatt R. *SEER Revision*. Greenwich International, 1969. Document no. ASDIRS 2650, Pentagon Library.

Sinaiko, H. Wallace; Guthrie, George M.; and Abbot, Preston S. *Operating and Maintaining Complex Military Equipment: A Study of Training Problems in the Republic of Vietnam*. IDA Research Paper P–501. Arlington, Va.: Institute for Defense Analyses, 1969.

Social Behavior Division, Combat Development and Test Center–Vietnam, JGS. *Report of the Study on Living Standards, Republic of Vietnam Armed Forces (Army)*. English translation. Saigon, 1969.

Special Studies Group, Office of the Chief of Staff of the Army. "Programs To Improve ARVN (PIARV)." December 1966. Document no. ASDIRS 2589, Pentagon Library.

Stires, Frederick H. *The U.S. Special Forces C.I.D.G. Mission in Vietnam: A Preliminary Case Study in Counterpart and Civil-Military Relationships*. Washington, D.C.: Special Operations Research Office, American University, 1964.

Thayer, Thomas C. "How To Analyze a War Without Fronts: Vietnam, 1965–72." *Journal of Defense Research*, Series B.: Tactical Warfare Analysis of Vietnam Data, 7B, no. 3 (Fall 1975).

Official Histories

Similar sources are the published histories prepared by defense agencies of their activities and related subject areas. These studies are normally authored by professional historians following rigorous academic standards in the use of evidence, balance, and objectivity. During the preparation of this volume, the author has consulted with other government historians on a regular basis and reviewed many of their works, some in draft form. Those cited in the text are noted below.

Allen, Alfred M. *Skin Diseases in Vietnam, 1965–72*. Medical Department, United States Army. Washington, D.C.: Office of the Surgeon General and the U.S Army Center of Military History, 1977.

Ballard, Jack S. *Development and Employment of Fixed-Wing Gunships, 1962–1972*. The United States Air Force in Southeast Asia. Washington, D.C.: Office of Air Force History, 1982.

Bergen, John D. *Military Communications: The Test of Technology*. United States Army in Vietnam. Washington, D.C.: U.S. Army Center of Military History, 1986.

Bowers, Ray L. *Tactical Airlift*. The United States Air Force in Southeast Asia. Washington, D.C.: Office of Air Force History, 1983.

Carland, John M. *Combat Operations, June 1965–October 1966.* United States Army in Vietnam. Washington, D.C.: U.S. Army Center of Military History, forthcoming.

Demma, Vincent H. *Advice and Support: The Middle Years, 1961–1965.* United States Army in Vietnam. Washington, D.C.: U.S. Army Center of Military History, forthcoming.

Futrell, Robert F., assisted by Martin Blumenson. *The Advisory Years to 1965.* The United States Air Force in Southeast Asia. Washington, D.C.: Office of Air Force History, 1981.

Hammond, William M. *Public Affairs: The Military and the Media, 1962–1968.* United States Army in Vietnam. Vol. 1. Washington, D.C.: The U.S. Army Center of Military History, forthcoming.

Hermes, Walter G. *Truce Tent and Fighting Front.* United States Army in the Korean War. Washington, D.C.: Office of the Chief of Military History, 1966.

Hunt, Richard A. *Pacification.* United States Army in Vietnam. Washington, D.C.: U.S. Army Center of Military History, forthcoming.

Sawyer, Robert K. *Military Advisors in Korea: KMAG in Peace and War.* Edited by Walter G. Hermes. Washington, D.C.: Office of the Chief of Military History, 1962.

Scoville, Thomas W. *Reorganizing for Pacification Support.* Washington, D.C.: U.S. Army Center of Military History, 1982.

Shulimson, Jack, and Johnson, Charles M. *U.S. Marines in Vietnam: The Landing and the Buildup, 1965.* Washington, D.C.: U.S. Marine Corps History and Museums Division, 1978.

Shulimson, Jack. *U.S. Marines in Vietnam: An Expanding War, 1966.* Washington, D.C.: U.S. Marine Corps History and Museums Division, 1982.

Spector, Ronald H. *Advice and Support: The Early Years, 1941–1960.* United States Army in Vietnam. Washington, D.C.: U.S. Army Center of Military History, 1983.

———. *Researching the Vietnam Experience.* Historical Analysis Series. Washington, D.C.: U.S. Army Center of Military History, 1984.

Whitlow, Robert H. *U.S. Marines in Vietnam: The Advisory and Combat Assistance Era, 1954–1964.* Washington, D.C.: U.S. Marine Corps History and Museums Division, 1977.

Published Accounts

To those cited in the text, the author has added only a few general works, with no intention of slighting the many other excellent studies available from the sea of literature produced by the war. More complete treatments of secondary sources can be found in the bibliographical works noted below, Spector's *Researching the Vietnam Experience* mentioned earlier, and the bibliographical essay in George C. Herring, *America's Longest War: The United States and Vietnam, 1950–1975* (New York: Wiley, 1979), currently the standard college text for the conflict.

Battreal, Raymond R. "Ky Binh Viet Nam—Muon Nam!" *Armor*, July–August 1974, pp. 8–14.

Berman, Larry. *Planning a Tragedy: The Americanization of the War in Vietnam*. New York: Norton, 1982.

Blaufarb, Douglas S. *The Counterinsurgency Era: U.S. Doctrine and Performance, 1950 to the Present*. New York: Free Press, 1977.

Burns, Richard Dean, and Leitenberg, Milton. *The Wars in Vietnam, Cambodia and Laos, 1945–1985*. War/Peace Bibliography Series, no. 18. Santa Barbara, Calif.: ABC-Clio Information Services, 1984.

Cochran, Alexander S., Jr. "American Planning for Ground Combat in Vietnam, 1952–1965." *Parameters* 14 (Summer 1984): 63–69.

Corson, William R. *The Betrayal*. New York: Norton, 1968.

Dillard, Walter Scott. *Sixty Days to Peace: Implementing the Paris Peace Accords, Vietnam 1973*. Washington, D.C.: National Defense University, 1982.

Fall, Bernard B. *The Two Vietnams: A Political and Military Analysis*. 2d rev. ed. New York: Praeger, 1967.

Fitzgerald, Francis. *Fire in the Lake*. Boston: Little, Brown, 1972.

Goodman, Allan E. "Dynamics of the U.S.–South Vietnamese Alliance: What Went Wrong." Paper delivered at Vietnam War Conference sponsored by the Woodrow Wilson's International Security Studies Program and the *Wilson Quarterly*, Washington, D.C., January 7–8, 1983.

——. The Lost Peace: America's Search for a Negotiated Settlement of the Vietnam War. Stanford, Calif.: Hoover Institution Press, 1978.

Greene, T. M., ed. *The Guerrilla—And How To Fight Him: Selections From the Marine Corps Gazette*. New York: Praeger, 1962.

Hackworth, David H. "Our Advisors Must Pass the Ball." *Army* 21 (May 1971): 61–62.

Hickey, Gerald Cannon. *Sons of the Mountains: Ethnohistory of the Vietnamese Central Highlands to 1954*. New Haven, Conn.: Yale University Press, 1982.

——. Free in the Forest: Ethnohistory of the Vietnamese Central Highlands, 1954–1976. New Haven, Conn.: Yale University Press, 1982.

Kowet, Don. *A Matter of Honor*. New York: Macmillan, 1984.

Lewy, Guenter. *America in Vietnam*. New York: Oxford University Press, 1978.

——. "Some Political-Military Lessons of the Vietnam War." *Parameters* 14 (Spring 1984): 2–14.

McCoy, Alfred W. *The Politics of Heroin in Southeast Asia*. New York: Harper and Row, 1972.

McMahon, Richard. "Saigon '75: The Inevitable Collapse." *The Retired Officer*, April 1985, pp. 18–22.

McNaugher, Thomas L. *The M16 Controversies*. New York: Praeger, 1984.

Moore, Robin. *The Green Berets*. New York: Crown, 1965.

Oberdorfer, Don. *Tet!* Garden City, N.Y.: Doubleday, 1971.

Peake, Louis A. *The United States in the Vietnam War, 1954–1975: A Selected, Annotated Bibliography*. New York: Garland, 1986.

Pike, Douglas. *Viet Cong: The Organization and Techniques of the National Liberation Front of South Vietnam*. Studies in International Communism, no. 7. Cambridge, Mass.: M.I.T. Press, 1966.

542

Piller, Geoffrey. "DOD's Office of International Security Affairs: The Brief Ascendancy of an Advisory System." *Political Science Quarterly* 98 (Spring 1981): 59–78.

Race, Jeffrey. *War Comes to Long An: Revolutionary Conflict in a Vietnamese Province.* Berkeley, Calif.: University of California Press, 1972.

Savage, Paul L., and Gabriel, Richard. "Cohesion and Disintegration in the American Army: An Alternative Perspective." *Armed Forces and Society* 2 (Spring 1976): 340–75.

———. *Crisis in Command: Mismanagement in the Army.* New York: Hill and Wang, 1978.

Shaplen, Robert. *The Lost Revolution: The U.S. in Vietnam, 1946–1966.* Rev. ed. New York: Harper and Row, 1966.

Simpson III, Charles M. *Inside the Green Berets: The First Thirty Years.* Novato, Calif.: Presidio Press, 1983.

Stanton, Shelby L. *The Green Berets at War: U.S. Army Special Forces in Asia, 1956–1975.* Novato, Calif.: Presidio Press, 1986.

Sugnet, Christopher L., and Hickey, John T. *Vietnam War Bibliography.* Lexington, Mass.: Lexington Books, 1983.

Summers, Harry G., Jr. *On Strategy: The Vietnam War in Context.* Carlisle Barracks, Pa.: Strategic Studies Institute, U.S. Army War College, 1981.

———. "Principles of War and Low-Intensity Conflict." *Military Review* 65 (March 1985): 43–49.

Trullinger, James W., Jr. *Village at War: An Account of Revolution in Vietnam.* New York: Longman, 1980.

Tuchman, Barbara W. *Stilwell and the American Experience in China, 1911–45.* New York: Macmillan, 1971.

Turley, G. H. *The Easter Offensive, Vietnam, 1972.* Novato, Calif.: Presidio Press, 1985.

Weller, Jac. "Good and Bad Weapons for Vietnam." *Military Review* 48 (October 1968): 56–64.

Westerman, George F. "Military Justice in the Republic of Vietnam." *Military Law Review* 31 (January 1966). DA Pamphlet 27-100-31.

List of Abbreviations

Am	American
ARVN	Army of the Republic of Vietnam
Asst	Assistant
AWOL	Absent without leave
Bde	Brigade
Bn	Battalion
CAP	Combined Action Program
CAT	Combat assistance team
Cdr(s)	Commander(s)
CG	Commanding general
CIA	Central Intelligence Agency
CIDG	Civilian Irregular Defense Group
CINCPAC	Commander in Chief, Pacific
CMH	U.S. Army Center of Military History
CO	Commanding officer
Co	Company
COAAR	Combat operations after-action report
CofS	Chief of Staff
CORDS	Civil Operations and Revolutionary Development Support
CRIMP	Consolidated RVNAF Improvement and Modernization Plan
CTZ	Corps Tactical Zone
DA	Department of the Army
DCG	Deputy commanding general
Dep	Deputy
DIA	Defense Intelligence Agency
DIOCC	District Intelligence Operations and Coordination Center
Div	Division
DMZ	Demilitarized Zone
DOD	U.S. Department of Defense
DRAC	Delta Regional Assistance Command
DS	U.S. Department of State
Elms	Elements

EMBTEL	U.S. Embassy, Saigon, telegram
FAC(s)	Forward air controller(s)
FFV	Field Force, Vietnam
FO	Forward observer
FRAC	First Regional Assistance Command
FULRO	*Front unifie de la lutte des races opprimees*
FY	Fiscal year
GVN	Government of Vietnam
HES	Hamlet Evaluation System
HRB	Historical Records Branch, CMH
HQ	Headquarters
ICS, SEA	Integrated Communications System, Southeast Asia
IMSTAF	International Military Security Task Force
ISA	International Security Affairs
J–1	Assistant chief of staff for personnel
J–2	Assistant chief of staff for intelligence
J–3	Assistant chief of staff for operations
J–4	Assistant chief of staff for logistics
J–5	Assistant chief of staff for plans
J–6	Assistant chief of staff for communications-electronics
JCS	Joint Chiefs of Staff
JGS	Joint General Staff
JSF	Joint support funds
JUSPAO	Joint U.S. Public Affairs Office
LLDB	*Lac Luong Dac Biet*
MAAG	Military Assistance Advisory Group
MACV	Military Assistance Command, Vietnam
MALTs	Mobile advisory logistics teams
MAP	Military Assistance Program
MATs	Mobile advisory teams
MATA	Military assistance training and advisory course
MCHC	U.S. Marine Corps Historical Center
MHI	U.S. Army Military History Institute
MIKE	Mobile Strike
MSS	Military Security Service
NARA	National Archives and Records Administration
NSA	National Security Affairs
NSDM 36	National Security Decision Memorandum 36
NSSM 1	National Security Study Memorandum 1

NSSM 36	National Security Study Memorandum 36
NTC	National Training Center
NVA	North Vietnamese Army

OJT	On-the-job training

PAVN	People's Army of [North] Vietnam
PFTC	Popular Forces Training Center
POW	Prisoner of war
PRAISE	Program Review and Analysis Improvement System
PRUs	Provincial Reconnaissance Units
PSDF	People's Self-Defense Force
PSYOPS	Psychological operations

RD	Revolutionary development
RFTC	Regional Forces Training Center
RG(s)	Record group(s)
ROK	Republic of Korea
RVN	Republic of Vietnam
RVNAF	Republic of Vietnam armed forces

SA	Systems Analysis
SACSA	Special Assistant for Counterinsurgency and Special Activities, JCS
SAME	Senior adviser monthly evaluation
SEAB	Southeast Asia Branch, CMH
SecDef	Secretary of Defense
SecState	Secretary of State
SEER	System for Evaluating the Effectiveness of RVNAF
SITS	Single Integrated Telecommunications System
SJS	Secretary Joint Staff, MACV
SOG	Studies and Observation Group, MACV
SRAC	Second Regional Assistance Command
SRAG	Second Regional Assistance Group
SSB	Staff Support Branch, CMH
SVN	South Vietnam

TAORs	Tactical areas of responsibility
TFES	Territorial Forces Evaluation System
TRAC	Third Regional Assistance Command

Und	Under
USAID	U.S. Agency for International Development
USARV	United States Army, Vietnam
USIA	U.S. Information Agency
USMACV	United States Military Assistance Command, Vietnam

VNAF	South Vietnamese Air Force

VC   Viet Cong
VCI   Viet Cong infrastructure

WNRC   Washington National Records Center, NARA

Index

Aaron, Col. Harold R., 381
Abrams, General Creighton W., Jr.
  and advisers, 209-10, 237-38, 368, 371, 380-
    84, 450-52, 505, 507-09, 511
  "one-war" campaign, 391-93, 396-97, 409,
    420-21, 424
  and reform measures, 216-17, 314, 319-20, 385
  and RVNAF modernization, 281, 284-85, 300-
    301, 519
  and South Vietnamese military performance,
    244, 247, 276, 327, 330, 332, 334, 336, 342,
    344, 378, 389-90, 471, 473, 502
  and Vietnamization, 352-53, 356-59, 361-62,
    365, 427-28, 430, 432, 435-37, 441, 443, 455-
    60, 466, 476, 478, 483-84, 487-88, 490-91,
    494, 499
  and withdrawal planning, 292, 303, 305, 347-
    51, 367, 371, 376, 475-76
Adjutant General, South Vietnamese, 26, 29, 39
Advisers, Nationalist Chinese, 30
Advisers, U.S., 25, 48, 151, 209, 303
  chain of command, 53-57, 236-40
  drawdown of, 355, 449-55, 489
  effectiveness of, 199, 497, 505-22
  functions of, 14, 53-78, 94, 187, 191, 210, 236,
    239, 321-23, 377-84, 417, 497
  organization, 49, 51, 210
  personnel strength, 55-56, 236, 372, 450, 452
  tactical role, 14, 57, 59-61, 65, 212, 236-37,
    321-23, 333, 368, 483, 486
  tour of duty, 62
  and training of South Vietnamese, 29, 377
Advisory Team 99, 55n, 67
Air Force Advisory Group, U.S., 54-56, 77, 210,
  217, 452, 462, 489
Air strikes, U.S., 96
  against North Vietnam, 14, 16, 108, 112, 145,
    291, 449, 506
  against Viet Cong in Laos, 145
Air support, U.S., 13, 59, 65, 137, 195, 322, 349,
  396, 401, 410, 416, 456, 472-73, 475, 482-83,
  485-86, 517
Airborne Brigade, U.S. 173d, 85, 116, 185, 395-
  96, 399
Airborne Command, South Vietnamese, 31, 57,
  210
Airborne Division, ARVN, 473-74, 487
Airborne Divisions, U.S.
  82d, 291, 406n
  101st, 393

Airborne units, ARVN, 26, 32, 42, 72, 111, 146,
  277, 279, 284, 379, 415-17, 480
  advisers to, 191-92
  combat effectiveness, 46, 84, 102, 116-17, 248
  role of, 177-78, 183, 218
Allen, Brig. Gen. Richard J., 396-97, 399
Ambassador, American. *See* U.S. Ambassador
  to Vietnam.
An Khe, 396
An Loc, 481-83, 485-87
An Quang sect, 479
Armed Combat Youth, 112
Armed Forces Congress, South Vietnamese,
  129, 131, 259, 262
Armor Command, South Vietnamese, 54, 57,
  210
Armor units, ARVN, 29, 34-37, 113, 132, 146
Armored Cavalry Regiment, U.S. 11th, 406n
Armored Cavalry Squadron, ARVN
  1st, 243
  3d, 134-35
Army Advisory Group, U.S., 450
Army Command and General Staff College,
  U.S., 24, 61, 159
Army, North Vietnamese. *See* North Vietnamese
  Army.
Army of the Republic of Vietnam (ARVN). *See*
  South Vietnamese Army.
Army Support Commands, U.S., 431-34
Army, United States. *See* United States Army,
  Vietnam (USARV).
Army War College, U.S., 61, 237
Arntz, Col. John P., 190
Artillery, South Vietnamese, 19, 29, 34-36, 39,
  282, 457, 494
Artillery Command, South Vietnamese, 54, 57,
  210
Artillery support, U.S., 195, 322, 349, 396, 398,
  400-401, 410, 414, 416, 420, 475
Attrition, U.S. strategy of, 108, 124, 145, 170,
  171, 195, 233, 362, 455, 497-98
Australian forces, 87, 91-92, 109, 123, 185, 303
Aviation Brigade, U.S. 1st, 442-43

Ba, Col. Ly Tong, 484
Ban Me Thuot, 71, 381, 397, 401
Barnes, Brig. Gen. John W., 399-400
Barrel Roll, 16
Bartholomees, Col. James B., 192

Barton, Col. George, 116
Ben Het–Dak To region, 401
Berry, Col. Sidney, 333
Bien Hoa, 27, 168, 366, 415, 433
Bien Hoa Province, 366
Bien Hoa Tactical Area Command, 411, 417
Binh Dinh Province, 331, 393, 396–97, 400, 481
Binh Duong Province, 185–86, 412–13, 415
Binh Thuy, 432
BLACKJACK, Operation, 206
Boi Loi Woods, 412
Bolton, Brig. Gen. Donnelly P., 210, 300–301
Bombing. *See* Air strikes, U.S.
Bradley, Lt. Col. W. Ray, 334–35
Brownfield, Brig. Gen. Albert R., 180, 191, 210
Bu Prang, 401
Buddhists, 8, 22, 110, 128–44, 248, 255, 259, 310, 334
BUDDY, Operation, 429–30, 432–34, 438–39
Buddy system, 409
Budget, Saigon, 75–76, 155, 225, 228, 352, 462–64
Budget, U.S. defense, 228–29
Bundy, McGeorge, 90, 104
Bundy, William P., 91
Bunker, Ellsworth, 225, 230, 274, 277, 502, 507
    and civilian regime, 261–66, 269
    and reforms, 211, 311, 313, 323, 381
    and withdrawal planning, 304–05, 332, 346, 356, 361, 366, 376, 382, 420, 486, 490–91
Buon Brieng, 74

Cam Ranh Bay, 427, 433
Cambodia, 6, 8, 113, 230, 357, 388, 431, 463
    border operations, 73, 205, 217, 302, 308, 334, 449
    operations in, 472–74, 476, 498, 508
    sanctuaries in, 363, 397, 405–25
Cambodians
    ethnic, in South Vietnam, 8, 201
    and Special Forces program, 71, 201
Camp Strike Force. *See* Civilian Irregular Defense Groups (CIDGs).
Can Tho, 27, 165, 432
Cang, Admiral Chung Tan, 154
Canh, General Vo Vanh, 364, 477
Cao Dai sect, 71, 201
Cao, General Huynh Van, 30, 136–38, 140–41, 143, 149, 212
CAP, 181, 391, 393
Capital Military Assistance Command, U.S., 411
Capital Military District, 24, 33, 44, 57, 111, 168, 250, 256, 308, 311, 313–14, 365, 411, 417, 478, 487
Capital Military Region, 24n
Capital Security Group, South Vietnamese, 32
Casualties, 108
    enemy, 48, 209, 233, 272, 308, 325–27, 336, 401
    South Vietnamese, 46, 48, 85, 97, 112, 117, 141, 161, 175, 274, 281, 293–94, 313, 325, 327–29, 401, 423n, 469, 473–74, 485

Casualties—*Continued*
    U.S. combat, 105, 122, 233, 274, 279, 325, 327
CAT, 323, 368, 372
Cat Lai, 225, 318, 432
Catholic Youth Corps, 36
Cavalry Division, U.S. 1st, 109, 117, 124, 393, 406n, 415–16, 444
Ceasefire, 279, 282, 292, 295, 302, 304–05, 332, 356, 383, 453, 490–93, 495–96, 499, 518
Central Highlands. *See* Highlands
Central Intelligence Agency, U.S., 31, 50, 105, 335–36, 380, 387, 389
    Combined Studies Division, 69–70
    critical evaluation of war, 341–42, 344, 346, 390–91
    and funding, 78
    role of, 54, 72
Central Intelligence Office, South Vietnamese, 31
Central Logistics Command, South Vietnamese, 27, 164–65, 222–25, 230, 453, 467, 511
Central Office, South Vietnam, 405
Central Training Command, South Vietnamese, 28–29, 37, 54, 98, 159–62, 210, 309, 317–18, 367, 378, 421, 514
Chaisson, Col. John R., 133
Chau, Tam, 128
Chau, Tran Ngoc, 479
Chief of Staff, United States Army. *See* Johnson, General Harold K.
Chinese, 8, 14, 30, 71, 495. *See also* Nungs.
Chinh, General Phan Trong, 47, 114–15, 188–93, 245–47, 265, 267–68, 309, 378, 421, 423
Chu Lai, 140–41
Chuan, General Nguyen Van, 113, 129, 133, 143
Chuong Thien Province, 366
CIDGs. *See* Civilian Irregular Defense Groups (CIDGs).
Civic action
    military, 31, 94
    and U.S. assistance, 14, 55, 60, 62, 69, 77, 157
Civil Guard, 37
Civilian Irregular Defense Groups (CIDGs), 76, 78, 111, 147, 170, 195, 321, 397, 412, 457–58
    effectiveness, 72–74, 196, 198–99, 248, 323, 401, 515–16
    role of, 37, 71, 175, 201–07, 217, 219, 362, 382
    strength, 38, 71, 200–201
Civil operations and revolutionary development support (CORDS). *See* CORDS.
Clearing operations, 93–94, 101, 106–07, 122, 183, 233, 237, 239, 362
Clifford, Clark, 291, 294–95, 298, 301
Co, Nguyen Huu, 36, 259
    and Buddhists, 136, 138
    chief, JGS, 51, 107
    and manpower problems, 97–98, 114, 120, 129, 131, 152
    minister of defense, 25, 51, 109–11, 140–41, 154, 192–93
    and revolutionary development, 177–78
Colby, William E., 366, 465

Collins, Lt. Gen. Arthur S., Jr., 368, 383–84, 401–02, 422–23, 477
Collins, Brig. Gen. James L., Jr., 89–90, 93, 97, 146
Combat assistance team. *See* CAT.
Combat Aviation Group, U.S.
  11th, 416
  164th, 442
Combat effectiveness, RVNAF, 46–48, 85, 97, 102, 106, 113–18, 162, 183–84, 241–54, 279, 284, 324–31, 342–46, 349, 387–90, 395, 402, 405, 418, 518
Combined Campaign Plan, U.S.–South Vietnamese
  1967, 179, 233, 278
  1969, 391
Combined command concept, 81–82, 84, 87–96, 124, 185, 212
Combined External Operations Studies Office, 72
Combined Military Interrogation Center, 149, 168
Combined Military Operations Studies Office, 72
Combined operations concept, 391–403, 405–25
Command and General Staff College, U.S. Army, 368
Command and Staff College, South Vietnamese, 29, 161
Commander-in-chief, Pacific. *See* McCain, Admiral John S., Jr.
Commercial Import Program, 75, 352
Commissary system, 30, 46, 155–56, 185, 224, 318–19, 352, 375, 503, 515
Commissions, South Vietnamese officer, 29
  battlefield, 154, 220
  and class bias, 163, 467
  Saigon policies on, 22, 40, 153–54
Committee of the Direction of the State. *See* Directory.
Communications system, South Vietnamese, 10, 285
Communications system, U.S., 59, 65, 296, 438
Communism, 5–6
  in South Vietnam, 7, 10–11, 21, 73, 129–35, 142–43, 259
  and U.S. policy in Vietnam, 106
Con Son, 320, 377
Congress, U.S., 7, 231, 464, 491–92, 498, 507
Conroy, Maj. Gen. Raymond C., 430
Conscription, South Vietnamese. *See* Draft, South Vietnamese.
Consolidated RVNAF Improvement and Modernization Plan (CRIMP). *See* CRIMP.
Constitution, South Vietnamese, 23, 127–28, 131–32, 259, 262
Contractors, civilian, 225, 296, 438, 453
Convention of 19 June 1965, 23
Corcoran, Lt. Gen. Charles A., 400–401
CORDS, 211–12, 214, 231, 234, 236, 239, 244, 250–54, 307, 331–33, 366, 369, 377, 379, 402, 408, 452, 510

Corps, U.S. Army XXIV, 382, 392, 422, 457
Corps Tactical Zone, I, 13, 20, 168, 481, 493
  advisers, 56, 113, 137, 176, 252, 342–43, 382, 400, 451, 476
  commander, 23, 25, 33, 149, 192, 248, 308, 364, 473
  buildup of forces in, 123, 457–58
  combined operations, 89, 175, 181, 392–93, 409, 422
  composition, 33
  revolt in, 128–44, 501
Corps Tactical Zone, II, 134, 145, 168, 176, 227, 248, 252, 331, 434
  advisers, 47, 56, 71, 162, 199, 342–43, 368, 399, 476–77, 484–85
  combined operations, 89, 205, 393–403, 422
  commander, 25, 114, 135, 138, 364, 367, 464, 477
  composition, 33, 123, 146, 458
Corps Tactical Zone, III, 156, 168, 176, 224, 432–33, 482–83
  advisers, 56, 185, 188–89, 201, 205–06, 244, 322, 333, 381, 431, 478
  capabilities, 114, 248–49, 252, 342–44
  combined operations, 405–06, 408–12, 417–18, 423
  commander, 25, 109, 230, 256, 313, 364–65, 367, 420, 478
  composition, 34, 123, 166, 460
Corps Tactical Zone, IV, 168, 364, 432–33, 439
  advisers, 57, 201, 206, 322, 333, 381, 385–86, 458, 476
  combat effectiveness, 116, 248, 252, 342, 366, 479
  combined operations, 405–08, 417–18, 423
  commander, 25, 192, 259, 477, 479
  composition, 34, 166, 460
Corruption, South Vietnamese, 44, 192
  in officer corps, 21–22, 28, 31, 47, 116, 249
  general analysis of, 73, 128–29, 154–55, 167, 229–31, 253, 283, 335–36, 355, 363, 487, 502–03
Counterinsurgency, 36, 397, 409
  and U.S. advisers, 12–15, 66, 69
  U.S. doctrine on, 14–15, 91
  U.S. training in, 62, 149
Counterintelligence, 24, 227, 450
Coups, 15, 24, 81, 260, 263–64, 307, 313, 435
Craig, Sfc. William T., 206
CRIMP, 356
Cu Chi, 188, 411–12
Cua, Col. Van Van, 310, 312
Cunningham, Col. Hubert S., 430
Cushman, Maj. Gen. John H., 386, 423–24, 458, 476, 479
Cushman, Lt. Gen. (USMC) Robert E., Jr., 392–93

Da Lat, 29, 55*n*, 159, 226
Da Nang, 27, 89, 105, 130–34, 136–38, 140–43, 165, 175, 393, 434, 483
Da Nang Air Base, 17, 131, 133

Dak Seang, 423

Dao, Col. Le Minh, 486

Darlac Province, 74, 103, 395

Davis, Brig. Gen. Franklin M., Jr., 246, 329–30

Davis, Lt. Col. Medley M., 196–97

Davison, Lt. Gen. Michael S., 478

Defense Language Institute, 62, 162

Deferments, South Vietnamese, 151, 386
  academic, 98, 467
  selling, 22, 41–42

Delta Force, 204–05

Demilitarized Zone, 7, 99–100, 206, 215–18, 277, 279, 302, 343*n*, 351, 356, 382, 481–82

Dependents, South Vietnamese, 44–45, 62, 84, 224, 300

DePuy, Maj. Gen. William E., 52, 60–61, 68–69, 102, 113, 117, 121, 185–86, 246

Desertions, South Vietnamese, 158, 161, 175, 226, 335–36, 354
  amnesty policy, 313, 315, 466
  factors contributing to, 44–45, 155, 343–44, 385
  and MACV's concern, 82–85, 97–98, 148, 151–53, 219, 293, 331, 343–46, 348, 363, 390, 467–69, 518
  rate of, 42–43, 112, 114–16, 216, 314, 331, 345–46, 348, 363, 385–88, 408

Desobry, Brig. Gen. William R., 248

Di An, 452

Dial Telephone Exchange System, 439

Diem, Ngo Dinh, 110
  government of, 6–7, 10–11, 13, 20, 22–24, 30, 36–37, 71, 133, 311
  fall of, 15–16, 27, 234, 263, 312, 408, 479, 501, 516

Dien Bien Phu, 105, 311, 364

Dinh, General Ton That, 28, 97, 133–34, 136–37, 140–41, 143

Dinh Tuong Province, 206

Directory, 99
  and civilian government, 129, 504
  composition, 23–25, 97
  functions, 24, 98, 225, 229, 245, 275, 277, 313
  generals, 24–25, 32, 51, 115, 246, 255, 257–59, 261–69, 365
  internal squabbles, 24–25, 109–11, 133–38, 141–43, 192–93

Dolvin, Lt. Gen. Welborn G., 457, 476

Don, General (Ret.) Tran Van, 259

Donald, Lt. Col. (USMC) William A., 331–32

Dong Ba Thin, 205

Dong, General Du Quoc, 32, 112, 117, 136, 191–93, 246, 365, 416, 475, 487

Dong Ha, 482–83

Dong, General Pham Van, 311–12

Dong Tam, 406, 432–33, 439

Dong Tien, 409–17, 443

Draft, South Vietnamese, 40–42, 48, 84–85, 98, 151, 216, 274–77, 293, 314, 377, 467

Duc Hoa, 189–90

Duc Lap, 401

Duquemin, Brig. Gen. Gordon J., 402

Dzu, General Ngo, 364–65, 464, 477–78, 484

Dzu, Truong Dinh, 264, 310, 479

"Easter" offensive, 449, 452, 455, 460, 463, 466, 468, 481–90, 493, 520

Eckhardt, Maj. Gen. George S., 478

Economic problems, in South Vietnam, 10, 76, 128, 156

Education, and RVNAF, 10, 29, 159, 220, 253, 336, 374, 514

Elections, Vietnamese, 6, 127–28, 133, 258–69, 274–76, 449, 479

Enclave strategy, 95, 99–100, 122

Engineer Battalion, U.S. 62d, 437

ENHANCE and ENHANCE PLUS, Projects, 453, 459, 489, 491, 500

Enoul, Y Bham, 73–74, 199–200

Ethnic groups, 10, 196–97
  minorities, 8, 36–37, 70–73, 201
  Vietnamese hostility toward, 8, 64, 71, 73, 201, 207, 323, 477, 516

Ewbanks, Maj. Gen. (USAF) John N., Jr., 185, 209–10

Ewell, Lt. Gen. Julian J., 381, 409–12, 415–17

Facy, Lt. Col. Kenneth B., 197

FAIRFAX, Operation, 250–51, 277, 391, 396, 400

Field Forces, Vietnam
  I, 56, 323, 393, 397, 399, 401, 409
  II, 56, 176, 185, 249, 381, 405, 409, 411, 415, 478

Filipino troops, 92, 495

Financial support, U.S., 74–78, 300, 352, 355–56, 462–63, 489, 511

Flanagan, Brig. Gen. Edward M., Jr., 210, 236–37

Forsythe, Maj. Gen. George I., 307

Four-Party Joint Military Commission, 495

"Freeze" agreement, 282, 294

Freund, Brig. Gen. John F., 132, 134–35, 137, 143, 146, 159–61, 179, 185, 210, 235, 250

FULRO, 73–74, 199–200, 381

General Political Warfare Department, South Vietnamese, 26, 30, 55, 149, 224

General Support Group, U.S., 29th, 432

Geneva Accords, 6

Geneva Conventions, 118–20, 167, 170, 320

"Ghosts," 21, 40, 159, 386, 469

Gia, Col. Vu Quoc, 479

Gia Dinh Province, 250–51, 366, 400

Giac, Ho, 134

Giai, General Do Ke, 245–46, 334, 364, 367, 478

Giai, General Vu Van, 476, 478, 483–84

Giam, Col. Nguyen Van, 308, 311

Greek-letter forces, 204–07, 248, 515

Gritz, Capt. James ("Bo"), 206

Guerrilla operations, 13–15, 69, 150, 198, 271, 363. *See also* under Viet Cong.

Hai, General Tran Van, 177, 308–09, 313, 479

Haig, General Alexander, 475, 490–91

Haines, Lt. Gen. Ralph E., 499
Hamblen, Col. Archelaus L., Jr., 137
Hamburger Hill, 393
Hamlet Evaluation System (HES). *See* HES.
Hamlets, 11, 27, 83, 112. *See also* Strategic Hamlet Program.
Hanh, Col. Nguyen Huu, 218
Hanh, Col. Vo Huu, 365
Harkins, General Paul D., 14, 17, 50, 52
Harriman, W. Averell, 139
Hau Nghia Province, 42, 47, 114, 185, 365, 411–12
Hawaii, 14, 50, 137, 145
Hayes, Col. Robert E., 408
Healy, Brig. Gen. Michael D., 485
Heintges, Lt. Gen. John A., 131, 145, 190–91, 199, 209, 247
Heiser, Maj. Gen. Joseph M., Jr., 429–30
Helicopters
  South Vietnamese, 166, 282
  and U.S. advisers, 65
  U.S. support, 13, 322, 409, 414, 420, 475
  and Vietnamization, 441–43
Helms, Richard M., 277
HES, 211–12, 253, 377, 387
Hewgley, Lt. Col. Clarence T., 206
Hickey, Gerald Cannon, 63–64, 464
Hiep, Col. Phan Hoa, 476
Hieu, General Nguyen Van, 364, 367, 396, 413–15, 476, 478, 484
Highlands, 8, 22, 25, 29, 33–34, 71–72, 74, 85, 104–05, 114, 198, 248, 309, 331, 369, 391–403, 422, 476, 481, 484
Ho Bo Woods, 412
Hoa Hao sect, 71
Hoang, General Nguyen Thanh, 367
Hoi An, 130
Hollingsworth, Maj. Gen. James F., 485–86, 510
Hollis, Maj. Gen. Harris W., 411–12
Hollis, Col. Joel M., 172
Honolulu conferences
  1965, 90–91
  1966, 128, 171–72, 174
  1968, 299
Housing, South Vietnamese dependent, 30, 44, 83, 155–56, 185, 224–25, 320, 331, 336, 376, 383, 390, 399, 464, 515
Hue, 113, 128–33, 136–38, 140–44, 334, 481, 483
Hung, Col. Le Van, 478, 485–86
Hunnicutt, Col. Cecil F., 188–93, 245, 309
Huong, Nguyen Van, 311
Huong, Tran Van, 311, 313

Ia Drang campaign, 124
Improvement and Modernization Plans, 300–304, 345, 348, 351, 354–57, 359, 428, 440, 442
Infantry Divisions, ARVN
  1st, 33, 113, 129, 132, 134, 136–37, 140–43, 215–16, 243, 248, 325, 329, 334, 364–66, 382, 392, 457, 473–74, 476, 481
  2d, 33, 113, 129, 136–37, 139–40, 142, 248, 364–65, 393, 400, 475–76, 486
  3d, 457, 467, 476, 481, 483

Infantry Divisions, ARVN—*Continued*
  5th, 34, 44, 47, 72n, 115–16, 156, 184–86, 243, 245–46, 265, 322, 333–34, 364, 412–15, 476, 478, 481, 485–86
  7th, 34, 116, 230, 243, 248, 252, 313, 364–67, 406
  9th, 34, 116, 248, 252, 329, 364, 366, 407, 409, 460
  10th, 85, 115–16, 185
  18th, 156, 243, 245, 252, 309, 334, 364–65, 367, 381, 411, 478, 486
  21st, 34, 116, 248, 252, 312, 364, 366, 460, 478, 482, 486
  22d, 33–34, 247, 323, 331–32, 364, 368–69, 396, 400–401, 413, 422, 423n, 477, 481, 483–84
  23d, 33–34, 74, 146, 215, 309, 331, 364, 397, 400, 477, 482, 484
  25th, 34, 42, 47, 55n, 67, 69, 114, 156, 184–85, 188, 245, 265, 309, 364, 411, 478
Infantry Divisions, U.S.
  1st, 109, 116, 184–85, 195, 206, 246, 406n, 412–15
  4th, 145, 203, 393–97, 399, 401, 423n
  5th, 393
  9th, 233, 307, 346, 351, 364, 406, 409, 411, 432
  23d, 248, 393
  25th, 145, 184–85, 406n, 249, 411
Infantry Regiments, ARVN
  7th, 115, 413
  42d, 33–34, 243, 397, 401, 422
  43d, 34
  44th, 397
  45th, 397
  46th, 189, 411
  47th, 401, 422, 423n
  48th, 34
  49th, 411
  50th, 189, 411
  51st, 33, 113, 129, 132, 334–35, 393
  53d, 397, 402
Infiltration, enemy, 31, 209, 233, 295, 302, 471, 490
Inflation, in South Vietnam, 45–46, 76–77, 155, 213, 215, 222, 318, 395, 464–65, 503
Inspector General,
  MACV, 229
  South Vietnamese, 26, 153, 230, 309, 367
Insurgency, 75
  internal, 7, 46, 119, 298, 302, 465, 471, 520
  North Vietnamese support of, 106, 108, 271, 498
  and U.S. Special Forces, 71
  Viet Cong, 12, 16, 33, 517
  Viet Minh, 6
Integrated Communications System, Southeast Asia (ICS, SEA), 438–40
Intelligence, South Vietnamese, 13, 15, 27, 38, 102, 149, 227, 400, 412, 426, 435
Intelligence support, U.S, 13, 65, 400, 456.
  and enemy POWs, 118, 170
International Military Assistance Office, 91
International Military Security Task Force (IMSTAF), 89–91

Jacobson, Col. George, 175
Johnson, General Harold K., 50, 62, 89, 198–99, 211, 237–38, 286, 441–42, 506
Johnson, Lyndon Baines, 128, 130, 149, 171–72, 179, 280, 298
  and air strikes against North Vietnam, 16, 506
  and American ambassadors, 50, 507
  and encadrement, 90–91
  and expanded combat, 17, 95–96, 102–04, 106, 233, 273
  second-term aspirations, 282, 291
  sensitivity to public opinion, 105, 271, 282, 291, 304
Joint Chiefs of Staff, U.S., 14, 17, 139, 156, 166, 507
  and clandestine operations, 72
  and expanded U.S. combat role, 95, 99, 233, 284, 420
  and RVNAF modernization, 300, 345, 352–56
  and objectives in Vietnam, 84, 95, 106–08, 120–21, 124, 145, 215–16, 335, 508
  and U.S. advisers, 16, 62, 489
  and U.S. troop withdrawal, 298, 302, 366–67, 387, 459–60, 472
Joint General Staff (JGS), 64, 68. *See also* General Political Warfare Department, South Vietnamese; Strategic Technical Directorate, South Vietnamese.
  and civilian government, 260, 266, 268
  and combined operations, 90–91, 180, 415, 435, 438
  components, 26–32, 37
  functions, 29, 177, 204, 226, 229, 256–57, 282, 440, 453, 462, 511, 516–17
  Logistics Directorate, 26–27
  and MACV, 52, 54, 179, 189, 210, 385–86, 430, 432–33, 499, 513, 518–19
  and manpower, 40, 42, 44, 85, 98, 111, 146–49, 151–58, 161–62, 216, 218–21, 244, 248, 251, 316–20, 455, 458–60, 466, 468–69
  Operations Directorate, 26
  Personnel Directorate, 26
  and POWs, 167
  Territorial Directorate, 214
  Training Directorate, 26, 55
  and U.S. withdrawal, 305, 347, 373–76, 453, 482, 488–89
Joint support funds (JSF), 75–76
Joint U.S. Public Affairs Office, 135, 191
Jorgensen, Gordon L., 105–06
Justice, military, 43, 98, 152, 230, 315, 466.

Kelly, Col. Francis J., 198–99, 204
Kennedy, Maj. Paul J., Jr., 325
Kerwin, Lt. Gen. Walter T., Jr., 209, 268–69, 333–34, 342–44, 372
Khang, General Le Nguyen, 24, 32, 102, 111, 188–89, 249, 256, 262, 308–11, 313, 334, 365, 475, 487
Khang, Maj. Tran Tien, 230
Khanh, General Nguyen, 312
Khe Sanh, 206, 473

Khiem, General Tran Thien, 310–11, 361, 366, 382, 420, 469, 479, 484, 487
Khuyen, General Dong Van, 467
Kien Tuong Province, 230
Kissinger, Henry A., 348, 350, 358, 428, 456, 459–60, 490–92, 499, 507–08
Kit Carson Scout force, 313, 320, 356
Knowlton, Brig. Gen. William A., 172, 252
Komer, Robert W., 266, 277, 333
  and ARVN security role, 176, 238, 254
  director, CORDS, 211–12, 214, 231, 235, 366–67, 465
  and South Vietnamese manpower problems, 149–50, 245, 247, 252, 274, 301, 311, 507, 509
  and pacification, 172, 211–12, 332
Kontum, 71, 103, 481–85
Kontum Province, 395, 399, 401
Korean conflict, 5, 87, 119, 357
Korean forces, 77, 92, 303, 495
Kraft, Brig. Gen. William R., Jr., 389
Kroesen, Maj. Gen. Frederick J., Jr., 484
Ky, Air Vice-Marshal Nguyen Cao, 23, 114, 378
  clique, 24–25, 32, 47, 149, 230, 256, 309–10, 313
  and counterintelligence activities, 31
  and general elections, 255–57, 259–69, 276, 479
  head of South Vietnamese Air Force, 23, 32, 51
  and internal political struggles, 74, 109–11, 127–36, 138, 140–41, 143, 199–200, 311, 501–02
  and reforms, 153–54, 192–93, 245, 310
  and shift in roles and missions, 124, 171–72, 178–79, 234, 277
  and unified command, 91

Laird, Melvin R., 347–48, 351–57, 359, 366, 369, 387, 421, 430, 456, 459–60, 464, 486, 488–90, 508
Lam, General Hoang Xuan, 114, 136–37, 139, 142–43, 248, 262, 308, 364, 382, 473, 475–76, 483–84
Lam Son (General Phan Dinh Thu), 423
LAM SON 719, 472–76, 483–84, 493
Lan, General Bai The, 487
Lan, General Lu Mong, 115, 309–10, 331, 364, 367, 393–99, 401, 477
Language training, 318, 432
  in English, 62, 64, 162, 440, 513
  in Vietnamese, 237–38
Lansdale, Edward G., 230
Lanthrom, Maj. Joseph R., 322
Laos, 6, 8, 106, 357, 456, 463
  air war over, 118
  border operations, 71, 105, 205–06, 217–18, 302, 308, 422, 424, 449
  operations in, 472–76, 493, 498, 508
  sanctuaries in, 363, 397
  U.S. military efforts in, 50
  and U.S. Special Forces, 69, 71

Leadership, South Vietnamese, 7, 11, 309
  military training for, 159, 163, 226, 280, 331,
    354
  quality of, 46–47, 115, 117, 193, 245–47, 253,
    283, 327, 335, 343, 348, 358, 363, 367, 385–
    86, 388–90, 423–24, 510
  and reforms, 151–54, 158, 213, 219, 345, 354–
    55
  U.S. policy of fostering, 59, 78, 83, 187, 514
  and Vietnamization, 471–96
Lee, Maj. Gen. Richard M., 162–63
Lieu, Col. Pham Van, 111, 134, 267
Light Infantry Brigade, U.S. 199th, 250–51,
    406n, 411
LLDB. See Special Forces, South Vietnamese.
Lloyd, 1st Lt. Charles R., 206
Loan, Col. Nguyen Ngoc, 24, 31, 33, 131, 134–
    35, 137, 141, 143, 256, 265, 310–13, 364n
Loc, Nguyen Van, 311
Loc Ninh, 481–82
Loc, General Vinh, 378
  ability of, 114, 249
  commander, II CTZ, 25, 33, 135, 138, 199–200,
    265, 267, 308–09, 393–95, 402
Lodge, Henry Cabot, 150–51, 192, 507
  and civilian regime, 257–58, 260
  and expanded U.S. combat role, 102–04, 109,
    273
  and MACV, 50, 211
  and Struggle Movement, 127, 130–37, 139,
    142–43
Logistical Command, U.S. 1st, 427, 429–32, 435
Logistics, RVNAF, 27–29, 46, 158, 163–65, 167,
    278–79, 328, 336, 363, 431, 453. *See also* Joint
    General Staff, Logistics Directorate.
Logistics, U.S. support to RVNAF, 13, 74, 81,
    140, 164, 166, 278–80, 300, 349, 416, 427–35,
    452–53, 463
Long An Province, 47, 190, 411
Long Binh, 427, 453
Long Binh Special Zone, 411
Long-range reconnaissance patrol (LRRP), 398
Long Thanh, 205
Luong, Col. Le Quang, 486–87
Luyen, Col. Hoang Van, 68

MAAG. *See* Military Assistance Advisory Group
    (MAAG).
McCain, Admiral John S., Jr., 353–54, 371, 382,
    420
McClellan, Brig. Gen. Stanley L., 378
McGarr, Lt. Gen. Lionel C., 14
McGiffert, Brig. Gen. John R., II, 486
McGovern, Brig. Gen. Donald H., 219–21, 275
McKean, Col. William A., 199
McNamara, Robert S., 156, 166, 245, 277, 291
  and civilian regime, 263, 265
  and expanded combat, 91, 98, 101–02, 109,
    112, 271, 273
  interest in war statistics, 506, 512
  and roles and missions changes, 96, 103–07,
    123–24, 176, 178, 212, 274–75, 284–85

McNaughton, John T., 91, 101, 108, 150
MACV. *See* Military Assistance Command,
    Vietnam (MACV).
MACV commander. *See* Abrams, General
    Creighton W., Jr.; Harkins, General Paul
    D.; Westmoreland, General William C.;
    Weyand, General Frederick C.
MALTs, 236, 321
Manh, General Nguyen Van, 114, 192, 262, 308–
    09
Manila Communique of 1966, 271, 302–03, 305
Manpower, South Vietnamese, 48, 85. *See also*
    under Joint General Staff (JGS); Komer,
    Robert W.; Westmoreland; General William
    C.
  and combat expansion, 84, 97–98, 111, 213–18
  pool, 41, 149, 151, 216
  problems, 40, 151–59, 198, 222, 384–87
Mao Tse-tung, 10
MAP. *See* Military Assistance Program (MAP).
Marine Amphibious Force, III, 56, 113, 382, 392
Marine Combined Action Program (CAP). *See*
    CAP.
Marine Corps Command, South Vietnamese,
    31
Marine Division, U.S.
  1st, 393
  3d, 89, 108, 393
Marine units, South Vietnamese, 42, 46, 84,
    102, 116, 146, 177–78, 183, 218, 248, 307, 325,
    329, 379, 407, 473. *See also* South Vietnam-
    ese Marine Corps.
Martin, Graham, 50
Materiel assistance, U.S., 13, 145, 228, 427
MATs, 236, 321, 452
May Plan, 294–99
Mekong Delta, 10, 25
Mekong River, 8
Metaxis, Col. Theodore C., 114
Midway Island conference, 351–54, 375
MIKE units, 72, 195–96, 203, 205–07, 248, 323,
    381
Military assistance, 6, 12, 38, 61–62, 210, 244
Military Assistance Advisory Group (MAAG), 7,
    14, 49, 302, 456
Military Assistance Command, Vietnam
    (MACV), 14–15, 84, 102, 493, 499. *See also*
    Abrams, General Creighton W., Jr.;
    Harkins, General Paul D.; Inspector Gen-
    eral; Studies and Observation Group
    (SOG); Westmoreland, General William C.;
    Weyand, General Frederick C.
  advisory role, 14, 49, 54–61, 64, 68, 70, 72–78,
    87, 210, 318, 321–37, 379, 465–68, 479, 483,
    489
  and civilian government, 255, 257–62, 266,
    268, 504
  and combined operations, 90, 93, 108, 392–93,
    400, 403, 472
  and defense budget, 75, 77, 229–31
  effectiveness of, 501–03, 505–20
  functions, 26, 28, 51, 75, 175

Military Assistance Command, Vietnam
  (MACV)—*Continued*
  operational role, 14, 49, 483
  organization, 49–51, 450
  plans to modernize RVNAF, 113, 166, 279–80,
    283, 285–87, 293–306, 309, 342, 344–55, 359,
    361, 417–18, 464, 476
  political pressure on, 271, 273
  and POWs, 168–70, 228
  and reform effort, 137, 145–62, 193, 209–26,
    229–31, 254, 316, 319, 335, 469, 487–88
  and RVNAF performance, 47, 113–18, 189,
    236–44, 513
  and RVNAF roles and missions, 93–96, 105,
    107, 172–74, 177, 213, 272, 277, 332, 397
  size of, 51–53
  and Special Forces programs, 195, 200–203,
    205
  Training Directorate, 54–55, 77, 159, 179, 210,
    236, 371, 450
  and Vietnamization, 359, 363–90, 424, 427,
    449–59, 462
Military Assistance Program (MAP), 55, 57, 59,
    75–77, 81–82, 94, 111, 156, 166, 210, 228, 244–
    45, 286, 450, 462
Military assistance training and advisory
    (MATA) course, 61–62, 64, 510
Military Council, South Vietnamese, 262, 310
Military Intelligence Battalion, U.S. 519th, 227
Military Intelligence Group, U.S. 135th, 435
Military schools, South Vietnamese, 7, 318, 377
Military Security Service (MSS), South Viet-
    namese, 31, 55, 131, 256, 265–66, 435
Militia forces. *See also* Territorial Forces.
  South Vietnamese, 19, 37, 71, 112
  Viet Cong, 12, 93
Milloy, Maj. Gen. Albert E., 413
Minh, General Duong Van, 263, 479
Minh, General Nguyen Van, 116, 248, 312, 478,
    485–86
Minh, General Tran Van, 91
Ministries, South Vietnamese
  Chieu Hoi, 436
  Defense, 19, 25, 41, 51, 76, 225, 266, 378, 484
  Economy, 156, 222
  Finance, 375
  Information, 31, 256
  Interior, 256
  Revolutionary Development, 172, 177, 230,
    234, 256, 264, 267–68, 309–10
  Security, 256
  Veterans Affairs, 225, 318
Minority groups. *See* Ethnic groups.
Mission Council, U.S., 50–51, 150, 173
Mobile advisory logistics teams (MALTs). *See*
    MALTs.
Mobilie advisory teams (MATs). *See* MATs.
Mobile Strike Force. *See* MIKE units.
Mobilization, South Vietnamese
  early measures, 41, 84, 98, 151, 216–17, 274–
    75, 277

Mobilization, South Vietnamese—*Continued*
  general (1968), 293, 300, 313–14, 323, 328, 335,
    345–46, 377, 384, 467
  service obligation, 85, 151, 216, 274–76, 314
Momyer, General William W. ("Spike"), 441,
    445
Montagnards, 13, 105, 249, 458, 464–65, 484
  and ethnic Vietnamese, 8, 64, 71, 73–74, 201,
    323, 477, 516
  and U.S. Special Forces, 64, 71, 196–204, 207,
    381
Montague, Col. Robert M., 254
Moorer, Admiral Thomas H., 367, 460
Morale, RVNAF, 17, 36, 39, 102, 115–16, 135,
    329–30, 335, 363, 462
  and discipline, 36, 83, 116, 226, 229
  factors contributing to, 45–46, 331, 405
  measures to improve, 30, 41, 97, 114, 153, 184,
    354–55, 385
  U.S. advisers role, 60, 63, 78, 83
Mountain Scouts, 72
Mueller, Col. Arndt, 188
Murray, Maj. Gen. John E., 433, 495
My Tho, 439

Nakhon Phanom Air Base, 495
Nam Bo, 405
Nam Dinh Reserve Officers School, 74
Nam, Col. Nguyen Khoa, 365
National Central Revolutionary Development
  Council, 172
National Defense College, Saigon, 226, 367
National Field Force Police, 131
National Liberation Front, 12, 259
National Materiel Management Agency, 453
National Military Academy, Da Lat, 29, 55n,
  159, 226, 318, 486
National Noncommissioned Officers Academy,
  Nha Trang, 29, 226, 267, 318
National Police, 37–38, 111–12, 129, 134, 137, 170,
  218, 256, 265, 313, 315, 353, 364n, 379
National Security Adviser. *See* Bundy,
  McGeorge; Kissinger, Henry A.
National Security Study Memorandum
  (NSSM). *See* NSSM.
Naughton, Col. Francis E., 117
Naval Advisory Group, U.S., 54–56, 77, 140,
  210, 217, 285, 452
Naval support, U.S., 13, 472, 488, 517
Navy Command, South Vietnamese, 26
New Horizons campaign, 372
Newport, 432
Nghi, General Nguyen Vinh, 486
Nha Trang, 27, 29, 70, 72, 165, 195, 433
Nhon, General Bui Huu, 27–28, 230
Nhuan, General Pham Xuan, 129, 131–32, 136–
  37, 140–43
Nhut, Col. Tran Van, 486
Nickerson, Lt. Gen. (USMC) Herman, Jr., 382
Nitze, Paul, 298, 302, 304
Nixon, Richard M., 341–42, 348, 351, 361, 420,
  449, 456, 459, 475, 488, 490–92, 498, 508

Nixon Doctrine, 359
Nol, General Lon, 418, 421
Noncommissioned officers, South Vietnamese, 29, 40, 45, 153–54, 159, 163, 220, 316, 468. *See also* National Noncommissioned Officers Academy, Nha Trang.
North Vietnam, 113, 119–20, 363, 472
  air war over, 118
  infiltration from, 209, 233, 295, 302, 471, 490
  and U.S. strategy, 106, 108, 205, 498
North Vietnamese Army, 7, 16, 102, 145, 169, 271, 304, 345, 348–49, 355, 357, 401, 420, 495, 520
NSSM
  1, 342, 344–47, 358, 363, 390, 517
  36, 348, 383, 417, 428
Nungs, 72, 205, 312
Nur, Paul, 199

O'Daniel, Lt. Gen. John W., 7
Officer Candidate School, Thu Duc, 29, 318
Offshore Training Program, U.S., 29, 54, 77, 162
Omega project, 204
"One-war" policy, 362, 392–403
On-the-job training programs, 430, 432–33, 435–36, 439–40, 444
"Open Arms" Program, 31, 320

Pacific Command, U.S., 14, 50, 145, 156
Pacification, 27, 110, 129, 211, 455
  campaign, 15, 20, 123, 170, 171–75, 239, 363, 397, 471
  evaluation of effort, 105, 114, 212, 342
  and U.S. advisers, 59, 66–67, 71, 210
  and U.S. objectives, 82–83, 93, 101, 103, 108, 123–24, 175, 177, 180, 233, 235, 258, 332, 362, 497, 507
"Pair-off" program, 396–97, 399–400, 409, 413, 443
Palmer, General Bruce, Jr., 52, 286, 441, 488
Paramilitary forces, 7, 12–13, 37, 70, 77, 123, 151, 356, 400
PARASOL-SWITCHBACK, 78
Paris peace talks, 359, 363, 382, 458, 490–93
Parmley, Lt. Col. Eleazar ("Lee"), IV, 203
Paschall, Col. Rod, 198
Peers, Lt. Gen. William R., 323, 331–33, 393–403, 409, 417
People's and Armed Forces Council, 259
People's Revolutionary Party, 12
People's Self-Defense Force, 19*n,* 314, 461, 466, 516
Phnom Penh, 420
PHOENIX program, 379
Phong, General Tran Thanh, 138, 140, 266, 268, 484
Phu Bai airfield, 136
Phu Bon Province, 74, 396
Phu, General Pham Van, 364–65, 476
Phu Quoc Island, 228, 320, 376
Phu Yen Province, 396

Phuoc Binh, 416
Phuoc, Lt. Col. Dao Ba, 250
Plan Six, 299–300, 302, 351
Platt, Brig. Gen. (USMC) Jonas M., 137
Plei Me, 207
Plei Mrong camp, 201
Pleiku, 71, 74, 103, 134, 168, 203, 401, 423*n*
Pleiku Province, 395
Police, civilian, 11–12, 43, 94, 104, 107, 152. *See also* National Police.
Police, military, 26, 29, 146, 152
Political stability, as U.S. concern, 81–96, 109, 127, 151, 193, 209, 255–69, 501, 505
Political warfare, 13, 30, 55, 97–98, 149, 226–27, 436
Political Warfare College, 149, 226
Popular Forces, 19*n. See also* Territorial Forces.
  desertion rate, 151
  pay rate, 45, 155, 167, 300
  role of, 37–38, 122, 132, 172, 181, 244, 516
  strength, 83, 112–13, 147–48, 213–14, 216, 317, 353, 355, 455–56, 461
Porter, William J., 137, 172, 175–76
Post exchange system, 30, 156, 185, 224, 503, 515
Postal system, military, 156–57, 374–75
Potts, Lt. Gen. William E., 435
PRAISE, 218–19
Presidential elections, South Vietnamese. *See under* Ky, Air Vice-Marshal Nguyen Cao; Thieu, General Nguyen Van.
Press, American, 231, 245, 247, 273, 276, 283, 287, 291, 347, 506
Prisoners of war, 146
  camps, 119–20, 167–69, 227, 320, 376–77
  enemy, 118–20, 228, 420
  repatriation of U.S., 302, 449, 490, 495, 499
Pritchett, Maj. Charles C., 321
Program Review and Analysis Improvement System (PRAISE). *See* PRAISE.
Project 640, 209
Project 981, 452
Project 982, 452
Project Delta, 72
Project Switch 1097, 432
Promotions, South Vietnamese policy on, 21, 24, 40, 84, 97, 153–54, 219–20, 316, 336, 343, 345, 373–74, 390, 468, 511, 513
Province chiefs, 28, 37, 161, 171, 233–34, 249, 253, 259, 267, 307, 466
Provincial Reconnaissance Unit (PRU). *See* PRUs.
PRUs, 379–80, 516
Psychological Operations Group, U.S. 4th, 436
Psychological warfare, 13–14, 29–31, 55, 60, 62, 77, 84, 98, 131, 149, 436
Public opinion, U.S., 122, 209, 271–72, 274–75, 279, 361

Quang Da Special Zone, 393
Quang, General Dang Van, 25, 34, 116, 154, 192–93, 259, 267, 311, 364*n*
Quang, General Doan Van, 36, 364

Quang Duc Province, 74
Quang Nam Province, 393
Quang Nam Special Zone, 129, 132, 140
Quang Ngai, 137, 393
Quang Ngai Province, 42
Quang Tin, 393
Quang, Tri (Thich), 128, 134–35, 137, 140–43, 310
Quang Tri, 143, 481–84
Quang Tri Province, 141, 393
Quang Trung Training Center, 230, 364
Que Son Valley, 486
Qui Nhon, 27, 143, 165

Radios, 10, 39, 59, 285
Ranger Battalions, ARVN
 11th, 140
 81st Airborne, 72n, 205, 461, 515
Ranger Command, South Vietnamese, 54, 57, 129, 177, 210, 308, 367, 458
Ranger Group, ARVN 5th, 250
Ranger units, ARVN, 34, 146, 284, 397, 482
 advisers to, 67, 465
 combat effectiveness, 102, 116
 role of, 13, 36, 177–78, 217–18, 279, 380
 training, 28
Rations, South Vietnamese, 45, 157–58, 251, 319, 352, 375–76, 383, 503
Recruitment, South Vietnamese, 40–42, 84–85, 98, 112, 151, 161, 175, 214, 314, 331, 384, 466
Red Cross, International, 170, 228, 320, 376
Reforms, 22. *See also under* Abrams, General Creighton W., Jr.; Leadership, South Vietnamese; Military Assistance Command, Vietnam (MACV); Westmoreland, General William C.
 advocated by MACV, 111, 137, 145–62, 193, 209–19, 221
 failure of, 218–31, 374, 469
Regional Communications Group, U.S. Army, 439
Regional Forces, 19n, 28, 37, 96, 224, 376. *See also* Territorial Forces.
 desertion rates, 151
 and Montagnards, 74, 201, 323
 pay rates, 45
 role of, 106, 122, 132, 172, 217, 380, 516
 strength, 37, 83, 111–12, 147–48, 213–16, 244, 294, 455, 459, 461
Religion, and factionalism, 7–8, 10, 21–22, 30, 110. *See also* An Quang sect; Buddhists; Cao Dai sect; Hoa Hao sect.
Republic of Vietnam Armed Forces (RVNAF). *See* South Vietnamese Armed Forces (RVNAF); individual services.
Resettlement programs, 12, 15, 76, 464–65
Resor, Stanley R., 372, 440
Revolutionary development, 211, 226–27, 271–73, 489
 cadre, 172, 174, 249, 356
 strategy, 172, 177–79, 183, 185, 212, 233–35, 238, 254, 256, 258, 450

Revolutionary Development Support Directorate, MACV, 172, 252
RF/PF. *See* Territorial Forces.
Rice, 46, 157, 352, 375, 503
Riley, Lt. Col. Evan F., 322
ROLLING THUNDER, 16, 108
Rosson, Lt. Gen. William B., 51, 105, 107, 109, 191, 248, 487
Rostow, Walter W., 277
Ruff-Puff. See Territorial Forces.
Rusk, Dean, 104, 129, 131, 137, 277

Saigon Terminal Transportation Command, 165, 433
SAME reports, 60, 189, 241, 243
Sang, General Nguyen Thanh, 114
Schiller, Lt. Col. William E., 322
Seaman, Lt. Gen. Jonathan O., 176, 185–86
Search-and-destroy operations, 93–94, 101, 103–04, 106–07, 123, 206, 237, 239, 328, 362
Second Armed Forces Congress, 127
Secretary of Defense, 50, 62. *See also* Clifford, Clark; Laird, Melvin R.; McNamara, Robert S.
Securing operations, 93–94, 99, 106–07, 122, 183, 412
Security, area
 and Pacification, 67, 171–72, 176–80, 193, 212
 and revolutionary development program, 233, 254, 271
 RVNAF role in, 33, 124, 183, 278, 301, 305, 307, 331, 333, 355, 395, 397, 405, 408, 424, 512
 and Territorial Forces, 37, 83
 as U.S. political and military strategy, 67, 101, 170, 233–54, 273, 278, 397, 424
 U.S. role in, 95, 175, 185, 212, 400
Security, internal, 7, 12–13, 20, 357, 362
SEER, 324–31, 335, 377, 387–90, 418
Seibert, Maj. Donald A., 67–69
Self-Defense Corps, 19n, 37
Senior adviser monthly evaluation (SAME) Reports. *See* SAME reports.
Sensor control and management platoons (SCAMPs), 435
Sharp, Admiral U.S. Grant, 50, 88–91, 98, 122–23, 245, 263, 274, 284–85
SHINING BRASS, 205
Shoemaker, Col. John O., 304
Sierra, Sfc. Adolf, 335
Sigma project, 204, 206
Signal Battalions, U.S.
 361st, 439
 369th, 439
Signal Brigade, U.S. 1st, 438–40
Signal Directorate, South Vietnamese, 438
Signal groups, 13, 27, 29
Signal School, South Vietnamese, 439–40
Simpson, Col. Charles M., III, 196
Single Integrated Telecommunications System (SITS), 440

Index

Snuol, 473, 486
Soldier's Saving Fund, 487
South Korean forces, 87, 89, 91–92, 109, 113, 123, 145, 284, 347, 391, 395, 400
South Vietnamese Air Force, 136, 141, 325, 329. *See also* Ky, Air Vice-Marshal Nguyen Cao.
  advisers, 54
  command and control, 32, 256
  logistics support, 27, 285–86
  strength, 20, 32, 217, 379, 441, 444–45, 458, 461–62
  training, 28–29
South Vietnamese Army (ARVN), 24, 54, 331, 445. *See also* South Vietnamese Armed Forces (RVNAF); Infantry Divisions, ARVN; Infantry Regiments, ARVN.
South Vietnamese Armed Forces (RVNAF), 7. *See also* Combat effectiveness, RVNAF; Leadership, South Vietnamese; Logistics, RVNAF; Mobilization, South Vietnamese; Morale, RVNAF; Reforms; Strength, RVNAF; Training, RVNAF.
  kill ratio, 48, 242, 327–28, 345, 388
  organization, 19–20, 26
  pay rate, 22, 45–46, 84, 222, 318
  and politico-military turmoil, 13, 16, 20, 34, 59, 85, 136
  roles and missions, 107, 121–24, 176–80, 455
  weapons captured-to-lost ratio, 48, 242, 345, 388
South Vietnamese Marine Corps, 19–20, 24, 27, 32, 54, 131, 136, 217, 248, 256, 285, 313, 325. *See also* Marine units, South Vietnamese.
South Vietnamese Navy, 19–20, 26–29, 32, 54, 154, 166, 217, 244, 285, 325, 329, 379, 461–62
Special Commissariat for Montagnard Affairs, 199
Special Forces, South Vietnamese, 22, 26, 248, 380–81, 516
  role of, 34, 36–37, 72, 178, 204, 207, 217
  training, 28
  and U.S. Army Special Forces, 64, 70–71, 73, 195–98, 204–05, 217
Special Forces, U.S. Army
  as advisers, 54, 56, 69–74, 78, 195, 203, 205, 211, 321, 505, 510
  criticism of, 198
  Group (Airborne), 5th, 49, 70, 78, 198–99, 201, 205, 207, 217–18, 323, 380
  intelligence-gathering mission, 72–73, 200–201
  organization of, 69–70, 210
  paramilitary role, 36–37, 73, 498
  reconnaissance missions, 204–05
  roles and missions, 13, 36, 70–74, 193, 195–99, 201, 204–07, 515
  and Vietnamese Special Forces, 64, 70–71, 73, 195–98, 204–05, 217
Special Tactical Zones, ARVN
  24th, 114, 397, 399, 401, 422
  44th, 218, 364–65, 458, 479
Special Warfare School, U.S. Army, 61
Spragins, Col. Charles E., 198
Sternberg, Maj. Gen. Ben, 97–98

Stevens, Lt. Col. Norman M., 378
Stilwell, Lt. Gen. Richard G., 50, 52, 342, 344, 392–93, 498
Strategic Hamlet Program, 15
Strategic Technical Directorate, South Vietnamese, 72, 205, 218, 435, 451
Strategy, U.S., 424. *See also* Attrition, U.S. strategy of; "One-war" policy; Pacification; Revolutionary development; Security, area.
  1964, 81–82, 93–94
  1965, 81–82, 84–92, 94–95, 97–108, 121–24, 171
  1966, 123, 150
  1967, 209, 233
  1968, 291, 307–08, 362
  1969, 498
Strength, enemy, 48, 102, 145, 345, 491, 495
Strength, RVNAF, 519
  1960–64, 12, 19
  1965, 19–20, 40, 83, 85, 98
  1966, 146–50
  1967, 213–18, 293–94, 300–01
  1968, 293, 314
  1969–70, 293, 295–96
  1970–73, 355–56, 455, 461
Strength, U.S. forces
  1960–64, 13, 109
  1965, 109, 112
  1966, 112, 145
  1967, 112, 233
Strikers. *See* Civilian Irregular Defense Groups (CIDGs).
Struggle Movement, 128–44
Studies and Observation Group (SOG), 72, 205, 218, 435
Sullivan, William H., 50
Support Activities Group, U.S., 495
Sutherland, Lt. Gen. James W., Jr., 422, 475–76
"Switchback," 428–29, 432–33
System for Evaluating the Effectiveness of RVNAF (SEER). *See* SEER.

Tactical areas of responsibility (TAORs), 95–96
Tam, Dr., 135
Tan Canh, 484
Tan Hung, 44
Tan Linh pagoda, 138, 141
Tan Son Nhut Air Base, 27, 415
Tank Battalion, ARVN 20th, 457, 481
Tanks
  enemy, 206, 283, 482
  South Vietnamese, 19, 34, 457
Task Force South, 397
Tat, Col. Pham Duy, 479
Tay Ninh, 412, 416
Tay Ninh Province, 47, 55n, 67
Taylor, Maxwell D., 17, 50–51, 85, 87, 90–91, 93, 95, 98, 102, 109, 121–22, 124, 507
Tchepone, 473
T-Day Plans, 302–03, 341, 346, 348, 428–29
Territorial Forces, 26, 71, 166, 235, 256–57, 325, 343, 399, 466. *See also* Regional Forces; Popular Forces; TFES.

559

Territorial Forces—*Continued*
  advisers to, 57, 180, 236, 411, 431, 452
  control of, 265–67
  role of, 19, 37, 106–07, 111, 122, 172, 174–75, 177, 217, 234, 416, 515
  strength, 112, 147, 200–201, 214, 221, 379, 455, 460
Territorial Forces Evaluation System (TFES). *See* TFES.
Terrorism, 15, 302
Tet offensive, 206, 286, 291, 293–94, 305, 308–09, 311, 313–17, 325, 327–29, 335–36, 343*n*, 345, 354, 363, 391, 471, 506
TFES, 387
Thailand, 50, 77, 113, 303, 349, 495
Thang, General Nguyen Duc, 24, 123, 172, 179, 230–31, 256, 264–69, 309
Thang, Col. Tran Van, 265
Thanh, General Nguyen Viet, 116, 313, 333, 365, 407, 420, 423–24, 471, 477, 479
Thayer, Thomas C., 514
Thi, Col. Lam Quang, 116
Thi, General Nguyen Chanh, 111, 267, 309
  commander, I CTZ, 23, 25, 33, 129–31, 134–37, 140–41, 143, 267
  and Struggle Movement, 129–31, 134–37, 140–41, 143, 154, 192–93, 255, 309
Thieu, General Nguyen Van, 375, 475, 486, 502
  chairman, Directory, 23–25, 51, 234
  clique, 25, 32, 47, 116, 191, 246–47, 477–78
  and elections, 255, 258–65, 267–69, 276, 479, 481
  and internal political struggles, 109–10, 112, 127–31, 138, 141, 143, 192, 309–13, 334, 413, 484, 501
  minister of defense, 23–24, 378
  and reforms, 153–54, 245, 307–09, 313–14, 316, 318, 364–67, 467–68, 487
  and shifts in roles and missions, 91, 124, 171–72, 178–79, 277, 293, 420–21
  and Struggle Movement, 127–31
  and U.S. troop withdrawal, 346, 351–52, 490–93, 500, 508
  and Vietnamization, 356, 358, 361, 382, 384, 424
Thinh Hoi pagoda, 138
Thinh, General Nguyen Xuan, 247, 364, 411, 478
Tho, General Lam Quang, 159, 364, 478, 486
Tho, Le Duc, 490
Throckmorton, Lt. Gen. John L., 52, 88–89, 91
Thu Duc, 149
Thu Duc Infantry School, 29, 41, 154, 220, 364, 367
Thu, General Phan Dinh [pseud. Lam Son], 423
Thua Thien Province, 141, 393
Thuan, General Pham Quoc, 47, 115, 245–47, 265, 334, 364, 367, 412–13
Thuc, Col. Truong Tan, 334–35
Tiger cages, 332, 377

TIGHT JAW, Operation, 435
Toan, General Nguyen Van, 142, 248, 364–65, 476, 483
Ton Le Chon, 195
Trailwatchers, 72
Training, RVNAF, 7, 466, 519–20
  facilities, 41, 85, 317–18, 354
  problems with, 159–63
  programs, 28–29, 98, 214, 377–79
  revolutionary development, 235, 252
Transportation system, South Vietnamese, 27, 164–65
Tri, General Do Cao, 138, 267, 310, 313, 333–34, 364–65, 408–10, 412–13, 415–17, 421, 423–24, 471, 478, 486
Tri, General Nguyen Bao, 24, 109–10, 114, 149, 185, 188*n*, 256, 268
Trien, General Le Ngoc, 364, 477
Truong, General Ngo Quang, 117, 138, 143, 248, 334, 364–65, 393, 469, 471, 479, 484
Tu, Le Van, 478
Tuan, Col. Vu Ngoc, 230

Ugalde, Col. Jesse G., 67–69
Unconventional warfare, 7, 13, 77. *See also* Guerrilla operations.
Unified command. *See* Combined command concept.
U.S. Air Force, 13–14, 138, 287, 442
  advisory role, 67, 167, 443
  headquarters, 49, 51, 441–42
  strength, 20, 51, 296
U.S. Agency for International Development (USAID), 50, 54, 60, 75, 156, 224–25, 352
U.S. Ambassador to Vietnam, 14, 51, 175, 367, *See also* Bunker, Ellsworth; Lodge, Henry Cabot; Taylor, Maxwell D.
U.S. Army, Special Forces. *See* Special Forces, U.S. Army.
U.S. Army, Vietnam (USARV), 78, 441–42. *See also* Logistics, U.S. support to RVNAF; Strategy, U.S.
  advisory role, 55–56, 443–44
  command structure, 14, 51
  post-ceasefire residual force, 296
  roles and missions, 93–96, 104, 106, 120–24, 171
  troop buildup, 17, 34, 60, 90, 109, 111, 120, 123, 209, 233
U.S. Department of the Army, 145, 439–510
U.S. Department of Defense, 77–78, 145, 156, 166, 284–85, 287, 342, 346, 349, 375, 388–89, 439–40, 458, 488, 508
U.S. Department of State, 130, 318, 342, 345–46
U.S. Embassy, Saigon, 54, 75, 94, 130, 134, 154, 172, 211, 228–30, 234, 239, 258, 266, 274, 280, 342, 345–46, 465, 479, 501–02, 504
U.S. Information Agency, 31, 50, 54, 142
U.S. Marine Corps, 129, 133, 138, 141, 145, 175, 180–81, 248, 291, 434

U.S. Marine Corps—*Continued*
  advisory role, 55–56
  early role, 16–17, 33, 85, 87
U.S. Navy, 13–14, 20, 167, 296, 345

Vann, John Paul, 66, 244, 246, 253, 357, 366, 386, 451–52, 458, 476–78, 484–86, 510
VER, Project, 453
Vien, General Cao Van
  chief, JGS, 109–11, 145, 256n, 313, 378
  and civilian regime, 258, 260, 262, 266–68
  commander, III CTZ, 25, 34, 114
  and manpower utilization, 153–54, 161, 185, 191, 213, 216, 221, 224–26, 231, 245–48, 250–51, 310–11, 313, 316, 396
  and revolutionary development, 177, 179, 212
  and security mission, 175–76, 234–35
  and Struggle Movement, 127, 131, 134–36, 138, 140–41
  and U.S. withdrawal, 282, 308, 379–80, 424, 456–58, 466, 475–76, 487, 499
Vien, General Linh Quang, 24, 256
Viet Cong, 11, 73, 84, 93, 105–06, 118, 179, 184, 196, 228, 271, 349. *See also* Strength, enemy.
  guerrillas, 12, 14, 105, 107, 117, 150, 169–70
  interdiction of transportation routes, 27–28
  politico-military strategy, 10–12, 14–15, 133–35, 143
  psychological operations against, 31
  recruitment by, 43, 72
  strength, 19
  supply lines, 16
Viet Minh, 6
Vietnamization, 341–59, 361, 363, 369, 382, 387, 390, 396, 399–403, 415, 417, 424, 427–45, 455, 476, 488, 498–99, 507, 512, 518–19
Vogt, General John W., Jr., 495
Vung Tau, 433, 439
Vung Tau Revolutionary Development School, 235
Vy, General Nguyen Van, 222, 231, 251, 266, 299, 378, 382, 487

Wagstaff, Maj. Gen. Jack J., 478
Walt, Lt. Gen. Lewis W., 113, 120, 132–33, 136–38, 140–41, 180–81
Warner, Lt. Col. Volney F., 234
WASHINGTON GREEN, Operation, 400
Weapons, North Vietnamese, 283
Weapons, South Vietnamese, 38–39, 166, 283
Westmoreland, General William C., 17, 292, 361–62, 390, 391, 442, 507
  and advisory programs, 56–60, 62, 78, 81, 187–88, 190, 210, 236–39, 505–07, 509–12

Westmoreland, General William C.—*Continued*
  and RVNAF image, 271–87
  and civilian government, 260–64, 266–69
  and Co, 25, 97–98, 109–11
  and combined operations, 81–96, 184–86, 273–74, 281, 396
  and expansion of U.S. combat role, 91, 95–96, 99, 103, 121–23, 233, 284
  National Press Club speech, 280, 282
  and organization of MACV, 50–52
  and POWs, 119–20, 168, 170, 228
  and reform effort, 145–48, 166–67, 170, 192–93, 229, 231, 257–58, 310–13, 318, 320, 325–29, 380–81
  and RVNAF effectiveness, 113–18
  and shift in roles and missions, 174–81, 183, 211–12, 233–35, 282, 286, 498–502
  and South Vietnamese manpower, 41, 77, 97–98, 112–13, 150–62, 213, 215–26, 242–48, 250, 313–14, 328, 336, 353, 358–59, 519
  and Special Forces, 72, 74, 195, 199–203, 210
  and strategy, 77, 81–96, 97–108, 209, 282, 284, 291, 305, 307–08
  and Vietnamese politico-military turmoil, 109–11, 127, 129, 131–41, 143
  and withdrawal planning, 282, 293–95, 299–300, 302, 309, 346, 363, 424
Wetherill, Maj. Gen. Roderick, 381
Weyand, General Frederick C., 185–86, 249, 452, 493–95
Wheeler, General Earle G., 237, 271, 276–77, 328
  chairman, JCS, 50
  and combined command, 87, 107, 274, 420
  and expanded U.S. combat role, 84, 91, 96, 99–102, 104, 109, 233, 273, 291, 506
  and internal politico-military turmoil, 139–40, 262
  and U.S. troop withdrawal, 282, 294–95, 303, 347–48, 350, 387, 389
WHITE STAR, 69
Williams, Lt. Gen. Samuel T., 7
Williamson, Maj. Gen. Ellis W., 411
Wilson, Col. Wilbur, 47
Withdrawal, U.S. troop, 294, 296–97, 300–301, 305–06, 382–84, 471, 493, 495. *See also* May Plan.
  contingency planning for, 449–69
  mutual U.S.–North Vietnamese, 271, 279, 282, 292, 295, 298, 302, 341, 346, 348
  unilateral U.S., 279–80, 299, 341–59, 387, 417
Women's Armed Forces Corps, South Vietnamese, 84

Xuan Loc, 411

Yeu, Col. Dam Quang, 132–34, 141

Zais, Maj. Gen. Melvin, 382
Zorthian, Barry, 135, 143

WIDENER UNIVERSITY
WOLFGRAM
LIBRARY
CHESTER, PA

PIN: 062275-00